CORPORATE FINANCE LAW

UNITED KINGDOM
Sweet & Maxwell
London

AUSTRALIA
LBC Information Services
Sydney

CANADA AND USA
Carswell
Toronto • Ontario

NEW ZEALAND
Brooker's
Auckland

SINGAPORE AND MALAYSIA
Thomson Information (S.E. Asia)
Singapore

CORPORATE FINANCE LAW

DERMOT CAHILL

B.C.L., LL.M. (National University of Ireland)
Diplôme Adv.Eur.Leg.Stud. (College of Europe)
Solicitor
Faculty of Law
University College Dublin

DUBLIN
ROUND HALL LTD
2000

Published in 2000 by
Round Hall Ltd
43 Fitzwilliam Place
Dublin 2, Ireland.

Typeset by
Gilbert Gough Typesetting, Dublin.

Printed by
MPG Books, Cornwall

ISBN 1–85800–131–5

A catalogue record for this book
is available from the British Library.

For Yvonne
and to my parents,
Frank and Joan

Foreword

As the new Millennium approaches, lawyers and corporate finance advisers are faced with an ever complex set of problems in their daily work on behalf of their clients. The financing of companies is becoming increasingly more complex. The globalisation of capital markets is increasing this complexity. Often the legal issues presented are highly complicated. An additional complicating factor is presented by often conflicting regimes of non-statutory legal principles, national laws, European Union laws and indeed, legislative structures of global application. These regimes present new challenges for the practitioner of Corporate Finance.

Given the ever complicated nature of the different legal frameworks used to facilitate corporate finance activity, *Corporate Finance Law* is indeed a most timely publication. The author approaches the subject by providing in-depth treatment of a number of major areas, rather than attempting to cover every possible conceivable area in light detail. This approach is to be commended, and the authority of the work enhanced.

Reading through the book, one of the things which was impressive was the author's clear and lucid attempts to bring order to areas where often there is legal uncertainty.

Also of note is the extensive and relevant citation and comment on foreign precedents where they are helpful in guiding us on problems arising nearer to home. Reference to analagous U.K. legislation in some of the chapters, such as Chapter 5 on Insider Dealing, I found particularly illuminating and helpful.

Mr Cahill's writing displays an author at ease with his subject. Whether he is considering the intricacies of case law, statutes or EC directives, the author is always mindful that the reader may not be as familiar with the subject as he. For example, Chapter 1, Listing Rules on the Stock Exchange, makes extensive cross-reference between the Yellow Book Rules and the EC Admissions, Listing Particulars and Public Offer Prospectus Directives, as well as relevant statutory instruments.

Chapter 2 gives exhaustive consideration to the vexed issue of what is an "offer to the public", with consideration given to a multitude of case law from several jurisdictions as well as relevant provisions of the Companies Acts. Chapter 3 on Liabilities Arising out of Prospectuses is similarly comprehensive, and considers the confluence and uneasy co-existence of 19th Century case law principles with modern day statutory rules.

Those involved in the charging of corporate book debts would be well advised to read Chapter 5 on Corporate Borrowing. Chapter 7 on Debt Factoring considers, from a historical perspective, the merging of Equity and Common law jurisdiction by the Judicature Act of 1877, and then brings us all the way up to modern-day debt factoring practices.

Chapter 8 on the Legal Framework of State-Provided Corporate Finance will particularly interest those who advise foreign companies seeking investment assistance from the State. Likewise, similarly comprehensive insights are offered in Chapter 9 on the Legal Regulation of Mergers which covers the respective regimes of the Mergers Acts 1978-1991, the Competition Acts 1991–1996 and the EC Merger Regulation 1989 (as amended in 1998).

This book is more than just an important addition to the practitioner's library. It also represents a valuable contribution to legal scholarship. I have little doubt but that this will be a valued text in the years ahead, not only for corporate finance lawyers, but also for the corporate finance community generally, whether as advisers or regulators. The fact that it is eminently readable distinguishes it from many legal text books.

I warmly congratulate Dermot Cahill on the publication of *Corporate Finance Law*. I have little doubt but that this text shall set a benchmark in the area for the years to come.

Peter D. Sutherland

Preface

Corporate Finance Law encompasses many different and varied elements. To one person, it is the law of corporate borrowing and security. To another, it could be the law pertaining to debt sub-ordination, or debt factoring. It may mean the admission rules of the stock exchange, or perhaps the laws on insider dealing or prospectuses. Others may define it to include the law of mergers and acquisitions, or even the law relating to the sources of State-provided corporate finance.

At the end of the day, company financing, and the legal frameworks devised to achieve this objective, are as various as human ingenuity. Therefore, rather than trying to meet all constituencies (and satisfy none) by giving every conceivable topic light treatment, instead I have sought to give comprehensive treatment to nine different areas of essential importance to the corporate finance practitioner. In doing so, I have also sought to strike a balance between information and analysis, which I hope will be of assistance to practitioner and student alike.

The book is written for more than just the corporate finance lawyer. Corporate financing structures involve a myriad of professionals, from bankers to corporate finance advisers, accountants to company directors, stockbrokers to public officials. In explaining issues at some length, I hope I do not lose the lawyer-readers' interest. Lawyers should never forget that the law does not just appear. It is the result of complex interaction of different human demands which eventually result in "law". Therefore, this work will also be of interest to corporate finance advisers, in all guises, who seek a better understanding of the law's impact on their activities in the corporate finance sphere.

While writing the book, one thing that struck me in particular is how the State needs to make greater efforts to reconcile the requirements of often incongruous legal regimes. For example, at various points in the text I point out how legislation and common law principles lie uneasily alongside each other. An acute problem arises when the implementation of European law is an issue. The State's practice of using clumsily drafted statutory instruments to implement EC Directives does neither the State, nor its corporate finance practitioners, any service.

Corporate Finance is also an area that demonstrates how we live in an interdependent world. In several areas, because of a dearth of domestic case law, we are often reliant on foreign case law precedents for guidance. Insider dealing is a case in point. In noting the relevance of precedents from other common law jurisdictions, we can appreciate how other jurisdictions often face similar problems to those we face nearer to home.

In 1993, I first offered Corporate Finance Law to the then newly launched Business and Legal studies degree in UCD. Since then, some 700 students have contributed to my lectures on this subject. I hope that you will find this work of use in your present careers.

As for my friends and family whose excellent company I have missed at times over the last few years due to my engagement with this work, I thank you for your encouragement.

When Mr Peter D. Sutherland graciously agreed to write the Foreword to this work, I was deeply honoured. I thank him most sincerely for his contribution, particularly given his unparalleled dual experience of law and finance whether as eminent lawyer, distinguished Commissioner and public servant, and now international financier.

Finally, I wish to thank Yvonne Hennessy. Without her encouragement and support, this work would not have been possible.

While I have made very effort to state the law correctly at the time of writing, legal responsibility for the accuracy of the contents herein is not accepted. This work does not constitute legal advice, which should always be sought whenever a legal issue arises.

Dermot Cahill
Faculty of Law
University College Dublin
November 1999

Acknowledgments

As the end of my work on this book approached, I engaged in an extensive consultation process with corporate finance law practitioners in various areas for the purpose of subjecting the work to their critical scrutiny. I readily acknowledge the benefit of their criticisms and observations. This was a most worthwhile process and the work is all the better for it.

While ultimately I take moral responsibility for the content of the book, I would nevertheless like to record my thanks to the following persons who gave so freely of their valuable time to read some of the chapters, and for their incisive and helpful comments: Declan Drislane, Stephen Hegarty and Padraig O' Riordain of Arthur Cox; Liam Carney of Bank of Ireland Corporate Banking and Noel Gaughran of Bank of Ireland Group Legal Advisers; Vincent Shannon B.L. and Daniel O'Keeffe S.C. of the Law Library; Orla Muldoon of McCann FitzGerald; Joseph Kelly of A&L Goodbody and David Walsh of Jones Day Reavis & Pogue, Brussels.

My colleagues in the academic world also commented on various chapters, offered insights or drew relevant authorities to my attention. In this regard I wish to thank Oonagh Breen, Blanaid Clarke, Declan Murphy, Jonathan Newman and Professor Nial Osborough of UCD Law Faculty. Eoin O'Dell of Trinity College Dublin provided me with a wealth of material on matters pertaining to restitution. Irene Lynch-Fannon of University College Cork advised me on some difficult examinership issues. Numerous officials from various Government departments, statutory agencies and state bodies assisted with my requests for information on several difficult and complicated matters. Rosario Cooney, Tony Eklof and Anne Cooney of the UCD Law Library gave tremendous assistance at all times over the years in chasing down obscure references.

I also wish to record my thanks to the publishers, Round Hall Sweet and Maxwell, in particular to Catherine Dolan whose professionalism (good at chasing reluctant authors) and dedication (slave-driver) to her authors' contentment and well-being is becoming legendary. Also I wish to acknowledge the excellent work put in by legal editor Kieran Lyons, whose positive and efficient assistance at all times was most appreciated. Terri McDonnell did excellent work on the book's cover design.

Table of Contents

Foreword vii
Preface ix
Acknowledgments.. xi
Table of Cases xxxi
Table of Statutes xxxvii

CHAPTER 1: ADMISSIONS, LISTING AND PROSPECTUSES

    Introduction 5
I. **The Stock Exchange and Listing Markets** 6
    A. Short History 6
        (1) The International Stock Exchange of the United
            Kingdom and RoI 6
        (2) The Investment Services Directive 7
        (3) Central Bank as regulator 8
            (a) Approved stock exchanges 8
            (b) Member Firms 10
    B. The Markets 14
    C. Domestic markets 14
    D. Foreign markets 16
II. **Admission Conditions – the Admissions Directive and
    Yellow Book Regime** 18
    (1) Admissions Directive and the Stock Exchange
        Listing Rules...19
        (a) Role of the Stock Exchange as "competent
            authority"...19
        (b) Powers of the Stock Exchange over Admission
            to Listing 20
            (i) Power to impose additional admission
                conditions or refuse admission 20
            (ii) Enforcement powers...21
            (iii)Judicial review 22
    (2) Admission Conditions 23
        (a) Applicant Conditions (shares)........................23

   (b) Debt Securities 26
  (3) Shares, Debt Securities or Issuers which Fall Outside
    the Admissions Directive 28
III. Different Methods of Listing Securities 29
 A. Methods 29
  (1) Offer for Sale or Subscription 29
  (2) Placing 30
  (3) Intermediaries Offer 32
  (4) Introduction 33
  (5) Rights Issue 33
   (a) Yellow Book Rules 33
   (b) Statutory pre-emption rights/Yellow Book 35
  (6) Open Offer 37
  (7) Acquisition or Merger Issue 37
  (8) Capitalisation Issue 37
  (9) Issue for Cash/Conversions of Securities of one
    class into securities of another class/Exercise of
    Options or Warrants to subscribe securities 38
IV. Listing 38
 A. Principles Underlying the Listing Particulars Directive/
   Yellow Book 38
  (1) The provision of certain limited minimum information
    and the Duty to Allow Informed Assessment 38
  (2) Principle of Mutual Recognition 40
 B. Contents of Listing Particulars 43
  (1) Corresponding Framework: Yellow Book and Listing
    Particulars Directive 43
   (a) Shares or convertible debt securities 44
   (b) Debt securities 47
   (c) Certificates representing shares 48
   (d) Responsibility statement and
     responsibility letters 49
 C. Approval of Listing Particulars 51
  (1) Principle of prior approval 51
  (2) Supplementary Particulars 52
 D. Exemption from Requirement to Publish Listing
   Particulars 53
  (1) Exemptions which may be granted 53
   (a) Previously published documents 53
   (b) Three years' admission to listing in another
     Member State 54
   (c) Admission of a DCM company 54
  (2) Exempt Listing Particulars 55
  (3) Exemptions available except in "exceptional

          circumstances" 56
      (4) Summary Particulars 57
      (5) Shelf Registration 48
      (6) Omission of information from the Listing
           Particulars...59
V. **Listing Application Procedures** 60
  A. Time for Application 60
  B. Publication and Circulation of Listing Particulars 61
VI. **The Legal Principles Underlying the Development of EC**
    Listings Legal Framework...63
  A. Mutual Recognition of Listing Particulars 63
  B. Listing Particulars and Prospectuses 66
    (1) Listing particulars and the Companies Act 1963 67
    (2) Mutual Recognition of prospectus as
       listing particulars...67
  C. Mutual Co-Operation 71
VII. **Prospectus Directive Regime** 72
  A. Overlapping Regimes...72
  B. Publication and Registration of Prospectus...........................75
  C. Content of Prospectus 76
  D. Omission of Information..78
  E. The Prospectus Directive and the Principle of Mutual
    Recognition 78
    (1) Mutual tecognition of prospectuses 78
    (2) Mutual Recognition of Prospectus as
       Listing Particulars 82
VIII. **Continuing Obligations of Listed Companies** 83
  A. Exchange has Oower to Set Additional or More Stringent
    Requirements 83
  B. Main Principles..84
  C. Additional Requirements in Specific Transactions 87

CHAPTER 2: PROSPECTUSES – OFFER TO THE PUBLIC

Introduction
  (1) Part III Companies Act 1963.....................................91
  (2) Council Directive 89/298/EEC 94
  (3) Council Directive 80/390/EEC 97
  (4) Part XII Companies Act 1963 98
A. **The Statutory Definition of a Prospectus** 100
  (1) Section 2(1) Companies Act 1963.............................. 100
  (2) Section 44(3) – prospectus must accompany "form of
    application".. 100

(3) Documents deemed to be a Prospectus 101
    (a) Where company issues shares "with a view to any or all
         of them being offered to the public" 101
    (b) Prospectus Directive 102
    (c) Listing Particulars Directive 103
B. Offer to "the Public" 103
    (1) Private companies 103
    (2) Statutory and judicial elaboration on the concept of
         'the public' 103
    (a) Statutory Definition 104
    (b) Exclusions 104
            (i) Offer either acceptable by offerees only, or
                 else a "domestic concern" 104
            (ii) Issues to members or debenture holders
                 by company prohibited from making
                 offers to the public 114
            (iii)Offers of debentures to professional
                 dealers 115
    (3) Offer for "subscription or purchase" 115
    (a) For subscription 115
    (b) For purchase 116
C. Relaxation of the Third Schedule Rules under the
    Companies Act 117
D. Offers for which Neither the Companies Act Nor the
    Prospectus Directive require a Prospectus 119
    (1) The Companies Act 1963 119
    (2) The Prospectus Directive 120

CHAPTER 3: LIABILITIES THAT MAY ARISE FROM THE
PROSPECTUS

Introduction 129
I. **Non-Statutory Investor Remedies** 131
    A. Action for Omission or Deceitful Misrepresentation 132
        (1) Omission 132
        (2) Deceit 134
        (3) Connection between maker of representation and
             those parties who relied upon it 136
        (4) Measure of damages 137
    B. Action for Negligent Misstatement or Omission 139
        (1) Tort of negligent misstatement 139
        (2) Irish recognition of *Hedley Byrne* 141

(3) Liability for negligent misstatements in aditor's
    accounts – a lesson for promoters 142
(4) New developments extending liability exposure 145
C. Action for Recission by Allottee of Share Purchase 148
(1) Preconditions before Recission can be granted 148
(2) Truthful disclosure of material information 149
D. Damages against Company? 151
II. **Statutory Investor Remedies** 152
A. Section 49 Untrue Statements 154
(1) Section 49 Companies Act 1963 Civil Liability for
    "Untrue Statements" in a Prospectus offering
    securities to the public for Subscription or
    Purchase 154
(2) Possible Section 49 defendants 155
(3) No Section 49 liability for company 155
(4) Section 49 plaintiffs 156
(5) Section 49 defences 157
    (a) Defences based on lack of consent 157
    (b) Belief in truth of statement defence 157
    (c) Statement fairly reflects expert's statement
        defence 158
    (d) Official statement defence 158
    (e) Expert's defence 158
B. Listing Particulars Directive Regulations 160
(1) Disapplication of some provisions of
    Companies Act 1963 160
(2) Duty on Persons to allow for "Informed
    Assessment" 160
(3) Damages for breach of the Listing Particulars
    Regulations 161
    (a) Issuer liability? 161
    (b) "Persons responsible for the listing particulars"
        liability 163
(4) Possible plaintiffs 164
C. Prospectus Directive Regulations 165
D. Section 44 omission 167
(1) Liability under Section 44 for mere omission 167
(2) Omission in the context of the Listing Particulars
    Regulations 168
(3) Omission in the context of the Prospectus
    Regulations 168
E. Liability of Stock Exchange or Registrar of Companies 172
III. **Criminal Liabilities** 173
A. Offences 173

(1) Companies Act 1963 173
   (a) Section 50 (untrue statements) 173
   (b) Section 44 (8) (contravention of Section 44(1)
       or (3))/Section 46 (violating expert's
       consent) 174
   (c) Section 47 (failure to register prospectus) 175
(2) Section 242 Companies Act 1990 175
(3) Listing Particulars Regulations 176
   (a) Regulation 6 (breach of professional secrecy/
       publication of false or misleading
       information) 176
   (b) Regulation 13 (late delivery of listing
       particulars) 176
   (c) Regulation 12(3) (failure to produce listing 176
       particulars/withdrawal of expert's consent/
       publication of untrue statement) 177
(4) Prospectus Regulations 177
   (a) Regulation 20 (breach of professional secrecy/
       publication of false or misleading
       information) 178
   (b) Regulation 21/Regulation 11 (failure to produce
       prospectus in conformity with Prospectus
       Regulations/failure to register prospectus/
       violation of expert's consent/publication of
       untrue statement) 178
(5) Larceny Act 1861 179
IV. **The Promoter and the Company** 179
  A. The Promoter/Company Fiduciary Relationship 180
    (1) Two Key Issues 180
       (a) Promoter Directors and the Sale of Promoters'
          Property to the Company 181
       (b) Whether Promoter Directors can release
          themselves from their Duty to Account 183
  B. Company Action against the Promoter who has
    made Secret Profit 185
    (1) Return of Secret Profit 185
    (2) Recission of the Company's Contract with the
       Promoter 186
  C. Promoters and PLCs 190
    (1) Companies (Amendment)Act 1983 190
       (a) Relevant person 190
       (b) Initial period 190
       (c) Size of transaction and valuer's report 191
       (d) Exclusion of certain transactions 191

(e) Sanctions for contravention 191
   (i) Where consideration does not include
      shares 191
   (ii) Where consideration does include shares 192

CHAPTER 4: INSIDER DEALING

I. Insider Dealing 199
  A. Introduction 199
  B. Common Law 200
  C. Statutory Regime 205
    (1) Dealing 206
      (a) Territorial scope 208
    (2) Securities 210
      (a) Recognised Stock Exchange 211
      (b) Off-market dealings in 'securities' 211
      (c) Securities issued or proposed to be issued,
         whether in the State or otherwise 212
      (d) Transactions involving professional
         intermediaries 213
    (3) Inside Information 214
      (a) Not Generally Available 215
      (b) Likely materially to affect the price of the
         securities 218
      (c) Information of a precise nature 220
      (d) The securities 223
    (4) Insiders 224
      (a) Primary Insiders 224
         (i) How must connected person have come
            into possession of information 225
         (ii) Connected to the company 226
         (iii) Mere "possession" sufficient 228
         (iv) The United Kingdom legislation
            (comparative overview) 228
      (b) Secondary Insiders ('Tipees') 230
         (i) No need for connection to the company 231
         (ii) Liability test 231
         (iii) "Directly or indirectly" 232
         (iv) The new United Kingdom legislation
            (comparative overview) 232
      (c) Causing and Procuring 233
      (d) Communication of inside information 235
         (i) Points of distinction 237

(e) Directors and securities options 238
(f) Companies as insider dealers 239
   (i) Chinese wall structures 240
   (ii) Mere information that company proposes
        to deal 241
   (iii) Company dealing in own securities 241
(5) Exempt Transactions 242
   (a) Section 110 exemptions 242
   (b) Section 108 exemptions 243
      (i) Execution-only agents 243
      (ii) Seven-day Window 244
(6) The Yellow Book's Model Code 245
(7) Grounds for liability under Part V 248
   (a) Civil liability 248
      (i) Compensation for loss 249
      (ii) Account for profit 251
   (b) Criminal liability 253
      (i) Offences 253
      (ii) Penalties 254
      (iii) Agents 254
      (iv) Unresolved issues 254
   (c) Enforcement of criminal liability 255
      (i)   Relevant Authority 255
      (ii)   Duty to report insider dealing 256
      (iii)   Direction to Relevant Authority to act 256
      (iv)   Investigation powers 256
      (v)   Role of court in determining ambit of
              investigation 257
      (vi)   Obligationof professional secrecy 257
      (vii) Duty to co-operate with other EC
              Stock Exchanges 258
      (viii) Annual Report of recognised
              Stock Exchange 258

II. **Manipulation of the Stock Market** 259
  A. Market Manipulation 259
   (1) How the market may be manipulated 259
   (2) Companies (Amendment) Act 1999 –
       Stabilisation Rules 260
      (a) Relevant Securities 260
      (b) Stabilising Periods 261
         (i) Within the State 261
         (ii) Outside the State 262
      (c) Preliminary Steps Before Stabilising Action 262
         (i) Reasonable belief 262

(ii) Modification where Stabilisation occurs
    outside the State 263
(iii) associated securities 263
(d) Stabilising Action 264
(e) Action ancillary to Stabilising Action 264
(f) Limits on Stabilisation Price 265
  (i) Relevant Securities and Certain Associated
      Companies 265
  (ii) Certain other Associated Securities 266
  (iii) Associated Call Options 267
(g) Termination of Stabilising Period 267
(h) Recording of Stabilisation Transactions 267
(i) Stabilisation Rules and the Companies Act 1990
    disclosure rules regarding relevant share
    capital 268
(3) Stock Exchange regime to prevent market
    manipulation 268

CHAPTER 5: CORPORATE BORROWING

I. Corporate Borrowing – Loans 275
What is a Loan 275
(1) Loan defined 275
(2) Loan instruments 277
(a) Loan facility agreement 277
(b) Overdraft 279
(c) Debentures... 279
II. Corporate Borrowing – Developments in *Ultra vires* 281
Overview of developments 281
A. Borrowing – "Power" or "Object" 282
(1) Trading company cannot have "borrowing" as
    an Object 282
(2) Drafting Devices which attempt to designate
    borrowing as a Corporate Object 284
(a) Main Objects Principle................................. 284
  (i) Cotman clause 285
  (ii) Bell Houses clause 286
(3) Restrictive judicial interpretation 287
(4) Benefit to the company....................................... 289
B. Borrowing Transactions Tainted by Abuse of Directors'
  Powers.. 290
(1) *Ultra vires* distinguished from abuse of directors'
    powers 291

(2) Transactions tainted by abuse of directors' powers 291
(3) Limitations of a general and specific nature
    distinguished 295
(4) Th issue of benefit to the company 296
C. Enforcing Loan Contracts against *Ultra Vires* Corporate
    Borrower 299
(1) Companies Act 1963, section 8(1) 299
    (a) Limitations on availability of section 8(1) 299
    (b) 'Actually Aware' 301
        (i) Judicial interpretation of section 8(1) 301
        (ii) Article 9 First Company Law Directive 304
        (iii) Regulation 6 of S.I. No. 163 of 1973 305
D. Recovery of Funds Loaned Pursuant to *Ultra Vires*
    Transaction 307
(1) *In personam* contractual and quasi-contractual
    remedies denied 307
(2) Quasi-contractual remedies rehabilitated 309
(3) Basis for recovery of funds loaned *ultra vires*
    the lender? 311
(4) Recovery of sums paid *ultra vires* the
    Revenue authorities 318
III. Corporate Borrowing – Authority of Corporate
    Borrower's Agents 320
    Overview 320
A. Types of Authority 321
(1) Actual Authority 321
(2) Ostensible Authority 322
    (a) Representation of authority 323
    (b) Representation by company 324
    (c) Reliance on representation 324
    (d) Intra vires transaction 324
    (e) No express limitation on agent's authority 324
B. Constructive Notice and Authority of
    Company Agents 325
(1) The rule in Turquand's case 325
    (a) Limitations on Turquand's rule 327
        (i) Deficiency on public record 327
        (ii) Where party not in good faith 327
        (iii) Where the company agent was acting outside
            usual authority 330
C. Agents Authority and the Impact of European
    Legislation 331
(1) Article 9(2) 331
(2) European Communities (Companies) Regulations

1973 331
    (a) Regulation 6 331
    (b) Impact on Turquand's rule/agency principles 332
        (i) Turquand's rule 332
        (ii) Agency principles 333
    (c) Limitations on availability of Regulation 6 333
IV. Corporate Borrowing – Charging Book Debts 335
  A. Types of Charges on Book Debts 335
    (1) What is a Book Debt 336
    (2) Statutory obligation to register charges on
        Book Debts 336
    (3) Advantages of being a fixed charge leader 342
  B. Feasibility of Attaching Floating or Fixed Charge on
    Book Debts 344
    (1) Floating charges on Book Debts 344
    (2) Fixed charges on Book Debts 345
    (3) Judicial methods for ascertaining true nature of
        charges over Book Debts 345
        (a) The constructionist approach 345
        (b) Consolidation of the constructionist approach 348
        (c) The importance of the terms of the designated
            account 349
    (4) Some possible implications of recent case law 352
  C. Book Debts, Charges and the Borrower's Examinership 353
    (1) Crystallised floating charges de-crystallise 355
    (2) Negative pledge covenants unenforceable 358
    (3) Lender realisation of debt charged prevented 359
    (4) Certified borrowings repayable in priority 359

CHAPTER 6: DEBT SUBORDINATION LEGAL FRAMEWORK AND
METHODS

I. Debt Subordination 363
  What is debt subordination? 363
  Why subordinate corporate debt? 364
    (1) The debtor company 364
    (2) The senior creditors 364
    (3) The junior creditors 364
  Some Possible Advantages of Debt Subordination to
  the Debtor Company 365
    (1) Breathing space 365
    (2) Circumvent borrowing limits 365
    (3) Group companies and group debtors 366

Subordinated Debt – Debt or Equity?.................................... 366
    (1) Similarities 366
    (2) Differences 367
Debt Subordination and Charges Distinguished 368
Debt Subordination and Assignment of Debt
Distinguished 370
II. **Legal Framework of main methods of debt
    subordination** 371
When Will the Subordination Take Effect?........................... 371
    (1) Complete subordination 371
    (2) Inchoate subordination... 372
Main Methods of Debt Subordination 373
    (1) Turnover subordination 373
        (a) Subordination trust: *advantages* 374
            (i) Junior creditor insolvency 374
            (ii) Avoiding debtor/junior creditor set-off 375
            (iii) Senior creditor double payment.................. 375
            (iv) Avoids privity concerns............................... 376
            (v) Avoids *pari passu* objections 376
            (vi) Proving the junior debt 377
            (vii) Breadth of turnover obligation 378
        (b) Subordination trust: *disadvantages* 379
            (i) Trust concept not universally
                 recognised 379
            (ii) Inadvertent creation of security interest 379
            (iii) Assignment by junior creditor.................... 382
        (c) Contractual turn-over subordination:
            advantages 383
            (i) Senior creditor may receive double
                 payment... 384
            (ii) Avoids *pari passu* concerns 384
            (iii) Avoids 'inadvertent' security concerns...... 384
            (iv) Contract concept more widely recognised 385
        (d) Contractual Turn-Over Subordination:
            disadvantages... 385
            (i) Senior creditor has no beneficial
                 interest 385
            (ii) Turn-over may breach company law 386
    (2) Contractual Contingent Subordination 386
        (a) Contractual Turn-Over Subordination
            distinguished 386
        (b) Compatibility with *pari passu*: the source of
            the confusion 387
        (c) The contingency 388

    (d) Judicial clarification 390
    (e) Legislative clarification....................................... 398
  (3) Turn-Over Subordinations and Contingent
      subordination: a comparison 400
III. Subordination: Some Company Law issues 402
  Fraudulent Trading 403
  Reckless Trading 404
  Fraudulent Preference 407

CHAPTER 7: DEBT FACTORING

I. Debt Factoring as a Source of Corporate Finance 413
II. Assignment of Debt – A Brief History 418
  Law and Equity – Two systems 418
  Choses in Action – Historical difficulties at
  Common Law 418
III. Debt Factoring – The Legal Framework 420
  Assignment in Law 420
    (1) "Absolute" assignment... 422
    (2) Express notice to debtor 424
    (3) Written requirement 428
    (4) Section 28(6) "Subject to Equities" 429
    (5) Notice of assignment and the rule in
       Dearle v. Hall 432
    (6) Failure to comply with section 28(6) and
       whether assignment may take effect
       in equity 433
  Assignment in Equity 433
    (1) Necessary requirements 434
    (2) Recommended requirements 435
      (a) Assignment in writing 435
      (b) Notice of assignment to debtor 435
IV. Competing Assignments – Priority Rules 437
  Priority nightmare 437
    (1) *Dearle v. Hall* 437
    (2) Section 28(6) and *Dearle v. Hall*................................. 439
  Case Study 440

Chapter 8: LEGAL FRAMEWORK OF MAIN SOURCES OF STATE-
PROVIDED CORPORATE FINANCE

I.   **Institutional Framework** 448
     (1) Forfás 448
     (2) The IDA 449
     (3) Institutional Reforms 451
          (a) Forbairt (1993) 451
          (b) Reform of Agency Framework and the
               establishment of Enterprise Ireland 452
II. **Part III Industrial Development Act, 1986 –**
     Industrial Incentives 456
     (1) Legal Framework of financial incentives 456
          (a) Fixed asset purchase grant 458
          (b) Additional persons employed grant 459
          (c) Leased fixed assets grant 460
          (d) Reduction of fixed asset loan interest grant 460
          (e) Fixed asset loan guarantee grant 460
          (f) Employment grants to service industries 461
          (g) Loan guarantees and Interest subsidies grant to
               promote corporate restructuring 461
          (h) Loan guarantees and interest subsidies grant to
               promote enterprise development 462
          (i) Training grants 462
          (j) Research and development grants 462
          (k) Technology acquisition grants 463
          (l) Acquisition of shares 463
          (m) Rent subsidies grant 465
          (n) Land acquisition grant 465
     (2) Statutory Limits on Aggregate of Certain grants.......... 465
     (3) Government's Power to Override grant Limits 466
III. **Grant Contract – Legal Framework and Terms** 466
     (1) Agreement 466
IV. **Other State Agencies** 468
     (1) County Enterprise Boards 468
     (2) ICC Bank plc 458
     (3) Údarás na Gaeltachta 469
     (4) FÁS 470
     (5) Shannon Development 470
     (6) EU 471
     (7) Sectoral agencies 471

CHAPTER 9: LEGAL REGULATION OF MERGERS

I. **The Different Legal Regimes** 477
II. **The Mergers Act Regime** 479
    (1) What is a Merger or Take-Over? 479
    (2) What criteria make a Merger or Take-Over notifiable
        under the Mergers Act? 482
    (3) Notification 482
        (a) Form 482
        (b) Contents 483
    (4) Power to request further information 485
    (5) Time limit for Ministerial consent or refusal 485
    (6) Courses of action open to Minister 485
        (a) Minister takes no action 485
        (b) Minister refers proposal to Competition Authority
            and makes Section 9 Order 486
        (c) Minister declines to make any order under
            Section 9 488
    (7) Appeal to High Court against Section 9 Order
        of Minister 488
    (8) Enforcement of Section 9 Orders 488
    (9) Title to shares or assets cannot pass unless Minister
        makes favourable decision within relevant period
        (or else makes no decision within that period) 489
        (a) Title cannot pass 489
        (b) Purported vendor has right to damages 489
    (10) Failure to notify 491
III. **The Competition Acts Regime** 491
    (1) The Competition Authority 492
    (2) Could a Merger or Take-Over be an anti-competitive
        arrangement contrary to section 4(1)? 494
    (3) 1997 Category Certificate 497
        (a) Authority's definition of a 'Merger' 498
        (b) Assessment of state of the market in which the
            Merger is located 498
            (i) The Hirfindahl/Hirschmann index (HHI) 499
            (ii) The Four-Firm Concentration Ratio (FFC) 502
            (iii) The HHI and FFC compared 502
            (iv) The HHI and FFC ignored 503
        (c) Category Certificate inapplicable 503
            (i) Dominant position created or strengthened
                by merger 503
            (ii) Actual level of competition in relevant market
                already weak 503

(iii) Ancillary restraints on competition 504
(4) Vertical Mergers 510
IV. **EC Mergers Regulation Regime** 511
The Merger Regulation: An Overview 511
(1) Concentrations 514
     (a) Acquisition of control or decisive influence 514
     (b) Joint Ventures as Concentrations: clarification
         or confusion 516
     (c) Extra-territorial Concentrations 518
(2) Notifiable concentrations – 'Community Dimension' 519
     (a) The original thresholds 519
     (b) Additional thresholds 520
     (c) Revised Turnover Rules for Credit and Financial
         Institutions 521
(3) "One-Stop Shop" 524
     (a) Exclusive Regulator 524
         (i) National Competition/Merger Law
              disapplied 524
         (ii) Notification-triggering event 525
         (iii) Suspensive effect 525
         (iv) Regulation deadlines and legal bases for
              Commission decisions 526
     (b) Appraisal test – compatible with the common
         market? 531
         (i) Collective Dominance 533
         (ii) Failing Firm Defence 537
         (iii) Full-Function Joint Ventures 537
     (c) Exceptions to exclusive regulation 538
         (i) The German clause 538
         (ii) Legitimate interests 543
         (iii) The Dutch clause 544
(4) Full-Function Joint Ventures 545
(5) Powers of Commission to enforce Regulation 550
V.   **The Takeover Panel Rules Regime** 552
A. Institutional Background 552
     (1) Replacement of London Panel 552
     (2) Irish Takeover Panel Act 1997 553
B. The Takeover Rules 554
     (1) General principles 554
     (2) Takeovers and Control 555
     (3) Influence of Principles on Rules 557
     (4) Restrictions on acquisitions 559
     (5) Exceptions 560
     (6) Mandatory Offer 561

(7) Interplay with Mergers Act/EC Merger Regulation
       Regimes 562
C. Substantial Acquisition Rules 563
    (1) Prohibition 563
    (2) Exceptions 565
    (3) Prompt Disclosure Obligation 566
D. The Panel 567
    (1) Composition and Legal Form 567
    (2) Powers of Panel 567
        (a) Rulings and Directions 567
        (b) Censure 568
        (c) Hearings 568
    (3) Judicial Review of Panel 569
    (4) Liability of Panel 571
E. The Proposed Takeovers Directive 572
    (1) Mandatory Bid 573
    (2) Defensive Measures 573
    (3) Cross-Border Takeovers and determination of
        Supervisory Authority Competency 574
    (4) Impact of the Directive on national
        appeal systems 575
    (5) Forms of Consideration in a Takeover 575
    (6) Information requirements 576

INDEX 577

Table of Cases

IRELAND

AIB v. Ardmore Studios International (1972) Ltd., unreported,
High Court, May 30, 1973 .... 5–41n
Atlantic Magnetics Ltd (in receivership), Re [1993] 2 I.R. 561 .... 5–69n, 5–71
Bank of Ireland Finance v. Daly [1978] I.R. 79 .... 5–57n
Bank of Ireland Finance Ltd v. Rockfield Ltd [1979] I.R. 21 .... 5–20n, 5–45n
Burke Clancy & Co Ltd, Re, unreported, High Court, Kenny J.,
May 23 1974 .... 5–01n, 5–17
Conlon & Coyle v. Carlow County Council [1912] II I.R.
(K.B.) 535 .... 7–02n, 7–06n, 7–10n, 7–10
Corran Construction v. Bank of Ireland Finance
[1976] I.L.R.M. 175 .... 6–79n
Cox v. Dublin City Distillery (No. 2) [1916] 1 I.R. 345 5–46
Creation Printing, Re [1981] I.R. 353 .... 5–59n
Daniel Murphy, Re [1964] I.R. 1 .... 5–59n
Dempsey v. Bank of Ireland, unreported, Supreme Court,
December 6, 1985... 5–68n
East Cork Foods v. O'Dwyer Steel [1978] I.R. 103 .... 5–26, 5–27
Brian Tucker, Re or Farrell v. Equity Bank [1990] 2 I.R. 549 .... 5–55n
Farm Fresh Frozen Foods Ltd, Re [1980] I.LR.M. 131 .... 5–57n
Farrell v. Equity Bank [1990] 2 I.R. 549 .... 6–33n
Flood v. Irish Provident Assurance Company [1912] 46 I.L.T.R. 5–26
Frederick Inns Ltd, Re
[1991] I.LR.M. 582 .... 5–12, 5–16n, 5–16, 5–18, 5–20,
5–23, 5–28, 5–29, 5–29n, 5–30, 5–52n
Glow Heating v. Eastern Health Board
[1988] I.R. 110 .... 5–68n, 6–54n, 6–56, 6–62
Hefferon Kearns, re [1993] 3 I.R. 191 .... 6–73n
Holidair, Re [1994] I.R. 481 .... 5–60n, 5–64, 5–66, 5–69, 5–70, 5–71
Hunting Lodges, re [1985] I.L.R.M. 75 .... 6–71n
International Factors (Ireland) Ltd. v. Midland Factors Ltd,
unreported, Lynch J., High Court,
December 9, 1993.................................. 6–43n, 7–02n, 7–12n, 7–16
Jackson v. Lombard & Ulster Bank [1992] I.R. 94 .... 5–55n
Keenan Bros, Re [1985] I.R. 401 .... 5–54, 5–61, 5–62, 5–63, 5–64
Kum Tung Restaurant (Dublin) Ltd [1978] I.R. 446 .... 5–55n
Kett v. Shannon and English [1987] I.L.R.M. 364... 5–34

Lakeglen Construction, Re (Kelly v. McMahon Ltd)
[1980] I.R. 347 5–61
Law v. Roberts [1964] I.R. 306 .... 5–29n
Lee v. McGrath [1882] 10 L.R. (Ir) 313 .... 7–13n, 7–21n
Lough Neagh Shipping Company, Re [1895] 1 I.R. 533 .... 5–26n
Lynch v. Ardmore Studios [1966] I.R. 133 .... 5–68n
Metro Investments Ltd, Re, unreported, High Court,
May 25,1977 .... 5–13, 5–18
Northern Bank Finance Corporation Ltd v. Quinn and
Achates Investments Co.
[1979] I.LR.M. 221 .... 5–12, 5–13, 5–21, 5–22n, 5–23, 5–52n
Northside Developments Pty v. Registrar General
[1990] 170 C.L.R. 146 5–44
Parkes and Sons Ltd v. Hong Kong and Shanghai Banking
Corporatation [1990] I.L.R.M. 341 5–16
PMPA v. PMPS , unreported, High Court, Murphy J., June 27, 1994 5–29
PMPA Garage (Longmile)Ltd. and Others (No. 2)
[1992] I.L.R.M. 349 .... 5–06, 5–17, 5–18, 5–27, 5–29
Ulster Investment Bank v. Euro Estates Ltd
[1982] I.L.R.M. 57 5–41
Welch v. Bowmaker (Ireland) Ltd [1980] I.R. 251 .... 5–57n, 5–59n, 5–60n
Wogan's Drogheda Ltd [1993] 1 I.R. 154 .... 5–63, 5–64

OTHER COMMON LAW JURISDICTIONS

ENGLAND

Abbey National Building Society v. The Building Societies
Commission [1989] B.C.C. 259 .... 2–28n
Akierhelm v.De Mare [1959] A.C. 789 2–28
A.L. Underwood Ltd v. Bank of Liverpool [1924] 1 K.B. 775 5–44
Allen v. Hyatt [1914] 30 T.L.R. 444 .... 4–04, 4–74n
Anglo-Overseas Agencies Ltd v. Green [1961] 1 Q.B. 1 5–09
Arnison v. Smith [1889] 41 Ch 348 2–28
Ashbury Railway Carriage and Iron Company v. Riche
[1875] L.R. 7 653 .... 5–06, 5–09n
Attorney General v. Great Eastern Railway [1880] 5 A.C. 473 .... 5–07, 5–18n
Bateman v. Hunt [1904] 2 K.B. 539 .... 7–12n
Bell Houses Ltd v. City Wall Properties Ltd [1966]
2 All E.R. 1045 .... 5–11, 5–12
Boardman v. Phipps [1967] 2 A.C. 46 .... 4–06n
Brightlife, Re [1987] W.L.R. 197 .... 5–58, 5–59n, 5–62, 5–63n, 5–64
British Eagle International Airlines Ltd v. Air France [1975]
2 All E.R. 390 .... 6–49n, 6–52, 6–53, 6–54n, 6–55n,
6–56, 6–57, 6–58, 6–59, 6–62
British and Commonwealth Holdings plc, re [1992] 1 W.L.R. 672 .... 6–31n
Brooks v. Blackburn Benefit Building Society [1884] 9 A.C. 857 5–04
Burlinson v. Hall [1884] 12 Q.B.D. 147 .... 7–11n

Carreras Rothmans Ltd v. Freeman Matthews Treasure Ltd
[1985] 1 All E.R. 155 .... 6–54, 6–62n
Charge Card Services Ltd, Re [1986] 3 All E.R. 289 .... 5–56, 5–58
CharterbridgeCorporation Ltd. v. Lloyd's Bank Ltd
[1970] Ch. 62 .... 5–13, 5–18n
Chase Manhattan Equities v. Goodman [1991] B.C.L.C. 897 .... 4–85n
Chow Yoonh Hong v. Choong Fah Rubber Manufacturer
[1962] A.C. 209 5–01
City of London Brewery Co Ltd. v. (IRC) [1899] 1 Q.B. 121 5–01
Clayton's case [1817] 1 Mer 572 .... 5–59n
Commissioner for Corporate Affairs v. Green [1978]
Vict. R. 505 4–29
Cotman v. Brougham [1918] A.C. 514 .... 5–10, 5–12, 5–16
Credit Suisse v. Allerdale BC [1997] Q.B. 306 .... 5–27n
Curran v. Newpark Cinemas Ltd [1951] 1 All E.R. 295 .... 7–12n
David Payne&Co Ltd., Re [1904] 2 Ch. 608 .... 5–16n
Dearle v. Hall [1824–1834] All E.R. 28 .... 7–17, 7–18, 7–23n, 7–24,
7–25, 7–26, 7–27, 7–28, 7–29
Denney Gasquet & Metcalfe v. Conklin [1913] 3 K.B.177 7–12
Destone Fabrics, Re [1941] 1 Ch. 319 .... 5–59n
Ernest v. Nicholls [1857] 6 H.L. Cas 401 .... 5–41n
Firth v. Staines [1897] 2 Q.B. 70 .... 5–46n
Fitzroy v. Cave [1905] 2 K.B.364 .... 7–06n
Forster v. Baker [1910] 2 K.B. 636 .... 7–10n
Freeman & Lockyer v. Buckhurst Park Properties (Mangal) Ltd
[1964] 2 Q.B. 480 .... 5–34, 5–51
General Auction Estate Co. v. Smith [1891] 3 Ch. 492 .... 5–07n
German Date Coffee Co Ltd [1882] 20 Ch. 169 .... 5–09n
Gorringe v. Irwell India Rubber and Gutta Percha Works
(1886) Ch.D. 128 .... 7–02n, 7–12n, 7–23n, 7–23, 7–26n
Government Stock and Other Securities Investment Co Ltd v.
Christopher and Others [1956] 1 All.E.R. 490 .... 2–20, 2–23n, 2–28, 2–29
Halt Garage Ltd, Re [1982] 3 All E.R. 1016 ....5–13n, 5–18n
Helstan Securities Ltd. v. Hertfordsire County Council [1978]
3 All E.R. 262 .... 7–02n
Hely-Hutchinson v. Brayhead Ltd [1968] 1 Q.B. 549 .... 5–34, 5–46n
Hilger Analytical Ltd v. Rank Precision Industries and Others
[1984] B.C.L.C. 301 5–05
Holt v. Heatherfield Trust [1942] 2 K.B. 1 .... 7–02n, 7–06n, 7–12, 7–16n,
7–20n, 7–23n, 7–26n
Hong Kong and Shanghai Banking Corp v. Kloeckner
& Co. A.G. [1990] 2 Q.B. 514 .... 6–24n
Horsley &Weight Ltd, Re [1982] 3 ALL E.R. 1045 .... 5–06, 5–10, 5–13, 5–18n
Hughes v. Pump House Hotel Co. [1902] 2 K.B. 190 .... 7–11n
Hutton v. West Cork Railway Co [1883] 23 Ch 672 .... 5–13n
IDC v. Cooley [1972] 2 All E.R. 162 .... 4–06n
Illingsworth v. Houldsworth [1904] A.C. 355 .... 5–60n
International Factors Ltd. v. Roderiguez [1979] Q.B. 351 7–01

International Sales and Agencies Ltd & Anor v. Marcus
[1983] 3 All E.R. 551 .... 5–52n
Introductions Ltd, Re [1968] 3 All E.R. 1221 .... 5–07, 5–10n, 5–12, 5–16n
Irvine v. Union Bank of Australia [1877] 2 A.C. 366 .... 5–01n, 5–17n, 5–42n
Joachimson v. Swiss Banking Corp [1921] 3 K.B. 110 CA 5–01
Johnstone v. Cox [1881] 16 Ch. Div. 571 .... 7–14n
Jon Beauforte (London) Ltd, Re [1953] 1 All E.R. 634 .... 5–06n
Kreditbank Cassell Gmbh v. Schenkers [1927] 1 K.B. 826 5–47
Lee Behrens, Re [1932] 2 Ch 46 .... 5–13n
Linden Garden Trust Ltd. v. Lenesta Sludge Disposals Ltd. & Ors
[1994] 1 A.C. 85 .... 7–02n
Marchant v. Morton, Down & Co [1901] 2 K.B. 829 .... 7–25n
Matthew Ellis Ltd, Re [1933] Ch 5–59n
Maxwell Communications Corporation plc, in re
[1993] 1 W.L.R. 1402 .... 6–31n, 6–42n, 6–49n, 6–57, 6–59
Morris v. Agrichemicals Ltd (1998) J.I.B.L. 115 .... 5–56n, 5–58n,
Morris v. Kanssen [1946] A.C. 459 .... 5–46n
Morris and Others v. Rayners Enterprises Incorporated [1996]
2 All E.R. 121 .... 5–56, 5–58
National Westminster Bank plc.& Anor v. I.R.C., Barclay's Bank plc
& Anor [1995] 1 A.C. 119 .... 2–29n
National Westminster Bank v. Halsowen Presswork and Assemblies
Ltd [1972] A.C. 785 .... 6–49n
New Bullas Trading, Re [1994] B.C.L.C. 485 .... 5–62n, 5–63, 5–64, 5–65
Newfoundland Government v. Newfoundland Railway Co
and Others [1888] 13 App Cas. 199 7–16
Northern Bank v. Ross [1990] B.C.C. 883 5–58
Percival v. Wright [1902] 2 Ch. 421 .... 4–03, 4–04, 4–05, 4–74n
Permanent Houses (Holdings) Ltd, Re [1988] B.C.L.C. 563 .... 5–58n
Pfeiffer Weinkellerei v. Arbuthnot Factors Ltd [1988]
1 W.L.R. 150 .... 6–35, 7–28
Regal (Hastings) v. Gulliver [1942] 1 All E.R. 378 4–06
Reisnod & Mica Products [1983] Ch 132 .... 5–57n
Rolled Steel Products Holding Ltd. v. British Steel Corp. [1985]
3 All E.R. 52 .... 5–07n, 5–10n, 5–13n, 5–15, 5–16, 5–17, 5–18n , 5–43
Roxburghe v. Cox [1881] 17 Ch. Div. 520 .... 7–16n
Royal British Bank v. Turquand [1856]
6 E. & B. 327 .... 5–41, 5–42, 5–43, 5–44, 5–46, 5–47, 5–50
Seldon v. Avison [1968] 2 All E.R. 755 5–01
Sherwell v. Combined Incandescent Mantles Syndicate
[1907] 23 T.L.R. 482 .... 2–20, 2–21n, 2–22n, 2–23n
Siebe Gorman & Co Ltd v. Barclays Bank Ltd [1977]
2 Lloyd's Reps 142 .... 5–61, 5–62
Sinclair v. Brougham [1914] A.C. 398 .... 5–25, 5–26, 5–27
Skipper & Tucker v. Holloway and Howard [1910] 2 K.B. 630 7–10
South of England Natural Gas, Re [1911] 1 Ch 573 2–20
Southern Brazilian Rio Grande do Sul Railway Co Ltd, Re
[1905] 2 Ch. 78 .... 5–01n

Swiss Bank Corporation v. Lloyds Bank Ltd and Others
[1982] A.C. 584 .... 6–32n
Tailby v. Official Receiver [1888] 13 A.C. 523 5–64
Tancred v. Dalagoa Bay & East Africa Railway Co. [1889]
23 Q.B. 239 .... 7–11n
TCB Ltd v. Gray [1986] 1 All E.R. 587 .... 5–52n
Telford Motors, Re, unreported, High Court, Hamilton J.,
January 29, 1978 .... 5–57n
Tolhurst v. Associated Portland Cement Manufacturers
[1990] A.C. 415 .... 7–09n
Torkington v. Magee [1902] K.B.D. 427 .... 7–09n
Victoria Housing Estates v. Ashpurton Estates Ltd. [1983] Ch. 110 .... 5–57n
Waite Hill Holdings v. Marshall [1983] 133 N.L.J. 745 .... 5–01n
Walter & Sullivan Ltd. v. J.Murphy & Sons Ltd [1955]
2 Q.B. 584 .... 7–02n, 7–10n
Welsh Development Agency v. The Export Finance Company Ltd.
[1992] B.C.L.C. 148 .... 5–56n
Westdeutsche Landesbanke Girozentrale v. Islington
London Borough Council [1996] A.C. 669 .... 5–25n, 5–27n, 5–28, 5–29
Whittingstall v. King [1882] 46 L.T. 520 .... 7–20n
William Brandt's Sons Ltd. v. Dunlop Rubber Company
[1905] A.C. 454 .... 7–15n, 7–19n, 7–21n, 7–23n
Williams, Re: Williams v. Ball [1917] 1 Ch. 1 .... 7–10n, 7–11n
Woolwich Building Society v. Inland Revenue Commissioners
(No. 2) [1992] 3 All E.R. 737 5–31
Yeovil Glove, Re [1965] Ch 148 .... 5–59n
Yorkshire Woolcombers Assoc Ltd (Houldsworth v. Yorkshire
Woolcombers Association Ltd) [1903] 2 Ch 284 5–60

AUSTRALIA

Attorney General of New Zealand v. McMillan & Lockwood Ltd
[1991] 1 N.Z.L.R. 53 .... 6–60n
Broken Hill Proprietary v. Bell Resources Ltd [1984] 58 A.L.J.R. 526 2–28
Coleman v. Myers [1977] 2 N.Z.L.R. 225 .... 4–04, 4–74n
Corporate Affairs Commission (South Australia) and Another v.
Australian Central
Crindle Investments and Others v. Wymes, and Others [1998]
2 I.L.R.M. 275 4–04
Credit Union [1985] 59 A.L.J.R. 785 .... 2–20, 2–22, 2–23n, 2–24
Horne v. Chester & Fein Property Developments Pty Ltd
[1987] A.C.L.R. 485 6–55
Kinsela v. Russell Pty (in liquidation) [1986] 4 N.S.W.L.R. 722 .... 5–20n
Kinwat Holdings Ltd. v. Platform Ltd [1982] Q.R. 370 4–19
Lee v. Evans [1964] 112 C.L.R. 276 .... 2–20, 2–21, 2–22, 2–23n
Mutual Home Loans Fund of Australia Ltd. v. Attorney General
NSW [1973] 130 C.L.R. 103 .... 2–12n

CANADA
Green v. Charterhouse Group Canada Ltd [1976] 68 D.L.R. 592 4–29

NEW ZEALAND
Kiwi Co-operative Dairies v. Securities [1995] 3 N.Z.L.R. 26 2–24
Orion Sound Ltd, re [1979] 2 N.Z.L.R. 574 .... 6–49n, 6–54, 6–55n
Walker Construction Co Ltd [1960] N.Z.L.R. 523 6–55

UNITED STATES
Johnson v. Wiggs [1971] 443 F.2d 803 (5th Cir.) 4–19
SEC v. Geon Industries Inc [1976] 531 F.2d 39(2d Cir.) 4–29
SEC v. Texas Gulf Sulphur [1968] 401 F.2d 833 (2d Cir.) 4–20
T.S.C. Industries Inc. v. Northway Inc [1976] 426 U.S. 438 4–24

NORTHERN IRELAND
Armagh Shoes, Re [1982] N.I. Reps 60 .... 5–62n

EUROPEAN COURTS

Case 13/61 Bosch v. Van Rijn [1962] E.C.R. 45 .... 9–31n
Case 6/72 Europemballage Corp. and Continental Can Co. Inc. v.
    Commission [1973] E.C.R. 215 .... 9–01n, 9–27n
Case 66/86 Ahmed Saed Flugreisen and Silver Line v. Z.B.U.W.
    [1989] E.C.R. 803 .... 9–31n
Cases 142 & 156/84 BAT and Reynolds v. Commission
    [1987] E.C.R. 4487 .... 9–01n, 9–19n
Case 68/94 & 30/95 France v. Commission [1998] E.C.R. I-1375 9–51
Case T-102/96 Gencor Ltd v. EC Commission, March 25, 1999 .... 9–35n

Table of Statutes

Bankruptcy Act 1988 .... 5–68n, 6–28
    s.75 .... 6–51n
Better Regulation of Stockbrokers (Ireland) Act 1799 39 Geo.III Chap. 40 1–02
Building Societies Act 1989 .... 9–02n
Central Bank Act 1989 .... 1–02, 1–04, 1–11, 9–01
    s.9 .... 9–02n
Companies Act 1963 .... 1–62, 5–10n, 6–09
    s.2 5–05
    s.2(1) 1–32n, 2–02n, 2–03n, 2–07n, 2–11, 2–12, 2–27, 2–29
    s.6 .... 5–06n
    s.8 .... 5–24, 5–28n, 5–30
    s.8(1) 5–06n, 5–19, 5–20, 5–21, 5–22, 5–23, 5–26
    s.8(2) 5–19n
    s.33(1)(c) 2–16n
    s.37 .... 5–45n
    s.43 .... 1–62n, 1–71n, 2–02n, 2–07n, 2–20
    s.43(4) 2–07n
    s.44 .... 1–24n, 1–34n, 2–03n, 5–05
    s.44(1) 1–63n, 1–71n, 2–02, 2–07n, 2–12, 2–31
    s.44(3) 1–71, 2–02, 2–07n, 2–12
    s.44(4) 2–02n, 2–07n
    s.44(4)(a) 2–30n
    s.44(4)(b) 2–16, 2–31n
    s.44(7) 1–32n, 2–02n
    s.44(7)(a) 2–18n, 2–23, 2–30n
    s.44(7)(b) 2–30n
    s.45 .... 1–62n, 1–71n, 2–02n
    s.45(1) 2–30n
    s.45(1)(a) 2–30n
    s.45(1)(b) 2–30n
    s.452(a) 2–30n
    s.46 .... 1–41n, 1–71n, 2–02n
    s.47 .... 1–62n, 1–72, 2–02, 2–13n
    s.49 .... 1–41n, 1–71n
    s.50 .... 1–41n, 1–62n, 1–71n
    s.51 .... 1–24n, 1–25n, 1–33n, 2–07n, 2–31
    s.51(1) 2–07n, 2–13, 2–31n
    s.51(2) 2–03n, 2–07n, 2–13, 2–31n

Companies Act 1963—*contd.*

s.51(2)(a) 2–13n
s.51(2)(b) 2–13n
s.52 .... 2–02n, 2–07n
s.56 .... 2–02n, 2–07n
s.57 .... 2–02n, 2–07n
s.60 5–20
s.61 .... 1–24n, 1–25n, 1–28n, 1–33n, 2–02n,
                                                          2–07n, 2–18, 2–22
s.61(1) 2–18, 2–19, 2–20, 2–22
s.61(2) 2–16n, 2–18, 2–20, 2–22, 2–23, 2–25
s.61(2)(a) 2–25
s.61(3) 2–26
s.72 6–09
s.77 6–09
s.81 5–05
s.98 .... 5–59, 5–64n, 6–10n
s.99 .... 5–05n, 5–55, 5–56, 5–57, 5–58, 7–29n,
                                              6–10n, 6–15, 6–32, 6–33, 6–67
s.99(1) 5–57
s.99(2) 6–33
s.100 .... 5–57n
s.106 .... 5–57n
s.155 .... 9–02n
s.155(5) 8–21n
s.194 .... 5–16n
s.241 .... 6–29n
s.275 .... 6–50n, 6–56, 6–60, 6–62
s.275(1) 6–49n, 6–60
s.285(2) 6–56n, 6–60, 6–61, 6–62
s.283 .... 6–28n, 6–51
s.284 .... 6–28n
s.285 .... 5–59n
s.285(7) 5–59n, 6–10n
s.286 .... 5–59, 6–09n, 6–79, 6–80, 6–81
s.286(5) 6–79n
s.288 .... 5–59n
s.288(1) 5–59n
s.294 .... 6–51n
s.297 .... 6–09n, 6–74, 6–76, 6–77, 6–78
s.297(1) 6–70, 6–72, 6–73
s.344 .... 2–02n
s.361(1) 1–62n, 1–71n, 2–10n
s.361(2) 1–62n, 1–71n
s.361(4) 2–10
s.361(5) 2–30n
s.361(8)(a) 2–30n
s.361(8)(b) 2–30n

Companies Act 1963—*contd.*

s.362 .... 1–62n, 1–71n, 2–30n
s.364 .... 1–62n, 1–71n, 2–10n
s.367(3) 1–71n, 2–10n
s.391 5–20
Third Schedule 1–62, 1–71, 1–77n, 2–02n,, 2–03, 2–06, 2–07n
Ninth Schedule 2–02n, 2–07n

Companies (Amendment) Act 1983

s.5(4) 5–098n
s.12 .... 1–18n
s.20 .... 1–29n
s.21 .... 2–16n
s.21(1) 2–16n
s.21(3) 2–16n
s.23 .... 1–29, 1–33
s.23(1) 1–29
s.23(3) 1–29n
s.23(4) 1–29
s.23(7) 1–29n
s.23(8) 1–29n
s.23(13) 1–29n
s.24 1–29
s.24(1) 1–29
s.24(2) 1–29
s.24(5) 1–29n
s.26(1) 2–28

Companies (Amendment) Act 1990 .... 5–66, 5–69, 5–71, 6–05, 6–73n

s.2 .... 5–66n
s.3 .... 5–66n, 5–67n
s.5 .... 5–66n, 5–67, 5–68, 5–70n
s.6 .... 5–67n
s.10 .... 5–71n
s.11 5–67
s.29 .... 5–71n

Companies Act 1990

s.3(2) 4–13n
s.30 4–57
s.30(3) 4–57
s.50 .... 1–42n
s.64 4–70
s.67 .... 1–85n, 4–110
s.79 .... 1–85n, 4–110
s.107 .... 4–08, 4–12, 4–12n, 4–13, 4–15, 4–16,
4–34n, 4–39n, 4–51n, 4–58n, 4–68, 4–86
s.108 .... 4–11, 4–15, 4–17, 4–23n, 4–27, 4–28,
4–32, 4–57, 4–63, 4–65, 4–67, 4–95
s.108(1) 4–18n, 4–31, 4–32, 4–33, 4–37, 4–39,
4–41, 4–43, 4–44, 4–47, 4–48, 4–49, 4–50, 4–51,
4–52, 4–59, 4–74, 4–75, 4–79n, 4–82, 4–83

Companies Act 1990—*contd.*
s.108(2) 4–32, 4–37, 4–39, 4–41, 4–43, 4–44, 4–47,
                                4–48, 4–49, 4–50, 4–51, 4–52, 4–59, 4–82
s.108(3) 4–33n, 4–41, 4–43, 4–45, 4–46, 4–47,
                                        4–50, 4–51, 4–52, 4–55, 4–85
s.108(4) 4–36n, 4–51, 4–56, 4–59n
s.108(5) 4–36n, 4–51n, 4–52, 4–53, 4–54,
                                          4–55, 4–56, 4–59n, 4–85
s.108(6) 4–58, 4–59, 4–60, 4–61, 4–62, 4–82
s.108(7) 4–60
s.108(8) 4–52, 4–61
s.108(9) 4–16n, 4–66, 4–68
s.108(10) 4–57, 4–69
s.108(11) 4–34, 4–36, 4–40, 4–69
s.108(12) 4–34n
s.108(13) 4–36, 4–42n, 4–51n, 4–52n
s.109 .... 4–02, 4–02n, 4–67, 4–73, 4–73, 4–74, 4–75
s.109(1) 4–74, 4–75, 4–76, 4–77, 4–79, 4–81
s.109(2) 4–78, 4–81
s.110 .... 4–63, 4–64
s.110(2) 4–64
s.110(3) 4–64
s.111 .... 4–82, 4–83
s.112 4–83
s.113 .... 4–67, 4–84
s.114 .... 4–67n, 4–84, 4–91
s.115 .... 4–87, 4–89
s.115(2) 4–87
s.115(3) 4–87
s.115(4) 4–87
s.115(5) 4–88
s.115(6) 4–88
s.115(7) 4–86
s.116 4–92
s.116(2) 4–92
s.117 .... 4–87n, 4–89
s.117(3) 4–89
s.117(5) 4–90
s.117(6) 4–90
s.118(1) 4–91
s.118(2) 4–91
s.132 .... 6–50n, 6–56n, 6–60
s.136 .... 5–59n
s.160(2)(c) 6–72n
s.180 4–64
s.223 4–62
s.251 .... 6–75n

Companies (Amendment) (No. 2) Bill 1999 (in progress) 5–66, 5–69
    s.5(b) 5–66n
    s.14 .... 5–66n
    s.14(b) 5–67n, 5–68, 5–70n
    s.18 .... 5–69n
    s.28 5–71
Companies (Amendment) (No. 8) Act 1999 .... 4–11, 4–11n, 4–95
    s.1(1) 4–98n
    s.3 4–110
Competition Act 1991 .... 9–05, 9–17
    s.4(1) 9–17, 9–18, 9–19, 9–20, 9–21, 9–23, 9–29, 9–30
    s.15(1) 9–02n
    s.17(4) 9–05n
    s.18 9–10
Competition Act 1996 .... 9–04n
Debtors (Ireland) Act 1840 5–29
Export Promotion Act 1959 .... 8–06n
Finance Act 1986 ....
    s.115 5–59
Finance Act 1992
    s.207 7–15
Finance Act 1995
    s.174 .... 5–59n, 6–10n
Industrial Development Act 1950 .... 8–04n
Industrial Development Act 1986 .... 8–03, 8–04, 8–08, 8–09
    s.2(1) 8–09
    s.3 .... 8–08n, 8–09, 8–10
    s.4 .... 8–10n
    s.14(3) 8–03n
    s.16 .... 8–23n
    s.16(1) 8–23
    s.16(1)(g) 8–23
    s.21 .... 8–22, 8–24
    s.21(1) 8–24n
    s.21(2) 8–10
    s.21(3) 8–10, 8–12, 8–17n, 8–21n, 8–22n
    s.21(4) 8–10, 8–12, 8–17n, 8–21n, 8–22n
    s.21(5)(a) 8–11n
    s.21(5)(b) 8–11n
    s.21(5)(c) 8–24n
    s.22 .... 8–12n, 8–24
    s.22(4) 8–12n
    s.23 .... 8–13n, 8–24
    s.24 .... 8–14n, 8–24
    s.25(4) 8–15n
    s.25 .... 8–09n, 8–15
    s.26 .... 8–16n
    s.27 .... 8–17n

Industrial Development Act 1986—*contd.*
    s.28 .... 8–18n
    s.29 8–19
    s.29(3)(b) 8–19n
    s.29(5) 8–19
    s.29(7) 8–19
    s.30 8–20
    s.31 .... 8–21n
    s.31(1) 8–21n
    s.31(1)(a) 8–21n
    s.31(1)(b) 8–21n
    s.31(4) 8–21n
    s.32 .... 8–22n, 8–24
    s.32(3) 8–22n
    s.33 8–24
    s.34 8–24
    s.35 8–25
    s.37 8–27
Industrial Development (Amendment) Act 1991 ....
    s.3 .... 8–21n
    s.7 .... 8–21n
    s.9 .... 8–11n
    s.9(d) 8–21n
    s.11 .... 8–21n
Industrial Development Act 1993 .... 8–02, 8–04n
    s.6 .... 8–02n
    s.6(1) 8–03
    s.6(2) 8–03n
    s.6(3) 8–03n
    s.7 8–05
    s.8 .... 8–04n
    s.9 .... 8–09n
    s.9(1) 8–04n, 8–23
    s.11 .... 8–03n
    s.12 .... 8–24n
    s.12(2) 8–09n, 8–15
    s.18 .... 8–04, 8–05n
Industrial Development Act 1995
    s. 3(3) 8–23
    s.4 8–21
    s.4(6) 8–21n
    s.4(8) 8–21n
    s.4(9)(a) 8–21n
    s.10 .... 8–28n
    s.10(3) 8–28
    s.10(4) 8–28
    s.10(5) 8–28

Industrial Development (Enterprise) Ireland
  Act 1998 .... 8–01n, 8–02n, 8–05, 8–07, 8–09n
    s.3 .... 8–07n
    s.4 .... 8–05n
    s.6 8–08
    s.7 .... 8–07n
    s.8 8–08
    s.9(2) 8–04n
    s.23 8–08
    s.25(1) 8–07
    s.26 .... 8–21n
    s.33 .... 8–03n
    s.34(1) 8–15n, 8–24n
    s.34(2) 8–09n
    s.34(2)(j) 8–21n
    s.35 .... 8–32n
    s.44(2) 8–04n
    s.44(3) 8–04n, 8–09n
    s.45(1)(a) 8–03n
    s.45(1)(c) 8–03n
    s.48(1)(b) 8–03n
Investment Intermediaries Act 1995 .... 1–03n, 1–08n
    s.37 4–51
Investor Compensation Act 1998 .... 1–06n
Irish Takeover Panel Act 1997 .... 9–01, 9–70, 9–73
    s.1(1) 9–72n, 9–73n
    s.1(2) 9–72n
    s.2 .... 9–79n
    s.3 .... 9–82n
    s.5 .... 9–72, 9–73, 9–86n
    s.6 .... 9–82n
    s.8 .... 9–73n
    s.8(2) 9–78
    s.8(3) 9–72n, 9–76n
    s.8(5) 9–72n
    s.9 9–83
    s.9(1) 9–83n
    s.9(2) 9–83n
    s.9(3) 9–83n
    s.10
    s.10(1) 9–84n
    s.10(2) 9–84n
    s.10(3) 9–84n
    s.10(4) 9–84n
    s.11(1) 9–85n
    s.11(2) 9–85n
    s.11(3) 9–85n
    s.11(5) 9–85n

Irish Takeover Panel Act 1997—*contd.*
        s.12(1) 9–83
        s.13(1) 9–86n
        s.13(3) 9–86n
        s.13(5) 9–86n
        s.13(7) 9–86n
        s.14 .... 9–86n
        s.17(2) 9–87n
        s.17(3) 9–87n
        s.20(1) 9–87n
        s.20(5) 9–87n
        s.25(1) 9–85n, 9–87n
        s.25(2) 9–85n, 9–87
        s.25(3) 9–85n, 9–87n
Local Government Act 1941 .... 9–02n
Mergers Act
        s.1(1) 9–02n
        s.1(3) 9–02
        s.2(1) 9–03
        s.2(5) 9–03
        s.3 9–16
        s.3(1) 9–09
        s.5 .... 9–04n, 9–53n
        s.5(1) 9–04, 9–16
        s.5(2) 9–06, 9–16
        s.5(3) 9–16
        s.5(4) 9–04
        s.6(1) 9–07
        s.7 .... 9–05, 9–10
        s.8(2) 9–05, 9–10
        s.9 .... 9–17n
        s.12 9–12
        s.13 9–13
        s.13(3) 9–13n
        s.13(4) 9–13n
        s.13(6) 9–13
Mergers, Takeovers and Monopolies (Control) Act 1978 9–01
National Development Corporation Act 1986 .... 8–21n
Shannon Free Airport Development Company Limited Act 1959 .... 8–32n
Statute of Frauds 1695
        s.6 7–22
Stockbrokers (Ireland) Act 1918 .... 1–02n
Stock Exchange Act 1995 .... 1–03, 1–04, 1–05, 9–69
        s.3 .... 1–02n
        s.3(1) 1–04n, 1–05n
        s.4 .... 1–02n
        s.8 .... 1–04n
        s.8(4) 1–04n

Stock Exchange Act 1995—*contd.*
   s.9 .... 1–04n
   s.9(5)(f) 1–04n
   s.9(5)(g) 1–07n
   s.9(13) 1–07n
   s.9(16) 1–07n
   s.10 .... 1–04n
   s.11 .... 1–04n
   s.13 .... 1–04n
   s.14 .... 1–04n
   s.16 .... 1–05n
   s.17 .... 1–05n
   s.18 .... 1–05n
   s.20 .... 1–05n
   s.20(3) 1–05n
   s.21 .... 1–05n
   s.22 .... 1–05n
   s.24 .... 1–06n
   s.26 .... 1–06n
   s.28 .... 1–04n
   s.28(5) 1–05n
   s.29 .... 1–08n
   s.38 .... 1–04n, 1–06, 4–111
   s.38(1) 1–06n
   s.38(3) 4–111
   s.57 .... 1–08n
Stock Transfer Act 1963 .... 5–05n
Supreme Court of Judicature(Ireland) Act 1877 .... 7–24n
   s.4 .... 7–07n
   s.5 .... 7–07n
   s.25 .... 7–09n
   s.25(6) 7–07n
   s.28(6) 6–35n, 7–02, 7–07, 7–08, 7–09, 7–10, 7–11,
        7–12, 7–13, 7–14, 7–15, 7–16, 7–18, 7–19, 7–21,
        7–22, 7–24, 7–25, 7–26, 7–27, 7–28, 7–29n
   s.27 .... 7–06, 7–07n
Taxes Consolidation Act 1997 .... 8–09n
   s.443 .... 8–09n, 8–15, 8–32n
   s.443(10) 8–09n
   s.445 ....8–09n, 8–32n
   s.446 .... 8–09n
Trade and Marketing Promotion Act 1991 .... 8–07n
Trade and Marketing Promotion Act 1994 .... 8–07n
Trustee Savings Bank Act 1989 .... 9–02n

STATUTORY INSTRUMENTS

Companies Act 1990 (Insider Dealing) Regulations 1992
(S.I. No. 131 of 1992) 4–11
Companies (Stock Exchange) Regulations 1995
(S.I. No. 310 of 1995) 4–13n, 4–86, 4–93n
European Communities (Companies) Regulations 1973
(S.I. No. 163 of 1973)
        Regulation 3 5–52
        Regulation 4 .... 5–49n
        Regulation 6 .... 5–06n, 5–22, 5–23, 5–28n, 5–48,
                                                        5–49, 5–50, 5–51, 5–52
        Regulation 10 5–49
European Communities (Stock Exchange) Regulations 1984
(S.I. No. 282 of 1984) 1–01n, 1–13n, 1–14n, 1–17n,
                                                        1–34, 1–41, 1–81n, 2–09
        Reg 3(1) 1–81n
        Reg 3(2) 1–14n, 1–81n, 1–86n
        Reg 4(1) 1–34, 1–43n
        Reg 4(2) 1–41
        Reg 4(3) 1–41
        Reg 7 .... 1–14n, 1–55n, 1–81n
        Reg 7(1) 1–14n, 1–34n, 1–42n
        Reg 8(1) 1–42n
        Reg 8(2) 1–42n
        Reg 10 1–17
        Reg 12(2) 1–62n, 2–08n, 2–10n, 2–15
        Reg 12(3) 1–62n, 2–08n, 2–15
        Reg 13(1) 1–42n, 1–56n
        Reg 13(3) 1–42n
        Second Schedule 1–21n, 1–22n, 1–38n
European Communities (Stock Exchange) (Amendment) Regulations 1991
(S.I. No. 18 of 1991) 1–01n, 1–14n, 1–34n, 1–35n, 1–59n
        Reg 3(3) 1–59n, 1–66n
European Communities (Transferable Securities and Stock Exchange)
Regulations 1992 (S.I. No. 202 of 1992) 1–01n, 1–14n, 1–36n, 1–61n,
                1–63n, 1–64n, 1–65n, 1–69, 1–77n, 2–04, 2–09, 2–10, 2–14n
        Reg 6 .... 1–69n, 2–02n, 2–12n, 2–14
        Reg 7(a) 2–32n
        Reg 7(b) 2–32n
        Reg 8 .... 1–71, 2–05, 2–10n
        Reg 8(1) 1–69
        Reg 8(2) 1–71n
        Reg 8(3) 1–71n
        Reg 8(4) 1–71n, 1–77n, 2–30n
        Reg 9(1) 1–72, 1–75n, 1–76n
        Reg 11 .... 1–72n
        Reg 12 .... 1–72n

European Communities (Transferable Securities and Stock Exchange)
Regulations 1992—*contd.*
Reg 13 .... 1–72n
Reg 19 .... 1–63n, 1–72n, 1–76n, 1–77n, 1–78n
Reg 21 2–09
Reg 21(3) 1–71, 2–02n, 2–05, 2–10n
Reg 21(4) 1–71, 2–05
Reg 22(3) 2–14, 2–30
Reg 22(4) 2–14, 2–30
Third Schedule 1–69n, 1–77n, 2–13n, 2–32n
para 3 .... 1–78n
para 4 .... 1–77n
para 5 .... 1–77n
European Communities (Stock Exchange) (Amendment) Regulations, 1994
(S.I. No. 234 of 1994) 1–01n, 1–14n, 1–34n, 1–36n, 1–46n, 1–49n, 1–60n
Industrial Development (Enterprise Ireland) Act 1998 (Establishment Day)
Order 1998 (S.I. No. 252 of 1998) 8–05n, 8–07n
Industrial Development (Service Industries) Order 1998
(S.I. No. 253 of 1998) 8–08n, 8–09n, 8–10n, 8–15n
Merger or Takeover (Notification) Fee Regulations
(S.I. No. 381 of 1996) 9–04n
Stock Exchange Act 1995 (Commencement) Order 1995
(S.I. No. 206 of 1995) 1–03n
Stock Exchange Act 1995 (Commencement) Order (No. 2) 1995
(S.I. No. 255 of 1995) 1–03n
Supervision of Credit Institutions, Stock Exchange Member Firms and
Investment Business Firms Regulations 1996
(S.I. No. 267 of 1996) 1–08n
Reg 2(1) 1–08n
Reg 3(2) 1–08n
Reg 4(2) 1–08n

UK LEGISLATION

Companies Act 1985 .... 5–58n
s.396 .... 5–56, 5–58, 5–58n
Companies Securities (Insider Dealing) Act 1985
s.3 .... 4–09n
Criminal Justice Act 1993
s.52(2) 4–51n
s.52(3) 4–14, 4–16n
s.53 .... 4–09n
s.53(2) 4–51n
s.56(1) 4–18n, 4–28n
s.57 4–40
s.57(1) 4–38, 4–39, 4–49n
s.57(2) 4–39, 4–49n

Criminal Justice Act 1993—*contd.*
  s.58(2) 4–18n, 4–22
  s.58(3) 4–18n, 4–22n
  s.63(2) 4–85
Factors Acts 1889, 52 & 53 Victoria 7–01n
Financial Services Act 1986 .... 1–02n, 1–12
Insolvency Act 1986
  s.40 5–64

Law of Property Act 1925, 15 Geo. 5 .... 7–07n
  s. 136 .... 7–09n, 7–29
  s.136(1) 7–09n, 7–12n, 7–13n, 7–28, 7–28n, 7–29

EUROPEAN TREATIES/LEGISLATION

EC Treaty
  Art 81 .... 9–01, 9–31, 9–34, 9–60, 9–61, 9–64
  Art 81(3) 9–64
  Art 82 .... 9–01, 9–31, 9–60

Regulations
Council Regulation 4064/89, 21 December, 1989 .... 9–01n, 9–31
Council Regulation 1301/97, 30 June, 1997 .... 9–01n

Directives
Admissions Directive - Council Dir 79/279/EEC,
  March 5, 1979 .... 1–13, 1–64n, 1–81n, 1–82, 1–86
    Art 1 1–14
    Art 2 .... 1–14n
    Art 3 1–14
    Art 4.2 .... 1–81n
    Art 5 1–14
    Art 5.2 .... 1–81n
    Art 5.3 .... 1–15n, 1–81
    Art 6 .... 1–15n
    Art 7 .... 1–14n
    Art 8 .... 1–14n, 1–22n, 1–81n
    Art 9 .... 1–14n
    Art 9(3) 1–15n
    Art 10 .... 1–14n, 1–15
    Art 11 .... 1–15n
    Art 12 .... 1–16n
    Art 13 .... 1–16, 1–81, 1–81n
    Art 14 .... 1–16n
    Art 15 .... 1–17n, 1–17
    Art 16 .... 1–20n
    Art 17 .... 1–81, 1–81n

Admissions Directive - Council Dir 79/279/EEC—*contd.*

Art 18 1–68
Art 18(1) 1–68n
Art(2) 1–68n
Art 20 .... 1–13n
Schedule A 1–18, 1–19
Schedule A(I) para. 1 .... 1–18n
Schedule A(I) para 2 .... 1–18n
Schedule A(I) para 3 .... 1–18n
Schedule A(I) para 4 .... 1–19n
Schedule A (II) para 1 .... 1–18n
Schedule A (II) para 2 .... 1–18n
Schedule A (II) para 3 .... 1–19n
Schedule A (II) para 4 .... 1–19n
Schedule A (II) para 6 .... 1–19n
Schedule A (II) para 7 .... 1–19n
Schedule B 1–21, 1–22
Schedule B (A)(I) 1–21n
Schedule B (A)(II) para 1 .... 1–22n
Schedule B (A)(II) para 2 .... 1–22n
Schedule B (A)(II) para 3 .... 1–22n
Schedule B (A)(II) para 4 .... 1–22n
Schedule B (A)(II) para 5 .... 1–22n
Schedule B (A)(III) para 1 .... 1–22n
Schedule B (A)(III) para 2 .... 1–22n
Schedule C 1–81
Schedule C para 2 .... 1–83n, 1–84n
Schedule C para 4 .... 1–83n, 1–84n
Schedule C para 5 .... 1–83n, 1–84n
Schedule C para 6 .... 1–84n
Schedule D 1–81
Schedule D(A) 1–81n
            para 1 .... 1–84n
            para 4 .... 1–85n
            para 5 .... 1–85n
Schedule D(B) 1–81n
Banking Directive - Council Dir 77/780/EEC 9–41n
Banking Directive - Council Dir 89/646/EEC 9–41n
Capital Adequecy Directive 93/6/EC, March 15, 1993 1–05
Insider Dealing Directive - Council Dir 89/592/EEC,
    November 13, 1989 .... 4–01, 4–07, 4–64n
Art 1.1 .... 4–17, 4–18, 4–23n, 4–26n, 4–30
Art 1.2 .... 4–12n
Art 2 4–31
Art 2.3 4–16
Art 3 .... 4–51n, 4–52
Art 4 4–46
Art 5 4–11
Art 6 .... 4–26, 4–53

Listing Particulars directive - Council Dir 80/390/EEC,
    March 17 1980 .... 1–01, 1–13, 1–34, 1–35, 1–36n, 1–38n, 1–42,
                                   1–46n, 1–51, 1–57, 1–59, 1–60, 1–64n, 1–67,
                                    1–70, 1–72, 1–73, 1–77, 1–78, 1–80, 2–08
        Art 1.1 ....1–34n, 1–63n
        Art 1.2 .... 1–34n
        Art 2 .... 1–34n
        Art 4 1–34
        Art 4.1 .... 1–41, 1–43n
        Art 4.2 1–41
        Art 5 .... 1–37n
        Art 5.1 1–34
        Art 6 .... 1–44, 1–49n
        Art 6.1 ....1–45n, 1–48n
        Art 6.4 .... 1–46n, 1–49n, 1–67n
        Art 6.5 .... 1–36n, 1–47n, 1–50n
        Art 7(a) 1–54n
        Art 7(b) 1–54n
        Art 11 .... 1–63n
        Art 13 4–71
        Art 17 .... 1–38n
        Art 18 .... 1–42n, 1–56
        Art 18(2) 1–56n
        Art 20 .... 1–52n, 1–56n, 1–57
        Art 22 .... 1–52, 1–56n
        Art 23 .... 1–43n
        Art 24 1–59, 1–60, 1–61, 1–64, 1–65, 1–66n, 1–67n, 1–80n, 1–81n
        Schedule A 1–34n, 1–37
        Schedule B 1–34n, 1–37, 1–39n, 1–40n
        Schedule C 1–34n, 1–37, 1–40n
Interim Reports Directive - Council Dir 82/121/EEC,
    February 15, 1982 .... 1–13, 1–14n
Investment Services Directive Council Dir
    93/22/EC 1–03, 1–05, 1–12, 4–111n
Investor Compensation Directive Council/EP Dir 97/9/EC,
    March 3, 1997 .... 1–06n
Prospectus Directive - Council Dir 89/298/EEC,
    April 17, 1989 .... 1–01, 1–12, 1–14n, 1–26, 1–28n, 1–33,
                                   1–61n, 1–63, 1–69, 1–71, 1–72, 1–77, 2–04, 2–05
        Art 1 .... 2–31, 2–32
        Art 1.1 ....2–05n, 2–07n, 2–09n, 2–14, 2–14n, 2–32
        Art 1.2 ....1–69n, 2–07n, 2–14n, 2–18n, 2–32
        Art 2.1 .... 1–25n, 2–06n, 2–32
        Art 2.2 2–32
        Art 3 ....2–07n, 2–32n
        Art 3(e)... 2–05n, 2–07n, 2–32n
        Art 4 .... 1–36n, 1–63n, 1–69n, 2–07n, 2–12, 2–31n, 2–32n
        Art 5 2–32

Prospectus Directive - Council Dir 89/298/EEC—*contd.*
      Art 6 1–77
      Art 7 .... 1–36, 1–64, 1–72n, 1–77, 1–78n, 1–80
      Art 8 .... 1–36n, 1–63n, 1–64, 1–72n, 1–77, 1–80
      Art 8.2 .... 1–77n
      Art 9 .... 1–72n
      Art 10 .... 1–78n
      Art. 11 .... 1–10n, 1–36n, 1–71, 1–73, 1–75, 1–78
      Art 11.2 .... 1–73n, 1–74n
      Art 11.4 .... 1–74n
      Art 11.7 .... 1–75n
      Art 11.8 .... 1–75n, 1–76n
      Art 12 .... 1–36n, 1–63n, 1–64, 1–77, 1–78n, 1–78n, 1–80
      Art 13 .... 1–72n, 1–76
      Art 13.1 .... 1–76n
      Art 13.2 .... 1–76n
      Art 14 .... 1–72n,
      Art 15 .... 1–72n
      Art 20 1–78
      Art 20.2 .... 1–80n
      Art 21 .... 1–77, 1–78
      Art 21.3 .... 1–78n
      Art 21.5 .... 1–77n
Council Dir 68/151/EEC,
   March 9, 1968 .... 5–21, 5–32n
      Art 9 .... 5–22, 5–23
      Ar t9(2) 5–48
Council Dir 77/780/EEC 1–05n
      Art 2 .... 2–32n
Council Dir 90/211/EEC,
   April 23, 1990 .... 1–01n, 1–14n, 1–34n, 1–36, 1–64n
      Art 2 .... 1–36n, 1–64n, 1–80n
Council Dir 87/345/EEC,
   June 22, 1987 .... 1–01, 1–14n, 1–34n, 1–35, 1–59, 1–59n, 1–60n, 1–67n
      Art 1 .... 1–64n
Council/EP Dir 94/18/EC,
   May 30, 1994 ... 1–01n, 1–14n, 1–34n, 1–35, 1–36n, 1–46, 1–49n, 1–60, 1–67
      Art 1 .... 1–46n, 1–49n, 1–50n
Council/EP Dir 95/26/EC 1–08

1

Admissions, Listing and Prospectuses

Introduction 5
I. The Stock Exchange and Listing Markets 6
   A. Short History 6
      (1) The International Stock Exchange of the United
          Kingdom and RoI 6
      (2) The Investment Services Directive 7
      (3) Central Bank as regulator 8
          (a) Approved stock exchanges 8
          (b) Member Firms 10
   B. The Markets 14
   C. Domestic markets 14
   D. Foreign markets 16
II. Admission Conditions – the Admissions Directive and
    Yellow Book Regime 18
    (1) Admissions Directive and the Stock Exchange
        Listing Rules 19
        (a) Role of the Stock Exchange as "competent
            authority" 19
        (b) Powers of the Stock Exchange over Admission
            to Listing 20
            (i) Power to impose additional admission
                conditions or refuse admission 20
            (ii) Enforcement powers 21
            (iii) Judicial review 22
    (2) Admission Conditions 23
        (a) Applicant Conditions (shares) 23
        (b) Debt Securities 26
    (3) Shares, Debt Securities or Issuers which Fall Outside
        the Admissions Directive 28
III. Different Methods of Listing Securities 29
    A. Methods 29
    (1) Offer for Sale or Subscription 29
    (2) Placing 30

    (3) Intermediaries Offer 32
    (4) Introduction 33
    (5) Rights Issue 33
        (a) Yellow Book Rules 33
        (b) Statutory pre-emption rights/Yellow Book...............35
    (6) Open Offer 37
    (7) Acquisition or Merger Issue 37
    (8) Capitalisation Issue 37
    (9) Issue for Cash/Conversions of Securities of one
           class into securities of another class/Exercise of
           Options or Warrants to subscribe securities 38

IV. Listing 38
  A. Principles Underlying the Listing Particulars Directive/
       Yellow Book 38
    (1) The provision of certain limited minimum information
           and the Duty to Allow Informed Assessment 38
    (2) Principle of Mutual Recognition 40
  B. Contents of Listing Particulars 43
    (1) Corresponding Framework: Yellow Book and Listing
           Particulars Directive 43
        (a) Shares or convertible debt securities 44
        (b) Debt securities 47
        (c) Certificates representing shares 48
        (d) Responsibility statement and
            responsibility letters 49
  C. Approval of Listing Particulars 51
    (1) Principle of prior approval 51
    (2) Supplementary Particulars 52
  D. Exemption from Requirement to Publish Listing
       Particulars...53
    (1) Exemptions which may be granted 53
        (a) Previously published documents 53
        (b) Three years' admission to listing in another
            Member State 54
        (c) Admission of a DCM company 54
    (2) Exempt Listing Particulars 55
    (3) Exemptions available except in "exceptional
           circumstances" 56
    (4) Summary Particulars 57
    (5) Shelf Registration 48
    (6) Omission of information from the Listing
           Particulars...59

V. Listing Application Procedures 60
  A. Time for Application 60

B. Publication and Circulation of Listing Particulars 61
**VI. The Legal Principles Underlying the Development of EC
     Listings Legal Framework** 63
A. Mutual Recognition of Listing Particulars 63
B. Listing Particulars and Prospectuses 66
     (1) Listing Particulars and the Companies Act 1963 67
     (2) Mutual Recognition of Prospectus as
          Listing Particulars 67
C. Mutual Co-Operation 71
VII. Prospectus Directive Regime 72
A. Overlapping Regimes...72
B. Publication and Registration of Prospectus 75
C. Content of Prospectus 76
D. Omission of Information...78
E. The Prospectus Directive and the Principle of Mutual
     Recognition 78
     (1) Mutual Recognition of prospectuses...................................78
     (2) Mutual Recognition of Prospectus as
          Listing Particulars 82
VIII. Continuing Obligations of Listed Companies 83
A. Exchange has Oower to Set Additional or More Stringent
     Requirements 83
B. Main Principles..84
C. Additional Requirements in Specific Transactions 87

1

Admission, Listing and Prospectuses

Introduction

1–01 Since the late 1970s European Community Directives have laid down a series of similar principles to further the objective of constructing a legal framework, the aim of which is to require Member States to ensure that certain minimum conditions are satisfied whenever an issuer of securities seeks to offer securities to the public or have them admitted to listing. In this regard, the legal regime put in place by the Admissions[1] Directive, the Listing Particulars[2] Directive and the Prospectus[3] Directive will be considered later in the Chapter. Undoubt-

---

[1] Council Directive 79/279/EEC of 5 March 1979 co-ordinating the conditions for the admission of securities to official Stock Exchange listing [1979] O.J. L66/21 (the "Admissions Directive") as implemented by the European Communities (Stock Exchange) Regulations 1984 (S.I. No. 282 of 1984).

[2] Council Directive 80/390/EEC of 17 March 1980 co-ordinating the requirements for the drawing up, scrutiny and distribution of the listing particulars to be published for the admission of securities to official Stock Exchange listing [1980] O.J. L.100/1 (the "Listing Particulars Directive") as implemented by the European Communities (Stock Exchange) Regulations 1984 (S.I. No. 282 of 1984) which came into effect on January 1, 1985; as amended by Council Directive 87/345/EEC of June 22, 1987 [1987] O.J. L.185/81 as implemented by the European Communities (Stock Exchange) (Amendment) Regulations 1991 (S.I. No. 18 of 1991); and as further amended by Council Directive 90/211/EEC of April 23, 1990 [1990] O.J. L.112/24 as implemented by the European Communities (Transferable Securities and Stock Exchange) Regulations 1992 (S.I. No. 202 of 1992); and as further amended by Council and European Parliament Directive no. 94/18/EC of May 30, 1994 [1994] O.J. L.135/1 as implemented by the European Communities (Stock Exchange) (Amendment) Regulations, 1994 (S.I. No. 234 of 1994).

[3] Council Directive 89/298/EEC of April 17, 1989 [1989] O.J. L.124/8 co-ordinating the requirements for the drawing up, scrutiny and distribution of the prospectus to be published when transferable securities are offered to the public, as implemented by the European Communities (Transferable securities and Stock Exchange Regulations) 1992 (S.I. No. 202 of 1992). Note that the types of offer to which the Prospectus Directive does, and does not, apply to are further considered in Chap. 2 in the context of "Offers to the Public". In this Chapter consid-

edly the European legislation has influenced domestic regulatory regimes, both statutory and non-statutory, ranging from the Companies
Acts to the listing rules of the Stock Exchange. The overall impression
is that this amalgam of European laws, domestic company laws and
non-statutory rules[4] have all combined to bring about a somewhat complicated legal framework, which both issuers of securities and regulatory authorities must utilise. However, before considering the salient
points and issues arising out of the European legal framework and its
translation into the domestic context, it may be useful to give a brief
account of the separation of the Irish and London Stock Exchanges, as
well as an overview of some of the different markets available to issuers of securities.

I. THE STOCK EXCHANGE AND LISTING MARKETS

A. SHORT HISTORY

(1)   The International Stock Exchange of the United Kingdom and RoI

1–02   A stock exchange has operated in Dublin since 1799 when the
Stock Exchange was established by Act of Parliament in 1799.[5] In 1971
the Dublin Exchange merged with an exchange which had operated in
Cork since the latter part of the last century, to form the Irish Stock
Exchange. Shortly afterwards in 1973, the Irish Stock Exchange and
the London Stock Exchange merged to form the International Stock
Exchange of the United Kingdom and the Republic of Ireland Limited.
The Irish part of the new Exchange was known as the Irish Unit of the
International Stock Exchange.[6]
    The supervision of the Irish Unit of the Stock Exchange was super-

---

eration of the Prospectus Directive will be largely confined to its role in the
promotion of mutual recognition as between prospectuses and listing particulars (see further sections V and VI of this chapter).
[4] *e.g.* Yellow Book listing rules of the Stock Exchange.
[5] An Act for the Better Regulation of Stockbrokers (Ireland) Act 1799 39 Geo.III
Chap. 40 (Ir.). This Act was expressly repealed by s.4 of the Stock Exchange Act
1995, as was the Stockbrokers (Ireland) Act 1918. The former Act set up the
Stock Exchange which initially concentrated on dealings in gilts and the latter
Act permitted the Stock Exchange to regulate the fixing of commission for gilt
dealings.
[6] Amongst the main attractions of the merger was that the Irish securities industry had access to the expertise of the London market, investors' confidence was
strengthened as the London Exchange operates one of the largest regulated markets in the world, and listed companies on the Irish Unit seeking investors were
perceived to be more internationally "acceptable" because of the Unit's links to
the London Exchange.

vised under the rules of the International Stock Exchange.[7] So far as local operational matters were concerned, the Irish Unit largely regulated its own affairs. The listing rules applied by the Irish Unit were the "Yellow Book" rules used by the London Exchange, with a supplement attaching for adaptation to Irish conditions and legal requirements, colloquially known as the "Green Pages."[8] Even after the separation of the two Exchanges in 1995, the Irish Stock Exchange continues to use the Yellow Book rules, with appropriately updated Green Pages for adaptation to local requirements.[9] One major effect brought about by the 1995 separation was that it established the Central Bank as the regulatory supervisory authority for the Stock Exchange in its regulation of member firms, and indeed for any other stock exchange[10] which may subsequently be established in Ireland. However the Stock Exchange is autonomous in so far as its functions as a listing authority are concerned.

(2) The Investment Services Directive: role in the separation

1–03 The main reason underlying the separation of the two Stock Exchanges can be found in the requirements of the European Community Investment Services Directive.[11] One of the main objectives of that Directive is to provide for the mutual recognition of authorisation and prudential supervision systems for investment services providers in the European Community. The grant of authorisation to an investment services firm in one Member State will allow that firm provide investment services throughout the Community's territory without the firm having to obtain separate authorisation in each Member State in which it wishes to operate.[12] This regime operates using the so-called 'Home State' supervision principle, which is often used in EC legal frameworks as a means of facilitating companies and firms to operate in other Member States. Once an undertaking's Home State supervisory body has authorised the undertaking to operate on the basis that it complies

---

[7] These rules were enacted into law by the U.K. Financial Services Act 1986, although they had no statutory application in Ireland.

[8] While the relevant Minister in Ireland has the power to approve the Green Pages, the Minister cannot require changes to be made.

[9] For an explanation of the background to the separation, see para. 1–03 below.

[10] Note however that the term "stock exchange" defined in subs. 3(1) of the 1995 Act does not include any exchange wholly or mainly in financial futures or options regulated by the Central Bank pursuant to the Central Bank Act 1989.

[11] The Investment Services Directive (Council Directive 93/22/EEC [1993] O.J. L.141) was implemented in relation to the Stock Exchange member firms by the Stock Exchange Act 1995; and in relation to other investment services providers by the Investment Intermediaries Act 1995.

[12] Either on a cross border basis or by establishing a branch.

with certain common minimum standards applicable under a relevant Directive, then the undertaking is authorised to provide services in other Member States without requiring fresh authorisation to operate in other Member States.[13]

As the regime created by the Investment Services Directive is dependent on Home State authorisation, a supervision and authorisation body is required in each Member State. This posed a difficulty in Ireland as the member firms of the Irish Exchange were supervised, not by a domestic supervisor, but by the Securities and Futures Authority [SFA] based in the United Kingdom.[14] While the Directive would not have prevented the member firms being regulated by two separate regulators, one in the United Kingdom and another in Ireland, the legal difficulties that could arise out of such a dual regime were thought to be considerable. Consequently, it was felt that as a proper operation of the Directive's Regime would require the designation of an autonomous compentent authority in the State, it was also considered appropriate that the separation of the two Exchanges should come about in order to facilitate the operation of this new regime, even though not strictly required by the Directive. Seen in this light, the 'split' from London was not driven so much by business reasons, as by the need to give legal certainty and efficacy. Accordingly, the Stock Exchange Act 1995 was enacted.[15] Under this Act, the Irish Stock Exchange became an autonomous entity, and the new supervisory authority for the Irish Stock Exchange and its member firms is the Central Bank.

(3) Central Bank as regulator

(a) Approved Stock Exchanges

1–04 The Stock Exchange Act 1995 defines a stock exchange as an organised financial market whose members provide an investment service[16] in respect of investment instruments,[17] but excluding any ex-

---

[13] Though of course, the undertaking will have to comply with any local requirements, provided they are compatible with E.C. law. (Note also that the term "undertaking" collectively includes companies and firms).

[14] Although the activities of the member firms would also come under the scrutiny of the Irish Stock Exchange's Regulation Department.

[15] Various provisions of the 1995 Act came into force by virtue of the Stock Exchange Act 1995 (Commencement) Order 1995 (S.I. No. 206 of 1995) and the Stock Exchange Act 1995 (Commencement) Order (No. 2) 1995 (S.I. No. 255 of 1995) with effect from August 1, 1995 and 29 September 1995 respectively.

[16] s.3(1) of the Stock Exchange Act 1995 defines "investment services" as *inter alia* dealings in investment instruments on behalf of others or on own account. "Investment instruments" is given an extensive definition and includes *inter alia* transferable securities, units or shares in UCITS, financial futures contracts, swaps, debentures, Government or public securities, etc. However, it does not

change involved wholly or mainly in financial futures or options falling within the Central Bank Act 1989. Under the Stock Exchange Act 1995, the new regulatory authority for the Irish Stock Exchange[18] is the Central Bank. The Central Bank is charged under the Act with administering the system of regulation and supervision of stock exchanges and their member firms in accordance with the Act in order to promote the maintenance of the proper and orderly regulation and supervision of approved Stock Exchanges, the orderly regulation of financial markets and the protection of investors.[19] No person shall operate or establish a stock exchange in the State unless it is an approved exchange.[20]

When considering whether to approve a proposed exchange, the Central Bank must be satisfied as to a wide range of matters, such as ensuring that the proposed exchange is a company incorporated under the Companies Acts, that it has the minimum level of capital set by the Central Bank, and that its controlling shareholders are "suitable" persons.[21] Furthermore the registered office and head office of the proposed exchange must be located in the State.[22] Its board must include a number of persons independent of the Stock Exchange and its member firms for the purposes of protecting the common good, investors and the maintenance of proper codes of conduct and practice.[23] The Central Bank may attach such conditions to a grant of approval as it sees fit.[24] A right of appeal to the Minister is also provided in the event that the Central Bank refuses approval to a proposed exchange.[25] The Central Bank may revoke the approval of an approved exchange, although in certain circumstances it must seek the approval of the High Court

---

include cheques or banker's drafts, banknotes or any instrument acknowledging or creating indebtedness for a contract to pay for goods or services. See further subs.3(1).

[17] *ibid.* for definition of "investment instruments."

[18] And also the member firms that work on the Stock Exchange: see further below.

[19] Stock Exchange Act 1995, s.28. S. 28 also provides that the Central Bank, in pursuing the above objectives, must be mindful of any guidelines issued by the Minister for Finance.

[20] Stock Exchange Act 1995, s.8. However, note that s.8(4) provides that "established in the State" excludes any stock exchange which provides services electronically to Irish clients where the exchange's head office or registered office is outside the State.

[21] For a comprehensive list of relevant factors that the Central Bank must be satisfied as to, see further s.9 of the Stock Exchange Act 1995.

[22] Stock Exchange Act, s.9(5)(f).

[23] Stock Exchange Act 1995, s.9, such codes of conduct being codes drawn up by either the Central Bank or the relevant Stock Exchange pursuant to s.38 of the Act.

[24] Stock Exchange Act 1995, s.11.

[25] Stock Exchange Act 1995, s.13.

before effecting the revocation.[26] The Irish Stock Exchange was deemed to be an approved exchange on the coming into force of the 1995 Act.[27]

(b) Member Firms

1–05   Member firms are defined as any person who is a member of an approved stock exchange and whose regular occupation or business is the provision of investment services on a professional basis on or off the floor of the exchange.[28] The Central Bank is the body in the State charged with member firm approval under the 1995 Act, as well as being designated as the "competent authority" for the purposes of the Investment Services Directive[29] and also the Capital Adequacy Directive.[30] The Act provides that it shall be unlawful to operate as a member firm unless duly authorised either by the Central Bank, or by a competent authority in another Member State pursuant to the Investment Services Directive.[31] Existing member firms at the time of the coming into force of the 1995 Act continue to be member firms unless the Central Bank revokes their authorisation.[32]

The Central Bank will not authorise a proposed member firm unless the firm is a company incorporated by statute or under the Companies Acts, a company formed under Royal Charter or a formally constituted partnership.[33] The Central Bank may make the authorisation subject to such conditions as it sees fit, or amend the terms of authorisation at any time.[34] When considering authorisation requests, the Central Bank must be satisfied as to a range of matters.[35] *Inter alia*, the

---

[26] As to the precise circumstances when the High Court's permission will be required, see s.14 of the Stock Exchange Act 1995.

[27] Stock Exchange Act 1995, s.10. The Exchange's full title is the Irish Stock Exchange Limited, a company incorporated under the Companies Acts pursuant to s.10 of the 1995 Act.

[28] For the precise parameters of this definition, see further s.3(1) of the Stock Exchange Act 1995.

[29] Council Directive 93/22/EC.

[30] Stock Exchange Act 1995, s.16. As part of its regulatory functions, the Central Bank is charged with ensuring that approved member firms satisfy the capital adequacy requirements of the Capital Adequacy Directive 93/6/EC of March 15, 1993 [1993] O.J. L.141.

[31] Stock Exchange Act 1995, s.17. Authorised by a competent authority in another Member State includes "credit institutions" (defined under Council Directive 77/780/EEC (as amended)) duly authorised in another Member State under the various E.C. Banking Directives to provide cross border services or establish branches in other Member States.

[32] Stock Exchange Act 1995, s.21.

[33] *ibid.*, s.18.

[34] *ibid.*, s.22.

[35] *ibid.*, s.18.

registered office and head office of the proposed member firm must be located in the State, its financial resources must be adequate to ensure solvency, its controlling shareholders must be "suitable" and the expertise of its management and staff must be acceptable.[36]

The Central Bank is obliged to co-operate with the relevant competent authorities in other Member States.[37] Where a member firm wishes to establish a branch business outside the State, it must notify the Central Bank which shall in turn communicate the information to the competent authorities in the other Member State(s) concerned.[38] Should the Central Bank refuse to communicate such information then the Central Bank is obliged to furnish reasons for the refusal[39] and a right of appeal to the courts is provided.[40]

1–06 The Central Bank has extensive powers to revoke a member firm's authorisation for a wide variety of reasons.[41] For example, a member firm may no longer comply with the terms of the initial authorisation, or perhaps its capital and solvency status raises concerns,[42] or perhaps it has breached a code of conduct or rule drawn up pursuant to Section 38 of the Act. Section 38 sets out a list of seven principles of proper practice for member firms and permits the Central Bank to draw up and issue a code of conduct based on these principles.[43] How-

---

[36] Stock Exchange Act 1995, s.18.

[37] *ibid.*, s.28(5).

[38] *ibid.*, s.20.

[39] *ibid.*, s. 20(3).

[40] Stock Exchange Act 1995, s.20. While the Act does provide grounds for refusal to communicate, presumably the Central Bank can refuse to communicate where it fears that the investment services provider already has a less than satisfactory record of compliance in this jurisdiction, or perhaps it considers that it is not adequately resourced to competently provide cross border services or establish a branch in another Member State.

[41] Stock Exchange Act 1995, s.24.

[42] For example, s. 26 of the Stock Exchange Act 1995 permits the Central Bank to specify various asset and liability ratios which authorised member firms must adhere to.

[43] These principles, set out in subs.38(1) are to ensure that a member firm (a) acts honestly and fairly in the best interests of clients and the integrity of the market (b) acts with due care, skill and diligence in the best interests of clients and the integrity of the market (c) has and employs effectively the resources and procedures that are necessary for the proper performance of its business activities (d) seeks from its clients information regarding their financial situation, investment experience and objectives as regards the services requested (e) makes adequate disclosure of relevant material information in its dealings with clients (f) makes a reasonable effort to avoid conflicts of interests and, when they cannot be avoided, ensures that its clients are fairly treated (g) complies with all regulatory requirements applicable to the conduct of its business activities so as to promote the best interests of its clients and the integrity of the market.

ever, section 38 also provides that where a Stock Exchange has its own set of conduct rules which reflect all of the section 38 principles, then the Central Bank shall not draw up a code of conduct for that exchange.

The Rules of the Irish Stock Exchange do indeed reflect these seven principles as they are included as part of member firms' general obligations under the Stock Exchange's own conduct of business rules for member firms. However, a difficulty arises as the Act does not provide any workable sanction for breach of any code or rules within the meaning of section 38, apart from permitting the Central Bank to revoke a member firm's authorisation as punishment for contravening a prescribed code of conduct. This is a drastic measure, and even if taken, would be of little solace to an aggrieved investor, as the Act does not appear to provide a civil liability remedy for breach of the code. While the Stock Exchange itself may discipline the member firm under its own internal disciplinary rules, resulting in detriment to the member firm, the Exchange does not provide the investor with a right of civil action for a compensatory civil remedy against the member firm.[44] The Exchange's own rules provide that a particular transaction will only be invalidated for failure to comply with its conduct of business rules where the Stock Exchange finds that the member firm acted intentionally, negligently, reckless or wilfully, and in circumstances where the Stock Exchange considers it necessary in the interests of fairness. In an appropriate case, the Exchange, at its discretion, can order the member firm to make restitution to the client.

1–07 The 1995 Act required approved exchanges to establish and maintain a complaints handling system, which approved exchanges must maintain for the proper investigation of complaints against either the Stock Exchange or its member firms.[45] The Minister for Finance may request a copy of the Exchange's report arising from any such investigations.[46] The Minister for Finance, however, shall not lay the report before the Houses of parliament without both the Minister

---

[44] Nor is there a civil liability remedy as such provided by the Investor Compensation Directive (Council and European Parliament Directive 97/9/EC of March 3, 1997 [1997] O.J. L.84, as implemented by the Investor Compensation Act 1998. That Directive obliges member firms to be members of limited compensation schemes for the purposes of compensating clients where the firm fails to return clients funds or client securities. However, the client is not entitled to full compensation, but to a certain measure of compensation as determined in accordance with the Directive and the 1998 Act's provisions.

[45] Stock Exchange Act 1995, s.9(13). The Irish Stock Exchange has established such a complaints procedure

[46] With the consent of the Minister for Enterprise and Employment: s.9(5)(g)(ii) of the Stock Exchange Act 1995.

and the Minister for Enterprise, Trade and Employment considering it is proper for the exigencies of the common good and having regard to the rights of any person referred to in the report.[47]

Should the Stock Exchange itself engage in a disciplinary hearing under its own conduct of business rules, then it can order a range of measures such as censure, substantial fines, payment of compensation, suspension or expulsion of the member firm from dealing on the Stock Exchange.

1–08 In certain circumstances, the Central Bank may revoke a member firm's authorisation or reject a proposed member firm's application for authorisation to pursue investment business pursuant to Regulations adopted under Council and European Parliament Directive 95/26/EC.[48] Where the Central Bank is of the opinion that "close links" exist between a member firm and other persons such that the existence of close links between the member firm and the persons would prevent the effective exercise of the Central Bank's supervisory functions, it shall refuse or revoke authorisation, as the case may be.[49] A member firm is in a "close links" situation where two or more persons are linked by "participation" or "control" in a permanent arrangement with one and the same person. Participation is defined as meaning the ownership (directly or by way of control) of 20% or more of the voting rights or capital of an undertaking. "Control" is defined as meaning the relationship between a parent undertaking and a subsidiary undertaking or a similar relationship between any person and an undertaking.[50]

Finally amongst the Central Bank's other substantial powers is the power to issue "directions" to member firms under the 1995 Act, as for example where it is concerned about the solvency of a member firm.[51] The Central Bank also has the right to ask the courts to appoint an inspector to investigate the affairs of a member firm where the Central Bank considers that it is in the best interests of the orderly regulation of markets or for the protection of investors.[52]

---

[47] Stock Exchange Act 1995, s.9(16).

[48] [1995] O.J. L.168 as implemented by the Supervision of Credit Institutions, Stock Exchange Member Firms and Investment Business Firms Regulations 1996 (S.I. No. 267 of 1996) with effect from September 10, 1996. Note that these regulations also concern "credit institutions" (within the meaning of the E.C. Banking Directives) and "investment business firms" within the ambit of the Investment Intermediaries Act 1995 (and the Investment Services Directive).

[49] reg. 3(2) and 4(2) (S.I. No. 267 of 1996).

[50] See further reg. 2(1) (S.I. No. 267 of 1996).

[51] Pursuant to s. 29 of the Stock Exchange Act 1995 the Central Bank may direct a member firm to suspend its activities for a wide variety of reasons.

[52] Stock Exchange Act 1995, s.57.

B. THE MARKETS

It is outside the scope of this work to engage in an in-depth detailed analysis of every possible conceivable market where Irish and overseas securities may seek a listing. The following is a brief overview of some of the more important listings markets for Irish securities.

(1) Domestic markets

1–09 The Irish Stock Exchange provides a market for a wide range of securities, ranging from government bonds, equities, investment funds, corporate bonds, and local authority securities. The number of member firms dealing on the Stock Exchange is less than twenty and the market is order, rather than quote, driven. However, there are six approved market makers (known as primary dealers) in the government bonds market, who are members of the Stock Exchange. The primary dealers are authorised by the National Treasury Management Agency. The Exchange also lists several hundred investments funds, many of whom are based in the International Financial Services Centre.[53]

The primary list for equities is the official list. There are approximately one hundred companies whose shares are currently listed on this list. The index of listed shares is known as the ISEQ index. The admission and listing requirements for companies seeking a listing are set out in the Yellow Book. These requirements are onerous and are considered in detail later in this Chapter. However, before proceeding to consider the Yellow Book, some mention should be made of the Developing Companies Market and the Exploration Securities Market.

1–10 For companies in the early growth stage, there is the Developing Companies Market [DCM]. The DCM market is for companies that seek a listing but which do not wish to undergo the full rigours of preparing for a full stock market listing. Such companies are likely to be smaller companies which are undergoing rapid expansion and growth, and which wish to seek access to a wider capital base. The DCM is a second tier market which imposes less rigorous disclosure requirements on companies seeking a listing. Separate admission rules therefore apply[54] which are not as rigorous as the full listing Yellow Book listing rules.

---

[53] The Stock Exchange's requirements with regard to investment funds are summarised in "Investment Funds: Listing Requirements and Procedures" rather than in Chap. 21 Yellow Book on "Investment Entities" (which deals with unit trusts, investment trusts and investment companies).

[54] The Developing Companies Market Rules.

In order for a company[55] to be admitted to the DCM market, it must normally have a minimum of one year's trading record,[56] although this may be waived in exceptional circumstances.[57] This should particularly suit some of the newer technology industries which have an appetite for significant amounts of capital based on their potential. A sponsor will be retained to advise the company on how to comply with the DCM admission and listing rules. The Exchange will require a DCM applicant to have a minimum amount of securities in public hands at the time of listing in order to ensure a sufficient market will exist once listing takes place.[58] The admission document will have to disclose a range of information about the company such as the identity of its directors and senior management, the nature and duration of its activities, the identity of its controlling shareholders, its trading accounts as well as other relevant information concerning the nature of the securities seeking admission. The Exchange will be required to approve the admission document though it does not accept any responsibility for its contents.[59]

Where securities are to be offered to the public, a prospectus complying with the Prospectus Directive and the Stock Exchange's rules will have to be published. Under the requirements of the Directive, all information will have to be disclosed which allows investors make an "informed assessment" of the assets, liabilities, and future prospects of the company.[60] Also it will have to detail the rights attaching to the securities as well as the company's profits and losses. The Exchange may allow omission of information from the prospectus where investors would not be likely to be misled by its omission. The directors of the applicant will have to attach a responsibility statement to the prospectus whereby they take responsibility for the information contained therein. Any person who has agreed to become a director will also be required to sign this statement.

1–11 For exploration companies there is the Exploration Securities Market ("ESM"). Currently this market lists less than twenty mineral or oil and gas exploration companies. This market has its own separate admission rules, the ESM Rules. An "exploration company" is defined

---

[55] para. 1.2 of the DCM Rules require the company to be incorporated as a public limited company according to the laws relevant to its place of incorporation.

[56] para. 1.3 DCM Rules.

[57] para. 1.4 DCM Rules.

[58] para. 1.11 requires at least 10% of each class of shares seeking to be admitted to be in public hands.

[59] para. 3.A.2 DCM Rules requires the company directors to attach a Responsibility Statement to the admission document.

[60] Art. 11 Prospectus Directive.

in the ESM Rules as a company the principal activity of which is, or is planned to be, the exploration for and/or the extraction of mineral resources, a material part of which is carried on in Ireland. The company is required to be a public limited company according to the laws in its place of incorporation. The ESM Rules require at least one year's trading accounts to be produced prior to application for admission to the ESM, and that a report be produced demonstrating that the company has engaged in some exploration activity. At least 10% of the shares of each class seeking admission must be in public hands at the time of admission unless the Exchange otherwise agrees. Where an exploration company seeks admission to the official list, then more onerous admission requirements will apply.

Companies that are involved only in exploration, which are not undertaking or proposing to undertake extraction on a commercial scale, are not suitable for listing on the official list.[61] Companies may be admitted to listing on this market without having to show three years trading records normally required of official list companies.[62] An exploration company's listing particulars must contain a "competent person's report". The purpose of this report is to independently substantiate evidence that there are mineral resources existing on the site from where proposed extraction of minerals will occur.

FINEX is a market for futures and options. It is not regulated by the Stock Exchange but independently by the Central Bank pursuant to the Central Bank Act 1989.

(2) Foreign markets

1–12 London and New York are the two most important markets where companies seek a listing outside of Ireland. London is one of the largest equity markets in the world. Irish companies could have a primary listing in London before the separation of the Dublin and London Exchanges in 1995. Since 1995, Irish companies who wish to obtain a primary listing in London may do so provided they satisfy the London Stock Exchange Rules. It is possible to obtain a secondary listing there also. The advantage for Irish companies of obtaining a listing in London is that the London capital pool is vastly larger than the Irish Exchange can offer. Also, from an admission and listing standpoint, corporate advisers are comfortable with the use of the Yellow Book

---

[61] Chap. 19 Yellow Book.

[62] para. 19.3 Derogation from para. 3.3(a) Yellow Book: par. 19.3 Yellow Book provides that the Exchange will be satisfied if the applicant can show that it has a visible plan for extracting mineral resources in a viable manner, and that it has proven reserves sufficient to maintain a level of extracting sufficient to support commercial trading for at least two years post admission to listing or extraction commencement, whichever date is the later.

rules, given their use domestically. The main pieces of United Kingdom legislation that may be of relevance are the United Kingdom Companies Acts and the Financial Services Act 1986.

For smaller companies the Alternative Investments Market [AIM] may be an attractive option. Like Dublin's Developing Companies Market, its admission and listing requirements are less stringent than for the official list. Consequently, access may be more cost effective for smaller companies. Recently, the London Exchange has relaxed the admission requirements in order to make AIM even easier to access, particularly for high growth companies such as technology and pharmaceutical applicants. Furthermore, there are tax breaks available to encourage investors to participate in AIM listed companies.

In New York the NASDAQ index is the index that is of most interest to Irish companies with several high profile Irish computer technology, aviation, telecommunications and pharmaceutical companies listing there in the last few years.[62a] Unlike the Irish Exchange, the NASDAQ does not occupy a fixed location. In effect it has no trading floor as it operates purely in the virtual world of computer trading. Trading is done by member firms using computer links to allow traders match buyers and sellers. Market makers are also involved and the quotation of securities is constantly displayed on the trading screens located in traders' offices. NASDAQ operates a National Market and a Smallcap market. The former being for large well known companies with large capitalisation and the latter being suitable for smaller emerging high growth companies seeking access to the United States' vast capital pool. In order to be admitted, a United States sponsor is required and the applicant will have to register with the Securities and Exchange Commission [SEC]. A prospectus has to be published which complies with both SEC and Irish legal requirements.

Significantly smaller is the European version, known as EASDAQ based in Brussels. This index is designed to permit authorised investment firms under the Investment Services Directive and credit institutions authorised under the various EC Banking Directives, to engage in trading. This Exchange uses a screen quotation system and computer technology to confirm and settle the trades. Market making is involved on this Exchange, and often companies quoted on NASDAQ also appear on EASDAQ. This European Exchange seeks to exploit the Prospectus Directive regime by allowing those seeking admission to draw up a prospectus that complies with the Prospectus Directive and any local requirements in the various Member States. The prospectus has to be approved by a Prospectus Directive "competent authority" in a Member State, and then the applicant must further satisfy EASDAQ

[62a]For more traditional industrial stocks, the New York Stock Exchange (NYSE) presents Irish industrials with the opportunity to access U.S. capital.

that the prospectus also satisfies local requirements in the various Member States. EASDAQ can relieve the applicant from having to prepare a prospectus where the applicant has recently published a prospectus, by requiring the publication of an updating prospectus only.

II. ADMISSION CONDITIONS – THE ADMISSIONS DIRECTIVE AND YELLOW BOOK REGIME

1–13 With the enactment of Council Directive 79/279/EEC, otherwise known as the "Admissions Directive",[63] the European Community sought to put in place an initial legal framework designed to achieve a partial measure of co-ordination throughout the Community territory with regard to, *inter alia*, minimum conditions for admission of securities to official listing. In the preamble to the Admissions Directive, the aspiration was expressed that the co-ordination of the conditions for the admission of securities to listings on stock exchanges operating in the Member States, would be likely to promote the objective of achieving a certain measure of protection for investors at Community level. Furthermore, it was stated that the Directive's promotion of the closer alignment of the admission rules of the Member States would facilitate admission to listing of securities listed in other Member States, the ultimate aim being the promotion of the interpenetration of national securities markets by facilitating the listing of securities in other Member States.[64] However, the Community also acknowledged that because of differences in the structures of securities markets from Member State to Member State, the adoption of this new legal framework was only a first step in facilitating admission to listing securities in more than one Member State. Consequently, the amount of desired co-ordination was limited to the establishment of minimum conditions regarding admission matters but without giving a right to listing. To complete this initial legal framework to pursue these objectives, the Community also adopted the Listing Particulars Directive[65] and the Interim Reports Directive[66] at around the same time.[67]

---

[63] Council Directive 79/279/EEC of March 5, 1979 co-ordinating the conditions for the admission of securities to official Stock Exchange listing [1979] O.J. L66/21 (the "Admissions Directive") as implemented by the European Communities (Stock Exchange) Regulations 1984 (S.I. No. 282 of 1984).

[64] Article 20 of the Directive provided for the establishment of a contact committee composed of Member State and Commission representatives whose mission was to facilitate the harmonised implementation of the Directive through regular consultation.

[65] Council Directive 80/390/EEC of March 17, 1980 co-ordinating the requirements for the drawing up, scrutiny and distribution of the listing particulars to be

(1) ADMISSIONS DIRECTIVE AND THE STOCK EXCHANGE LISTING RULES

(a)   Role of the Stock Exchange as "competent authority"

1–14   Article 1 of the Admissions Directive provides that the Directive concerns securities admitted to official listing or those which are the subject of an application for admission. However, not all securities or issuers fall within the scope of the Directive. A number of optional exceptions are provided, and Ireland has opted to take them.[68]

Article 3 of the Directive provides that Member States shall ensure that securities may not be admitted to official listing on any Stock Exchange situated or operating within the territory unless the conditions

---

published for the admission of securities to official Stock Exchange listing [1980] O.J. L.100/1 (the "Listing Particulars Directive") as implemented by the European Communities (Stock Exchange) Regulations 1984 (S.I. No. 282 of 1984); as amended by Council Directive 87/345/EEC of June 22, 1987 [1987] O.J. L.185/81 as implemented by the European Communities (Stock Exchange) (Amendment) Regulations 1991 (S.I. No. 18 of 1991); and as further amended by Council Directive 90/211/EEC of April 23, 1990 [1990] O.J. L.112/24 as implemented by the European Communities (Transferable Securities and Stock Exchange) Regulations 1992 (S.I. No. 202 of 1992); and as further amended by Council and European Parliament Directive no. 94/18/EC of May 30, 1994 [1990] O.J. L.135/1 as implemented by the European Communities (Stock Exchange) (Amendment) Regulations, 1994 (S.I. No. 234 of 1994).

[66] Council Directive 82/121/EEC of February 15, 1982 on information to be published on a regular basis by companies the shares of which have been admitted to official Stock Exchange listing [1982] O.J. L. 48/26 (the "Interim Reports Directive") as implemented by the European Communities (Stock Exchange) Regulations 1984 (S.I. No. 282 of 1984).

[67] This initial legal framework was further enhanced throughout the 1980s and 1990s by the adoption and implementation of further Directives considered later below in this chapter, *i.e.* various directives amending the Listing Particulars Directive; and the Prospectus Directive.

[68] Ireland has opted not to apply the Directive to units issued by collective investment undertakings other than the closed end type (defined in art. 2) and also securities issued by a Member State or its regional or local authorities: see second sched. para. 1 of the implementing regulations (S.I. No. 282 of 1984). Furthermore, Ireland has opted to disapply certain parts of the Directive to issuers of securities falling within the terms of art. 8 of the Directive, *i.e.* securities issued by a company or other legal person who is a national of a Member State and who is set up, governed by or managed pursuant to a special law whereby repayments on those securities are guaranteed by the State: see second sched. para. 2 of the implementing regulations (S.I. No. 282 of 1984). However, note that just because Ireland has opted not to apply the Directive to certain types of securities or issuers, this does *not* mean that the Stock Exchange's Yellow Book Rules will not apply to such securities should they apply to be admitted to listing on the Irish Exchange.

laid down by the Directive are satisfied and that issuers are made subject to the obligations provided for by the Directive's Schedules.[69]

Ireland implemented the Directive by way of S.I. 282 of 1984 and designated the Irish Stock Exchange as the "competent authority" for the purposes of the Directive.[70] Furthermore, the 1984 regulations also provide that nothing shall prevent the Irish Stock Exchange from requiring admission conditions, or from imposing obligations on issuers once admitted to listing,[71] which are more onerous that those permitted by the Directives.[72] Consequently, an examination of Chapter 3 of the Yellow Book illustrates how the Directives principles are reflected in the Stock Exchange's admission to listing rules.[73]

(b) Powers of the Stock Exchange over Admission to Listing

(i) *Power to impose additional admission conditions or refuse admission*

Article 5 of the Admissions Directive provides that nothing in the Directive shall prevent a Member State from imposing more stringent admission requirements or obligations imposed on issuers, provided that certain parameters are respected. This is reflected in the domestic implementing regulations[74] which provide that the Stock Exchange[75] is not prevented from imposing more stringent or additional conditions for admission to listing or continuing obligations on the issuers

---

[69] Of which there are four, the first two, Schedules A and B applying to admission conditions regarding shares and debt securities respectively; the second two, Schedules C and D detail continuing obligations of the issuers of such securities once admitted to listing. Schedules A and B are considered at paras 1–18—1–22 below, and C and D at paras 1–81—1–86 below.

[70] reg. 7(1) European Communities (Stock Exchange) Regulations 1984 (S.I. No. 282 of 1984).

[71] For an overview of Continuing Obligations that may be imposed on an issuer admitted to listing, see further at paras 1–81—1–86 below.

[72] reg. 3(2) (provided of course that any such conditions or obligations do not violate the Directive's principles).

[73] See further paras 1–18—1–22 below. Note that additional and alternative conditions for listing are set out in Chaps 17 to 26 of the Yellow Book dealing with overseas companies, property companies, mineral companies, scientific research based companies, investment entities, public sector issuers, issuers of specialist securities (including specialist certificates representing shares) and miscellaneous securities, and venture capital trusts. A consideration of the minutae of those rules are outside the scope of this work and are further elaborated upon in the Yellow Book.

[74] reg. 3(2). See also art. 10 of the Directive.

[75] reg. 7 provides that the Irish Stock Exchange is designated as the "Exchange" for the purposes of the Directive (Art. 9).

of securities admitted to listing,[76] provided that any such conditions or obligations

– apply generally for all issuers or particular classes of issuers, and
– are published before application for admission of such securities is made, and
– are not otherwise inconsistent with the Directive.[77]

1–15 Article 10 also permits the Stock Exchange to make the admission of securities to listing subject to any special condition which it considers appropriate in the interests of protecting investors and of which the Stock Exchange has explicitly informed the applicant.[78] However, the Stock Exchange may also dispense with or modify its requirements where it deems it appropriate.[79]

The Directive also invokes the principle of non-discrimination by providing that Member States cannot make admission of securities issued by nationals or companies of other Member States subject to the condition that the securities seeking admission are already listed in another Member State.[80] However this in turn is further qualified as the Directive also provides that the Stock Exchange may refuse to admit to listing a security already officially listed in another Member State where the issuer fails to comply with the obligations resulting from admission in that Member State.[81] The Directive also provides that the Stock Exchange may refuse admission to listing where the issuer's situation is such that admission would be detrimental to investors' interests.[82] An issuer unhappy with any of the aforegoing decisions may appeal to the Stock Exchange's Listing Committee.

(ii) Enforcement powers

1–16 The Stock Exchange also has extensive enforcement powers. For example, the Admissions Directive provides that it may, without preju-

---

[76] For an overview of the Continuing Obligations that an issuer is subject to once admitted to listing, see further paras 1–81—1–86 below.
[77] In similar fashion, art. 7 of the Directive provides that any derogations from the conditions for the admission of securities to official listing which may be authorised in accordance with Schedules A and B of the Directive must apply generally for all issuers where the circumstances justifying them are similar.
[78] para. 3.1 Yellow Book so provides.
[79] Admissions Directive art. 5(3); para. 1.3 Yellow Book.
[80] Admissions Directive art. 6.
[81] Admissions Directive art. 11; reg. 7(1); para. 1.4(b) Yellow Book.
[82] Admissions Directive Art. 9(3); para. 1.4(a) Yellow Book. Or furthermore, if the Stock Exchange considers that the applicant does not or has not complied with the Yellow Book listing rules or indeed any "special condition" imposed pursuant to para. 3.1 Yellow Book.

dice to any other sanction at its disposal, make public the fact that an issuer is failing to comply with obligations resulting from admission to listing.[83] Also, Article 13 provides that an issuer whose securities have been admitted to official listing is obliged to furnish all information which the Stock Exchange considers appropriate in order to protect investors or the smooth operation of the market. Where the Stock Exchange so requires, the issuer may be requested to publish this information. If it fails to do so the Stock Exchange may publish the information after having given the issuer the chance to be heard on the matter.[84]

Also, the Directive permits the Stock Exchange to suspend a listing of a security where the smooth operation of the market is, or may be, temporarily jeopardised, or the protection of investors so requires.[85]

Furthermore, the Stock Exchange may discontinue a listing of a security where it is satisfied that, due to special circumstances, normal dealing in a security can no longer be possible.[86] Paragraph 1.7 of the Yellow Book provides that unless the smooth operation of the market or the protection of investors so requires, the Stock Exchange will not take any of the aforementioned decisions without first having given advance notice to the issuer to allow representations be made to the Stock Exchange committee considering the matter.[87]

(iii) *Judicial review*

1–17 However, in order to maintain balance, the Directive also provides that the decision of the Stock Exchange either refusing admission to listing, or discontinuing a listing must be subject to the issuer's right to judicial review.[88] Regulation 10[89] amplifies this right to judicial review by providing that the issuer's right of appeal is to the High Court which shall confirm the Stock Exchange's decision unless satisfied that the procedures laid down, or the requirements of the regulations,[90] have not been complied with in some material respect. It further provides that in such event, the High Court shall set aside the decision of the Stock Exchange and remit the matter back to the Stock Exchange for reconsideration.

---

[83] Admissions Directive art. 12.
[84] para. 1.5 and 6 Yellow Book.
[85] Admissions Directive art 14; para. 1.19-21 Yellow Book.
[86] Admissions Directive art 14; para. 1.22-26 Yellow Book.
[87] Either the listings committee or the investments funds committee, as the case may be.
[88] Admissions Directive art. 15.
[89] S.I. No. 282 of 1984.
[90] *i.e.*, S.I. No. 282.

Article 15 of the Directive provides that an applicant for admission of a security to listing must be given a decision by the Stock Exchange within six months of the furnishing of the admission information, or within six months from the furnishing of further information requested within the initial six month period. Failure by the Stock Exchange to deliver a decision to the applicant upon the expiry of the aforegoing period is deemed to be a negative decision, in which event the right to appeal to the court arises.

In addition to suspension or discontinuance of a listing, the Stock Exchange may also censure the issuer, or any director found to be responsible for contravention of the rules. Such censure may be published.

(2) ADMISSION CONDITIONS

(a) Shares

1–18 Schedule A of the Admissions Directive sets out the conditions for applicants who seek the admission of shares to official listing on a Stock Exchange.[91] The Yellow Book elaborates upon the Directives terms, as appropriate. The Directive provides that the legal position of the applicant company must be in conformity with the laws and regulations to which it is subject, both as regards its formation and its operation.[92] It also provides that the minimum market capitalisation of the shares for which admission to listing is sought must be at least one million euros, although Member States may provide for admission to listing even when this condition is not met provided that the Stock Exchange is satisfied that there will be an adequate market for the shares.[93] The Yellow Book implements this provision by providing that the minimum aggregate market value of all shares to be listed must be

---

[91] Note that while Chap. 3 of the Yellow Book deals with the conditions for admission to listing of securities, these are modified where the securities are considered to be "specialist securities" and the admission conditions for such securities are found in Chap. 23 of the Yellow Book. "Specialist securities" are defined by Chap. 23 to mean securities which are traded by a limited number of specialist investors who are particularly knowledgeable in investment matters.

[92] Admissions Directive sched. A (I) para. 1. Para. 3.2 of the Yellow Book provides that if the applicant is a company incorporated in Ireland, it must not be a private company or an "old public limited company" as defined in s.12 Companies (Amendment) Act 1983.

[93] Admissions Directive sched. A (I) para. 2. Ireland has opted to facilitate this derogation: see second sched. to S.I. No. 282, para. 3.

at least £700,000,[94] though it may admit shares of lower value where satisfied there will be an adequate market for the shares.[95]

Both the Directive[96] and Yellow Book[97] further provide that the minimum market capitalisation will not apply to admission to listing of a further block of shares of the same class as those already admitted. A company seeking admission must have filed its annual accounts in accordance with national law in the three years prior to application for admission,[98] though it is recognised that derogation may be allowed from this requirement where the Stock Exchange is satisfied that it is in the interests of the company and of investors and that investors are in possession of sufficient information about the company to arrive at an informed judgment on the applicant company and its shares.[99] It is interesting to note that the guidance note accompanying the recent thirteenth amendment to the Yellow Book notes that in the case of high tech companies, the three year requirement for trading accounts may be derogated from where the applicant seeking admission is able to otherwise satisfy the Stock Exchange as to its business. This is a recognition that the Stock Exchange must not deter high growth companies from gaining admission to listing merely because their life has been a short one.

1–19 Schedule A of the Admissions Directive then proceeds to elaborate conditions relating to the shares for which admission to listing is sought. There are seven conditions, and these are for the most part elaborated upon in the Yellow Book.

First, the shares must be in conformity with the laws and regulations to which they are subject.[100] Second, the shares must be freely negotiable.[101] Third, where a public issue precedes admission to listing, the first listing may only be made after the end of the subscription

---

[94] para. 3.16(a) Yellow Book.
[95] para. 3.17 Yellow Book.
[96] Admissions Directive sched. A(I) para 2.
[97] para. 3.16 Yellow Book.
[98] Admissions Directive sched. A(I) para. 3. Para. 3.3 of the Yellow Book requires audited accounts drawn up according to applicant's national law and with U.K., Irish or U.S.A. generally accepted accounting principles (although leeway is allowed for companies incorporated outside the Republic of Ireland to satisfy the Stock Exchange as to the accounting procedures: see para. 17.3). Also para. 3.3 requires that the latest accounts be in respect of a period ending not more than six months before the date of the listing particulars and that the accounts have been independently audited.
[99] para. 3.4 Yellow Book. Although in practice, such derogations are rarely granted.
[100] Admissions Directive sched. A(II) para. 1; para. 3.14 Yellow Book.
[101] Admissions Directive sched. A(II) para. 2; para. 3.15 Yellow Book.

period.[102] Fourth, a sufficient number of shares must be distributed to the public in one or more of the Community's Member States not later than time of admission.[103] A "sufficient number" of shares is deemed to have been distributed where either at least 25% of the subscribed capital represented by the class of shares concerned is in "public hands",[104] or where a lower percentage is in the hands of the public and the market will operate properly.[105]

Fifth, the application for admission to listing must cover all the shares of the class already issued.[106] Paragraph 3.22 of the Yellow Book elaborates by providing that an application for listing shares of any class must relate to all shares in that class, issued or proposed to be issued. Furthermore, if shares of that class are already issued, then it must relate to all further shares of that class, issued or proposed to be issued.

Sixth, where shares have a physical form, it is necessary that they comply with the laws and regulations governing that form in the Member State of the shares' nationality at the time of application for admission to listing in another Member State.[107] Where the physical form does not comply with the requirements in the latter, then the Stock Exchange is obliged to make that fact known to the public.[108]

Seventh, where shares are issued by a company which is a non-Member State national and the shares are neither listed in the country

---

[102] Admissions Directive sched. A(II) para. 3.

[103] Admissions Directive sched. A(II) para. 4; paras 3.18-21 Yellow Book. Although the Directive qualified this by providing that where shares are to be distributed through the Stock Exchange, this condition does not apply. Instead, admission to listing will only be granted if the Stock Exchange is satisfied that a sufficient number of shares will be distributed through the Stock Exchange within a short period. Note that sched. A (I) para. 4 provides separate paras for shares admitted to listing in non-Member States, and para. 3.18 Yellow Book provides that account may be taken of holders in one or more non-Member States, if the shares are listed in such State.

[104] "Public hands" is further elaborated upon in para. 3.20 Yellow Book where certain holdings will not be regarded as being in public hands, *e.g.*, shares held by a director of the applicant; shares held by trustees of employee pension scheme, etc.

[105] Admissions Directive sched. A (II) para. 4; para. 3.19 Yellow Book. However, note that para. 3.21 provides that where the percentage of shares held in public hands falls below the minimum permitted (whether 25% or a lower permitted percentage as the case may be), that may result in a suspension or cancellation of the listing if necessary to protect investors or the smooth operation of the market.

[106] Admissions Directive sched. A (II) para. 7.

[107] Admissions Directive sched. A (II) para. 6; para. 3.14 Yellow Book.

[108] The physical form of shares issued by companies which are nationals of non-Member States must afford sufficient safeguard for the protection of investors.

of origin nor the country in which a major proportion of the shares is held, then the Stock Exchange may refuse admission to listing if investor protection would be at risk.[109]

1–20 Apart from the aforegoing which are provided for by the Directive, the Yellow Book itself provides for other conditions. For example, paragraph 3.23 provides that in the absence of exceptional circumstances, the issue of warrants or options to subscribe for equity shares must be limited to not more than 20% of the issued equity share capital of the applicant at the time of issue of the warrants or options. Rights under employees' share schemes will not be included for the purpose of this 20% limit. Also paragraphs 3.6 – 3.13 require further information to be furnished to the Stock Exchange on various matters such as:

– the working capital[110];

– relationship between issuer and controlling shareholders[111] (if any);

– demonstration of management responsibility;

– whether directors have conflicts of interest[112]; and

– nature and duration of issuer's business activities.[113]

Where an application is made to list certificates representing shares, paragraph 3.31 Yellow Book provides that the application will be dealt with as if the application were an application for the listing of shares.[114] In such event, the issuer of the certificates must satisfy a modified version of the admission rules.[115]

(b) Debt Securities

1–21 Schedule B of the Admissions Directive sets out the admission conditions for applicant undertakings and their debt securities.[116] It

---

[109] Admissions Directive sched. A (II) para.7.

[110] paras 3.10–11 Yellow Book.

[111] para. 3.12 Yellow Book. Para. 3.13. defines a "controlling shareholder" as a person (or persons) who is (are) entitled to exercise, directly or indirectly 30% or more of the applicant's voting rights at a.g.m., or who is (are) able to control the appointment of the directors capable of exercising a majority of votes at board meetings.

[112] paras 3.8–9 Yellow Book.

[113] paras 3.6–6A Yellow Book.

[114] Art. 16 of the Admissions Directive provides that applications to admit certificates representing shares to official listing should only be permitted where the Exchange is satisfied that the issuer is offering adequate safeguards for the protection of investors.

[115] paras 3.31–3.37 Yellow Book elaborate further.

[116] Note that while Chap. 3 of the Yellow Book deals with the Conditions for ad-

provides for only one condition as to the undertaking seeking admission to listing. The undertaking must be in conformity with the laws and regulations to which it is subject as regards its formation and operation.[117] However, just as with issuers of shares,[118] the Yellow Book goes further, as it provides that the three years' audited accounts requirement also applies to issuers of debt securities which are companies,[119] although it permits a derogation from this requirement where the Stock Exchange is of the view that it is in the interests of investors and they have sufficient information about the issuer to make an informed judgment.[120]

1–22 Schedule B of the Admissions Directive sets out the following conditions for the admission of debt securities to official listing on a Stock Exchange. The first three conditions (legal position of the securities[121]; negotiability[122]; and, public issue preceding issue[123]) are the same as those that the Directive applies to shares.[124] Also the condition as to physical form is similar to that imposed by the Directive regarding shares.[125]

There are other additional conditions imposed by the Directive. First, the minimum amount of the loan may be not less than 200,000 euros[126]

---

mission to listing of debt securities, these are modified where the securities are considered to be "specialist debt securities" and the modified admission Conditions for such securities are found in Chap. 23 of the Yellow Book. "Specialist debt securities" are defined by Chap. 23 to mean debt securities which are traded by a limited number of specialist investors who are particularly knowledgeable in investment matters.

[117] Admissions Directive sched. B(A) (I); para. 3.2 Yellow Book.
[118] See para. 1–18 above.
[119] para. 3.3 Yellow Book.
[120] para. 3.4(a) Yellow Book. Or alternatively, where the guarantor in respect of guaranteed debt securities has published or filed three years of audited accounts in the period immediately prior to application for admission (para. 3.4(b); or where, the obligations in respect of the debt securities are fully secured (para. 3.4(c)). In the case of specialist debt securities, two years' audited accounts will be acceptable (para. 23.4 Yellow Book) unless the Exchange permits a derogation on the basis that this is not necessary.
[121] Admissions Directive sched. B (A) (II) para. 1; para. 3.14 Yellow Book.
[122] Admissions Directive sched. B (A) (II) para. 2; para. 3.15 Yellow Book.
[123] Admissions Directive sched. B (A) (II) para. 3 (subject to the caveat that this condition does not apply in the case of tap issues of debt securities when the closing date for subscription is not fixed). However, this condition does not appear to be replicated in Chapter 3 of the Yellow Book in so far as debt securities are concerned.
[124] See para. 1–19 above.
[125] Admissions Directive sched. B(A) (II) para. 5 (subject to the additional requirement that the physical form of debt securities issued in a single Member State must conform to the standards in force in that State).
[126] Admissions Directive sched. B (A) (III) para. 1, although this is stated not to be

although derogation from this minimum is permissible where the Stock Exchange is satisfied there will be a sufficient market for the debt securities.[127] Second, the application for admission to listing must cover all debt securities ranking *pari passu*.[128] Third, convertible or exchangeable debentures, and debentures with warrants may only be admitted to listing if the related shares are already listed on the same Stock Exchange or on another regulated, regularly operating recognised open market or are so admitted simultaneously.[129]

However, the Stock Exchange may allow a derogation from this condition if satisfied that the holders have sufficient information at their disposal to form an opinion as to the value of the shares to which the debt securities relate.[130]

(3) SHARES, DEBT SECURITIES OR ISSUERS WHICH FALL OUTSIDE THE ADMISSIONS DIRECTIVE

1–22 Although Schedule B of the Admissions Directive has separate requirements relating to admission to listing of debt securities issued by the State or regional or local authorities, Ireland has opted to disapply the Directive to all securities issued by such entities, whether of the share or debt variety.[131]

However, the Yellow Book does apply certain admission rules to such securities, albeit in limited form.[132] Furthermore, Ireland has also

---

applicable in the case of tap issues where the minimum amount of the loan is not fixed; para. 3.16(b) Yellow Book.

[127] Admissions Directive sched. B (A) (III) para. 1. Ireland has opted to permit this derogation: second sched. to S.I. No. 282 para. 4; para. 3.17 Yellow Book

[128] Admissions Directive sched. B (A) (II) para. 4. Para. 3.22 Yellow Book provides that an application for listing of a class of securities must relate to all securities in that class, issued or proposed to be issued, and if part of the class is already issued, must relate to all further securities of that class, issued or proposed to be issued.

[129] Admissions Directive sched. B (A) (III) para. 2; para. 3.25 Yellow Book

[130] Admissions Directive sched. B (A) (III) para. 2. Ireland has opted to permit this derogation: see second sched. to S.I. No. 282 para. 5; para. 3.26 Yellow Book.

[131] See second sched. to S.I. No. 282 para. 1. For other instances where Ireland has opted to disapply the Directive see para. 1–14 above.

[132] para. 23.4 Yellow Book provides that the following conditions apply to admission to listing applications by such entities: para. 3.14 requires the securities to conform with the law in the applicant's place of incorporation; para. 3.15 requires the securities to be transferable; para. 3.16 requires the securities, except where of the same class already listed, to have an expected aggregate market value of all securities to be at least £700,000 for shares and £200,000 for debt securities (though there is no minimum limit in the case of tap issues where the amount of the debt securities is not fixed); para. 3.17 provides that securities of lower value may be admitted where the Exchange is

opted not to apply the Schedule B conditions to "companies and other legal persons" seeking admission to listing of debt securities where such entities are nationals of a Member State and are set up, governed by or managed pursuant to a special law where repayments and interest payments in respect of those securities are guaranteed by a Member State or one of its federal states.[133]

III. DIFFERENT METHODS OF LISTING SECURITIES

A. METHODS

1–23 There are several different methods of bringing securities to listing provided in Chapter 4 of the Yellow Book. Only the first four methods about to be described may be used by applicants without equity shares already listed,[134] whereas all methods may be used by applicants with equity shares already listed.[135] Applicants in the former category must comply with the requirements of paragraphs 4.2 and 4.3. The first paragraph requires that in all cases the securities in issue must be sufficiently widely held in order to ensure that their marketability, when listed, can be assumed. The second paragraph provides that, whatever method is used, no shares may be placed with connected clients either of the sponsor or of any securities house or other intermediary assisting with the offer unless placed with a market maker or fund manager for the purpose of its business as such.

(1) Offer for Sale or Subscription[136]

1–24 An offer for sale is an invitation to the public by, or on behalf of,

---

satisfied there will be an adequate market; and, para. 3.22 requires whole classes of securities to be listed.
[133] This option is provided by art. 8 of the Admissions Directive and adopted by Ireland in second sched. S.I. No. 282 of 1984 para. 2.
[134] para. 4.2 Yellow Book (or also any "other method as may be accepted by the Exchange either generally or in any particular case": this is how the "catch-all" category is described in para. 4.2(f) Yellow Book). The same applies under the DCM and ESM Rules respectively.
[135] Except the introduction method: para. 4.1 Yellow Book. Note that the "catch-all" category (any "other method as may be accepted by the Exchange either generally or in any particular case") also applies: see para. 4.1(m) Yellow Book. For consideration of how the DCM and ESM Rules respectively apply in the situation where equity shares are already listed, the respective Rules should be consulted.
[136] Whether an offer constitutes an "offer to the public" is considered in detail in Chap. 2 below where the parameters of ss.44; 51; and 61 Companies Act 1963 are considered.

a third party, to purchase securities of the issuer already in issue or allotted.[137] An offer for subscription is an invitation to the public by, or on behalf of, a third party to subscribe for securities of the issuer not yet issued or allotted.[138] Either type of offer may be in the form of an invitation to tender at or above a stated minimum price.

In the case of an offer for sale, the company allots the shares to an intermediary who in turn makes the offer to the public. In this type of offer, the intermediary acts as a principal and not as agent of the company. Consequently as the intermediary is bearing much of the risk, this is a common method preferred by companies. The intermediary will of course have entered into agreements with subunderwriters to minimise its risk associated with the offer.

In the case of an offer for subscription, the intermediary does not act as a principal but rather as an agent of the company, which remains the principal. The company will enter into underwriting arrangements to minimise its risk. Consequently, this method is not as popular with companies.

Sometimes, a company may decide to offer by way of a combined offer for sale and subscription. This allows existing shareholders of the company to use the occasion of listing to sell their shares to the public once listing occurs. The company itself can offer further shares to the public.

In an offer for sale the intermediary profits in that it takes the premium between the price it subscribed to the company initially for the securities and the price it sells to the public. Alternatively, it may charge an underwriting commission in an offer for subscription.

Paragraph 4.6 Yellow Book provides that in an offer for sale or subscription the issuer must ensure that letters of allotment or acceptance are all issued simultaneously and numbered serially. Where the securities may be held in uncertificated form, the issuer must ensure that there is equality of treatment between those who elect to hold the securities in certificated form and those who elect to hold them in uncertificated form. Letters of regret must be posted at the same time or not later than three business days thereafter.

(2) Placing

1–25 A placing will not normally constitute an offer to the public as only a relatively small number of investors, usually of the institutional variety, will be offered the securities. Paragraph 4.7 of the Yellow Book defines a placing as a marketing of securities in issue but not yet listed,

---

[137] para. 4.4 Yellow Book.
[138] para. 4.5 Yellow Book.

or not yet in issue, to specified persons or clients of the sponsor or any securities house assisting in the placing, which does not involve an offer to the public or to existing holders of the issuer's securities generally. In order to protect investor interests and ensure smooth operation of the market, paragraph 4.8 provides that an applicant may not bring securities to listing by way of a placing where the securities are equity securities and are of a class already listed if the placing price is to be at a discount of more than 10% to the "middle market" price of those securities at the time of the placing, unless the Stock Exchange is satisfied that the issuer is in severe financial difficulties or that there are other exceptional circumstances.[139]

In a placing, the issuer will avail of the services of an intermediary, such as a merchant bank or corporate finance house, to place large blocks of the shares (whether new or existing) with the interested investors. Underwriting arrangements with third parties will generally not be necessary as the sponsoring intermediary will have given the company a commitment that it will secure buyers for all of the securities, and in any event, it will be likely to have "lined up" firm commitments to purchase from the selected investors. Given the nature of a placing, the costs associated with a placing are much lower than with an offer for sale or subscription. The placing could take the form of a "best efforts" placing, whereby the intermediary commits to secure purchasers, and if any securities are not taken up, the intermediary will take them up itself. Alternatively, a "reasonable efforts" placing could take place, whereby the intermediary will not be liable to take up unsold securities. To cater for this eventuality, independent underwriting arrangements should be put in place by the company. Another form of placing is "clawback" placing, whereby the intermediary places the securities conditionally with placees on condition that if the company's shareholders wish to take them up, then the placees lose the right to take up the securities.

A more exotic form of placing is known as "vendor consideration placing", which the Yellow Book rules specifically provide for in paragraph 4.29.[140] A vendor consideration placing is a marketing by or behalf of vendors of securities that have been allotted as consideration for an acquisition. Paragraph 4.30 requires that all vendors must have an equal opportunity to participate in the placing; paragraph 4.8 must be respected in the case of a placing involving equity securities already

---

[139] The DCM and ESM Rules make similar provision.

[140] Note that "vendor consideration placing" should be distinguished from "vendor consideration issue" as described in para. 4.27 Yellow Book and further considered below at para. 1–31.

listed; and, paragraphs 4.2[141] and 4.3[142] must be respected in the case of placing involving equity shares of a class not already listed.

Whether or not a placing requires a prospectus all depends on the circumstances surrounding the placing. A placing with the intermediary's clients where no stock market listing is involved is unlikely to require a prospectus as it is unlikely to be categorised as an offer to the public.[143] This is colloquially known as a "private placing". Where a placing forms part of a listing whereby shares will be available for offer or subscription, then a prospectus may well be required.[144]

(3) Intermediaries Offer

1–26   An intermediaries offer is defined as a marketing of securities already or not yet in issue by means of an offer by, or on behalf of, the issuer to intermediaries for them to allocate to their own clients.[145] "Intermediaries" are defined in the Yellow Book as being an intermediary who is independent of both the sponsor of the offer and who does not assist in any way with the marketing of the offer. The Exchange may require the names of the intermediaries to whom the securities were

---

[141] The securities must be sufficiently widely held in order to ensure that their marketability when listed can be assumed: see para. 1–23 above.

[142] No shares may be placed with connected clients either of the sponsor or securities house or intermediary assisting with the offer unless placed with a market maker or fund manager: see para. 1–23 above.

[143] Though the point is not free from doubt in several respects. First, the clients of a firm may be a "section of the public" within the meaning of s. 61 Companies Act 1963 unless the offer is a "domestic concern of the persons making and receiving it". Furthermore, it may be that a prospectus may be required if the shares are allotted "with a view to them being offered to the public" within the meaning of s. 51 Companies Act 1963. It provides that where shares are offered to the public within two years of their initial allotment or agreement to allot, it is presumed that they were originally allotted with a view to them becoming available to the public. This presumption also arises where at the date the offer was made, the whole consideration for the allotment or agreement to allot, had not been received by the company. And finally, the Prospectus Directive requires a prospectus to be published whenever securities are "offered to the public for the first time", though in this latter instance it is probably not the placing that would be deemed to be the offer to the public because the Directive (Art. 2.1) provides that an offer to a "restricted circle of people" shall not constitute an offer to the public within the scope of the Directive), but the subsequent offer. However, as the Directive does not define "restricted circle" with any precision, the possibility remains that, notwithstanding the Directive, the placing itself may constitute an offer to the public.

[144] See further Chap. 2 below where "offer to the public" is considered in detail and the situations where the Companies Acts or the Prospectus Regulations will, or will not, require a prospectus in some form.

[145] para. 4.10 Yellow Book.

allocated and in turn the names of the clients of the intermediaries who were allocated the securities.[146]

(4) Introduction

1–27 An introduction is a method of bringing securities to listing that are already issued and widely held by the public.[147] For example, it may be used by well known companies that already have a listing on the United Kingdom Alternative Investments Market or the Irish Developing Companies Market. Also, it may be favoured by overseas companies whose securities are traded internationally, and who wish to obtain a secondary listing on the Irish Exchange. The Stock Exchange will only admit securities to listing by way of an Introduction where it is satisfied that the shares are so widely held that their marketability can be assumed.[148] No capital is raised by the applicant as the purpose of the Introduction is merely to list its securities rather than make an offering to the public. The Yellow Book provides that this method cannot be used by companies that already have an equity listing.

(5) Rights issue[149]

(a)   *Yellow Book rules*

1–28 A rights issue is defined in the Yellow Book as an offer to existing holders of securities to subscribe or purchase further securities in proportion to their holdings made by means of the issue of a renounceable letter (or other negotiable document) which may be traded (as "nil paid" rights) for a period before payment for the securities is due.[150] To encourage existing shareholders to take up the offer,

---

[146] para. 4.11 Yellow Book.

[147] para. 4.12 Yellow Book.

[148] para. 4.13 Yellow Book.

[149] Whether or not a rights issue is an offer to the public requiring a prospectus all depends on the form of renouncement letter. Where no right to renounce, then the offer is likely to be regarded as a non-public offer as it would appear to be a "domestic concern of the persons making and receiving it" within the meaning of s.61 of the Companies Act 1963 such that a prospectus would not be required under the 1963 Act. (However, notwithstanding, a prospectus may be required pursuant to the Prospectus Directive if the offer is deemed to be an "offer to the public for the first time" of "transferable securities" which are not already listed in the Exchange: see futher Chap. 2). On the other hand, if the rights issue is renounceable, then all may depend on the precise form of the letter of provisional allotment. In such circumstances, the members of the company might be deemed to be a "section of the public" such that the rights issue would be an "offer to the public" pursuant to s.61: see further para. 2–23 below.

[150] para. 4.16 Yellow Book. Para. 9.19 provides that in a rights issue a company

the offer is usually made at a deep discount in order to encourage the members to take up the offer. A merchant bank may underwrite the issue, and any securities not taken up or sold will be taken up by the underwriter. The offer is accompanied by a circular detailing the offer, a provisional letter of allotment, and a renounceable letter which allows the shareholder renounce their right to allotment in favour of another party should they so wish.[151] The offer must remain open for at least 21 days.[152] The use of provisional letters of allotment means that a trade can occur in the securities even before the end of the offer period has expired, even though no subscription monies have yet been paid over to the company.[153] Where the Stock Exchange grants a listing for the rights issue in "nil paid" form, then upon the securities being paid up and the allotment becoming unconditional in all respects, the listing in nil paid form will be amended without any need for further application for a listing of fully paid up securities.[154]

The shareholder to whom a rights offer is made has a number of choices:

— Allotment may be taken up;

— or, a renouncement of the rights in favour of another may be made;

— or, the shareholder may split the rights, such that some are taken up and others are renounced;

— or, the rights could be allowed to lapse in which event the merchant bank or sponsoring broker may sell the securities and pay over any premium earned to the shareholder.

Where existing holders do not take up their rights, special rules apply.[155] Such rights must be offered for subscription or purchase on terms that any premium obtained over the subscription or purchase price (net of expenses) is to be for the account of such holders, save that if the proceeds for an existing holder do not exceed £3, the proceeds may

---

need not comply with proportional entitlement parameters with respect to securities representing fractional entitlements, or securities which the directors of the company consider necessary or expedient to exclude from the offer on account of either legal problems under the laws of any territory or the requirements of a regulatory body.

[151] If no renounceable letter is used, then the offer becomes an "open offer" in which event different Yellow Book rules apply. See para. 1–30 below.

[152] para. 4.21(a) Yellow Book.

[153] Hence the reference in para. 4.16 Yellow Book to rights which may be "traded (as "nil paid" rights) for a period before payment for the securities is due."

[154] para. 4.18 Yellow Book.

[155] para. 4.19 Yellow Book.

be retained by the company.[156] Furthermore, if on the expiry of the subscription period no premium (net of expenses) has been obtained, the securities may be allotted or sold to underwriters.[157] Finally, no excess application may be permitted without the prior permission of the Stock Exchange.[158]

The Yellow Book also makes specific provision for placing of rights before the start of official dealing.[159]

(b) Statutory pre-emption rights / Yellow Book

1–29   In the case of equity securities, section 23(1) Companies (Amendment) Act 1983 provides for a statutory right of pre-emption. This means that where a company proposes to offer new unissued equity securities[160] in return for cash, it must first offer to its existing members in proportion to their existing holdings. Such offer must remain open for acceptance for at least 21 days and may not be withdrawn before the end of that period.[161] During that time, the Act permits an existing member to renounce their rights in favour of another party.[162] Where the offer is for consideration otherwise than wholly in cash, section 23 does not apply as subsection (4) provides that the statutory right of pre-emption does not apply where the equity securities are wholly or partly paid up otherwise than in cash.

---

[156] para. 4.19(a) Yellow Book.

[157] para. 4.19(b) Yellow Book.

[158] para. 4.19(c) Yellow Book also provides that a director of an issuer will not, save in exceptional circumstances, be permitted to subscribe for or purchase excess securities without those securities being offered to other existing holders on the same terms.

[159] para. 4.17 Yellow Book provides that in a placing of rights arising from the issue before the official start of dealings, certain conditions must be satisfied. For example, the placing must relate to at least 25% of the maximum number of securities offered, or such lesser amount as agreed by the Stock Exchange. Also, the price paid by the placees must not exceed the price at which the securities the subject of the rights issue are offered, by more than one half of the calculated premium over that offer price.

[160] "Equity securities" for the purposes of s.23 of the Companies (Amendment) Act 1983 are defined in subs. 23(13) to mean company shares or securities which may be converted into shares but does not include bonus shares; or shares shown in the Memorandum to have been shares taken by a subscriber to the Memorandum; or shares which as respects dividends and capital carry restricted distribution participation rights; or shares which are held under an employee share scheme; or which, although not yet allotted, are to be allotted pursuant to such a scheme.

[161] Companies (Amendment) Act 1983, s.23(8).

[162] Companies (Amendment) Act 1983, s.23(3): such other party having the right to be admitted as a member of the company, subject to any restrictions in the company's Memorandum and Articles.

Section 24 of the 1983 Act permits the disapplication of section 23's statutory pre-emption rights.[163] Section 24(1) permits the directors of the company to have the power to either disapply section 23(1) or modify its application where either an appropriate provision in the company's Articles or a shareholders' special resolution so permits. Furthermore, section 24(2) allows the members of the company by way of a special resolution to resolve that section 23(1) be either disapplied or modified in its application to a specific allotment.[164] Before the special resolution under section 24(2) can be proposed, it must have been recommended by the company's directors and advance notice have been given to the members setting out: the directors' reasons for making the recommendation; the amount to be paid to the company for the securities; and, the directors' justification of the amount.[165]

While the Yellow Book requires companies to apply pre-emption rights (paragraph 9.18) when issuing securities in return for cash, it also recognises that shareholders may permit the company to ignore pre-emption rights. Paragraph 9.20 provides that where the shareholders give section 24 permission to disapply statutory pre-emption rights, issues by a company of equity securities for cash, made otherwise than to existing shareholders in proportion to their existing holdings, will be permitted in accordance with that authorisation. The Yellow Book further provides that a circular in connection with a resolution proposing to disapply statutory pre-emption rights must include a statement of the maximum amount of equity securities which the disapplication will cover. Furthermore, in the case of a general disapplication in respect of equity securities for cash made otherwise than to existing shareholders in proportion to their existing holdings, the circular must give an indication of the percentage which the amount generally disapplied represents of the total ordinary share capital in issue, as at a date not more than one month prior to the date of the circular.[166]

---

[163] In the case of *private* companies, s.23(7) of the Companies (Amendment) Act 1983 provides that the s.23(1) right of statutory pre-emption can be excluded in the case of private companies by the insertion of an appropriate provision in the company's Memorandum or Articles.

[164] Under both s.24(1) and (2) Companies (Amendment) Act 1983, in either case, the directors must already have been granted a general power of allotment pursuant to s.20 of the 1983 Act. S. 20 provides that the directors may not allot securities unless authorised by the company's Articles or by way of resolution of the company in general meeting.

[165] Companies (Amendment) Act 1983, s.24(5).

[166] para. 14.8 Yellow Book.

(6) Open Offer

1–30   An open offer is an invitation to existing holders of securities to subscribe or purchase securities in proportion to their holdings.[167] However, it is not made by means of a renounceable letter or other negotiable document. This is what distinguishes it from a rights issue. Paragraph 4.23 Yellow Book provides that an open offer must be made using assignable or transferable application forms, with splitting facilities. Furthermore, it may be made in conjunction with other methods of issue. A director may not, save in exceptional circumstances, apply for excess securities without those securities being offered to other existing shareholders on the same terms. The timetable for an open offer must ensure that valid claims through the market are satisfied promptly and special paragraphs are provided to achieve this aim.[168] An open offer may not be made where the securities are equity securities and are of a class already listed if the price is to be at a discount of more than 10% to the middle market price of those securities at the time of announcing the terms of the open offer, unless the Stock Exchange is satisfied that the issuer is in severe financial difficulties or that there are other exceptional circumstances.[169]

(7) Acquisition or Merger Issue

1–31   An acquisition or merger issue (or vendor consideration issue) is defined in the Yellow Book as an issue of securities in consideration for an acquisition of assets, or an issue of securities on an acquisition of, or merger with, another company as consideration for the securities of that company.[170] A company could use this method where it did not wish to finance an acquisition by means of borrowings or a rights issue.

(8) Capitalisation Issue

1–32   A company may opt to issue bonus shares to its existing members in proportion to their existing holdings rather than paying dividends, or for any other reason.[171] Such an issue is known as a

---

[167] para. 4.22 Yellow Book.
[168] para. 4.24 Yellow Book.
[169] para. 4.26 Yellow Book.
[170] para. 4.27 Yellow Book. As to whether an offer of securities in return for non-cash consideration may constitute a "subscription or purchase" such that the offer requires a prospectus, see Chap. 2 below where relevant caselaw is considered.
[171] A prospectus is not required where a bonus issue is made as there is no requirement for the allottee to "subscribe or purchase" the shares within the meaning of s.2(1) Companies Act 1963. Also see s.44(7) Companies Act 1963.

capitalisation or bonus issue and does not involve the company raising any capital, as the funds to finance the issue come from company
reserves.[172] In a capitalisation issue other than one in lieu of dividend,
if a shareholders' entitlement includes a fraction of a security, that fraction must be sold for the benefit of the holder, save that if its value (net
of expenses) does not exceed £3 it may be sold for the company's benefit. Such sales are required to be made before listing is granted.[173]

(9) Issue for Cash/Conversions of Securities of one class into securities of another class/Exercise of Options or Warrants to subscribe securities

1–33   An issue for cash is an issue of securities for cash to persons
who are specifically approved by shareholders in general meeting, or
an issue pursuant to a general disapplication of section 23 Companies
(Amendment) Act 1983 approved by shareholders in general meeting.[174] Such an issue will not be regarded as a placing where the subscribers are small in number and are named in general meeting.[175]

Paragraph 4.34 of the Yellow Book provides that securities of a class
already listed may be granted a listing if they arise from an issue for
cash, an exchange for, or a conversion into, another class of securities
or an exercise of options or warrants to subscribe for securities (including options under an employees' share scheme).

IV.   LISTING

A. PRINCIPLES UNDERLYING THE LISTING PARTICULARS DIRECTIVE / YELLOW BOOK

(1) The provision of certain minimum information and the Duty to Allow Informed Assessment

1–34   Where a company proposes to list its securities on the official
list, a listing particulars document must be prepared in compliance
with the requirement of Article 3 of Council Directive 80/390/EEC
otherwise known as the "Listing Particulars" Directive.[176] Ireland im-

---

[172] para. 4.31 Yellow Book.
[173] para. 4.32 Yellow Book.
[174] para. 4.33 Yellow Book. For further reading on s.23, see para. 1–29 above.
[175] para. 4.33 Yellow Book. Though whether a prospectus is required will all depend on whether the issue to such a restricted circle, is an offer to the public.
See further ss. 44; 51 and 61 of the Companies Act 1963 and the Prospectus
Directive considered in Chap. 2 below.
[176] Article 3 provides that Member States shall ensure that the admission of secu-

plemented the Directive by way of S.I. 282 of 1984 and designated the Irish Stock Exchange as the "competent authority" for the purposes of the Directive.[177] The Directive applies to securities which are the subject of an application for admission to official listing on a stock exchange situated or operating within a Member State.[178]

Article 4 is a key provision. It provides that listing particulars shall contain the information which, according to the particular nature of the issuer and of the securities, is necessary to enable investors and their investment advisers to make an "informed assessment" of the assets and liabilities, financial position, profits and losses, and prospects of the issuer and of the rights attaching to the securities. Regulation 4(1) of S.I. No. 282 of 1984 implements this obligation into domestic law by providing that the obligation to disclose all information in order to permit "informed assessment", shall be imposed on all persons (human or legal) responsible for the listing particulars or parts thereof.[179] The Yellow Book provides in its opening statement in Chapter 5 on "Listing Particulars" that issuers are reminded that they are under a general duty to disclose information which investors and their advisers would reasonably require or expect to receive for the purposes of making an informed assessment of the issuer's current posi-

---

rities to official listing on a Stock Exchange situated or operating within their territories is conditional upon the publication of an information sheet, referred to as a "listing particulars". Council Directive 80/390/EEC of March 17, 1980 co-ordinating the requirements for the drawing up, scrutiny and distribution of the listing particulars to be published for the admission of securities to official Stock Exchange listing [1980] O.J. L.100/1 (the "Listing Particulars Directive") as implemented by the European Communities (Stock Exchange) Regulations 1984 (S.I. No. 282 of 1984) which came into effect on January 1, 1985; as amended by Council Directive 87/345/EEC of 22 June 1987 [1987] O.J. L.185/81 as implemented by the European Communities (Stock Exchange) (Amendment) Regulations 1991 (S.I. No. 18 of 1991); and as further amended by Council Directive 90/211/EEC as implemented by the European Communities (Transferable Securities and Stock Exchange) Regulations 1992 (S.I. No. 202 of 1992); and as further amended by Council and European Parliament Directive 94/18/EC of May 30, 1994 [1994] O.J. L.135/1 as implemented by the European Communities (Stock Exchange) (Amendment) Regulations, 1994 (S.I. No. 234 of 1994).

[177] reg. 7(1) European Communities (Stock Exchange) Regulations 1984 (S.I. No. 282 of 1984).

[178] Art. 1.1. However, art. 1.2 further provides that the Directive does not apply to units issued by collective investment undertakings other than the closed-end type, nor to securities issued by a State or by its regional or local authorities. These terms are further defined in art. 2 of the Directive.

[179] Also the Directive and the Yellow Book Rules require the persons responsible to sign a Responsibility Statement and append same to the listing particulars: see further para. 1–41 below and also Chap. 2 where Responsibility Statements are further considered.

tion and future prospects. It provides[180] that where an issuer of securities applies for listing of its securities, listing particulars must be prepared in accordance with the Yellow Book rules, and submitted and approved by the Stock Exchange.

The preamble to the Listing Particulars Directive recognises that investors are hindered by the different listing particulars disclosure requirements from Member State to Member State. While it does not seek to eliminate such differences by making the disclosure requirements completely uniform, it does seek to achieve an "adequate degree of equivalence in the safeguards required in each Member State to ensure the provision of information which is sufficient and as objective as possible for actual or potential security holders." Consequently, article 5.1 of the Directive provides that without prejudice to the obligation to disclose all information as is necessary to allow investors make an "informed assessment", Member States shall ensure that at least the listing particulars contain the information required by Schedules A, B and C to the Directive.[181]

(2) The Principle of Mutual Recognition

1–35 In time, the legal framework created by the original Listing Particulars Directive in 1980 had its ambit widened by virtue of several subsequent amendments, all of which were designed to further the objective of market interpenetration. The legal principle used as the basis for this expansion was a much used principle of European Community legal harmonisation, the principle of mutual recognition.

First the Directive was amended in 1987 by Council Directive 87/345/EEC. This provided for the mutual recognition of listing particulars in circumstances where an application is made to admit the same securities to listing in two or more Member States at the same time or within a short interval of each other.[182]

---

[180] para. 5.1(b) Yellow Book.
[181] Schedule A sets out the Listing Particulars Directive's requirements for the layout of listing particulars where shares are to be admitted to the official list; Schedule B the requirements for the layout of listing particulars where debt securities are to be admitted to the official list; Schedule C the requirements for the layout of listing particulars where certificates representing shares are to be admitted to the official list. See further paras 1–37—1–40 below. Articles 8–17 elaborate further regarding the contents of listing particulars in specific cases.
[182] Council Directive 87/345/EEC of June 22, 1987 amending Directive 80/390/EEC co-ordinating the requirements for the drawing up, scrutiny and distribution of the listing particulars to be published for the admission of securities to official Stock Exchange listing, as implemented by the European Communities (Stock Exchange) (Amendment) Regulations 1991 S.I. No. 18 of 1991 which came into effect on March 1, 1991.

Second, a further amendment came about in 1994 by virtue of Council and European Parliament Directive 94/18/EC. This provided that where securities have been officially listed in one Member State for not less than three years, then the competent authorities in another Member State may exempt the issuer from having to publish listing particulars when it applies to be admitted to the list in the latter State.[183]

1–36 A third amendment was brought about in 1990. Council Directive 90/211/EEC provided that where a public offer prospectus is approved in one Member State to Listing Particulars Directive standards, then it must be recognised as a listing particulars in any other Member State in which an application to list the securities is either contemporaneous with (or made within three months of) the public offer in the first State.[184]

The European legal framework set in place for achieving this objective employs similar principles to those employed in the other two expansions noted immediately above. Just as the Listing Particulars Directive had required of listing particulars, the Prospectus Directive[185] required a certain common minimum of information to be available to investors throughout the Community whenever prospectuses were published in respect of public offers of securities. Member States were required to ensure that whenever an issuer was proposing to offer securities to the public for the first time, a prospectus would have to be published which included a certain minimum level of information.[186]

---

[183] Council and European Parliament Directive 94/18/EC of May 30, 1994 [1994] O.J. L.135/1 as implemented by the European Communities (Stock Exchange) (Amendment) Regulations 1994 (S.I. No. 234 of 1994) which came into effect on August 1, 1994. Directive 94/18/EC also provided that similar relief may be provided for companies whose securities have been traded on a second-tier market for at least two years in another Member State by inserting such a provision into art. 6(5) of the Listing Particulars Directive. However, this is only available where the applicant seeking admission to the official list has been trading on a second-tier market in the same State.

[184] Council Directive 90/211/EEC of April 23, 1990 [1990] O.J. L. 112/24 amending the Listing Particulars Directive 80/390/EEC in respect of the mutual recognition of public offer prospectuses as stock exchange listing particulars, as implemented by the European Communities (Transferable Securities and Stock Exchange Regulations) 1992 (S.I. No. 202 of 1992) which came into effect on September 1, 1992.

[185] Council Directive 89/298/EEC of April 17, 1989 [1989] O.J. L.124/8 coordinating the requirements for the drawing up, scrutiny and distribution of the prospectus to be published when transferable securities are offered to the public, as implemented by the European Communities (Transferable Securities and Stock Exchange Regulations) 1992 (S.I. No. 202 of 1992) which came into effect on September 1, 1992.

[186] Art. 4 Prospectus Directive (though where the issuer does not intend to seek a listing, less onerous prospectus disclosure requirements apply: art. 11). Note

Furthermore, the Prospectus Directive also employed the principle of mutual recognition. Not only did it provide for the mutual recognition of prospectuses,[187] but it also provided the basis for a link-up to be established with the Listing Particulars Directive's regime. *Inter alia* the Prospectus Directive required public offer prospectuses to be drawn up to Listing Particulars Directive disclosure standards whenever securities were also seeking contemporaneous admission to listing. For example, article 7 of the Prospectus Directive provides that where a public offer relates to transferable securities which at the time of the offer are the subject of an application to admission to official listing on a Stock Exchange operating within the same State, the contents of the prospectus and the procedures for scrutinising and distributing it shall be, subject to adaptations appropriate to the circumstances of a public offer, be determined in accordance with the disclosure requirements of the Listing Particulars Directive.[188] Consequently, the Yellow Book provides that where an issuer applies for listing of its securities which are to be offered to the public for the first time before admission, a prospectus prepared in accordance with the provisions of Chapter 5 of the Yellow Book must be submitted and approved by the Stock Exchange.[189] In other words, the contents of such a prospectus, and the procedures for submission to and approval by the Stock Exchange, are the same as those applicable to listing particulars, subject to adaptation as may be appropriate to the circumstances of the public offer.[190] It shall be seen how this demand for similar levels of disclosure ultimately facilitates the mutual recognition of listing particulars and prospectuses between Member States.[191] This interrelationship between

---

however that the Prospectus Directive does not cover all offers as it only applies to offers of "transferable securities", as further elaborated upon in Chap. 2 below.

[187] See below paras 1–77—1–78 when mutual recognition of prospectuses is considered further.

[188] The Prospectus Directive also provides in art. 8 that where an issuer of a public offer prospectus in one Member State intends to list the securities in another Member State, then the issuer should have the opportunity to draw up the prospectus in the first State to Listing Particulars Directive standards. Furthermore, art. 12 permits issuers to draw up public offer prospectuses to Listing Particulars standards if they so wish, even where no admission to listing is contemplated. These matters are given further consideration at paras 1–77 and 1–80 below.

[189] para. 5.1(a) and (b) Yellow Book.

[190] para. 5.1(d) Yellow Book; Art. 7 Prospectus Directive.

[191] Article 24b of the Listing Particular Directive (inserted by art. 2 of Council Directive 90/211/EEC of 20 April 1990 [1990] O.J. L. 112/24 amending the Listing Particulars Directive 80/390/EEC in respect of the mutual recognition of public offer prospectuses as stock exchange listing particulars, as implemented by the European Communities (Transferable securities and Stock Exchange Regulations) 1992 (S.I. No. 202 of 1992).

listing particulars and prospectuses, which grew out of the expanding European Community legal framework in the area will be considered in greater detail below.[192]

B. CONTENTS OF LISTING PARTICULARS

(1) Corresponding framework: Yellow Book and Listing Particulars Directive

1–37 According to Chapter 6 of the Yellow Book, the Yellow Book rules, which set out the information that a listing particulars must contain, vary according to the nature and circumstances of the applicant and the type of security being listed.[193] Required information must be set out in factual form, in as easily and analysable a form as possible.[194] There are restrictions on the use of pictures, charts, graphs, or other illustrations unless the Stock Exchange is satisfied they are the only way in which the relevant factual information can be clearly and fairly presented. The Exchange may also require such additional information as it considers appropriate in any particular case.[195]

Additional information will be required in the case of property companies, mineral companies, scientific research based companies, investment entities, public sector issuers, issuers of specialist securities (including specialist certificates representing shares) and miscellaneous securities, and venture capital trusts.[196]

Chapter 6 of the Yellow Book is divided into three subsections, each one corresponding to the Listing Particulars Directive's three Schedules:

1. information required for the admission to listing of shares or convertible debt securities (Schedule A)[197];

2. debt securities (Schedule B)[198]; and

3. certificates representing shares (Schedule C).[199]

---

[192] See paras 1–59—1–66 and 1–69—1–80.

[193] para. 5.6(a) Yellow Book. To facilitate this, a number of Tables are appended to appendix 1 to Chap. 5 Yellow Book. These Tables detail the level of Chap. 6 Yellow Book disclosure required in specific instances.

[194] Art. 5 Listing Particulars Directive; para. 5.7 Yellow Book.

[195] para. 5.6(c) Yellow Book.

[196] As required by Chapters 18-26 Yellow Book: para. 5.6(b) Yellow Book.

[197] paras 6.A–G (inclusive) Yellow Book.

[198] paras 6.H–N (inclusive) Yellow Book.

[199] paras 6.O–P (inclusive) Yellow Book.

The Appendix 1 Tables to Chapter 5 of the Yellow Book indicate the specific level of Chapter 6 information required in any particular type of application for listing.

(a) Shares or convertible debt securities

1–38   Chapter 6 Yellow Book sets out the information required for the admission to listing of shares[200] or convertible debt securities[201] to include the following.[202]

To begin with, information concerning the persons responsible for listing particulars such as auditors, bankers, legal advisers, and sponsors will be required.[203] In particular, it is required that any auditor's refusal or qualification of the issuer's accounts in the preceding three years be reproduced, and explained in full.

Also, a vast amount of information must be disclosed regarding the

---

[200] In so far as para. 6 refers to the listing of shares, it is based on schedule A of the Yellow Book. However for practical purposes, the precise level of Chap. 6 Yellow Book information required to be disclosed by the issuer of shares seeking a listing is determined by Table I to Appendix 1 to Chap. 5 Yellow Book which specifically indicates the categories of Chap. 6 information required, depending on whether the issuer is a new applicant, or an issuer with shares already listed.

[201] Table III ("Issue of Debt Securities Convertible into Shares of the Issuer") to appendix 1 to Chap. 5 Yellow Book specifically indicates the categories of Chap. 6 Yellow Book information required where an issuer is seeking listing for debt securities that are convertible into shares of the issuer, with varying requirements depending on whether the issuer is a new applicant, or an issuer with shares already listed. Table IV ("Issue of Convertible Debt Securities (where the issuer of the convertible debt securities is not the issuer of the shares into which they are convertible)") to Appendix 1 to Chap. 5 specifically indicates the categories of Chap. 6 information required where the issuer of the convertible debt securities seeking listing is not the issuer of the shares into which they are convertible, with varying requirements for the issuer of the convertible debt securities (depending on whether the issuer is a new applicant or an issuer with shares already listed), and the issuer of the shares. See also Table VI ("Issue of Debt Securities (including convertible debt securities) Guaranteed by a State or by a Federated State") to Appendix 1 to Chap. 5 on the level of Chap. 6 information required where an issue of debt securities (including convertible debt securities) guaranteed by a State or a Federated State seeks a listing, with varying requirements for the issuer and the guarantor (art. 17 Listing Particulars Directive). Also, depending on the circumstances, the appendices to Chaps 22 (public sector issuers of debt securities); 23 (specialist debt securities) and 24 (miscellaneous securities) may be of relevance.

[202] Note that what follows is an overview of some of the more important requirements, and that where one wishes to ascertain exactly what level of disclosure is required in any particular situation, Chap. 6 Yellow Book and the tables to the appendices of Chaps 5, 22, 23 and 24 should be consulted, where relevant.

[203] para. 6.A Yellow Book; sched. A Chap. 1 Listing Particulars Directive.

shares[204] for which application to listing is being made. For example, a statement that an application for admission in respect of the shares has been made to the Stock Exchange seeking admission to the official list must be provided. Furthermore, a statement that a copy of the listing particulars has been delivered to the Registrar of Companies is required, as well as an indication of the size and number of the issue, the rights attaching to the shares, the price at which the shares were placed (if any) and whether pre-emption rights have been disapplied.

So far as the issuer and its capital[205] are concerned, again a vast amount of information may be required on matters as various as:

- the laws governing the incorporation and operation of the issuer (if a foreign issuer),

- the existence and nature of material contracts, audited accounts of the issuer for the past two years,

- the amount of the issuer's authorised and issued share capital,

- the names of those who control the issuer and whether the issuer is satisfied that it will be capable of carrying out its business independently of the controlling shareholder(s)' influence,

- assurances that all transactions with the controlling shareholder(s) will be at arm's length, and,

- information on any options that a controlling shareholder(s)[206] may have over the issuer's capital.[207]

Where the issuer is part of a group then information on the group's activities[208] will be required. For example, what may be required here

---

[204] para. 6.B Yellow Book; sched. A Chap. 2 Listing Particulars Directive.

[205] para. 6.C Yellow Book; sched. A Chap. 3 Listing Particulars Directive.

[206] By virtue of para. 9 second sched. S.I. No. 282 of 1984. Ireland has set the threshold at 5% of the issuer's capital for the purposes of determining what constitutes a controlling shareholders. However, in this regard, para. 6.C.16 Yellow Book (somewhat differently) requires:

"In so far as is known to the issuer, the name of any person other than a director who, directly or indirectly, is interested in 3% or more of the issuer's capital, together with the amount of each person's interest or, if there are no such persons, an appropriate negative statement. While it is acknowledged that there is no legal requirement on shareholders in Irish registered companies to notify an interest below 5%, if such shareholder makes a notification of an interest of 3% or more, this interest should be disclosed."

[207] Also note that para. 6.C Yellow Book goes further as it requires names of any holders of an option, not just those of controlling shareholders (it does not however require names where all holders of a class of securities have options, or where employees have options under an employees share scheme.

[208] para. 6.D Yellow Book; sched. A Chap. 4 Listing Particulars Directive.

is a description of the products or services that the issuer provides, the location of the issuer's group's principal places of business, and a breakdown of net turnover during the preceding three years by activity and geographical market. Also information must be disclosed pertaining to any legal proceedings either pending or which involved the group in the preceding 12 months which might adversely affect the issuer's financial position. Furthermore, information concerning the principal investments the group has made in other undertakings within the preceding three years is required, as well as information regarding any investments that the group is proposing to make, or in respect of which it has made firm commitments.[209]

On the topic of the issuer's assets and liabilities, financial position, profits and losses,[210] again a wide range of information may be sought, ranging from:

– the preceding three years' accounts (or consolidated accounts in the case of a group of which the issuer is part),

– dividends paid in that period, profit and loss each year,

– the accounting principles by which the accounts were determined,

– the total amount of all total loan capital outstanding, or all borrowings and indebtedness in the nature of borrowings,

– as well as all contingent liabilities, or guarantees given.

So far as the management is concerned,[211] information must be provided demonstrating an indication of the management's expertise and experience, in particular to include a history of the directors of the issuer and information as to matters such as: whether they have been involved in liquidations or receiverships or examinerships of companies whilst a director of any such company; whether personally involved in any partnership which dissolved; whether personally bankrupted or voluntarily so arranged; whether subject to public criticism by any statutory or regulatory authority; or, whether disqualified by a court from acting in the management of any company. Also, the total aggregate of the remuneration paid to, and benefits in kind granted to, the directors of the issuer by any member of the issuer's group during that last completed financial year must be disclosed, as well as holdings held by any director in the issuer or any company in the issuer's group. Furthermore, any loans or guarantees granted by any mem-

---

[209] Although this does not include interests being acquired in other undertakings (para. 6.D).

[210] para. 6.E Yellow Book; sched. A Chap. 5 Listing Particulars Directive.

[211] para. 6.F Yellow Book; sched. A Chap. 6 Listing Particulars Directive.

ber of the group in favour of any director must be disclosed. Some details of directors' service contracts must also be provided.[212]

Finally, so far as the recent development and prospects of the group are concerned,[213] this may require information to be furnished concerning any special trade factors or risks not mentioned elsewhere in the listing particulars which might affect the group's prospects and which is unlikely to be known to, or anticipated by, the general public and which could materially affect profits.

(b) Debt securities

1–39 Chapter 6 Yellow Book requires similar categories of information for the admission to listing of debt securities as that required in respect of shares or convertible debt securities,[214] with of course necessary adaptation as appropriate for debt securities.[215] The precise level of disclosure required in each category will depend on the precise circumstances surrounding a particular application to list.[216] The main headings under which information is required are as follows:

– the persons responsible for listing particulars, in particular the auditors and the audited accounts for the last three years[217];

---

[212] According to the Yellow Book definition, a director's service contract is every contract of services, and variation thereof, of which a copy or written memorandum is required to be kept by s. 50 Companies Act 1990. Furthermore, the Yellow Book definition provides that subs.50(9) (which provides that any such contract which may expire within 3 years is not subject to s.50) is to be read for the purposes of the listing paragraphs as if subs.50(9) read "12 months".

[213] para. 6.G Yellow Book; sched. A Chap. 7 Listing Particulars Directive.

[214] See para. 1–38 immediately above, though note that in some instances the information required to be disclosed may vary: see further para. 6 Yellow Book where appropriate.

[215] In so far as it relates to debt securities, para. 6 is based on Schedule B Listing Particulars Directive.

[216] Accordingly, Table II to Appendix 1 to Chap. 5 Yellow Book specifically indicates the categories of Chap. 6 Yellow Book information required depending on whether the issuer of debt securities is a new applicant, or a listed issuer. See also Table VI ("Issue of Debt Securities (including convertible debt securities) Guaranteed by a State or by a Federated State") to Appendix 1 to Chap. 5 on the level of Chap. 6 information required where an issue of debt securities (including convertible debt securities) guaranteed by a State or a Federated State seeks a listing, with varying requirements for the issuer and the guarantor. Also the appendices to Chaps 22 (public sector issuers of debt securities); 23 (specialist debt securities) and 24 (miscellaneous securities) may be of relevance depending on the circumstances of the issue. (So far as debt securities convertible into the shares of the issuer, or debt securities convertible into shares issued by another party are concerned, Table III and IV to Appendix 1 to Chap. 5 Yellow Book should be consulted).

[217] para. 6.H Yellow Book; Sched. B Chap. 1 Listing Particulars Directive.

- extensive information about the debt securities for which application for listing is being made[218];

- detailed information about the issuer and its capital[219];

- details of the group's activities regarding the operation of its business and further investment prospects[220];

- wide-ranging information on the issuer's assets and liabilities, financial position and profits and losses[221];

- information on the management[222] and

- information on recent developments and prospects of the group.[223]

In some of the aforementioned categories, the level of information required about the issuer and the debt securities is as extensive as that
required when the corresponding analogous categories were considered above *vis a vis* the listing of shares/convertible debt securities,[224]
although some categories are less so.

(c) Certificates representing shares

1–40   Finally, Chapter 6 also sets out the information required for the
admission to listing of certificates representing shares.[225] The disclosure requirements in this instance relate to both the shares and their
issuer,[226] and also general information about the issuer of the certificates,[227] and basic information about the certificates.[228] Information
on the financial position of the issuer of the certificates is not required
when the issuer is a "credit institution"[229] which is a national of a Mem-

---

[218] para. 6.I Yellow Book; Sched. B Chap. 2 Listing Particulars Directive.
[219] para. 6.J Yellow Book; Sched. B Chap. 3 Listing Particulars Directive.
[220] para. 6.K Yellow Book; Sched. B Chap. 4 Listing Particulars Directive.
[221] para. 6.L Yellow Book; Sched. B Chap. 5 Listing Particulars Directive.
[222] para. 6.M Yellow Book; Sched. B Chap. 6 Listing Particulars Directive.
[223] para. 6.N Yellow Book; Sched. B Chap. 7 Listing Particulars Directive.
[224] See para. 1–38 immediately above.
[225] In so far as it relates to certificates representing shares, para. 6 is based on
schedule C Listing Particulars Directive.
[226] To the extent required by Table VII ("Issue of Certificates Representing Shares")
to Appendix 1 of Chap. 5 Yellow Book detailing the level of Chap. 6 Yellow
Book disclosure required.
[227] para. 6.O Yellow Book; Sched. C Chap. 1 Listing Particulars Directive.
[228] para. 6.P Yellow Book; Sched. C Chap. 2 Listing Particulars Directive.
[229] "credit institution" is defined in art. 2(b) of the Listing Particulars Directive as
"an undertaking whose business is to receive deposits or other repayable funds
from the public and to grant credits for its own account". Furthermore, information on the financial position of the issuer of the certificates is not required
where either that issuer is a subsidiary, 95% or more of which is owned by a

ber State and is set up or governed by a special law, or pursuant to such a law is subject to public supervision designed to protect savings.[230] Furthermore, it is provided that in the case of certificates issued by a securities transfer organisation, or by an auxillary institution set up by such an organisation, the Stock Exchange may dispense with the publication of general information about the issuer of the certificates.[231]

(d) Responsibility Statement and Responsibility Letters

1–41   Article 4.2 of the Listing Particulars Directive provides that Member States shall ensure that the Article 4.1 obligation to disclose sufficient information to allow investors make an "informed assessment" is incumbent upon the persons responsible for the listing particulars. Schedules A and B of the Directive require such responsible persons to declare in a responsibility statement that, to the best of their knowledge, the information given in the part of the listing particulars for which they are responsible, is in accordance with the facts and contains no omissions likely to affect the impact of the information. The implementing regulations[232] reflect this regime, as regulation 4.2 provides that the "obligation referred to in Article 4.1 of the Listing Particulars directive shall be incumbent on the persons referred to in Article 4.2 of that directive."

The Yellow Book[233] provides that a listing particulars must include a "responsibility statement" signed by the "directors" of the issuer. "Director" shall include any persons who have authorised themselves to be named in the listing particulars as persons who agreed to become directors.[234] However, the Stock Exchange may also insist on the statement being signed by a person who either has been, or will be, invited to become a director of the issuer, or whose appointment as a director is otherwise in contemplation.[235] Furthermore, the Stock Exchange may

---

credit institution, the commitments of which towards the holders of the certificates are unconditionally guaranteed by that credit institution and which is subject to the same supervision. Nor is it required where the issuer is an "Adminstratiekantoor" in the Netherlands, governed for the safe custody of the original securities, by special regulations laid down by the competent authorities (see pars. (b) and (c) of Table VII ("Issue of Certificates Representing Shares") to appendix 1 of Chap. 5 Yellow Book).

[230] Table VII para. (a) ("Issue of Certificates Representing Shares") to Appendix 1 of Chap. 5 Yellow Book.

[231] Table VII.

[232] S.I. No. 282 of 1984.

[233] para. 5.2.

[234] para. 5.2 Yellow Book.

[235] *ibid.*

require responsibility to be extended to "additional persons", in which case the statement must be adapted accordingly.[236]

Where the listing particulars relate to certificates representing shares, then the directors of the issuer of the shares (not the directors of the issuers of the certificates) must accept responsibility for all of the information in the listing particulars.[237] However, where the listing particulars relate to securities issued in connection with a merger or takeover of either a listed company or a DCM company and the directors of the other company accept responsibility for the information given on that company in the listing particulars, then the directors of the issuer may accept responsibility only for the rest of the information in the listing particulars and the responsibility statement will be adapted accordingly.[238]

The issuer must provide the Stock Exchange with a responsibility letter signed by every director confirming that the listing particulars include all information within their knowledge (or which it would be reasonable for them to obtain by making enquiries) which investors and their professional advisers would reasonably require and reasonably expect to find, for the purpose of allowing an informed assessment of the prospects and position of the issuer to be made.[239] Responsibility letters will not be required in respect of a person who either has been, or will be, invited to become a director, if the Exchange has agreed to relieve such person from the obligation to make a responsibility statement.

The domestic implementing regulations (S.I. No. 282 of 1984) provide for a number of criminal offences in the event that the listing particulars is published in contravention of the regulations.[240] Regulation 4(2) provides for a number of defences in the event of non-compliance with, or contravention of, the obligation to make disclosure sufficient to permit an informed assessment to be made. However, as will be seen when liabilities are considered further in Chapter 3 below, these defences are not absolute, particularly as regulation 4(3) provides that:

> "Nothing in this Regulation shall be construed so as to limit or diminish any liability which any person may incur under the law of the State apart from these Regulations."[241]

---

[236] para. 5.4 Yellow Book.
[237] para. 5.3(a) Yellow Book. Although if the Stock Exchange so agrees, this may be limited in certain situations. See further para. 5.3(a).
[238] para. 5.3(b) Yellow Book.
[239] para. 5.5 Yellow Book.
[240] See further Chap. 3 below.
[241] For example, s. 46 of the Companies Act 1963 (experts' liability); s. 49 and s. 50 of the Companies Act 1963 (civil and criminal liability for mis-statements in prospectus) may apply, as may common law forms of action: see further Chapter 3 below.

C. APPROVAL OF LISTING PARTICULARS

(1) Principle of Prior Approval

1–42 The Listing Particulars Directive provides for the principle of prior approval of listing particulars.[242] No listing particulars may be published until they have been approved by the competent authorities, who shall "approve" the publication of the listing particulars only if they are satisfied that the particulars satisfy all of the requirements set out in the Directive.[243] In order to facilitate this process mandated by the principle of prior approval, the Yellow Book requires three copies of the draft listing particulars to be submitted to the listing department of the Stock Exchange at least 10 clear business days prior to the intended publication date.[244] Where an applicant has never listed before, or where there are complex issues to be resolved, then at least 20 clear business days must be allowed.[245] In practice, applicants tend to give the Exchange more time (than the minimum time set by the Yellow Book) to examine the draft particulars.

---

[242] Approval must be given prior to publication: Art. 18 Listing Particulars Directive and para. 5.12 Yellow Book. The Stock Exchange is designated as the competent authority by reg. 7(1) of S.I. No. 282 of 1984 for the purposes of the Directive.

[243] Art. 18(3) Listing Particulars Directive. The Stock Exchange is the competent authority for approval of the listing particulars and the Registrar of Companies is the competent authority for the purpose of registration of the listing particulars: S.I. No. 282 of 1984. However, note that the Stock Exchange does not verify the veracity or correctness of the information submitted to it in the particulars (under the Yellow Book rules that is the responsibility of the directors and the sponsor who undertakes to ensure that the listing requirements are satisfied by the issuer). Interestingly, art.18(4) of the Directive provides that the Directive shall not affect the competent authorities' liability, as that is a matter which shall continue to be governed solely by national law. In this regard, reg. 8(1) of S.I. No. 282 of 1984 provides that neither the Stock Exchange nor its agents shall be liable in damages by reason only of non-compliance with or contravention of any obligation imposed by, or by virtue of the regulations implementing the Directive, nor shall it or its agents be liable in respect of anything done or omitted to be done by them in connection with the exercise of the Stock Exchange's functions as competent authority unless the act or omission was done in bad faith. Furthermore, reg. 8(2) provides that no transaction shall be void or voidable by reason only of the fact that it was entered into in contravention of, or not in conformity with, the regulations.

[244] para. 5.9 Yellow Book (although shorter periods may also be allowed if the Exchange so agrees). Note that these days are exclusive of the submission day and the approval day according to the January 1999 notes to the Yellow Book, and also note that they are significantly shorter than the periods previously allowed, which were 14 and 28 days respectively. In practice, the Stock Exchange will accept one copy.

[245] para. 5.10 Yellow Book.

The submission deadlines are necessary in order for the Stock Exchange to examine the draft documents and consider whether they require any further elaboration or amendment in order that they may be resubmitted by the applicant to the Stock Exchange in final form for formal approval. When any amendments have been made, the amended listing particulars (as well as a long list of various documents[246]) must be submitted to the listing department of the Stock Exchange seeking formal approval. The Stock Exchange will only give formal approval where it considers that the information in the particulars is "complete".[247] A copy of the listing particulars shall also be delivered by the issuer to the Registrar of Companies either on or before the day of publication.[248] Should the Prospectus Directive also apply, there are additional registration formalities.[249]

(2) Supplementary Particulars

1–43 Prior approval and publication of supplementary listing particulars is required in the event that in the period between formal approval of the listing particulars and the commencement of dealing in the relevant securities, there has either been a significant change affecting a matter contained in the main listing particulars, or, a significant new matter has arisen which would have warranted inclusion in the main particulars had such matter arisen at the time.[250]

A matter is regarded as "significant" where it is a matter that would be relevant to an investor attempting to make an "informed assessment"[251] of the issuer.[252] A copy of any such supplementary particulars must be delivered to the Registrar of Companies.[253] The supplementary particulars must contain a statement to the effect that, save as disclosed, there has been no significant change and no significant new matter has arisen since the publication of the previous particulars.[254]

---

[246] *ibid.*

[247] para. 5.12 Yellow Book.

[248] reg. 13(1) S.I. No. 282 of 1984. Failure to comply is an offence (reg.13(3)). For consideration of advertisement and circulation of the listing particulars, see para. 1–56—1–58.

[249] See further para. 1–72 below.

[250] Art. 23 Listing Particulars Directive; para. 5.14 Yellow Book.

[251] Art. 4(1) Listing Particulars Directive; reg. 4(1) S.I. No. 282 of 1984; Chap. 5 Yellow Book.

[253] para. 5.15 Yellow Book.

[253] para. 5.16(d) Yellow Book.

[254] para. 5.16(c) Yellow Book.

D. EXEMPTION FROM REQUIREMENT TO PUBLISH LISTING PARTICULARS

1–44 Article 6 of the Directive allows the Stock Exchange to provide for the partial or complete exemption from the obligation to publish listing particulars in several situations. The Yellow Book has had regard to this article as follows.

First, it provides for three instances where an exemption "may" be granted.[255] Appendix 2 to Chapter 5 of the Yellow Book sets out in detail the specific information required in each of the three instances. Such information will be required to be published in a document known as an "exempt listing particulars".

Second, the Yellow Book provides for a number of situations (seven) where a listing particulars is not required, save in "exceptional circumstances."[256] In these seven situations, the issuer of the shares has shares or issues of certificates representing shares, already listed.

(1) Exemptions which may be granted

(a) Previously published documents[257]

1–45 The first situation where exemption may be granted is in respect of securities which either have been:

1. the subject of a public issue, or;

2. issued in connection with a takeover offer, or;

3. issued in connection with a merger involving the acquisition of another company or the formation of a new company, or the division of a company, or the transfer of all or part of an undertaking's assets and liabilities, or as consideration for the transfer of assets other than cash.

In order for the Stock Exchange to be able to consider granting an exemption in any of the aforegoing situations, the Yellow Book requires that in the previous 12 months before admission of the securities, a document must have been published which in the opinion of the Stock Exchange contained equivalent information to that which would otherwise be required to be included in listing particulars by the Stock Exchange.[258]

---

[255] Art. 6 Listing Particulars Directive; para. 5.23A Yellow Book.
[256] para. 5.27 Yellow Book. See further para. 1–51 below.
[257] For the exempt listing particulars content requirements in this instance, see para. 1–48 below.
[258] Art. 6.1 Listing Particulars Directive; para. 5.23A(a) Yellow Book.

(b) Three years' admission to listing in another Member State[259]

1–46   The second situation where exemption may be granted is where
the securities have been listed in another Member State(s) for not less
than three years, and the competent authorities in such other Member
State(s) have confirmed that the issuer has complied with all of the
Directive's requirements there.[260] This effectively permits the Stock Exchange to exempt an applicant from having to publish a listing particulars where the applicant already has, in the eyes of the listing
authorities in another Member State(s), an existing history of listing
compliance. This exemption has its legislative origin in Council and
European Parliament Directive 94/18/EC of 1994.[261]

   However the applicant will still have to publish a certain level of
information such as information about the number and class of shares,
any listing particulars or prospectus or equivalent document that it
may have published in the past 12 months, latest annual accounts, etc.[262]

(c) Admission of a DCM company[263]

1–47   The third situation where the Stock Exchange may consider
granting an exemption is where the issuer's shares have been trading
on the Developing Companies Market in the State for a period cover-
ing at least the preceding two years and the securities for which application is made for admission to the official list are those shares, or are
those shares and any other securities of the issuer which have been so
traded for such a period.[264]

---

[259] For the exempt listing particulars content requirements in this instance, see
para. 1–49 below.

[260] para. 5.23A(b) Yellow Book. And also that, in the case of any Member States
where the securities have been listed for less than three years, that the competent authorities in those States also confirm that the issuer has complied with
all of the Directive's requirements.

[261] Arts. 6(4) (a) and (b) of the Listing Particulars Directive. Art. 6(4) was inserted
into the original Listing Particulars Directive 80/390/EEC by art. 1 of Council
and European Parliament Directive 94/18/EC of May 30, 1994 [1994] O.J. L.135/
1 as implemented by the European Communities (Stock Exchange) (Amendment) Regulations, 1994 (S.I. No. 234 of 1994).

[262] Art. 6(4) (c)–(e) Listing Particulars Directive, as inserted by art. 1 of Council
and European Parliament Directive 94/18/EC of May 30, 1994 [1994] O.J. L.135/
1 as implemented by the European Communities (Stock Exchange) (Amendment) Regulations, 1994 (S.I. No. 234 of 1994).

[263] For the exempt listing particulars content requirements in this instance, see
para. 1–50 below.

[264] Art. 6(5) Listing Particulars Directive, as inserted by art. 1 of Council and European Parliament Directive No. 94/18/EC of May 30, 1994 [1994] O.J. L.135/1
as implemented by the European Communities (Stock Exchange) (Amendment)
Regulations, 1994 (S.I. No. 234 of 1994).

In order for the Stock Exchange to be able to consider granting an exemption, it must be of the opinion that information equivalent in substance to that required by the Directive is available to investors before the date on which admission to listing becomes effective.[265]

(2) Exempt Listing Particulars

1–48 Where any of the aforegoing three exemptions (in paragraphs 1–45—1–47 above) are permitted by the Stock Exchange, then a document known as an exempt listing particulars must be published.[266]

In practice, what this means in the case of the first category above (previously published document),[267] is that the exempt listing particulars must contain details of material changes that have occurred in the meantime since the date of publication of the relevant document, a brief description of the number and class of the securities applying to be listed, and a responsibility statement by the directors.[268]

1–49 In the case of the second category (admission of a company listed in another Member State),[269] the exempt listing particulars must be in English or accompanied by an English translation[270] and contain general information about the company, including its latest set of annual accounts, and any listing particulars, prospectus or equivalent document it may have published in the last 12 months before applying to the Stock Exchange for admission to listing. Also, it must provide details of any significant changes in the interim period, a description of the securities and the rights attaching thereto, as well as a description of how Irish resident holders of the company's securities will be treated for tax purposes, and a responsibility statement by the directors.[271]

---

[265] para. 5.23A(c) Yellow Book.

[266] para. 5.24 Yellow Book.

[267] *i.e.* securities which have been the subject of a public issue, or which have been issued in connection with a takeover offer, or which have been issued in connection with a merger or restructuring of a company. Provided that in the case of each of the aforegoing, a document has been published in the preceding 12 months which is equivalent in content to a listing particulars (art. 6.1 Listing Particulars Directive; para. 5.23A(a) Yellow Book).

[268] For a more complete and specific description of each of the items requiring elaboration, see further para. 1 of Appendix 2 to Chap. 5 Yellow Book.

[269] Arts. 6(4) (a),(b) and (c) Listing Particulars Directive (as inserted by Council and European Parliament Directive 94/18/EC, art. 1); para. 5.23A(b) Yellow Book.

[270] Art. 6a of the Listing Particulars Directive, as inserted by Directive 94/18/EC, permits English to be specified as the language of choice of the Stock Exchange.

[271] For a more complete and specific description of each of the items requiring elaboration, see further para. 2 of appendix 2 to Chap. 5 Yellow Book. Also see art. 6.4(c) Listing Particulars Directive, as inserted by art 1 of Directive 94/18/

1–50 Finally, in the case of the third category (admission of a DCM company),[272] the exempt listing particulars must contain the latest three years annual accounts, any prospectus or equivalent document the company may have published in the last 12 months before applying for admission to listing, details of any significant changes in the interim period, a statement of indebtedness, a working capital statement, a statement detailing when the shares will be admitted to listing and when dealings will commence, as well as general information about the securities and their rights, and a responsibility statement.[273] Overseas[274] DCM companies are advised to contact the Stock Exchange at an early stage to ascertain whether extra information is required.

(3) Exemptions available except in "exceptional circumstances"

1–51 There are a number of situations (seven) where pursuant to article 6 of the Listing Particulars Directive the Stock Exchange has indicated that it will not require a listing particulars, except in "exceptional circumstances".[275] These seven situations are as follows:

– where shares are allotted by way of a capitalisation issue to the holders of shares already listed (*i.e.* bonus shares);

– where shares result from the conversions of convertible debt securities already listed;

– where shares result from the exercise of rights under warrants already listed;

– where shares are issued in place of shares already listed, provided there is no increase in the nominal value of the share capital as a result;

EC of May 30, 1994 [1994] O.J. L.135/1 as implemented by the European Communities (Stock Exchange) (Amendment) Regulations 1994 (S.I. No. 234 of 1994).

[272] *i.e.* a company operating in the State on a second tier market regulated and supervised as required by Art. 6.5 Listing Particulars Directive, as inserted by Art. 1 of Council and European Parliament Directive 94/18/EC.

[273] For a more complete and specific description of each of the items requiring elaboration, see further para. 3 of Appendix 2 to Chap. 5 Yellow Book; art. 6.5 Listing Particulars Directive, as inserted by art. 1 of Council and European Directive 94/18/EC.

[274] For the purposes of the Yellow Book, an "overseas company" is normally a company incorporated outside the Republic of Ireland (though note that for certain purposes of Chap. 17 Yellow Book (which deals with Overseas Companies) an Irish company with a primary listing on an exchange and its primary market outside Ireland, may be treated as an overseas company.

[275] The Yellow Book does not define what "exceptional circumstances" are.

- where shares would increase the shares of a class already listed by less than 10%;

- where shares are allotted to employees and shares of the same class are already listed;

- where certificates representing shares are issued in exchange for the shares, provided that certificates of the same class are already listed and that there is no increase in the nominal value of the company's share capital as a result.

In these seven situations just outlined, shares are already listed, and no listing particulars is required unless in the opinion of the Stock Exchange exceptional circumstances exist.

However, certain information must nevertheless be published.[276] Paragraph 5.28 provides that, if in any of the first four situations immediately above the shares would increase the shares of the relevant class by more than 10%, then a certain amount of information about the shares must be published, in accordance with Chapter 6 of the Yellow Book.[277] All such information must be notified to the Company Announcements Office of the Exchange.[278] However, if the shares would increase the shares of the relevant class by less than 10%, then merely the number and type of securities to be admitted, and the circumstances of their issue, need be published.[279] In the case of the final three types of issue considered above, no 10% threshold applies. In such issues, merely the number and type of securities to be admitted and the circumstances of their issue need be published.[280]

(4) Summary Particulars

1–52   Article 22 of the Listing Particulars Directive gives the applicant the option of not circulating a listing particulars. This is not an

---

[276] Such information (as described in para. 5.28) must be published in accordance with Chap. 8 Yellow Book as if the document comprised listing particulars, and must be notified to the Company Announcements Office, such notification stating where the information can be obtained: para. 5.29 Yellow Book.

[277] para. 5.28(a) Yellow Book.

[278] para. 5.29 Yellow Book.

[279] para. 5.28(b) Yellow Book. All such information to be notified to the Company Announcements Office: para. 5.29 Yellow Book. Note that para. 5.30 further provides that, in the case of the fifth situation detailed above ("shares which would increase the shares of a class by less than 10%"), where such shares are listed in connection with the acquisition of assets, further information may be required to be notified to the Company Announcements Office, and in some cases a circular to shareholders may be necessary.

[280] para. 5.28(b) Yellow Book. para. 5.29 Yellow Book requires all such 5.28 information to be notified to the Company Announcements Office.

exemption situation *per se*,[281] but rather a situation where the listing particulars need not be circulated. Instead, a summary particulars may suffice.[282] The Yellow Book provides that summary particulars may be circulated instead of full listing particulars and may accompany or be included in any circular sent to holders of listed securities.[283] In such cases, issuers must draw up full listing particulars, and have them approved by the Stock Exchange and published in accordance with the usual Yellow Book rules regulating the publication of listing particulars.

However, only the summary particulars are circulated. Before they are circulated, the summary particulars must be authorised by the Stock Exchange[284] (but they do not require approval by the Exchange, as the full listing particulars will already have been approved). Summary particulars must not contain any material information not contained in the listing particulars.[285] It must indicate that listing particulars have been published, and also where the listing particulars may be inspected[286] or obtained free of charge.[287]

(5) Shelf Registration

1–53   The Yellow Book rules provide that an issuer whose shares have been listed for more than 12 months, or which has issued its first annual accounts as a listed issuer, whichever is the earlier, may prepare a document known as a shelf document.[288] A shelf document is a document containing the categories of information that one would expect to find in a listing particulars (*i.e.* Chapter 6 Yellow Book information).[289]

The purpose of such a document is to facilitate a listed issuer should it subsequently wish to admit shares to listing within a specified pe-

---

[281] Exemption instances were considered above at paras 1–44—1–51.
[282] para. 5.32 Yellow Book. See also Art. 20 Listing Particulars Directive.
[283] para. 5.32 Yellow Book.
[284] para. 8.24 Yellow Book.
[285] para. 5.33 Yellow Book.
[286] Available for inspection at the Companies Announcements Office (para. 5.33(c) (ii) Yellow Book).
[287] From the issuer's registered office and the office of any paying agent and any other address as the issuer may determine (para. 5.33(c) (i) Yellow Book).
[288] paras 5.35–41 set out the Yellow Book rules pertaining to shelf registration documents.
[289] Table 1A of Appendix 1 to Chap. 5 Yellow Book sets out the specific level of Chap. 6 information required. The January 1999 notes to the Yellow Book observe that a guide will be published shortly to assist issuers and advisers with the procedures involved in this new system of shelf registration which will clarify a number of unspecified matters raised as a result of consultations which took place in late 1998 between the London Stock Exchange and interested parties.

riod, as its existence relieves the issuer from having to publish a fresh listing particulars. The specified period is the period during which the shelf document remains "current", and is defined by the rules as the earlier of either the publication of the issuer's next annual accounts, or the date 12 months from the date the shelf document is published on the Stock Exchange website, or the date the shelf document is removed from the Website at the written request of the issuer.[290]

In essence, the shelf document, together with a further document known as an "issue note" which is compiled just in advance of the listing, will be deemed to comprise a listing particulars. If any significant changes have occurred since the preparation of the shelf document, then the issue note will detail such changes.[291] Both shelf document[292] and issue note[293] have to be submitted in draft form to the Stock Exchange and once any required adjustments are made, require to be resubmitted to the Stock Exchange for formal approval prior to their publication.[294]

(6) Omission of information from the Listing Particulars

1–54 The Directive recognises that there will be situations where the Stock Exchange may authorise omission from the listing particulars of certain information. It provides that information may be omitted where it is of minor importance and will not influence investor assessment of the prospects and position of the issuer.[295] Furthermore, information may be omitted where disclosure would be contrary to the public interest or seriously detrimental to the issuer. However, with regard to detriment to the issuer, the Directive further provides that such omission must not be likely to mislead the public with regard to facts and circumstances, knowledge of which is essential for the assessment of the securities in question.[296]

Where an issuer wishes to omit information, a request in writing must be made to the Stock Exchange, identifying the information in question, and explaining why it should be omitted.[297] Specific provision is also made for the omission of material contracts to be withheld from public inspection if any of the aforegoing criteria are satisfied.

---

[290] para. 5.35 Yellow Book.
[291] para. 5.36 Yellow Book.
[292] para. 5.38 Yellow Book.
[293] para. 5.39 Yellow Book.
[294] para. 5.40 Yellow Book.
[295] Art. 7(a) Listing Particulars Directive; para. 5.18 (a) Yellow Book.
[296] Art. 7(b) Listing Particulars Directive; para. 5.18(b) and (c) Yellow Book.
[297] para. 5.21 Yellow Book.

Again application seeking permission for the omission must be made to the Stock Exchange in writing.[298]

V. LISTING APPLICATION PROCEDURES

A. TIME FOR APPLICATION

1–55 As already seen earlier above,[299] the applicant seeking admission to listing must submit the draft listing particulars to the Stock Exchange for approval at least 10 business days before the intended publication date. Assuming approval is obtained, Chapter 7 of the Yellow Book sets out the procedures which are to be followed by the issuer when applying formally for a listing.[300] Admission becomes effective only when the decision of the Stock Exchange to admit the securities to listing has been announced by the Stock Exchange's electronic communication systems with member firms.[301] Two days before the application is to be considered, a number of documents referred to as the "48 hour documents" must be delivered to the Stock Exchange for consideration. These include two copies of the listing particulars,[302] a copy of the newspaper advertisement relating to the offer, a copy of the applicant's board resolution, and other miscellaneous documents.[303]

Paragraph 7.7 Yellow Book details items to be lodged on the day that the Stock Exchange is to consider the application. These include the appropriate Exchange fees and a pricing statement. The Yellow Book also provides for a range of documentation to be lodged with the Stock Exchange shortly afterwards including, where applicable, items such as the names and addresses of clients with whom securities were placed in an intermediaries offer and a statement of the number of securities which were in fact issued.[304]

---

[298] para. 5.22 Yellow Book.
[299] para. 1–42.
[300] Additional and alternative procedures are set out for public sector issuers, issuers of specialist securities, and miscellaneous securities. For the specific level of detail required, Chaps. 22–44 Yellow Book should be consulted in this regard.
[301] para. 7.1 Yellow Book.
[302] para. 7.5(b) Yellow Book (or eight copies in the case of a new applicant).
[303] In the case of a new applicant, para 7.5(g) Yellow Book requires the Certificate of Incorporation to be lodged, as well as Letters of Compliance from the company's legal advisers to the effect that the Articles of Association of the company comply with the requirements of Appendix I to Chapter 13 Yellow Book.
[304] And where different from the number the subject of the application, the aggregate number of that class in issue.

Where an issuer issues securities on a regular basis[305] and in circumstances which do not require the production of listing particulars, the rules provide for a simplified form of application, being either a "block listing" (where the issuer makes an application for a specified number of securities which may be issued in a particular case[306]) or a "formal application" (where the issuer may adopt a simplified application procedure for each issue[307]). The Yellow Book sets out the simplified form of application and documents that require to be furnished.

B. PUBLICATION AND CIRCULATION OF LISTING PARTICULARS

1–56 The opening paragraphs of Chapter 8 Yellow Book reflect the Article 18 principle of prior approval demanded by the Listing Particulars Directive. Neither listing particulars nor supplementary listing particulars can be published, advertised or circulated, until they have been formally approved by the Stock Exchange in its role as competent authority.[308]

The Directive sets out requirements regarding publication of the listing particulars[309] which paragraph 8.4 of the Yellow Book reflects. It provides that listing particulars and shelf documents must be published by making them available to the public for inspection at the Company Announcements Office, and free of charge at the registered office of the issuer and its paying agents (if any). The listing particulars must also be delivered to the Registrar of Companies for registration, on or before their date of publication.[310]

The date for the publication of the listing particulars is determined by paragraph 8.8. It provides that it must be published at least two business days before the expected date of the consideration of the application for admission to listing. However, the Stock Exchange may also allow listing particulars to be published no later than the day on which dealings are expected to commence provided a written request from the sponsor is received. Qualifying applicants are:

---

[305] *e.g.* pursuant to an employees share scheme.

[306] para. 7.10(b) and 7.12 Yellow Book. Reg. 7, S.I. 282 of 1984.

[307] para. 7.10(a) and 7.12 Yellow Book.

[308] Art. 18(2) Listing Particulars Directive; para. 8.1 Yellow Book (although para. 8.3 does permit draft listing particulars to be circulated without approval for the purpose of arranging a placing, a syndication or underwriting or for marketing an intermediaries offer). Note that "approval" by the Exchange is not a warranty as to the listing particulars accuracy: see para. 1–42 above.

[309] Art. 20.

[310] reg. 13(1) of S.I. No. 282 of 1984.

1. a company transferring to the official list from the DCM by means of an introduction,[311] or

2. an overseas company already listed on an overseas exchange in respect of securities being admitted to listing by way of introduction,[312] or

3. a listed company in respect of securities of a class new to listing.[313]

Copies of the listing particulars must be available for inspection to the public during normal business hours for at least 14 days from the earliest of:

- the day on which the text of the listing particulars or the formal notice,[314] offer notice[315] mini-prospectus[316] or other advertisement is inserted in a national newspaper;

- the business day following the date of dispatch, in cases where the listing particulars are dispatched to holders of securities of the issuer or of another company;

- the business day on which admission to listing is expected to become effective.[317]

The content of formal notices and offer notices must be "approved" by the Stock Exchange before their issue[318] whereas the mini-prospectus, summary particulars, issue notes or any other advertisement announcing the admission to listing must be "authorised for issue by the Stock Exchange before their issue".[319]

---

[311] Unless it is the subject of a reverse takeover: para. 8.9(a) Yellow Book.

[312] para. 8.9(b) Yellow Book.

[313] para. 8.9(c) Yellow Book.

[314] A "formal notice" is not a listing particulars but is an advertisement giving the name of the company, the amount and title of the securities seeking listing, information as to where the listing particulars can be inspected and other information as set out in para. 8.10 Yellow Book.

[315] An "offer notice" is defined in para. 8.11 Yellow Book as not being a listing particulars, but has attached to it all of the information that a "formal notice" would contain and also an application form.

[316] A mini-prospectus is defined in para. 8.12 Yellow Book as not being a listing particulars, but as having an application form attached to it and containing more information than would be contained in either a "formal notice" or "offer notice."

[317] para. 8.5 Yellow Book.

[318] para. 8.23 Yellow Book; Art. 22 Listing Particulars Directive.

[319] para. 8.24 Yellow Book. para. 8.25 Yellow Book provides *inter alia* that in the case of "any other advertisement" which is to be issued by or on behalf of the issuer for the purposes of announcing the admission, it must contain a state-

1–57 Article 20 of the Listing Particulars Directive sets out the requirements for advertising. This is put into effect by paragraph 8.7 Yellow Book which provides that a formal notice must be inserted in at least one national newspaper no later than the next business day following publication of the listing particulars, unless the securities are of a class already listed. In the case of an offer for sale or subscription, the issuer may opt instead to insert an offer notice, listing particulars or mini-prospectus in a national newspaper.

1–58 So far as circulation of the listing particulars is concerned, the extent and manner of circulation all depends on the nature of the listing. The Yellow Book provides different requirements depending on whether the listing involves a rights issue or open offer,[320] a takeover or merger,[321] a reverse takeover,[322] or other circumstances.[323]

   Also, as discussed earlier above, an issuer may opt to circulate summary particulars instead of the listing particulars itself.[324]

VI. THE LEGAL PRINCIPLES UNDERLYING THE DEVELOPMENT OF EC LISTINGS LEGAL FRAMEWORK

A. MUTUAL RECOGNITION OF LISTING PARTICULARS

1–59 Under the Listing Particulars Directive 80/390/EEC, a minimum common level of disclosure in listing particulars was demanded throughout the Member States. The original article 24 provided that competent authorities should co-ordinate to the maximum extent possible where an applicant was proposing to list in two or more Member States either simultaneously or within a six month period. However, mutual recognition of listing particulars from one Member State to the next was still some way off. Council Directive 87/345/EEC[325] took the

---

ment that it has been authorised by the Exchange without approval of its contents. Also note that para. 8.26 Yellow Book provides that press releases and other advertisements that merely include a reference to admission or a public offer are not required to be submitted to the Stock Exchange.

[320] para. 8.14 Yellow Book.

[321] para. 8.15-17 Yellow Book.

[322] para. 8.18 Yellow Book.

[323] para. 8.19 Yellow Book.

[324] Summary particulars are considered above at para. 1–52.

[325] Council Directive 87/345/EEC of June 22, 1987 amending Directive 80/390/ EEC co-ordinating the requirements for the drawing up, scrutiny and distribution of the listing particulars to be published for the admission of securities to

initial necessary steps in this regard by replacing article 24 with a more comprehensive provision.

The replacement article 24 provides that where an issuer makes an application to list the same securities in two or more Member States either simultaneously or within a short interval,[326] then listing particulars shall be drawn up to the Listing Particulars Directive's standards. Furthermore, such Listings Particulars must be submitted to, and approved by, the competent authority in the State where the issuer has its registered office.[327] Article 24a[328] builds on the foundation laid down by article 24 by providing that once a listing particulars is approved by a competent authority in a Member State, then the particulars must[329] be recognised by the other Member States in which the admission to official listing has been applied for.[330]

The Directive recognises that the competent authorities in such States may however require that listing particulars include information specific to the local market of the country of admission. In particular, information may be required as to the income tax system, the financial organisations required to act as paying agents for the issuer in that country, and the way in which notices to investors will be published.[331] Ireland has implemented this provision by providing that only issuers of listing particulars who have their registered office in a Member State of the Community may take advantage of this mutual recognition regime.[332]

---

official Stock Exchange listing, as implemented by the European Communities (Stock Exchange) (Amendment) Regulations 1991 S.I. No. 18 of 1991.

[326] para. 17.68(b) (i) regards a "short interval" as being normally not more than three months.

[327] The State of the registered office will also be one of the States where an application to list is being made. However, in the event that it is not, then article 24 (and para. 17.68(c) Yellow Book) further provides that in such event, the issuer must choose as the approving authority, the competent authority of one of the States where the application to list is being made.

[328] Inserted by Directive 87/345/EEC.

[329] Subject to any translation into local language, *i.e.* English: art. 24a(1) Listing Particulars Directive.

[330] Note that while this means that the other Member State's competent authority cannot require the applicant to obtain "approval" from it for the already approved document, it does not give the applicant an automatic right to be admitted to listing. So far as this matter is concerned, the competent authority retains the power to assess the applicant's suitability for admission by reference to the Admissions' Directive criteria.

[331] Art. 24a(1) Listing Particulars Directive; para. 17.68(e) Yellow Book.

[332] Art. 24a(5) Listing Particulars Directive gives Member States this option which Ireland adopted by way of reg. 3(3) European Communities (Stock Exchange) (Amendment) Regulations 1991 of S.I. No. 18 of 1991. The Stock Exchange's Yellow Book rules appear to be more permissive in this regard as they allow (para. 17.68(a)) an overseas company to be able to take advantage of the mu-

1–60 The Directive further provides that listing particulars approved by a competent authority in one Member State must be recognised in another Member State in which application to listing is being made even if partial exemption or derogation has been granted pursuant to the Listing Particulars Directive.[333] In order for this to be so, article 24a(2) provides that the partial exemption or derogation must be of a type that is recognised in the rules of the other Member State(s) concerned, and also that the conditions that justify the exemption or derogation also exist in the other Member State(s).[334]

From a practical point of view, the Directive provides that the system will function on the basis that the competent authority who has the approving responsibility will furnish a certificate of approval to the competent authority(s) in the other concerned Member State(s).[335] Where partial exemption or derogation has been permitted, then the certificate shall state the reasons for the exemption or derogation.[336] The applicant will forward the draft listing particulars which it intends to use at least 10 days prior to intended publication[337] and must submit the final form of the particulars at least two business days prior to consideration of the application for admission to listing by the Stock Exchange.[338] Where the Stock Exchange is of the view that, listing particulars have been duly approved by a competent authority in another Member State and they satisfy any local requirements, then none of the provisions of Chapter 5 Yellow Book apply.[339] In that event the

---

tual recognition regime even where it does not have its registered office in another Member State, but either has securities listed on an overseas stock exchange market or the Stock Exchange is satisfied that the company can properly be regarded as a company of international standing and repute.

[333] Art. 24a(2) Listing Particulars Directive.
[334] These conditions are replicated in para. 17.68(f) Yellow Book. Although these conditions are not absolute, as art. 24a(2) also provides that even if these conditions are not fulfilled, the Member State may allow the competent authority to recognise the listing particulars approved by another competent authority, if they so wish.
[335] Although para. 17.70 Yellow Book puts the responsibility for furnishing the foreign competent authority's certificate on the overseas company itself. The certificate must be furnished 10 clear business days prior to the intended publication date.
[336] Art. 24a(3) Listing Particulars Directive; para. 17.70 Yellow Book.
[337] Art. 24a(4) Listing Particulars Directive. para. 17.69 Yellow Book requires that the overseas company must submit a draft to the Stock Exchange's listing department 10 clear business days prior to the intended publication of that document, or at the time of the company's application for admission to listing in the other Member State. In practice, submission will be made earlier than 10 days.
[338] para. 17.71 Yellow Book.
[339] Except its paras that relate to the publication of supplementary particulars: para. 17.76 Yellow Book. For a consideration of the Yellow Book rules concern-

foreign approved particulars (or an English translation of it), as amended for local conditions, may be published by the applicant, once the Stock Exchange gives written confirmation.[340]

Finally article 24c *inter alia* provides that where an application for admission to official listing is made for securities which have been listed in another Member State less than six months previously, the competent authorities to whom application is made shall contact the competent authorities which have already admitted the securities to official listing and shall, as far as possible, exempt the issuer of those securities from the preparation of new listing particulars, subject to any need for translation or updating or modification to meet local requirements such as taxation issues.[341] However, in a sense this provision has been overtaken by events as article 6(4)(a) which was inserted into the Directive by Directive 94/18/EC in 1994[342] now provides that where securities have been listed in a Member State for three years, then the competent authority in another Member State may exempt the issuer from having to publish a listing particulars when the issuer applies to be admitted to listing in the latter State.[343]

B. LISTING PARTICULARS AND PROSPECTUSES

1–61   In enacting a legal framework which facilitated the mutual recognition of listing particulars, the European Community had done much. Yet further work remained to be completed. In particular, the Community desired to put in place a legal framework which could achieve the wider objective of allowing mutual recognition of public offer prospectuses as listing particulars. The legal tool used to realise this objective, the Prospectus Directive,[344] will shortly be considered below.

---

ing supplementary particulars, see further above at para. 1–43. On Chapter 5 of the Yellow Book, see paras 1–34—1–39 and 1–40—1–54.

[340] para. 17.76 Yellow Book.

[341] Art. 24c(3). Art 24c was inserted into the Listing Particulars Directive by Directive 87/345/EEC.

[342] Council and European Parliament Directive of May 30, 1994 [1994] O.J. L.135/1 as implemented by the European Communities (Stock Exchange) (Amendment) Regulations, 1994 (S.I. No. 234 of 1994).

[343] And para. 5.23A(b) Yellow Book so provides also. Also, it provides that the Exchange may accept a shorter listing period (*i.e.* less than three years).

[344] Council Directive 89/298/EEC of 17 April 1989 [1989] O.J. L.124/8 co-ordinating the requirements for the drawing up, scrutiny and distribution of the prospectus to be published when transferable securities are offered to the public, as implemented by the European Communities (Transferable securities and Stock Exchange Regulations) 1992 S.I. No. 202 of 1992.

(1) Listing Particulars and the Companies Act 1963

1–62 Where listing particulars have been appoved of by the Stock Exchange in conjunction with an offer to the public for subscription or purchase of securities, a prospectus within the meaning of the Companies Act 1963 (*i.e.* Third Schedule document) will not be required provided the form of application has the listing particulars attached or indicates where they may be inspected.[345] The approved listing particulars is deemed to be a prospectus for the purposes of the Companies Act[346] thereby obviating the need to publish a Companies Act 1963 Third Schedule document which is not therefore required.[347]

(2) Mutual recognition of Prospectus as Listing Particulars

1–63 Where an issuer proposes to offer "transferable securities"[348] to the public for the first time in advance of admission to listing, then a prospectus is required by the Prospectus Directive.[349] The prospectus must be published, and contain a certain minimum level of information.[350] *Inter alia* the Prospectus Directive requires public offer prospectuses to be drawn up to Listing Particulars Directive disclosure standards whenever securities are also seeking contemporaneous admission to listing.[351] As Warren has observed, the regime:

> ". . . is designed to integrate the disclosure requirements applicable to the public offer and sale of both listed and unlisted securities."[352]

---

[345] Reg. 12(2) S.I. No. 282 of 1994.

[346] Reg. 12(3) S.I. No. 282 of 1984. Also reg. 12(3) disapplies several provisions of the Companies Act 1963 such as ss.43, 44(1), 45, 47, 361(1) (b), 361(2), 362 and 364. However, note that neither s.46 (liability for experts' statements) nor s.49 (civil liability for mis-statements in prospectus) nor s.50 (criminal liability for mis-statements in prospectus) are disapplied, nor is liability at common law precluded (*e.g.* negligence, deceit, etc.). These matters are given further consideration in Chap. 3 below.

[347] Reg. 12(3) S.I. No. 282 of 1984. For examples of situations under the Companies Act 1963 itself where the Stock Exchange can exempt an issuer from having to publish a Third Schedule prospectus, see further Chap. 2 below where consideration is given to s.45 (certificate of exemption where in the opinion of the Stock Exchange a Third Schedule prospectus would be "unduly burdensome") and s. 44(7) (b) (where requirement for Third Schedule is obviated where issue of securities is uniform with a listed issue made in the preceding two years).

[348] The meaning of "transferable securities" is considered at Chap. 2 below.

[349] Art 4 Prospectus Directive – indeed this obligation applies whenever securities are offered for the first time, irrespective of whether there will be a subsequent application to admit the securities to listing: Art. 1.1 Prospectus Directive.

[350] Art. 4 Prospectus Directive.

[351] Although, where the issuer does not intend to seek a listing, less onerous prospectus disclosure requirements apply: Art. 11.

[352] Warren, "The Common Market Prospectus" (1989) 26 C.M.L. Rev. 687 at p. 694.

Such a prospectus must be prepared to the same disclosure standards as a listing particulars document and must be submitted to and approved by the Stock Exchange in its role as the "competent authority."[353]

Article 7 of the Prospectus Directive provides that where a public offer relates to transferable securities which at the time of the offer are the subject of an application to admission to official listing on a Stock Exchange operating within the same State, the contents of the prospectus and the procedures for scrutinising and distributing it shall, subject to adaptations appropriate to the circumstances of a public offer, be determined in accordance with the disclosure requirements of the Listing Particulars Directive.[354] The Yellow Book reflects this as it explicitly provides that the contents of such a prospectus, the procedures for submission to and approval by the Stock Exchange, and for the publication of the prospectus, are the same as those applicable to listing particulars, subject to adaptations appropriate to the circumstances of the public offer.[355] Consequently, the Yellow Book provides that such a prospectus must be drawn up in accordance with the requirements of Chapters 5 and 6 Yellow Book (which set out the Listing Particulars contents requirements, and which require submission to and prior approval by, the Stock Exchange).[356] The prospectus must be published in accordance with Chapter 8 Yellow Book.[357] In practice, most of the listing particulars regime therefore applies to the prospectus as the contents of such a prospectus, and the procedures for submission to and approval by the Stock Exchange, are the same as those applicable to listing particulars, subject to adaptation as may be appropriate to the circumstances of the public offer.[358]

1–64 This article 7 process of similar disclosure levels, prior scrutiny and approval, ultimately provides the basis for facilitating the mutual recognition of listing particulars and prospectuses between Member

---

[353] Art. 7 Prospectus Directive; the Stock Exchange is designated as competent authority for the purposes of *inter alia* art. 7 by reg.19 S.I. No. 202 of 1992.

[354] The Prospectus Directive also provides in article 8 that where a public offer is made in one Member and the issuer applies to list the same securities in another Member State, then the issuer of the public offer prospectus in the first State should have the opportunity to draw up the prospectus to Listing Particulars standards. Furthermore, art. 12 permits Member States to opt to permit issuers generally to draw up public offer prospectuses to Listing Particulars standards, even where no admission to listing is contemplated: Ireland availed of this option by way of para. 3 of S.I. No. 202 of 1992. See further immediately below where both arts. 8, 12 (and 7)'s role in the overall regime is considered.

[355] para. 5.1(d) Yellow Book.

[356] para. 5.1(a) Yellow Book.

[357] Art. 4 Prospectus Directive; para. 5.1(c) Yellow Book.

[358] para. 5.1(d) Yellow Book; Art. 7 Prospectus Directive.

States.[359] More immediately in this respect, article 8 of the Prospectus Directive provides that where a public offer is made in one Member State and the issuer has also applied to admit the securities to listing in another Member State, then the public offer prospectus in the first State may be drawn up to Listing Particulars standards. Furthermore, article 12 permits issuers to draw up public offer prospectuses to Listing Particulars standards if they so wish, even where no admission to listing is contemplated). In any of these three situations (*i.e.* arts. 7, 8 or 12) article 24b(1) of the Listing Particulars Directive as amended[360] provides that where application for admission to official listing is made in one or more Member State(s) and the securities have been the subject of a public offer prospectus drawn up and approved in any Member State in accordance with either Arts. 7, 8 or 12, in the three months preceding application for admission, then the public offer prospectus shall be recognised[361] as a listing particulars in the Member State or States in which the application for admission to listing is made.[362]

1–65 However, the Directive does make an allowance in that it provides that the competent authorities may require that the prospectus include information specifically local to the market of the country where admission is sought, and in particular, information concerning the income tax system, the financial organisations retained to act as paying agents for the issuer in the country, and the ways in which notices to investors are to be published.[363]

---

[359] Article 24b of the Listing Particular Directive (inserted by art. 2 of Council Directive 90/211/EEC of April 20, 1990 [1990] O.J. L. 112/24 amending the Listing Particulars Directive 80/390/EEC in respect of the mutual recognition of public offer prospectuses as stock exchange listing particulars, as implemented by the European Communities (Transferable securities and Stock Exchange Regulations) 1992 S.I. No. 202 of 1992.

[360] Art. 24b(1) was inserted into the Listing Particulars Directive by art. 2 of Council Directive 90/211/EEC of 23 April 1990, replacing the former 24b(1) inserted by art. 1 of Council Directive 87/345/EEC which in turn had amended the original Art. 24 Listing Particulars Directive 80/390/EEC. Directive 90/211/ EEC was implemented by the European Communities (Transferable Securities and Stock Exchange) Regulations 1992, S.I. No. 202 of 1992.

[361] Subject to any translation requirements: Art. 24b(1).

[362] para. 17.68(b) (ii) Yellow Book provides that the Stock Exchange will recognise such a prospectus as a listing particulars, subject to translation and local requirements (para. 17.68(e)). It should be noted also that although the competent authority (the Stock Exchange) cannot require the applicant to submit a fresh document to it for approval, mutual recognition does not confer an automatic right to be admitted to listing. In this regard, the Stock Exchange still retains the right to assess the applicant's suitability for listing by reference to the Admissions' Directive criteria.

[363] Ireland has opted to implement this option by providing that the following

From an operational point of view, article 24b(2) provides that the operational provisions of article 24a(2)–(5)[364] (which oblige Member States to recognise partially or completely exempted listing particulars where so approved in another Member State) shall equally apply to partially or completely exempted prospectuses seeking mutual recognition as listing particulars pursuant to article 24b(1).[365] Thus for example, if the competent authority which approved the prospectus permitted partial exemption or derogation to the applicant relieving the applicant of the obligation to publish a full prospectus, then the other Member State(s) competent authorities must accept this, unless the same conditions do not pertain in the latter State(s).[366]

The Yellow Book rules mirror this regime by providing that the Stock Exchange will recognise partially exempted prospectuses approved in other Member States as listing particulars provided that the exemption or derogation granted by the approving authority is recognised in Ireland, and furthermore that the circumstances that justify the exemption or derogation also exist here in Ireland.[367] The Exchange will require the draft prospectus seeking recognition as a listing particulars to be furnished to it at least 10 business days in advance of the intended publication of that document or at the time of the company's application for admission in another Member State.[368] Also the Stock Exchange will require a certificate from the competent authority in the other Member State to be furnished to it certifying approval of the document and also certifying the reasons justifying any derogations permitted by the competent authority in the other Member State.[369]

1–66 Paragraph 17.76 provides that where the Stock Exchange is of the view that the overseas approved prospectus satisfies the requirements set out above, then none of the provisions of Chapter 5 Yellow Book apply, except that relating to the publication of supplementary

---

local information will be required: (a) a summary of the tax treatment of Irish resident holders of the securities; (b) the names and addresses of the paying agents for the securities in Ireland (if any); (c) a statement of how notice of meetings and other notices from the issuer of the securities will be given to Irish resident holders of the security (S.I. No. 202 of 1992, Third Schedule, para. 4). Also see para. 17.68(e) Yellow Book which reflects this.

[364] Considered above at para. 1–59 when mutual recognition of listing particulars was considered.

[365] Art 24b(2) Listing Particulars Directive provides that the art 24a(2)–(5) partial exemption/derogation regime that applies to listing particulars seeking mutual recognition as listing particulars also applies to prospectuses seeking recognition as listing particulars.

[366] Art. 24a(2) Listing Particulars Directive.

[367] para. 17.68(f) Yellow Book.

[368] para. 17.69 Yellow Book.

particulars.[370] Such prospectus, as amended and translated to meet local conditions, can be published as a listing particulars once written confirmation is given by the Stock Exchange.

Again, it is noteworthy that, just as with the listing particulars and the notion of mutual recognition, Ireland has opted, where prospectuses seek recognition as a listing particulars, to confine availability of the mutual recognition regime to the situation where the issuer of the prospectus has its registered office in the European Community Member State,[371] although the Yellow Book rules appear more relaxed in this regard.[372]

C. MUTUAL CO-OPERATION

1–67 In order to foster the development of the expanding Community legal framework, the various Directives also require the competent authorities to co-operate with one another. For example, the Listing Particulars Directive obliges the competent authorities to co-operate with one another whenever necessary for the carrying out of their duties. They are obliged to exchange information required for this purpose.[373] In particular, where an application for admission to official listing is made for securities which have been admitted to listing in another Member State in the previous six months, then the competent authorities to whom application is made shall contact the competent authority in the other State which has already admitted the securities to listing. Furthermore, the competent authorities are obliged to exempt the applicant as far as possible from the obligation to prepare new listing particulars, subject to any need for updating, translation or the issue of supplementary particulars.[374]

---

[369] para. 17.70 Yellow Book.

[370] Supplementary Particulars are considered at para. 1–43 above.

[371] Art. 24a.5 Listing Particulars Directive gives Member States this option, and Ireland took it by implementing reg. 3(3) European Communities (Stock Exchange) (Amendment) Regulations, 1991 (S.I. No. 18 of 1991).

[372] para. 17.68(a) allows an overseas company to apply for mutual recognition even if they only have securities traded on an overseas Stock Exchange, or are in the Stock Exchange's opinion, a company of international standing and repute.

[373] Art. 24c(1) Listing Particulars Directive as inserted by Council Directive 87/345/EEC of 22 June 1987.

[374] Art. 24c(3) Listing Particulars Directive as inserted by Council Directive 87/345/EEC of 22 June 1987. Also see Art 24c(2). However, this has to a large extent been "overtaken" by Art.6(4) Listing Particulars Directive as inserted by Directive 94/18/EC which provides that competent authorities may exempt an issuer from having to publish listing particulars when applying for admis-

1–68   Article 18 of the Admissions Directive also promotes co-operation between competent authorities as it provides that the competent authorities shall cooperate wherever necessary for the purpose of carrying out their duties and shall exchange any information required for that purpose.[375]

It also provides that where applications for admission are to be made simultaneously or within short intervals of one another for the admission of the same securities to official listing on Stock Exchanges in more than one Member State, or where an application for admission is made in respect of a security already listed on an exchange in another Member State, then the competent authorities shall communicate with each other and make arrangements as may be necessary to expedite the procedure and simplify as far as possible the formalities and any additional conditions required for admission of the security concerned.[376]

VII. PROSPECTUS DIRECTIVE REGIME

A. OVERLAPPING REGIMES

1–69   The Prospectus Directive applies to public offers of securities made to the public for the first time,[377] which have not been admitted to listing in the Member State. It provides that Member States shall ensure that, subject to exceptions,[378] any offer of "transferable securities"[379] offered to the public within their territories is subject to the publication of a prospectus by the person making the offer.[380] The Di-

---

sion to list where the applicant has been listed for the previous three years in another Member State.

[375] Art. 18(1) Admissions Directive.

[376] Art. 18(2) Admissions Directive.

[377] Although art.1.2 allows Member States to opt not to require a prospectus where part of the securities will be offered to the public at a time subsequent to the initial public offer of the other part of the securities. In such circumstances, it will not be necessary to publish a prospectus in respect of the subsequent offer. Ireland has implemented this option in para. 1 Third Schedule of S.I. No. 202 of 1992.

[378] Although certain offers are excluded from its scope. See further Chap. 2 below where these are considered.

[379] "Transferable securities" does not include all securities: see further Chap. 2 below.

[380] Art. 4 Prospectus Directive. Warren, "The Common Market Prospectus" (1989) 26 C.M.L.Rev. 687 at p. 697 observes that when the Prospectus Directive was first proposed, only five Member States – France, Belgium, Luxembourg, Ireland and the U.K. – required a prospectus to be published in connection with a public offering of securities.

rective has been implemented by the European Communities (Transferable Securities and Stock Exchange) Regulations 1992.[381] The Directive seeks to ensure that a certain minimum level of information is available to investors throughout the EC when public offers of transferable securities occur.[382] Regulation 8(1) provides that every such prospectus shall contain information which, according to the particular nature of the issuer and of the securities concerned, is necessary to enable an "informed assessment"[383] to be made of the assets and liabilities, financial position, profits, losses, prospects of the company, and of the rights attaching to the securities.

1–70 However, the level of disclosure required will all depend on whether the securities will also be applying for admission to listing or not. In the event that a listing will take place, then the Listing Particulars Directive standard of disclosure will be required of the prospectus.[384] In other words the Yellow Book rules shall apply to the prospectus, subject to any necessary adaptations. In effect therefore, the extent of disclosure is similar for both a prospectus and a listing particulars if a company is making an offer of securities in the State using both non-listed and listed avenues. Alternatively, in the event that a public offer is being made, but no listing is contemplated, a high level of disclosure is still required by the Prospectus Directive, though it is not as extensively detailed or as onerous as the Listing Rules.[385]

1–71 So far as the relationship between the Prospectus Directive and the Companies Act Third Schedule regime is concerned, the position is that the Prospectus Directive (where applicable) subsumes the Third Schedule regime. Regulation 8 provides that a prospectus must contain at least the matters specified in article 11 of the Directive, as well as any matter that may additionally be required by the requirements of the Third Schedule to the Companies Act 1963.[386] A comparison with the requirements of article 11 and the Third Schedule will reveal, that not only are the Third Schedule's requirements as to prospectus content replicated to a large extent by article 11, but furthermore, in

---

[381] S.I. No. 202 of 1992.

[382] Reg. 6 provides that it shall be unlawful to issue any form of application for the transferable securities of a company unless a prospectus is issued which complies with the regulations.

[383] Art. 11 Prospectus Directive.

[384] See paras 1–63—1–66 above.

[385] Though of course, at all times this is subject to the overriding requirement that disclosure be made of all matters necessary to enable investors reach an "informed assessment" of the issuer's position.

[386] reg. 8 S.I. No. 202 of 1992.

many instances more extensive disclosure demands are made by article 11.[387] Consequently, the regulations provide that the Third Schedule requirements are only required to the extent that they are "not already required" by article 11.[388] However, in a key respect, the Prospectus Directive has rendered the requirements of the Third Schedule (should the Schedule apply) less demanding. In this regard, Regulation 8(3) provides that the Third Schedule requirement for five years' accounts be reduced to three years.

A prospectus complying with the 1992 regulations (and therefore the Directive) obviates the section 44(3) Companies Act declaration that it is unlawful to offer securities to the public without a Third Schedule document accompanying the offer.[389] In order to give legal certainty in this respect, regulation 21(4) provides that a prospectus drawn up in conformity with the regulations implementing the Directive, shall be deemed to be a prospectus for the purposes of the Companies Act, and regulation 21(3) provides that a Third Schedule document is not required.[390]

---

[387] Art. 11 is considered in detail below at para. 1–73. The main heads under which information are required under the Third Schedule are (a) the capital of the company (b) the number of securities and rights and privileges attaching (c) the names of the directors and proposed directors (d) the number and amount of shares issued in the past five years (e) property to be purchased with the proceeds of the offer (f) expenses paid in connection with the offer (g) material contracts and the parties thereto (h) the names of the auditors (i) declaration of any interests held by directors in the property to be acquired by the company or any interest held by any director in any firm providing services to the company. Also various reports need to be attached, such as an auditors report, on various specified matters.

[388] reg. 8(2) (b) S.I. 202 of 1992. However, note that even in this situation, Regulation 8(4) permits the Stock Exchange to relieve the issuer of the burden of complying with any such Third Schedule requirements if it would be "unduly burdensome".

[389] reg. 21(3) S.I. No. 202 of 1992. However note that if the offer is for subscription or purchase of securities of a type which are not eligible to be classified as "transferable securies" such that the Directive (and hence the Regulations) is not applicable, then s.44(3) continues to apply such that a Third Schedule document is required in order to comply with the Companies Act 1963. (Note, as will be further elaborated in Chap. 2 below, a Third Schedule type prospectus in this instance will not be required if the prospectus was first issued or published in the U.K.: Companies Act 1963, s.367(3).

[390] In which event ss. 43, 44(1), 45, 361(1) (b), 361(2), 362 and 364 of the Companies Act 1963 are disapplied. However, note that neither s.46 (liability for experts' statements) nor s.49 (civil liability for mis-statements in prospectus) nor s.50 (criminal liability for mis-statements in prospectus) are disapplied, nor is liability at common law precluded (*e.g.* negligence, deceit, etc.). These matters are given further consideration in Chap. 3 below.

B. PUBLICATION AND REGISTRATION OF PROSPECTUS

1–72 The Prospectus Directive[391] provides that a prospectus must be communicated, before its publication, to the bodies designated for that purpose in each Member State in which the transferable securities are offered to the public for the first time. The Registrar of Companies is the designated body for this purpose under the regulations, and every prospectus must be registered with the Registrar on or before its date of publication in compliance with section 47 Companies Act 1963.[392]

Where no listing is contemplated, then the prospectus must be registered with the Registrar of Companies[393] and made available to the public not later than the time the offer is made to the public[394] either by notice in one or more national daily newspapers circulating in the State, and in the form of a brochure available free of charge to the public at the registered office of the issuer and at the offices of the financial organisation retained to act as the issuer's paying agent.[395] Before the prospectus will have been registered with the Registrar, it will have been submitted to the Stock Exchange in order that consent can be granted where any omission of information otherwise required is sought to be made. Regulation 9(1) of S.I. No. 202 of 1992 so designates the Stock Exchange for this purpose.[396]

However, where admission to listing is also contemplated then not only must the prospectus be registered with the Registrar of Companies,[397] but also the Stock Exchange has a designated role. Wherever an issuer seeks to use a prospectus as the basis for admission to listing (either in the State[398] or in another Member State[399]) then the prospec-

---

[391] Art. 14 Prospectus Directive.

[392] *inter alia*, s.47 requires all experts' consents to be attached to the prospectus as well as all material contracts. Also it will require the prospectus to state on its face that a copy has been delivered to the Registrar for registration, and a copy must be signed by every director of proposed director.

[393] reg. 11 S.I. No. 202 of 1992; Art. 14 Prospectus Directive.

[394] reg. 13 S.I. No. 202 of 1992; Arts. 9 and 15 Prospectus Directive.

[395] reg. 12 S.I. No. 202 of 1992.

[396] See para. 1–76 below where Art. 13 Prospectus Directive is considered in this regard.

[397] reg. 11 S.I. No. 202 of 1992 requires that a copy of the prospectus must be delivered to the Registrar of Companies on or before its date of publication in accordance with s.47 Companies Act 1963.

[398] Article 7 Prospectus Directive.

[399] Article 8 Prospectus Directive (though this will only apply where Ireland is the State where the issuer has its registered office, the public offer is taking place here, and the applicant wishes to use the prospectus approved here as the basis for seeking a listing in another Member State by utilising the mutual recognition regime. On the other hand, if the prospectus has been approved by a com-

tus must be drawn up to Listing Particulars Directive standards[400] and the Stock Exchange is designated as the competent authority for the purpose of prior scrutiny and approval of the prospectus by the implementing regulations.[401] In this event, the Yellow Book rules apply to determine the prospectus's content, scrutiny, time of publication[402] and distribution to the public, just as if it were a listing particulars, subject to any necessary adaptations as are appropriate to the circumstances of the offer.[403]

C. CONTENT OF PROSPECTUS

1–73 So far as the specific content of a prospectus is concerned, it all depends on whether the public offer will also involve a contemporaneous application for admission to listing. Where listing is contemplated, then the Listing Particulars Directive and Yellow Book rules apply,[404] subject to any adaptations as are necessary to the circumstances of the public offer.[405] However, where no application to listing is contemplated, then article 11 of the Prospectus Directive provides that where a public offer relates to transferable securities[406] the prospectus must contain information on at least the following matters.

First, information on those responsible for the prospectus, including declarations that to the best of their knowledge the information contained in the prospectus is in accordance with the facts, and that the prospectus makes no omission likely to affect its import.[407]

Second, extensive information on the securities being offered, including the number being issued and the rights attaching, any restrictions on their transferability, the identity of paying agents (if any), methods of payment, etc.[408]

---

petent authority in another Member State, the Exchange has no approval role *viz.* the prospectus, other than to ensure that it has received a certificate from the foreign competent authority to that effect, and also the Exchange will require the applicant to satisfy local requirements as to tax and other matters).
[400] See paras 1–63—1–64.
[401] reg. 19 S.I. No. 202 of 1992.
[402] While reg. 13 of S.I 202 of 1992 provides that the prospectus must be published not later than the time that the offer is made available to the public, the application of the Yellow Book rules may require publication at an earlier time.
[403] para. 5.1 Yellow Book.
[404] Art. 5(1) (a) Yellow Book.
[405] See paras 1–63—1–64.
[406] These categories of securities that are, and are not, "transferable securities" are considered in Chap. 2 below.
[407] Art. 11(2) (a) Prospectus Directive.
[408] *ibid.*, art. 11(2) (b).

Third, information on the issuer, including the composition of the issuer's capital, the amount and nature of any debt securities, convertible debt securities, or exchangeable debt securities, information relating to the group of which the issuer is part (if any), an indication of the identity of the shareholders who control the issuer (in so far as they are known).[409]

Fourth, information on the issuer's principal activities and information on any factors that may affect such activities as well as information on investments in progress or any legal proceedings which may adversely affect the issuer.[410] Fifth, information on the issuer's assets and liabilities, financial position, profits and losses, and consolidated accounts (where available), as well as any auditor's qualifications to the accounts (if any).[411]

Sixth, information on the issuer's administration, management and supervisory bodies.[412] Seventh, information on recent developments which may have an impact on the issuer's business.[413]

1–74   Where a public offer relates to convertible or exchangeable debt securities or debt securities with warrants attaching or to the warrants themselves, information must also be given with regard to the shares to which they confer entitlement. Where the issuer of the shares or debt securities is not also the issuer of the debt securities or warrants, the information (specified in article 11 above) must also be given in respect of the issuer of the shares or debt securities.[414]

1–75   Should the public offer also involve either of the two following types of offer, then article 11 of the Directive provides that the Stock Exchange may allow the omission of certain of the above categories of information on the basis that investors are otherwise sufficiently informed as a result of Stock Exchange disclosure requirements. The first situation is where shares are offered on a pre-emptive basis to members of the issuer on the occasion of their admission to the stock market. In this case, the Stock Exchange may allow some of the information specified above in the fourth, fifth and sixth paragraphs above to be omitted on the basis that investors already have equivalent information as a result of Stock Exchange disclosure.[415] The second situation is where a class of shares has been admitted to dealing on a Stock Ex-

---

[409] *ibid.*, art. 11(2) (c).
[410] *ibid.*, art. 11(2) (d).
[411] *ibid.*, art. 11(2) (e).
[412] *ibid.*, art. 11(2) (f).
[413] *ibid.*, art. 11(2) (g).
[414] Art. 11(4) Prospectus Directive.
[415] Art. 11(7) Prospectus Directive; reg. 9(1) S.I. No. 202 of 1992.

change and the number or estimated market value or the nominal value[416] of the shares offered amounts to less than 10% of the number (or of the corresponding value) of the shares of the same class already admitted to dealing. In this case, provided that as a result of stock exchange disclosure investors already possess up to date information about the issuer equivalent to that required by the seven article 11 paragraphs, then the Stock Exchange may authorise either a partial or complete exemption from the obligation to publish an article 11 prospectus.[417]

D. OMISSION OF INFORMATION

1–76   Article 13 of the Directive permits the competent authority to allow the omission of information from an article 11[418] prospectus where it is of only minor importance and not likely to influence an informed assessment of the issuer, or if disclosure would be contrary to the public interest or seriously detrimental to the issuer.[419] Regulation 9(1) of S.I. No. 202 of 1992 designates the Stock Exchange as the competent authority for this purpose.[420]

E. THE PROSPECTUS DIRECTIVE AND THE PRINCIPLE OF MUTUAL RECOGNITION

(1)   Mutual Recognition of Prospectuses

1–77   A major objective of the Prospectus Directive was not only to insist on the provision of a common minimum level of information throughout the European Community, but also to reduce the need to publish a fresh prospectus in certain circumstances. For example, arti-

---

[416] Or in the absence of nominal value, the accounting par value of the shares offered: Art. 11(8).

[417] Art. 11(8) Prospectus Directive; reg. 9(1) S.I. No. 202 of 1992.

[418] See above para. 1–73.

[419] Provided that in the latter case, omission would not be likely to mislead investors: Art. 13(1). Art. 13(2) also allows the Stock Exchange to allow omission of information in circumstances where the initiator of the offer is neither the issuer nor a third party acting on their behalf, where such information would not normally be in the initiator's possession.

[420] Note that while the Stock Exchange is designed as the authority with power to grant exemption from Article 11 prospectus content requirements, it otherwise is not generally charged with "approving" public offer prospectuses. It only is charged with such a role where an application to listing forms part of the offer process: Reg. 19 S.I. No. 202 of 1992.

cle 6 of the Prospectus Directive provides that where a "full prospectus" has been published in a Member State within the previous 12 months, the "following prospectus" drawn up by the same issuer in the same State, but relating to different transferable securities, may indicate only those changes likely to influence the value of the securities which have occurred since publication of the full prospectus.[421]

However, the Directive also had grander ambitions. Principally, it sought to use the principle of mutual recognition as a means of facilitating the mutual recognition of prospectuses as between Community Member States. The way that it sought to achieve this was to build on articles 7, 8 and 12 of the Directive. To recap,[422] article 7 provides that where a public offer is being made in a Member State and at the same time the securities are also subject to an application for listing in that State, then the prospectus shall be drawn up to Listing Particulars standards and subject to the same procedures for scrutiny and distribution as would a listing particulars.[423] Article 8 provides that where a public offer is made in one Member State and admission to listing is sought in another, then the person making the public offer shall have the opportunity, in the Member State where the public offer is taking place, to draw up the prospectus to Listing Particulars Directive standards and subject it to the same procedures for scrutiny and distribution as would a listing particulars, subject to such adaptations as are necessary for the circumstances of a public offer. [424] In so far as the last mentioned Article is concerned, article 12, it merely gives an issuer the option to meet Listing Particulars Directive standards even where there is no intention on the issuer's part to apply for admission to listing.

---

[421] Yellow Book para. 5.23 reflects this provision in the sense that where an issuer applies for admission to listing of securities that are to be offered to the public in Ireland for the first time before admission, and has published a full prospectus in the 12 months preceding the date the offer is first made, then the prospectus may contain only those differences that have arisen since the date of the publication of the full prospectus. In order for this concession to be available, the prospectus must either be accompanied by or refer to, the full prospectus which will have been previously approved by the Stock Exchange.

[422] From paras 1–63 and 1–64.

[423] The Stock Exchange is the body which oversees this process (reg. 19 S.I. No. 202 of 1992). Para. 5.1 Yellow Book provides that the contents of a prospectus, and the procedures of admission to and approval by the Exchange, and for the publication, of a prospectus, are the same as those applicable to listing particulars, subject to adaptations appropriate to the circumstances of a public offer. In such circumstances application would be made to the Stock Exchange pursuant to reg. 8(4) S.I. No. 202 of 1992 to request that the applicant be relieved from the burden of having to publish matters required by the Third Schedule Companies Act 1963 on the grounds that it would be "unduly burdensome."

[424] Art. 8(2) Prospectus Directive provides that this only applies in Member States which in general provide for prior scrutiny of public offer prospectuses.

Using the aforegoing three articles as a basis for further expansion of the regime, article 21 of the Prospectus Directive built on the foundation provided by these Articles. It provides that where for the same transferable securities, public offers are made either simultaneously or within a short interval[425] in one or more Member State, then the Member States must recognise a prospectus approved in one of the Member States, and cannot have the right to approve the prospectus or require any additional information to be included in it.[426] Article 21 recognises that the other Member State may require translation, and also that the prospectus include information specific to the market in the Member State. Ireland has implemented this provision as follows. The implementing regulations provide that, where the prospectus approved by another Member State competent authority does not already include local information on the following matters, then the Stock Exchange shall require such information to be added to the approved prospectus:[427]

1. a summary of the tax treatment of Irish resident holders of the securities;

2. the names and addresses of the paying agents for the securities in Ireland, and

3. a statement of how notices of meetings and other notices from the issuer of the securities will be given to Irish resident holders of the securities.

1–78 However, in order for an issuer to be able to take advantage of the article 21 mutual recognition of prospectuses regime, article 20 must be satisfied. It requires that the prospectus seeking mutual recognition be drawn up and approved by a competent authority to Listing Particulars Directive standards.[428] Consequently, an article 11 Prospectus

---

[425] Defined as normally not more than three months: para. 17.72(b) (i) Yellow Book.

[426] Art. 21(5) permits Member States to restrict the application of this Article to prospectuses concerning transferable securities of issuers who have their registered office in a Member State. Ireland has opted to accept this restriction: para. 5 Third Sched. S.I. No. 202 of 1992. Although the Stock Exchange in the Yellow Book rules appears to be more permissive as it allows (para. 17.68(a)) an overseas company to be able to take advantage of the mutual recognition regime even where it does not have its registered office in another Member State, but either has securities listed on an overseas stock exchange market or the Stock Exchange is satisfied that the company can properly be regarded as a company of international standing and repute.

[427] para. 4 Third Sched. to S.I. No. 202 of 1992

[428] para. 17.72(b) (ii) Yellow Book. Reg. 19 S.I. No. 202 of 1992 designates the Stock Exchange as the competent authority for the purpose of scrutiny of prospectuses pursuant to arts. 7, 10 and 12 of the Prospectus Directive.

will not be able to take advantage of this mutual recognition regime because the level of disclosure required by that article is not up to the Listing Particulars Directive standards.[429] The competent authority for the purposes of approving the prospectus shall be that of the Member State where the issuer has its registered office if the public offer is made in that State.[430] Where an overseas company is seeking to have its prospectus recognised as such in Ireland, the Yellow Book rules require overseas companies to submit the approved prospectus to the Stock Exchange at least 10 days prior to the intended publication date.[431] Also, evidence that competent authority approval has been granted by another Member State competent authority must be furnished by the overseas company to the Stock Exchange.[432] Such a prospectus must be recognised by the Exchange even if partial exemption or derogation was permitted by the approving competent authority, provided that the exemption or derogation is of a type recognised in the listing rules, and that the circumstances that justify the exemption or derogation also exist in the State.[433] Once the Stock Exchange is satisfied that all the aforegoing requirements are satisfied, it shall issue written confirmation, after which the prospectus may be published.

1–79 The Yellow Book provides a separate set of rules[434] to deal with the situation where an issuer proposes to make a public offer (but no application to listing) in this State and intends to make a public offer, in another Member State. In this situation, the issuer may request the Stock Exchange to assume the role of approval authority for the purpose of approving the prospectus. The prospectus approved by it can

---

[429] Unless the issuer opted to avail of Article 12 of the Prospectus Directive which permits the person making the public offer to have the possibility of drawing up a prospectus in accordance with the Listing Particulars Directive standards, even though no application for admission to listing was contemplated. Ireland has opted to permit this option to be possible: para. 3 Third Sched. S.I. No. 202 of 1992.

[430] Art 20 provides other paragraphs where the issuer may have to choose a supervisory authority elsewhere in certain circumstances and these are elaborated upon in para. 17.68(d) Yellow Book.

[431] Art 21.3 Prospectus Directive; para. 17.73 Yellow Book.

[432] para. 17.73A Yellow Book requires this to be furnished at least 10 business days prior to intended publication.

[433] para. 17.73A Yellow Book requires that details of any such derogation or exemption be supplied as well as the grounds of justification. Art. 21 further provides that Member States may deem a prospectus to comply with its laws even of they do not satisfy either of these two conditions.

[434] These separate rules, entitled Rules for Approval of Prospectuses Where No Application for Listing is Made, provide that the listing requirements of Chaps 5 and 6 apply in modified fashion.

then be used as the basis of a public offer or application for admission to listing in another Member State within the terms of article 8 of the Prospectus Directive.

(2) Mutual Recognition of Prospectus as Listing Particulars

1–80   The foundation laid by articles 7, 8 and 12 in the Prospectus Directive has now been the site of yet further construction. Article 24b(1) of the Listing Particulars Directive (as amended by Council Directive 90/211/EC) provides that where application for admission to official listing is made in one Member State, and the securities which are the subject of the application have been the subject of a public offer prospectus drawn up and approved in any Member State in accordance with articles 7, 8 or 12 of the Prospectus Directive in the three months[435] preceding the application for admission, then the public offer prospectus shall be recognised as a listing particulars in the Member States where the application for listing is made.[436] The Yellow Book provides that approval must be given by the competent authority of the issuer's Home State if public offers are made in two or more Member States (and both a public offer and an application to list are made in the issuer's Home State), or, either a public offer or an application to list is made in the issuer's Home State (and the Home State) provides in general for the prior scrutiny of public offer prospectuses.[437] It will not be necessary to obtain the approval for the document from the competent authorities in the other Member State(s) in which application for admission to listing will be made, nor will they be able to require additional information.[438] However, article 24b(1) does provide that translation into local language may be required. Also article 24b(1) al-

---

[435] Both art. 24b(1) and para. 17.68(b) (ii) Yellow Book provide a three month limit.

[436] Art 24b(1) Listing Particulars Directive as amended by art. 2 of Council Directive 90/211/EC.

[437] para. 17.68(d) Yellow Book, which additionally provides that in any other case, the approval must be given by the competent authority chosen by the company from among the Member States in which the offer is made and which provide in general for the prior scrutiny of public offer prospectuses (see art 20(2) Prospectus Directive).

[438] para. 17.68(e) Yellow Book reflects this regime, setting out identical requirements. Furthermore paras 17.68(f)–17.71 Yellow Book, which applies to listing particulars seeking mutual recognition, will also apply to prospectuses approved in one State seeking recognition as listing particulars in another. Paras 17.68(f)–71 reflect the provisions of art. 24a(2)-(4) Listing Particulars Directive inclusive, which deal with partial exemptions or derogations allowing a less than "full" listing particulars to be published. As art. 24b(2) declares that this exemption/derogation regime shall apply equally to prospectuses seeking mutual recognition as listing particulars in other Member States, hence these Yellow Book rules apply equally to prospectuses seeking mutual recognition as listing particulars under art 24b(1). (To see how these paragraphs apply in

lows the Stock Exchange to require inclusion of (so far as not already included) information concerning matters such as:

1. a summary of the tax treatment of Irish resident holders of the securities;

2. the names and addresses of the paying agents for the securities in Ireland, and

3. a statement of how notices of meetings and other notices from the issuer of the securities will be given to Irish resident holders of the securities.

VIII. CONTINUING OBLIGATIONS OF LISTED COMPANIES

A. EXCHANGE HAS POWER TO SET ADDITIONAL OR MORE STRINGENT REQUIREMENTS

1–81 Once admitted to listing, the company is obliged to ensure that the company complies with the requirements of Schedules C and D of the Admissions Directive.[539] Schedule C sets out the obligations of *companies* whose shares are admitted to official listing on a Stock Exchange in a Member State, and Schedule D the obligations of *issuers*[440] whose debt securities shares are admitted to official listing on a Stock Exchange in a Member State.[441] However, for the purposes of this section of the chapter, the terms "company" and "issuers" shall include the other (unless otherwise indicated) for ease of reference. In effect, these obligations are what the Yellow Book recognises as "Continuing Obligations" incumbent on listed companies.[442]

---

an analogous fashion to listing particulars, see above earlier in this chapter where Mutual Recognition of Listing Particulars was considered).

[439] Council Directive 79/279/EEC of March 5, 1979 co-ordinating the conditions for the admission of securities to official stock exchange listing [1979] O.J. L66/21 (the "Admissions Directive") as implemented by the European Communities (Stock Exchange) Regulations 1984 (S.I. No. 282 of 1984).

[440] The term "Issuers" is used instead of "Companies" as Sched. D concerns not only debt securities issued by companies (Sched. (D) part (A)) but also those issued by "a State or its regional or local authorities or by a public body international body."

[441] Note that in the case of debt securities issued by a State or its regional or local authorities or by a public body international body, less onerous continuing obligations may apply: Sched. D (B) and art. 8 Admissions Directive.

[442] Note that additional and alternative conditions relating to Continuing Obligations, are set out in Chaps. 17, 18, 21 to 24 and 26 of the Yellow Book dealing with overseas companies, property companies, investment entities, public sector issuers, issuers of specialist securities (including specialist certificates representing shares), miscellaneous securities, and venture capital trusts.

Articles 13 and 17 of the Directive provide the legal basis for these obligations as follows. A company whose securities are admitted to official listing shall provide the competent authorities with all information which the authorities consider appropriate in order to protect investors or ensure the smooth operation of the market.[443] The information which companies are obliged to make available to the public under Schedules C and D shall be published in one or more national newspapers or else it shall be widely advertised as to where such information may be obtained.[444] The issuers of securities admitted to listing must fulfil the obligations set out in the two Schedules, as applicable.[445]

However, the Directive also provides that Member States may make issuers of listed securities subject to more stringent or additional conditions than those set out in the two Schedules.[446] Accordingly, the implementing regulations permit the designated competent authority, the Stock Exchange,[447] to impose obligations on the issuers of securities admitted to listing, provided that any such conditions or obligations:

– apply generally for all issuers or particular classes of issuers, and

– are published before application for admission of such securities is made, and

– are not otherwise inconsistent with the Directive.

Article 5.3 provides that derogations may be granted from these additional or more stringent requirements, provided they apply generally for all issuers and the circumstances justifying them are similar.

B. MAIN PRINCIPLES

1–82 The Yellow Book reflects the Admissions Directive's Continuing Obligations requirements by implementing the main principles behind the Continuing Obligations in Chapter 9. In succeeding Chapters 10–16, the Yellow Book sets out more additional and stringent require-

---

[443] Art. 13 Admissions Directive. As will be seen below, the Yellow Book rules for the most part require that information be disclosed to the Company Announcements Office.

[444] Art. 17 Admissions Directive.

[445] Art. 4(2) Admissions Directive; reg. 3(1) S.I. No. 282 of 1984.

[446] Art. 5(2) Admissions Directive; reg. 3(2) S.I. No. 282 of 1984.

[447] reg. 7 S.I. No. 282 of 1994 provides that the Irish Stock Exchange is designated as the "competent authority" for the purposes of the Directive.

ments to those set out in the two Schedules, in respect of specific transactions.[448] In its opening statements in Chapter 9 the Stock Exchange provides that observance of the Continuing Obligations is essential to the maintenance of an orderly market in securities and to ensure that all users of the market have simultaneous access to the same information. Failure to comply with any applicable Continuing Obligation may result in the Stock Exchange either censuring an issuer, censuring an issuer's directors, or ordering a suspension or cancellation of an issuer's listing.[449]

1–83 The first major principle reflected in Chapter 9 is the general obligation of disclosure for companies. Paragraph 9.1 Yellow Book provides that a company must notify the Company Announcements Office of the Exchange without delay of any major new developments in its sphere of activity which are not public knowledge and which may have a substantial effect on the movement of the price of its listed securities[450] or, in the case of debt securities which may affect its ability to meet its commitments.[451] The rules further elaborate to provide that matters in negotiation need not be disclosed unless the company becomes aware there has been, or is likely to be, a breach of confidence such that the price of the securities will, or is likely to be, substantially affected. It is open to the company to request the Stock Exchange to grant a derogation from the obligation to disclose where – in the company's view – its legitimate interests might be prejudiced.

1–84 Another important principle is the principle of equivalence. This means that a company whose securities are listed on stock exchanges operating in different Member States must ensure that equivalent information is made available at the same time to the Stock Exchange and to the other markets.[452] The well established principle of equal treatment of shareholders or debt securities holders is also recognised. Under this principle, equality of treatment must be ensured for all those in the same position.[453] For example, in this regard pre-emption rights

---

[448] See immediately below.

[449] Chapter 1 Yellow Book: see further above at para. 1–16.

[450] para. 9.1(a) Yellow Book; Admissions Directive Sched. C. para. 5.

[451] para. 9.1(b) Yellow Book; Admissions Directive Sched. D.(A) para. 4.

[452] By way of notifying the Company Announcements Office: para. 9.9 Yellow Book; Admissions Directive Scheds. C. para. 6 and D.(A) par 5 respectively. Note that Chap. 17 Yellow Book sets out similar obligations for "overseas" companies which maintain a secondary listing on the Stock Exchange in this jurisdiction.

[453] paras 9.16 and 17 Yellow Book respectively; Admissions Directive Scheds. C. para. 2 and D.(A) para. 1 respectively.

must be respected, where applicable.[454] Also, the Directive obliges companies to ensure that all necessary facilities and information are available to securities holders to allow them exercise their rights to participate in the company with regard to matters such as the holding of meetings, the right to vote, the publication and distribution of circulars concerning the payment of dividend and interest, the issue of new securities, and the redemption or repayment of securities.[455]

1–85   Another major principle is the principle that alterations to capital structure must be notified without delay.[456] Thus any changes in proposed capital structure including the structure of listed debt securities must be notified, or any change in rights attaching to securities. Furthermore, if any person has acquired a substantial interest[457] in the company (or has reduced or ceased to have such interest), notification must be made without delay to the Company Announcements Office once the company has been so notified or has become otherwise aware.[458]

Finally, Chapter 9 sets out various other miscellaneous obligations, the two most important being (1) that the issuer must notify at least two national newspapers in the event that the Company Announcements Office is closed at the time it is obliged to notify the relevant information[459] and (2) a company must inform the Stock Exchange in writing without delay if it becomes aware that the proportion of any class of listed securities in the hands of the public has fallen below 25% of the total issued share capital of that class.[460]

---

[454] paras 9.18–20 Yellow Book.

[455] para. 9.24 *et seq.* Yellow Book; Admissions Directive Scheds. C. para. 2 and D.(A) para. 1 respectively.

[456] para. 9.10 Yellow Book; Admissions Directive Scheds. C. pars. 4 and 5, and D.(A) para. 4 respectively.

[457] Pursuant to ss.67–79 Companies Act 1990.

[458] para. 9.11–14 Yellow Book. Note that 9.13 provides that the requirement to make a notification will be deemed to have been discharged where the relevant interest has been notified to the Company Announcements Office pursuant to the Takeover Panel's takeover code or rules governing substantial acquisitions of shares.

[459] para. 9.15 Yellow Book.

[460] para. 9.37 Yellow Book: or where applicable such lower percentage as the Stock Exchange may permit.

C. ADDITIONAL REQUIREMENTS IN SPECIFIC TRANSACTIONS

1–86 The Yellow Book sets out additional and more stringent requirements to those required by the Admissions Directive.[461] These requirements are often of a highly technical nature, some involving mathematical calculations of some complexity. It is beyond the scope of this work to consider them to the same depth and breadth as the treatment given them in the Yellow Book itself, and the reader is recommended to consult the relevant chapters of the Yellow Book for more specific information. In brief, Chapter 10 details how a listed company's transactions (principally acquisitions and disposals) are classified, what are the requirements for the making of announcements to the Company Announcements Office in respect of such transactions, and whether a circular or shareholder approval is required. It sets out additional requirements for takeovers and mergers.

Chapter 11 concerns the Yellow Book rules concerning safeguards to prevent "related parties" such as directors, substantial shareholders or their associates taking advantage of their position. Where any transaction is proposed between a listed company or its subsidiaries and a related party, a circular and the prior approval of the company in general meeting will normally be required. Any circular sent to shareholders in connection with the transaction must provide sufficient information to enable the recipient evaluate the effects of the transaction on the company. Where the transaction involves the acquisition or disposal of property of an unlisted company, the valuation requirements of Chapter 18 will be relevant.

Chapter 12 sets out the types and categories of financial information which may be required to be included in listing particulars and circulars, depending on the particular circumstances. Chapter 13 sets out documents not requiring approval by the Stock Exchange. For example, trust deeds relating to the purchase of debt securities or documents relating to employee share schemes and long term incentive schemes need not be notified provided they otherwise comply with the requirements of Chapter 13. The onus is placed on the company to ensure that any such documents meet the requirements of the Chapter.

Chapter 14 sets out the general requirements applying to all company circulars sent by a company to holders of its listed securities, such as requirements concerning content and approval requirements. Chapter 15 sets out the rules applying to a company proposing to pur-

---

[461] As permitted by art 5.2 Yellow Book; reg. 3(2) S.I. No. 282 of 1984.

chase its own listed securities. The requirements mainly relate to the notification of proposed or actual purchases. Chapter 16 imposes obligations relating to directors, including rules as to disclosures a company must make about its directors and about dealings in securities of the company by directors and persons connected with them. Appended to the Chapter is a Model Code for transactions in securities by directors, certain employees and persons connected with them.[462]

---

[462] The Model Code is further considered in Chap. 4 below on Insider Dealing.

Prospectuses – Offer to the Public

Introduction
    (1) Part III Companies Act 1963 91
    (2) Council Directive 89/298/EEC 94
    (3) Council Directive 80/390/EEC 97
    (4) Part XII Companies Act 1963 98
A. **The Statutory Definition of a Prospectus** 100
    (1) Section 2(1) Companies Act 1963 100
    (2) Section 44(3) – prospectus must accompany "form of
         application" 100
    (3) Documents deemed to be a Prospectus 101
        (a) Where company issues shares "with a view to any or all
            of them being offered to the public" 101
        (b) Prospectus Directive 102
        (c) Listing Particulars Directive 103
B. **Offer to "the Public"** 103
    (1) Private companies 103
    (2) Statutory and judicial elaboration on the concept of
         'the public' 103
        (a) Statutory Definition 104
        (b) Exclusions 104
            (i) Offer either acceptable by offerees only, or
                else a "domestic concern" 104
            (ii) Issues to members or debenture holders
                by company prohibited from making
                offers to the public 114
            (iii)Offers of debentures to professional
                dealers 115
    (3) Offer for "subscription or purchase" 115
        (a) For subscription 115
        (b) For purchase 116
C. **Relaxation of the Third Schedule Rules under the
    Companies Act** 117

D. Offers for which Neither the Companies Act Nor the Prospectus Directive require a Prospectus 119
(1) The Companies Act 1963 119
(2) The Prospectus Directive 120

┌───┐
│ 2 │
└───┘

Prospectuses – Offer to the Public

Introduction

2–01   In this chapter the issue of what is an "offer to the public" will be considered in detail. Whether an offer of securities is to "the public" (or not) is an essential question in the context of the application of the disclosure obligations applicable to offers to the public as regulated by domestic and European Community laws. These legal regimes impose heavy disclosure obligations on the company, as well as heavy responsibilities on those responsible for issuing the prospectus.[1]

The question of whether or not there has been an "offer to the public" is therefore an important matter. In order to place it in its proper context, a brief overview of the somewhat convoluted regulatory framework for prospectuses must first be undertaken.

(1) Part III Companies Act 1963

2–02   Part III Companies Act 1963, section 44(3), provides that it shall not be lawful to issue a form of application[2] for shares or debentures[3]

---

[1]   These regimes will not ordinarily apply to private companies (because they are not supposed to make offers to the public). However, should a private company make such an offer, then the full rigours of those regimes will apply to the private company as if were a public company: see further paras 2–16 and 2–25 below.

[2]   The use of the term "form of application" would seem to preclude purely oral offers from requiring a prospectus in the form prescribed by the Third Schedule Companies Act 1963. (Note that the implementing regulations for the Prospectus Directive, S.I. 202 of 1992, reg. 6 similarly confines the application of the Prospectus Directive, notwithstanding that the Directive contains no such limitation itself: see further para. 2–12 below).

[3]   s.2(1) of the Companies Act 1963 defines "shares" as "share in the share capital of a company, and includes stock except where a distinction between stock and shares is expressed or implied" and "debentures" as "including debenture stock, bonds and any other securities of a company whether a charge on the assets of a company or not."

in a company[4] unless the form is accompanied by a prospectus, which section 44(1) states must contain all of the matters specified in the Act's Third Schedule. Such a prospectus must be registered with the Registrar of Companies in accordance with the requirements of section 47 Companies Act 1963.[5] The obligation to produce a Third Schedule form of prospectus only applies where there is an offer to "the public"[6], and there are a number of exceptions where such a form of prospectus will not be required.[7]

The main heads under which information is required under the Third Schedule are (a) the capital of the company (b) the number of securities and rights and privileges attaching (c) the names of the directors and proposed directors (d) the number and amount of shares

---

[4] "Company" means a company incorporated and registered under the Companies Act 1963 or a company existing at the date of the 1963 Act's enactment. Note that the Ninth Schedule to the 1963 Act also applies s.44 to "unregistered companies" (*e.g.* trustee savings banks: s.344 Companies Act 1963). Other key sections of Part III concerning prospectuses are similarly applied to unregistered companies, i.e., ss.43, 45-52, 56, 57, 61 and the 1963 Act's Third Schedule. In the case of companies incorporated outside the State, the 1963 Act provides that where such a company makes an offer for subscription within the State, a Third Schedule prospectus in the form required by Part XII Companies Act 1963 will be required (unless the Prospectus Directive applies, in which event a prospectus in the form required by the Directive's regime will be required): Part XII is considered below at par.2.10.

[5] s.47 Companies Act 1963 provides that a copy of the Third Schedule form of prospectus signed by every director or proposed director (or agent authorised in writing) must be registered with the Registrar of Companies on or before the date of its publication. Additionally s.47 requires that such prospectus must contain any experts' consents (required pursuant to s.46 of the Act) and copies of material contracts (as defined in par. 14 Third Schedule). Furthermore, such prospectus must contain a statement on its face that it has been delivered for registration pursuant to s.47, and specify any documents that are required by the Act to be appended to it.

[6] "the public" is considered below at paras 2–16—2–29. Although the phrase "the public" does not actually appear in s. 44(1) or (3), it must be read into those subsections by reference to s.44(4) which provides that the s.44(1) and (3) requirement for a Third Schedule prospectus is not applicable when the offer is *not* to the public: therefore, by implication an offer that is to the public is subject to the ss.44(1) and (3) requirement for a Third Schedule Prospectus to be published.

[7] e.g, s.44(7)(b) (issue of shares or debentures in all respects uniform with similar securities issued within previous two years which are now traded on a stock exchange does not require a prospectus); nor does s.45 (issue of shares which are proposed to be listed on the stock exchange and the exchange certifies that compliance with the Third Schedule would be "unduly burdensome"); nor does reg. 21(3) S.I. 202 of 1992 (issue of "transferable securities" (as defined in Prospectus Directive) where a prospectus complying with S.I. 202 is published). These, and other exceptions, are considered further at para. 2–30 below.

issued in the past five years (e) the property to be purchased with the proceeds of the offer (f) the expenses paid in connection with the offer (g) material contracts[8] and the parties thereto (h) the names of the auditors (i) the declaration of any interests held by directors in the property to be acquired by the company or any interest held by any director in any firm providing services to the company. Also various reports need to be attached, most importantly an auditor's report (which is a most onerous obligation) pertaining to various specified matters over a five year period.

2–03 The Companies Act does not require a Third Schedule prospectus in all circumstances when an offer to the public is contemplated. This is because "prospectus" is defined[9] to mean a document which offers shares or debentures to the public *for subscription or purchase*.[10] Effectively, this confines the application of the 1963 Act requirement for a Third Schedule prospectus to the situation where new shares or debentures are being offered to the public.[11] Consequently, if shares or debentures were initially issued by way of a non-public offer (e.g., by way of a private placing), and were after some time offered to the public, the Companies Act requirement for a Third Schedule form of prospectus would not apply to the subsequent offer, because such an offer would not be an offer for subscription.[12]

2–04 Since the adoption of the Prospective Directive[13] in 1992 (as im-

---

[8] Par. 14 Third Schedule defines "material contracts" as meaning contracts not involving the ordinary business of the company which the company either is carrying on, or intends to carry on, or a contract entered into more than five years before the date of issue of the prospectus.

[9] The definition of "prospectus" contained in s.2(1) of the Companies Act 1963 defines "prospectus" to mean "any prospectus, notice, circular, advertisement or other invitation, offering to the public for subscription or purchase any shares or debentures of a company."

[10] Author's emphasis added. As to what "subscription or purchase" may mean in specific instances, see further pars. 2–27—2–29 below.

[11] Hence, secondary offers of securities do not require a Third Schedule form of prospectus.

[12] Although a key qualification arises if the circumstances are such that s.51(2) Companies Act 1963 applies: *inter alia* 51(2) provides that it will be presumed that an allotment (or agreement to allot) was made with a view to offering securities to the public for subscription (requiring a Third Schedule) should any of the securities be offered to the public within two years of their initial allotment (or the agreement to allot). If this circumstance pertains, then a Third Schedule prospectus would be required for the offer to the public notwithstanding s.44.

[13] Council Directive of April 17, 1989 coordinating the requirements for the drawing up, scrutiny and distribution of the prospectus to be published when transferable securities are to be offered to the public (89/298/EEC) [1989] O.J. L. 124/8 (the "Prospectus Directive").

plemented by S.I. No. 202 of 1992)[14] the form of prospectus required under the Directive has largely supplanted the Third Schedule form of prospectus.[15] However, notwithstanding this development, in certain circumstances the Third Schedule continues to be relevant. The interplay between the Third Schedule and the Prospectus Directive (and S.I. No. 202 of 1992) will now be considered.[16]

(2) Council Directive 89/298/EEC (the "Prospectus Directive")

2–05   Council Directive 89/298/EEC (the "Prospectus Directive")[17] requires a prospectus in the form specified by that Directive to be published whenever "transferable securities[18]. . . are offered to the public for the first time . . . provided that these securities are not already listed on a stock exchange situated or operating in that Member State".[19]

In requiring a prospectus to be published in accordance with the form required by the Prospectus Directive whenever securities are offered to the public for the first time, this clearly also includes initial offers for subscription. The domestic implementing regulations (S.I. 202 of 1992) for the Prospectus Directive address this matter, but in a less than clear manner. Regulation 21(4) provides that where a prospectus is published in conjunction with an offer for subscription or purchase of securities in compliance with the Prospectus Directive's requirements (as implemented by S.I. No. 202 of 1992), it shall be deemed to be a prospectus within the meaning of the Companies Act

---

[14] The Directive was implemented in Ireland by the European Communities (Transferable Securities and Stock Exchange) Regulations 1992 (S.I. No 202 of 1992) with effect from September 1, 1992.

[15] Provided the offer is of "transferable securities" to which the Directive applies. See further para. 2–05 below. (For a description of certain transferable securities and certain types of offers of such securities to which the Prospectus Directive *does not apply*, see further par. 2–32 below).

[16] Next in para. 2–05.

[17] Council Directive of April 17, 1989 coordinating the requirements for the drawing up, scrutiny and distribution of the prospectus to be published when transferable securities are to be offered to the public (89/298/EEC) [1989] O.J. L. 124/8 (the "Prospectus Directive"). The Directive was implemented in Ireland by the European Communities (Transferable Securities and Stock Exchange) Regulations 1992 (S.I. No 202 of 1992) with effect from 1 September 1992.

[18] Article 3(e) of the Prospectus Directive defines "transferable securities" to mean shares in companies and other transferable securities equivalent to shares in companies, debt securities having a maturity of at least one year and other transferable securities equivalent to debt securities, and any other transferable security giving the right to acquire any such transferable securities by subscription or exchange. For a description of certain transferable securities and certain types of offers of such securities to which the Prospectus Directive *does not apply*, see further para. 2–32 below.

[19] Art. 1.1 Council Directive 89/298/EEC.

1963. Furthermore, Regulation 21(3) provides that in such event, no Third Schedule form of prospectus is required. Hence, a prospectus in the form required by the Prospectus Directive would appear to supplant the Third Schedule prospectus. However, a closer reading of the regulations is required. Regulation 8 provides that a prospectus in the form required by the Directive must contain Third Schedule information where any such information is not required under the Prospectus Directive itself. Although regulation 8 further provides that application can be made to the Stock Exchange for exemption from such obligation where compliance with the requirements of the Third Schedule would be "unduly burdensome",[20] nevertheless the fact remains that in substance cognisance still has to be taken of the Third Schedule's requirements when drawing up a Prospectus Directive form of prospectus.

Notwithstanding this confusion, a major advantage flowing from the application of the Prospectus Directive to any particular offer is that only three years' previous audited accounts need be published.[21]

2–06 In another key respect, the Third Schedule regime is not defunct either. It should not be forgotten that the Prospectus Directive only applies where "transferable securities" are being offered to the public for the first time. The Directive defines a number of such securities, and offers of same, to which the Prospectus Directive will not apply.[22] Where such securities or offers of same are made to the public for subscription, the Part III regime therefore continues to apply: i.e., a Third Schedule form of prospectus will be required.[23]

2–07 While both Part III[24] and the Directive[25] are predicated upon

---

[20] Reg. 8(4) S.I. 202 of 1992.

[21] Reg. 8 S.I. 202 of 1992. By contrast, in the case of any offers for subscription to which the Third Schedule continues to apply by virtue of the Directive's inapplicability (such as where the securities offered are not of the "transferable securities" variety) *five years* previous audited accounts are required: par. 19 Third Schedule Companies Act 1963.

[22] For a more detailed description of certain securities and certain types of offers to which the Prospectus Directive does not apply, see further art. 2 Prospectus Directive and par. 2–32 below.

[23] Unless one of the exceptions specified in the 1963 Act apply (see par. 2–02 above and also further below at par. 2–30). If the company concerned is a foreign incorporated company, the form of Third Schedule prospectus it must publish will be published in accordance with the requirements of Part XII Companies Act 1963 (though cf. 1964 derogation from this requirement for prospectuses first published or issued in the U.K.: see further below par. 2.10 below when Part XII is considered.)

[24] ss. 44(1); (3); and (4)(b) of the Companies Act 1963 when read together.

[25] Articles 4 and 1 read together.

an "offer to the public", there are however also differences between Part III and the Directive. It may be useful to set out the chief differences here.

First, Part III concerns an offer of "shares or debentures",[26] whereas the Directive concerns offers of "transferable securities",[27] a term which the Directive clearly intends to cover a much wider range of securities than mere shares or debentures.

Second, Part III only applies to offers by "a company or in relation to an intended company"[28] whereas the Directive does not confine issuing entities of "transferable securities" to mere "companies".[29]

Third, Part III's regime concerns the situation where shares are being offered "with a view to . . . them being offered for sale to the public. . . .",[30] whereas the Directive applies whenever shares are offered to the public "for the first time".[31] This final point of distinction is of interest because it is generally accepted that once shares have been issued, secondary offers of those shares do not ordinarily attract the attention of Part III.[32] However, this is not necessarily the case under the Directive. If shares have been issued by way of a private offer, and

---

[26] s.44(3) Companies Act 1963. S. 2(1) of the Act defines a debenture as "including debenture stock, bonds and any other securities of a company whether constituting a charge on the assets of the company or not"; a share is defined as a "share in the share capital of a company, and includes stock except where a distinction between stock and shares is expressed or implied."

[27] As defined in Article 3(e) Prospectus Directive "transferable securities" mean shares in companies and other transferable securities equivalent to shares in companies, debt securities having a maturity of at least one year and other transferable securities equivalent to debt securities, and any other transferable security giving the right to acquire any such transferable securities by subscription or exchange. (For a description of certain securities and certain types of offers to which the Prospectus Directive *does not apply*, see further par. 2–32 below).

[28] s.43 Companies Act 1963. The relevant provisions of Part III (being ss.43-52, 56, 57, 61 and the Third Schedule) also apply to "unregistered companies" as per Ninth Schedule Companies Act 1963.

[29] Article 3 Prospectus Directive defines "issuers" as companies and other legal persons and any undertakings the transferable securities of which are offered to the public.

[30] ss. 51(1); 43(4); and 51(2) of the Companies Act 1963.

[31] Article 1.1 Prospectus Directive 89/298/EEC. However, Article 1.2 of the Directive further provides that where an offer to the public is for part only of the transferable securities from a single issue, the Member State need not require that another prospectus be published if the other part is subsequently offered to the public. See further para. 3–32 of this Chapter below.

[32] Unless of course there has been a deliberate attempt to circumvent the prospectus regime of Part III Companies Act 1963 by issuing shares non-publicly with a view to making them available to the public at a later time. See above para. 2–03 where s.51 deals with this situation by putting anti-avoidance measures in place, and also further at paras 2–13 and 2–31 below.

subsequently their holders decide to offer them to the public, then such a secondary transaction will constitute an offer to "the public for the first time" of the securities and therefore will require a prospectus to be issued pursuant to the Directive.[33]

(3) Council Directive 80/390/EEC ("The Listing Particulars Directive")

2–08   Where an application for listing on the Stock Exchange is involved, then listing particulars will have to be published as required by Council Directive 80/390/EEC ("the Listing Particulars Directive") and the Stock Exchange's Yellow Book.[34] The implementing regulations for this Directive provide, that where the Stock Exchange has approved the listing particulars, then the form of application need not have a Third Schedule form of prospectus attached to it.[35]

Although fully considered above in Chapter 1, it should be briefly mentioned at this point (for the sake of completeness) that the Prospectus Directive has created a mutual recognition regime in order to facilitate the *mutual recognition* in different EU Member States of Prospectus Directive form of prospectuses, *and* also the *mutual recognition* of prospectuses as listing particulars. The fact that the contents requirements of listing particulars and prospectuses required under the respective Listing Particulars and Prospectus Directives are quite similar, facilitates the operation of the mutual recognition regime.[36]

In so far as mutual recognition of listing particulars *per se* is concerned, the Listing Particulars Directive itself provides for the mutual recognition of listing particulars.[37]

2–09   Due to less than clear drafting of the domestic Prospectus Directive Regulations (S.I. No. 202 of 1992), a somewhat unfortunate situation has arisen. As one may recall, the Prospectus Directive applies whenever there is an offer to the public for the first time of transferable

---

[33] Article 1.

[34] See Chapter 1 above generally on the listing particulars regime.

[35] Regulation 12(2) S.I. 282 of 1984 provides that a Third Schedule form of prospectus will not be required where a listing particulars complying with requirements of the Directive and S.I. 282 is published, and reg. 12(3) deems such listing particulars to be a prospectus within the meaning of the Companies Act 1963 whenever there is an offer for subscription or purchase of securities admitted to official listing.

[36] As described in Chapter 1 above, this reflects the EU's objective of ensuring that the level of disclosure made to investors was comparable irrespective of whether securities were being offered to "the public" via the stock exchange or otherwise. see further Chapter 1 above, particularly paras 1–59—1–80.

[37] See paras 1–59—1–60 in Chapter 1 above.

securities where such securities are not already listed in the State.[38]
However, one would have expected S.I. No. 202 of 1992 not to apply
where a company was going to offer to the public *in the context of* an
application for admission to listing, on the grounds that the onerous
level of disclosure required by the Listing Particulars Directive implementing Regulations (S.I. 282 of 1984) and Yellow Book regime would
render unnecessary the need to comply with the Prospectus Directive
regime. However, regrettably, on grounds of caution, many legal advisers take the view that a prospectus must be drawn up in compliance with the Prospectus Directive implementing regulations
notwithstanding compliance with the Listing Particulars Directive and
Yellow Book listing regimes. This is because Regulation 21 of S.I 202 of
1992 *inter alia* refers to applications for admission to listing *and* listing
particulars approved by the Stock Exchange and therefore is open to
the interpretation that whenever securities are being admitted to listing *and* they have not already been offered to the public for the first
time, then the Prospectus Regulations must be complied with *in addition to* the (properly applicable) Listing Particulars regulations and
Yellow Book regime.[39] As a result of this peculiar form of drafting
employed in the Regulations, many practitioners adopt an understand-
ably cautious approach by having the particulars comply with the Prospectus Regulations also.

(4) Part XII Companies Act 1963

2–10   Part XII Companies Act 1963 provides a separate prospectus
regime for companies incorporated outside the State. Overall, Part XII's
legal framework is quite similar to Part III in many respects. Essentially what Part XII provides is that it shall not be lawful for any person to issue, circulate or distribute a prospectus in the State offering
for subscription shares in or debentures of a company *incorporated*[40]
outside the State unless it contains the information required by the Companies Act 1963 Third Schedule. Section 361(4) further adds that it shall
be not be lawful for any person to issue to any person in the State a

---

[38] Art. 1.1 Prospectus Directive.

[39] The background to this matter is provided by less than precise drafting in S.I.
202 of 1992 (the Prospectus Regulations). In sum, several paragraphs of Regulation 21 refer to "these Regulations" rather than to "this Regulation" as appropriate. Consequently, the Regulations give the impression that the Prospectus
Regulations' regime must be complied with when an application for admission
to listing is being made under the Listing Regulations' regime (S.I. No. 282 of
1984).

[40] s.361(1)'s prohibition also applies to companies not yet incorporated outside
the State, and also irrespective of whether the company has established, or will
establish, a place of business in the State.

form of application for shares or debentures of such a company[41] unless the form of application complies with Part XII and the requirements of the Third Schedule. The prospectus must be registered with the Registrar of Companies in Dublin.[42]

A derogation from the aforegoing prohibitions is provided in the case of a prospectus or form of application for shares or debentures first published or issued in a country which complies with the law of that country, provided that such country is a "recognised" country for this purpose. Only the United Kingdom has been so recognised by the Minister thus far for this purpose.[43] Maintaining such a derogation in favour of one State only may be contrary to EC law. Admittedly, the recognition afforded the U.K. is understandable in the sense that it took place in 1964 prior to Ireland joining the EC in the early 1970's, and was appropriate given the similarity of the prospectus regimes applicable in both jurisdictions. However, in light of more recent developments, particularly the enactment of the Prospectus Directive which has harmonised the common minimum disclosure conditions applicable in offers of transferable securities to the public throughout the EC, confining this recognition to the U.K. may well constitute a violation of Articles 54 EC on the grounds that it works against the stated EC objective of facilitating the interpenetration of Member States' capital markets.

A further derogation is provided by section 367(2). It provides that an offer of shares or debentures by a foreign company for subscription or sale to any person whose ordinary business it is to buy or sell shares or debentures (whether as principal or agent), shall not be an offer to the public for the purposes of Part XII.

However, notwithstanding the section 361(4) prohibition, should a company incorporated outside the State issue a form of application for securities accompanied by a Prospectus Directive form of prospectus (*i.e.*, complying with S.I. 202 of 1992), it need not have attached to it a prospectus in the form required by section 361(4).[44]

---

[41] Or intended company: s.361(4).

[42] s.364 of the Companies Act 1963: the prospectus must be registered on or before the day of publication; state on its face that it has been delivered for registration; contain all required experts' consents; have copies of all "material contracts" attached; and, be signed by the Chairman and two directors of the company.

[43] Companies (Recognition of Countries) Order 1964 (S.I. No. 42 of 1964) adopted pursuant to s. 367(3) of the Companies Act 1963.

[44] Regulation 21(3) S.I. 202 of 1992. Of course, while a Prospectus Directive form of prospectus is much more detailed than a Third Schedule form of prospectus, as a matter of reality the former will often duplicate the type of information one would find contained in a Third Schedule form of prospectus, though with im-

Where the Listing Particulars Directive's regime is applicable (S.I. 282 of 1984) and satisfied, section 361(4) does not apply in that regime either.[45]

Finally, there may be one further significant difference between Part III and Part XII. Part III (where applicable) requires a Third Schedule prospectus only if there is an offer to the public. While the point is not free from doubt, a strict reading of Part XII does not suggest that Part XII is similarly so confined. If this is correct, then Part XII (where applicable) will require a Third Schedule form of prospectus whenever a company incorporated outside the jurisdiction (or anyone acting on their behalf) makes an offer in the State, whether to the public or not.[45a]

A. THE STATUTORY DEFINITION OF A PROSPECTUS

(1) Section 2(1) Companies Act 1963

2–11   Section 2(1) Companies Act 1963 states:

> "prospectus means any prospectus, notice, circular, advertisement or other invitation, offering to the public for subscription or purchase any shares or debentures of a company."

(2) Section 44(3) Companies Act 1963: Prospectus must accompany "form of application"

2–12   In Part III of the 1963 Act, section 44(1) provides that every prospectus must state the matters that require disclosure as specified in the Third Schedule of the Companies Act 1963. Section 44(3) provides, *inter alia,* that it shall not be lawful to issue any form of application for shares without a prospectus. As section 44(3) requires a prospectus where there is "a form of application" issued for shares or debentures, it is submitted that an oral offer would not constitute such a "form of application" within the meaning of the Act. However, this may not be the case under the Prospectus Directive, Article 4 of which states that:

> "Member States shall ensure that any offer of transferable securities to the public within their territories is subject to the publication of a prospectus by the person making the offer."

---

portant modifications (e.g., three years' audited accounts rather than five years accounts: see reg. 8 S.I. 202 of 1992).
[45] Reg. 12(2) S.I. 282 of 1984.
[45a]Unless one of the derogations noted above apply (or any of the other derogations provided in Part XII, e.g. rights issues; issues to underwriters etc.).

The reference to "any offer" would suggest that all offers – whether oral or in writing – require a prospectus.[46]

It would appear from the section 2(1) definition of "prospectus" that no distinction should rest on whether the section 44(3) "form of application" is an invitation capable of leading to a binding arrangement or merely an invitation to show interest. In other words, the distinction that is made in the law of contract between "an offer" (the acceptance of which constitutes a legally binding contract) and an "invitation to treat" (which does not of itself amount to "an offer") should not apply in the context of prospectuses. Otherwise, companies could merely solicit expressions of interest, retain the right to reject such expressions, and consequently argue that their invitation does not amount to a "prospectus" because it never made an offer capable of leading to a binding contract for the purchase of securities. It is submitted that such an argument is not tenable for two reasons. First, were it to be so, companies could use it to evade the application of the prospectus provisions, with consequent risks to the public investment market. Second, the definition of "prospectus" used in section 2(1) Companies Act 1963 makes it clear that an ". . . invitation, offering to the public ... any shares or debentures . . ." can be a prospectus. There is no indication that such an invitation need be one that amounts to "an offer" in the contractual sense. When faced with this issue, courts have tended to take the view that all the circumstances of the issue should be taken into account, rather than merely looking at the initial advertisement and considering whether it is "an offer" in the contractual sense.[47]

Finally, a further distinction must be drawn between an offer or invitation and the mere giving of information. Where a document merely gives information but does not offer or invite expressions of interest, it is not a prospectus as the definition in section 2(1) requires that a "prospectus" makes either an offer or an invitation.

(3) Documents deemed to be a Prospectus:

(a) Where a company issues shares "with a view to any or all of them being offered to the public"

2–13 Section 51(1) Companies Act 1963 provides that where a company allots or agrees to allot any "shares or debentures" in the com-

---

[46] Curiously however, reg. 6 of the domestic implementing regulations (S.I. No. 202 of 1992) provides that it shall not be lawful to issue any *form of application* (emphasis added) for transferable securities unless a prospectus is issued. In this respect therefore, reg. 6 may not be adhering to the objectives of the Directive.

[47] *Mutual Home Loans Fund of Australia Ltd v. Attorney General NSW* [1973] 130 C.L.R. 103.

pany "with a view to all or any" of them being offered for sale to the public, then any document by which the offer for sale to the public was made shall be deemed to be a prospectus issued by the company. In an anti-avoidance measure, section 51(2)(a) provides that where shares or debentures are offered to the public within two years of their initial allotment (or agreement to allot), it is presumed (unless rebutted) that they were initially allotted or agreed to be allotted "with a view to [them] being offered for sale to the public".[48] Consequently any document that accompanied the offer will be deemed to be a "prospectus" and therefore will have to comply with the regulatory requirements for prospectuses.[49]

(b) Where the Prospectus Directive applies

2–14   Article 1.1 of the Prospectus Directive requires a prospectus to be published whenever "transferable securities" are offered to the public for the first time and are not already listed in the State.[50] Regulation 6[51] provides that it shall not be lawful to issue any form of application for transferable securities of a company unless a prospectus is issued that complies with the Directive. It is further provided in regulation 22(3) that a Part III (*i.e.* Third Schedule) form of prospectus will not be required where an offer is accompanied by a prospectus which complies with the Directive.[52] Regulation 22(4) deems such a prospectus to be a prospectus within the meaning of the Companies Act 1963. The regulations set out the disclosure requirements and other relevant details required for such a prospectus.[53]

---

[48] s. 51(2)(a). S. 51(2)(b) raises a similar rebuttable presumption where at the date the offer was made, the whole of the consideration for the shares was not received by the company.

[49] And of course, in addition, the authorisers of such a "prospectus" will also have to be concerned with potential exposure to a s.49 Companies Act 1963 compensation action if there are "untrue statements": see Chap. 3 below. As seen above in para. 2–02, a Third Schedule form of prospectus must be registered with the Registrar of Companies pursuant to s. 47 of the Companies Act 1963.

[50] Also note that "first time" includes where the securities were originally issued and then subsequently offered to the public (art. 1.1). Hence it is conceivable that the vendor of the shares would be liable to issue a prospectus if their subsequent offer genuinely constituted an offer to "the public". However, note that art. 1.2 provides that (in the case of so-called "split issues") where an offer to the public is for part only of the securities from a single issue, then it shall not be necessary to publish another prospectus if the other part is subsequently offered to the public (implemented by para. 1 of third schedule to S.I. No. 202 of 1992).

[51] S.I. No. 202 of 1992 (the Prospectus Directive implementing regulations).

[52] Or indicates where such particulars may be obtained or inspected.

[53] See further Chap. 1, paras 1–72—1–76 above where contents and registration requirements of Prospectus Directive prospectuses are considered.

(c) *Where the Listing Particulars Directive applies*

2–15   Regulation 12(2) of the Listing Particulars Directive implementing regulations (S.I. No. 282 of 1994) provides that a form of application for securities need not have attached to it a Part III (*i.e.* Third Schedule) prospectus if accompanied by a listing particulars approved by the Stock Exchange, or alternatively if it indicates where they may be inspected. Regulation 12(3) deems such a listing particulars to be a prospectus, thereby obviating the need for the publication of a separate Part III prospectus.[54]

B. OFFER TO "THE PUBLIC"

(1) Private companies[55]

2–16   Section 44(4)(b) makes it clear that a prospectus is not required where shares or debentures are not offered to the public. Furthermore, it is clear that, although private companies are companies that, *inter alia*, are prohibited from offering shares to the public,[56] nevertheless, a private company is capable of making such an offer,[57] with the consequence that a prospectus will be required. Therefore, irrespective of the status of the company, the central issue that arises in any proposed issue of shares or debentures in a company is whether or not the offer is intended to be to "the public".[58]

(2) Statutory and judicial elaboration

2–17   Precisely what "the public" constitutes is not defined in easy language in the Companies Act 1963. Indeed, the Prospectus Directive states in its preamble that " . . . so far, it has proved impossible to furnish a common definition of the term 'public offer' and all its constituent parts" which could be used throughout the European Union. As the Directive makes no attempt to define "the public", the obtuse

---

[54] See further Chap. 1, paras 1–56 and 1–62 above where the listing particulars regime is considered.

[55] See also para. 2–25 of this chapter below.

[56] s. 33(1)(c) of the Companies Act 1963. S. 21 of the (1) Companies (Amendment) Act 1983 further makes it a criminal offence for the company and any of its of officers to either offer any shares or debentures to the public, or to allot or agree to allot any shares or debentures with a view to any of them being offered for sale to the public. S. 21(3) states that s. 21(1) does not in any way affect the validity of any allotment or sale or any agreement to allot or sell.

[57] Whether deliberately or inadvertently.

[58] See further para. 2–25 (private company offers) below when s. 61(2) Companies Act 1963 is considered and paras 2–16 and 2–24 (offers to the public).

language of the Companies Act 1963 falls to be examined for the purpose of attempting to define what the parameters of the elusive concept of "the public" might be.

(a) Statutory definition

2–18 Section 61 Companies Act 1963, while it attempts to define "the public", does not succeed in providing an all-embracing definition that lends itself to easy elucidation. It is neither an easy definition to apply, nor is it one that appears to be conclusive, in the sense that its phraseology does not seem to indicate that it is an exhaustive definition of "the public".

According to section 61(1), an offer to the public shall include offers of shares or debentures:

> ". . . to any section of the public, whether selected as members or debenture holders of the company concerned or as clients of the person issuing the prospectus or in any other manner. . . ."

Clearly section 61(1) intends that 'the public' may include a selected group of offerees, *i.e.* a "section of the public" such as a group selected by virtue of being the most likely persons to be interested in an offer (*e.g.* a broker's clients).[59] Also, the subsection provides that a group selected by virtue of their being members or debenture holders of the company concerned may be a "section of the public". In this regard therefore, a rights issue may well be an offer to a "section of the public".[60] Also, a group "selected . . . in any other manner" can be a "section of the public". Hence, in order for an offer to such groups to fall outside the prospectus requirement, clearly something more must be present before they will be deemed not to constitute "the public". In order to determine this additional element, section 61(1) must be read in conjunction with section 61(2) which is considered next.

(b) Exclusions

(i) Offer either acceptable by offerees only, or else a "domestic concern of the persons making and receiving the offer"

2–19 Section 61(2) provides that an offer will not be an offer to the public if, either it is not calculated to result in persons acquiring the

---

[59] Note that Art. 2.1 of the Prospectus Directive does not require a prospectus if the offer is to a "restricted circle of persons". However it does not elaborate any further on the point. Therefore, s. 61 will have to be looked at for guidance.

[60] Unless it remains within the parameters of s. 61(2) (though even if it does constitute an offer to the public a Third Schedule prospectus may not be required if s. 44(7)(a) applies). See further para. 2–23 of this chapter below.

shares other than those receiving the offer or alternatively, if the offer can properly be regarded as a "domestic concern of the persons making and receiving the offer." The specific form of wording used in section 61(2) provides that consideration should be given to whether the offer or invitation can:

> "... properly be regarded, in all the circumstances, as not being calculated to result, directly or indirectly, in the shares or debentures becoming available for subscription or purchase by persons other than those receiving the offer or invitation, or otherwise as being a domestic concern of the persons making and receiving it."

As subsections 61(1) and (2) must be read together, interesting issues arise as to many of the phrases used, such as, "the public", "section of the public", "... not being calculated to result, directly or indirectly, in the shares or debentures becoming available [to] persons other than those receiving the offer . . .", "domestic concern" , "subscription or purchase". An examination of relevant caselaw is of assistance in understanding the ambit of such phrases.

2–20 In *Sherwell v. Combined Incandescent Mantles Syndicate*[61] a company printed 1,000 copies of an offer document and it was circulated by one of the directors amongst 200 of his friends. The offer document was marked "strictly private and confidential: not for publication". One issue that arose was whether there had been an offer to "the public". Warrington J. held that there had been no offer to the public on two grounds. First, the relevant legislation at the time required that an offer, to be a public one (if at all), had to be circulated by the company. However, the learned judge found that the director had circulated the prospectus, not on the company's, but on the directors' behalf. It is questionable whether such a distinction would be drawn today given that sections 43 and 44 of the 1963 Act refer to invitations or offers "... by or on behalf of a company".[62]

However, the second ground of the court's decision is much more important as it was held that in circulating the prospectus to their friends, the directors' intention was to keep the share capital in the company to themselves and friends whom they would like to have as members of the company. Accordingly, the court held that there had been no offer to the public, as an offer to the public was one "to anyone

---

[61] [1907] 23 T.L.R. 482 (Chancery Div.).
[62] It seems that a key point in this case was that the judge took the view that the director's activities did not fall within the legislation that existed at the time which seemed to require that the circulation of a prospectus had to be an act of the company, rather than an act on its behalf.

who should choose to come in".[63] The court took the view that the director's offer was not such an offer. Warrington J.'s formula has been cited with approval in many more modern cases, as discussed below.

Although this judgment indicated that in order for an offer to be an offer to "the public" it must be an offer capable of acceptance by any person who chose to take up the offer, it was still unclear whether this would be the position where, for example, an offer was made to a group of persons most likely to take up the offer. This issue arose in *Re South of England Natural Gas*,[64] where a promoter of a newly incorporated gas company circulated a document to shareholders of several other gas companies, inviting them to subscribe in the newly incorporated company and informing them that the offer was only being made to them. Furthermore, it was marked "for private circulation only". It was not publicly advertised and only 3,000 copies were sent out. In all only 200 shares were applied for on foot of the offer document and, of these, 180 were applied for by the directors of the company. Some months later, the company issued a second offer. However, that offer was publicly advertised. The court was called upon to consider whether the first offer had been an offer to the public. The company contended that the offer had not been to the public as the prospectus was only sent to a limited class of persons, was marked "private" and was intended by the promoter to be taken up only by those to whom it was sent.

However, the court took the view that the document did constitute an offer to the public. After hearing the evidence, Swinfen-Eady J. took the view that, merely because the offer document was sent to those *most likely* to take up the offer, that does not mean that it was not an offer to "the public". It is clear therefore, that although an offer document inviting subscribers may be marked "private" and advertised only amongst a selective group, the courts will nevertheless consider whether the offer could constitute an offer to the public. The judge having examined the evidence, evidently[65] took the view that it was open to persons other than the shareholders in the other gas companies, to subscribe to the offer if presumably they somehow had access to a copy of the prospectus from one of the original offerees.

Barwick C.J., agreeing with the decision in *Re South of England Natural Gas*, commented in the High Court of Australia in *Lee v. Evans*:[66]

> "I do not regard [Re South of England] as an instance of an invitation which is shown to be an invitation to the public by the circumstances of

---

[63] [1907] 23 T.L.R. 482 at 483.
[64] [1911] 1 Ch 573.
[65] The author uses the word "evidently" as the report of the case is quite terse.
[66] [1964] 112 C.L.R. 276 at 285.

its issue but rather as a case where an invitation to the public does not cease to be such because it is given a restricted or selective issue."

In other words, merely because an offer is made to a group selected on the basis that they are the persons most likely to be interested in the investment opportunity does not mean that therefore the offer cannot be an offer to "the public".

In another Australian decision, *Corporate Affairs Commission (South Australia) and Another v. Australian Central Credit Union*, Brennan J. observed that, when attempting to ascertain whether a selected group of offerees constitute a "section of the public" or not, " . . . the criterion of distinction cannot be simply whether the offerees have some special interest in the subject-matter of the offer."[67] The learned judge emphasised that:

> "A group of offerees who are not a 'section of the public' are not to be distinguished from a group who are a 'section of the public' by reference merely to the manner in which they are selected to receive the offer."

These sentiments are reflected in section 61(1) of the Companies Act 1963 which provides that an offer to a select group ("a section of the public") is capable of constituting an offer to "the public". Section 61(1) provides that notwithstanding that offerees are selected whether as clients, members, debenture holders or in any other manner, the offer may still be an offer to "the public". The fact that such persons were selected on the basis that they would be most likely to take up the offer does not render the offer a non-public offer. In order for offers to such selected offerees to be non-public offers, clearly something further is required i.e., that section 61(2) is satisfied.[68]

Re South of England can be contrasted with *Government Stock and Other Securities Investment Co Ltd v. Christopher and Others*.[69] In the latter decision, Wynn-Parry J. held that where a company offered shareholders in two other companies (it wished to take over) the opportunity to exchange their shareholdings in exchange for shares in it, this did not constitute an offer to "the public". The court took the view that as only the shareholders of the two target companies could possibly accept the offer, it was not an offer capable of acceptance by "the public". According to the court:

> " . . . the test is not who receives the circular, but who can accept the offer

---

[67] [1985] 59 A.L.J.R. 785 at 789.

[68] *i.e.* either the offer is demonstrated not to be calculated to result in the shares or debentures becoming available to any persons other than those receiving the offer, or, the offer is a domestic concern of the persons making and receiving the offer. This is considered shortly below.

[69] [1956] 1 All E.R. 490 (Chancery Div.)

put forward. In this case it can only be persons legally or equitably interested as shareholders in the shares of [the two companies]".[70]

An additional factor that bolsters this conclusion was the fact that those
shareholders who would accept the offer would be issued with
non-renounceable letters of allotment. Accordingly, they could not have
renounced their entitlements in favour of any third party at the time of
allotment. This certainly supports the conclusion that the offer was
only capable of acceptance by those to whom it was made, and not by
any others.

2–21   In *Lee v. Evans*,[71] the High Court of Australia elaborated upon
the qualities that an offer had to have in order to be to "the public".
Although this case was not concerned with the interpretation of that
term in Australian securities law, nevertheless the judgments are extremely helpful in assisting an understanding of the concept of "the
public".[72] Barwick C.J. stated that in order for an offer to be to 'the
public', the offer must be "general" in nature.[73] What this means is
that it must be capable of acceptance by any member of the public who
should choose to accept it.[74] Furthermore, he stated that in order for
the offer to be "general", it is not necessary that it be "universal" in the
sense that it is advertised to all the world. In other words, an offer does
not cease to be "general" merely because it is addressed to a particular
segment in the community.[75] The segment of the community to whom
the offer is made does not have to be any particular number: what is
important is whether the offer was "general" or not and in this regard
the question to be asked is whether the offer is, "an offer of shares to
anyone who should choose to come in".[76] Furthermore, the learned
judge stated that merely because an invitation is sent to those who
have a special relationship with the offeror will not of itself prevent
the invitation being to the public.[77]

Kitto J.[78] added some interesting observations on the question of

---

[70] *ibid.* at 493.
[71] [1964] 112 C.L.R. 276 at 285.
[72] The case was concerned with the Registration of Business Names legislation
which prohibited the use of registered business names in connection with invitations to "the public" to deposit or lend money to the registered business name
firm.
[73] [1964] 112 C.L.R. 276 at 285.
[74] [1964] 112 C.L.R. 276 at 285.
[75] *ibid.*
[76] The learned judge cited Warrington J. in *Sherwell v. Combined Incandescent Mantle Syndicate* in support of this conclusion at p. 286 of the judgment.
[77] [1964] 112 C.L.R. 276 at 286.
[78] *ibid.* at 286–289.

whether an invitation to one individual could ever be an offer to the public. The learned judge took the view that such an invitation may be an offer to the public "when considered in the light of all the circumstances". He cited an example of this to be where the offer to one individual was merely the first step in the communication of the offer to the public generally. The learned judge explained that what he envisaged in this circumstance would be a situation whereby that individual could pass the invitation on to a stranger. If the terms of the offer were such that the stranger regarded the terms of the offer as being such that he could accept it, just as the original invitee could have done, then it is capable in this circumstance of being an offer to "the public". At page 287 of the judgment the learned judge stated:

> "I am not intending to hold, however, that the size of the immediate audience is necessarily conclusive of the question whether the invitation is an invitation to the public. That is a question of the true scope of the invitation. While it may be answered conclusively in one case by the terms in which the invitation was expressed, it may require in another case a consideration both of the words in which it was expressed and of the circumstances in which they were used. I see no reason to doubt that the statement of an invitation even to one person only may be seen, when considered in the light of all the circumstances, to be part of, even though only the first step in, the communication of the invitation to the public generally, so that if the lone hearer were to tell some stranger of it the stranger would be right in treating it as open to acceptance by him no less than by the hearer. But . . . I think it is going too far to say that proof of an invitation given to a person as a member of the public is necessarily proof of an invitation to the public. If a person, wishing to obtain a loan, makes his request to a stranger whom he picks at random in the street, it remains, I think, a question of fact whether his invitation is to the public or to the selected individual only. In many cases the answer may be easy, but that does not mean that the question is not there to be answered; and in considering the answer the distinction must not be overlooked between the case of an invitation which itself is open to acceptance by a specific individual only but, if declined by him, is likely to be followed by similar invitations to other specific individuals in succession until an acceptor is found. The first of these is a case of an invitation to the public; the second, in my opinion, is not."

Taylor J. also elaborated stating that, what was essential in determining whether an offer was public, was what was the "essential character" of the invitation.[79] In other words, was the invitation one that was particular to the invitee or could it be accepted by another (a stranger) if it was passed onto them? The learned judge also emphasised that it is not how the invitation is communicated that is important (*i.e.* was it

---

[79] [1964] 112 C.L.R. 276 at 290.

advertised to all the world or merely to a select group; or was the offer stated to be "private" or not) but whether the invitation in character is one that is capable of acceptance by such a stranger.

2–22   In *Corporate Affairs Commission (South Australia) and Another v. Australian Central Credit Union*[80] the High Court of Australia was called upon to consider the meaning of "section of the public" in the relevant provisions of the Companies (South Australia) Code.

The facts of the case were that a credit union offered its members *alone* the opportunity to purchase units in a unit trust set up by the credit union. The credit union was in the process of buying a building for its business and it wished to give its members the opportunity to acquire units in the trust. Once the building was acquired, ownership of the building would be transferred to the trust. A crucial difference between this case and *Lee v. Evans* was that in *Lee v. Evans*, the relevant legislation in that case did not deem offerees, who were the *only* persons capable of accepting the offer, to be "the public". However, in the present case, the Companies (South Australia) Code expressly contemplated that such a group could be "the public" even though the credit union was making the offer only to its members and only they could accept it. *Inter alia*, section 5(4) of the Code provided that an offer can be to "the public",

> "notwithstanding that the offer is capable of acceptance only by each person to whom it is made or that an offer or application may be made pursuant to the invitation only by a person to whom the invitation is issued."[81]

The court therefore had to decide if the credit union members were a "section of the public". It was crucial for the High Court to determine the meaning of "section of the public" because the Australian legislation being considered expressly provided that an offer to a "section of the public" was an offer to "the public" even though it was made to a group who were the only persons who could accept the offer. If the offerees were deemed to constitute such a group, then the offer would have been a "public" offer notwithstanding that only the invitees could have accepted it. Section 61 of the Companies Act 1963 however is different in that 61(2) provides, *inter alia*, that where an offer is not calculated to result in the shares becoming available to persons other than those to whom the offer is made, then it will not be an offer to "the

---

[80] [1985] 59 A.L.J.R. 785.

[81] Hence, the Companies Code legislation was expressly negativing both the *Lee* and *Sherwell* decisions on this point in the context of South Australian Companies legislation.

public".[82] Notwithstanding this key difference the judgment is still relevant as it considers not only the common term "section of the public" but also the related concept of "domestic concern".

The court held that if a stranger had made the offer to the members of the credit union, they would constitute a "section of the public" because there was nothing to distinguish them from the rest of the public. The court stated that there would be:

> "no rational connection between the characteristic which sets the members of the group apart and the nature of the offer to them. . . . However, [if] there is some subsisting special relationship between the offeror and members of the group and the offer made to them, the question whether the group constitutes a section of the public for the purposes of the offer will fall to be determined by reference to a variety of factors of which the most important will be: the number of persons comprising the group, the subsisting relationship between the offeror and the members of the group, the nature and content of the offer, the significance of any particular characteristic which identifies the members of the group and any connection between that characteristic and the offer."[83]

The court held that although the number of members (23,000) would militate in favour of a conclusion that the offer was an offer to a section of the public, nevertheless the court held that the offer was not such an offer. It held that the credit union's offer (units in the trust) to its members had a perceptible and rational connection with their membership. It would involve extending to those members an opportunity to share in the beneficial ownership of the premises which the union intended to use. Furthermore, where members acquired such a direct interest (*i.e.* units), their indirect ownership of the building (through their membership of the credit union) would diminish correspondingly. Consequently, the court held the offer to the members was an offer to them in their "domestic and private capacity as members"[84] which

> "would arise from their membership, would relate to property in which they would be already indirectly interested as members and would have a perceptible and rational connection with that membership".[85]

Accordingly, the offer was not an offer to a "section of the public."

---

[82] S.61(2) of the Companies Act 1963 provides that an offer to a "section of the public" is not an offer to "the public" if it can be shown either that, the offer was not calculated to result in the shares or debentures becoming available for subscription or purchase by persons other than those receiving the offer, or it can be shown that the offer was a domestic concern of the persons making and receiving the offer.
[83] [1985] 59 A.L.J.R. 785 at 787, 788.
[84] *ibid.* at 788.
[85] *ibid.*

This is a most interesting decision. It illustrates a clear example of a situation where an offer, made to a select group and which can only be accepted by them alone, is not an offer to the public because it is regarded as being of domestic and private concern to those to whom the offer was made. Because section 61(2) of the Companies Act 1963 uses similar language,[86] this judgement and its principles are directly relevant when attempting to understand what characteristics an offer would have to have in order to be of "domestic concern".

Brennan J. delivered a separate judgment in an effort to further consider the implications of a provision such as section 5(4) of the Companies (South Australia) Code. In so doing, his judgment gives helpful guidance on whether an offer to a group is an offer to a "section of the public", or not. According to the learned judge, whether a group of persons selected to receive an offer is a "section of the public", depends on whether there exists some particular relationship between the offeror and the group whom he has in contemplation as offerees which is apt to distinguish the group from a section of the public. Also, this relationship must exist before the offer is made.[87] The learned judge then elaborated by stating the importance of the antecedent relationship:

> "[are] the offerees . . . members of a group who, by virtue of their antecedent relationship with the offeror, have an interest in the subject matter of the offer substantially greater than or substantially different from the interest which others who do not have that relationship would have in the subject matter of the offer."[88]

2-23 In light of all of the preceding analysis, the issue arises as to whether a company can select its members or debenture holders as a group to whom an offer is to be made, without running the risk that the offer is to "the public". It is clear that if an offer is made to the company's existing members or debenture holders in circumstances which remain within the parameters set by 61(2) of the Companies Act 1963, then the offer will not be to "the public", *i.e.* either the offer is not calculated to result in the shares or debentures becoming available to any person other than those who receive the offer,[89] or the offer is a

---

[86] s. 61(2) makes it clear that where an offer is of "domestic concern" of the persons making and receiving the offer, then the offer is not an offer to the public.

[87] [1985] 59 A.L.J.R. 785 at 789.

[88] *ibid.* at 790.

[89] s. 61(2); *Lee v. Evans* [1964] 112 C.L.R. 276; *Sherwell v. Combined Incandescent Mantle Syndicate* [1907] 23 T.L.R. 482; *Government Stock v. Christopher* [1956] 1 All E.R. 490; and c.f. *Corporate Affairs Commission v. Central Australian Credit Union* [1985] 59 A.L.J.R. 785.

domestic concern of those making and receiving the offer.[90] Thus, for example, where a company makes a rights issue with non-renounceable letters of allotment, such an offer cannot normally be said to be calculated to result in the shares becoming available to persons other than those receiving the offer. Consequently, the offer cannot be said to be an offer to "the public".

However, somewhat confusingly section 44(7)(a) of the Companies Act 1963 unduly complicates matters. It provides that any prospectus or form of application issued to a company's existing members or debenture holders in respect of shares or debentures of the company need not comply with the section 44 requirement of a Third Schedule prospectus. This is stated (by s.44(7)(a)) to be irrespective of whether an applicant for the shares or debentures will or will not have the right to renounce in favour of other persons. The question therefore arises as to whether the company has to be concerned with section 61 at all in such circumstances? It is submitted that section 44(7)(a) has to be read in light of section 61 where the offer is accompanied by a certain type of renouncement letter.

In other words, while the point remains to be judicially clarified by the courts, it may be that a proper construction of section 44(7)(a) does not render all letters offering securities to existing members or debenture holders outside the requirement for a Third Schedule prospectus, as the offer may well be found to be an offer to "the public" and thus fall outside the terms of section 44(7)(a).

In this regard a distinction must be drawn between renouncement letters that permit the addressee to renounce the right to be allotted securities on one hand, and on the other, letters which merely permit the addressee to renounce his right to securities that he has already agreed to accept. In the former situation, the offer constituted by the letter has now become open to acceptance by any person to whom the addressee has transferred his right to allotment. That means that the original addressee has never had any form of title to the securities and consequently the offer, which originally appeared to be of domestic concern to a distinct group only, is in fact capable of acceptance by a much wider circle. However, in the latter situation, the letter does not constitute a public offer as what has been renounced is not a right to allotment, but rather the right to purchase securities from an allottee. In other words, it is not the right to be allotted the securities that has been renounced, but rather title to the securities has been assigned to the third party by the addressee, the initial allottee. While the point is

---

[90] s. 61(2); *Corporate Affairs Commission v. Central Australian Credit Union* [1985] 59 A.L.J.R. 785.

not free from doubt, it is submitted that section 44(7)(a) only relates to the latter situation and not to the former.

2–24 Finally, some consideration should be given to the observations of Brennan J. in *Corporate Affairs Commission (South Australia) and Another v. Australian Central Credit Union.* The learned judge observed that:

> "relationships, particularly commercial relationships, are various and not every relationship between an offeror and a group will suffice to take an offer to a group out of [the Companies Code] . . . [as] . . . some relationships may have no connection or only a tenuous connection with the subject-matter of the offer. . . ."[91]

An example of such a situation arose in the New Zealand decision *Kiwi Co-Operative Dairies v. Securities*[92] where the Court of Appeal in New Zealand had to consider whether an offer by a dairy co-operative to "supplying shareholders" inviting them to deposit funds in the co-op was an offer to "the public" under the New Zealand Securities Act 1978. The 1978 Act provided that offers to "relatives or close business associates" are not offers to the public. However, the court held that an offer to the public was made. According to the court, the relationship between the offerees (the supplying shareholders) and the offeror (the co-op) was not sufficiently intimate as each shareholder did not have access to up-to-date financial information on the co-op's status. Therefore, in this situation although the offerees were selected as members of a group, their antecedent relationship with the offeror was not such as to give them such a special interest in the subject matter of the offer that they could be regarded as not being a "section of the public". Hence the offer was found to be an offer to "the public".

(ii) Issues to members or debenture holders by company prohibited from making offers to the public

2–25 A private company's articles will prohibit it from offering shares or debentures to "the public". This raises the issue of whether such a company runs the risk that when it issues securities to its members or debenture holders, it may be offering to "the public". Section 61(2)(a) deals with this situation. It provides that although the company's articles may prohibit it making offers to the public, that will not be taken to mean that it is prohibited from offering shares or debentures to its members or debenture holders. According to section 61(2)(a), such an offer will not be an offer to the public provided it can be "properly be regarded as aforesaid" – in other words, it respects the parameters set

[91] [1985] 59 A.L.J.R. 785 at 789.
[92] [1995] 3 N.Z.L.R. 26.

in 61(2) as noted above. Thus, for example, a rights issue to existing members would normally be expected to "properly be regarded" as not being an offer to "the public". Notwithstanding however, it is clear from section 61(2)(a)'s wording that the possibility remains that an offer to members or debenture holders may yet constitute an offer to the public if the offer cannot "properly be regarded" as a purely private offer. All will ultimately depend on the circumstances of each case.

(iii) Offers of debentures to professional dealers

2–26 Section 61(3) Companies Act 1963 provides that where an offer of debentures, repayable within five years, is made to persons whose business it is to buy or sell shares or debentures, such an offer shall not be deemed to be an offer to the public.[92a]

(3) Offer for Subscription or Purchase

2–27 Section 2(1) of the 1963 Act describes a prospectus *inter alia* as an ". . . invitation offering to the public for subscription or purchase any shares or debentures of a company". Section 61(2) of the 1963 Act also uses the phrase "subscription or purchase". The question therefore arises as to the likely meaning of the term "subscription or purchase".

(a) For Subscription

2–28 In *Government Stock and Other Securities Investment Co Ltd v. Christopher and Others*[93] Wynn-Parry J. was called upon to consider whether an offer by one company, to the shareholders in two other companies, to exchange their shares in return for shares in it, was an offer for "subscription or purchase" within the meaning of the United Kingdom Companies legislation. The learned judge held that the phrase "subscription" in the equivalent United Kingdom Companies legislation meant "taking or agreeing to take shares [or debentures] for cash".[94] *Inter alia*, the learned judge stated that subscription involves the "notion of payment in cash"[95] and relied upon the decision of *Arnison v. Smith*[96] as support for this conclusion.

[92a]Note that Part XII of the 1963 Act, s.367(2) provides a significantly wider exemption for foreign companies. It provides that an offer of shares or debentures for subscription or sale in the State by a foreign company, to persons whose ordinary business it is to buy and sell shares or debentures, shall not be deemed to be an offer to the public.

[93] [1956] 1 All E.R. 490.

[94] *ibid.* at p.492.

[95] *ibid* at p.493.

[96] [1889] 41 Ch. Div. 348, where it was held that "subscribed" means "subscribed for cash."

In *Akierhelm v. De Mare*[97] the Privy Council ruled that it would not follow *Arnison v. Smith* on this point as it took the view that the ordinary meaning of "subscribed" also includes shares acquired for consideration other than money. The Australian courts have also taken this approach. Hampel J. in *Broken Hill Proprietary v. Bell Resources Ltd*[98] held that persons who received an offer of an exchange of shares need protection in just the same manner as persons who were to receive shares in return for money. Refusing to follow *Christopher*, Hampel J. held that the object of prospectus legislation is to protect the investing public and therefore there is no basis for confining that protection to situations where shares are being offered for money consideration and not where offered for other consideration. As Part III of the Companies Act 1963 has a similar objective – to protect the public – it is submitted that the phrase "subscription" in the 1963 Act should be similarly construed such that *Christopher* would not be followed on this point. *Ussher* takes a similar view where he states that *Christopher* should be regarded as "faulty" on this point since shares have always been subscribable for non-cash consideration, and furthermore he adverts to section 26(1) of the Companies (Amendment) Act 1983 which provides that shares can be paid for by "money or money's worth".[99]

(b) For Purchase

2–29   In *Government Stock and Other Securities Investment Co Ltd v. Christopher and Others*, Wynn-Parry J. held that "purchase" in the equivalent U.K. Companies legislation meant that where a circular proposed an exchange of unissued shares (in the bidder company) for issued shares in the target companies, this could not constitute an offer for "purchase" within the meaning of the United Kingdom equivalent of section 2(1) 1963 as the shares to be acquired were as yet unissued and thus could not be the subject of a "purchase". While the judgment may well be correct on this point, it does not of course cover situations where securities have been issued.[100] Hence, where securities have been is-

---

[97] [1959] A.C. 789.

[98] [1984] 58 A.L.J. 526; [1984] 8 A.C.L.R. 609.

[99] *Company Law in Ireland* (Sweet & Maxwell, London, 1986), p. 392. *cf. Abbey National Building Society v. The Building Societies Commission* [1989] B.C.C. 259 (Ch. Div.) which interpreted the phrase "subscribe" in U.K. Building Society legislation in a manner consistent with *Government Stock and Other Securities Investment Co Ltd v. Christopher and Others*.

[100]Interestingly, the House of Lords has recently elaborated on the issue of when are shares to be regarded as "issued", ruling that shares are issued when ownership has been entered on the Register: *National Westminster Bank plc.& Anor. v I.R.C., Barclay's Bank plc. & Anor. v. I.R.C.* [1995] 1 A.C. 119; [1994] 3 All E.R. 1. While an enforceable contract may well exist before that event, the shares will

sued, they can be the subject of an offer for purchase. It is submitted that, if the view that "subscription" covers subscription for money and also money's worth,[101] is wrong, then "purchase" must have that wider meaning. Otherwise the protection intended by the Act would be limited to the narrow situation of where an offer was made in return for money consideration only. Bearing in mind concerns[102] regarding protection of the public, such a narrow construction of the 1963 Act is not a reasonable one.

C. RELAXATION OF THE THIRD SCHEDULE RULES UNDER THE COMPANIES ACT

2–30   There are seven situations where Part III of the Companies Act 1963 does not require a prospectus in the form of the Act's Third Schedule. It should be noted that in some of these situations, the offer may be an offer to the "public", yet there is good reason for not requiring a Third Schedule prospectus.

The first situation is where the form of application was issued in connection with a *bona fide* invitation to a person to enter into an underwriting agreement in respect of the shares or debentures.[103] The law does not require a prospectus in the form of the Third Schedule level of disclosure as the underwriter is regarded as being a sophisticated party who has voluntarily assumed the underwriting risk presumably on the basis that such a party has access to all relevant information before assuming the risk.

The second situation is where a company issues a prospectus or form of application to its existing members or debenture holders relating to its shares or debentures and the applicants may or may not have the right to renounce in favour of other persons.[104] In this situation, even though the offer may be an offer to "the public" (particularly where the offer is accompanied by renounceable letters of allotment[105]), nevertheless a Third Schedule prospectus may not be required as the initial offer and allotment is to persons who are familiar with the company's affairs.[106]

---

not be regarded as 'issued' under English companies legislation until entry has been made on the register.

[101] See immediately para. 2–28 above.

[102] See immediately para. 2–28 above.

[103] s. 44(4)(a) of the Companies Act 1963; s.361(5) in the case of a company incorporated outside Ireland.

[104] s. 44(7)(a) of Companies Act 1963; s.361(8)(a) in the case of a company incorporated outside Ireland.

[105] See para. 2–23 of this chapter above.

[106] Though the precise nature of the renounceable rights is all important in this

Although not stipulated in the Act, the third situation is where an issue of bonus shares is made. It does not require a Third Schedule prospectus as such an issue can hardly be said to be for "subscription or purchase".

The fourth situation where a Third Schedule prospectus is not required is where regulation 22(3) of S.I. No. 202 of 1992 applies. This provides that a Third Schedule form of prospectus will not be required where an offer is accompanied by a prospectus which complies with the Prospectus Directive. Regulation 22(4) deems such a prospectus to be a prospectus within the meaning of the 1963 Act.[107]

The fifth situation is where the Listing Particulars Regulations (S.I. No. 282 of 1984) apply. Regulation 12 of S.I. No. 282 provides that a Third Schedule form of prospectus will not be necessary where a listing particulars is published in compliance with the Listing Particulars Regulations.

In the sixth and seventh situations, the legislation recognises that relaxation of the Third Schedule requirements is justified where the more rigorous disclosure rules of the Stock Exchange either have been recently met by an earlier issue[108] or will be met by a proposed issue.[109] In the case of where there has been an earlier recent issue, the Act provides that a Third Schedule prospectus will not be required where a prospectus or form of application is made relating to shares or debentures which are, or are to be, in all respects uniform with shares or debentures issued within the preceding two years and which are quoted on a recognised Stock Exchange.[110] In the case of a proposed issue, where it is proposed to issue shares or debentures to the public generally[111] on a recognised Stock Exchange,[112] the applicant may request the Stock Exchange for a certificate of exemption from having to comply with the requirements of the Third Schedule on the grounds that compliance would be "unduly burdensome".[113] Such an applica-

---

regard. See further para. 2–23 of this chapter above where this point is further considered.

[107] Although, as discussed at para. 2–05 above, application will have to be made to the Stock Exchange to relieve the issuer from having to include Third Schedule-type information in the Prospectus Directive form of prospectus: reg. 8(4) S.I. No. 202 of 1992.

[108] s.44(7)(b) of the Companies Act 1963; s.361(8)(b) in the case of a company incorporated outside Ireland.

[109] Companies Act 1963, s.45.

[110] s.44(7)(b) of the Companies Act 1963 (meaning the Irish Stock Exchange).

[111] s.45(1)(a) of the Companies Act 1963 refers to shares or debentures "issued to persons who are not existing members or debenture holders of the company".

[112] Companies Act 1963, s.45(1)(b).

[113] s.45(1) of the Companies Act 1963; s. 362 in the case of a company incorporated outside Ireland.

tion may rest on a variety of grounds which range from the size of the proposed issue; the number and class or persons to whom the offer is to be made; or any other circumstances.[114] The Companies Act 1963 goes on to provide that where a certificate of exemption is granted, then the documents published in connection with the application to have the proposed issue quoted or dealt on the Stock Exchange will be deemed to be a Third Schedule prospectus.[115]

D. OFFERS FOR WHICH NEITHER THE COMPANIES ACT 1963 NOR THE PROSPECTUS DIRECTIVE REQUIRE A PROSPECTUS

(1) The Companies Act 1963[115a]

2–31 A prospectus is not required where the form of application related to shares or debentures not issued to "the public".[116]

Another situation where a prospectus is not required is not enumerated in Part III as such, but it is appropriate to make reference to it here. A prospectus will not be required for genuine secondary transactions in shares or debentures. Section 44(1) only requires a prospectus to be issued "by or on behalf of a company, or by or on behalf of any person who is or has been engaged or interested in the formation of the company." Therefore, in normal circumstances, a secondary transaction in shares or debentures will not pose a situation where a prospectus is required. However, at the same time, the provisions of section 51 should not be overlooked. Section 51 provides that where shares are allotted[117] with a view to all or any of them being made available to the public, then any document published in connection with the offer will be deemed to be a prospectus. The Act further provides in this respect that where shares or debentures are made available to the public within two years of allotment,[118] it is presumed unless rebutted that the original allotment was made "with a view to all or any of those shares or debentures being offered for sale to the public".[119]

As already noted elsewhere,[120] it would seem that an oral offer does

---

[114] Companies Act 1963, s.45(1).
[115] Companies Act 1963, s.45(2)(a).
[115a] For foreign companies, see para. 2–10 above where Part XII Companies Act 1963 is considered.
[116] Companies Act 1963, s.44(4)(b).
[117] Or agreed to be allotted.
[118] Or agreement to allot, see s.51(2) of the Companies Act 1963.
[119] s. 51(1) of the Companies Act 1963. See para. 2–03 and 2–13 above, where s.51 is further considered.
[120] See paras 2–02 and 2–12 above (cf. Prospectus Directive, article 4).

not warrant the publication of a prospectus in the form prescribed by the Third Schedule because of the absence of a "form of application".

(2) *The Prospectus Directive*

2–32 The Prospectus Directive provides for four groups of situation where the Directive does not require a prospectus.

The first situation is provided for by article 1 of the Directive. Article 1.1 requires that whenever "transferable securities"[121] are offered to the public "for the first time", then a prospectus which meets the disclosure levels set out in the Directive must be published by the person making the offer.[122] Thus it is clearly possible that, unlike Part III Companies Act 1963, genuine secondary transactions could require a prospectus under the Directive if shares had been initially allotted in a non-public offer and perhaps held for several years before subsequently being offered to the public "for the first time".

However, Article 1.2 provides that Member States may opt not to require a prospectus under the Directive where there is a split issue, *i.e.* where only part of the issue is offered to the public initially and the remaining part is offered subsequently, Member States may opt not to require a prospectus to be published in respect of the remaining part. Ireland has opted to take this route.[123]

The second situation is provided for by article 2.1. It provides that the Directive does not apply to offers of transferable securities:

– to persons in the context of their trades or professions;
– to a restricted circle of persons;
– where the selling price of all the securities offered does not exceed 40,000 euros;
– where the securities can only be acquired for a consideration of at least 40,000 euros per investor.

Unfortunately, the first and second offer examples are vague. The Directive gives no further assistance as to what such terms might mean. For example, does offer "to persons in the context of their trades or professions" mean offers to professional dealers in securities and market operators only, or does it have a wider meaning such that offers to

---

[121] Art. 3(e) Prospectus Directive defines these as meaning shares in companies and other transferable securities equivalent to shares in companies, debt securities having a maturity of at least one year and other transferable securities equivalent to debt securities, and any other transferable security giving the right to acquire any such transferable securities by subscription or exchange.

[122] Art. 4 Prospectus Directive.

[123] S.I. No. 202 of 1992, Third Schedule, par. 1.

any person made in the guise of being associated with their own personal trade or profession should also be included? It is submitted that, although the Directive does not make this clear, the narrower interpretation is the correct one given that professional dealers require lesser protection than other offerees. The phrase "restricted circle of persons" is similarly left unexplained. Here again it is not clear what such a phrase means. What does "restricted" mean? Does it relate to the size of the circle of offerees? Or, is it the case that, given the difficulties that have arisen in the caselaw considered earlier in this chapter on the issue of whether an offer is one that can be accepted by anyone who chooses to accept it, similar principles apply to determine whether an offer is "restricted". The domestic implementing regulations do not elaborate upon any of the above concerns.[124]

The third situation is provided for by article 2.2.[125] It provides that the Directive does not apply to offers of the following types of transferable securities:

– Securities offered in denominations of at least 40,000 euros.
– Units issued by collective investment undertakings[126] other than of the closed-end type.[127]
– Securities offered by the State or local authorities.
– Securities offered on a take-over bid or merger.
– Bonus shares.
– Shares or equivalent securities that are offered in exchange for shares in the same company provided that the offer of the new shares does not increase the company's overall issued share capital.
– Securities offered by employer or affiliated undertaking to employees or former employees.
– Securities resulting from the conversion of convertible debt securities or from the exercise of warrants or shares offered in exchange for exchangeable debt securities (provided a public offer prospectus or listing particulars was published in the same State in respect of the convertible or exchangeable debt securities or warrants).
– Securities offered by non-profit making bodies.
– Securities offered by building societies or credit unions or industrial or provident societies.

---

[124] reg. 7(a) of S.I. No. 202 of 1992 is silent.
[125] Again reg. 7(a) of S.I. No. 202 of 1992 implements this provision without any further elaboration.
[126] Defined in article 3 Prospectus Directive.
[127] *ibid.*

– Euro-securities[128] which are not the subject of a generalised campaign of advertising or canvassing.

The fourth situation is provided for by article 5 of the Directive. It permits Member States to opt to permit partial or complete exemption from the obligation to publish a prospectus where transferable securities are being offered to the public where:

– the securities are debt securities or equivalent thereto which are issued in a continuous or repeated manner by credit[129] or other financial institutions equivalent to credit institutions which regularly publish their accounts, and are either set up or governed by a special law or are subject to public supervision intended to protect savings, or

– the debt securities or equivalent securities are issued by companies and other legal persons who are nationals of a Member State and which, in carrying out their business, benefit from State monopolies and are set up or governed by special law or have their borrowings irrevocably guaranteed by the State or local authorities, or

– debt securities issued by legal persons (other than companies), which are nationals of a Member State, were set up by a special law and whose activities are governed by that law and consist solely in raising funds under State control through the issue of debt securities for the purpose of financing production. Finally, such debt securities must be regarded under national law applicable to admission to listing, to be considered as securities that are issued or guaranteed by the State.

Without any detailed elaboration, Ireland has implemented article 5 into Irish law by simply providing that there is no obligation under the Directive to publish a prospectus whenever any of the securities listed in article 5 are offered to the public. In other words, Ireland has opted for the complete rather than the partial exemption option.[130] Re-

---

[128] "Euro-securities" mean transferable securities which:
  – are to be underwritten and distributed by a syndicate at least two of the members of which have their registered offices in different States, and
  – are offered on a significant scale in one or more States other than that of the issuer's registered office, and
  – may be subscribed for or initially acquired only through a credit institution or other financial institution.
[129] Defined in article 3 Prospectus Directive to mean an undertaking the business of which is to receive deposits or other repayable funds from the public and to grant credits for its own account, including credit institutions such as those referred to in Article 2 of Directive 77/780/EEC (as amended).
[130] reg.7(b) of S.I. No. 202 of 1992.

grettably, some of article 5's terms are more than a little vague, and the definitions given to explain them in the Directive are not that much clearer.

3

Liabilities that may arise from the Prospectus

Introduction 129
I. Non-Statutory Investor Remedies 131
    A. Action for Omission or Deceitful Misrepresentation 132
        (1) Omission 132
        (2) Deceit 134
        (3) Connection between maker of representation and
            those parties who relied upon it 136
        (4) Measure of damages 137
    B. Action for Negligent Misstatement or Omission 139
        (1) Tort of negligent misstatement 139
        (2) Irish recognition of *Hedley Byrne* 141
        (3) Liability for negligent misstatements in aditor's
            accounts – a lesson for promoters 142
        (4) New developments extending liability exposure 145
    C. Action for Recission by Allottee of Share Purchase 148
        (1) Preconditions before Recission can be granted 148
        (2) Truthful disclosure of material information 149
    D. Damages against Company? 151
II. Statutory Investor Remedies 152
    A. Section 49 Untrue Statements 154
        (1) Section 49 Companies Act 1963 Civil Liability for
            "Untrue Statements" in a Prospectus offering
            securities to the public for Subscription or
            Purchase 154
        (2) Possible Section 49 defendants 155
        (3) No Section 49 liability for company 155
        (4) Section 49 plaintiffs 156
        (5) Section 49 defences 157
            (a) Defences based on lack of consent 157
            (b) Belief in truth of statement defence 157
            (c) Statement fairly reflects expert's statement
                defence 158
            (d) Official statement defence 158

(e) Expert's defence 158
B. Listing Particulars Directive Regulations 160
   (1) Disapplication of some provisions of
       Companies Act 1963 160
   (2) Duty on Persons to allow for "Informed
       Assessment" 160
   (3) Damages for breach of the Listing Particulars
       Regulations 161
       (a) Issuer liability? 161
       (b) "Persons responsible for the listing particulars"
           liability 163
   (4) Possible plaintiffs 164
C. Prospectus Directive Regulations 165
D. Section 44 omission 167
   (1) Liability under Section 44 for mere omission 167
   (2) Omission in the context of the Listing Particulars
       Regulations 168
   (3) Omission in the context of the Prospectus
       Regulations 168
E. Liability of Stock Exchange or Registrar of Companies 172
III. **Criminal Liabilities** 173
A. Offences 173
   (1) Companies Act 1963 173
       (a) Section 50 (untrue statements) 173
       (b) Section 44 (8) (contravention of Section 44(1)
           or (3))/Section 46 (violating expert's
           consent) 174
       (c) Section 47 (failure to register prospectus) 175
   (2) Section 242 Companies Act 1990 175
   (3) Listing Particulars Regulations 176
       (a) Regulation 6 (breach of professional secrecy/
           publication of false or misleading
           information) 176
       (b) Regulation 13 (late delivery of listing
           particulars) 176
       (c) Regulation 12(3) (failure to produce listing 176
           particulars/withdrawal of expert's consent/
           publication of untrue statement) 177
   (4) Prospectus Regulations 177
       (a) Regulation 20 (breach of professional secrecy/
           publication of false or misleading
           information) 178

         (b) Regulation 21/Regulation 11 (failure to produce
            prospectus in conformity with Prospectus
            Regulations/failure to register prospectus/
            violation of expert's consent/publication of
            untrue statement) 178
      (5) Larceny Act 1861 179
IV. The Promoter and the Company 179
  A. The Promoter/Company Fiduciary Relationship 180
  (1) Two Key Issues 180
      (a) Promoter Directors and the Sale of Promoters'
            Property to the Company 181
      (b) Whether Promoter Directors can release
            themselves from their Duty to Account 183
  B. Company Action against the Promoter who has
    made Secret Profit 185
  (1) Return of Secret Profit 185
  (2) Recission of the Company's Contract with the
      Promoter 186
  C. Promoters and PLCs 190
  (1) Companies (Amendment)Act 1983 190
      (a) Relevant person 190
      (b) Initial period... 190
      (c) Size of transaction and valuer's report 191
      (d) Exclusion of certain transactions 191
      (e) Sanctions for contravention 191
         (i) Where consideration does not include
             shares 191
        (ii) Where consideration does include shares 192

Liabilities that may arise from the Prospectus

Introduction

3–01 Inviting the public to subscribe for securities in a company can give rise to many interesting legal issues. In this chapter four major areas of potential liability for those involved in the issue of a prospectus are analysed.

The first section of the chapter examines common law investor remedies. Depending on the circumstances, various common law remedies can be sought by investors aggrieved by virtue of the quality of the information presented in the prospectus. In this regard, omission constituting misrepresentation, deceitful misrepresentation, negligent misstatement and the action for recission are examined. The review of these remedies indicates that while the criteria for invoking these remedies are often quite strict, the traditional view that the prospectus serves only to provide information to initial subscribers or allotees, may no longer be as persuasive as it once was. As will be seen, the courts in the U.K. are making their way around this area in light of changing commercial practices, although the Irish courts have yet to be presented with a suitable opportunity.

The second section of this chapter concerns the various remedies arising from Part III of the Companies Act 1963, as well as the statutory instruments which implement the EC Listing Particulars and Prospectus Directives. The reader may find the material in this section of the chapter turgid, and often highly qualified. This is because the legislation on public offers is incoherent and unclearly worded. Until there is legislative reform in the area, many of the issues discussed will remain arguable and unclear. This is evident when one looks at the legal framework set out in Part III of the 1963 Act. Using often unclear and convoluted language, Part III sets out the requirements for a Third Schedule form of prospectus whenever a public offering of new securities takes place. In the interim period, the EC Listing Particulars Directive 80/390 (which sets out the requirements for listing particulars) has been implemented into Irish Law (1984), as has the EC Prospectus Directive 89/298 (1992) which sets out the requirements for public offerings of securities (which may include not only Third Schedule-type offerings in certain circumstances, but also secondary offerings if made to the public for the first time).[1] Both of these Directives have been implemented by way of domestic Regulations in the form of Ministerial Statutory Instruments. The layout and wording of these Statutory Instruments is quite unsatisfactory, being often unhelpfully cryptic on vital matters, as well as being difficult, in general, to interpret.

Whenever a public offering is contemplated, whether with or without a listing, the busy practitioner and indeed student in this area, runs the risk of "prematurely greying". Facing the prospect of attempting to comprehensively reconcile the demands of Part III Companies Act 1963, the Prospectus Directive, the Listing Particulars Directive as well as the appallingly worded domestic implementing Regulations thrown in for good measure, is not a happy task.

When called upon to implement an EC Directive, Member States are obliged to implement domestic laws which give meaning to the objectives set out in the particular Directive. A Directive by its very nature, is merely a framework document. The purpose of the domestic implementation measure is to put flesh on the Directive's skeleton. However, regrettably, in the instance of the implementation of the Listing Particulars and Prospectus Directives, the draughtsman somehow lost sight of this objective. In any event, a radical overhaul of the disparate pieces of legislation in the area of public offers is urgently needed. The time for consolidation and clarification of the existing legislation has arrived. Otherwise, legal uncertainty on many issues in this area will continue. Unless consolidation occurs soon, those using the services of lawyers in the preparation of public offerings of securities will never cease to be amazed at the byzantine extremes that their lawyers have to go to in order to ensure that their clients are satisfying the requirements of a most unclear legal regime. As already noted above, section two of this chapter will itself demonstrate how unmanageable this amalgam of Companies legislation, Directives and Statutory Instruments, has become. Finally, spare a thought for the investor who wishes to invoke a statutory remedy in circumstances where it is alleged that the prospectus was deficient in some key respect. As will become evident, the already difficult waters have become more perilous due to often incomprehensible legislation.

The third section of this chapter concerns the criminal liabilities that may arise out of the prospectus. A review of the somewhat light penalties in this area is overdue.

---

[1] These directives are considered in Chaps. 1 and 2 above, as well as in section II of this chapter below.

Finally, the fourth section of this chapter concerns the fiduciary duties of the promoter, to the newly formed company. It concentrates particularly on the fiduciary duties of the promoter owed to the company, as well as the asset valuation rules applicable to transactions involving promoters and plcs.

I. NON-STATUTORY INVESTOR REMEDIES

Introduction

3–02 Common law remedies for the aggrieved investor will be considered in this section of the chapter. Despite the fact that statutory intervention in this area has provided the investor who suffers loss as a result of a defective prospectus with some forms of remedy, nevertheless the common law remedies continue to be relevant. This is for chiefly three reasons.

First, the common law remedies have not been supplanted by statutory intervention in this area.

Second, there are limitations to the ambit of the statutory remedies. For example, the section 49 Companies Act 1963 action (for compensation resulting from an untrue statement in the prospectus) cannot be invoked against the company because the section does not mention the company itself as a possible defendant.[2] Furthermore, as will be seen below in section two of this chapter, it is not conclusively certain from the language used in the Prospectus Regulations (which implement the Prospectus Directive) that the Regulations provide a right to seek damages in the event that the prospectus does not respect the EC requirement that sufficient information be disclosed such as would allow the investor make an "informed assessment" of the company's prospects. Furthermore, to add to the investor's difficulties, immunity from damages is provided to the issuer in certain circumstances under the Regulations, and also a number of statutory defences are provided. The aggrieved investor may not be able to overcome such obstacles.

Third, the aforegoing forms of statutory remedy do not apply to non-public offers of securities, in which event the common law remedies will be all that an aggrieved investor will be able to rely upon.

---

[2] See paras 3–23 *et seq.* below.

A. ACTION FOR OMISSION OR DECEITFUL MISREPRESENTATION

3–03   The investor who has suffered loss as a result of a deceitful misrepresentation in a prospectus can attempt to recover damages against the persons who were responsible for issuing the prospectus. A right of action in damages does not appear to be possible against the company itself at common law,[3] (though it may be, where the prospectus takes the form of a listing particulars (or prospectus with the meaning of the Prospectus Regulations)).[4]

In the caselaw about to be discussed,[5] it will be seen how at common law, the misrepresentation must be deceitful for a damages remedy to be granted. In order to obtain damages for deceitful misrepresentation at common law, the court will require that the deceit was in the form of an "active misrepresentation", and furthermore that it affected the judgment of the unsuspecting investor. Furthermore, loss must be shown to have resulted from reliance on such a misrepresentation.

The term "misrepresentation" implies the positive act of a statement made. However, the courts are also willing to classify "omission" as an "active misrepresentation", in certain circumstances.[6]

In light of the foregoing, three issues require further examination: (1) What constitutes an active misrepresentation? (2) What constitutes deceit? and (3) What relationship must exist between the maker of such a representation and the party who relied upon it?

(1) "Omission"

3–04   Mere omission of material facts will not cause a right in damages for misrepresentation to arise automatically.[7] In this regard, Lord Cairns stated in *Peek v. Gurney*[8] that mere silence could not provide the basis for an action for damages for misrepresentation. However, he elaborated by explaining that the situation is otherwise if an omission had the effect of making what had been disclosed absolutely false. The dicta of Palles C.B. in *Components Tube Co v. Naylor*[9] emphasise

---

[3] *Houldsworth v. City of Glasgow Bank* [1880] 5 A.C. 317. See below, para. 3–21.
[4] Their statutory forms of action are considered separately below at paras 3–35 and 3–38.
[5] See paras 3–04—3–07 below.
[6] See para 3–04 below.
[7] Though it might well give rise to grounds for seeking recission: see paras 3–17—3–20 below where recission is considered.
[8] [1873] 6 H.L. 377.
[9] [1900] 2 I.R. 1.

that where misrepresentation by omission is alleged, the court will consider the substantive effect of the omission, to determine whether such an omission was of information which would have had a bearing on the truth of the statements made in the prospectus, had it been disclosed.

Palles C.B. stated that while mere concealment does not amount to an actionable omission where damages is the remedy sought, the position alters when the omission

> ". . . may upon the construction of the entire document, render false a statement which would have been true had the omitted statement been contained in the document; and that, where the omission is of this character, the deceived party has a right not only to rescind the contract, which he would have been entitled to do even had the representation not been of this character, but in addition he can treat it as an active misrepresentation, as distinguished from mere concealment, and therefore make it the ground of an action for damages for deceit – an action which mere concealment would not be sufficient to maintain."[10]

The learned judge continued:

> ". . . concealment, to be sufficient, must be such as to make some material statement in the prospectus untrue, that is, must amount to active misrepresentation . . .".[11]

In *Peek v. Gurney*,[12] it was held that the suppression of the existence of arrangements which, had they been revealed to exist, would have affected the truth and meaning of optimistic statements made in the prospectus about the health of the firm, was an omission that amounted to an actionable misrepresentation. The court took the view that, suppression of information which would render what was stated to be false, being more than mere omission, amounts to an active misrepresentation where the context and meaning of other statements are altered by the absence of the suppressed information. Lord Cairns summarised the position as follows:

> "Mere non-disclosure of material facts, however morally censurable, however that non-disclosure might be a ground in a proper proceeding at a proper time for setting aside an allotment or a purchase of shares, would in my opinion form no ground for an action in the nature of an action for misrepresentation. There must, in my opinion, be some active misstatement of fact, or, at all events, such a partial and fragmentatery statement of fact, as that the withholding of that which is not stated makes that which is stated absolutely false."[13]

---

[10] *ibid.* at 59, 60.
[11] *ibid.* at 60.
[12] *op.cit.*
[13] *ibid.* at 403.

Therefore, although mere omission of material information cannot give rise to an action for damages for misrepresentation, (though it may permit recission),[14] an action for damages may arise where the omission has the effect of altering the complexion of what has been disclosed, so as to render it false.

Modern corporate finance practice would appear to reflect the sentiment running through the judgments discussed above. The directors' responsibility statement, which the Prospectus Directive requires all prospectuses issued in connection with an offer to the public for the first time to contain, typically provides that to the best knowledge and belief of the directors no information has been omitted from the prospectus which would be likely to affect the import of the information disclosed in the prospectus. Such a statement imposes a heavy responsibility on the directors to ensure that no information is omitted if such information would affect the meaning of the information disclosed. Consequently, the risk that material information would be ommitted is significantly reduced in modern practice, as on one hand, the Prospectus Directive demands a vast range of information be disclosed, and on the other, modern verification practices help ensure that all relevant information is furnished in the prospectus to support statements made. As a result, the risk that important information, that would have a bearing on what is published, would be omitted, is significantly reduced.

(2) "Deceit"

3–05   In *Derry v. Peek*,[15] the meaning of deceit was considered by the House of Lords. The Lords were of the view that in order to establish deceit, fraud must be shown. "Fraud" in the context of deceit was held to mean that the promoters must have made a statement either knowing it to be false, or without belief in its truth, or without caring whether it was true or false. Furthermore, the Lords held that where a false statement is made, while it may be evidence of fraud, it is not fraud merely because it was made carelessly or because there were no reasonable grounds to believe it was true (on the part of those who made it). The Lords emphasised that what was important in determining

---

[14] Note that an action for recission will be possible even if the omission is not tantamount to a misrepresentation actionable in damages as it is not required that it be shown that the omission changed the character of what was represented, but rather than the omission was of a material fact: per Lord Herschell in *Derry v. Peek* [1889] 14 A.C. 337 at 359. See paras 3–17—3–20 below.

[15] [1889] 14 A.C. 337.

fraud was, whether the makers of the statement had honestly believed what they stated to be true.[16]

In this case a prospectus stated that a tramway company had the right to use steam power (which was much faster than horse transport). Subscribers bought shares in the company and then sued for damages in deceit when the company was refused consent to use steam power by the Board of Trade. It was held that the defendants – the directors– were not liable in deceit as it was found that at the time they made this statement in the prospectus, they honestly believed that the company would be able to use steam power. On the facts of the case it was demonstrated that the directors believed that at the time the information was published they would obtain the requisite consent from the Board of Trade to use steam. The Board of Trade, as it turned out, refused consent, but because the directors believed that such consent was forthcoming, the Lords took the view that they had acted honestly, rather then fraudulently. Hence, from this decision it is clear that an honest, albeit mistaken belief, does not constitute the requisite degree of fraud or falsity in order for deceit to be established. As Lord Herschell stated:

> "...in order to sustain an action in deceit, there must be proof of fraud, and nothing short of that will suffice ... fraud is proved when it is shewn that a false representation has been made (1) knowingly, or (2) without belief in its truth, or (3) recklessly, careless whether it be true or false ... to prevent a false statement being fraudulent, there must, I think, always be an honest belief in its truth."[17]

The learned judge continued:

> "In my opinion making a false statement through want of care falls far short of, and is a very different thing from, fraud, and the same may be said of a false representation honestly believed though on insufficient grounds."[18]

While some of the statements quoted from *Derry v. Peek* might appear unduly restrictive (in that either knowledge or recklessness is required to establish fraudulent deceit), modern corporate finance practice does much to eliminate the kind of problem such as arose in *Derry v. Peek*. Modern due diligence and verification practices help ensure that all facts stated in the prospectus are true and not misleading. Furthermore, the verification process helps ensure that all opinions expressed in the prospectus are soundly based and therefore genuinely held.

---

[16] The judgment of Lord Herschell goes through the authorities at great length on this point.

[17] *ibid.* at 374.

[18] *ibid.* at 375.

Therefore, provided that systematic due diligence and verification takes place, the risk of directors leaving themselves open to an action alleging deceit is greatly reduced. Typically, the verification process will involve lawyers going through the draft prospectus line-by-line in order to ensure that someone in the company (or their advisers) takes responsibility for statements made, or facts quoted. In this way, statements likely to mislead are weeded out of the final draft of the prospectus.

(3) Connection between maker of representation and those parties who relied upon it

3–06   The case of *Peek v. Gurney*[19] demonstrates how, before the investor can succeed in establishing deceit arising out of a prospectus, it must be demonstrated that the maker of the statement knew that the investor would rely on the statements. In other words, the aggrieved investor must be able to show that the promoters intended that their representations would be relied upon by him. *Peek v. Gurney* demonstrates that, unless the plaintiff can show that the company had some direct connection with the investor such as where it directly communicated the prospectus to him, he will not be able to show a direct connection with the prospectus and thus will be unable to maintain an action for deceit.

On the facts of the case, the applicant was found not to be an initial subscriber to whom the prospectus was sent but a subsequent purchaser from an allottee. Accordingly, the court held that, because the applicant could not demonstrate that there was some "direct connection" between the directors of the company and him when they communicated the prospectus, he could not be viewed in the same way as would original allottees, *i.e.* parties whom the makers of the statements would have had in mind. Consequently, subsequent purchasers of the shares could not fall within the group of persons that the promoters should be aware would rely on the prospectus statements.

The Court took the view that once the initial allotment has been made on foot of the prospectus, then the purpose of the prospectus had ceased and therefore, parties who subsequently acquire the shares from initial allottees cannot be persons whom the promoters should have had in mind when publishing the prospectus. In a way, this is reasonable as otherwise the promoters might be responsible to parties to whom they would never have known would have access to the prospectus. Also because allegations of fraud may be involved, such a confinement may be justified to protect the rights of the directors or

---

[19] [1873] 6 H.L. 377.

promoters from unfair accusations. However, notwithstanding such concerns, *Peek v. Gunney* was decided well over a hundred years ago. The question may be asked whether the court's view is sustainable in light of modern market practices where shares change hands almost immediately once they are allotted. Perhaps it is not unreasonable for the promoters to contemplate that immediate subsequent purchasers of the shares will have access to and rely upon the prospectus. In this respect, the action for deceitful misrepresentation at common law has, to some extent, been overtaken by developments in the Law of Negligence, where the courts are more willing to expand the class of potential plaintiffs. However, as deceit implies dishonesty, whereas negligence does not, the more restrictive approach to confining the class of plaintiffs in deceit actions, is likely to continue.[20]

(4) Measure of damages?

3–07   Where deceit is established, the remedy of the aggrieved investor is the recovery of damages. The quantum is the equivalent to the diminution of the price paid[21] for the shareholding, which the investor was induced to acquire by the fraudulent representation. In *McConnel v. Wright*[22] an investor was found to have invested in a company on foot of prospectus representations that the company owned high-yielding shares in other reputable companies. This was in fact untrue as the company did not acquire such shares until some days after the investor's purchase of shares in the company. Subsequently, the company went into liquidation and the plaintiff lost his investment. The Court of Appeal was called upon to consider, when damages would come to be assessed, whether the fact that the company had actually succeeded in acquiring the high-yielding share assets should be taken into account.

The Court held that the time for assessing damage was at the time the investor's shares were allotted. Consequently, the fact that the company had only subsequently acquired the high-yielding shares was irrelevant at that time, according to the Court. Therefore, prima facie the measure of damage was the difference between the value of the company's shares as represented by the prospectus, and the company's value without the ownership of the high-yielding share assets at the time of allotment to the investor, (*i.e.* the real value of the company).

---

[20] On the issue of whether the purpose of the prospectus can be regarded as having ceased once the initial allotment has been taken up, *cf.* recent developments in the field of negligent misrepresentation at paras 3–08—3–16 below.

[21] *McConnel v. Wright* [1903] 1 Ch. 546; *Potts v. Miller* [1940] 64 C.L.R. 282

[22] [1903] 1 Ch. 546

For the purposes of this assessment, the Court was prepared to hold that the prima facie value of the shares should be the price that was paid for them when purchased by the investor.

Using these criteria therefore, the measure of the damages awarded in a successful action would be the difference between the price at which the shares were purchased (the value the prospectus represented the company to have) and the value the company's shares would have had, had the high-yielding share assets been excluded from the value of the company. Such assessment is based on the date of the acquisition of the shares by the investor.

However, apart from concluding that there was prima facie evidence of damage to the plaintiff, the Court of Appeal did not go further and actually assess the damage because it was not required to do so.[23] However, Collins M.R. did venture somewhat *obiter* as follows.[24] The learned judge stated that because it was an action for deceit (as the plaintiff was "tricked out of certain money in his pocket"[25] for the shares) the maximum damages that the plaintiff could potentially recover in such an action was the loss of the entire of what he paid for the shares. The learned judge continued to state that where the assets of the company were worth an equivalent to what was paid, then the investor would be at no loss, and in so far as they might fall short of that equivalent, the investor suffered damage and should recover proportionately to the diminution in value of the shareholding. Clearly implicit in this reasoning is the proposition that the investor will not be awarded the entire price he paid, but merely the diminution in value, such that the defendant shall receive credit for the fair or real value of the shares estimated at the time of allotment or purchase.[26]

Whether or not *McConnel* provides a sound basis for assessing damages in deceit actions remains to be seen. Lord Atkin in the House of Lords stated in *Clarke v. Urquhart; Stacey v. Urquhart*[27] that: "The formula in *McConnel v. Wright* may be correct or it may be expressed in too rigid terms. I reserve the right to consider it if it should ever be in issue in this House." In other words, perhaps the measure of damages should be assessed on a case-by-case basis, rather than be confined by the strict parameters of the *McConnel* formula, such that in an appropriate case, other consequential damages should also be recoverable.

---

[23] This was not the court's role as the court was not called upon to determine damages – that was up to a lower court.

[24] *McConnel v. Wright* [1903] 1 Ch. 546 at 554, 555.

[25] *ibid.* at 554.

[26] *Peek v. Derry* [1887] 37 Ch. D. 541 and *per* Dixon J. in *Potts v. Miller* [1940] 64 C.L.R. 282 at 297.

[27] [1930] A.C. 28 at 67.

Dixon J. in the High Court of Australia decision, *Potts v. Miller*[28] also comments on *McConnel*. While he did not disapprove of the decision, the learned judge held that when applying the *McConnel* formula, it may be necessary to look to subsequent events so that an injustice to defendants would not occur. What the learned judge was referring to was the fact that a company's losses might have resulted from factors that were extrinsic to, and had no connection with, the inducement. In such circumstances, it would not be proper to award an investor compensation for diminution in value that resulted from such extrinsic circumstances that had no connection with the inducement. In this respect therefore, it may be appropriate to inquire into events prevailing around the time of the acquisition of the securities and events subsequent thereto in order to assess whether the inducement was the cause of the entire diminution in value or not.

B. ACTION FOR NEGLIGENT MISSTATEMENT OR OMISSION

3–08 Although the landmark decision of *Donoghue v. Stevenson*[29] revolutionised the law, it was not until the *Hedley Byrne Co v. Heller and Partners Ltd*[30] decision in the U.K. and *Securities Trust v. Hugh Moore and Alexander Ltd*[31] in Ireland, that the courts acknowleged that not only does one owe a duty of care to others that they do not suffer physical harm resulting from one's physical actions, but also, there is a duty of care owed to others who suffer economic harm resulting from one's *statements*.

(1) Tort of negligent misstatement

3–09 Before *Hedley Byrne & Co. v. Heller and Partners Ltd*[32] and *Securities Trust v. Hugh Moore and Alexander Ltd*,[33] the courts would not ground liability for monetary loss resulting from negligent misstatements unless there was a contractual or fiduciary relationship between the parties. The "neighbour" principle of *Donoghue v. Stevenson*[34] was not sufficient to create liability for economic loss flowing from a negligent misstatement – there also had to be some form of contractual or fiduci-

---

[28] (1940) 64 C.L.R. 282 at 298, 299.
[29] [1932] A.C. 562.
[30] [1964] AC 465.
[31] [1964] I.R. 417.
[32] [1964] A.C. 465.
[33] [1964] I.R. 417.
[34] [1932] A.C. 562.

ary relationship between the plaintiff and defendant. While neither *Hedley Byrne* nor *Securities Trust* involved promoters or prospectuses *per se*, the principles that these cases have established are now beginning to enter the domain of the promoter in such a way that promoters need to be aware of their own potential liability in negligence to prospective investors in respect of statements or omissions made in the prospectus. While the boundaries of such liability has yet to be clearly established, it is submitted that recent judicial utterances are clearly leaning in the direction of finding a duty of care in appropriate cases. Furthermore, the fact that the Prospectus Directive requires directors to make a responsibility statement in the prospectus (accepting responsibility for information in the prospectus and stating that they have taken all reasonable care to ensure its accuracy and that they have taken similar care to ensure that no relevant information has been omitted that might affect the import of the disclosed information) signifies that directors must not act negligently in publishing the prospectus information. If they do, then they may find an action in negligence taken against them by a party who claims to be owed a duty of care. As shall be discussed, the courts have recently had to consider whether a duty of care was owed to investors who relied on financial forecasts by a company; of a prospectus issued by a company; or auditor's reports. While the courts are reluctant to open the floodgates, there are increasing signs evident in the caselaw which demonstrate that the purpose of the documents is all important in determining whether the requisite degree of proximity exists in order for a court to find that a duty of care is owed. In order to consider this purpose-based approach, first it is appropriate to consider *Hedley Byrne* and its adoption into Irish law.

3–10 In *Hedley Byrne*, the House of Lords held that, in principle, negligent misstatement should give rise to liability for ecomonic harm where the maker of the statement knew or ought to have known that the plaintiff was a party who was relying upon the skill of the maker of the statement. Although some of the judgments in the case indicated that before liability in negligence can arise, the relationship between the parties should at least be one that is "equivalent to contract", nevertheless the judgments emphasised that it is not a prerequisite that the relationship *be contractual* in nature. The Irish courts have adopted the principles set out in *Hedley Byrne* and do not require that the parties' relationship be based in contract or circumstances "equivalent to contract", when considering whether a duty of care should arise.[35] Ac-

---

[35] *e.g., Tulsk v. Ulster Bank Ltd,* unreported, High Court, Gannon J., May 13, 1983; *Towey v. Ulster Bank Ltd* [1987] I.L.R.M. 142, High Court, O'Hanlon J.; *Kelly v. Boland, t/a Haughey Boland* [1989] I.L.R.M. 373, High Court, Lardner J.

cordingly, where one person is relying on another's skill in making a statement, and the latter knew or ought to have known that there would be reliance on that statement by the former, then liability in negligence may arise if the statement is made negligently.

In order for such principles to apply in an action between a promoter and an aggrieved shareholder, the plaintiff would have to demonstrate the following:

- that the maker of the statement (whether as promoter, director, expert etc) owed a duty of care to the person because he knew or ought to have known that that person would rely upon the statement;

- that the statement constituted a breach of that duty of care;

- that the plaintiff suffered loss as a consequence of the breach of the duty of care.

(2) Irish recognition of *Hedley Byrne*

3–11   The decision in *Securities Trust* demonstrates how the scope of the range of parties to whom the duty is owed is not as extensive as might first appear. In this case, there was a mistake in the defendant company's articles of association, a copy of which had been requested by a shareholder. The shareholder happened to be the managing director of the plaintiff company which, on foot of the defendant company's articles, invested in the defendant and thereby suffered loss. The plaintiff company sued for negligent misstatement. The action failed on the grounds that when the company supplied the articles to the managing director, it was not aware that he was seeking them in a capacity other than as a shareholder. Accordingly, it was not possible for the plaintiff company to succeed in demonstrating that the defendant should have been aware that the plaintiff company would be relying on the articles when making its investment decision.

Hedley Byrne was cited before the High Court and Davitt P. held that the company did not owe a duty of care to the world at large. However, the obvious implication from the judgment is that if the circumstances had been such that the company should have been aware that the plaintiff would also rely on the statement (the articles), then a duty of care may well have arisen towards the plaintiff.[36]

---

[36] *cf.* contrast with the restrictive approach to confining the range of potential plaintiffs employed by the House of Lords in an action for damages for deceitful misrepresentation (not negligence) in *Peek v. Gurney* above at para. 3–06.

(3) Liability for negligent misstatements in auditor's accounts – a lesson for promoters by analogy ?

3–12 In the absence of a specific Irish judicial decision on the issue of liability of promoters for misstatements in a prospectus, it is interesting to consider the liability principles adopted in 1989 in *Kelly v. Boland t/a Haughey Boland*, the High Court decision of Lardner J. involving auditors' liability for alleged misstatements in company accounts. It is submitted that the criteria adopted in that decision for the determination of auditors' liability are appropriate for application by analogy to the determination of promoters' liability, at least to initial allottees, or perhaps in appropriate circumstances to other investors.

Before looking at that decision, it is interesting to first consider a contemporaneous U.K. House of Lord's decision. In *Caparo Industries Plc v. Dickman*,[37] the House of Lords held that the auditors of a public company's accounts owed no duty of care to members of the public at large who might rely on the audited accounts when buying shares in the company. The Lords held that in order for a duty of care to arise where there has been a negligent misstatement, it must be foreseeable that someone would rely on the statement before a duty of care can arise; furthermore, that there must be some nexus or relationship between the maker of the statement and the person who relied upon it; and finally, the court would have to consider the reasonableness of imposing such a duty. Effectively, therefore, the Lords were holding that even if it was forseeable that others might rely on one's statements, there was insufficient proximity unless the maker of the statement, when he made it, made it for *the purpose* of communicating it to another so that they might rely on it in a specific transaction or transactions of a particular kind.

This case concerned an attempt by investors to establish liability in negligence on the part of the company's auditors. However the court refused to impute a duty of care on the grounds that auditor cannot be held to owe a duty to the world at large, particularly to potential investors in the company who are not already shareholders in the company. Merely because they might get access to the auditor's reports does not thereby imply that a duty of care relationship has arisen. While this may be a reasonable limitation on the scope of liability, the Lords went further, ruling that the necessary relationship did not exist either between the auditors and the company's existing shareholders. This ruling was based on the reasoning that although the auditors are obliged in law to report to the general body of shareholders, there is not sufficient proximity between the auditors and individual shareholders as

---

[37] [1990] 2 A.C. 605.

the purpose of the auditor's report is not to allow individual shareholders be better informed so that they could increase their stake in the company, but rather its purpose is to provide them with information as a general body so that they can better exercise control over the affairs of the company.[38]

3–13 The view could be taken that perhaps this judgment beats a retreat on the wider principles of the *Hedley Byrne* decision as the House of Lords referred to the purpose of the documents containing the statements as being all-important in determining the scope of the class of persons owed a duty of care. In some quarters it was considered this might herald a return to a requirement of a "relationship equivalent to contract" before a duty of care could be imputed.[39] However, it would not appear to be the case, as the Lords continued to state that the required relationship may exist where the auditors of a company suspect or know that the company will supply particular plaintiffs with a copy of the auditor's reports.[40]

The courts in Ireland would appear to take this more broad-based approach, being less saddled with theoretical distinctions. In *Kelly v. Boland, t/a Haughey Boland*, Lardner J. expressly adopted the remarks of Woolf J. in *JEB Fastners v. Marks, Bloom and Co.*[41] as stating the law in Ireland in the context of auditors liability. It is submitted that the relevance of these judicial observations to promoters' liability, by analogy, should not be underestimated:

> ". . . the appropriate test for establishing whether a duty of care exists appear in this case to be whether the defendants knew or reasonably should have forseen at the time the accounts were audited that a person might rely on those accounts for the purpose of deciding whether or not to take over the company and therefore could suffer loss if the accounts were inaccurate. Such an approach does place a limitation on those enti-

---

[38] Lord Oliver of Alymerton's judgment is particularly illuminating at pp. 629–654. His Lordship's concluding comment is noteworthy: "In my judgment, accordingly, the purpose for which the auditor's certificate is made and published is that of providing those entitled to receive the report with information to enable them to exercise in conjunction those powers which their respective proprietary interests confer upon them and not for the purpose of individual speculation with a view to profit . . . the duty of care is one owed to the shareholders as a body and not to individual shareholders. . . . I can see no sensible distinction, so far as as a duty of care is concerned, between a potential purchaser who is, *vis-à-vis* the company, a total outsider and one who is already the holder of one or more shares [in the company]."

[39] For example, Lord Oliver referred (at p. 650) to the importance of a "special relationship".

[40] *per* Lord Roskill at p. 629; *per* Lord Oliver at p. 638.

[41] [1981] 3 All E.R. 289, the remarks of Woolf J. appearing at 296.

tled to contend that there had been a duty owed to them. First of all, they must have relied on the accounts and, second, they must have done so in circumstances where the auditors either knew that they would or ought to have known that they might. If the situation is one where it would not be reasonable for the accounts to be relied on, then, in the absence of express knowledge, the auditor would be under no duty. This places a limit on the circumstances in which the audited accounts can be relied on and the period for which they can be relied on. The longer the period which elapses prior to the accounts being relied on, from the date on which the auditor gave his certificate, the more difficult it will be to establish that the auditor ought to have forseen that his certificate would, in those circumstances, be relied on."[42]

Applying this test in Ireland, Lardner J. held that a company's auditors, who knew that the plaintiffs had entered into an agreement to purchase the company, owed the plaintiffs a duty of care when they furnished them with audited accounts in respect of the company.[43] Lardner J.'s judgment, although not explicitly so stated, uses the purpose approach (*Caparo v. Dickman*) as it is clear that the existence of the duty was predicated upon the auditors either having known (or ought reasonably to have known) that the purchasers would rely on their reports. However, it may well be the case that the Irish courts will utilise this approach less stringently than their U.K. counterparts as the Irish courts have not, in general, shown the same zeal for restricting liability to the extent that has been evident in the U.K. courts in recent years.

3–14 It is submitted that, by analogy, the formula adopted by Lardner J. could equally apply to promoters or directors in circumstances similar to those outlined in the *JEB Fastners* liability test above. Directors are required to certify that reasonable care has been taken in the compilation of every statement in the prospectus, that they accept responsibility for the accuracy of such statements, and that to the best of their knowledge and belief no information has been omitted from the prospectus which might affect the import of the information disclosed. Clearly any person whom the directors could reasonably foresee (due to surrounding circumstances) would rely on the prospectus, is owed a duty of care. Also, Lardner J.'s test also implicitly contemplates that the duty of care may subsist for a period after publication of the prospectus. This raises difficult issues which shall now be considered.

---

[42] [1989] I.L.R.M. 373 at 386, 387.

[43] However, although the court held a duty of care was owed and there was evidence of negligent practice by the auditors, ultimately the plaintiffs action failed as they were unable to prove that key contentious statements had been incorrectly formulated.

(4) New developments extending liability exposure?

3–15 Given that the law often develops more slowly than the world of corporate finance, the question that arises for consideration is whether the courts are likely to apply negligence principles in a narrow fashion – such that only *initial* allottees on foot of a propectus could claim to be owed a duty of care – or whether the courts are willing to extend the range of persons to whom a duty of care is owed to a wider range of persons such as investors who acquire the allottees' shares very shortly after their allotment.[44]

In other words, under what circumstances might promoters of a company be liable to subsequent allottees in respect of statements made in the prospectus? It would appear from the principles expressed in the dicta cited above[45] that a promoter, by analogy, could be held to owe a duty of care to those whom he knew or ought to have known would receive and rely upon the prospectus.

As for subsequent purchasers, while the courts are anxious not to open the floodgates, a duty of care may nevertheless arise in specific instances.

This issue has arisen recently in several cases in the U.K., though not in substantive decisions but rather in preliminary hearings. The U.K. Courts have used the "purpose of the prospectus" approach adopted in *Caparo v. Dickman* as a device for deciding whether the requisite proximity (giving rise to a duty of care) exists between the parties. In *Al Nakib Investments (Jersey) Ltd v. Longcroft*[46] it was held that the purpose of a prospectus published by a company in connection with a rights issue of shares was to assist persons in relation to that specific issue, not subsequent purchasers[47] of the shares in the market. This seems a reasonable decision in view of the fact that a rights issue was involved. However, in *Morgan Crucible Co plc v. Hill Samuel Bank*[48] it was held by the Court of Appeal, *per* Slade L.J. (again deciding a preliminary issue) that a company which has identified itself as the only bidder in a contested takeover bid, is entitled to attempt to claim

---

[44] As has been seen already at para. 3–06, *Peek v. Gurney* would lean against such an extension in so far as the action for deceit was concerned.

[45] at paras 3–12—3–14

[46] [1990] 3 All E.R. 321.

[47] Even if they were existing shareholders of the company. Mervyn-Davies J. (Ch. Div.) explained that the purpose of the prospectus was to give information to the shareholders who wished to subscribe in the rights issue. In this circumstance, a duty of care is owed. However, where such shareholders subsequently acquired further shares in the market, and they relied on the original rights issue prospectus, no duty of care arose as the purpose of the prospectus was confined to the original rights issue.

[48] [1991] 1 All E.R. 148.

in law that it is owed a duty of care by the target company if the target publishes over-optimistic financial forecasts intending that the bidder would rely on such information, and knows that the bidder will rely on such information. The Court of Appeal took the view that it was arguable that there was sufficient proximity between the parties in such circumstances because the target published the information for the purpose of persuading the bidder to make the most attractive bid possible.

In light of these developments, it is almost inevitable that *dicta* in *Peek v. Gurney*[49] – authority for the proposition that the purpose of a prospectus is finished once the initial allotment had been made such that subsequent purchasers cannot rely on it in actions in deceit – are not definitive in all situations.[50] In other words, can such a proposition prevail in the face of the more recently developed tort of negligent misstatement?[51]

That such reappraisal is necessary is supported by yet another decision on a preliminary hearing, *Possfund Custodian Trustee Ltd &Anor v. Diamond & Ors.*[52] Lightman J. had to consider whether subsequent purchasers of a company's shares in the "After Market" on the unlisted securities market (USM) in London were owed a duty of care by the company? In this case, the plaintiffs claimed that a prospectus was intended by the company's directors to be relied upon by post-allotment purchasers of the shares as it had become modern commercial practice for promoters and directors of companies who list on that market to foster an after-allotment market.[53] The rationale behind such a practice is to create an effective trade in the securities in the post allotment period. Hence, it is difficult to argue that the promoters are not aware that subsequent purchasers may rely on such a prospectus for the period of the after-market when the purpose of the prospectus appears to contemplate that such purchasers may rely on it. Lightman J. considered the authorities, as well as developments in statute law, and concluded that if it was so that commercial practice in the market now regarded the prospectus in this different light, both from the point of view of the issuer and investors, then *Peek v. Gurney* may no longer

---

[49] On the issue of the purpose of the prospectus.

[50] See para. 3–06 above where purpose of the prospectus is considered in *Peek v. Gurney* in the context of an action for deceit.

[51] Lightman J. in *Passfund Custodian Trustee Ltd & Anor. v. Diamond & Ors* [1996] 2 All E.R. 774 could see no reason why the issue of proximity should depend on whether the representation was negligent or fraudulent.

[52] [1996] 2 All E.R. 774.

[53] *ibid.* at 786: affidavits were cited to suport this contention, and were accepted by the defence.

be accurate in so far as it is authority for the proposition that the purpose of the prospectus is over once initial allotment has taken place.[54]

It is interesting that the learned judge was prepared to come to this view notwithstanding that the Financial Services Act 1986 (U.K.), expressly allowed a statutory right of action for either initial or after-market purchasers of listed securities, whereas the Act did not extend this to the USM market. *Al-Nakib* and *Peek* were distinguished on the grounds that in those cases there was no intention that the prospectus was intended to be relied upon post-allotment. Thus the learned judge held that it is arguable that investors are owed a duty of care where they could establish that they reasonably relied upon representations made to them in a prospectus having reasonably believed that the promoters of the prospectus intended them to rely on the prospectus, where it can be established that there was such an intention on the part of the representors. In such a situation, a sufficient direct connection (*i.e.* proximity) would exist, giving rise to a duty of care between the purchaser and the representor. The learned judge was prepared to regard this proximity criterion as being satisfied where the representor intends subsequent purchasers in the after-market to rely on the prospectus, and this in fact occurs.

3–16 It is arguable at least, that given the Irish courts apparently flexible attitude in general to the establishment of the requisite proximity, promoters may be held to owe a duty of care to post-allotment purchasers where the circumstances so warrant.[55] In this regard, the limiting of liability factors referred to in the formula adopted by Lardner J. in *Kelly v. Boland, t/a Haughey Boland* may become highly relevant. For example, did the promoters know or ought they have known that certain parties post-allotment would rely on the prospectus? Or has the period of time that has elapsed between publication of the prospectus, and reliance on it, been insufficient such that the promoter is precluded

---

[54] [1996] 2 All E.R. 774 at 788/789.
[55] Of the U.K. Courts somewhat more cautious attitude, Gower's *Principles of Modern Company Law* (6th ed, London, 1989) (Davies, ed.) observes at p. 439 that: "While *Caparo* is part of a more general move in the Law of Tort to restrict liability for negligent statements causing purely economic loss, it has to be said that the consequence in this area of drawing a distinction between subscribers and market purchasers in the immediate period after dealings commence, is in commercial terms, highly artificial. Companies have an interest not only in the issue being fully subscribed but also in a healthy after-market developing so that subscribers can easily dispose of the shares, if they so wish. . . . Perhaps the way forward in the common law would be for the courts to take a more inclusive view of the issuer's purposes."

from arguing that he ought to have forseen that reliance would be placed on it during such period?[56]

C. ACTION FOR RECISSION BY ALLOTTEE OF SHARE PURCHASE

3–17   The shareholder may wish to rescind[57] the contract under which shares were acquired from the company on the basis that the promoter or the company in some way induced the investor to invest by furnishing information that was incorrect in some key respect. This could arise in a variety of ways. Information may have been furnished that was downright fraudulent; or misrepresentative, in that its true meaning was materially distorted by the suppression of other relevant information; or perhaps the suppression of material information *simpliciter*. In all of these circumstances, recission of the investor's contract to buy shares may be granted provided that the conditions for the grant of the remedy of recission are satisfied.

It is not necessary that actual fraud be proven as the courts are willing to grant recission even where no fraud[58] but merely some untruth in the information provided to the investor materially induced him to invest. However, as will be seen below, where there is an element of fraud, then the courts are less likely to allow the company or its promoters to raise as a defence arguments that would otherwise be successful barriers to a grant of recission. Where the remedy is granted, the investor will be entitled to a rectification of the company's register of shareholders,[59] return of the purchase price and interest on that sum. Where however the misrepresentation was merely of an innocent nature, then recission is unlikely to be granted once the share transfer has been executed in the name of the investor.[60]

(1) Preconditions before recission can actually be granted

3–18   There are a number of prerequisites that require to be satisfied

---

[56] Apart from the possibility of liability in negligence, investment intermediaries should also bear in mind that they may be in breach of the Central Bank's Code of Conduct under the Investment Intermediaries Act 1995 if they publish information and thereby knowingly create a false market in a company's shares: see further Chap. 4 below.

[57] Unlike s. 49, which provides for compensation, and the actions for deceit and negligence which give rise to damages, recission is a different remedy.

[58] *Components Tube v. Naylor per* Palles C.B,. *op. cit.; Peek v. Gurney, per* Lord Cairns *op. cit.* at para. 3–04 above.

[59] Companies Act 1963, s.122.

[60] *Seddon v. North Eastern Salt Company* [1905] 1 Ch. 326.

before a court will award the remedy of recission. The first is that the party making the representation must have been aware that the applicant would subscribe for shares on foot of that representation. Second, the misrepresentation must have been responsible for inducing the investor to invest. Third, the applicant investor seeking the remedy must have acted promptly and without delay to seek recission once the misrepresentation came to light. Fourth, *restitutio in integrum* must still be possible.[61] Where any of these criteria cannot be met, then the court is likely to regard this as a barrier to the grant of recission.

(2) Truthful disclosure of material information

3–19   Lord Justice Fitzgibbon proclaimed in *Aaron's Reef Ltd v.Twiss*,[62]

> "In my opinion, a company inviting money on the faith of a prospectus is bound to state every known fact which, if disclosed, would prevent a prudent man from taking shares at all. And also every known fact which materially qualifies or alters the effect of the previous representations made to induce persons to subscribe."

Thus the investor is entitled to truth and material disclosure when invited to subscribe by either the company or its promoter.[63] In order to obtain recission of the contract to buy the shares, the investor will have to demonstrate that either of these aforementioned two duties owed to the investor by the company/promoter were not respected in some material fashion. Furthermore, however, the investor will also have to demonstrate that the four prerequisites[64] to a grant of recission are satisfied, particularly that there has not been excessive delay and that it is possible to put the parties back in their original position *(restitutio in integrum)*.

In *Aaron's Reef Ltd v.Twiss*,[65] a prospectus offering investors the opportunity to subscribe for shares in a gold mine gave the impression that the subscription funds would be used to buy machinery for the mine. Furthermore, the impression was conveyed that dividends of 100 per cent per annum would be paid once mining got underway. Twiss invested on foot of these representations, but when the call on his shares became due one year later, he refused to pay on the basis that the prospectus was untrue in several material respects. Twiss argued that while it had been disclosed that the promoters had sold the

---

[61] The Supreme Court refused to order rescission in *Northern Bank Finance Corp. v. Charlton & Ors.* [1979] I.R. 149 on the grounds that *restitutio in integrum* was not possible.

[62] [1895] 2 I.R. 207; [1896] A.C. 273.

[63] Ussher *op. cit.*

[64] See para. 3–18 above.

[65] *op. cit.*

mine to the company and had to be paid for it, it was not disclosed that the money that would be used to pay for the mine would be the subscribed investor capital. However, the prospectus had given the impression that the subscribed funds would go towards obtaining machinery to work the mine. Accordingly he argued that the promoters had not revealed their interest truthfully. The court held (affirmed by House of Lords) that Twiss was entitled to rescind notwithstanding that he had subscribed for the shares for an entire year before he had raised an objection.

Several interesting points arise out of this decision. Although one of the prerequisites for the granting of recission is that there has been no excessive delay by the applicant, where there is an element of fraud then time does not begin to run until the fraud comes to light. As Twiss did not realise what the promoters had done until the litigation commenced, the court pointed out that time only began to run from the time that he discovered that something was amiss. Furthermore, a barrier often to the granting of recission arises if it emerges that the applicant had in fact affirmed the contract in the eyes of the law whether by conduct[66] or by the passage of time. However, in Twiss's case he had not affirmed the contract as he had never honoured the call on the shares.

Components Tube v. Naylor[67] is another instructive decision. In that case a company brought an action to enforce a call on shares purchased by Naylor. Naylor's defence was that the shares had been allotted to him on foot of a dishonest and fraudulent prospectus, which had induced him to invest (the prospectus had concealed the fact that the company had purchased its business from the promoters who now stood to gain handsomely). Accordingly, he argued, by refusing to honour the call he had repudiated the contract within a reasonable time and could not be regarded as having affirmed it. The court held that where promoters make actual misrepresentations and suppressed material facts, a shareholder who invests on foot of such a prospectus, if he takes no benefit under the contract he may repudiate it within a reasonable time after he becomes aware of the fraud. The fraud can be relied upon as a defence in an action for calls and the contract can be rescinded.

This case raises the further issue of whether recission would be available if the investor had, in ignorance of the fraud or suppression of material information, affirmed the contract to purchase shares by paying for the shares fully, received dividends, etc. It is submitted that

---

[66] *e.g.*, acceptance of dividends or sale of some of the shares by the shareholder.
[67] [1900] 2 I.R. 1.

recission may still be possible in these circumstances provided the investor acted quickly once the true position became known.[68] However, in the absence of some element of fraud or wilful suppression of material information, the courts may well refuse to grant recission of the contract on the basis that the contract has been affirmed and there has been a passage of time.[69]

3–20 Finally, it should be noted that there is authority for the proposition that recission cannot be granted to an investor where the company has commenced winding up as otherwise third party rights might be prejudiced. In other words, other parties such as creditors may be prejudiced if a grant of recission is made after winding-up as they may well have done business with the company on the basis that the investor was a shareholder in the company. Accordingly, if the shareholder was now permitted to obtain recission, its subscribed capital would no longer be available to satisfy the creditors' claims on the company.[70]

D. DAMAGES AGAINST COMPANY?

3–21 Until this point, all remedies that lead to damages have focused on the promoter (or directors)/investor relationship. The reason why the company has not been the focus of attention is because of the controversial decision of the House of Lords, *Houldsworth v. City of Glasgow Bank*.[71] This is authority for the proposition that investors who have been misled into investing in the company cannot sue the com-

---

[68] Although Gower (*Gower's Principles of Modern Company Law*) (6th ed., London, 1989) (Davies, ed.) at p. 440 points out that in the U.K., s.1(b) Misrepresentation Act 1967 removed the bar that was once thought to exist such that an executed contract could not be rescinded, Gower also observes that notwithstanding "the investor is still well advised to act quickly once the truth is discovered".

[69] In *Seddon v. North Eastern Salt Co.* [1905] 1 Ch. 326, a shareholder claimed that as the victim of an innocent misrepresentation made to him about the health of the company, his shares were worth considerably less than he would have otherwise believed. The court refused recission on the grounds that had there been an element of fraud he could easily have rescinded, but as there was not, he could only obtain recission if there had been a total failure of consideration, which there was not.

[70] *Oakes v. Turquand* [1867] 2 H.L. 325. Note however that Ussher, *op. cit.* (p. 397) takes the view that winding-up should not be a barrier to recission if the company would, even after recission, be able to satisfy its creditors.

[71] [1880] 5 A.C. 317. Note that s.131 of the U.K. Companies Act 1989 effectively abolished Houldsworth in that jurisdiction by providing that a shareholder is not debarred from obtaining damages from a company by reason only of his being a shareholder.

pany itself for damages. Although recission may be sought,[72] damages cannot. In this case, the plaintiff was fraudulently induced to subscribe for shares by the directors of a company. Recission was not available as a remedy because the defendant had already commenced winding up.[73] The ratio of the case appears to be that a shareholder cannot seek damages against a body of which he himself is a member. In order for such a party to be able to seek damages, first he would have to rescind the contract for the purchase of the shares. Forde[74] criticises this case trenchantly, stating that it runs against the fundamental rule of a company's separate legal personality and considers that the real basis of the court's decision should have been that, just as with recission, damages could not be awarded on the basis that the company had commenced winding up. In such circumstances, it would be unfair to the company's creditors to allow the aggrieved shareholder deplete the company's assets, upon which the creditors would be looking to, to settle their claims in the event of liquidation. The learned author submits that if the company's creditors would not be prejudiced by an award of damages to an aggrieved investor, then it should be permitted notwithstanding the *Houldsworth* decision.

II. STATUTORY INVESTOR REMEDIES

3–22 Whether an aggrieved investor can pursue statutory remedies against the company or the promoters (whether promoters in the strict sense, or directors, or experts) is dependant on whether they invested in circumstances which amounted to an "offer to the public". If the offer is not an 'offer to the public', a prospectus is not required and thus only the non-statutory remedies are available.

Section 44(3) of the Companies Act 1963 makes it unlawful to offer shares to the public for subscription by way of a form of application unless a prospectus has been published. Normally therefore, an "offer to the public"[75] can be expected to be by way of a prospectus.[76] Where

---

[72] In *Houldsworth v. City of Glasgow Bank* itself the House of Lords so conceded (although it was not available as a remedy in the case itself).
[73] Rescission is not available as a remedy in these circumstances: *Oakes v. Turquad* [1867] 2 H.L. 325.
[74] *Company Law* (2nd ed., Mercier Press, Dublin 1992), p. 202.
[75] As seen in Chapter 2, it is not often easy to determine whether an offer is an "offer to the public".
[76] However, note that an offer to the public, constituted by merely a verbal offer, may not require a prospectus and therefore the statutory remedies may not be available. See Chapter 2 where this issue is considered in the context of s. 44(3) of the Companies Act 1963, though *cf.* Article 4 of the Prospectus Directive which

a prospectus is published, common law *and* statutory remedies are available to the aggrieved investor. Thus, whether a prospectus has been published has an important bearing on the range of remedies potentially available. For example, where there has been a misstatement in the prospectus, the shareholder potentially may invoke not only common law remedies against the promoters, but also an action for compensation pursuant to section 49 of the Companies Act 1963 which provides a statutory right of action for compensation in respect of untrue statements against every person who authorised the issue of the prospectus.[77]

However, because in practice many companies will prefer their offer to qualify as an offer within the meaning of the Prospectus Directive (as this means they only have to publish three years' accounts instead of five under the 1963 Act) liability provisions based on the Prospectus Regulations may apply. Where the securites are to be listed, the Listing Particulars Regulations implementing the Listing Particulars Directive will apply. Both of the regimes are considered further below. For the moment, in order to avoid confusion, section 49's regime will be considered on its own.

Under the Companies Acts, private companies are companies whose articles prevent them from offering shares to the public,[78] and furthermore, it is an offence for a private company to make such an offer, and its officers shall be guilty of an offence.[79] Normally, therefore, as there will be no "offer to the public", the statutory remedies will not be available to an aggrieved private company investor. However, on the other hand, were a private company to contravene section 33 in the sense that its offer constituted an "offer to the public", then the statutory remedies would be also available to the aggrieved investor in addition to the common law remedies.[80]

---

would appear to require a prospectus for all offers to the public, irrespective of the form in which they were made.

[77] See para. 3–24 as to who may be such a person.

[78] s. 33(1)(c) Companies Act 1963 states that a private company is a company whose articles of association, *inter alia*, prohibit the company from offering shares to the public.

[79] s. 21 of the Companies (Amendment) Act 1983. S. 21(3) provides however that no allotment shall be void merely because it contravenes the prohibition.

[80] Therefore, while contravention of s. 33 does not result in the company losing its private status (if, as a by-product of the offer the company acquired a total or more than 50 members, it would lose its private status in any event), now the company and its promoters would have to contemplate facing not only common law actions, but also, statute-based actions.

A. SECTION 49 UNTRUE STATEMENTS

(1) Section 49 Companies Act 1963 civil liability for "untrue statements" in a Prospectus offering securities for Subscription or Purchase

3–23   Where there are untrue statements in the prospectus, then as well as invoking a range of common law remedies, the aggrieved investor may take an action for mis-statement in a prospectus pursuant to section 49. Under section 49(1), where a prospectus invites persons *to subscribe*[81] for shares or debentures in a company, then a wide range of named persons can be found liable to compensate all persons who subscribed for shares or debentures in the company on the faith of a prospectus for loss or damage they may have sustained by reason of any "untrue statement" in the prospectus that was material to their investment decision. An "untrue statement" is any statement included in a prospectus which is misleading in the form and context in which it is included.[82] Thus, a statement, even though correct by itself, may yet be "untrue" if the context in which it appears in the prospectus distorts its meaning. Similarly, a statement may be "untrue" where relevant information has been suppressed or not disclosed thereby placing a different interpretation on the statement.

   One advantage of this form of action over say, a common law action, is that it is not required that the investor be in a position to identify the party responsible for the untrue statement. Merely because the statement deemed to be 'untrue' is included in the prospectus is sufficient for liability to arise (unless one of the statutory defences is invoked successfully). The burden of proof is effectively reversed, as once it is established that an untrue statement was made, the onus shifts onto the defendants to convince the court that one of the statutory defences to section 49 applies to preclude their liability.

   A limitation of section 49's scope of application is that it only ap-

---

[81] Because s. 49 can only apply to offers for subscription (because the definition of "prospectus" is so confined in the 1963 Act) it is not available as a remedy in the case of secondary offers. In this respect, the investor will have to rely on the Prospectus Directive Regime (assuming the Directive is applicable to the particular offer) for a remedy (or the general common law remedies, if invocable). The Prospectus Directive applies to public offers "for the first time" which in certain circumstances may be a secondary offer, such as where securities were allotted and only subsequently offered to the public for the first time: see further Chap. 2 above, para. 2–07 (and para. 2–32 for those offers to which the Prospectus Directive does not apply).

[82] s. 52(a) of the Companies Act 1963. S. 52(b) defines a statement as being included in the prospectus if it is contained therein or it appears on the face of the prospectus or was incorporated therein by reference or issued therewith.

plies to prospectuses issued by "companies". Therefore, a non-company issuer would escape its application. In such event, however, the Prospectus Directive regime may apply (such that a remedy under its regime may be invocable) as it applies to "issuers" which is a wider class than "companies".[83]

(2) Possible section 49 defendants

3–24 Before looking at the defences to a section 49 action, first it is necessary to look at the range of parties who can be found liable in respect of untrue statements in a prospectus:

– directors of the company at the time of issue of the prospectus[84] or every person who has authorised himself to be named and is named in the prospectus as a director or as having agreed to become a director either immediately or after an interval of time;[85]

– every person being a promoter of the company[86]; and

– every person who has authorised the issue of the prospectus.[87]

Interestingly, section 49 also provides that, for the purposes of section 49, a "promoter" includes any person who was a party to the preparation of the prospectus, but it does not include any person who acted in a professional capacity for the persons engaged in setting up the company.[88] In this way professional advisers such as lawyers and accountants are excluded from liability.[89]

(3) No section 49 liability for company

3–25 Significantly, the company itself is not named as a party who may be exposed to section 49 liability. This is a lacuna in the legislation

---

[83] Although, note that the Prospectus Directive only applies if the offer is of "transferable securities" offered to the public for the first time: the meaning of transferable securities excludes several types of securities (see further Chap. 2 above, para. 2–32).

[84] s. 49(1)(a).

[85] s. 49(1)(b).

[86] s. 49(1)(c).

[87] s. 49(1)(d).

[88] s. 49(8).

[89] Furthermore, s. 49(6) provides that the directors of a company shall be liable to indemnify any person whose name appears in the prospectus and who either being a director had withdrawn his consent before the issue of the prospectus (or having agreed to being a director has withdrawn his consent to being so appointed). It also provides an indemnity in respect of a person whose consent is required under s. 46 (expert) and he either did not give it or had withdrawn it before the issue of the prospectus.

which should surely be remedied. While the absence of the company as a named section 49 defendant may help concentrate the minds of errant promoters, it must be questioned whether such an omission serves any useful purpose if the overall purpose of the remedy is to ensure that investors can obtain compensation. This lacuna is even more significant when one considers that, at common law, an investor who is misled into investing in a company does not have the right to obtain damages against the company.[90]

(4) Section 49 plaintiffs

3–26   Another interesting issue arises as to who may invoke section 49. Section 49(1) states that:

> ". . . where a prospectus invites persons to subscribe for shares in or debentures of a company, [certain persons][90a] shall be liable to all persons who subscribe for shares or debentures on the faith of the prospectus for the loss or damage they may have sustained by reason of any untrue statement. . .".

However, the precise meaning of this paragraph is less than clear. Does it mean that only persons to whom the prospectus was specifically addressed are to have the right to invoke section 49, or does it have a wider meaning in the sense that any person who relied on the prospectus (even though it was not sent to them) and subscribed for the shares, may rely on it also? If it was intended to exclude the latter group of subscribers then, surely the phrase "all such persons" would have appeared in order to confine the offer strictly to invitees, rather than the phrase "all persons" which is used instead. If this interpretation is the correct one, it would seem that any person who *subscribes* will have the right to invoke section 49. Whichever meaning is correct, it would appear that all persons who actually subscribe are within section 49.

It is also submitted that whatever uncertainties exist on this matter, those who fall within the terms of section 51 of the 1963 Act also may invoke section 49. Section 51(1) provides that where a company allots or agrees to allot shares or debentures with a view to all or any of them being offered for sale to the public, then the document by which they are offered is deemed to be a prospectus; all laws relating to the contents of prospectuses shall apply whether enacted laws or rules of law; and those who accept the offer are deemed to be "subscribers". One consequence of this is that such offerees, being deemed to be subscribers on foot of a prospectus, have the right to invoke section 49 (and other statutory/non-statutory) remedies.

---

[90] *Houldsworth v. City of Glasgow Bank* [1880] 5 A.C. 317. See para. 3–21 above.
[90a] See para. 3–24 above for such potential defendants.

Furthermore, even if securities were not apparently issued by way
of a public offer for subscription first day, but are subsequently offered to "the public", then the initial allotees are entitled to regard themselves as section 49 plaintiffs if any untrue statements were made in
any document accompanying the initial offer. In this regard section
51(2) is instructive.[91] This provision is designed to ensure that where a
company issues shares to an intermediary, that fact will not prevent
those who subsequently purchase the shares from the intermediary
from being able to invoke remedies such as section 49.

(5) Section 49 defences

3–27 Section 49(3) provides a number of defences to a section 49(1)
action:

(a) Defences based on lack of consent

3–28 There are three defences that can be raised which are based on
withdrawal of consent. Where a person is a *director*, such a person has
a good defence if he can show that he withdrew his consent before the
issue of the prospectus, and that it was issued without his authority or
consent.[92] In the case of *any* person who falls within section 49(1), it
shall be a good defence to show that the prospectus was issued without that person's knowledge or consent and, that upon becoming aware
of its issue, that person gave reasonable public notice that it was issued without his knowledge or consent.[93] Another defence open to such
a person is if it can be demonstrated that after the issue of the prospectus and before any allotment thereunder, that person on becoming
aware of the untrue statement, withdrew his consent and gave reasonable public notice of the withdrawal and the reason for it.[94]

(b) Belief in truth of statement

3–29 Another defence is that of reasonable belief in the truth of a statement. Any person liable to be a section 49(1) defendant can raise the
defence that up to the time of the allotment of shares or debentures,
that person believed the untrue statement to be true. The test is an

---

[91] s. 51(2)(a) stipulates that where an allotment is made, or an agreement to allot,
and within two years the shares or debentures or any of them become available
to the public, then it shall be presumed that the allotment or agreement to allot
was made with a view to the shares being offered to the public. Being presumed
to be an offer to the public, such an offer will attract s. 49 jurisdiction.
[92] s. 49(3)(a).
[93] s. 49(1)(b).
[94] s. 49(1)(c).

objective test as there is a requirement for a "reasonable ground" for the person's belief to be demonstrated.[95] Where a due diligence and verification exercise is done thoroughly, and all directors have indicated that they are satisfied with the outcome, then in such circumstances the directors will probably be in a position to advance firm grounds for belief in the truth of any particular statement as the due diligence/verification process will have provided supporting evidence for statements made in the prospectus.

(c) Statement fairly reflects expert's statement

3–30   Another defence that a defendant facing a section 49(1) action may raise concerns a statement of an expert which turns out to be untrue. Where a statement is included in the prospectus and it either purports to have been made by an expert or purports to be a copy or extract from an expert's report, then the defendant may raise the defence that the statement, or the extract from it, fairly represented the expert's statement. In order to invoke this defence, the defendant will have to further show that he had reasonable ground to believe up to the time the prospectus was issued, the expert was: competent to make the statement; had not withdrawn consent to the inclusion of the statement in the prospectus before registration of the prospectus; and had not, to the defendant's knowledge, withdrawn the statement before allotment.[96]

(d) Official statement defence

3–31   A section 49(1) defendant may raise the defence that a statement deemed to be untrue was either a statement purporting to be made by a public official or was contained in what purported to be a copy of or extract from an official public document, and that it was a correct and fair representation of the official's statement, or the copy of, or extract from, the official document.[97]

(e) Expert's defence

3–32   Where one is an expert whose statements are included in the prospectus, then liability under section 49 can arise as follows. An expert is any person whose profession gives authority to the statement made by him.[98] Section 46(1) of the Act provides that a prospectus which

---

[95] s. 49(1)(d)(i).
[96] s. 49(3)(d)(ii).
[97] s. 49(3)(d)(iii).
[98] s. 46(3).

contains the statement of an expert cannot be issued unless certain conditions are satisfied.

The expert must have given written consent to the issue of the prospectus containing his statement and such consent must not have been withdrawn before delivery of the prospectus for registration.[99] Also, it is required that a statement outlining the aforementioned appears in the prospectus.[100] The question arises whether an expert's consent to the issue of the prospectus containing his expert statement could be deemed to constitute authorisation in respect of the entire prospectus such that the expert might thereby be exposed to liability under section 49(1) in the same way that a promoter or director would be? Section 49(2) clarifies this matter by providing that an expert's consent shall not expose him to liability as a person who authorised the issue of the prospectus except in so far as any statement made by the expert is untrue.

Section 49(5) provides a number of defences to the expert.[101] First, the expert may plead that he gave written withdrawal of his consent before delivery of the prospectus for registration.[102] Second, the expert may plead that upon becoming aware of the untrue statement between the time of registration of the prospectus and before any allotment, he gave written withdrawal of his consent in writing and gave reasonable public notice of his reasons for withdrawal of consent.[103] Third, the expert may plead that he was competent to make the statement and had reasonable grounds for believing it to be true up to the time of allotment.[104] Section 49(6) goes on to provide that where an expert's consent was never given to the issue of the prospectus, or was but was withdrawn before the issue of the prospectus, then the directors of the company and any other person who authorised the issue of the prospectus shall be liable to indemnify the expert against all damages costs and expenses that the expert might incur by reason of his name or his statement appearing in the prospectus. This is most interesting as it would appear that it is the issue of the prospectus that is the critical time by which the expert must have withdrawn consent.

---

[99] s. 46(1)(a).
[100] s. 46(1)(b).
[101] s. 49(4) makes it clear that the expert cannot invoke ss.(3) defences.
[102] s. 49(5)(a).
[103] s. 49(5)(b).
[104] s. 49(5)(c).

B. LISTING PARTICULARS DIRECTIVE REGULATIONS

(1) Disapplication of some Companies Act 1963 provisions

3–33 Regulation 12(2) of S.I. No. 282 of 1984[105] provides that a form of application for shares or debentures of a company need not have attached to it a prospectus in the form required by the 1963 Act if a listing particulars approved by the Stock Exchange is attached. Regulation 12(3) deems the listing particulars[106] published in connection with an offer for subscription or purchase approved by the Stock Exchange to be a prospectus within the meaning of the 1963 Act. Consequently several provisions of the Act are disapplied. For example, section 44(1) (which prohibits the issue of securities to the public for subscription or purchase unless accompanied by a Third Schedule-type document detailing relevant information about the company's affairs) is disapplied.

(2) Duty on persons to allow for "informed assessment"

3–34 Article 4(1) of the Listing Particulars Directive requires listing particulars to contain the information which is necessary to enable investors and their advisers to make an "informed assessment" of the financial position and prospects of the issuer. Given its importance, the text of Article 4(1) is reproduced for ease of reference:

> "Article 4.1: The listing particulars shall contain the information which, according to the particular nature of the issuer and of the securities for the admission of which application is being made, is necessary to enable investors and their investment advisers to make an informed assessment of the assets and liabilities, financial position, profits and losses, and prospects of the issuer and of the rights attaching to such securities."

Article 4(2) of the Directive stipulates that Member States must ensure that those who are responsible for the listing particulars, or parts thereof, are under the obligation described in Article 4(1) of the Listing Particulars Directive. Accordingly, Regulation 4(1) (without further elaboration) states that the obligation of Article 4(1) shall be incumbent on

---

[105] European Communities (Stock Exchange) Regulations, 1984 implementing, *inter alia*, the Listing Particulars Directive, Council Directive 80/390/EEC of March 17, 1980.

[106] Council Directive 80/390/EEC of March 17, 1980 coordinating the requirements for the drawing up, scrutiny and distribution of the listing particulars to be published for the admissions of securities to official stock exchange listing [1980] O.J. L100/1 as implemented by the European Communities (Stock Exchange) Regulations 1984 (S.I. No. 282 of 1984). Note that the Directive has been amended on several occasions. See further Chap. 1.

those referred to in Article 4(2), *i.e.* those responsible for the listing particulars or part thereof. Undoubtedly this responsibility falls on the directors, as they are responsible overall for the contents of the particulars (and they will have expressly accepted responsibility in the Responsibility Statement required to be included by the Yellow Book Rules). However, Article 4(2) contemplates that "persons responsible for the particulars, or parts thereof", should also be subject to the Article 4(1) obligation. Consequently, it is submitted that this could mean that the promoters, directors and experts[107] may also be under this obligation. The imposition of the Article 4(1) obligation can vary from one Member State to another. For example, in some states, it is the company itself that must accept the Article 4(1) responsibility. In Ireland, as outlined, the responsibility appears to rest principally on the directors' shoulders. However, as shall further be discussed below, notwithstanding the use of highly ambiguous wording in Regulation 4, it further seems that the *issuer* may have a liability in damages if the "persons responsible" breach the obligation placed upon them.

(3) Damages for breach of the Listing Particulars Regulations?

(a) Issuer liability?

3–35 While the Listing Particulars Regulations do not specify that damages will be the remedy against those who breach the Article 4(1) obligation, Ussher suggests that this must be implied as damages can be a remedy for breach of statutory duty.[108] In order to consider this issue, it is worthwhile considering the text of Regulation 4 in full.

Regulation 4(1) provides that:

> "The obligation referred to in Article 4.1 of the Listing Particulars directive shall be incumbent on the persons referred to in Article 4.2 of that directive."

Regulation 4(2) provides that

> "In the event of non-compliance with or contravention of the obligation referred to in Article 4(1) of the Listing Particulars directive, a person referred to in Article 4.2 of that directive shall not incur any liability by reason of the non-compliance or contravention if—
> (a) in relation to any matter not disclosed, he proves that he did not know it, or
> (b) he proves that the non-compliance or contravention arose from an honest mistake of fact on his part, or

---

[107] It would appear that the expert is responsible only for the part of the prospectus that relates to the expert's report given that Article 4 refers to persons responsible for the issue of the particulars or part thereof.

[108] Ussher, *op. cit.* at p. 402.

(c)   the non-compliance or contravention was in respect of matters which
      in the opinon of the court dealing with the case were immaterial or
      was otherwise such as ought, in the opinon of the court, having re-
      gard to all the circumstances of the case, reasonably to be excused.

Regulation 4(3) provides that:

"Nothing in this Regulation shall be construed so as to limit or diminish
any liability which any person may incur under the law of the State apart
from these Regulations."

Regulation 4(4) provides that:

"An issuer shall not be liable in damages by reason only of the non-compliance with, or contravention of, the provisions of these Regulations
(other than paragraph (1) of this Regulation): Provided that any such
non-compliance or contravention does not give rise to any liability under any provision of the Companies Act, 1963."

Breach of Regulation 4(1) would be tantamount to a breach of statutory duty. Regulation 4(4) is curious in that it provides that *an issuer*
(meaning the company[109]) shall not be liable in damages merely because the Regulations are breached. However, it also provides[110] – by
way of specific exception – that this immunity from damages granted
to the issuer who breaches the Regulations will not apply where the
issuer fails to make available information necessary to enable an "informed assessment" to be made.[111] This is significant as it implies that
where Listing Particulars do not meet the "informed assessment" standard, then the company may be liable in damages. Thus one can envisage a situation whereby a company itself can be held liable in damages
under this test although no such liability exists under section 49 of the
Companies Act 1963 (as the company is not mentioned as a possible
defendant in a section 49 misstatement action).

Interestingly also, regulation 4(4) further provides that, while apart
from a breach of regulation 4(1), the issuer will not be liable in damages where it is in breach of the Regulations, "provided that any such
non-compliance or contravention does not give rise to any liability

---

[109] See Art. 2(c) of the Directive.
[110] Admittedly in very unclear and convoluted language.
[111] Although the wording used in Reg. 4(4) is highly obtuse (because the earlier
    Reg. 4(1) refers to "persons" while Reg. 4(4) (which cross-references to Reg.
    4(1)) refers to "issuer", and furthermore due to confusing use of the phrase
    "(other than para. (1) of the Regulation)"), nevertheless, it is submitted that as
    the central core obligation is the duty to make informed disclosure, such obli-
    gation would be largely meaningless if Reg. 4(4)'s convoluted language was
    interpreted to mean that liability in damages, could not arise (on the part of the
    issuer).

under any provision of the 1963 Act". What does this awkwardly-worded provision mean? It would appear that it means that regulation 4(4) does not preclude the grounding of liability under any provision of the Companies Act and furthermore, that there may be a right to damages for breach of the Regulations themselves where such breach could also constitute a breach occasioning liability under the Companies Act.[112] It should also be noted of course, that regulation 4(3) *inter alia* means that common law remedies are not affected by the Regulations, and so those responsible for issuing listing particulars should bear in mind that those remedies continue to be available to aggrieved investors also.

(b) "Persons responsible for the Listing Particulars" liability?

3–36 Although the Listing Particulars Regulations do not explicitly provide a right to damages against the promoters (or more particularly the directors) for loss arising out of their failure to live up to the duty imposed on them to publish listing particulars that satisfy "informed assessment", it is submitted that there is nothing in the Regulations which precludes the availability of such a remedy. Regulation 4(1) imposes a duty on persons responsible for the listing particulars or parts thereof (i.e. Article 4(2) persons). Regulation 4(4) (which provides limited immunity for issuers to a damages action) is not extended to such Article 4(2) "persons". While they are provided with other defences by regulation 4(2), they are not provided with a specific immunity to a damages action for breach or non-compliance with the Regulations.[113] Therefore it is submitted, that while the point has not been resolved judicially, it is conceivable that a court would so interpret the Regulations as to permit damages to be awarded against directors, who bear the primary responsibility for the listing particulars, and perhaps also against other persons responsible, such as promoters or experts.[114] Although (by comparison with section 49 which explicitly grants a right of action for compensation to persons who suffer from untrue statements in prospectuses to which section 49 applies) the Listing Particulars Regulations do not explicitly grant a right of action, it is submitted that a damages remedy is the most appropriate remedy, given the objective of Article 4 of the Listing Particulars Di-

---

[112] This appears somewhat superfluous given that regulation 4(3) specifically states that nothing in regulation 4 shall be construed so as to limit or diminish any liability which any person may incur under any other law of the State.

[113] See above at para. 3–35 where the position of issuers is considered.

[114] Although in the case of experts, their liability would be confined to their own brief.

rective, which is to impose a duty on "persons responsible" to enable investors make an informed assessment.[115]

Regulation 4(2) provides that liability under the Regulations shall not be incurred if:

— the person can prove that he did not know of the matter that was not disclosed, or

— the person can prove that the non-compliance or contravention arose from an honest mistake on his part, or

— if, in the view of a court, the non-compliance or contravention was in respect of matters which were not material or excusable.

(4) Possible plaintiffs

3–37   Finally, it should be noted that the Listing Particulars Regulations do not confine plaintiffs to initial subscribers and there appears to be nothing in the Regulations that prevents subsequent purchasers from pursuing the action for breach of statutory duty against either the company or the persons responsible for the issue of the listing particulars. This raises the issue of whether the issuers intended that listing particulars were only to be relied upon by the initial subscribers, or, did they intend subsequent purchasers to rely on them also, at least for a period of time after the initial subscribers have taken up the offer? As will be seen above,[116] recently the courts appear to be coming to the view that the purpose of the prospectus/listing particulars has changed since the era of *Peek v. Gurney* such that now in some modern stock launches, the promoters may well intend the listing particulars to be a guide for subsequent purchasers also for a specified period post-initial allotment of the shares in order to help foster a steady post launch trade in the shares. It remains to be seen what view will be taken by the courts in Ireland on this issue, particularly as we do not as have an

---

[115] Article 4(1) of Council Directive 80/390/EEC (the Listing Particulars Directive) provides that:

> "The Listing particulars shall contain the information which, according to the particular nature of the issuer and of the securities for the admission of which application is being made, is necessary to enable investors and their investment advisers to make an informed assessment of the assets and liabilities, financial position, profits and losses, and prospects of the issuer and of the rights attaching to such securities."

Art. 4.2 further provides that:

> "Member States shall ensure that the obligation referred to in paragraph 1 is incumbent upon the persons responsible for the listing particulars. . .".

[116] See paras 3–15—3–16.

equivalent to the Financial Services Act 1986 (U.K.), which has expressly recognised the right of subsequent purchasers to be compensated if they suffered loss arising out of reliance on a misleading statement in listing particulars.

C. PROSPECTUS DIRECTIVE REGULATIONS[117]

3–38   It is submitted that a prospectus within the meaning of the Prospectus Directive[118] may give rise to similar liability issues as those outlined immediately above in relation to Listing Particulars Regulations.[119] The Prospectus Regulations[120] likewise disapply section 44(1) of Part III Companies Act 1963 concerning prospectuses and deems that a form of application to which the Prospectus Directive applies need not have attached to it a prospectus in the form required by the Companies Act 1963 provided it has a Prospectus Directive form of prospectus attached.[121] Furthermore, where any offer for subscription or purchase to which the Directive relates is accompanied by a Prospectus Directive form of prospectus, it is deemed to be a prospectus within the meaning of the Companies Act 1963.[122]

Regulation 8(1) of the Prospectus Regulations states:

> "Every prospectus issued by or on behalf of an issuer shall contain the information which, according to the particular nature of the issuer and of the securities concerned, is necessary to enable an informed assessment to be made of the assets and liabilities, financial position, profits and losses and prospects of the company and of the rights attaching to the securities."

In this regard, the requirement for "informed assessment" to be facilitated makes regulation 8(1) similar to regulation 4 of the Listing Particulars Regulations except that the obligation is placed on the issuer rather than persons responsible for issuing the prospectus. In other words, regulation 10 of the Prospectus Regulations is similar to regulation 4 of the Listing Particulars Regulations, apart from the fact that it does not contain an analogous provision to regulation 4(1) of the Listing Particulars Regulations. As one may recall, regulation 4(1) is

---

[117] So far as possible plaintiffs under the Prospectus Regulations are concerned, the same considerations apply as were discussed in relation to Listing Particulars: see para. 3–37 above.
[118] Council Directive no. 89/298/EEC as implemented by S.I. No. 202 of 1992.
[119] S.I. No. 282 of 1984; see above paras 3–34—3–37.
[120] S.I. No. 202 of 1992, reg. 21(4).
[121] Reg. 21(3).
[122] Reg. 21(4)

the provision that places responsibility for making "informed assessment" on the shoulders of "persons responsible."[123] The omission of
an analogue to regulation 4(1) is significant because it means that the
obligation to make proper disclosure falls on the "person making the
offer" (*i.e.* the issuer or owner of the securities) rather than on the directors. Regulation 10(1) Prospectus Regulations provides a similar list
of defences to "the person making the offer" as regulation 4(2) Listing
Particulars Regulations; also regulation 10(2) Prospectus Regulations
(just as regulation 4(3) Listing Particulars Regulations does) provides
that nothing in Regulation 10 shall limit or diminish any liability which
any person may incur under the law of the State apart from the Prospectus Regulations; and regulation 10(3) Prospectus Regulations (just
as regulation 4(4) Listing Particulars Regulations does) provides that
an *issuer* shall not be liable in damages by reason only of the non-compliance with or contravention of the Regulations, and (as does regulation 4(4) Listing Particulars Regulations) it *specifically*[124] provides that
this does not apply in the case of non-compliance or contraventions
which breach the duty to make an "informed assessment" as required
by the Prospectus Directive. It is submitted therefore, that promoters
who act on behalf of an issuer promoting a prospectus pursuant to the
Prospectus Regulations may well find themselves liable to a damages
action for breach of statutory duty, as may the issuer itself, where there
has been a failure to make the standard of disclosure required by regulation 8(1) Prospectus Regulations (and the Prospectus Directive[125]) if
they are deemed to be "the person making the offer". Furthermore, if
the offer is of existing securities, rather than new securities, the term
"person making the offer" and "issuer" may mean the offeror, rather
than the issuer of the securities.[126]

As has been elaborated in detail in Chapter 2, while section 49 of
the Companies Act 1963 only applies to offers for subscription for new
securities, the Prospectus Directive applies to a potentially wider range
of public offers as it can also apply to an offer of existing shares (to the
public for the first time). Therefore, the damages action for breach of
statutory duty will be available in instances where section 49 would
not.

---

[123] See paras 3–35 and 3–36 above.
[124] In less than clear language.
[125] Arts. 4 and 11 Prospectus Directive. Art 11 Prospectus Directive specifically
refers to the requirement for disclosure sufficient to permit investors to make
an informed assessment of the issuer's financial position.
[126] See further para. 3–42 below where a sensible interpretation of the rather im-
precise wording of the Regulation is attempted.

D. SECTION 44 OMISSION

3–39   As described elsewhere in this chapter above[127] omission of material information will allow one to pursue a section 49 remedy where the omission changes the true meaning of disclosed information.[128]

(1) Liability under section 44 for *mere* omission ?

3–40   Although, in practice, most companies will prefer to satisfy the Prospectus Regulations rather than the Companies Act 1963 Third Schedule regime (principally because under the former regime only three year's audited accounts are required to be published, where five year's accounts are required under the latter) nevertheless, there may be circumstances where a company cannot fall within the Prospectus Directive and thus it must satisfy the Third Schedule regime. Hence, section 44 Companies Act 1963 which may be thereby applicable, deserves consideration.[129] Section 44(1) Companies Act 1963 provides that a public offer prospectus must have attached to it the information contained in the Third Schedule. Furthermore, section 44(3) states that it shall not be lawful to issue a prospectus unless it complies with the Act. However, no obvious civil sanction is provided under the section for *mere* omission of Third Schedule information from the prospectus.[130]

However, some kind of liability is envisaged as a number of defences are provided for directors and any other person responsible for the prospectus. Section 44(5) provides that a director or other person responsible for the issue of the prospectus shall not incur any liability by reason of non-compliance or contravention of section 44 if:

(i)   he proves he did not know of the disclosed matter;

(ii)   he proves that the non-compliance or contravention arose from an honest mistake on his part; or

---

[127]   para. 3–23. Omission may also provide a cause of action in relation to omission in the context of listing particulars (see para. 3–41 below) and in the context of the Prospectus Regulation Prospectuses (see para. 3–42 below).

[128]   Omission may also provide a cause of action at common law such as negligent misstatement (provided omission constitutes negligence) or deceit (where the suppression of information thereby causes fraud). However, *mere* omission, *without more*, does not permit either a s. 49 action or either of the aforementioned actions to proceed. It may however provide grounds for recission.

[129]   See further Chap. 2.

[130]   *i.e.,* omission which does not constitute a s.49-type situation, *i.e.* an omission which does not render what is stated in the prospectus "untrue" within the meaning of s.49 (see para. 3–23 above where s.49 and meaning of "untrue statements" are considered).

(iii) the non-compliance or contravention was in respect of matters which, in the opinion of the court were immaterial or reasonably excusable bearing in mind the circumstances of the case.

Thus, while a number of defences are provided, no contravention or sanction is explicitly specified by the section other than a fine of £500 for breach of sections 44(1) or 44(3).[131] The question therefore arises as to whether breach of section 44 could give rise to some form of action for compensation or an action in damages for breach of statutory duty (on the part of a director or person responsible), even though the section does not explicitly provide such a right. As against this possibility, there are two arguments, neither of which are conclusive. First, to read a right to compensation into section 44(5) would do some violence to the legislative intent, as a specific right to compensation is provided (by section 49) for "untrue statements" in the prospectus and clearly an omission which rendered a statement "untrue" would be actionable under section 49. Therefore, it is arguable that mere omissions (*i.e.* omission that does not go so far as to render prospectus statements "untrue") were not intended to be actionable by way of a civil compensation remedy. Second, it is difficult to argue that section 44(5) implicitly recognises a right to some form of damages or compensation action in the absence of an explicit provision to that effect in section 44(5), particularly when the common law actions do not provide for damages in *mere* omission situations.[132]

Also of interest is the fact that the section does not appear to envisage the company itself being a possible defendant to an omission action under section 44 as it only refers to "directors or other persons responsible".[133]

(2) Omission in the context of the Listing Particulars Directive Regulations

3–41 Pursuant to the Listing Particulars Directive,[134] as enacted by the Listing Particulars Regulations, persons responsible for the listing particulars are under a duty to ensure that all information is published

---

[131] s.44(8).

[132] Note that while s. 44(9) provides that "Nothing in this section shall limit or diminish any liability which any person may incur under the general law or this Act apart from this section", the common law remedies such as deceit or negligence would not appear to give any assistance to the investor unless the omission either constituted deceit or negligent omission.

[133] Though it may be a defendant to a non-statutory action for recission.

[134] Art. 4 Council Directive 80/390/EEC [1980] O.J. L100/1 as implemented by S.I. No. 282 of 1984.

such as would be required to enable investors make an "informed assessment" of the issuer. An omission of material information from the document could constitute a breach of the duty imposed on persons responsible for the issue of the prospectus. Like section 44(5) Companies Act 1963, regulation 4(2) of the Listing Particulars Regulations provides a number of defences where a breach of the Regulations is alleged on the part of any person responsible for a Listing Particulars.[135] However, in contrast to section 44, the Listing Particulars Regulations, although clumsily worded, appear to contemplate damages being a remedy where those responsible for publishing a listing particulars have failed to permit "informed assessment". [136] Furthermore, it also appears that *issuers* may be exposed to a similar liability in damages under the Regulations.[137] If this is correct,[138] then a listed company can be sued for omission under the Regulations, whereas (as seen above)[139] to imply a similar right into section 44(5) is more difficult and in any event section 44(5) makes no reference to "company" but only to "persons" thereby implying that, if any remedy (at all) is available for breach of section 44, it can only be obtained against the persons responsible and not the company itself. As a consequence, awaiting judicial resolution of the matter, it may be that a damages action for loss caused by omission may be easier to sustain where based on the Listing Particulars Regulations. Those who only have section 44 to rely on (*i.e.* non-listed or non-Prospectus Directive public offers) may find arguing for a right to damages more difficult in the absence of legislative clarity on the matter.

(3) Omission in the context of the Prospectus Directive Regulations

3–42 The adoption of Prospectus Regulations in 1992[140] pursuant to the Prospectus Directive[141] has had a further impact on the issue of omission. Whenever a public offer falls within the terms of the Prospectus Regulations, it is submitted that the failure of section 44 of the Companies Act 1963 to explicitly provide either a right to action in

---

[135] The Listing Particulars Regulation's defences are worded very similarly to the defences in s. 44(5): see para. 3–35 above.

[136] See above paras 3–33—3–36 where this issue was considered in the context of the Listing Particulars Regulations.

[137] See above paras 3–35—3–36 where this issue was considered in the context of issuers.

[138] The writer readily concedes that the Regulations' text is highly unreadable.

[139] para. 3–40.

[140] European Communities (Transferable Securities and Stock Exchange) Regulations, 1992, (S.I. No. 202 of 1992).

[141] Council Directive 89/298/EEC O.J. [1989] L.124/8 implemented by S.I. No. 202 of 1992.

damages for omission, nor to name the company itself as a possible defendant, has been overcome by virtue of the Regulations.

Regulation 10(1) provides that:

"In the event of non-compliance with or contravention of the obligation referred to in Article 4[142] of the Prospectus Directive, the person[143] making the offer shall not incur any liability by reason of the non-compliance or contravention if–

(a) in relation to any matter not disclosed, he proves that he did not know it, or

(b) he proves that the non-compliance or contravention arose from an honest mistake of fact on his part, or

(c) the non-compliance or contravention was in respect of matters which in the opinon of the court dealing with the case were immaterial or was otherwise such as ought, in the opinon of the court, having regard to all the circumstances of the case, reasonably to be excused."

Regulation 10(2) provides that:

"Nothing in this Regulation shall be construed so as to limit or diminish any liability which any person may incur under the law of the State apart from these Regulations."

Regulation 10(3) provides that:

"An issuer shall not be liable in damages by reason only of the non-compliance with, or contravention of, the provisions of these Regulations (other than paragraph (1) of this Regulation) provided that any such non-compliance or contravention does not give rise to any liability under any provision of the Companies Act, 1963."

This Regulation is, in many ways, similar to the equivalent regulation in the Listing Particulars Regulations.[144] For example, regulation 10(2) makes it clear that nothing in the Regulations shall limit or diminish a person's liability under any other law of the State. Hence neither common law nor statutory actions are precluded from being invoked where applicable. Furthermore, the defences provided for the "person making the offer" in regulation 10(1) are similar to those provided for 'persons responsible for the Listing Particulars' under regulation 4(2) of the Listing Particulars Regulations. Finally, it is clear that an action in damages, although not explicitly provided for under the Regulations,

[142] Article 4 (read together with Article 1) provides that the Member States shall ensure that a prospectus is published containing certain information whenever securities are offered to the public for the first time where they have not already been listed on an exchange operating in that Member State.

[143] The Directive (Art. 4) place the obligation on "the person making the offer".

[144] Reg. 4, S.I. No. 282 of 1984 (see para 3–35 above).

is contemplated for the same reasons as were suggested when the Listing Particulars Regulations were discussed above.[145]

However, upon closer inspection of these highly obtusely worded Regulations a key difference emerges. The immunity afforded to issuers by regulation 10(3) is expressed (obtusely!) *not to* extend to situations where a violation of *regulation 10(1)* has occurred. Thus, it is contemplated that an issuer of a prospectus cannot invoke the regulation 10(3) immunity in damages where the regulations are breached by virtue of the omission of a matter that should have been disclosed under regulation 10(1). Although "the person making the offer" may invoke the defences listed in regulation 10(1), is an "issuer" such a person? Therefore, the question arises as to what is the significance, if any of the use of the term "person making the offer" in regulation 10(1) and "issuer" in regulation 10(3). It is submitted that in the case of an offer of *new* shares for subscription, the person making the offer is also the issuer. In this event, the issuer could invoke regulation 10(1) defences. However, in the case of the offer of *existing* securities to the public for the first time, it is submitted that the "person making the offer" is the owner of the securities and that "issuer" be so interpreted. To allow "issuer" mean the actual issuer in this circumstance would be a patent absurdity as the issuer no longer owns the securities. The whole rationale behind the regulations is to make the *offeror* (whether issuer or alternatively owner) of the securities *at the time of the first public offer* be the party responsible for publishing a prospectus. This is but another example of how the poor wording employed in the regulations can cause grief to the practitioner and student alike. Consequently, if this interpretation of the regulation is correct, then both the company (or its agents) or the subsequent owner (or its agent) ("as the case may be"), although not liable in damages for mere omissions where section 44 of the 1963 Act applies), may well suffer such a liability where the Prospectus Regulations apply.[146]

Finally, regulation 10(2) should not be overlooked. It provides (in effect) that nothing in the Prospectus Regulations shall limit any exposure under any other law of the State. Hence, common law and statutory liabilities will continue where relevant to apply.

---

[145] See above paras 3–33—3–38.
[146] Chap. 2 above considers in more detail the circumstances in which either the Third Schedule regime or the Prospectus Directive Regulations apply.

E. LIABILITY OF STOCK EXCHANGE OR REGISTRAR OF COMPANIES

3–43 The staff of the Stock Exchange will be guilty of an offence if they violate regulation 6(1) of the Listing Particulars Directive's[147] implementing regulations, the Listing Particulars Regulations.[148] Regulation 6(1) provides that employees (including former employees) are bound by professional secrecy and may not divulge any confidential information received by them in the course of their professional duties, except as permitted by law.[149] Failure to comply with regulation 6(1) is an offence punishable by a maximum £1,000 fine. The Prospectus Regulations[150] (which implement the Prospectus Directive)[151] provide a similar prohibition against divulging confidential information by employees of the Exchange. However, it provides not only for a possible £1,000 fine, but also for imprisonment of up to 12 months.[152]

3–44 So far as liability in damages is concerned, regulation 8(1) of the Listing Particulars Regulations[153] provides that neither the Stock Exchange nor any employee, officer, committee or any person asked to advise it, shall be liable in damages by reason only that there has been non-compliance with or contravention of, any obligation imposed by the Regulations. It is further provided that liability will not be incurred either where anything was done, or omitted to be done, by such persons in connection with the exercise by the Exchange of its functions as "competent authority" under the Regulations. However, the aforegoing immunity from damages is not an absolute one for two reasons. First, regulation 8(1)'s wording only seems to preclude liability from damages where the contravention was a breach of the Regulations. This would seem to suggest that if liability for damages could be established on other grounds (e.g. tort) then regulation 8(1) would not preclude damages. Second, regulation 8(1) explicitly provides that where the act or omission under the Regulations was done in bad faith, the immunity from damages cannot apply.

---

[147] Directive 80/390/EEC (note that S.I. No. 282 of 1984 is also the implementing Regulation for the Admissions Directive 79/279/EEC.
[148] S.I. No. 282 of 1984.
[149] In this regard, both Art. 18 Admissions Directive and Art. 25 Listing Particulars Directive provide that this prohibition does not apply to the Exchange sharing information for the purposes of either Directive with other similar bodies in other member States.
[150] S.I. No. 202 of 1992, reg. 20.
[151] Directive 89/298/EEC.
[152] S.I. No. 202 of 1992, reg. 21.
[153] S.I. No. 282 of 1984, reg. 8(1).

3–45 The Prospectus Regulations[154] expressly adopt regulation 8(1) of the Listing Particulars Regulations in so far as the Exchange (or its employees or persons asked to advise or assist it) seek immunity from damages in regard to dealings with prospectuses under the Prospectus Regulations.

3–46 The Prospectus Regulations[155] provide that the Registrar of Companies shall not be liable in damages in respect of his activities under the Prospectus Regulations. The conditions governing the availability of this immunity from damages are along similar lines to those set out in regulation 8(1) governing the activities of Stock Exchange personnel under the Listing Particulars Regulations.[156]

3–47 Finally, an issue arises as to whether a transaction may be void on the basis that it was entered into in contravention of the Listing Particulars or the Prospectus Regulations. In this regard, both sets of implementing Regulations provide that no transaction shall be void or voidable by reason only of the fact that it was entered into in contravention of, or not in conformity with, the respective Regulations.

III. CRIMINAL LIABILITIES

A. OFFENCES

(1) Companies Act 1963

3–48 The Companies Act 1963 provides for the following offences in connection with a prospectus which offers securities for subscription or purchase.

(a) Section 50 (untrue statements)

3–49 Section 50 of the Companies Act 1963[157] provides that where a prospectus includes any untrue statement,[158] any person who authorised the prospectus shall be liable upon summary conviction to a prison term not exceeding six months or a fine not exceeding £500, or both. Upon conviction on indictment, the person shall be liable to a term not

---

[154] S.I. 202 of 1992, reg. 9(2).

[155] S.I. No. 202 of 1992, reg. 15.

[156] See para. 3–44 above.

[157] Fines increased by Sched. I of the Companies (Amendment) Act 1982 (No. 10 of 1982).

[158] s. 52 defines an "untrue statement" to be a statement that "is misleading in the form and context in which it is included".

exceeding two years or a fine not exceeding £2,500, or both. A defence is provided if the person can prove that either the statement was immaterial, or he had reasonable ground to believe, and did, up to the time of the issue of the prospectus, that the statement was true.[159] Section 50(2) provides that where one has authorised the issue of a prospectus pursuant to Section 46 in the capacity of expert, that alone shall not deem such a person to have authorised the prospectus for the purposes of the aforementioned offences.

(b) Section 44(8) (contravention of sections 44(1) or 44(3)/section 46 (violating expert's consent)

3–50 Section 44(8) of the Companies Act 1963 makes a person who acts in contravention of Section 44(1) or (3) liable to a fine not exceeding £500. Section 44(1) requires every prospectus issued in connection with an offer for subscription or purchase of new securities to include Third Schedule information.[160] Section 44(3) makes it unlawful to issue any form of application for shares unless the form is accompanied by a prospectus which complies with Part III of the 1963 Act, and the issue of which does not violate the requirements of section 46. Section 46 provides *inter alia* that it shall be an offence to publish a prospectus containing the consent of an expert, where either the expert did not consent to the issue or, having given it he withdrew it. Section 46(2) imposes a fine not exceeding £500 on the company and every person who is knowingly a party to such issue.

Although section 44(8) does not make specific reference to section 44(5) (defences to mere omissions), presumably a person who is charged with an offence under section 44(8) can attempt to invoke section 44(5)(c) as a defence. This allows a director or any person responsible for the prospectus to plead that the contravention of section 44 was in respect of matters which a court may decide was immaterial, such that having regard to all the circumstances, the court could reasonably excuse the accused from liability. Also presumably the section 44(5)(a) (no knowledge of matter not disclosed) defence and the section 44(5)(b) (honest mistake) defence are also invocable as section 44(5) states that ". . . a director or other person responsible for the issue of the prospectus shall not incur any liability by reason of non-compliance or contravention" of section 44 where any of the aforementioned defences are successfully invoked.

---

[159] s. 50(1).

[160] However, as described further below in this paragraph, s. 44(1) does not extend to prospectuses complying with either the Prospectus or Listing Particulars Regulations; in particular, s. 44(1) does not extend to offers of existing securities.

Note however, that section 44(3) does not have to be satisfied where the form of application for securities is issued with a document which takes the form of either a prospectus complying with the Prospectus Regulations[161] or a Listing Particulars complying with the Listing Regulations.[162] In either case, the relevant Regulations deem the prospectus or listing particulars to be a prospectus within the meaning of the Companies Act 1963 where an offer for subscription or purchase of the securities is made, in which event section 44(1) is disapplied.[162a]

(c) Section 47 (failure to register Prospectus)

3–51　　Failure to register a prospectus with the Registrar of Companies on or before the date of its publication will render the company and every person knowingly a party to the issue of the prospectus liable to a fine not exceeding £500. Section 47 makes many demands including requiring that the prospectus be, at the time it is offered up to the Registrar, duly signed by all directors or proposed directors (or their authorised agents), endorsed with any experts consents, and, in the case of prospectuses issued generally[163] that relevant Third Schedule requirements such as memoranda giving full dates of "material contracts" binding the company etc. be attached to the prospectus.

As will be seen below when liabilities under the Prospectus Regulations are considered, every prospectus issued under the Prospectus Regulations must also be registered with the Registrar of Companies in conformity with section 47's requirements.[164]

(2) Section 242 Companies Act 1990

3–52　　Where a person knowingly or recklessly makes a statement or delivers a document, which is false in some material respect, in compliance with any requirement under the Companies Acts, the person shall be guilty of an offence. If the court takes the view that the act, omission or conduct constituting the offence has either defrauded other persons, or caused a company to become insolvent, or impeded a winding-up, then the court can impose on indictment a fine of up to £10,000 or imprisonment for up to seven years, or both.

---

[161] or, alternatively where such document may be obtained and inspected: S.I. No. 202 of 1992, reg. 21(4).

[162] or, alternatively where such document may be obtained and inspected: S.I. No. 282 of 1984, reg. 12(3).

[162a] See paras 3–33 (listing particulars) and 3–38 (Prospectus Directive prospectuses above.

[163] Defined under s. 45 as an issue to persons not already members or debenture holders of the company.

[164] see para. 3–59 below.

(3) Listing Particulars Regulations

3–53 The Listing Particulars Regulations provide for the following offences. Regulation 6(4) provides that the Minister shall prosecute the offences.

(a) *Regulation 6 (breach of professional secrecy or publication of false or misleading information)*

3–54 Article 25 of the Listing Particulars Directive[165] provides that all persons employed or formerly employed by the Stock Exchange shall be bound by professional secrecy such that confidential information received in the course of their duties may not be divulged to any person or authority except as laid down by law.[166] Regulation 6(2) of the Listing Particulars Regulations provides that it shall be an offence punishable on summary conviction to a fine not exceeding £1,000 where there has been a failure to comply.

Regulation 6(2) further provides that any person who knowingly publishes any information required to be published by the Directives which is false or misleading in any material respect shall be guilty of an offence and shall be liable on summary conviction to a fine not exceeding £1,000.

Regulation 6(3) provides that where an offence under the Regulations is committed by a body corporate and is proved to have been committed with the consent or connivance of, or was attributable to any neglect on the part of, any director, manager, secretary or other officer or person purporting to act in such capacity, he shall be guilty of an offence.

(b) *Regulation 13 (late delivery of Listing Particulars)*

3–55 Where a copy of listing particulars have not been delivered to the Registrar of Companies for registration on or before the date of their publication, regulation 13(1) provides that the issuer and every person who knowingly is a party to the publication shall be guilty of an offence and liable on summary conviction to a fine not exceeding

---

[165] Art. 25 of Directive 80/390 [1980] O.J. L100/1 as amended by Council Directive 87/345/EEC of 22 June 1987 [1987] O.J. L185/81 as implemented by S.I. No. 18 of 1991. Article 25 elaborates by providing that this obligation shall not preclude the competent authorities in different Member States from exchanging information in the manner provided by the Directives.

[166] Art. 18(1) Admissions Directive does likewise (Council Directive 79/297/EEC of 5 March 1979 coordinating the conditions for the admission of securities to official stock exchange listing [1979] O.J. L66/21).

£1,000.[167] Regulation 13(2) requires the document to state conspicuously that a copy has been duly delivered to the Registrar.

(c) Regulation 12(3) (failure to produce Listing Particulars; withdrawal of expert's consent; publication of "untrue statement")

3–56 Regulation 12(3) provides that while several provisions of the Companies Act 1963 are disapplied[168] to an offer for subscription or purchase of securities which are accompanied by a listing particulars (which is deemed to be a prospectus within the meaning of section 44 of the 1963 Act), it does not disapply section 44(8), 46 or 50. Thus these criminal provisions may apply to a listing particulars in circumstances where securities are offered for subscription or purchase and the listing particulars serves as a prospectus. Thus, a failure to publish a listing particulars (in compliance with the Listing Particulars Regulations) incurs criminal liability pursuant to section 44(8) and makes a person responsible subject to a fine of £500. Where an expert's opinion is contained in a listing particulars, and the expert never gave consent or has withdrawn consent before publication, an offence is committed by those responsible, being the company and every person who knowingly was a party to the issuing of the listing particulars in such circumstances.[169] Where a listing particulars contains "untrue statements" within the meaning of section 50, then a criminal offence has occurred.[170]

(4) Prospectus Regulations

3–57 The Prospectus Regulations provide for the following offences. Regulation 20(4) provides that the Minister shall prosecute the offences.

---

[167] s. 47 of the Companies Act (which requires prospectuses to be registered) does not apply to listing particulars *per se*: Reg. 12(3) S.I. No. 282 of 1984 expressly disapples s. 47. However, this may be otherwise where a listing particulars are issued in conjunction with an offer to the public for subscription or purchase which falls within the terms of the Prospectus Regulations. Reg. 21(4) S.I. No. 202 of 1992 provides that where a prospectus complying with the Prospectus Regulations is published in conjunction with an offer for subscription or purchase, then any listing particulars issued in connection with the offer shall be deemed to be a prospectus within the meaning of the Companies Act 1963 – in which event s. 47 will presumably apply (as Reg. 11 S.I. No. 202 of 1992 provides that "Every prospectus under these Regulations shall be registered . . . in compliance with s. 47. . . .").

[168] *i.e.*, ss. 43, 44(1), 45, 47, 361(1)(b), 361(2), 362 and 364.

[169] s. 46(2).

[170] See further para. 3–49.

(a) *Regulation 20 (breach of professional secrecy or publication of false or misleading information)*

3–58   Regulation 20 provides that breach of the Prospectus Directive's obligation of professional secrecy[171] by employees or former employees of the Stock Exchange shall be an offence punishable on summary conviction by imprisonment for a term not exceeding 12 months or a fine not exceeding £1,000, or both.[172] The professional secrecy obligation is framed in similar terms to that found in Article 25 of the Listing Particulars Directive.[173]

Any person who knowingly publishes any information required to be published by the Directive which is false or misleading in any material respect shall be guilty of an offence and shall be liable on summary conviction to up to 12 months in jail, or to a fine not exceeding £1,000 or both.[174]

The Prospectus Regulations are markedly more severe than the Listing Particulars Regulations as the latter make no provision for jail terms.[175]

Regulation 20(3) provides that where an offence under the Regulations is committed by a body corporate and is proved to have been committed with the consent or connivance of, or was attributable to any neglect on the part of, any director, manager, secretary or other officer or person purporting to act in such capacity, such person shall be guilty of an offence, subject to the penalties outlined above.

(b) *Regulation 21/Regulation 11 (failure to produce Prospectus in conformity with Prospectus Regulations; failure to register prospectus; violation of expert's consent; untrue statements)*

3–59   Regulation 21(4) deems a prospectus issued in connection with an offer of securities for subscription or purchase and which meets the requirements of the Prospectus Regulations to be a prospectus for the purposes of the 1963 Act. It disapplies[176] certain provisions of the 1963 Act accordingly. However, this does not preclude the application of sections 44(8), 46, 47 or 50 to such a prospectus.[177] The Listing Particu-

---

[171] Art. 23 Prospectus Directive 89/298/EEC.
[172] Reg. 20(2).
[173] Or in Art. 18 Admissions Directive 79/279/EEC: see para. 3–54 above.
[174] Reg. 20(2).
[175] Although certain provisions of the Companies Act, where applicable, may: see para. 3–56 above.
[176] ss. 43, 44(1), 45, 361(1)(b), 361(2), 362 and 364.
[177] The offences specified in ss. 44(8), 46, 50 apply, and are set out above, in para. 3–56 when listing particulars were considered. It is not proposed to reiterate them here.

lars Regulations expressly disapply section 47,[178] but the Prospectus Regulations do not.[179] In fact, regulation 11 of the Prospectus Regulations expressly provides that every prospectus issued under the Prospectus Regulations shall be registered with the Registrar of Companies in compliance with section 47 of the Companies Act. Failure to do so in an offence, subjecting persons who knowingly issued the prospectus to a maximum fine of £500 each.

(5) Larceny Act 1861

3–60   Section 84 of the Larceny Act 1861 provides for a prison term of up to seven years where a director, manager or other officer of a company knowingly *inter alia* issues or is a party to the making or circulating of a prospectus which is false with the intent to induce anyone to become a member of a company. In *R. v. Kyslant*,[180] a company chairman was convicted under this section.

IV. THE PROMOTER AND THE COMPANY

Introduction

3–61   In this section of the chapter, the legal relationship between the promoter and a company in formation will be considered, in particular the regime governing the sale of property by the promoter to the fledgling company. Both common law and statutory regimes may be relevant in this relationship. For the non-plc, common law rules apply. For the plc, the Companies (Amendment) Act 1983 will also be relevant. The 1983 Act sets out rules concerning the *valuation* of property sold by the promoter to the plc. However, notwithstanding the enactment of the 1983 Act, the common law continues to be relevant to promoter/ plc transactions, as the common law compliments the statutory regime. Therefore, it is appropriate to begin this section of the chapter by examining the common law regime, and conclude by considering the statutory regime.

Although the Companies legislation does not define who a promoter may be, it is clear from the case law on the subject of promoters that a promoter (in the context of a company in formation) is someone whose endeavours are directed towards getting a company formed

---

[178] Though *cf.* para. 3–55 above.
[179] Although there is nonetheless an obligation to register Listing Particulars with the Registrar, but this is pursuant to reg. 13(1) (S.I. No. 282 of 1984) rather than s. 47. Failure to do so is an offence (reg. 13(3)).
[180] [1932] 1 K.B. 442.

and running. The promoter may enter into contracts on behalf of the company even before the company comes into existence, as Section 37 Companies Act 1963 provides that such contracts[181] can be adopted by the company once it comes into existence, and furthermore the company will be bound to such a contract as if the company had been in existence at the time of the contract. Until such time that the company adopts the transaction as its own, the promoter remains personally liable on foot of it.[182] Such a person is in a fiduciary relationship to the company[183] which means that should the promoter behave improperly in his dealings with the company, he may run the risk of incurring liabilities to the company. In the following paragraphs, the extent of the promoter's fiduciary duty to the company being promoted will be considered, as will some consideration be given to the kinds of legal action that the company may pursue against the errant promoter.

A. THE PROMOTER/COMPANY FIDUCIARY RELATIONSHIP

(1) Two key issues

3–62 All companies start life from modest beginnings. An individual or individuals who go about setting up and forming a company will be engaged in a wide range of activities, ranging from the location, and perhaps, selling of start-up assets to the company on the one hand, to efforts designed to attract suitable investor capital, on the other. A difficulty for the promoter is that the law regards the promoter as being in a fiduciary relationship with the company being promoted.[184] Consequently, the promoter is under a duty to disclose any conflict of interest to the company.[185] Particularly, the promoter is under a duty to disclose to the company any advantage that the promoter has obtained by virtue of promoting the company. Failure to disclose any of these matters will constitute a breach of fiduciary duty. Thus for ex-

---

[181] Known as pre-incorporation contracts.

[182] And will remain so if the company decides not to adopt the transaction.

[183] *Erlanger v. New Sombrero Phosphate Co.* [1878] 3 A.C. 1218 (H.L.).

[184] *Components Tube Co Ltd v. Naylor* [1990] 2 I.R. 1; *Erlanger v. New Sombrero Phosphate Co* [1878] 3 A.C. 1218 (HL).

[185] *Erlanger v. New Sombrero Phosphate Co.* [1878] 3 A.C. 1218 (H.L.) where several of the directors of the company had breached their fiduciary duty as they had not revealed to the company that they were also the agents of the vendor of property sold to the company; in *Gluckstein v. Barnes* [1900] A.C. 240 the promoter-directors had breached their fiduciary duty as they had not revealed that they had made a secret profit out of property they had sold to the company.

ample, where the promoter gains financially arising from promotion activities, the promoter is under a duty to disclose such gains to the company, and furthermore is under a duty to account for such gains to the company unless the company's board of directors permits the promoter to retain the disclosed gains.

This necessity for disclosure and accountability arising from the fiduciary position of the promoter may cause the promoter to seek to find a means by which to avoid his (otherwise fiduciary) obligations. Given the promoter's close relationship with the fledgling company, this course of action, if pursued, may not always have happy consequences for the promoter. Apart from the fact that the promoter is a fiduciary with all the attendant obligations that being a fiduciary entails, there is the further complication that often promoters will be the sole company directors and members in the first instance. In this situation, two key issues will often arise for consideration.

The first issue is whether promoters may sit as a board and adopt on behalf of the company transactions with themselves.

The second issue, is whether the promoters in such circumstances may release themselves from their duty to account to the company for any advantage that may have accrued to themselves arising out of their promotion efforts.

Both of these issues will now be considered in turn.

(a) Promoter directors and the sale of promoters' property to the company

3–63 Where promoters are proposing to sell property to the company which they have formed, they must ensure that, in doing so, they do not compromise the position of the board of the company. For example, the promoters must disclose full information about the transaction to the board of directors charged with considering the adoption of the transaction on behalf of the company. Should this not occur, then the contract by which the property was sold to the company may be susceptible to being rescinded at later date by the company, when the true state of affairs becomes known.

In order to best protect themselves, promoters should therefore appoint an independent board of directors to the company. The promoters should disclose their ownership of the property to the board, and furnish all relevant information necessary to enable the directors to be able to make an informed judgement as to the market value of the promoter-owned property being acquired by the company.

However, in practice, the initial directors of a company are often either the promoters, or the promoters' agents. Therefore the question arises as to whether promoters (or their agents) can sit on the company board and adopt on behalf of the company, transactions with the promoters themselves. Although the dicta of Lord Cairns in the House of Lords in *Erlanger v. New Sombrero Phosphate Co.*[186] would appear to give the impression that promoters cannot sit on the board in such circumstances, when he observed:

> "I do not say that the owner of property may not promote and form a joint stock company, and then sell his property to it, but I do say that if he does he is bound to take care that he sells it to the company through the medium of an independent board of directors who can do and do exercise an independent and intelligent judgement on the transaction, and who are not left under the belief that the property belongs, not to the promoter, but to some other person."

it is submitted that this judicial statement should not be taken to mean that the promoters cannot themselves sit as a board in order to adopt transactions between themselves and the company.[187] In the subsequent Court of Appeals decision, *Lagunas Nitrate Co v. Lagunas Syndicate* Lindley M.R. stated that Lord Cairns remarks in *Erlanger* were not authority for the proposition that promoters could not sit on the board themselves for the purpose of adopting on behalf of the company a transaction concerning the sale of property by them to the company. In that case the Court of Appeals held that "[Erlanger] does not require or indeed justify the conclusion that if a company is avowedly formed with a board of directors who are not independent, but who are stated to be the intended vendors, or agents of the intended vendors, of property to the company, the company can set aside an agreement entered into by them for the purchase of such property simply because they are not an independent board."

Lindley M.R. felt compelled to so hold because the directors in *Lagunas* had openly admitted they were also promoters.

However, the danger in such a scenario (as ultimately turned out to be the case in *Lagunas*) is that while the promoters (sitting as direc-

---

[186] [1878] 3 A.C. 1218 (H.L.) at 1236.

[187] What Lord Cairns was really directing his attention to was the danger for promoters who pack the board with their own agents, where neither such fact nor their ownership of the property being acquired, is disclosed to the other independent directors. The problem in *Erlanger* arose from the fact that several of the directors charged with ratifying the transaction were undisclosed agents of the promoters. This was unknown to the independent directors, and furthermore, material details concerning the true market value of the property as well as the true identity of the vendors was not disclosed either. Hence, because of both in its flawed constitution (directors who did not disclose they were acting for the promoters) and the lack of disclosure of relevant information to the bona fide members (that the vendors were really the promoters), the board was not in a position to make an intelligent and independent appraisal of the wisdom of entering the transaction.

tors) can adopt the transaction between themselves and the company, they may run into difficulties subsequently when they seek to issue a prospectus for the purpose of attracting capital into the company. At this juncture, the new shareholders attracted in to the company, may seek to have the promoters/company transaction rescinded, alleging (for example) that the promoter dominated board of directors acquired the property on behalf of the company at an over-value. In this way, the new shareholders could seek recission of the contract on that ground (rather than the board's lack of independence *per se*) or perhaps seek the return of profit made by the promoters on the transaction.

Remedies such as recission and return of secret profit will be considered shortly below. However, before considering such matters, at this point it is first appropriate to consider whether promoters, who dominate the company board, may release themselves from their fiduciary duty to account to the company, for any advantage that may have accrued to them arising out of their promotion efforts.

(b) Whether the promoter-directors can release themselves from their duty to account to the company for any benefits accruing from the promotion activity

3–64   The promoters are fiduciaries in relation to the company. Hence, the issue arises as whether the promoters can have the board relieve them of their duty as fiduciaries to account to the company for any profits they may have made on transactions with the company. Where the promoters make full disclosure to an independent board, the board may decide to allow the promoters keep the profit. In this event, provided there has been no misrepresentation by the promoters, and the independent board acts bona fide, the promoters get effective release. However, in most company start-ups, the promoters will dominate the board, and so the question arises as to whether they can get a valid release from a board dominated by either themselves or their agents.

It is clear that promoters cannot release themselves from their fiduciary duties[188] merely by assembling as a board and voting on the matter.[189] Clearly the promoter directors' interests would have to be approved at a general meeting of the company's shareholders in order for them to be released from their fiduciary duty to account. Where the promoters control the board, disclosure to such a board for the purposes of being released from their duty to account for secret profit will not be deemed in law to be disclosure to an "impartial" board. Such a

---

[188] *Regal Hastings Ltd v. Gulliver* [1942] 1 All E.R. 378; *Gluckstein v. Barnes op. cit.*
[189] Normally a board of directors can release fiduciaries from their responsibilities, but not where the entire board consists of the fiduciaries seeking release.

board cannot release the promoters from their fiduciary duty to account for secret profit. The courts have insisted that in order to be released from fiduciary obligations in a manner consistent with law, disclosure must be made to a board that is made up of impartial directors who are not dominated by the promoters. In *Gluckstein v. Barnes* it was held that when the syndicate members who formed the company also constituted the board, disclosure of secret profits to such a board would not constitute effective disclosure as it would not have been disclosure to an impartial board. According to the Earl of Halsbury L.C.:

> "It is too absurd to suggest that a disclosure to the parties to this transaction is a disclosure to the company of which these directors [the syndicate members] were the proper guardians and trustees. They were there to do the work of the syndicate, that is to say, to cheat the shareholders. . . ."[190]

Lord MacNaghten added:

> "'Disclosure' is not the most appropriate word to use when a person who plays many parts announces to himself in one character what he has done and is doing in another. To talk of disclosure to the thing called the company when as yet there were no shareholders is a mere farce. To the intended shareholders there was no disclosure at all. On them was practised an elaborate system of deception."[191]

Thus, in order to release the promoters from their fiduciary duty to account, disclosure must be to an impartial board before disclosure can be effective in law, and any decision to release the promoters by a board consisting of promoters/directors or their agents cannot be accepted as effective release in law.[192]

Therefore, given these dilemmas for the promoter, the promoter might instead attempt to have the company ratify what the promoter has done, by getting ratification from the members of the company at a shareholders general meeting. This may be acceptable in law provided that certain parameters are respected. In *Salomon v. Salomon & Co.*[193] the promoter of a company formed it specially for the purpose of acquiring his own business from himself. However, the consideration offered by the company was probably significantly more than the business's real market value. Salomon held the bulk of the shares and the remaining shareholders were family members who owned a share

---

[190] [1900] A.C. 240 at 247.

[191] ibid. at 249.

[192] *Gluckstein v. Barnes* (1900) A.C. 240 at 249, *per* Lord MacNaghten; *Hopkins v. Shannon Transport Systems Ltd*, unreported, High Court, January 10, 1972.

[193] [1897] A.C. 22.

apiece. Salomon had the members, including himself, ratify the transfer *in full knowledge* of the terms of the transaction. It was held that, although the other shareholders were under the direction of Salomon (who in any event held the majority of the shares), nevertheless the approval of the transfer amounted to effective disclosure to the company and acceptance by it of the terms of the deal. Effectively therefore, Salomon's duty to account to the company for any excessive profits that he may have realised on the deal had been effectively disclosed, and released. This was because the other shareholders, being fully conversant with the terms of the transaction, approved it. Thus, it is clear that promoters of a company can form a company and sell property to it, realise a profit, and they will not be in breach of their fiduciary duties provided they have truthfully informed the company members about the transaction details and obtained their consent. However, interestingly, the House of Lords did intimate that release by shareholders in general meeting in such circumstances will only constitute effective disclosure to the company, *provided that* it is not envisaged that new outside shareholders will be encouraged to invest in the company shortly thereafter or in the future. Where any such new shareholders are invited in, they may attempt to have the transaction overturned.[194] As Keane succinctly puts it:

> "Where the company is formed as a "one man company", *i.e.* where virtually all the shares are owned by the promoter and he also nominates the directors, the duties owed by the promoter are of little importance. Where there are other investors – and most importantly of all where the public is invited to subscribe – his duties are of more significance."[195]

B. COMPANY ACTION AGAINST PROMOTER WHO HAS MADE SECRET PROFIT

(1) Return of secret profits ?

3–65 Company action against the promoter who has made a secret profit is unlikely to occur while the promoter dominates the company. However, the position may change when the promoters no longer have control over the board's functions, or where new shareholders, not under the influence of the promoter, invest in the company and start asking awkward questions. In *Gluckenstein v. Barnes*[196] promoters

---

[194] This was recognised by Lindley M.R. in *Lagunas Nitrate Co. v. Lagunas Syndicate* [1899] 2 Ch. 392 at 428.

[195] *Company Law in the Republic of Ireland* (2nd ed., Butterworths, Dublin, 1991), p. 68.

[196] *op.cit.*

formed a company and then sold an asset to the company without making full disclosure of all profit made by them in respect of the asset. When the company subsequently went into liquidation, the promoters were held to be accountable for such secret profits to the company on the basis that, as fiduciaries, they were bound to disclose all such profits.[197]

(2) Recission of the company's contract with the promoter?

3–66 Another remedy that may be open to the company would be to seek recission of the original contract under which the company originally purchased over-inflated assets from the promoters. However, in order to successfully obtain this remedy, the company must be in a position to satisfy somewhat onerous prerequisites, such as the abscence of *laches* and the possibility of *restitutio in integrum*.[198]

A case where recission of the contract between the company and the promoters was successfully obtained was *Erlanger v. New Sombrero Co.*[199] The promoters had purchased an island for mining purposes, and subsequently they sold the island to a company that had been specially formed by the promoters for the purpose of purchasing the island from them. The promoters' agents had dominated the initial board of the newly-formed company and adopted the transaction on behalf of the company. Subsequently, new shareholders were invited to subscribe in the company and it became apparent in due course to the new shareholders that full disclosure of the history of the acquisition of the island had not been made to them. They replaced the promoters' puppet directors with impartial directors, who then instituted legal action to rescind the contract for the purchase of the island.

It was held by the House of Lords that the company was entitled to repudiate the contract as the company never had had the opportunity of exercising, through independent directors, an independent mind on the transaction because the promoters' puppet directors had not revealed to the other directors on the board that they were agents of the vendors (the promoters) at the time the contract was concluded. Lord Penzance proclaimed:

---

[197] As seen above at para. 3–64, the promoter directors could not claim in law that because they had been both vendors and directors, they had made effective disclosure of such secret profits (so that they could effectively have regarded themselves as released from the duty to account for secret profits): see *dicta* of Halsbury L.C. and Lord MacNaghten above at para. 3–64.

[198] *Laches* and *restitutio in integrum* are considered in greater detail above at paras 3–17—3–20 when investor attempts to rescind a contract of allotment are considered.

[199] [1878] 3 A.C. 1218 (H.L.).

> "Can a contract so obtained be allowed to stand? The bare statement of facts is, I think, sufficient to condemn it. From that statement I invite your Lordships to draw two conclusions: first, that the company never had the opportunity of exercising, through independent directors, a fair and independent judgment upon the subject of the purchase; and secondly, that this result was brought about by the conduct and contrivance of the vendors themselves they were, as it seems to me, bound according to the principles acted upon in the Courts of Equity, if they wished to make a valid contract of sale to the company, to nominate independent directors and fully disclose the material facts."[200]

Furthermore, the House of Lords held that the company was not bound by laches from seeking recission merely because the shareholders had not instituted legal action immediately. The shareholders could not be faulted for having first sought information from the company; appointing a committee of inspection; and appointing new directors, before resolving to institute legal action promptly once appraised of the full facts.

It is interesting to note that while this case was referred to approvingly in *Lagunas Nitrate Co v. Lagunas Syndicate*,[201] it was distinguished on the basis that in the *Lagunas* case, the promoter-directors had made no secret of the fact that they were agents of the promoter, Lagunas Syndicate, nor of their express purpose (which was to ensure that the newly-formed *Lagunas Nitrate Company* acquired mine assets from the promoter).

Two distinct situations are involved. In *Erlanger* the promoter-dominated directors concealed their links to the vendor thereby enabling the company to subsequently repudiate the contract they had caused the company to enter. Whereas in *Lagunas*, the company formed by promoter-directors had entered into a transaction where the promoters had made no attempt to conceal their status as vendors of the asset to the company, and consequently, there were no grounds for recission *on this ground* as the directors had not concealed their dual status. In *Lagunas*, the court emphasised that the situation would be otherwise if the promoter-directors had misrepresented material facts, or had been fraudulent at the time of the contract as to their dual role.

3–67 *Lagunas* is an interesting case for other reasons. Although the court found that there was no breach of fiduciary duty when the promoter-directors had adopted the contract on behalf of the newly-formed company, it went on to find that there had not been full disclosure in the subsequently published prospectus that the promoters had issued

---

[200] [1878] 3 A.C. 1218 (H.L.) at 1229.
[201] [1899] 2 Ch. 392 at 425 *per* Lindley M.R.

inviting subscribers to invest in the company's shares. Accordingly, the court held that the company would be entitled in such circumstances to seek to rescind the contract on the basis that the promoter-directors had never represented a frank view of the mines' prospects to the company. This seems curious as one would have expected that it would be the shareholders and not the company that would be seeking relief.[202] At first glance this seems to contradict what the court had earlier held, but it does not. The court distinguished between the promoters not disguising from the company their role as vendors at the time of the contract (hence no breach of fiduciary duty) and, on the other hand, the promoters not disclosing full information on the mines to the company. The court explained how, although the promoters had full knowledge about the mines in their capacity *qua* promoters (former owners of the mine), such information could not be imputed to the company merely because they also were the directors as they had not acquired the information *qua* directors. Consequently, there had not been full disclosure to the company (breach of fiduciary duty) and furthermore the breach was compounded by the prospectus which the court found gave misleading[203] information about the mines. Accordingly, the company had grounds upon which to seek to rescind the contract.

However, before recission will be granted, certain prerequisites have to be satisfied, such as *laches* and *restitutio in integrum*. In *Erlanger* the issue arose as to whether the doctrine of *laches* would prevent the company from seeking recission on the basis that the company did not take legal action at an earlier time. The court acknowledged that although slothness of action is often fatal to recission being granted, this is not the position when the company was not in a position to take action until it had an independent will. Once the company acquired such a will, then action should be taken and delay should not be excessive.

Ultimately, this is where the action in *Lagunas* failed. There will be situations where the court is unwilling to grant recission either because the interval between the date of the impugned transaction and the company resolving to take action may be such that delay is excessive, or because *restitutio in integrum*[204] is no longer possible. In *Lagunas*, recission was not granted because the mines, sold by the promoters to

---

[202] It is interesting to note that Lindley M.R. noted that no shareholder had ever alleged that the prospectus was misleading – the court so found as a result of its own examination of the prospectus.

[203] Though not fraudulent.

[204] In *Northern Bank Finance Corp. v. Charlton & Ors.* [1979] I.R. 149, the Supreme Court refused to order recission where *restitutio in integrum* was not possible.

the company, had been so transformed by company mining operations that it would no longer be possible to place the parties back in their original position as required by a strict interpretation of the *restitutio* requirement. However, the dissent of Rigby L.J. is noteworthy. The learned judge was in favour of granting recission, taking the view that that any alteration of the mines was due principally to promoter-motivated company action as the promoters had initially controlled the company's actions for a time. Furthermore, he rejected the view that there had been undue delay (*laches*), again on the basis that the promoter-directors had dominated the company initially. Therefore, the learned judge took the view that time did not begin to run until the influence of the promoters over the company had ceased. Accordingly, in the learned judge's view, the delay should not be regarded as that of a company whose shareholders had always been fully familiar with the promoters' deeds. Furthermore, the fact that the mines had been worked on, such that *restitutio in integrum* was therefore no longer possible, was no barrier to a grant of recission according to the learned judge. The learned judge was of the view that the appropriate remedy would be a grant of recission accompanied by a measure of compensation to the promoter in respect of the changed asset. Rigby's dissent was referred to approvingly, albeit in a somewhat different context in *O'Sullivan v. Management Agency and Music Ltd*[205] where it appears that the court adopted the view that the court exercising equitable jurisdiction should, if the justice of the case so requires, not necessarily feel compelled to refuse a grant of recission, merely because *restitutio* is not strictly attainable. In that case the court looked at the merits and equity of the situation before it which involved an unconscionable contract which unduly favoured a young musician's management, to the detriment of the musician. In such a situation, the court was prepared to grant recission of the contract, accompanied by an award of compensation for the musician to reflect lost royalties, and a measure of compensation for the management to compensate for their efforts in promoting the musician's career. The compensation reflects the fact that the parties could no longer be returned to their original position. By analogy, if such an approach were to be taken today in the context of promoters' liability, perhaps the strict authority of *Lagunas* might not be followed where the justice of the case would be better satisfied by a grant of recission accompanied by a measure of compensation for one or either parties to reflect changes to the asset, their position, etc. However, where there has been excessive delay, the court would still be entitled to refuse recission.

---

[205] [1985] 3 All E.R. 351.

C. PROMOTERS AND PLC's

(1) Companies (Amendment) Act 1983

3–68 In 1983, the Companies (Amendment) Act introduced provisions which are designed to prevent, *inter alia*, certain[206] promoters of the company from taking advantage of the company by selling it assets at an over-inflated value. Unfortunately there is no similar provision for non-plc's. The Act obliges the plc to comply with independent valuation and reporting requirements in respect of sizeable[207] transactions concerning "non-cash assets". A non-cash asset[208] is defined as any property or interest in such property, other than cash.

(a) "Relevant person"

3–69 Section 32(1) provides that a plc shall not enter into an agreement to purchase non-cash assets with relevant persons for a sum equal in value to at least one-tenth of the nominal value of the company's issued share capital unless the requirements of section 32 have been satisfied. A "relevant person" means, in the case of a company formed as a plc, any person who was a subscriber to the memorandum of the company.[209] In the case of a company re-registered as a plc or a company registered as a plc pursuant to section 18 (joint stock companies), it means any person who was a member of the company on the date of re-registration[210] or registration,[211] respectively. Effectively therefore, a promoter who does not fall within any of these three categories will not be caught by this regime.

(b) "Initial period"

3–70 Section 32 only applies, if at all, to transactions made within the "initial period", which is defined as, in the case of a company formed as a plc, two years from the date from which it is entitled to do business.[212] In the case of a company which was re-registered as a plc the initial period is two years from the date of re-registration, and in the

---

[206] The phrase "certain" is used because, as the paragraph below on "Relevant Persons" demonstrates, not all promoters will be "relevant persons".

[207] According to s. 32(1), a transaction is of the requisite size where it is equal in value to at least one tenth of the nominal issued share capital of the company.

[208] s.2.

[209] s.32(2)(a).

[210] s.32(2)(b).

[211] s.32(2)(b).

[212] s.32(2)(a).

case of a joint stock company registered as a plc under section 18, two years from the date of such registration.[213]

(c) Size of transaction and valuer's report

3–71 Where the transaction satisfies both the relevant person and initial period requirements, it then has to be considered whether the transaction is sufficiently sizeable. In other words, is the non-cash asset being transferred to the company at least equal in value to one-tenth of the company's issued nominal capital.[214] Where this is so, the section requires that the non-cash asset be independently valued and a copy of the valuer's report given to the company in the six months prior to the date of the agreement to acquire the asset.[215] In addition, it is required that the terms of the agreement must be approved by the members by ordinary resolution, and the members must have the valuer's[216] report furnished to them in advance of the meeting to vote on the resolution.[217] The valuer's report will be expected to contain statements on several matters including, *inter alia*, the method and date of valuation; the amount to be paid by the company; a statement that the asset is not less than the value of the consideration being paid by the company; where other persons assisted in the valuation, a statement explaining why it was reasonable for the valuer to accept their assistance.[218]

(d) Exclusion of certain transactions

3–72 This section, however, excludes the acquisition of key assets from its scope of application. Section 32(4) provides that, *inter alia*, where it is part of the normal course of a company's business to acquire or arrange for others to acquire assets of a particular description, then any such agreement shall fall outside section 32.

(e) Sanctions for contravention

(i) Where consideration does not include shares

3–73 Where a plc enters into an agreement to acquire an asset in contravention of section 32 and *either* the relevant person has not received the valuer's report *or* some contravention of section 32 had occurred

---

[213] s.32(2)(b).
[214] s.32(1).
[215] s.32(3).
[216] ss.(5) specifies the qualifications that the valuer must have.
[217] s.32(3).
[218] For further and more detailed particulars of how the valuer is to operate, see ss. 30(5)(7) and (8) which are incorporated by reference into s. 32.

which he knew or ought to have known amounted to a contravention, then section 32(7) provides for the following consequences. First, the company will be entitled to recover from the relevant person any consideration given by the company under the agreement or an amount equivalent to its value at the time of the agreement.[219] Secondly, the transaction will be void in so far as it has not been carried out.[220]

(ii) Where consideration does include shares

3–74   Where, however, the agreement entered into by the company in contravention of section 32 was an agreement which involved the company allotting shares in itself to the relevant person, either as part or all of the consideration for the acquisition of the non-cash asset, then section 32(7) sanctions shall not apply to the part of the agreement that concerns consideration in the form of the company's shares.[221] Instead, that part of the sale agreement will be treated as if it constituted a breach of section 30 of the Act.[222] Accordingly, instead of section 32(7) sanctions being relevant to the part of the agreement for which company shares were the consideration,[223] section 32(8) treats such an agreement as being in contravention of section 30 of the Act, in which event sections 26(4) and 30(10) become applicable.

Under section 30, a company shall not allot shares in itself for non-cash consideration unless they have been subjected to an independent valuation. Where this valuation scheme has not been conducted in accordance with the Act's requirements, then section 30(10) provides that the allottee shall be liable to pay the company an amount equal to the nominal value of the shares, together with the whole of any premium and interest. Section 26(4) provides a defence to such liability in respect of *subsequent* purchasers for value of the shares who either were not actually aware that an earlier owner of the shares had contravened Section 30, or, had acquired the shares from another *bona fide* purchaser. However, if the subsequent purchaser cannot invoke these defences, joint and several liability applies such that the subsequent purchaser could be liable to pay whatever amount the contravener was liable to pay to the company.

Thus, it can be seen how, where shares form part of the consideration for the acquisition of the non-cash asset made in contravention of section 32, the Companies Act allows the transaction to be enforced,

---

[219] s.32(7)(a).
[220] s.32(7)(b).
[221] s.32(8)(a).
[222] s.32(8)(b).
[223] (a) void in so far as not carried out, and (b) the company being entitled to recover any consideration given, or an equivalent amount.,

but with recompense to the company. On the other hand, where section 32(7) applies, the transaction will be rendered void in so far as it has not been carried out, and there will also be recompense to the company (as would be the case if section 32(7) applied in its entirety).[224]

---

[224] s.30 is also considered at Ussher *op. cit.* pp. 310–315; Forde *op. cit.* p. 195 and paras 6.57–59; and Keane, *Company Law in the Republic of Ireland* (2nd ed., Butterworths, Dublin, 1991), at pp. 90–91.

4

Insider Dealing

I. **Insider Dealing** 199
   A. Introduction 199
   B. Common Law 200
   C. Statutory Regime 205
      (1) Dealing 206
         (a) Territorial scope 208
      (2) Securities 210
         (a) Recognised Stock Exchange 211
         (b) Off-market dealings in 'securities' 211
         (c) Securities issued or proposed to be issued,
             whether in the State or otherwise 212
         (d) Transactions involving professional
             intermediaries 213
      (3) Inside Information 214
         ·(a) Not Generally Available 215
         (b) Likely materially to affect the price of the
             securities 218
         (c) Information of a precise nature 220
         (d) The securities 223
      (4) Insiders 224
         (a) Primary Insiders 224
            (i) How must connected person have come
                 into possession of information 225
            (ii) Connected to the company 226
            (iii) Mere "possession" sufficient 228
            (iv) The United Kingdom legislation
                 (comparative overview) 228
         (b) Secondary Insiders ('Tipees') 230
            (i) No need for connection to the company 231
            (ii) Liability test 231
            (iii) "Directly or indirectly" 232
            (iv) The new United Kingdom legislation
                 (comparative overview) 232
         (c) Causing and Procuring 233
         (d) Communication of inside information 235

       (i) Points of distinction 237
     (e) Directors and securities options............................... 238
     (f) Companies as insider dealers 239
       (i) Chinese wall structures 240
       (ii) Mere information that company proposes
           to deal 241
       (iii) Company dealing in own securities 241
  (5) Exempt Transactions 242
     (a) Section 110 exemptions 242
     (b) Section 108 exemptions 243
       (i) Execution-only agents...................................... 243
       (ii) Seven-day Window 244
  (6) The Yellow Book's Model Code.................................... 245
  (7) Grounds for liability under Part V 248
     (a) Civil liability... 248
       (i) Compensation for loss 249
       (ii) Account for profit 251
     (b) Criminal liability 253
       (i) Offences... 253
       (ii) Penalties 254
       (iii) Agents.. 254
       (iv) Unresolved issues 254
     (c) Enforcement of criminal liability 255
       (i)   Relevant Authority.. 255
       (ii)   Duty to report insider dealing 256
       (iii) Direction to Relevant Authority to act........... 256
       (iv) Investigation powers 256
       (v)   Role of court in determining ambit of
            investigation 257
       (vi) Obligationof professional secrecy.................. 257
       (vii) Duty to co-operate with other EC
            Stock Exchanges 258
       (viii) Annual Report of recognised
            Stock Exchange 258
II. **Manipulation of the Stock Market** 259
  A. Market Manipulation 259
   (1) How the market may be manipulated........................... 259
   (2) Companies (Amendment) Act 1999 –
       Stabilisation Rules 260
     (a) Relevant Securities 260
     (b) Stabilising Periods.. 261
       (i) Within the State.. 261
       (ii) Outside the State.. 262
     (c) Preliminary Steps Before Stabilising Action 262

       (i) Reasonable belief 262

       (ii) Modification where Stabilisation occurs
           outside the State 263

       (iii) associated securities 263

   (d) Stabilising Action 264

   (e) Action ancillary to Stabilising Action 264

   (f) Limits on Stabilisation Price 265

       (i) Relevant Securities and Certain Associated
           Companies 265

       (ii) Certain other Associated Securities 266

       (iii) Associated Call Options 267

   (g) Termination of Stabilising Period 267

   (h) Recording of Stabilisation Transactions 267

   (i) Stabilisation Rules and the Companies Act 1990
       disclosure rules regarding relevant share
       capital 268

(3) Stock Exchange regime to prevent market
    manipulation 268

Insider Dealing

INSIDER DEALING[1]

INTRODUCTION

4–01 Part V of the Companies Act 1990 provides a statutory regime for regulating insider dealing for the first time in Ireland. Apart from government's desire to have such legislation in place,[2] the enactment of Part V was also motivated by Ireland's obligation to implement EEC

---

[1] On Insider Dealing in Ireland, see Ashe and Murphy, *Insider Dealing* (Round Hall Press, Dublin, 1992); Keane, *Company Law in the Republic of Ireland* (2nd ed., Butterworths, Dublin, 1991), Chap. 36; Forde, *Company Law* (2nd ed., Mercier Press, Dublin, 1992) at pp. 162–166; MacCann, "Liability for Insider Dealing" (June & July 1991 issues) I.L.T., pp. 130 and 151; Rider and Ashe, "The Insider Dealing Directive" in Rider and Ashe (eds.), *The Fiduciary, the Insider and the Conflict* (Brehon Sweet and Maxwell, Dublin, 1995) at pp.15-50; McCormack, *The New Companies Legislation,* (Round Hall Press, Dublin, 1991), Chap. 7; Binchy and Byrne, *Annual Review of Irish Law* (Round Hall Press, Dublin, 1990) at pp. 81–88; Flynn, "Insider Trading in Ireland: the new regime" (1991) 11 I.C.C.L.R. 361; Dudley and Casey, "Ireland" in Wegen and Heinz-Dieter Assman (eds.), *Insider Trading in Western Europe: Current Status* (Graham and Trotman, London, 1994), Chap. 9.

On various insider dealing issues internationally, see Herne, "Inside Information: Definitions in Australia, Canada, The U.K., And the U.S." (March 1986) 88 Journal of Comparative Business and Capital Markets Law, 1; White, "Towards a Policy Basis for the Regulation of Insider Dealing" 90 L.Q.R. 494; Lowry, "The International Approach to Insider Trading: the Council of Europe's Convention" (1990) J.B.L. 460; Ashe, "Insider Dealing" (1990) 11 Company Lawyer 127; Alcock, "Insider Dealing: an unholy mess" (1993, January 8 issue) N.L.J. 21.

For economic analyses, see Grossman, "An analysis of the role of 'Insider Trading' on Futures Markets" (1986) 59 Journal of Business no. 2 (part 2) S129; Givoly and Palmon, "Insider Trading and the Exploitation of Inside Information: Some Empirical Evidence" (1985) 58 Journal of Business (no. 1) 69; Haddock, "Regulation on demand: a private interest model with an application to Insider Trading" (1987) 30 Journal of Law and Economics 311.

[2] Though *cf.* Keane, *Company Law in the Republic of Ireland* (Dublin, 1991), p. 394 where that learned author considers whether the relatively small Irish market justifies legislation of such complexity.

Directive 89/592 on Insider Dealing.[3] The Directive's preamble states that the Community wished to ensure that co-ordinated rules were adopted on insider dealing throughout the Member States. The aim of such co-ordination is to ensure the smooth operation of the market, the combating of transfrontier insider dealing, and the promotion of investor confidence in the market. Accordingly, the Directive laid down a set of requirements which all Member States were obliged to ensure were reflected in their domestic law. Part V of the 1990 Act implemented the Directive in Ireland, with effect from December 27, 1990.[4]

COMMON LAW

4–02   Before examining the impact of the statutory regime set out in Part V of the Companies Act 1990 in detail, it is first necessary to consider the common law principles applicable to insider dealing. This is necessary for several reasons. To begin with, the statutory regime only applies to insider dealing in securities in respect of which the Stock Exchange provides dealing facilities.[5] Hence, the common law remains relevant as the applicable law to insider dealing in non-quoted securities and therefore has not been rendered obsolete by the enactment of the statutory regime in so far as such securities are concerned. Furthermore, even in relation to dealings in securities to which Part V applies, the Act recognises that the civil remedy provided by section 109[6] of the Act is "without prejudice to any other cause of action."[7] In this respect, the common law may – even if somewhat inadequately – supplement the statutory regime. Finally, an understanding of the relevant common law principles facilitates a more complete appreciation of the impact of the statutory regime on insider dealing law in Ireland.

Traditionally, the common law has not been of much assistance to

---

[3]   Council Directive of 13 November 1989 co-ordinating regulations on insider dealing (89/592 E.E.C.), [1989] O.J. L334/30 (18.11.89). See Hopt, "The European Insider Dealing Directive" (1990) 27 C.M.L. Rev. 51; Davies, "The European Community's Directive on Insider dealing: from Company Law to Securities Markets Regulation?" (Spring 1991) Oxford Journal of Legal Studies 92; Wymeersch, "The Regulation of Insider Dealing within the European Community" (October 1990) Conference Paper, Irish Center for European Law. On the Directive's implementation in Ireland by Part V, see Rider and Ashe (eds.), *The Fiduciary, the Insider and the Conflict* (Brehon Sweet and Maxwell, Dublin, 1995), pp. 31–50 and see n. 1 generally above.

[4]   S.I. No. 336 of 1990.

[5]   s.107.

[6]   To compensate aggrieved shareholders and account to the company for any profits that the insider dealer makes.

[7]   s.109(1).

shareholders who felt cheated by insider dealing. Little protection was provided by the common law in respect of the use of inside information *per se*. An aggrieved shareholder would have to attempt to invoke other remedies such as deceit, which are traditionally difficult to prove.[8] Although company directors were under fiduciary duties to their company, no such duties were ordinarily owed to shareholders of the company. Thus, directors could use inside information to enrich themselves at the expense of the company's shareholders without fearing that they were breaching any fiduciary duty to the shareholders. Where shareholders had been unfairly taken advantage of by company insiders, the law only afforded protection if special circumstances were found such that a fiduciary relationship was deemed to have arisen between the insider and the shareholder. Cases where insiders would have to compensate investors were rare, and the attaching of criminal liability was not an undue concern in the minds of insiders. In the ordinary course of events, the courts were unwilling to recognise the existence of a fiduciary duty between the *company insider* and the shareholder. Given such a judicial climate, it is not difficult to appreciate how reluctant the courts were to recognise any such relationship or duty between *non-company insider dealers* and aggrieved shareholders.

Finally, were the shareholder to attempt to take a personal action against the company for the diminution in the value of the shareholding arising out of insider dealing, it would be unlikely to succeed as the courts would analyse the dispute in the context of whether the insiders, when they acted as they did, subjectively felt that their actions were in the best interests of the company. Invariably, unless mala fides could be demonstrated, such a view would be upheld.

4–03 *Percival v. Wright*[9] is authority for the proposition that even though the directors are under a fiduciary duty to the company when they engage in insider dealing, they are under no such duty to any affected shareholder in that company.[10] In this judgment, shareholders in a company offered to sell their shares to the directors of the company. The directors bought the shares at a certain price from the shareholders. However, unknown to the shareholders, at the time the directors acquired their shares, the directors were engaged in takeover negotiations with a third party interested in acquiring the company's shares at a higher price. Although ultimately the takeover did not take

---

[8] See Chap. 3 above.
[9] [1902] 2 Ch. 421.
[10] More than any other, this decision demonstrated the rather unsympathetic view the courts adopted when considering legal actions brought by shareholders aggrieved by company insiders' dealing activities.

place, the shareholders sought recission of the sale of their shares to the directors, on the ground that the directors as company insiders should have revealed to them that the takeover negotiations were in progress. The shareholders' action failed for three reasons.

First, the court held that if a general obligation were to be imposed on directors, before they brought the shares, to disclose that negotiations were in progress, then this would stifle corporate activity. Second, the court held that the directors owe a duty to the company to manage its affairs as best they think fit, and the circumstances of the case were not such as to warrant an exception so that a similar duty be owed to the shareholders. The court elaborated by stating that the shareholders, being familiar with the company's memorandum and articles of association, are well aware of the scope and extent of the directors' powers. Therefore, they are fixed with the knowledge that the directors could be involved in exercising any of those powers at the time of dealing with the shareholders, such as negotiating the sale of the company to a third party. Third, there was no question of the directors having acted unfairly as it was the shareholders who had approached the directors offering their shares for sale, and not the other way around.[11]

4–04   After *Percival v. Wright* it was clear that the courts were not willing to be receptive to shareholder legal action seeking redress against company insiders who clearly had used insider information to profit personally at the shareholders' expense. *A fortiori,* an aggrieved shareholder could expect even less sympathy where a *non-company* party had used inside information to profit at the expense of the shareholder. However, the harshness of *Percival v. Wright* has been ameliorated somewhat by *Allen v. Hyatt*[12] where the Privy Council distinguished *Percival v. Wright*.

In the *Allen* decision it was found that the directors had approached their shareholders and encouraged the shareholders to sell options on their company shares to them. This was at a time when takeover negotiations were secretly going on behind the scenes involving the board and third parties. Later the directors exercised the options and profited handsomely. The Privy Council held that, by approaching the shareholders, the directors had in effect become their agents. In an agent/principal relationship fiduciary duties are owed. In this case,

---

[11] Had the company in question been a public company whose shares had dealing facilities provided for them on a recognised Stock Exchange post–1990, then the result of the case would be very different as s.108 of the Act would deem the directors' action to be insider dealing.

[12] [1914] 30 T.L.R. 444.

the shareholders were entitled to assume that, as the directors had made the initial approach, the directors were acting in their interests. Consequently, the court would permit the shareholders to sue the insiders for any profits they had made on the transaction, because agents must account to principals for all profits under normal agent/principal principles. Thus the court was able to distinguish this situation (and thus allow recovery of profits) from *Percival v. Wright* where the transaction was at arm's length.

In *Coleman v. Myers*[13] the New Zealand courts further distinguished *Percival v. Wright*, holding that in an appropriate situation fiduciary duties could arise as between shareholders and directors dealing in the company's securities in circumstances where it was obvious that the shareholders put their trust in the directors for advice and the directors unfairly exploited that position. In such a situation, the courts may be willing to imply that the directors had assumed fiduciary responsibilities to the shareholders. *Coleman v. Myers* concerned a dispute in a small family company where the insider, the managing director, had kept the true value of the company's assets (and hence the true value of the company's shares) from the shareholders. From the facts of the case, it was clear that the shareholders relied heavily on the managing director to give them accurate information about the company. The shareholders sold their shares to the managing director, who profited from the transaction. The Court of Appeal distinguished *Percival v. Wright*, holding that fiduciary duties can arise between shareholders and company insiders in circumstances where the insider could be regarded as having assumed responsibilities towards the shareholders.

The circumstances in which such a fiduciary duty can arise were summarised by Woodhouse J.[14] as follows:

> "It is... an area of the law where the courts can and should find some practical means of giving effect to sensible and fair principles of commercial morality in the cases that come before them; and while it may not be possible to lay down any general test as to when the fiduciary duty will arise for a company director or to prescribe the exact conduct which will always discharge it when it does, there are nevertheless some factors that will usually have an influence upon a decision one way or the other. They include, I think, dependence upon information and advice, the existence of a relationship of confidence, the significance of some particular transaction for the parties and of course, the extent of any positive action taken by or on behalf of the director or directors to promote it."

---

[13] [1977] 2 N.Z.L.R. 225 and 298.
[14] *ibid.* at p.325.

This statement was expressly quoted approvingly by Keane J. in the Irish Supreme Court in *Crindle Investments and Others v. Wymes, and Others*[15] in 1998. Although the matter before the Supreme Court was not an insider dealing matter as such,[16] nevertheless it must be taken as an authoritative statement of the present day courts more circumspect view of *Percival v. Wright*, as Keane J. elaborated:

> "There can be no doubt that, in general, although directors of a company occupy a fiduciary position in relation to the company, they do not owe a fiduciary duty, merely by virtue of their offices, to the individual members. That was the effect of the decision in the leading case of *Percival v. Wright* [1902] 2 Ch. 421 but it has been emphasised in subsequent decisions that, in particular circumstances, a company director may indeed be in a position where he owes a fiduciary duty to individual shareholders. A helpful example is the decision of the New Zealand Court of Appeal in *Coleman v. Myers* 2 N.Z.L.R. 225 which is referred to in the judgment under appeal [to this court]."[17]

Although on the facts of the case, the Supreme Court found that there were no circumstances such as those described by Woodhouse J. that might give rise to the imputation of a fiduciary duty,[18] the authoritative statement by Keane J. clearly indicates that the Irish courts will impute a fiduciary duty into the director/shareholder relationship where the circumstances so warrant.

4–05 Therefore, at common law, while *Percival v. Wright* is still authority to the extent that company directors normally owe no fiduciary duties to the shareholders where their acts of non-disclosure are relevant to the value of the company's securities,[19] the application of *Percival v. Wright* appears to be limited in two key respects. First, it may well be otherwise if the facts of the particular situation give rise to the imputation of a fiduciary duty, such that the directors are held to have impliedly assumed some sort of responsibility for the shareholders' interests.[20] Second, where dealing facilities are provided for securities by the Stock Exchange, then *Percival v. Wright* cannot be relied upon to prevent liability for insider dealing arising. This is because,

---

[15] [1998] 2 I.L.R.M. 275.

[16] The case concerned *inter alia* the issue of whether the directors of a company owed a fiduciary duty to shareholders of a company in circumstances where the directors refusal to compromise litigation claims was frustrating the settlement of litigation against the company.

[17] [1998] 2 I.L.R.M. 275 at 286.

[18] As the Court found that the relationship between the parties had never been one of mutual trust or confidence in the events that led to the litigation.

[19] Forde; McCormack, *op. cit.* at n.1 both agree with this view.

[20] Ashe and Murphy, *op. cit.* at n.1, p.53.

under the statutory regime, it is not a prerequisite for the grounding of liability that a fiduciary duty be found to exist. Instead, liability is grounded upon the occurrence of insider dealing.

4–06 Even if the company insider manages to avoid common law liability to aggrieved shareholders, nevertheless, the insider will still have breached fiduciary duties owed to the company. Company insiders are under a fiduciary duty to the company not to abuse their position by personally profiting from their privileged position *vis-à-vis* the company.[21] *Regal (Hastings) v. Gulliver*[22] is authority for the proposition that this fiduciary duty is applicable even where the directors' actions were bona fide for the good of the company. Consequently, applying such principles where company insiders use inside information when dealing in company securities, it is clear that insiders are under a fiduciary duty to account to the company for any secret profits thereby made (unless the company permits them to retain the profit). However, while the company itself could pursue the insider, this will often be unlikely to occur as the insiders may control the company.

Even if the company is willing to take action against the insider, there are several unsatisfactory aspects with such a course of action from the aggrieved shareholder's perspective. Any insider profit recovered will be for the benefit of the company, not the aggrieved shareholders. Furthermore, the company's attempt may only be half-hearted. Even if a shareholders' derivative action is mounted in the name of the company, the shareholders' position is not that much assuaged as again, even if such an action was 'successful', it may be difficult to demonstrate any measurable loss to the company itself – and if any such loss could be proved, any award would be in the company's favour, not the shareholders'.

THE STATUTORY REGIME

4–07 The enactment of Part V of the Companies Act 1990,[23] heralded a dramatic improvement from the relatively weak legal protection that

---

[21] For a general illustration of the operation of fiduciary principles generally, see *Boardman v. Phipps* [1967] 2 A.C. 46. For examples of situations where company directors were held to have abused their positions to personally profit by appropriating for their own benefit opportunities offered to their companies, see *IDC Ltd v. Cooley* [1972] 2 All E.R. 162 and *Canadian Aero Services Ltd v. O' Malley* [1974] S.C.R. 592.

[22] [1942] 1 All E.R. 378.

[23] Part V was brought into effect by S.I. No. 336 of 1990 with effect from December 27, 1990.

the common law afforded to the victims of insider dealing. However, as already noted above, this statutory regime only applies in respect of securities for which dealing facilities are provided by a "recognised stock exchange."[24] Part V was implemented in response to the obligations imposed by EEC Directive 89/592 on Insider Dealing.[25] Unlike comparable United Kingdom legislation[26] which only provides for criminal liability, Part V of the 1990 Act provides for both civil and criminal liability. Before proceeding to examine the specific prohibitions in Part V, it is first necessary to be familiar with the scope of certain key terms that are used in the legislation.

(1) "Dealing"

4–08   Section 107 defines dealing as follows:

> "dealing" in relation to securities, means (whether as principal or agent) acquiring, disposing of, subscribing for or underwriting the securities, or making or offering to make, or inducing or attempting to induce a person to make or to offer to make, an agreement –
>
> (a) for or relating to acquiring, disposing of, subscribing for or underwriting the securities; or
> (b) the purpose or purported purpose of which is to secure a profit or gain to a person who acquires, disposes of, subscribes for or underwrites the securities or to any of the parties to the agreement in relation to the securities.

In order for Part V to apply there must be "dealing" in relation to any of the defined "securities".[27] Unfortunately, while section 107 defines "dealing" very extensively, the wording and physical layout of the definition is very poor and does not read logically unless it is reconstructed as follows. It is necessary to break the definition into two limbs. The first is that one who is acquiring, disposing of, subscribing for, or underwriting[28] the securities (whether as principal or agent) can be

---

[24] Defined in s.107 to mean securities issued or proposed to be issued, whether in the State or otherwise, for which dealing facilities will be provided on a recognised Stock Exchange. See further para 4–13 below.

[25] For further analysis of the Directive's provisions and legislative history see Hopt, "The European Insider Dealing Directive" (1990) 27 C.M.L. Rev. 51; Davies, "The European Community's Directive on Insider dealing: from Company Law to Securities Markets Regulation?" (Spring 1991) Oxford Journal of Legal Studies 92; Wymeersch, "The Regulation of Insider Dealing within the European Community" (October 1990) Conference Paper, Irish Center for European Law; Ashe and Murphy, *op. cit.* and Ashe and Rider, *op.cit* (both at n. 1 above).

[26] U.K. Criminal Justice Act 1993, Part V(ss. 52–64) brought into force on March 1, 1994 by S.I. No. 242 of 1994.

[27] Defined below in "Securities" at para. 4–12.

[28] Defined to include sub-underwriting.

"dealing". The second limb defines "dealing" as also including making or offering to make, inducing or attempting to induce a person to make or to offer to make, an agreement either

(a) for or relating to acquiring, disposing of, subscribing for or underwriting the securities, or

(b) the purpose or purported purpose of which is to secure a profit or gain to a person who acquires, disposes of, subscribes for, or underwrites the securities or to any of the parties to the agreement in relation to the securities.

4–09   Seen in this light, this definition is extremely wide. Furthermore, a cursory initial reading of the definition in the Act might suggest that the transaction must, as a prerequisite, have as its purpose or purported purpose the securing of a profit or gain, in order to constitute "dealing". Paragraph (b) appears to have such a requirement but it is not conclusive from the wording of the entire definition that this is in all cases a prerequisite for "dealing". For example, the first limb of the definition (as reconstructed) does not have any such profit requirement, and indeed paragraph (a) of the second limb has no such requirement either.[29] McCormack notes that the "purpose or purported purpose requirement" in paragraph (b) might have been intended to reflect the aim of an exemption in corresponding United Kingdom legislation which permits individuals in possession of inside information to nevertheless deal in the securities if their motive[30] was not to make a profit or avoid a loss on the transaction, but to meet other obligations such as tax liabilities. In this regard, it is interesting to note Chapter 16 of the Yellow Book Model Code paragraph 9 of which provides that a director of a listed company who is otherwise prohibited from dealing pursuant to Chapter 16's Model Code, may be permitted by the company to sell (but not purchase) securities owned by the director in the company in order to meet a "pressing financial commitment on the part of the director that cannot otherwise be satisfied". McCormack

---

[29] Ashe and Murphy, *op. cit.* at n. 1 above, p. 74, paraphrase the definition in similar fashion (without commenting). *cf.* McCormack, *op. cit.* at n. 1 above, p. 119, who does not appear to break the definition into two limbs, instead reading the definition as all the one (though he does note that the full text is badly phrased). That author concludes that there are several difficulties with paragraph (b) as he states (at p. 120) that, "The question of what test the courts will apply remains within the realm of conjecture. ...To the uninitiated, at least, this choice or words implies that an insider dealer could adduce a non profit making purpose with impunity."

[30] U.K. Companies Securities (Insider Dealing) Act 1985, s.3. Note that this exemption has been retained in the U.K. Criminal Justice Act 1993, s.53.

concludes that an exemption of such nature is unsatisfactory as:

> "Although an individual's motive may have been otherwise than to make
> a profit or avoid a loss, the timing of the transaction may be influenced
> by the possession of inside information. Furthermore, the unscrupulous
> are prone to adduce some spurious rationale for their actions."[31]

4–10 Another curiosity with the definition of dealing is that it would
appear from the wording used that a positive act is required, such that
a decision not to acquire or dispose of securities based on the possession of inside information does not constitute "dealing".[32]

(a) Territorial scope

4–11 Potentially the greatest deficiency with the scope of "dealing"
arose from the adoption of the Companies Act 1990 (Insider Dealing)
Regulations 1992[33] which confined the application of Part V's prohibition to securities' dealings which take place within the State. Regulation 2 stated that the statutory prohibition on insider dealing set out in
section 108 did not apply to dealing outside the State in securities. The
reason why Ireland adopted the 1992 Regulations was in order to ensure that stabilisation efforts put into effect outside the State (and which
would presumably be adequately regulated by insider dealing rules in
the other jurisdiction), were not inadvertently jeopardised by the application of section 108. While such an objective was a proper one, the
difficulty that thereby arose was that a party, accused of illegal dealing outside the State, could invoke the 1992 Regulations as a defence
when challenged.

The minimum obligation required of the State in this respect is set
out in Article 5 of the Directive.

Article 5 states that the Member States must ensure that the Directive applies, at a minimum to:

> "actions undertaken within [the State's] territory to the extent that the
> transferable securities concerned are admitted to trading on a market of
> a Member State."

It continues to state that each Member State shall regard a transaction
as carried out within its territory if it is carried out on a market as
defined in Article 1(2)[34] *in fine*, situated or operating within that terri-

---

[31] McCormack, *op. cit.* at n.1 above, p.119.
[32] McCormack, *op. cit.* at n. 1 above, p.120.
[33] S.I. No. 131 of 1992 (repealed by s.6 of the Companies (Amendment) Act 1999
(No. 8 of 1999).
[34] Market according to Article 1.2 means a market that is regulated and super-

tory. By effectively confining the application of section 108's prohibitions to "dealing" in securities which takes place within the State, Ireland had satisfied the minimum requirement required by the Directive in this regard,[35] but had unwittingly given the insider dealer dealing outside the State a "free run".

In 1994, the Company Law Review Group[36] recommended that the legislation be amended to cover, insofar as it would be possible and appropriate, attempts to circumvent the application of Part V by the conduct of all or part of dealings outside the jurisdiction of the State. In other words, the Review Group was not recommending necessarily that the legislation cover extraterritorial dealings in securities as a matter of course,[37] but rather that the legislation have the capacity for such reach in circumstances where parties were deliberately using the restricted territorial application of Part V as a means of circumventing the application of Part V.

Section 2(b) of the Companies (Amendment) Act 1999[38] endorses the approach of the Review Group's Report in the following manner. It provides that any action taken during a stabilising period[39] by a person outside the jurisdiction for the purpose of stabilising or maintaining the market price for securities shall not be regarded as a contravention of Section 108 *provided* that any such action is in accordance with all relevant local requirements[40] applicable to such action in the jurisdiction where the action is affected. In effect therefore, it is recognised that foreign stabilisation actions do not violate Section 108 where they comply with Section 2(b)'s conditions. Consequently, the original rationale for the 1992 Regulations' blanket disapplication of Section 108 to dealings outside the State is no longer necessary.[41] Accordingly the 1992 Regulations were revoked by the 1999 Act.[42] A knock-on con-

---

vised by authorities recognised by public bodies and which operates regularly and is accessible directly or indirectly by the public.

[35] This will include off-market dealings too. See further below.

[36] First Report (December 1994) at para. 5–17.

[37] As the Group recognised that insider dealing laws in the other jurisdiction where all or any of the dealing was taking place might well apply.

[38] Companies (Amendment) Act (No. 8) 1999.

[39] On the new 1999 stabilisation regime generally, see part II of this chapter below where manipulation of the stock market is considered.

[40] Such as rules or regulatory requirements of the stock exchange in the other jurisdiction if the shares are listed in that other jurisdiction (s.2(b)).

[41] As discussed earlier above, such rationale was that s.108 had to be disapplied to dealings outside the State in order to protect the legality of foreign stabilisation actions. Clearly, a blanket disapplication of s.108 to achieve this worthy objective was too broad a measure, as it allowed insider dealers who dealt outside the State to deal without fear of application of s.108.

[42] s.6 Companies (Amendment) Act (No. 8) 1999 revokes S.I. 131 of 1992.

sequence of this revocation is that, a person who deals *outside* Ireland in securities listed in Ireland, can no longer hide behind the camouflage that the 1992 Regulations unwittingly afforded when Section 108 (pursuant to the 1992 Regulations) was disapplied to *all* dealings outside the State. As a matter of practical reality however, such a party may be difficult to prosecute where insider dealing outside the State is suspected. Typically, such a party will use an offshore nominee company, based in a foreign haven which has strict company secrecy laws. This may make it extremely difficult, or even impossible in many instances, to ascertain the identity of the human actor behind the offshore company.

(2) "Securities"

4–12 Part V applies to unlawful dealings in "securities" which are defined by section 107 to include any of the following[43] interests in respect of which dealing facilities are, or are to be, provided by a recognised Stock Exchange:

(a) shares, debentures or other debt securities, issued or proposed to be issued, whether in the State or otherwise;

(b) any right, option or obligation in respect of any of the securities in (a);

(c) any right, option or obligation in respect of any index relating to the securities in (a);

(d) any interests as may be prescribed by the Minister.

Apart from the obvious securities that will come within the above categories, types of securities that fall within the categories are, *inter alia*, Government stocks in paragraph (a)[44]; the reference to "obligation" contracts in paragraph (b) ensures that futures contracts are "securities"[45]; also the reference to any options or rights in respect of any securities as defined in (a) are also "securities"; index contracts, whereby investors speculate on a range of stocks, are covered by paragraph (c).

---

[43] Article 1.2 of the Directive lists similar (though not identical) categories of security to categories (a) to (c) listed in s.107.

[44] According to the Minister, Government stocks fall within the phrase 'other debt securities' (see Dáil Debates, January 9, 1990, Special Committee, Col. 344). Also see McCormack, *op. cit.* at n.1, p.121, and Ashe and Murphy, *op.cit.* at n.1, p.81.

[45] Article 1.2 of the Directive explicitly so states. Also the Minister made reference to futures contracts as falling within the scope of this provision at Special Committee, *Dáil Debates*, January 9, 1990, Special Committee, Col. 344.

(a) "Recognised Stock Exchange"

4–13   An important limitation on the scope of "securities" (and hence the application of Part V) is that trading facilities must be provided (or are to be provided)[46] on a "recognised stock exchange". According to section 107, a "recognised stock exchange" for the purposes of Part V includes, in particular, any exchange as designated by the Minister which provides facilities for the buying and selling of rights and obligations to acquire stock.[47] At the time of writing, the only exchange designated as a recognised Stock Exchange by the Minister is the Irish Stock Exchange.[48]

(b) "Off-market" dealings in "securities"

4–14   Neither the definition of "dealing" nor "securities" excludes "off-market" dealings in "securities" for which dealing facilities are (or are to be) provided by a recognised exchange.[49] Consequently, off-market dealing in securities will come within the scope of Part V.[50] In this

---

[46] In this respect Part V is wider than the Directive. Part V appears wider in the sense that "securities" for the purposes of Part V are, *inter alia,* defined as being securities for which dealing facilities are provided on a recognised Stock Exchange, or are to be provided. Presumably "are to be provided" covers securities which either (a) are dealt with on the "grey market" in the period between admission and first listing of the securities on the Stock Exchange List (as seen in the Telecom flotation in July 1999) or (b) which have been admitted to listing but dealing has not yet commenced (*i.e.* listed but trading not yet commenced, although this would be unusual as often listing and trading occur on the same date). Furthermore, it covers listed securities which are not being traded on the stock exchange at all. Article 1.2, by contrast, does not appear to be as wide. It requires that securities *are admitted* to trading on a market which is regulated and supervised by authorities recognised by public bodies, operates regularly and is accessible to the public directly or indirectly. While this would presumably cover "grey market" dealings in the period between admission and listing, it probably does not cover the situation where securities have been admitted to listing, but in respect of which trading has not yet commenced.

[47] s. 3(2) of the 1990 Act defines 'recognised stock exchange' as an exchange as prescribed by the Minister.

[48] Regulation 3(c) of the Companies (Stock Exchange) Regulations 1995 (S.I. No. 310 of 1995) (replacing S.I. No. 337 of 1990) prescribes the Irish Stock Exchange (as defined in Section 3(1) of the Stock Exchange Act 1995) as a 'recognised stock exchange' for the purposes of ss. 107, 112, 115, 116, 117, 118 and 120 of Part V of the 1990 Act.

[49] According to para. 5–13 of the Company Law Review Group (First Report, December 1994) "off-market" means dealing not on the exchange or not through a professional intermediary.

[50] Interestingly, note that Chap. 16, par. 19, Yellow Book subjects "off-market" dealings to the Chapter 16 Model Code on directors' dealings in securities of listed companies, thereby indicating that off-market dealings are not permitted

respect it is noteworthy that, while the Company Law Review Group (First Report)[51] agreed that off-market transactions should remain within the scope of application of Part V so that persons would not have an easy means to circumvent Part V, it did recommend that the Minister consider granting exemptions for specific situations and proposed that the legislation be amended to facilitate this.[52]

By contrast, Section 52(3) of the United Kingdom Criminal Justice Act 1993, provides that all transactions on a regulated market come within that legislation, as well as all transactions involving a professional intermediary.[53] The obvious implication of this must be that off-market transactions, not involving a professional intermediary, fall outside the United Kingdom legislation.

(c) "Securities" "issued or proposed to be issued, whether in the State or otherwise"

4–15   Section 107 states that "securities", *inter alia*, are securities which have been "issued, or are proposed to be issued, whether in the State or otherwise" in respect of which dealing facilities are (or are to be) provided on a recognised Stock Exchange. Section 108 goes on to instance several situations where dealing in securities of a "company" is unlawful and prohibited. At first glance, the above might appear to mean that dealings which take place in the State in the securities of foreign incorporated companies, quoted on a recognised exchange in the State will fall within the scope of Part V. However, it was submitted by the Company Law Review Group in 1994[54] that this cannot be the position for the following reason. The Group noted that the definition of "company" for the purposes of Part V did not appear to include companies that are not incorporated in the State. Section 2(1) of the Companies Act 1963 defines "company" as a company formed and registered under that Act, or an existing company. The Group therefore considered that although the definition of "securities" does cover securities whether issued in the State or otherwise, the definition of

---

under the Yellow Book Rules if the director of a listed company, in so dealing, would breach the terms of the Model Code (see further para. 4–70).

[51] December 1994.

[52] Such as where persons who have inside information deal with each other (but do not otherwise take advantage of the information), *e.g.* where directors sell holdings to each other. Another example considered would be where directors make recommendations on takeover bids. The Review Group recommended that the legislation be amended so that the Minister could have power to exempt such specific situations (and others as may arise) from the prohibition in Part V (see paras 5–12—5–14 of the First Report).

[53] Whether acting on their own or another's behalf.

[54] First Report (December, 1994) at para. 5–16.

"company" was not extended for the purposes of Part V to mean more than its normal meaning, *i.e.* effectively it is restricted to mean companies incorporated in the State. Hence, the Group was concerned that dealings in the securities of foreign incorporated companies whose securities were quoted and traded in this State might fall outside the scope of Part V.

It is submitted that this concern is a valid one. Although the term "company" is not used in the definition of the term "dealing" or "securities," it is used extensively in section 108 which instances the situations where one is prohibited from "dealing" in the "securities" of a company. Thus, even though a foreign incorporated company's securities may well be "securities" for the purposes of Part V of the 1990 Act, the Act prohibits dealings in the "securities" of "a company" – and as such a foreign incorporated company is not a section 2(1) "company" – the Act does not prohibit dealing in its securities even though they are quoted and traded in the State. Consequently, "dealings" in such securities fall outside the 1990 Act as currently drafted. The Group recommended that the Act be amended to clarify that the term "company" shall include all bodies corporate whose shares are quoted and traded on a recognised exchange in the State, whether they are incorporated in the State or not. Such an amendment would be sensible and fill the lacuna in the existing legislation. While it could be argued that such an amendment could be contrary to the spirit of the "home-State regulation" principle laid down under the Investment Services Directive (whereby primary responsibility for investigating allegations of insider dealing would lie with the authority of the home-State where the foreign-incorporated company has its head office) it is submitted that the coherency of the domestic legal framework prohibiting insider dealing is unnecessarily weakened unless such amendment is adopted.

(d) "Transactions involving professional intermediaries"

4–16 It would appear that Part V's application is wider in scope than the Insider Dealing Directive in the following sense. Section 107's definition of "dealing" and "securities", both being so broad, will bring within the scope of Part V all dealings in quoted securities, including off-market trades.

On the other hand, while Article 2.3 of the Directive, first paragraph, states that the prohibition on insider dealing contained in the Directive shall apply to any acquisition or disposal effected through a professional intermediary,[55] the second paragraph goes on to provide

---

[55] In this respect it is similar to s.107 which provides that 'dealing' can be carried out whether as principal or agent. Note that s.108(9) provides an exemption for agents who merely execute their principal's instructions without giving advice

that Member States may exempt dealings not effected by a professional intermediary which take place "outside a market".[56] It is not immediately clear what precisely is meant by the Directive here as the Directive does not specify whether "outside a market" is synonymous with "off-market" transactions. This suggests that what is intended is that the Directive is allowing Member States the option of taking off-market trades outside the Directive, provided that a professional intermediary is not involved. If this is correct, then Part V's arena of application is wider than the Directive as Ireland has not taken up this option.[57]

Another complication also arises with this second paragraph of Article 2.3. The reference to "outside a market" is complicated by the link to "professional intermediary". A literal reading of this would suggest that if a professional intermediary were involved in an outside market transaction, then Member States could not exempt it from the application of the Directive.[58] Again, this would narrow the scope of application of the Directive when compared to Part V's scope of application.

(3) "Inside Information"[59]

4–17   According to the Act, dealing is prohibited if a party in possession of inside information engages in any of the types of insider dealing listed in section 108. Therefore, before considering whether someone has engaged in any of these insider dealing situations, it must first be established that they were in possession of inside information. Section

---

on the transaction (though *cf.* s.113 under which the agent can nevertheless be guilty of insider dealing if it had reasonable cause to believe or ought to have known that the transaction was unlawful insider dealing).

[56] Article 1.2 refers to a market as being a market that is regulated and supervised by authorities recognised by public bodies and which operates regularly and is accessible directly or indirectly by the public.

[57] Conversely. the U.K. would appear to have taken this option. By contrast to Part V, the U.K. Criminal Justice Act 1993 has specifically provided for dealings involving professional intermediaries in the following respect. Subsection 52(3) specifically states that insider dealing falls within the statutory prohibition in that jurisdiction if either it takes place on a regulated market or else involves a professional intermediary (whether the intermediary is acting for another or on its own behalf). One consequence of this is that if a professional intermediary is involved in an off-market deal, then the deal will (by implication) fall within the U.K. insider dealing legislation (a situation which was not the case under the former U.K. legislation). On the other hand, if an intermediary is not involved, then the transaction will fall outside the U.K. Act.

[58] *cf.* though Wymeersch, *op. cit.* at n.3 above, pp. 11 and 12 suggests that this cannot be a proper interpretation of the Directive.

[69] Note that this term does not appear in Part V Companies Act 1990 as such. Instead the Act refers to "information". The Directive refers to "inside information" (Article 1.1).

108 defines such information as being *information that is not generally available, and which if it were so available, would be likely materially to affect the price of the securities.*

In effect therefore, any person who qualifies as an insider within the meaning of section 108 is prohibited from "dealing" if they are in possession of information which, had it been generally available, would affect the price of the relevant securities in a material fashion.

(a) "Not Generally Available"

4–18 Article 1.1 of the Directive *inter alia* defines inside information as information "which has not been made public".[60] "Not generally available"[61] represents the Irish implementation of this criterion. Unfortunately, the 1990 Act does not give any further assistance as to what criteria or test should apply to determine when information is, or is not, "generally available". Compared to the Irish legislation, the United Kingdom legislation does something which is very useful in that it defines situations, by way of a non-exhaustive list, where information *will*[62] be regarded as being "public", and where information *may*[63] be regarded as being "public".

The following are examples of information that *will* be public:

- where information is published in accordance with the rules of a regulated market for the purpose of informing investors and professional advisers, or;

- where contained in records that by enactment are open to inspection by the public, or;

- where information can be readily acquired by those likely to deal in the securities (i) to which the information relates, or (ii) of an issuer to which the information relates, or;

- where information is derived from information which has been made public.

The following are situations where information *may* be public:

- where information can be acquired only by persons exercising diligence or expertise, or;

---

[60] The U.K. Criminal Justice Act 1993 also uses a form of wording similar to that used in the Directive in this respect: s.56(1)(c) refers to information that ". . . has not been made public . . .".

[61] s. 108(1) of the Companies Act 1990.

[62] U.K. Criminal Justice Act 1993, s.58(2).

[63] *ibid.*, s.58(3).

– where information is communicated to a section of the public and not to the public at large, or;

– where information can only be acquired by observation, or;

– where information is communicated only on payment of a fee, or;

– where information is published outside the United Kingdom.

This is something that the Irish legislation would have been wise to have provided for given that the 1990 Act does not give any examples to illustrate what "generally available" might, or might not, mean. On the other hand however, although several of the United Kingdom categories are clear enough to be obviously helpful, several of them are ambiguous and will require clarification by the United Kingdom courts as to their parameters. One thing is clear: in the absence of further legislative clarification or judicial pronouncement in the Irish courts, it seems that "generally available" in the Irish context must be presumed to have a wide meaning and so, in this, as in so many other respects, the Irish legislation is probably considerably stricter than its current United Kingdom counterpart.

4–19 Case law from other jurisdictions may also be instructive. In an Australian decision, *Kinwat Holdings Ltd v. Platform Ltd* [64] it was held that information was "generally available" where it was pleaded in court proceedings and published in a newspaper. In this case, two companies had directors common to both companies. When one company attempted to take over the other, the target company sought an injunction to restrain the predator on the basis that the common directors had inside information in their possession to the effect that the assets of the target were undervalued. It was held that as the information had been pleaded in support of the injunction, revealed to the Stock Exchange and also published in a local newspaper, it was now "generally available". In an American decision, *Johnson v. Wiggs*[65] it was considered that information was in the public arena as it had been reported in the local papers and also on a local television station which reported financial news items.

4–20 However, merely because information has been published, may not mean that it has yet become "generally available" for the purposes of Part V. As Wymeersch[66] notes, the publication of a specialized local

---

[64] [1982] Q.R. 370. See further Herne, "Inside Information: Definitions in Australia, Canada, The U.K., And the U.S.", *op. cit.* at n. 1 above.
[65] [1971] 443 F.2d 803 (5th Cir.).
[66] *op. cit.* at n.3.

bulletin or a confidential newsletter circulated to a couple of hundred clients would not be sufficient for the purposes of the Directive. That author adds that some United States judicial decisions have gone even further by requiring that even after information is initially released, insiders should continue to abstain from using the information for a sufficient period to allow the market to assess fully the significance of the information.[67] Given the incredible revolution in the provision of 'instant' information to the markets facilitated by massive advances in communications technologies, the issue arises as to whether information may be acted upon by the insider as soon as it 'hits the screens', or whether a period of public assimilation must be 'waited out'. The 1990 Act is silent on this issue. One group of commentators taken the view that

> "... the Irish legislation ... requir[es] the information to be accessible and does not appear merely to require the release of a press statement. This probably achieves the objective of the Directive which places investor confidence on the assurance to investors that they are on an equal footing in the market."[68]

However, in light of modern communications assisting the dissemination of company announcements over the regulatory news service as well as continuous media commentary on the markets, it may be that as a matter of pragmatism it is unrealistic to expect parties not to deal until some time after the information "hits the screens". If this is an accurate view, then case law from the 1960's and 70's concerning the issue of when does information that is publicly available becomes "generally available" for the purposes of "dealing", may now appear somewhat dated. (For example, in *SEC v. Texas Gulf Sulphur*[69] it was held that insiders cannot act on information just because it has been made available to the public: such information may require consideration and evaluation in order to be understood by investors so that a certain amount of time should pass before information which is "available", but which requires evaluation by the investing public, is acted upon by the insider.[70])

4–21 The insider dealing code of best practice of the Irish Association of Investment Managers (IAIM) recommends that investors who come into possession of inside information should not deal or recommend others to deal, until the information has been published on the regula-

---

[67] *op. cit* at n. 3, p.15.

[68] Rider and Ashe, *op. cit.* at n.1, p.35.

[69] [1968] 401 F.2d 833 (2d Cir.).

[70] In *Reynolds v. Texas Gulf Sulphur* [1970] 309 F. Supp. 548 (D.Utah) it was held that 20 days was a reasonable period.

tory news service of the Stock Exchange. While this is prudent, in light of the aforementioned concerns raised by the 'generally available' test, further delay before acting on the information may be advisable where the information is such that it will require a reasonable amount of time for the market to digest the implications or meaning of the information.

4–22 As noted already, the United Kingdom Criminal Justice Act 1993 appears at first sight to be more lenient to insiders on this issue, *e.g.* section 58(2)(a) states that information is "made public" if published in accordance with the rules of a regulated market. One commentator is of the view that this now means that, in the United Kingdom at any rate, the insider can 'hair trigger trade', *i.e.* trade immediately once the information is released through the Company Announcements Office of the Stock Exchange before the market has had time to absorb the information.[71] If this is correct, then it is submitted that a divergence may exist between the United Kingdom legislation and the Irish "generally available" test. Although, the writer concedes that even under the new United Kingdom legislation, the matter is not so clear because that legislation also stipulates situations where information "may" be "public" (where, for example it is information that may be acquired only by persons exercising diligence or expertise, or where information is communicated to a section of the public and not to the public at large[72]). Thus, it may be that, notwithstanding section 58(2)(a), the hair trigger insider may have to take cognizance of these latter provisions, (or the case law principles on the issue of assimilation of the information, considered above).

(b) "Likely to materially affect the price of the securities"

4–23 The Directive[73] provides that *inter alia* inside information is information that, if it were made available, would be "likely to have a significant effect on the price of the securities". The 1990 Act requires that in order to be inside information, information must *inter alia* be "likely to materially affect the price of the securities".[74] No definition as to the actual meaning of "materially" is given in the Act. While, information that is not likely to have any effect on the price of securities cannot be inside information under this definition, on the other hand, this lack of legislative guidance as to what "materially" means is unhelpful.

---

[71] Alcock, "Inside Information", in Rider and Ashe (eds.), *op. cit.* at n.1, p.87.
[72] These two situations are listed in s.58(3)(a) and (b) of the 1993 U.K. Act.
[73] Article 1.1.
[74] s.108

While the lack of definition may be considered advantageous from a deterrence point of view, uncertainty for brokers and investors may be the consequence. In the parliamentary debates the Minister stated that a price movement of 10% would be indicative of a material effect.[75] The Code of the Irish Association of Investment Managers suggests a somewhat stricter test of material effect. It considers that the price of a liquid equity security would be likely to have been materially affected if, had the information in question been generally available, the price of the security would have been less than 95%, or more than 105%, of the market price on the day that dealing occurred.

4–24 Herne usefully analyses United States case law on the issue of 'materiality'. The courts focus on whether a 'reasonable investor' would have attached significance to the information, had it been revealed, and not on whether the price of the securities would have been affected. Several difficulties arise with this approach. What is a reasonable investor? How much information should such an investor be reasonably entitled to in any event? And finally, to what degree would the information have impacted on such an investor's decision? In *T.S.C Industries Inc v. Northway Inc*[76] the United States Supreme Court opted for the following test: would there be a substantial likelihood that a reasonable investor would consider the information important when deciding how to act or, would there be a substantial likelihood that the disclosure of such information would in the mind of such an investor alter considerably their view of the mix of information available?

4–25 The United Kingdom insider dealing legislation, on the other hand, considers whether the information would be "likely to have a significant effect on the price of any securities". This is similar to the Directive formulation and different from the 1990 Act formula ("material"). Unless a court determines otherwise, it would seem from a literal interpretation that the term "material" may have a much wider reach than the term "significant" such that non-significant likely effects on price (which would cause the transaction to fall outside the United Kingdom legislation) might yet be 'material' for the purposes of the Irish legislation. Furthermore, in this regard, it should be noted that although the Directive refers to 'significant effect', Article 6 of the Directive permits Member States to lay down more stringent provisions than the Directive itself requires. Therefore, it would appear that an Irish court would not be obliged to interpret "material" as meaning "significant".

---

[75] Dáil Debates, January 16, 1990, Special Committee, Col. 387.
[76] [1976] 426 U.S. at 438.

(c) "Information of a precise nature"

4–26   The Directive[77] defines inside information as *inter alia* information of a "precise nature". In considering the meaning of 'precise' in the Directive, Hopt observes:

> "It has been introduced in order to leave out mere rumours and speculations at the stock exchange. This restriction is indispensable. Without rumours and speculations the market is not alive."[78]

Expressing a similar view Wymeersch states that:

> "[While] [i]t is not very clear how far this criterion can be used in practice, . . . it can help to avoid the classical pitfall of including market rumours in the 'inside information' definition."[79]

Section 108 however has no "precise" requirement. This "omission" can be approached in a number of ways. On the one hand, it can be argued that the requirement that the information be precise should be read into section 108 as domestic legislation must be interpreted in light of Community law (though of course the meaning of the term "precise" is not resolved by such an approach). Alternatively, it can be argued that the "omission" is quite deliberate and permissible as Article 6 of the Directive permits each Member State to adopt more stringent provisions if they so wish. By omitting the "precise" requirement, it is arguable that Ireland has opted to define inside information more widely than the definition given in the Directive. As the Directive permits Member States to adopt provisions more stringent than the Directive itself, the latter alternative is possible. However, it does not follow as a matter of logic that the omission of the "precise" requirement potentially could mean that mere rumour, unfounded in fact, could constitute inside information. Were this to be so, then Irish insider dealing legislation would potentially render any information – even rumour – capable of being inside information if a court were to take the view that such information was information likely to have a material effect on the price of the securities. Although technically, the legislative definition is not so narrowly defined as to exclude the possibility that mere baseless rumour could be held to constitute information which would be likely to materially affect the price of the securities, it is submitted that such a construction would not be a correct conclusion.

4–27   It is therefore submitted that the omission of 'precise' is insignificant, as a proper construction of section 108 will exclude rumour in any event. Under the wording of the section, the courts will (a) focus

---

[77] Article 1.1.
[78] *op. cit* at n. 3, p.59.
[79] *op. cit*. at n. 3, p.16.

on whether the information would be likely to have the required material effect on the price of the securities. In order to consider this question, the court would also have to (b) consider the information itself, in order to consider what consequences are *likely* to flow from the information. These two questions cannot be divorced from each other. It is clear from the rather vague and generalised phraseology of this definition that, rather than focusing on the nature of the information itself in order to determine whether it is inside information, this legislative definition instead defines information as inside information which will be likely to have a material effect on the price of the securities. Mere baseless rumour should ordinarily be excluded from such a definition.

4–28 Finally, interestingly, the analogous United Kingdom legislation requires that inside information be *inter alia* "specific or precise"[80] about particular securities/issuers of securities. It appears that the United Kingdom government adopted this particular choice of words specifically to exclude rumour from the definition of inside information.[81] It is submitted that this does not present a serious divergence between the Irish and United Kingdom legislation in this regard, if one accepts the view that, even without the 'precise' requirement, section 108 will exclude rumour.

4–29 The issue of mere baseless rumour aside, a further issue which arises concerns the quality information must have before it can become inside information. For example, can an opinion or an inference drawn from other information constitute inside information? Or more particularly, as inside information is often most sensitive in the context of secret merger or takeover negotiations, is information about the progress of the negotiations capable of being inside information even though the outcome is still not definitive? Again this is a question that cannot be asked in isolation as it must be linked, in the case of dealings

---

[80] s.56(1)(b). The term 'specific' does not appear in the Directive. As Fortson observes (1993 C.L.S.A. vol. 3, Chap. 36 at p. 113) at standing committee (Standing Comm. B, Col. 175, June 10, 1993) the U.K.'s Economic Secretary to the Treasury stated:
> "I suggest that if somebody were to say during a lunch. . . . 'Our results will be much better than the market expects or knows,' that would not be precise. The person would not have disclosed what the results of the company were to be. However, it would certainly be specific because he would be saying something about the company's results, and making it pretty obvious that the information had not been made public. In such circumstances, it should not have been disclosed. It would be insider information because it would be specific."

[81] Fortson notes this point in his annotation of the Criminal Justice Act 1993 at 1993 C.L.S.A. vol. 3, Chap. 36 at pp. 57–58.

in Ireland at any rate, to the issue of whether there is likely to be a material effect on the price of the securities. What foreign precedents demonstrate is that it is a question of degree in each particular case whether the information is information that, by its nature, would be likely to either affect share price or the investment decisions a reasonable investor might make.[82] In other words, before a court would come to the conclusion that the information would be likely to affect the price of the securities, first the court would have to consider the actual "information".

After reviewing these authorities it would seem that, although the information need not be definitively[83] final in nature, it must have some of the following qualities. In *Commissioner for Corporate Affairs v. Green*[84] it was held in Australia that information is capable of constituting inside information if it allows an inference to be drawn as to other matters: "In many cases a hint may suggest information or may enable an inference to be drawn as to information".[85] In *Green v. Charterhouse Group Canada Ltd*[86] it was held in Canada that knowledge of takeover negotiations which had reached the stage where the bidder had revealed its bid price to the company was sufficiently precise to constitute inside information. Although the existence of takeover negotiations is not *per se* inside information, the court took the view that the negotiations had reached such a stage that knowledge of them could be regarded as inside information. Similarly in the United States case *SEC v. Geon Industries Inc*[87] it was held that knowledge of takeover negotiations constituted inside information even though it was not certain whether the negotiations would succeed or not. The court held that knowledge of the negotiations at a time before it became clear that the merger would not proceed was material inside information, as at that time it appeared probable that the deal would go ahead. What is interesting about the last two decisions referred to is that in both instances, the courts in Canada and the United States were of the view that the negotiations had not reached a stage in either case to warrant a company announcement, yet in both cases the court considered that knowledge that the negotiations were continuing was inside information. This is interesting as it demonstrates that mere adherence to the Stock Exchange disclosure and announcement rules will not necessarily protect one from

---

[82] Herne, *op. cit.* at n.1 above.
[83] Flynn *op. cit.* at n. 1 above is of the view that information which is not of a definite nature, such as opinion, may well fall within the meaning of 'information' for the purposes of s.108.
[84] [1978] Vict. R. 505.
[85] *ibid. per* McInerney J. at 511.
[86] [1976] 68 D.L.R. (3d) 592.
[87] [1976] 531 F. 2d 39 (2d Cir.).

an allegation that nevertheless, they were in possession of inside information. Ashe and Murphy suggest that although some courts may
approach the matter by confining 'information' to facts rather than in-
ferences, the Irish courts are unlikely to take such a view since the quality of the information requires that it be likely to materially affect the
price of the securities. They suggest as examples of types of information that could have that result as including facts, intentions, opinions
and data leading to an inference concerning the shares.[88]

(d) "The securities"

4–30   Finally, Article 1.1 of the Directive refers to inside information
as being *inter alia* information "relating to one or several issuers of transferable securities or to one or several transferable securities". An issue
arises as to whether this confines information to information specific
to those securities' issuers – or – whether information not specific to
those securities but which will nevertheless have an impact on their
price, is also capable of being insider information.

Different views have been expressed on this issue. Some commentators take the view that the information must be specific to a company such that (for example) a proposed change of bank interest rates,
even though it will affect the company and thus its share price, cannot
be said to relate to such a company at all and thus is not inside information.[89] Other commentators take a broader view, such that the definition of what can be inside information is much more wide-ranging.
Thus (for example), the decision of the European Central Bank to cut
interest rates, being information which is likely to influence the entire
market, is also meant to be included in the definition of inside information under the Directive. On this view, the distinction of political
from purely economic news is not possible so that items such as the
death of a leader, the imminence of war, a decision of a court or the
electoral success of a party which is hostile to business could all constitute inside information within the meaning of the Directive.[90] Then,
there is the intermediate view. This suggests that the formula used in
the Directive distinguishes between information relating to specific issuers on one hand and securities (though not necessarily their issuers)
on the other. Such a distinction differentiates between internal company information (specific issuers) and advance information about a
particular market (specific securities). For example, information concerning the likelihood of takeovers in a particular market involving
securities, and not necessarily their issuers. Under the intermediate

---

[88] Ashe and Murphy, *op. cit.* at n. 1 above, p.99.
[89] *ibid.*, *op. cit.* at n. 1 above, p.48.
[90] Hopt, *op. cit.* at n. 1 above, p.59.

view, both types of information are inside information, though in the case of advance information, while information about future market conduct is thought to be included, it is questionable whether general information that will affect most or all securities in a market, such as the outbreak of war or the death of a world leader, constitutes inside information.[91]

4–31 Section 108(1) of the 1990 Act refers *inter alia* to information which, had it been generally available would be likely to materially affect the price of securities of the company to which the insider is 'connected'.[92] Thus, the Irish legislation avoids the problems arising out of the Directive's formulation (discussed immediately above at para. 4–30) in the sense that any information that is likely to materially affect the price of the company's securities is inside information.[93] Therefore, even general political or economic information is capable of being inside information. However, this does not mean that any person in possession of such information is automatically prohibited from dealing. Under section 108, in order for a person in possession of such information to be an insider – a party prohibited from dealing – the information must have come into their possession either directly or indirectly by virtue of their "connection"[94] to the company.[95] In this sense, Part V reflects Article 2 of the Directive which lays primary responsibility on persons connected with the company not to deal.

(4) Insiders

(a) Primary Insiders[96]

4–32 Section 108 defines two types of primary insider.[97] Section 108(1)

---

[91] Wymeersch, *op. cit.* at n.1 above, p.15.

[92] s. 108(1); or the information is related to another company with which the insider's company is engaged (s.108(2)).

[93] By contrast, the 1993 U.K. legislation elaborates upon the Directive definition by *inter alia* defining inside information as information which relates to particular securities or to a particular issuer of securities or to particular issuers of securities and not to securities generally or to issuers of securities generally.

[94] Defined below at para. 4–34.

[95] Or if a tippee (unconnected to the company) they must have known, or ought to have known that the information came originally from a person connected to the company.

[96] Note: the term "primary insider" is not actually used in the Act but has been adopted extensively in the literature to differentiate between primary and secondary insiders (*i.e.* tipee(s)).

[97] While the insider connected to the company is the focus of attention, it should not be overlooked that where securities are issued by the State then 'State' should be inserted to replace 'company' in ss. 108(1), (3), (4) and (5). See further s.108(13), considered at para. 4–36 below.

provides that a person must not deal in securities of the company if he is, or was at any time in the preceding six months "connected to the company"[98] where he is in possession of inside information[99] by reason of his so being connected to the company. Section 108(2) provides that a person must not deal in securities of another company if he is, or was in the previous six months "connected" to a company which was proposing to enter[100] into a transaction with the other company and the connected person had inside information relating to that transaction by reason of his "connection".[101] As both types of primary insider definition have many elements in common, they will be considered together.

(i) How must the connected person have come into the possession of information

4–33 It appears that in order for a person's actions to come within either subsection, the inside information must have come to the insider by virtue of his 'connection' to the company. Although the wording of section 108(1) is less than clear on this point, it appears to provide that the connected person acts unlawfully if he deals in the company's securities "if by reason of his so being, or having been [at any time in the preceding six months], connected with that company he is in possession of information . . . likely materially to affect the price of those securities."[102]

Some commentators have interpreted these words used in the Act

---

[98] Defined below at para. 4–34. Note that the Directive, although not using the term, applies the main prohibition on insider dealing to persons who are in what one would describe as 'connected to the company' type situations. See Article 2 of the Directive.

[99] Such information is defined in s.108(1) to mean information which is not generally available, but if it were would be likely materially to affect the price of the securities.

[100] Or no longer enter (s.108(2)).

[101] s.108(2) states, *inter alia*, that the information can relate to "any transaction (actual or contemplated) involving both those companies or involving one of them and securities of the other, or to the fact that any such transaction is no longer contemplated." According to McCormack *op. cit.* at n. 1 above, p.124, a deficiency with this definition is that if a person, while his company is negotiating a transaction with another company, finds out inside information about a transaction that involves the other company but not his own, then he can deal in such information safely (s.108(2) will not apply) unless, of course the tippee rules are applicable to his behaviour. This surely is an unfortunate lacuna in the legislation.

[102] In so far as s.108(2) is concerned, it is similarly worded to the extent that it appears that the person connected with company A is prohibited from dealing in the securities of company B if he has acquired information about company B by reason of his connection to company A.

to mean that were a person 'connected' with the company to obtain inside information about the company otherwise than by virtue of his connection to the company, then he would fall outside the primary insider prohibition as he would not have obtained his information by reason of his connection to the company.[103] An alternative view is that merely being 'connected' to the company renders the primary insider subject to the dealing prohibition. Under this view, the insider would be deemed to be prohibited from dealing because of his connection to the company, regardless of how he acquired the inside information. If the former view is the correct one, then there would appear to be an unfortunate lacuna in the legislation as a primary insider who acquired inside information about his company *via* his connection to the company would be precluded from dealing, whereas a primary insider who acquired his information by another route could attempt to deal, unless the tipee prohibition applies.[104]

Notwithstanding, the former view is probably the proper interpretation of the legislation as it stands. It is submitted that even though the former view is less than satisfactory, the second view cannot be correct because the spirit of the legislation is to prevent insiders abusing inside information obtained *from their association with* their company to enrich themselves or others. Were the second view to prevail, company insiders would be harshly treated as they could effectively never deal in securities of the company to which they were connected.[105] Clearly this second view does not reflect the intention of the legislation, particularly when one considers how wide the category of persons 'connected' to the company is defined.

(ii) "Connected to the company"

4–34   It is necessary at this point to consider the statutory phrase "connected to the company". Section 108(11) defines a person as being connected to a company if, being a natural person,[106] the person is:

(a) an officer[107] of the company or of a related company;[108]

---

[103] McCormack, *op. cit.* at n. 1 above, p.123; Ashe and Murphy, *op. cit.* at n. 1 above, p.85.
[104] s.108(3), discussed below at paras 4–42—4–50.
[105] Chap. 16 of the Yellow Book's Model Code is constructive in this regard, as it provides that a director or employee of the company may deal in company securities provided clearance to do so is granted by the company chairman (although it prohibits dealings during certain periods (such as in advance of release of the company's trading results).
[106] Companies cannot therefore be 'connected' persons.
[107] "Officer" is defined in s.107 as being any person who, in relation to a company is either a director, a secretary, an employee, a liquidator, any person adminis-

(b) a shareholder in the company or in a related company;[109] or

(c) a person who occupies a position (including a public office[110]) that may reasonably be expected to give him access to information of a kind to which subsections [108](1) and (2) apply, by virtue of –

    (i) any professional or business or other relationship existing between himself[111] and that company or a related company, or,

    (ii) his being an officer of a substantial shareholder[112] in that company or in a related company.

The distinction between categories (a) and (b) on one hand, and (c) on the other, are as follows. Any person who is either an "officer" or a "shareholder" is automatically "connected to the company", whereas by contrast, in category (c) one is "connected" to the company only if one occupies a position of the kind described in category (c) and provided it is one which can reasonably be expected to give the holder access to inside information about the company or about a related company.[113]

Thus for example, a civil servant who has communication with a company will only be deemed to be 'connected' to the company as a primary insider if his position is one that can reasonably be expected to give him access to inside information about the company (or by virtue of that position of contact he has access to information about a transaction which a related company is negotiating). Similarly, a person working in an unrelated company which has dealings with the company, may or may not fall into this category depending on the

---

tering a compromise or arrangement between the company and its creditors, an examiner, an auditor and a receiver.

[108] s.107 defines a 'related company' as a company which is a holding company or a subsidiary of the company, or a subsidiary of the holding company.

[109] *ibid.*

[110] s.107 defines 'public office' as an office or employment which is remunerated out of the Central Fund or out of moneys provided by the Oireachtas or money raised by local taxation or charges, or an appointment to or employment under any commission, committee, tribunal, board or body established by the Government or any Minister of the Government or by or under any statutory authority.

[111] Or his employer or a company of which he is an officer (see n. 107 above for definition of "officer").

[112] s.108(12) defines a 'substantial shareholder' as a person who holds shares in a company above the notifiable percentage specified in s.70 which is stated to be "5 per cent, or such other percentage as may be prescribed by the Minister . . ."

[113] Chap. 16 Yellow Book Model Code employs a somewhat similar distinction as while directors are presumed to be in possesion of inside information about the company (by virtue of their position), company employees on the other hand are only restricted from dealing in the company's securities by the Model Code's terms where they are likely to be in possession of inside information by virtue of their office or employment in the company.

nature of his position. Paragraph (c)(ii) deals with officers of substantial shareholders in the company or related companies. They too may be connected to the company if their position within the substantial shareholder can reasonably be expected to give them access to inside information about the company.

4–35 It should not be overlooked that Part V does not require that the primary insider actually knows that he is an "insider", *i.e.* that he is or was in the last six months "connected to the company". The Act is quite strict in this respect. "Connection" may not be obvious, for example, to an employee or shareholder or company officer who is involved in only one of a complicated group of related companies.

4–36 Finally, one can also be "connected" to the State. Section 108(13) makes it quite clear that where one has inside information relating to securities issued by the State, then no party who is connected to the State may deal in those securities either at the time or within six months of such connection ceasing.[114] For the purposes of defining whether one is connected to the State, paragraph (c) of section 108(11)[115] is determinative.

(iii) Mere "possession" sufficient

4–37 Another key aspect of the legislation so far as primary insiders are concerned is that neither section 108(1)–(2) requires that the primary insider actually make use of the inside information when dealing during the prohibited period. This makes the scope of the prohibition very wide indeed. Primary insiders cannot resist liability by claiming that, although they had inside information, it was never actually used by them when dealing. Mere possession is enough to bring the otherwise qualified insider within the primary insider prohibitions as subsections (1) and (2) refer to dealing while "in possession" of inside information.

(iv) The comparable United Kingdom legislation

4–38 It is interesting to note that the comparable United Kingdom legislation, the Criminal Justice Act 1993 has now defined "insider" in

---

[114] Neither may one who is a mere tipee deal in State securities: s.108(13). Also s. 108(4) and (5) apply to dealings in State securities (these are considered at 4–51 and 4–52 below). Furthermore, the exemptions and prohibitions that apply to the behaviour of agents who deal in company securities on behalf of others on a purely 'execution-only basis' apply equally to agents' dealings involving State securities.

[115] As set out above in para. 4–34.

terms that are significantly different to the Irish legislation. Section 57(1)(a) of that Act defines an insider as one who knows that the information in his possession is inside information. Thus, the United Kingdom law is now radically different from the comparable Irish law. In Ireland, it is not required that the primary insider knows that the information is actually inside information before liability for unlawful insider dealing is incurred. Consequently, the Irish primary insider dealing regime is much stricter than its United Kingdom counterpart.

4–39 The United Kingdom legislation is also very different in another key respect. Section 57(1)(b) of the 1993 Act further requires that the insider knows that the information came "from an inside source". Section 57(2)(a) clearly states that a person has information 'from an inside source', if and only if he has it through

(i) being a director, employee or shareholder of an issuer of securities[116]; or,

(ii) having access to the information by virtue of his employment, office or profession.

The 'connection to the company' requirement, which previously existed in the previous United Kingdom legislation, has effectively been dropped from the current United Kingdom legislation. While (i) could be said to have retained an element of the 'connection to the company' theme, this category is not as extensively defined as its Irish counterpart.[117] More importantly, (ii) makes it clear that one can be an insider where one acquires information merely by virtue of one's job or profession.

This provision is critical in several key respects and markedly differs from the Irish legislation. For example, doubts – adverted to already above – concerning the section 108(1)–(2) "connected to the company" formula are not a feature of the United Kingdom legislation. As noted already, under section 108(1)–(2) information must be acquired by reason of one's connection to the company. In contrast, the United Kingdom section 57 makes it definitively clear that, *inter alia*, if one has access to inside information by virtue of one's position, then one is an insider prohibited from dealing.[118] It is not also necessary to show that one is "connected" to the company to which the in-

---

[116] This is a much more restrictive list of persons than those listed in s.107 of the 1990 Act under the definition 'officer'.

[117] Note the wide definition of 'officer' in s.107 of the 1990 Act: see para. 4–34 above.

[118] Provided of course that the person also knows that the information is inside information (s.57(1)(a)).

formation relates. In this sense therefore the United Kingdom legislation is wider, as the Irish primary insider provisions require that the
information concern the company to which one is connected.[119]

4–40 Section 57 is also much wider than the equivalent Irish provisions in another key respect. Before a party (who is neither an officer, a
shareholder, or an officer of a substantial shareholder, of the company)
can be a primary insider under the Irish legislation, they must be demonstrated to be 'connected' to the company by satisfying the terms of
section 108(11)(c)(i). There are several prerequisites to be satisfied before this can be established. First, the person's position must be one
that can reasonably be expected to give them access to inside information about the company.[120] By contrast, the United Kingdom provision has no such 'reasonably be expected' requirement. Second, the
person must have acquired the information by virtue of dealings between the person (or their employer) and the company.[121] Again, this
is not required by the United Kingdom legislation.

4–41 Furthermore, under the Irish provision the information must
concern the company one is dealing with,[122] whereas under the United
Kingdom legislation, the information can relate to any company. Thus
for example, analysts, if they know that they have inside information
and know that they came into possession of it by virtue of their job, are
insiders under the United Kingdom legislation even if they have no
dealings with the company to which the information relates. By contrast, the analyst in Ireland cannot be a primary insider if they have no
dealings with the company. The analyst in this situation will, if at all,
only be subject to the jurisdiction of the secondary insider dealing rules
(section108(3)) if she can be shown to be aware or ought to be aware of
facts and circumstances by virtue of which the original source of the
information was precluded from dealing by sections 108(1) or (2).

(b) Secondary Insiders

4–42 A secondary insider is often referred to as a 'tipee'.[123] Such a

---

[119] s.108(1). Or another company which is dealing with the company to which one
is connected where s.108(2) applies. (Of course if an insider in Ireland has information about a company other than by virtue of his connection to it, he
may still be prohibited from dealing if the tipee prohibition applies (s.108(3)).
[120] s.108(11)(c).
[121] s.108(11)(c)(i).
[122] Or any s.108(2) company.
[123] Note: neither term "secondary insider" or "tipee" is actually used in the legislation but have been adopted extensively in the literature for ease of reference.

person is, pursuant to section 108(3), prohibited from dealing in securities of a company[124] when in possession of information which is not generally available but if it were would be likely materially to affect the price of securities, where this information was received,[125] directly or indirectly, from another person and where the tipee is aware or ought reasonably to be aware of facts or circumstances by virtue of which that other person is precluded from dealing under section 108(1) or (2).

(i) No need for connection to the company

4–43 Unlike the primary insider dealing prohibitions in section 108(1)–(2), in order to be a tipee, there is no requirement that one be "connected" to the company, and therefore (as a matter of logic) no six month time limit applies. As with the primary insider, the Act merely demands that in order for liability to arise, the tipee need merely be "in possession" of inside information at the time of dealing. It is not required that the inside information was actually made use of in the particular transaction in order for section 108(3) to be infringed.

(ii) Liability test

4–44 However, there is a critical difference between the primary and secondary insider tests. The liability test for the tipee has an additional element. This is that the tipee be ". . . aware or ought reasonably to be aware of facts or circumstances by virtue of which [the source was] then himself precluded by section 108(1) or (2) from dealing in the relevant securities." It is submitted, that its ordinary meaning must be that the tipee is required to be aware or ought reasonably to be aware that the reason that the source is precluded from dealing is because the source is somehow involved with the particular company to which the suspect information relates. This is subtly, but importantly different from the tipee merely being aware that the information is inside information. In other words, because of the reference in the subsection to the tipee's awareness of ". . . facts or circumstances by virtue of which that other person is then himself precluded by section 108(1) or (2) from dealing in those securities", it appears that in order for a person

---

[124] Or securities of the State: see s.108(13).
[125] By using the word 'received' s.108 avoids the argument made in *Fisher's* case [1989] (*A.G.'s Reference*, No. 1 of 1988) A.C. 971 where it was argued that the word 'obtained' in the old U.K. insider dealing legislation was confined to meaning that the tipee must have actively sought out the information. However, the argument was unsuccessful as the House of Lords held that 'obtained' meant that the tipee was liable whether he actively sought out the information or merely came by it without having made any positive steps to acquire it.

to be caught as a tipee, they must have some level of awareness that the information is coming from a primary insider.[126]

4–45   A further question arises as to precisely what does 'aware' mean. Does it mean 'knowledge' in the sense of subjective understanding, or, is it a more objective concept given its accompaniment by the reference "or ought reasonably to be aware"? Again, in the absence of definitive judicial interpretation, this issue is not quite clear. Section 108(3) refers to the tipee either being aware or ought reasonably to be aware of facts or circumstances by virtue of which the source was himself precluded from dealing. So far as the "aware" criterion is concerned, it would seem that the tipee must have actual understanding of the 'facts and circumstances' by which the source was precluded from dealing, before liability can arise. Alternatively, so far as the "ought reasonably to be aware" criterion is concerned, if the tipee should have been aware of such facts or circumstances, then in this circumstance the tipee will be deemed 'ought reasonably to be aware' of such facts and circumstances. Read in this way, the subsection provides a subjective test (aware) and an objective test (ought), should the circumstances so warrant.

4–46   Article 4 of the Directive provides that tipees can be subject to insider dealing legislation if they are persons who with full knowledge of the facts possess inside information, the direct source of which could not be other than a primary insider. It is not clear what 'full knowledge of the facts' refers to. As is evident, section 108(3)'s tortuous implementation of this otherwise straightforward definition leaves much to be desired.

(iii) "Directly or indirectly"

4–47   The phrase "directly or indirectly" used in section 108(3) is designed to catch the tipee's tipee. In other words, 'indirectly' caters for the situation where the primary insider source provides inside information to a tipee, who then passes it on to another tipee. Provided that the tipee's tipee was aware or ought to have been aware that the inside information originated from a source that was precluded from dealing under section 108(1) or (2), then liability will be incurred if the tipee's tipee deals.

(iv) The comparable United Kingdom legislation

4–48   The Irish legislation sets out a significantly different test to the

---

[126] Even if indirectly: see para. 4–47 below under the tipee's tipee is discussed.

United Kingdom legislation. The 1993 United Kingdom legislation[127] demands that the tipee "knows" that the original source of the inside information was a primary insider. Whereas section 108(3)'s use of the "ought" criterion makes the Irish test substantially wider: if the tipee merely ought reasonably to be aware of facts or circumstances by virtue of which the original source was a party precluded from dealing under section 108(1) or (2), then liability will be incurred.

4–49 Also there is a difference in respect of the tipee's tipee. The Irish legislation differs from the United Kingdom legislation as the latter confines liability to the situation where the tipee actually knew[128] that the original source was either directly or indirectly[129] a primary[130] insider, whereas the Irish legislation sets out a wider test, *i.e.* liability is incurred where the tipee's tipee was either aware *or ought reasonably to be aware* of facts or circumstances by virtue of which the original source was a party precluded from dealing under section 108(1) or (2).

4–50 Another distinction is that the tipee under the United Kingdom legislation has to know that the information is inside information, whereas under the Irish legislation, as discussed above, the object of focus under section 108(3) is somewhat different.

(c) Causing or Procuring

4–51 Section 104(4) provides that a person precluded from dealing in a company's securities by 108(1), (2) or (3) acts unlawfully where he causes or procures any other person to deal in those securities.[131]

It would seem that the mere fact of causing or procuring another to deal is sufficient to attract the jurisdiction of the subsection.[132] Hence, the insider in possession of inside information will need to be very careful that their actions do not cause or procure another to deal, particularly given that the provision does not require that the inside information be revealed[133] to the other party.[134]

---

[127] Criminal Justice Act 1993, s.57(1).

[128] s.57(1)(b).

[129] s.57(2)(b).

[130] As defined in s.57(2)(a) to mean either he has it through being:
   (i) a director, employee or shareholder of an issuer of securities; or,
   (ii) a person having access to the information by virtue of his employment, office or profession.

[131] Or the State's securities in the case of a person precluded from dealing in such securities by subss. 108 (1) or (3): s. 108(13).

[132] Flynn *op. cit* at n. 1, at p. 365.

[133] If inside information is revealed, then an insider accused of 'causing or procuring' will also be likely to be accused of "communicating" inside information

An area where company officers need to be particularly vigilant concerns the issue of a prospectus. If the prospectus is misleading, because (for example), it contains false statements or material omissions, this may create a false market in the securities. The company officers who are in possession of the correct or full information may well be liable in this scenario on section 108(4) grounds. Furthermore, the corporate finance house involved in the arrangements may find itself accused of a breach of the Central Bank Code of Conduct (issued pursuant to section 37 of the Investment Intermediaries Act 1995) if found to have knowingly or without due care contributed to the creation of the false or misleading impression thereby arising.

Section 108(4) does not specify whether liability is incurred on the part of the insider in circumstances where the insider causes another party, A, to cause another party, B, to deal in the securities. Although this is not expressly provided for in the provision, it cannot be ruled out that a court would interpret the provision expansively as the provision refers to causing or procuring "any other person" to deal in the relevant securities.[135]

Finally, it should be noted that the corresponding United Kingdom provisions differ significantly from section 108(4).[136]

---

contrary to s.108(5).This is considered below, as are significant differences between both provisions.

[134] Neither does the Directive, suggests Hopt *op. cit.* at n. 1, p. 70. Article 3(b) of the Directive provides that "Each Member State shall prohibit any person . . . [from] . . . recommending or procuring a third party, on the basis of that inside information, to acquire or dispose of transferable securities. . . ." Hopt suggests that recommending or procuring can occur even if no inside information is communicated to the other party. If this is correct then serious issues arise. For example, "recommending" does not seem to be reflected in the Irish legislation. S.108(4) speaks of 'cause or procure' which means that dealing must have resulted, whereas recommending does not necessarily. If this is correct, then the terms of s.108(4) are unduly narrow, particularly as it cannot be argued that "recommending" has been implemented into Irish law by s.108(5). S.108(5) deals with the communication of inside information – recommending (at least, it appears) can take place even if the inside information is not communicated, in which event neither s.108(4) or (5) would seem to have implemented Article 3 properly in this respect.

[135] Furthermore, in this regard, it should be noted that the definition of dealing in s.107 is defined to include dealing whether as principal or agent.

[136] s.52(2)(a) U.K. Criminal Justice Act 1993 provides that a person who has information as an insider is guilty of insider dealing if he encourages another person to deal in securities that are (whether or not that other knows it) price-affected securities in relation to the information, knowing or having reasonable cause to believe that the dealing would take place. S.53(2) provides a defence where the encouraging party can either show that he did not expect the dealing to result in a profit attributable to the information, or he believed on reasonable grounds that the information had been or would be disclosed widely

(d) Communication of inside information

4–52 Section 108(5) provides that it shall be unlawful for a person precluded from dealing in a company's[137] securities under 108(1), (2) or (3) to communicate inside information to any third party, where he knows or ought reasonably to know, that the third party will use the inside information to deal or will cause or procure another to deal. Section 108(5) raises two serious issues, both problematical. The first is whether section 108(5) is a proper implementation of the Directive's requirements. The second is whether section 108(5), on its own terms, prohibits the mere communication of inside information *per se*?

4–53 The first question raises the following issue. Article 3(a) of the Directive provides that each Member State shall prohibit any person who possesses inside information by virtue of their being connected to the company concerned whether as an officer, member or by virtue of his employment, profession or duties, from disclosing that information to any third party unless such disclosure is made in the normal course of the exercise of that person's employment, profession or duties.

Two immediate difficulties arise with section 108(5) in light of Article 3(a). First, section 108(5) has no similar exclusion to excuse disclosure made in the normal course of one's employment, profession or duties.[138] Second, Article 3(a) appears to set out a prohibition on inside information communication *per se*. As section 108(5) appears to link communication of inside information with subsequent use of the information in dealing, the issue arises of whether the subsequent use requirement constitutes an improper implementation of Article 3(a). Such a requirement as a precursor to proving 'communication' would seem contrary to the spirit of the Directive.[139]

---

enough so that those dealing would not be prejudiced by not having it, or that he would have done what he did even if he had not had the information.

[137] Or the State's securities in the case of a person precluded from dealing in such securities by s.108 (1) or (3). See s.108(13).

[138] While it is arguable that Article 6 permits Ireland not to legislate this "watering-down" provision into Irish law, nevertheless the omission to legislate these three exclusions into the Act is unfortunate as it will undoubtedly create genuine difficulty for many parties, such as company insiders who are negotiating a possible takeover of their company and in so doing reveal inside information to the other side for the purposes of the negotiations. It is situations like this that the Directive intended to excuse. However, Part V has no such exemption.

[139] It is arguable that the addition of the subsequent use requirement does not constitute a "more stringent or additional requirement" which Member States may impose (under Article 6) as the real effect of it is to "water-down" the application of Article 3(a) by making it more difficult for liability to be established against the insider.

Also Article 3(b) is relevant. Article 3(b) *inter alia* prohibits recommending another, on the basis of inside information, to acquire or dispose of securities. It is arguable that this prohibition is violated even if dealing does not take place.[140] If this is correct, then this too supports the argument that Section 108(5) is not a proper implementation of the Directive's minimum objectives.

4–54 The second question raised by section 108(5) raises the issue of whether the terms of 108(5) actually require that use be made of the information at all, such that mere communication is prohibited *per se*? Commentators appear to differ on this point. According to some, it is not necessary that use be made of the information before liability can arise.[141] Others take the contrary view.[142] This is a critical issue as the former view would render mere communication (without actual use of the information) a breach of the Act, whereas the latter view requires that actual use be made of the information. It is submitted that, although the wording of the provision is less than clear, the terms of 108(5) must be read so that it requires that use be made of the information before liability can be incurred. As noted already above,[143] such a reading appears contrary to the Directive.

4–55 Leaving aside objections based on the Directive – or indeed assuming they proved groundless – what might the likely implications be if section 108(5) was deemed properly to require use of the information in dealing in order for liability for "communication" to arise? In other words, what if 108(5) is a legitimate implementation of the Directive? Were this to be so, then liability could not be imposed for mere communication. Something additional would be required, *i.e.* subsequent use of the communicated information. It could be argued that had the legislature intended to prohibit the mere communication of inside information *per se*, it should have attempted to do so in a clearer fashion, but did not. Corporate players would breath a sigh of relief, as they would not be living constantly in fear of a section 108(5) challenge merely because they discussed their company's affairs as they could argue that such information was never used for dealing by anyone.

Should the aforegoing view prove correct, a curious situation could then arise. Assume an insider communicates inside information to a tipee who subsequently deals. The tipee is liable as he was dealing

---

[140] See "Causing or Procuring" at para. 4–51 above where "recommending" is considered.
[141] McCormack, *op. cit.* at n. 1, p. 125.
[142] Flynn, *op. cit.* at n. 1, p. 365.
[143] At para. 4–53.

while in possession of inside information (and provided that he was aware or ought to have been of facts or circumstances by virtue of which the source was a primary insider precluded from dealing).[144] The tipee would be liable under section 108(3) even if he made no use of the communicated information when dealing.[145] Curiously, however, the insider who communicated the information[146] would only be liable under section 108(5) for 'communicating' if he knew or ought to know that use would be made of the information. Thus, it would appear that the insider would escape liability if the tipee made no use of the inside information, whereas the tipee would be liable under section 108(3) merely by dealing while being in possession of the inside information.

(i) Points of distinction

4–56 As already noted when considering section 108(4) above, an insider accused of 'communicating' is also likely to face claims that he 'caused or procured' dealing contrary to 108(4). Although this is likely, it should be borne in mind that there are several key points of distinction between the two provisions.

First, unlike section 108(4), section 108(5) requires that the information is actually disclosed to the other party by the insider. Second, unlike section 108(4), section 108(5) does not appear to impose a strict liability test as the test of liability is "knows or ought reasonably to know" that the third party will act on the information. Third, section 108(5) appears to require that the information was in fact so used, whereas this is not required in respect of section 108(4). This is therefore somewhat anomalous as it appears that the insider who communicates inside information in circumstances where he can demonstrate he did not know or ought to know that it would be used, will escape section 108(5) "communicating" liability even though dealing takes place using the information. Whereas, on the other hand, the insider who does not communicate any inside information at all, but yet who causes or procures another to deal, will incur liability under section 108(4). Fourth, the insider who communicates inside information where he knew or ought to have known that the other person would use the information for the purpose of *inter alia* causing or procuring another person to deal, will be guilty of 'communicating'.[147]

Finally, it should be noted by comparison that the corresponding United Kingdom provisions differ significantly from section 108(5). [148]

---

[144] s.108(3).
[145] As s.108(3) liability is based on possession, not use.
[146] Either a primary or secondary insider.
[147] s.108(5).
[148] s.52(2)(b) of the U.K. 1993 Act provides that a person who has information as

(e) Directors and securities options

4–57 Although one may presume company directors to be constantly in possession of inside information about the company by virtue of their position, section 108 does not automatically prohibit them from dealing in the company's shares.[149] Like any other party, a director is not prohibited by the 1990 Act if he is not in possession of inside information material to the securities' price.[150] Even where the director is in possession of inside information he may yet be able to deal if he satisfies the requirements provided by section 108(10)'s "seven-day dealing window" mechanism, considered further below.[151]

Section 30 of the Companies Act 1990 prohibits directors from dealing in certain types of share or debenture options even though they may not be in possession of any inside information.

Under section 30 of the 1990 Act, a company director commits an offence if he either buys

- a right to call for delivery at a specified price[152] and within a specified time of a specified number of relevant shares or specified amount of relevant debentures, or

- a right to make delivery at a specified price and within a specified time of a specified number of relevant shares or specified amount of relevant debentures, or

- a right (as he may elect) to call for delivery at a specified price and within a specified time or to make delivery at a specified price and within a specified time, of a specified number of relevant shares or specified amount of relevant debentures.

However, section 30(3) provides that nothing in section 30 will prohibit a person from buying a right to subscribe for shares or deben-

---

an insider is guilty of insider dealing if he discloses the information, otherwise than in the proper performance of the functions of his employment, office or profession, to another person. S.53(3) provides a defence where the disclosing party either did not at the time expect that dealing would take place or that although he had such expectation, he did not expect that a profit would result which would be attributable to the information.

[149] Nor does the Yellow Book provided they follow Chap. 16's Model Code. See further para. 4–70 below.

[150] Although in practice, he may be prevented from dealing by para. 7 of Chap. 16 Yellow Book Model Code which provides that a director shall not receive clearance to deal from the company chairman in a variety of circumstances including during a period when a company announcement might be required in respect of a matter of which the director may have no knowledge: see para. 4–70 further below.

[151] See para. 4–69.

[152] According to s.30(4), price can be money or money's worth.

tures in a body corporate, nor from buying debentures that confer on
the holder a right to subscribe to, or convert the debentures (either in
whole or in part) into shares of the body. Thus not all options fall within
the prohibition in section 30.

For the purposes of the prohibition, section 30(2) defines "relevant
shares" to mean shares in the company or in any other body corporate, being its subsidiary, its holding company or a subsidiary of the
holding company and for which dealing facilities are provided on a
recognised Stock Exchange, whether in the State or elsewhere. "Relevant debentures" means debentures in the company or in any other
body corporate, being its subsidiary, its holding company or a subsidiary of the holding company and for which dealing facilities are
provided on a recognised Stock Exchange, whether in the State or elsewhere.

Finally, a person who enters into any of the transactions in section
30(1) at the instigation of a director shall also be guilty of an offence.
The term director includes shadow director.[153]

(f) Companies as insider dealers

4–58   Section 108(6) provides that it shall not be lawful for a company
to deal in any securities when at that time an "officer" of the company
is precluded from dealing in those securities (the officer could be either a primary insider or a secondary insider). In effect therefore this
imputes the officer's inside information to the company and precludes
it from dealing. This is an extremely wide prohibition as, for example,
company A could be guilty of breaching section 108(6) by dealing in
another company's shares merely because, say, one of its employees
was precluded from dealing in that other company's shares by virtue
of being a tipee.[154] By enacting section 108(6), Irish insider dealing legislation has gone much further than its United Kingdom counterpart.

4–59   As section 108(6) specifically prohibits companies from dealing
if any of their "officers" are so precluded, then the question arises as to
whether companies are also intended to be "persons" for the purpose
of the primary insider dealing provisions as in section 108(1) or (2).
Although it is not entirely conclusive, it would appear that companies
are not intended to be "persons" for the purpose of the primary insider dealing provisions. In this regard, it has been pointed out[155] that
it would appear that the enactment of section 108(6) as a specific in-

---

[153] As defined in s.27 of the Act.
[154] s.107 defines 'officer' to include employees of the company: see further para.
4–34 above for full definition of 'officer'.
[155] Ashe and Murphy *op.cit.* at n. 1, p.88.

sider dealing prohibition for companies, as well as the language of section 108(1)–(2), would support the conclusion that companies are not intended to be "persons" for the purpose of the primary prohibitions. However, notwithstanding the enactment of section 108(6), it is less clear that companies cannot be regarded as tipees in their own right within the meaning of section 108(3), as section 108(6) is expressly stated to be "Without prejudice to section [108] (3). . . ."[156] Section 108(6) is qualified by three provisions of the Act in a number of key respects. These will now be considered.

(i) "Chinese wall" structures

4–60   Section 108(7) sets out the first qualification to section 108(6). In effect, it provides that section 108(6) will not preclude the company from dealing if:

(a) the decision to deal was taken by a person other than the officer in possession of the inside information, and

(b) written "chinese wall" arrangements can be demonstrated to have been in position such that the insider officer would not have been able to communicate the inside information to the decision-maker in the company, nor give any advice to such person in relation to the transaction, and

(c) that such arrangements were effective as a matter of fact.

A criticism of section 108(7) is that the company cannot invoke it unless a "chinese wall" formally and factually has been demonstrated to have been in operation within the company itself. The formal requirement should not be overlooked as the wording of the provision does not appear to allow a company claim it has satisfied section 108(7) merely because the officer who was in possession of the inside information had no part in the transaction and did not communicate the information nor bring it to the attention of the decision-maker in any way. The subsection requires that it must be demonstrated that chinese wall structures were already formally in place. According to one commentator, it is difficult to see how chinese walls can be effective in Ireland given that firms by their nature are small by international standards and employees within the same company usually tend to know each other and will interact at work and socially.[157] Other commenta-

---

[156] In which event, a company could also commit the offences of 'causing' or 'procuring' others to deal (s.108(4)) or "communicating" inside information (s.108(5)).

[157] McCormack, *op. cit.* at n. 1, p. 127.

tors observe that, apart from specialist multifunctionary securities firms – of which there are few in Ireland – few firms are likely to have continuing and effective non-porous chinese wall structures in operation.[158]

(ii) Mere information that company proposes to deal

4–61　The second qualification to section 108(6) is set out in section 108(8). It provides that the company will not be precluded from dealing in the securities of another company by reason only that one of the officers of the first-mentioned company had, in the course of his duties, come into possession of information to the effect that the company proposed to deal in the securities of the second-mentioned company. This provision was inserted to make it clear that merely because a company officer was aware, through his work, that his company was about to enter into a transaction involving the securities of another company, this should not of itself cause the company to violate the prohibition contained in section 108(6).

(iii) Company dealing in own securities

4–62　The third qualification to section 108(6) is provided by section 223 of the 1990 Act.[159] Section 223 provides that section 108(6) will not preclude a company from dealing in its own securities by reason merely that an officer of the company had information at the time, provided that the decision to deal was:

(a) taken by an officer of the company other than the officer who had the inside information; and

(b) there was no communication of the inside information to the decision-maker; and

(c) the party in possession of the information gave no advice to the decision-maker in relation to the transaction.

Unlike section 108(6), section 223 does not appear to require that a "chinese wall" formally be in existence.[160] The mere fact of non-communication or interaction between the information possessor and the decision-maker is sufficient to satisfy the section. A company which contravenes section 223 shall be guilty of an offence.[161]

---

[158] Ashe and Murphy, *op. cit.* at n. 1, p. 86.

[159] ss.206–234 were brought into effect by S.I. No. 117 of 1991.

[160] *i.e.* there is no requirement that the "chinese wall" arrangements exist in writing.

[161] s.234(1).

(5) Exempt Transactions:

4–63 Section 110 sets out three categories of transaction which are exempt from the application of section 108's prohibitions. Section 108 itself provides a further two categories.

(a) Section 110 exemptions

4–64 The first category that section 110 declares exempt are:

– acquiring securities under a will[162]

– acquiring securities pursuant to an approved employee profit sharing scheme[163]

In the case of the latter, "approved" means approved by the Revenue Commissioners and the company in general meeting. Also, all permanent employees in the company must have equal participating rights in the scheme in order to meet the exemption's requirements.

The second category of transactions declared exempt are those listed in section 110(2). Under this subsection, the following transactions are declared exempt, provided that they are entered into in good faith:

– a director's share qualifications under Section 180 of the 1990 Act

– a transaction entered into by a person pursuant to his underwriting obligations[164]

– a transaction entered into by a person in his capacity as personal representative of a deceased person, a trustee, a liquidator, a receiver, or examiner in performance of functions of office

---

[162] s.110(1)(a).
[163] s.110(1)(b).
[164] Pursuant to the Companies Act 1990 (Insider Dealing) Regulations 1991 (S.I. No. 151 of 1991) the Minister provided (in order to facilitate the operation of the section) that a person who has entered into a transaction as part of his underwriting obligations, shall be regarded as having entered in good faith if he enters in good faith
  (a) an agreement to underwrite securities; or
  (b) an agreement, in advance of dealing facilities being provided by a recognised Stock Exchange for securities, to acquire or subscribe for a specified number of those securities; or
  (c) negotiations with a view to entering an agreement referred to in paragraph (a) or (b); or
  (d) a transaction in accordance with such person's obligations under an agreement referred to in paragraph (a) or (b).
S.6 of the Companies Act 1999 (No. 8 of 1999) revoked S.I. No. 151 and s.4 of the Act expressly incorporated S.I .No. 151's terms into s.110 of the 1990 Act as s.110(2A).

– a transaction by way of, or arising out of, a mortgage of or charge on securities or a mortgage, charge, pledge or lien on documents of title to securities.

The third category of transactions declared exempt by section 110 are to be found in section 110(3).[165] It provides that transactions entered into in pursuit of monetary, exchange rate, national debt management or foreign reserve policies by any Minister, or the Central Bank, or any person on their behalf, are declared exempt from the application of Part V.

(b) Section 108 exemptions

4–65 Two exemption situations are set out in Section 108.

(i) Execution-only agents

4–66 The first situation arises under section 108(9). It provides that one is not precluded from dealing in securities (or rights to same) in the capacity of an agent for another if (a) he enters the transaction as agent acting on another's specific instruction, and (b) he has not given any advice regarding the particular class of securities concerned, or the securities of the company which fall into that class, to the principal.

An agent who remains within the parameters set out in section 108(9) by merely executing a transaction without any deeper involvement is known as an "execution-only" agent. Such an agent will normally be exempt from liability for insider dealing should it eventually turn out to be the case that the principal was an insider dealer.

4–67 Notwithstanding this, liability for insider dealing under Part V may arise even in respect of such an agent should section 113 apply. Section 113 provides that where a person who is dealing as agent has reasonable cause to believe or ought to conclude that the deal would involve insider dealing prohibited under section 108, he is prohibited from dealing, and will be guilty of an offence if he does deal in such circumstances.[166] The Act is silent as to whether, in such an event, the agent would additionally be exposed to statutory civil liabilities which section 109 of the Act imposes on the insider principal. Perhaps, the agent may be regarded in these circumstances as a tipee, and thus incur statutory civil liability to compensate affected investors or return profits to the company.

---

[165] Similar to article 2.4 of the Directive.
[166] s.114.

4–68 Where an agent is more than a mere "execution-only" agent, the agent cannot invoke section 108(9) as a defence as that subsection is only available to execution-only agents. It cannot be invoked by agents whose role in the transaction also involves an advisory element. In this regard, such agents should be mindful that the definition of "dealing" under section 107 includes where one acts as agent.

(ii) Seven-day window

4–69 The second exemption provided by section 108 is to be found in section 108(10). It provides that a person "connected" to the company within the meaning of section 108(1),[167] who does not otherwise take advantage of inside information which relates to the securities of a company, may deal in such securities notwithstanding the fact that he is in possession of such information, provided:

– he gives the Stock Exchange 21 days notice of his intention to deal, and

– the dealing takes place in the period beginning seven days after, and ending 14 days after, publication of the company's interim or final results, and

– the Stock Exchange immediately publishes the notification upon receipt.

This mechanism appears particularly designed to enable persons who are continuously in possession of inside information about a company, such as company directors, to deal legally provided they do not ". . . otherwise take advantage . . ." of the inside information. Of this provision Mac Cann comments,

> "This is a curious provision…section 108(10) enables [the director] to deal in shares for a limited period each year provided that in so doing he ignores any price sensitive information which he may possess. This is a somewhat unreal and metaphysical concept which will be extremely difficult to apply in practice."[168]

The drawback for the person in possession of inside information hoping to make use of this mechanism is that the time-frame is very short – only seven days – and will probably only arise twice a year.[169] According to the recommendations of the Company Law Review Group,[170]

---

[167] Connected persons are defined in s.108(11) and considered at para. 4–34 and s.108(1) persons are considered at para. 4–32.
[168] *op. cit.* at 132.
[169] Unless the company decides to publish interim results on a more regular basis.
[170] First Report (December 1994) at para. 5–15.

section 108(10)'s wording is not sufficiently clear. It suggested that the wording be amended to reflect the notion that a person who deals does not violate Part V (although they might gain) if they deal for some reason other than to take advantage of the inside information and would have done so even if they did not have the information. It is submitted that the final element suggested would clarify the scope of the exemption as the phrase "whilst not otherwise taking advantage" would then be more concrete.

(6) The Yellow Book's Model Code

4—70 Chapter 16 of the Yellow Book Model Code imposes restrictions on directors' dealing[171] in securities[172] *of their own company*. The purpose of the Code is to ensure that directors, or connected persons[173] neither abuse price sensitive information[174] nor place themselves in a position where they might come under such suspicion. It applies in similar fashion to "relevant employees".[175] Paragraph 4 of the Model Code provides that a director must not deal in any securities of the

---

[171] The Model Code defines "dealing" to include any sale or purchase of, or agreement to sell or purchase, any securities in a company and the grant, acceptance, acquisition, disposal, exercise or discharge of any option (whether for the call, or put, or both) or other right or obligation, present or future, conditional or unconditional, to acquire or dispose of securities, or any interest in securities, of the company.

[172] The Model Code defines "securities" as meaning any listed securities, and where relevant, securities which have been listed or admitted to dealing on, or have their prices quoted on or under the rules of NASDAQ or any investment exchange in a Member State which provides facilities for the buying and selling of securities.

[173] Par. 16.13 Yellow Book defines "connected persons" as meaning persons defined in s.64 Companies Act 1990 (*i.e.* spouses and children) whose interests in the company are treated as those of the director, and such interests are, along with the director's interests in the company, notifiable interests pursuant to s.53 of the 1990 Act.

[174] The Model Code defines "unpublished price-sensitive information" as per s.108(1) of the 1990 Act (*i.e.*, "not generally available" and "likely materially to affect the price of securities") but with the additional element that it must be "specific or precise" (reflecting the wording of the EC Insider Dealing Directive) and also that it must be information relating to "particular securities or to a particular issuer or issuers and not to securities generally or to issuers of securities generally".

[175] The Model Code defines "relevant employees" as any employee of the company, or director or employee of a subsidiary undertaking or parent undertaking who, because of his office or employment in the company, subsidiary or parent, is likely to be in possession of unpublished price-sensitive information in relation to the company. Par. 21 Model Code provides that relevant employees must comply with the terms of the Code as though they were directors.

company at any time when he is in possession of unpublished price-sensitive information in relation to the company's securities.

Where a director proposes to deal in the company's securities, Paragraph 6 of the Model Code provides that he must not deal unless he has first advised the chairman (or director designated for this purposes) of his intention to deal. Furthermore, he must obtain clearance to deal from such party. Should clearance not be obtained, the director cannot deal. A written record must be kept by the company of any clearance requests made by directors, and of any clearance given in response.[176] The Model Code is particularly concerned with ensuring that directors are not granted clearance to deal during "prohibited periods". There are three such periods specified under Paragraph 7 Model Code. These are as follows.

The first situation where clearance must not be given is during a "close period."[177] Such period is the period of two months preceding the preliminary announcement of the company's annual results.[178] Where the company reports on a half-yearly basis, a two month close period similarly applies, or one month in the case of a company which reports on a quarterly basis.[179]

The second situation where clearance must not be given is during any period when there exists any matter which constitutes unpublished price-sensitive information in relation to the company's securities and the proposed dealing would, if permitted, take place after the time when it has become reasonably probable that a company announcement will be required in relation to the matter.[180] This applies whether or not the director himself has knowledge of the price-sensitive matter. It may apply at any time of the year.

The third situation where clearance must not be given is where the chairman or designated director responsible for the clearance decision has reason to otherwise believe that the proposed dealing would be in breach of the Model Code.[181]

In exceptional circumstances, where according to the Model Code, "it is the only reasonable course of action available to the director", clearance may be given to the director to sell (but not to purchase) securities when he would otherwise have been prohibited from doing so by the Code. Paragraph 9 of the Model Code cites "a pressing financial commitment on the part of the director that cannot otherwise be

---

[176] Par. 8 Model Code.
[177] Par. 7(a) Model Code.
[178] Or if shorter, the period from the relevant financial year end up to and including the time of the announcement: par.3 Model Code.
[179] Par. 3 Model Code.
[180] Par. 7(b) Model Code.
[181] Par. 7(c) Model Code.

satisfied" as an example of an exceptional situation. Ultimately, the Model Code leaves the decision as to what is an exceptional situation to the chairman (or designated director) responsible for considering clearance requests.[182]

The Model Code permits the chairman (or designated director) to permit the director to exercise options or rights under an employee share scheme or convert a convertible security, where the date for exercising such rights fall during a prohibited period, on the grounds that the director could not reasonably have been expected to exercise such rights at an earlier time when he was free to deal.[183]

Not only is a director obliged to respect the Model Code, but the Model Code also obliges the director to "seek to prohibit" (so far as is consistent with his duties of confidentiality to the company) any dealing by or behalf of persons connected with him during a close period, or at any time when he is in possession of unpublished price-sensitive information.[184] This also applies to investment managers who either act on the director's behalf or on behalf of any person connected with the director.[185]

For the avoidance of doubt, the Model Code also specifies a number of transactions that fall within the Model Code,[186] and a number that fall outside the Model Code.[187]

---

[182] Par. 9 Model Code.

[183] Par. 14 Model Code: although Par. 15 Model Code goes on to provide that where clearance to exercise such rights is granted, such clearance cannot permit the director to go on and sell the securities acquired pursuant to such clearance.

[184] Par.11 Model Code.

[185] Par. 11 Model Code makes two significant exceptions to this prohibition (on dealing by investment managers on behalf of a director or a connected person). First, the prohibition does not apply to dealings concerning a trust where the director is a bare trustee (and not also a beneficiary under the trust) and the other trustees deal without any involvement or advice from the director trustee (Par. 10 Model Code). Second, where the director enters into a personal equity plan or regular savings scheme to buy shares in the company, the director may do so provided that he (a) does not commence the plan during a prohibited period (ie. a Par. 7 Model Code period, as considered above), and (b) does not cancel the plan during a prohibited period, and (c) obtains clearance (in accordance with Par. 6 Model Code) before he first enters, or cancels, the plan.

[186] Par. 19 Model Code provides that the following fall within the Code: dealings between directors and/or relevant employees of the company; off-market dealings; transfers for no consideration by a director other than transfers where the director retains a beneficial interest under the Companies Acts 1963-1990.

[187] Par. 20 Model Code provides an extensive list of dealings (too numerous to exhaustively detail here) such as (for example) undertakings or elections to take up entitlements under a rights issue; undertakings to accept, or the acceptance of, a takeover offer; dealing by a director with a person whose interest

Listed companies are obliged by Chapter 16 to ensure that the Model Code[188] (or a more stringent version of it as the company may choose[189]) is in operation in the company.

(7) Grounds for liability under Part V

4–71 Article 13 of the Directive provides that each Member State shall determine the penalties to be applied for infringement of the measures enacted pursuant to the Directive. It will be seen how, in the case of Ireland, Part V of the 1990 Act has provided a comprehensive range of sanctions, both civil and criminal, in respect of insider dealing.[190] However, as noted earlier in this chapter, Part V does not of course apply to dealings in unlisted securities.

(a) Civil liability

4–72 Some consider that insider dealing is a "victimless" event. Keane disagrees with this view stating that the person who is unaware of the information is at a loss as he may be getting less for his shares than if he knew all of the facts of which the insider is aware.[191] The view could also be taken that the law cannot adequately provide the means or mechanisms in which to provide an adequate legal framework for the provision of such a basis of liability. For example, comparable United Kingdom legislation does not provide for statutory civil liability. United Kingdom legislators felt that it would be too difficult as a matter of proof to attempt to establish liability between the insider and the innocent investor.

4–73 By contrast, section 109 provides for two civil causes of action which, if pursued successfully, will render the party who dealt in securities while in possession of inside information civilly liable, either as a primary insider[192] or secondary insider.[193] Those who "cause or

---

in securities is to be treated by virtue of s.64 Companies Act 1990 (extension of s.53 Companies Act 1963 to spouses and children) as the director's interest; dealings in connection with a Revenue Commissioners approved share option scheme (with the exception of a disposal of securities received by a director as a participant), or any other employees' share scheme approved by the Revenue under the Finance Act 1986; "bed-and-breakfast" dealings; transfers of shares by means of matched sale and purchase into director's personal equity plan or pension scheme, etc. (for the complete list, the reader is advised to consult the Model Code).

[188] Par. 16.19 Yellow Book.
[189] Par. 16.19 Yellow Book.
[190] See paras 4–72—4–92 below.
[191] *op. cit.* at n.1 at 397.
[192] Within the meaning of s.108(1) or (2).
[193] Within the meaning of s.108(3).

procure"[194] or "communicate"[195] may also incur these liabilities. Presumably companies which deal contrary to section 108(6) can also be subject to section 109 liability. In the first type of action, the investor who suffers at the hands of the insider dealer can seek statutory compensation[196] from the insider for loss. In the second type of action, the insider will be statutorily liable to account to the company[197] for any profit made on the transaction.

(i) Compensation for loss

4–74 As already alluded to, the first right of action provided for by section 109 is the right of the investor to be compensated for loss.[198] Section 109(1)(a) represents a major development as insider liability is no longer predicated upon the establishment of circumstances that would give rise to the existence of a fiduciary duty.[199] Consequently, section 109(1)(a) imposes civil liability on a much wider variety of operator than even the 'exceptions'[200] countenanced by modern day courts to *Percival v. Wright*.

Section 109 liability is stated to be "without prejudice" to any other forms of civil action that may be taken against the offending party.[201] This means that the availability of a section 109 remedy will not preclude other forms of action being taken, although given that difficulties of a *Percival v. Wright* nature may obstruct a common law action against the insider, a section 109 action will usually be the preferred choice of legal action. Even so, for reasons to be set out below, section 109 is not without its difficulties.

4–75 Section 109(1)(a) states that where a person deals in securities in

---

[194] s.108(4).

[195] s.108(5).

[196] s.109(1)(a).

[197] s.109(1)(b).

[198] The limitation period for a s.109(1)(a) civil action is two years after the date of completion of the transaction in which the loss occurred (s.109(4)).

[199] Though only in respect of dealings in Part V 'securities': Part V has not affected the application of *Percival v.Wright* [1902] 2 Ch. 421 to dealings in non-Part V securities (see paras 4–02—4–06 above).

[200] Such exceptions recognised that if there were special circumstances, a company insider could assume fiduciary duties to a shareholder, see above paras 4–04 and 4–05 where *Allen v. Hyatt; Coleman v. Myers* are considered. In these cases, the insider had been a company officer who had abused a position of trust.

[201] "Without prejudice" allows for the possibility that a disgruntled investor may prefer to attempt a common law action for recission and damages. Also it does not preclude the possibility of other forms of legal action such as actions based in fraud or negligence.

contravention of Section 108 whether by primary or secondary insider activity, or by causing or procuring others to deal, or by communicating inside information, then such person shall be liable to compensate:

> "... any other party to the transaction who was not in possession of the relevant information for any loss sustained by reason of any difference between the price at which the securities were dealt in in that transaction and the price at which they would have been likely to have been dealt in in such a transaction at the time when the first-mentioned transaction took place if that information had been generally available."

Hence, the requirement for some sort of a fiduciary duty to be inferred before the law will allow the investor recover for personal loss against the insider is irrelevant in a section 109 action.

4–76 Upon closer examination, there are several points of difficulty with this remedy. One is that the wording[202] does not make it entirely clear as to whether only those who dealt directly with the insider can recover under section 109(1)(a), or, whether all investors including those who did not deal directly with the insider, but who were dealing contemporaneously in the market at the time the insider was dealing, could claim that section 109(1)(a) permits them also to have the right of statutory action against the insider. If the latter is permitted by the subsection, then great difficulties of proof sufficient to satisfy a court of law may arise.[203] It would appear that the better view is that the wording of the section limits its use only to parties who dealt directly with the insider.[204] Binchy and Byrne[205] query this limitation on the scope of the remedy by considering the arguments for and against allowing civil sanction in respect of insider dealing. On one hand, they ponder as to why the law should permit any party to have the right to recover against the insider if the other party to the transaction was never aware that the insider had inside information. On the other hand, if recovery should be allowed, why should not all investors affected by the insider's actions on the market be allowed by section 109 to recover (irrespective of whether they had dealings specifically with the insider or not)?

4–77 Another difficulty with the remedy is the meaning of "loss". On an initial reading of section 109(1)(a), it might appear to quantify "loss" in definite terms by meaning that the compensatable "loss" is the difference in price between the price the shares were dealt at and the price

---

[202] "... liable to compensate any other party to the transaction ..."
[203] McCormack, *op. cit.* at n. 1, p.129.
[204] McCormack *ibid.*; Rider and Ashe, *op. cit.* at n. 1.
[205] *op. cit.* at n. 1, p.85.

they would have been dealt at, had the information been generally available.[206] However, a closer reading of the subsection also provides a possible alternative interpretation. It is arguable that "loss" means loss that the innocent party sustained "by reason of" that difference.[207] Under this interpretation, "loss" and price differential are not synonymous. The issue that arises out of these two possible interpretations is an important one. Either it means that the "loss" is the price differential (assuming such amounts to a loss) or else the loss must be demonstrated to have arisen by reason of the differential. It is not clear from the wording used which alternative is the proper interpretation of the provision. Accordingly, this uncertainty may make investor action less attractive to emback upon.[208]

4–78 This uncertainty as to the scope of "loss" also impacts on the further difficulty raised by section 109(2). Section 109(2)(a) provides that the loss for which the insider will be liable is the loss sustained by the person claiming the compensation. But section 109(2)(b) goes on to provide that if a person so liable has already been found by a court to be liable to pay an amount or amounts to any other person or persons by reason of the same act or transaction, then the amount of loss for which they are liable shall be the loss for which they are liable less the amount or the sum of the amounts for which that person has already been found to be liable. Thus, whether the meaning of "loss" is 'price differential' or otherwise may become very relevant to the outcome of such calculations where the plaintiff is not the first person to have been awarded sums against the insider. The net point appears to be that even if a section 109(1)(a) "loss" can be demonstrated by the investor, reduced compensation may be payable by the insider if section 109(2)(b) applies.

(ii) Account for profit

4–79 Section 109(1)(b)[209] makes the insider liable to compensate the company in respect of whose securities he either dealt (as a primary or secondary insider),[210] or "caused or procured" or "communicated".[211]

---

[206] s.109(1)(a).

[207] s.109(1)(a).

[208] Rider and Ashe, *op. cit.* at n.1, p.48 prefer the second interpretation and state that if it is the correct one, then loss may be very difficult to establish in most cases.

[209] The limitation period for a s.109(1)(b) action is two years after the date of completion of the transaction in which the profit occurred (s.109(4)).

[210] Contrary to s.108(1), (2) or (3).

[211] Contrary to s.108(4) and (5) respectively.

Here the plaintiff is not the investor. It is the company in whose shares the insider dealt. The liability is to return profit, made on the dealings, to the company.

Compared to section 109(1)(a), this provision is considerably clearer. It is clear that there can be only one plaintiff – the company. It is also clear that the insider will be liable for profit made on the transaction. At common law, a person who was under a fiduciary duty to the company was always under a duty to account to the company if he made a profit by virtue of his position. In this sense therefore, section 109(1)(b) does not represent an entirely new ground of liability. However, unlike the common law action, the statutory basis for liability to account provided for in section 109(1)(b) applies to a much wider class of potential defendants. At common law, only fiduciaries were under a duty to account for profit made by virtue of their position. However section 109(1)(b) applies to anyone who breaches section 108. Accordingly (for example), tipees, who do not owe any fiduciary duty to the company in the way that its directors would, can now be statutorily liable to account to the company for profit made from insider dealing in the company's securities. Thus, unlike the common law action, Part V does not require the existence of an implied fiduciary relationship as a prerequisite to legal action against the insider for the recovery of profit made from insider dealing.

4–80 Although this lack of necessity to prove the existence of a fiduciary relationship as a prerequisite to legal action represents a great leap forward, nevertheless, one of the old obstacles that was presented by the common law has not been removed by this statutory form of action. As adverted to earlier in this chapter[212] when the actions at common law were examined, a difficulty – and it may be a considerable one – is whether the company will pursue the insider. This obstacle – getting the company to take legal action for return of profit against the profiteer – may remain even in this statutory action. The company may be unwilling to pursue the insider dealer either because it is partial to the insider, or because it does not want to publicise the fact that (perhaps) one of its own directors or employees was insider dealing in the company's own securities. While a derivative action (*Foss v. Harbottle*) may be contemplated, this approach is fraught with difficulties.

4–81 Another difficulty is that it is not clear whether "profit" is to be the insider's net or gross profit.[213] Furthermore, it should be noted that

---

[212] at para. 4–06.

a limiting provision on the amount of profit that a person may have to account for applies, just as it does in respect of a section 109(1)(a) compensation action for loss. Section 109(1)(b) provides that the "profit" for which the insider is liable is the profit made by the insider on the transaction. But section 109(2)(b) goes on to provide that if a person so liable has already been found by a court to be liable to pay an amount or amounts to any other person or persons by reason of the same act or transaction, then the amount of profit for which he shall be liable shall be that profit less the amount or the sum of the amounts for which that person has already been found to be liable. Thus, the correct meaning of "profit" will become pertinent to the outcome of such calculations where the plaintiff (the company) is not the first person to have been awarded sums against the insider. The net point is that, even if section 109(1)(b) "profit" can be demonstrated, the insider will only be liable to hand over reduced profit if section 109(2)(b) applies.

(b) Criminal liability

(i) Offences

4–82 Section 111 provides that a person who deals in securities in a manner declared unlawful by section 108 shall be guilty of an offence. From a cursory reading of this provision, one might assume therefore that all activity declared 'unlawful' in section 108 would thus constitute a criminal offence for the purposes of section 111. However, this does not appear to be the case. This is because Section 111 refers to dealing that is declared unlawful under section 108. While both primary and secondary activity (section 108(1)–(3)) constitutes such "dealing", neither section 108(4) "causing or procuring" nor section 108(5) "communicating" fall within the definition of "dealing". Although both of the latter are declared "unlawful" by section 108, neither constitutes "dealing" and hence they fall outside section 111. Consequently, neither incurs criminal liability under section 111.[214] Although section 111 does not explicitly refer to companies, presumably companies who deal contrary to section 108(6) will also fall within the section 111 prohibition.

---

[213] Also, as the provision provides liability for 'profit', presumably no s.109(1)(b) action can be attempted where the insider makes a loss.

[214] The First Report of the Company Law Review Group in December 1994 recommended that this lacuna be remedied (see para. 5–20) but to date no such action has been taken. Note that Rider and Ashe, *op. cit.* at n.1 submit that 'causing or procuring' could be prosecuted summarily under the Petty Sessions (Ireland) Act 1851, s.2 or on indictment under the Accessories and Abettors Act 1861, s.8; however, 'communication' would not appear to be susceptible to prosecution as a criminal matter.

(ii) Penalties

4–83   Section 114 sets out the maximum fines upon successful prosecution of any activity that is declared an offence by Part V. The criminal sanctions range from not more than 12 months in jail and/or a fine not exceeding £1,000 on summary conviction to not more than 10 years in jail or a fine not exceeding £200,000 upon conviction on indictment.

Under section 112(1) there is an additional penalty. A person convicted of an offence under section 111 shall be automatically banned from dealing for 12 months from the date of conviction. To breach this ban is a further offence,[215] for which the insider will be subject to section 114 penalties, and furthermore to a further 12 month ban.[216] However, the ban is not absolute as section 112(2) provides that if a primary insider within the meaning of section 108(1) has initiated a transaction before the date of his conviction and some element of performance remains to be completed, then section 108(1) shall not prohibit him completing it if the Stock Exchange indicates in writing to all parties to the transaction that it is satisfied that

- the transaction had commenced before the date of conviction, and

- not to conclude it would prejudice third parties, and

- the transaction would not be unlawful under any other provision of Part V.

(iii) Agents

4–84   Section 113 provides a specific offence for agents. Where an agent has reasonable cause to believe or ought to conclude that the deal would be unlawful under section 108, then not only is the agent prohibited from dealing under section 113(1), but also to breach such a ban is a criminal offence under section 113(2). The penalties are those described above in section 114.[217]

(iv) Unresolved issues

4–85   One issue that the legislation leaves unresolved is whether transactions tainted by insider dealing are void or voidable. Unlike the United Kingdom Criminal Justice Act 1993 section 63(2) of which states that no contract shall be void or unenforceable by reason of it constituting an offence under the United Kingdom legislation, Part V has no corresponding equivalent. Commentators appear to be of the view that

---

[215] s.112(3).
[216] s.112(1).
[217] See para. 4–83 above.

the absence of a corresponding provision in Part V should not be interpreted to mean that insider-tainted transactions in Ireland do not have
such protection.[218] Another unresolved issue is whether some element
of *mens rea* is required before one can be convicted of an offence under
either sections 111, 112 or 113. While commentators appear to differ, it
is submitted that given the strict terms in which the prohibited activities are defined in section 108, there does not appear to be strong
grounds for importing any kind of *scienter* requirement into the offences, apart perhaps from section 108(3) or (5) where at least some
degree of *scienter* appears to be required with regard to certain elements of the proscribed activity. By contrast, it is worth noting that the
United Kingdom legislation requires knowledge of several key elements[219] and further provides for situations where even a person in
possession of such *scienter* can avoid liability.[220]

(c) Enforcement of criminal liability

(i) Relevant Authority

4–86   Under Part V, the primary role for the investigation and reporting of suspected insider dealing rests with the relevant authority of a
recognised Stock Exchange.[221] Section 107 defines the relevant authority as either the manager of an exchange, or its board of directors, management committee or other management body. Section 115(7) provides
that the relevant authority will only be liable in damages for its actions
or omissions in the conduct of its functions under Part V where it acts,
or omits to act, in bad faith.

---

[218] Flynn, *op. cit.* at n.1, at p. 366 submits that otherwise the markets would be
thrown into chaos; Rider and Ashe, *op. cit.* n. 1, p.47 submit that as the statute
penalises insiders by making them subject to criminal and civil liability, it does
not purport to attack the validity of the affected transaction. However, note
that in *Chase Manhattan Equities v. Goodman* [1991] B.C.L.C. 897 Knox J. held an
contract to transfer securities, which had still not been transferred, was unenforceable against the purchaser as it was tainted by the fact that the original
transferor of the shares had been in possession of price-sensitive information.
Although the U.K. legislation in force at the time (the Companies Securities
(Insider Dealing) Act 1985) provided that stock market transactions could not
be unravelled because of insider dealing, Knox J. held that such a provision did
not oblige the court to enforce a contract that had still not been completed.

[219] *e.g.* U.K. Criminal Justice Act 1993, s.57 requires *inter alia* that the insider knows
he has inside information and *knows* that it is from an inside source.

[220] U.K. Criminal Justice Act 1993, s.53.

[221] At the time of writing the only recognised Stock Exchange is the Irish Stock
Exchange Limited, as *per* S.I. No. 310 of 1995 (Companies (Stock Exchange)
Regulations 1995).

(ii) Duty to report insider dealing

4–87   Under section 115, the relevant authority of a recognised Stock Exchange is under a duty to report suspected Part V offences to the Director of Public Prosecutions; to provide information regarding same;[222] to allow access to documents and provide facilities for inspecting same. Section 115(2) imposes a duty on members of the Exchange to report suspected offences to the relevant authority. Section 115(3) provides that if in the course of legal proceedings it appears to a court that an offence under Part V has been committed and no report had been made in respect of it by the relevant authority, then it may direct the relevant authority to make a report to the Director of Public Prosecutions if it had not already done so. Section 115(4) provides that if the Director of Public Prosecutions having received a report decides to initiate prosecutions, then the relevant authority, the officers of the company concerned and any other person who may have relevant information (apart from the defendant) are under a duty to give all reasonable assistance to the Director of Public Prosecutions.

It would seem from the scheme of section 115 that, once it appears to the relevant authority that an offence has been committed, it is obliged to report the matter to the Director of Public Prosecutions, and in so doing it would appear that the relevant authority (*i.e.* the Stock Exchange) ceases to have any further investigation role in the (as yet) alleged offence.

(iii) Direction to Relevant Authority to act

4–88   Pursuant to section 115(5) and (6), the Minister may direct the relevant authority to use its Part V powers of investigation or make a report to the Director of Public Prosecutions, where the Minister concludes that the relevant authority has not done so in circumstances where the Minister concludes the relevant authority "ought" to do so. The relevant authority shall communicate the results of its investigations or a copy of its report, as the case may be, to the Minister.

(iv) Investigation powers

4–89   Section 117 provides for the appointment of an "authorised person". Such person is a person approved by the Minister whose role it

---

[222] In practice, once the Exchange reports the suspected offence to the DPP, the DPP takes an initial view on whether the file discloses a case it may wish to prosecute. If so, then the file is passed to the gardaí to investigate. In order that such follow-up investigation be as comprehensive as possible, consideration should be given to amending the legislation so that the gardaí have explicit investigation powers similar to those available to "authorised persons" pursuant to s.117 (considered at para. 4–88 below).

will be to investigate the suspected insider dealing contrary to Part V. This person can be either the manager of a recognised exchange or a person nominated by a relevant authority of a recognised exchange. Section 117(3) sets out the authorised person's powers. It provides that such person may require any person whom he, or the relevant authority, has reasonable cause to believe to have dealt or have any information about such dealings, to divulge such information as the investigator may reasonably require, in regard to:

—the securities concerned;

—the issuer of the securities;

—the person's dealings in such securities; or

—any other information the authorised person reasonably requires in relation to such securities or dealings.

A person being investigated is required to grant the authorised person access to and use of facilities for inspecting and taking copies of documents as he may reasonably require.

The authorised person's investigation results are furnished to the relevant authority for the purposes of discharging the relevant authority's functions under section 115 (i.e. with a view to the relevant authority reporting a suspected offence to the Director of Public Prosecutions).

(v) Role of court in determining ambit of investigation

4–90 Section 117(5) allows either the authorised person, or the investigated party, to go to court seeking a declaration that the information requested should, or should not, be divulged. In exercising this power, section 117(6) requires the court to exercise its discretion in the matter on the basis of the exigencies of the common good. If the court orders the investigated party to comply with the authorised person's request, and that party fails to comply with such request, the authorised person may verify the fact of such failure to comply, and the court may punish the investigated party as if he had been guilty of contempt of court.

(vi) Obligation of professional secrecy

4–91 Section 118(1) provides that, except in accordance with law, neither the relevant authority, an authorised person or any person employed (or formerly employed) by a recognised exchange, may divulge any information obtained by virtue of the exercise of any functions under Part V. Contravention of this obligation of professional secrecy shall constitute an offence, the penalties for which are contained in section 114. Section 118(2) explicitly provides that the aforegoing shall not prevent a relevant authority from disclosing any information to the Minister, or to a similar authority in another Member State of the European Community.

A difficulty which arises with this statutory obligation of secrecy in practice, is that if the Part V investigation suggests that offences other than those under Part V may have been committed, the investigating authority is effectively precluded by the obligation of secrecy from passing on such information to the relevant authorities (other than a section 118(2) body).

(vii) Duty to co-operate with other EC Stock Exchanges

4–92   Section 116 provides that a relevant authority of a recognised exchange shall cooperate with a similar authority from another European Community Member State which is exercising its powers under any Community enactment relating to unlawful dealing within the meaning of Part V, whether in the State or elsewhere. This provision is intended to facilitate mutual co-operation between exchanges in different Member States where one exchange requires another to provide it with information. Section 116(2) obliges the relevant authority, in so far as it is reasonably able to do so, to make use of its powers of investigation provided by Part V and provide the relevant information requested.

However, before it furnishes the information to the foreign authority, the relevant authority is obliged to inform the Minister of the request, and the Minister may direct the authority to refuse to provide all or any of the information requested. The Minister may direct the relevant authority to refuse the request where one of the following applies:

—communication of the information might affect the sovereignty, security or public policy of the State

—civil or criminal proceedings in the State have already been commenced against a person in respect of any of its acts in relation to which a request for information has been received

—any person has been convicted in the State of a criminal offence in respect of any such acts.

(viii) Annual report of Recognised Stock Exchange

4–93   Recognised stock exchanges[223] are obliged to make an annual

---

[223] At the time of writing the Irish Stock Exchange Limited is the only "recognised" Stock Exchange: S.I. No. 310 of 1995.

report to the Minister on the exercise of the relevant authority's functions. The Report shall include

– the number of written complaints received regarding possible contraventions of Part V

– the number of reports made to the Director of Public Prosecutions under Part V

– the number of instances in which, following the exercise of powers of authorised persons under this Part, reports were not made to the Director of Public Prosecutions

– any other information as may be prescribed.

A copy of the report shall be laid before the houses of the Oireachtas. However, if the Minister, after consultation with the relevant authority, is of the opinion that the disclosure of any information in any such report would materially injure or unfairly prejudice the legitimate interests of any person, or if there is any other good reason for not divulging information, the Minister may lay the report before the Oireachtas with such information deleted.

II. MANIPULATION OF THE STOCK MARKET

MARKET MANIPULATION

(1)   How the market may be manipulated

4–94   While this chapter has concentrated on insider dealing, it is appropriate to briefly consider rigging or manipulation of the stock market as a related theme. Manipulation of the market can be achieved in a number of ways. For example, a member firm of the Stock Exchange or its employees could attempt to manipulate the market by attempting to create a false market in particular securities by advising clients that the securities were good value or bad value, when clearly they thought otherwise privately. Alternatively, clients could be advised that certain securities should be purchased when the real objective unknown to the client was to cause the clients to buy the securities in the hope that they might rise in value and thereby enrich the encouraging party who had earlier quietly bought the securities at a lower price. Another way to manipulate the market would be to attempt to 'effect' false transactions whereby the appearance of changes in ownership of securities is created in order to encourage other investors into the market with the objective of causing the market to either rise or fall. Spreading false rumours can also be a way of rigging the market.

(2) Companies (Amendment) Act 1999[224] – Stabilisation Rules

4–95 Another classic form of manipulation is where one attempts to stabilise the market price of securities at a particular level, such as where all securities offered at a price lower than the desired price would be acquired by the manipulator in order to give the impression that the securities' price was holding steady.[225] However, it is recognised that in certain circumstances market manipulation in the form of market stabilisation may be justified. Consequently, the Companies (Amendment) No. 8 Act 1999 has provided that action taken to stabilise an issue or offer of securities either inside or outside the State is permissible, provided it is conducted in accordance with the Stabilisation Rules contained in the Schedule to the Act.[226]

According to the stabilisation regime set forth in the 1999 Act, nothing done in the State for the purpose of stabilising or maintaining the market price of securities shall violate Section 108 of the Companies Act 1990 provided it conforms with the 1999 Act's Stabilisation Rules.[227] Furthermore, stabilising action undertaken outside the State will not violate Section 108 provided it is permitted in the other jurisdiction and is in accordance with all relevant requirements applicable to such action in the jurisdiction where the action is effected.[228]

(a) Relevant Securities

4–96 Rule 2 of the Stabilisation Rules provides that the Rules apply to issues or offers of "relevant securities"[229] which means

— an issue of securities for cash

---

[224] No. 8 of 1999.

[225] Note that under the Exchange's rules, market stabilisation is permitted where a new issue takes place for the first 30 days post-issue date. The Stock Exchange must be informed of any such transactions. This compliments the statutory regime with the recent enactment of the Companies (Amendment) (No. 8) Act 1999.

[226] The 1999 Act was enacted in order to ensure that stabilisation action could be undertaken, if required, in connection with the initial public offering which took place in July 1999 when the State offered the general public the right to subscribe in the national Telecommunications operator, Telecom Éireann (now known as Eircom).

[227] s.2(a) Companies Act 1999.

[228] s.2(b) Companies Act 1999, and this includes the rules of the stock exchange in that other jurisdiction if the securities are listed in that other jurisdiction.

[229] For the purposes of the definition of "relevant securities", "securities" are defined as in s.107 Companies Act 1990 (as set out above in para. 4–12).

— an offer of securities for cash for which securities dealing facilities are not already provided by a recognised stock exchange, and

— an offer of securities for cash for which securities dealing facilities are already provided by a recognised stock exchange, if the total cost of the securities which are the subject of the offer is at least £15,000,000 (or the equivalent in the currency or unit of account in which the price of the securities is stated)

and which is made other than in connection with a takeover offer[230] and at a specified price and which securities may be dealt in on a recognised stock exchange without a formal application, or in respect of which application has been made to a recognised stock exchange for the securities to be dealt in on that exchange.

(b) Stabilising Periods

(i) Within the State

4–97   So far as stabilising action in this State is concerned, the "stabilising period" for securities (not being debentures or other debt securities) is defined[231] as the period beginning with the date on which the "earliest public announcement"[232] of the issue or offer for sale which states the "issue price"[233] or offer price (as the case may be) is made, and ending with the "relevant day."[234]

---

[230] The Stabilisation Rules define "takeover offer" as meaning an offer made generally to holders of shares in a company to acquire those shares or a specified proportion of them, or to holders of a particular class of those shares to acquire the shares of that class or a specified proportion of them.

[231] Rule 1 Stabilisation Rules.

[232] The Stabilisation Rules define "public announcement" to mean any communication made by or on behalf of the issuer or the stabilising manager, being a communication made in circumstances in which it is likely that members of the public will become aware of the communication.

[233] The Stabilisation Rules (Rule 1) define "issue price" to mean the specified price at which the relevant securities are issued without deducting any selling concession or commission.

[234] The Stabilisation Rules (Rule 1) define "relevant day" to mean the 30th day after the closing date, or, where before the 30th day after the closing date, the date the stabilising manager has determined that he or she would take no further action to stabilise or maintain the market price of the relevant securities and has notified the Irish Stock Exchange Limited accordingly pursuant to Rule 8 of the Stabilisation Rules (see further para. 4–108 and 4–109 below). Rule 1 defines "closing date" to mean, in the case of an issue of securities, the date on which the issuer of the securities receives the proceeds of the issue or, where the issuer receives those proceeds by way of instalments, the date on which it receives the first instalment. On the other hand closing date has a different meaning for an offer for sale of securities. In this instance it means the date on

So far as the stabilising period for debentures or other debt securities is concerned, it is the period beginning with the date on which the earliest public announcement of the issue is made (whether or not that announcement states the issue price) and ending with the relevant day.[235]

(ii) Outside the State

4–98   So far as stabilising action in a jurisdiction outside the State is concerned, the stabilising period is defined[236] as the period beginning on the date on which the earliest public announcement of such offer is made which states the issue price or the offer price (as the case may be) for those securities (not being an issue of debentures or other debt securities). The period ends on the expiration of the day which is either 30 days after the closing date,[237] or on a day prior to the expiry of that period on which the stabilising manager[238] shall have notified a stock exchange on which the stabilising action was being conducted as the day on which the manager determined that the manager would take no further action to stabilise or maintain the market price of the securities concerned.

So far as the stabilising period for debentures or other debt securities outside the State as concerned, it means the period beginning on the date on which the earliest public announcement of the issue was made (whether or not that announcement states the issue price) and ending on the earlier of the dates applicable to the stabilising of non-debenture securities (as described in the previous sentence).[239]

(c) Preliminary Steps Before Stabilising Action

(i) Reasonable belief

4–99   Before the stabilising manager can take any stabilising action,

---

which the offeror, or as the case may be, the offerors, receive the proceeds of the offer for sale, or where the offeror(s) elect to receive the proceeds in instalments, the date on which the first instalment is received by the offeror(s).

[235] Rule 1 Stabilisation Rules.

[236] s.1(1) Companies (Amendment) Act (No. 8) 1999.

[237] Rule 1 defines "closing date" to mean, in the case of an issue of securities, the date on which the issuer of the securities receives the proceeds of the issue or, where the issuer receives those proceeds by way of instalments, the date on which it receives the first instalment. On the other hand closing date has a different meaning for an offer for sale of securities. In this instance it means the date on which the offeror, or as the case may be, the offerors, receive the proceeds of the offer for sale, or where the offeror(s) elect to receive the proceeds in instalments, the date on which the first instalment is received by the offeror(s).

[238] Appointed by the issuer or the offeror (as the case may be).

[239] *ibid.*

first the manager must have a "reasonable belief" that the preliminary steps required by Rule 5 have been taken. Rule 5 requires that from the beginning of the "introductory period"[240] any electronic screen-based statement or announcement intended for publication in any newspaper, or any other announcement of a public nature, invitation telex or equivalent document which refer to the issue, published on behalf of the issuer or the stabilising manager, shall include a reference to either the prospectus, the future prospectus or the word "Stabilisation."[241] Furthermore, any preliminary offering circular/prospectus, final offering circular/prospectus relating to the issue of the securities concerned shall include a statement to the effect that stabilising action may or may not be effected during the stabilisation period.[242]

(ii) Modification where stabilisation occurs outside the State

4–100 Where stabilising action will be effected in a jurisdiction outside the State, Rule 5 recognises that the requirement that reference be made to the possibility that stabilisation may occur, may have to be modified. This is in order to ensure that the stabilising manager in the other jurisdiction(s) does not commit any breach of any legal rule or requirement in respect of any communication or announcement made, or advertisement or document issued, in that jurisdiction.[243]

(iii) Associated securities

4–101 The Stabilisation Rules may impact not only on relevant securities, but also on "associated securities". "Associated securities" are *inter alia* securities which are in all respect uniform with the relevant securities, or for which the relevant securities may be exchanged or converted.[244] Where the price of associated securities is higher than

---

[240] The Stabilisation Rules (Rule 1) define "introductory period" as the period starting at the time of the first public announcement from which it could reasonably be deduced that the issue was intended to take place in some form and at some time, and ending with the beginning of the stabilising period.

[241] Rule 5(1)(a) Stabilisation Rules.

[242] Rule 5(1)(b) Stabilisation Rules. Rule 5(3)(a) further provides that (other than the documents mentioned above), Rule 5 shall not apply to any communication, advertisement or document. In this regard, Rule 5(3)(b) specifically excludes allotment telexes; pricing telexes; contract notes; short form or image advertisement, including any newspaper, radio or television advertisement designed to generate interest in the issue of the securities concerned and any marketing brochure as long as it does not constitute a preliminary offering circular or preliminary offering prospectus.

[243] Rule 5(2)(b) Stabilisation Rules.

[244] For a complete definition of the several different varieties of "associated security", see further Rule 1 Stabilisation Rules in the Schedule to the 1999 Act.

the relevant securities due to the actions of persons, who the manager knows or ought reasonably to know created a false or misleading impression in the market as to the value of the associated securities, Rule 5 provides that the stabilising manager must be satisfied that the issue price of the relevant securities is no higher than it would have been had that third party action not been performed, or that course of conduct not been engaged in.[245]

(d) Stabilising Action

4–102   The stabilising manager may take what it defined in the Act as "permitted stabilising action."[246] This is defined to mean that the manager may purchase, agree to purchase or offer to purchase any of the relevant securities.[247] Alternatively, the manager may purchase, agree to purchase or offer to purchase any associated securities.[248] The manager can only engage in any of the aforegoing described stabilising actions provided that the manager "reasonably believes" that Rule 5 (preliminary steps before stabilising action) has been satisfied.[249]

It should be noted that in the case of certain types of associated securities, stabilisation action is not permitted. In this regard, Rule 6 provides that no stabilising action shall be taken in any associated securities of those relevant securities which are debentures or other debt securities where such associated securities are associated securities because:

(a)   the relevant securities may be exchanged for or converted into the associated securities, or

(b)   the holders of the relevant securities have a right to subscribe for or to acquire the associated securities

unless the terms on which the relevant securities may be exchanged for or converted into the associated securities, or the rights of holders of the relevant securities to subscribe for or to acquire the associated securities, have been finally settled and been made the subject of a public announcement.

(e) Action ancillary to Stabilising Action

4–103   Rule 4 permits the stabilising manager to take action ancillary

---

[245] Rule 5(1)(c) Stabilisation Rules.
[246] Rule 3 Stabilisation Rules.
[247] Rule 3(1)(a) Stabilisation Rules.
[248] Rule 3(1)(b) Stabilisation Rules.
[249] See paras 4–99—4-101 above.

to stabilising action, provided that the manager "reasonably believes" that the Rule 5 preliminary steps before stabilising action have been fulfilled.[250] What ancillary action means is that the manager may, with a view to effecting stabilising actions, either make allocations of a greater number of relevant securities than will be issued, or offer to sell, or agree to sell a greater number of relevant securities or associated securities than the stabilising manager has available for sale.[251] The manager may further choose to purchase, offer to purchase or agree to purchase relevant securities or associated securities in order to close out or liquidate any position established pursuant to the aforegoing.[252]

Additionally, the stabilising manager may also choose to sell, offer to sell, or agree to sell relevant securities or associated securities in order to close out or liquidate any position established by stabilising action.[253]

So far as certain types of associated securities are concerned, because there is a restriction on the taking of stabilising action in respect to them,[254] ancillary actions are likewise not permitted.[255]

(f) Limits on Stabilisation Price

4–104 The limits imposed on the manager's freedom of action with regard to the price at which the manager may intervene are imposed by Rule 7. This provides that no stabilising action shall be effected by the manager at a price higher than *the relevant price* determined in accordance with Rule 7.

(i) Relevant Securities and certain Associated Securities

4–105 In the case of relevant securities and associated securities which are in all respects uniform with the relevant securities (not being debentures or other debt securities), the relevant price for the initial stabilising action is the issue price.[256]

For subsequent stabilising actions, where a deal was done at a higher price than the initial stabilising price on the relevant exchange[257] and

---

[250] Rule 4(2) Stabilisation Rules.
[251] Rule 4 Stabilisation Rules permits the manager to do either, or both, as required.
[252] In which event, Rule 4(4) provides that a transaction of this type may be effected without regard to the requirements as to purchasing price limits set out in Rule 7 (these are considered at paras 4–104—4–106 below).
[253] Whether or not those actions were in accordance with Rule 3 (on permitted stabilising action).
[254] Rule 6 Stabilisation Rules, as discussed at para. 4–102 above.
[255] Rule 4(1) Stabilisation Rules.
[256] Rule 7(2)(a)(i) Stabilisation Rules.
[257] Rule 7 defines "relevant exchange" for the purposes of Rule 7 as being the stock exchange which the stabilising manager reasonably believes to be the

this deal was not done on the manager's instructions, then the relevant price shall be the issue price or the price at which that deal was done, which ever is the lower.[258] Where no such deal was done, then the relevant price is the issue price or the initial stabilising price, whichever is the lower.[259]

(ii) Certain other Associated Securities

4–106 In the case of associated securities (not being debentures or other debt securities, or associated securities which are in all respects uniform with the relevant securities, or associated call options) the relevant price shall be, for the initial stabilising action, the market bid price of the associated securities at the beginning of the stabilising period.[260]

For subsequent actions, where there has been a deal at a price above the price at which the initial stabilising action took place on the relevant exchange[261] and this deal was not done on the manager's instructions, then the relevant price shall be the market bid price of the associated securities at the beginning of the stabilising period or the price at which that deal was done, whichever is the lower.[262] Where there has been no such deal done, then the relevant price shall be the market bid price of the associated securities at the beginning of the stabilising period or the initial stabilising price, whichever is the lower.[263]

---

principal exchange on which those securities (or options, as the case may be) are dealt in at the time of the transaction.

[258] Rule 7(2)(a)(ii)(I) Stabilisation Rules.

[259] Rule 7(2)(a)(ii)(II). Note that Rule 7(3)(b)(i) provides that where the price of any relevant securities or associated securities on the relevant exchange is in a currency other than the currency of the price of the securities to be stabilised, stabilising actions may be made at a price that reflects any movement in the relevant rate of exchange, but this shall not permit stabilising action under Rule 7(2)(a) at a price above the equivalent in the other currency on the relevant exchange.

[260] Rule 7(2)(b)(i) Stabilisation Rules. Note that Rule 7(3)(b)(iii) provides that where no market bid price is quoted in respect of the associated security concerned at the beginning of the stabilising period, the relevant price shall be the closing quotation price in respect of such securities on the previous business day as published in the relevant stock exchange list.

[261] Rule 7 defines "relevant exchange" for the purposes of Rule 7 as being the stock exchange which the stabilising manager reasonably believes to be the principal exchange on which those securities (or options, as the case may be) are dealt in at the time of the transaction.

[262] Rule 7(2)(b)(ii)(I) Stabilisation Rules.

[263] Rule 7(2)(b)(ii)(II) Stabilisation Rules.

(iii) Associated Call Options

4–107   In the case of associated call options,[264] the relevant price for the initial stabilising action shall be the market price of the associated call option at the beginning of the stabilising period.[265]

For subsequent actions, where there has been a deal at a price above the price at which the initial stabilising action took place on the relevant exchange[266] and this deal was not done on the manager's instructions, then the relevant price shall be the market bid price of the associated call option at the beginning of the stabilising period or the price at which that deal was done, whichever is the lower.[267] Where there has been no such deal done, then the relevant price shall be the market bid price of the associated call option at the beginning of the stabilising period or the initial stabilising price, whichever is the lower.[268]

(g) Termination of Stabilising Period

4–108   The stabilising period will last for 30 days after the closing date.[269] However, it can also end prior to that where, at a date before the 30th day after the closing date, the stabilising manager determines that no further action will be taken to stabilise or maintain the market price of the relevant securities. In this event, the manager shall notify the Stock Exchange without delay of this decision. The Exchange is required to publish this information.[270]

(h) Recording of Stabilisation Transactions

4–109   The Stabilisation Rules require the manager to establish a Register[271] of transactions in which the manager shall record information

---

[264] Note that Rule 7(3)(b)(ii) provides that any convertible bond which is both a debenture or other debt security and an associated call option, shall be treated as a debenture only.

[265] Rule 7(2)(c)(i) Stabilisation Rules.

[266] Rule 7 defines "relevant exchange" for the purposes of Rule 7 as being the stock exchange which the stabilising manager reasonably believes to be the principal exchange on which those securities (or options, as the case may be) are dealt in at the time of the transaction.

[267] Rule 7(2)(c)(ii)(I) Stabilisation Rules.

[268] Rule 7(2)(c)(ii)(II) Stabilisation Rules.

[269] See para 4–97 above where "closing date" and related matters pertinent to the stabilising period are considered.

[270] Rule 8 Stabilisation Rules.

[271] Rule 5 Stabilisation Rules requires the manager to establish a Register as one of the preliminary steps before any stabilising action may be undertaken.

in relation to any Rule 3 (stabilising action) or Rule 4 (action ancillary to stabilising action) transactions.[272]

The details to be recorded are[273] the date and time of each transaction; the names of the persons to whom relevant securities were allocated or issued, and the respective amounts allocated or issued to each person; a description of the securities; the price of the securities; the number of securities; and, the identity of the counterparty to the transaction.

(i) Stabilisation Rules and the Companies Act 1990 disclosure rules regarding relevant share capital

4–110 Section 3 of the 1999 Act provides that the acquisition or disposal of interests in relevant share capital by a person during the stabilisation period which is done for either:

(a) the purpose of stabilising or maintaining the market price of the securities, and

(b) is so done in conformity with the Stabilisation Rules

shall be disregarded during the stabilisation period for the disclosure purposes of sections 67 to 79 of the Companies Act 1990.

Section 3 further provides that any interest in relevant share capital which was acquired by a person during the stabilising period for the purpose of stabilising or maintaining the market price of securities in accordance with the Act and which continues to be held by such person at the end of the stabilising period, shall be treated for the purposes of sections 67–79 as having been acquired by such person on the first day following the end of the stabilising period (not being a Saturday, Sunday or public holiday).

(3) Stock Exchange regime to prevent market manipulation

4–111 Part V of the Companies Act 1990 does not prohibit market manipulation and neither does the Stock Exchange Act 1995. Consequently, as there are no statutory remedies, only the common law can provide a remedy to an aggrieved investor such as deceit, recission or fraud. These may be difficult to pursue on evidential grounds. In an attempt to give investors a measure of protection, section 38 of the Stock Exchange Act 1995 provides that the Stock Exchange should lay down a code of practice for its member firms in order to ensure that they act honestly and fairly in the best interests of both their clients

---

[272] Rule 9 Stabilisation Rules.
[273] Rule 9(2) Stabilisation Rules.

and the integrity of the stock market. In this regard Section 38[274] set out seven principles which the Exchange's rules of conduct for member firms now reflect. These aim to ensure that member firms:

(a) act honestly and fairly in conducting their business activities in the best interests of clients and the integrity of the market;

(b) act with due skill, care and diligence, in the best interests of clients and the integrity of the market

(c) have and employ effectively the resources and procedures that are necessary for the proper performance of their business activities

(d) seek from their clients information regarding their financial situation, investment experience and objectives as regards the services requested

(e) make adequate disclosure of relevant information in their dealings with clients

(f) make a reasonable effort to avoid conflicts of interests and, when they cannot be avoided, ensure that clients are fairly treated, and

(g) comply with all regulatory requirements applicable to the conduct of business activities so as to promote the best interests of their clients and the integrity of the market.

Section 38(3) allows for the rules of conduct to be applied in such a way as to take account of the "status or experience" of the particular user of the member firm's services, and it is permissible for the rules of conduct to allow different categories of investor to be distinguished for this purpose.

Consequently, the Stock Exchange has (for example) provided in its rules of conduct that a member firm shall not knowingly and without due care do anything which might create a false impression of the market. Furthermore, the rules provide that the member firm is obliged to publish corrective statements promptly if it appears that a client has published a materially inaccurate statement about a transaction involving the client and the member firm. However, in leaving it to the Stock Exchange to lay down such a code of practice, the Stock Exchange Act 1995 does not impose civil liability on a member firm which transgresses the rules. Instead, it will be up to the Stock Exchange to decide if the transgressing firm has violated the rules, and if so, what sanction should be imposed. Section 24 of the Stock Exchange Act 1995 pro-

---

[274] The s.38 principles set out hereafter reflect those set out in Council Directive 93/22/EC, the Investment Services Directive.

vides that that the High Court may revoke the approval of a member firm on the application of the Central Bank, so perhaps this may act as some measure of deterrent to ensure that member firms comply with the Exchange's Rules of Conduct.

The Stock Exchange's rules also seek to counter member firm manipulation in other ways. For example, they provide that where a member firm is providing clients with recommendations based on research analyses, the firm must not deal either on its own account or on the accounts of its employees or connected persons until its clients have had an appropriate amount of time to absorb and deal with the information presented. However, if it can demonstrate that non-porous "chinese walls" exist, then the firm may deal. Another way in which the rules attempt to counter abuses is to require member firms to maintain in-house rules and structures for the recording of all transactions undertaken on the personal accounts of their employees or connected persons.

4–112   Finally, another practice that the rules seek to prevent is known as "churning". This is not so much manipulation of the market, but rather manipulation of the client directly. This is where the broker initiates an excessive or unnecessary level of transactions in order to extract a higher level of commission fees from a client's account. The rules provide that the onus is on the broker to demonstrate that the level of transactions was not excessive.

Corporate Borrowing

I. **Corporate Borrowing – Loans** 275
    What is a Loan 275
        (1) Loan defined 275
        (2) Loan instruments 277
            (a) Loan facility agreement 277
            (b) Overdraft 279
            (c) Debentures.. 279
II. **Corporate Borrowing – Developments in *Ultra vires*** 281
    Overview of developments 281
    A. Borrowing – "Power" or "Object" 282
        (1) Trading company cannot have "borrowing" as
            an Object 282
        (2) Drafting Devices which attempt to designate
            borrowing as a Corporate Object 284
            (a) Main Objects Principle... 284
                (i) Cotman clause 285
                (ii) Bell Houses clause 286
        (3) Restrictive judicial interpretation 287
        (4) Benefit to the company 289
    B. Borrowing Transactions Tainted by Abuse of Directors'
        Powers 290
        (1) *Ultra vires* distinguished from abuse of directors'
            powers 291
        (2) Transactions tainted by abuse of directors' powers 291
        (3) Limitations of a general and specific nature
            distinguished... 295
        (4) Th issue of benefit to the company................................ 296
    C. Enforcing Loan Contracts against *Ultra Vires* Corporate
        Borrower 299
        (1) Companies Act 1963, section 8(1) 299
            (a) Limitations on availability of section 8(1) 299
            (b) 'Actually Aware'... 301
                (i) Judicial interpretation of section 8(1) 301
                (ii) Article 9 First Company Law Directive 304
                (iii)Regulation 6 of S.I. No. 163 of 1973 305

D. Recovery of Funds Loaned Pursuant to *Ultra Vires*
        Transaction 307
    (1) *In personam* contractual and quasi-contractual
        remedies denied 307
    (2) Quasi-contractual remedies rehabilitated 309
    (3) Basis for recovery of funds loaned *ultra vires*
        the lender? 311
    (4) Recovery of sums paid *ultra vires* the
        Revenue authorities 318
III. **Corporate Borrowing – Authority of Corporate**
    Borrower's Agents.. 320
    Overview 320
    A. Types of Authority.. 321
    (1) Actual Authority 321
    (2) Ostensible Authority 322
        (a) Representation of authority 323
        (b) Representation by company 324
        (c) Reliance on representation.. 324
        (d) Intra vires transaction... 324
        (e) No express limitation on agent's authority 324
    B. Constructive Notice and Authority of
        Company Agents.. 325
    (1) The rule in Turquand's case 325
        (a) Limitations on Turquand's rule 327
            (i) Deficiency on public record 327
            (ii) Where party not in good faith 327
            (iii) Where the company agent was acting outside
                usual authority 330
    C. Agents Authority and the Impact of European
        Legislation 331
    (1) Article 9(2) 331
    (2) European Communities (Companies) Regulations
        1973 331
        (a) Regulation 6 331
        (b) Impact on Turquand's rule/agency principles 332
            (i) Turquand's rule 332
            (ii) Agency principles.. 333
        (c) Limitations on availability of Regulation 6............. 333
IV. **Corporate Borrowing – Charging Book Debts** 335
    A. Types of Charges on Book Debts 335
    (1) What is a Book Debt 336
    (2) Statutory obligation to register charges on
        Book Debts.. 336
    (3) Advantages of being a fixed charge lender.................... 342

B. Feasibility of Attaching Floating or Fixed Charge on
    Book Debts 344
    (1) Floating charges on Book Debts....................................... 344
    (2) Fixed charges on Book Debts 345
    (3) Judicial methods for ascertaining true nature of
        charges over Book Debts 345
        (a) The constructionist approach 345
        (b) Consolidation of the constructionist approach 348
        (c) The importance of the terms of the designated
            account 349
    (4) Some possible implications of recent case law 352
C. Book Debts, Charges and the Borrower's Examinership.... 353
    (1) Crystallised floating charges de-crystallise 355
    (2) Negative pledge covenants unenforceable 358
    (3) Lender realisation of debt charged prevented 359
    (4) Certified borrowings repayable in priority.................... 359

Corporate Borrowing

CORPORATE BORROWING – LOANS

WHAT IS A LOAN

(1) Loan defined

5–01 As a matter of business definition, a loan is a sum borrowed which must be repaid at some time in the future. From a legal perspective, a loan is a contract under which one party advances or otherwise makes available to another a sum of money in consideration of a promise, implied or express, to repay the sum involved, whether or not at a premium and with or without interest.[1] From the aforegoing definition, it appears that the obligation to repay at some time in the future is at the very core of the loan concept in law. The obligation to repay will usually be express, although it may be implied (in this event, the onus will be on the recipient of the funds to prove otherwise).[2] Where no stipulation as to repayment can be implied, the transaction would not appear to be a loan. Money provided without any stipulation as to repayment constitutes a present debt, which is generally repayable on demand without any prior demand being required.[3]

Whether a particular financial transaction constitutes a "loan" in law, or alternatively some other type of transaction, can often be a difficult question to answer. Many transactions may look like loans, but are not such in law. For example, a purchase on credit is not a loan.[4] Fuller points out that it is common for companies to borrow through the issue of perpetual or irredeemable securities expressed to be re-

---

[1] *Chitty on Contracts* (23rd edition, Sweet and Maxwell, London). This is also the definition favoured by Burgess, *Corporate Finance Law* (1993, 2nd edition, Sweet and Maxwell, London).

[2] *Seldon v. Avison* [1968] 2 All E.R. 755.

[3] Burgess, *op. cit..* Though in the case of overdrawn bank accounts, a prior demand must be made: *Joachimson v. Swiss Banking Corp* [1921] 3 K.B. 110 CA.

[4] *Chow Yoonh Hong v. Choong Fah Rubber Manuacturer* [1962] A.C. 209; nor is a sale of book debts which are payable by instalments: *Olds Discount Co. Ltd v. John Playfair Ltd* [1938] 3 All E.R. 275.

[5] *Corporate Borrowing: Law and Practice* (1995, Jordans, Bristol) at p. 4.

payable only in the winding up of the company or at the company's option.[5] The issue therefore arises as to whether a transaction constitutes a loan if the obligation to repay is only contingent in nature. There appear to be two views on the matter. One view is that where repayment is conditional, then the fund-raising only constitutes a loan if the event on which repayment is conditional is bound to happen.[6] The other view is that a transaction is not prevented from being classified as a loan in law merely because the repayment is dependent upon the happening of a contingent event.[7] Fuller considers that securities which are expressed to be irredeemable are still nevertheless loans if, on their true construction, they are irredeemable only so long as the company continues to trade and become repayable on a winding-up.[8]

Whether or not a particular financing transaction constitutes a "loan" can be an important issue from two perspectives.

The first perspective is that of the lender. The lender of the finance will wish to be satisfied that the loan constitutes a form of borrowing that is *intra vires* the borrowing company, not *ultra vires*.

The second perspective is that of the borrowing company's board of directors. The directors will be concerned to ensure that any limits imposed on the company's borrowing abilities are not breached. Such limits can arise either from the terms of the company's articles (*e.g.*, specified borrowing ceilings, or borrowings/share capital ratios) or from the terms of existing loan agreements that the company is party to (*e.g.* negative pledges).

So far as limits imposed by the articles are concerned, where these limits are in danger of being exceeded, the directors will wish to be satisfied as to whether a particular financing option being considered by the company would breach those limits. Where this may occur, the directors will have to consider whether to obtain the finance by some other instrument or method which does not constitute a "loan". Alternatively, they may seek the permission of the members of the company to have the articles amended in order to extend the borrowing ceilings, or have any breach of the borrowing ceiling ratified.[9]

So far as limits imposed by existing loan arrangements are concerned, the directors will have to ensure that their attempts to raise fresh finance respect such limits. Otherwise, they may cause the company to default on existing loans. This could arise where existing loan arrangements provide that the company's debt position must not be exacerbated by the taking on of further loan obligations. Directors

[6] *City of London Brewery Co Ltd. v. (IRC)* [1899] 1 Q.B. 121.
[7] *Waite Hill Holdings v. Marshall* [1983] 133 N.L.J. 745.
[8] *Re the Southern Brazilian Rio Grande do Sul Railway Co Ltd* [1905] 2 Ch. 78.
[9] *Re Burke Clancy & Co Ltd*, unreported, High Court, Kenny J., May 23 1974; *Irvine v. Union Bank of Australia* [1877] 2 App. Cas. 366.

placed in such a dilemma should seek to renegotiate such existing restrictions, or obtain the consent of existing lenders to allow the company procure fresh loan finance without going into a default situation.

(2) Loan instruments

5–02 Loans for corporate entities can be obtained using a variety of different legal instruments. While it is impossible to describe all possible instruments by which a company may raise loan finance, if for no other reason than that the possibilities are only constrained by the ingenuity of the borrower and lender, nevertheless the main features of the main types of loan instrument used in Ireland will be described.

(a) Loan facility agreement

5–03 The most common instrument by which loans to companies are arranged is the bank facility document[10] issued by a bank lender. This letter will set out the terms and conditions under which the lender is prepared to make funds available to the borrower. While the content of every facility document will vary with the transaction concerned, the essential elements are a description of the maximum and minimum amounts that will be advanced, the repayment date and arrangements, the interest rate applicable, and any security to be given in return.[11]

The loan facility can take many forms. For example, the facility document may describe a "standby facility" whereby the lender is prepared to make certain finance available over a stated period, should the company so require. Alternatively, the facility letter may describe a "term facility" whereby the finance will be advanced immediately or in tranches over a period, repayable within a stated timeframe. Another variation is the "revolving facility", whereby the lender will continue to make certain sums available to the company on an on-going basis, provided that the company adheres to an on-going repayment schedule in respect of sums already obtained under the facility. The aforegoing examples, being the most common type of bank facility, are merely illustrative, as many different types of facility can be provided depending on borrower and lender negotiations.

Common to all arrangements will be the specification of conditions precedent that the lender requires to be satisfied in advance of the drawdown of funds. Usually, the borrower will be required to specify that all such conditions precedent have been fulfilled. Normally such conditions will concern the lender's desire to ensure that the borrower has the requisite corporate capacity to borrow the funds, and that all

---

[10] Or "facility letter" as it is also known.
[11] Separate documents will be drawn up where security is to be provided.

company formalities required to be fulfilled under the memorandum and articles have been satisfied. Until such conditions precedent have been fulfilled, the lender's obligation to lend the funds will not arise.

A well drafted loan agreement will also contain conditions subsequent which take the form of warranties by the borrower. For example, a warranty to the effect that the borrower's financial condition has not adversely changed since its last published accounts.[12] What this means is that if the borrower's condition drastically changes for the worse, the warranty being breached will constitute a default event, in which event the bank can foreclose on the loan.[13] Other examples of conditions subsequent include the obligation not to exceed certain specified asset/borrowings ratios, as well as negative pledges by the borrower that it will not create superior security interests over its assets which could take priority over any security taken by the lender.

Where corporate borrowing requirements involve large funding needs, a syndicated loan arrangement will be put into effect. This involves one bank, the "agent bank", forming a syndicate of other banks interested in making funds available to the borrower. Although as a matter of law, the borrower has a separate contractual relationship with each member of the syndicate, for practical purposes the borrower only deals with the agent bank who will be responsible for negotiating a common form loan agreement with the borrower. Subject to the borrower, and each of the individual lenders being satisfied with the agent bank's efforts in this regard, the borrower will enter into a separate contract with each lender member of the syndicate along the lines of the common form agreement. So far as security is concerned, the borrower will grant security to the agent bank who holds it as trustee for all syndicate members.

Syndicate members are happy to be involved in syndicated loan arrangements for several reasons. For example, the time and effort spent in investigating the borrower as a credit risk will have been expended by the agent bank, not by the members of the syndicate. Also syndicate members are in a position to make funds available to a borrower with whom they might not otherwise have a relationship. Furthermore, the agent bank undertakes other responsibilities on behalf of syndicate members such as ensuring that conditions precedent and subsequent in the loan agreements are observed. Also, it will be the task of the agent bank to monitor the observance of repayment covenants.

Funds obtained through a syndicated loan arrangement (as described) are normally transferred from the syndicate members to the

---

[12] Such a warranty can be a condition precedent at the moment of drawdown, but can also become a condition subsequent where drawdown is made in stages, as it will represent a fresh warranty at the time of each drawdown of funds.

[13] And also perhaps have a remedy in damages for breach of warranty.

agent bank, who then transmits the funds on to the borrower, as the borrower requires. However, it is open to the parties to agree that the borrower's drawdown requests shall be met by direct syndicate members/borrower fund transfers.

(b) Overdraft

5–04　A company may also obtain a loan by way of an overdraft. In law, an overdraft constitutes a loan as, in effect, it constitutes a payment by the bank to the customer with either express or implied conditions that the overdraft amounts will be repaid with interest.[14] While an overdraft is payable on demand, there must be a prior demand by the bank before the obligation to repay arises. However, in practice, the company and the bank will have agreed overdraft terms, defining overdraft ceilings, as well as agreeing repayment arrangements.

(c) Debentures

5–05　An instrument that is commonly used by corporate borrowers in order to obtain loan finance is the debenture. A debenture is essentially a written acknowledgment by the borrower that the debt exists, and contains a promise to repay the debt and interest over a certain period. The debenture may, or may not, also grant security[15] over the borrower's assets.

The Companies Acts do not provide a comprehensive definition of what is a debenture other than to provide in section 2 of the Companies Act 1963 that a debenture "includes debenture stock, bonds and any other securities of a company whether constituting a charge on the assets of the company or not."

Debentures can be issued as a single debenture or as part of a series of debentures. Where issued as a series, they may constitute "an offer to the public." Consequently, only public companies can issue a series of debentures, as private companies risk acting unlawfully if they issue debentures to "the public" contrary to the Companies Acts.[16]

---

[14] *Brooks & Co v. Blackburn Benefit Building Society* [1884] 9 App. Cas. 857 (H.L.).

[15] Under subs. 99(8) of the Companies Act 1963, where a charge is over a series of debentures ranking *pari passu*, the relevant time for registration shall be 21 days from the date of execution of the debenture trust deed, if there is one, and if not, within 21 days of the date of execution of the first debenture in the series. S.99(2)(a) provides that, "a charge for the purpose of securing any issue of debentures" is registrable within 21 days of the date of its creation by the company: it is debatable whether a charge to secure a *single* debenture falls within this registration requirement (though it may well fall within one of the other s.99 categories of registrable charge).

[16] See Chap. 2 on the issue of what constitutes "an offer to the public."

Debentures can be transferred by mere delivery if they are bearer debentures. In the case of non-bearer debentures, all depends on the terms of the debenture. Under section 81 of the Companies Act 1963, the transfer cannot be registered unless the instrument of transfer, duly executed, has been delivered to the company.[17]

Although section 28(6) of the Supreme Court of Ireland (Judicature) Act 1877 provides that when a debt owed by another is assigned, the assignee takes ownership of the debt subject to all equities, it is common practice when a debenture is assigned for the debenture to specify on its face that it is assigned free of any prior equities that affected the transferor's title.[18] Consequently, debentures incorporating such a term are more easily marketable.

Debentures can take several different forms. A company will issue a single debenture when it is borrowing from one lender. However, where public companies wish to raise moneys from the public or a number of lenders, the single debenture is unsuitable. Instead the company will instead opt to issue either a series of debentures, or alternatively, debenture stock.

Where there are multiple sources of finance being sourced, the company will issue a series of debentures rather than a single debenture to each lender. All such debentures, being issued contemporaneously as part of a series rank *pari passu* for repayment purposes. Consequently, no debenture in the series can have priority to repayment over any other debenture in the series.

The series can take the form of either loan stock debentures or non-loan stock debentures. The disadvantage with the non-loan stock debenture is that the "units" in which the debentures are expressed may not suit all investor requirements. For example, the units may be too large for the smaller lender, and too small for the larger lender.

Consequently, a series of debenture loan stock may be more preferable. Although the stock may be issued in "bundles", such bundles are divisible into smaller amounts of loan stock, thus suiting different sizes of lender more easily than non-loan stock debentures. Another advantage of the debenture loan stock is that the stock is easily transferable, either in whole or in part. With a non-loan stock debenture this is not possible, as either the debenture is transferred in whole, or not at all.

It is common for a trust to be set up whenever a series of debentures are being issued. When issuing the debentures, the company will issue the debentures to the trust's trustees, not the individual debenture holders as such. The reason why a trust is used is because of the

---

[17] The Stock Transfer Act 1963 introduced a simplified transfer form for securities such as debentures.

[18] *Hilger Analytical Ltd. v. Rank Precision Industries and Others* [1984] B.C.L.C. 301.

sheer number of debenture holders. Rather than the company having to deal with each and every debenture holder, the company only has to deal with the trustees who act on behalf of the holders. The attraction for the holders is that the *pari passu* ranking of their individual claims are assured, because all of the debentures in the series are only issued to one entity (the trust).

When the company issues the debentures, each holder does not receive a debenture as such, but rather a certificate indicating what is held on their behalf by the trustees. The company covenants with the trustees to repay the debenture debt at some time in the future, and in the meantime assures a guaranteed rate of annual interest repayment on the debenture sum. Furthermore, any security that is part of the debenture arrangements will be granted by the company to the trustees on behalf of the debenture holders. Not alone are the administrative advantages of this arrangement self-evident, but also the advantage for the holders is that professional trustees will be acting in their interests.

II. CORPORATE BORROWING – DEVELOPMENTS IN *ULTRA VIRES*

Overview of developments

5–06 The "object" of a company is the purpose for which the company has been formed.[19] As a company may only pursue its corporate objects, it has no capacity to pursue activities which are unrelated to its objects. Such actions are *ultra vires* the company's corporate capacity.

Historically, actions that were *ultra vires* the company's corporate capacity were deemed void and unenforceable at common law.[20] Any outside party dealing with a company was deemed to be constructively aware of the company's objects.[21] Consequently, an outsider

---

[19] s.6 of the Companies Act 1963 provides that every company registered under the Act must have its objects detailed in its memorandum of association. The objects of a company need not be commercial in nature: "The objects of a company need not be commercial; they can be charitable or philantropic; indeed, they can be whatever the original incorporators wish, provided that they are legal. Nor is there any reason why a company should not part with its funds gratuitously or for non-commercial reasons if to do so is within its stated objects." *per* Buckley L.J. in *Re Horsley & Weight Ltd* [1982] 3 All E.R. 1045 at 1053 when commenting on whether a company could have as an object the paying of pensions to employees.

[20] *Ashbury Railway Carraige and Iron Company v. Riche* [1875] L.R. 7 H.L.C. 653.

[21] *Re Jon Beauforte (London) Ltd* [1953] 1 All E.R. 634; [1953] Ch. 131.

transacting with a company in ignorance of the fact that the company was acting *ultra vires* its objects could not enforce the transaction against the company. Thus, for example, where a company borrowed a loan for an *ultra vires* purpose, the innocent lender was deemed to be aware that the company was borrowing for an *ultra vires* purpose. However, in more recent times, this harsh position has been ameliorated in several key respects.

First, although a transaction may be *ultra vires* the company, nevertheless the transaction may be *enforceable* against the company in certain circumstances due to legislative intervention.[22]

Second, quasi-contractual remedies may be available to the outsider, thereby allowing the outsider recover sums loaned (or paid) to an *ultra vires* borrower.[23]

Third, developments have taken place, which may allow the company (that has itself acted *ultra vires*) *recover* sums loaned by it to third parties.[24]

However, before considering the aforegoing developments in the context of their relevance to loans, security-granting and corporate borrowing generally, it is first necessary to consider a number of issues that have been the subject of much debate and controversy.

A. BORROWING – "POWER" OR "OBJECT"

(1) Trading company cannot have "borrowing" as an Object

5–07 Apart from banks or corporate entities whose business it is to arrange loans, a trading company cannot have as its object the borrowing of funds, or the granting of security for such borrowings, *per se*. In other words, trading companies when borrowing, may not borrow as an object in itself, but for a purpose, that purpose being the attainment of the company's objects. As Buckley J. stated in *Re Introductions*[25]:

> "Now to borrow money, by itself, without intending to use the money for any purpose, would be a senseless operation. If the company were to borrow money and, like the servant in the parable,[26] were to bury it in

---

[22] See s.8(1) of the Companies Act 1963 and Regulation 6 of S.I. No. 163 of 1973 considered further below at paras 5–19—5–23.
[23] Considered below at paras 5–24 *et seq.*
[24] *Re PMPA Garage (Longmile) Ltd. and Others (No. 2)* [1992] I.L.R.M. 349. See below paras 5–27 to 5–30.
[25] *Re Introductions Ltd.: Introductions Ltd. v. National Provincial Bank Ltd* [1968] 3 All E.R. 1221 at 1227.
[26] The learned judge was making reference here to the Bible, St. Matthew, ch. 25, verse 25.

the ground until the creditor returned and demanded repayment, then to disinter it and pay it back again, the whole procedure would be senseless. Borrowing is only a sensible activity if it is associated with some use to which the borrowed money is proposed and intended to be put. . . ."

Affirming Buckley J's judgment on appeal, Harman LJ agreed, stating that

". . . a power or an object conferred on a company to borrow cannot mean something in the air: borrowing is not an end in itself and must be for some purpose of the company. . . ."[27]

Only banks or other entities whose business it is to make loans can properly have the making of loans, borrowings, and the taking of security, as their corporate object.[28] However, any trading company with properly drafted constitutional documents will have the express *power* to borrow (and to grant security for such borrowings) in its articles of association.[29] This power to borrow, not being an object itself, is a mere power to facilitate the achievement of the company's objects. Therefore, like all corporate powers, it should only be exercised for borrowings that are entered into in pursuit of the company's objects. In the event that a company's constitutional documents do not provide an

---

[27] [1969] 1 All E.R. 887 at 889 (Court of Appeal).

[28] Although Slade L.J. in *Rolled Steel Products Holding Ltd. v. British Steel Corp.* [1985] 3 All E.R. 52 (note that *Rolled Steel Products Holding Ltd. v. British Steel Corp.* is also reported at [1986] Ch. 246) at p. 81 stated that, "Counsel has submitted, and I agree, that there is no reason in principle why a company should not be formed for the specific purpose, *inter alia*, of giving guarantees, whether gratuitous or otherwise, rather unusual though such an object might be." However, in that decision itself (and in the case law generally), courts usually find, on a construction of a company's memorandum and articles, that such an objective is not an object in itself but merely a power to give guarantees to facilitate the company's trading objectives. In that sense therefore, Slade's *dictum* should not be overwidely interpreted. That this is so is evident from the comment of Murphy J. *In Re PMPA (Longmile) Ltd* [1992] I.LR.M. 337 at 340/341 where the learned judge stated: ". . . counsel did not seek to claim that the provisions in the memoranda of the debtor companies dealing with guarantees constituted a 'separate and independent object' of any of those companies. Whilst the decision of the Court of Appeal in England in *Rolled Steel Products (Holdings) Ltd. v British Steel Corporation* (1986) Ch. 246 has demonstrated (in my view correctly) how a clause dealing with the provisions of guarantees or even the making of gratuitous payments could constitute a valid and separate independent object of a company formed under the Companies Acts, it seems to me that the nature of the business carried on by the debtor companies and more particularly the terms of their respective memoranda would defeat any such inference in the present case."

[29] Art. 79 First Schedule, Table A, Part I, Companies Act 1963, if adopted by the company, provides an express, albeit restrictive, borrowing power. It is common for companies to adopt a less restrictive borrowing power than this model.

express power to borrow, the courts will imply a power to borrow.[30] Just as with the express power, the implied power will be exercisable by the company for purposes that are reasonably incidental to the attainment of the company's objects.[31]

(2) Drafting devices which attempt to designate borrowing/security-granting as a corporate Object?

5–08 Notwithstanding clear judicial dicta on the matter,[32] some corporate borrowers will continue to clothe their power to borrow in the language of an object in order to attempt to permit the company to borrow funds (and/or grant security) *as an object in itself*. To further this aim, a company can use a number of devices in the company's memorandum of association. First, the company may attempt to list several different items as company objects in the memorandum. Second, the company may insert a *Cotman* clause[33] in the memorandum in an attempt to designate each listed object as a separate and independent object of the company. Third, the company may insert a *Bell Houses* clause[34] into the memorandum, in an attempt to permit the directors enter into any business that is, in their opinion, advantageous for the company.

In response, the courts developed techniques to limit the legal efficacy of these devices.

(a) Main Objects Principle

5–09 The first response of the courts was the enunciation of the "main objects" principle as a countermeasure to companies' attempts to list several different items as company objects in the memorandum. Under this approach, the court would scrutinise the many paragraphs of the objects clause, and decide that one of the listed objects constituted the main object of the company. Usually this "main object" would be found in the first paragraph of the memorandum's list of objects. Then the court would declare that all other clauses in the objects clause were in fact mere powers, and consequently they could only be exercised in furtherance of the company's main object (as found by the court).[35]

---

[30] *Attorney General v. Great Eastern Railway* [1880] 5 App. Cas. 473.
[31] *General Auction Estate Co. v. Smith* [1891] 3 Ch. 492.
[32] See para. 5–07 above.
[33] See paras 5–10—5–12 below.
[34] See paras 5–11—5–12 below.
[35] *Ashbury Railway Carraige and Iron Company v. Riche* [1875] L.R. 7 H.L.C. 653; *Re German Date Coffee Co Ltd.* [1882] 20 Ch. D. 169; *Anglo-Overseas Agencies Ltd v. Green* [1961] 1 Q.B. 1.

The main objects principle constituted a set-back to those who wished a company to have multiple objects. In order to attempt to circumvent this limitation on the scope of the company's objects, lawyers employed two further devices in an effort to defeat this judicial strategy, the *Cotman* clause and the *Bell Houses* clause.[36]

(i) *Cotman clause*

5—10 When inserted into a company's memorandum, an "independent objects" clause (or "*Cotman*" clause as it is also known) typically states that all items listed as objects are to be construed as independent objects of the company in their own right. The aim of such a clause is to attempt to prevent a court from ruling that some of the items designated as objects are only mere powers, subservient to the main object. The validity of such a clause was upheld by the House of Lords in *Cotman v. Brougham*[37] as being a means of obviating the main objects rule *provided* that the objects clause, on its construction, supports such a conclusion.

Notwithstanding *Cotman v. Brougham*, the two chief reasons why the courts are reluctant to allow the *Cotman* device to elevate the power to borrow to that of an independent object in itself are:

(a) the fact that a company cannot be formed to do things which are by their very nature *incapable* of constituting objects of the company properly so called,[38] and,

(b) reluctance to allow an item to be designated as an independent object when a proper *construction* of the company's entire memorandum and articles would regard the item as something that is more properly in the nature of a mere power.[39]

---

[36] The courts cannot outlaw such clauses outright because subs.5(4) of the Companies (Amendment) Act 1983 provides that where the Registrar of Companies registers a company's memorandum and issues a certificate of incorporation, the certificate shall be "conclusive evidence" that the registration requirements of the Companies Act 1963 have been complied with. Of course, this does not prevent the courts from *construing* such clauses, when they arise for judicial interpretation.

[37] [1918] A.C. 514.

[38] *e.g.*, corporate borrowing as an object in itself (*Re Introductions Ltd.: Introductions Ltd. v. National Provincial Bank Ltd.* [1968] 3 All E.R. 1221 (dicta of Buckley J.) and (on appeal affirming Buckley J.) *dicta* of Harman L.J. in *Re Introductions Ltd.: Introductions Ltd. v. National Provincial Bank Ltd.* [1969] 1 All E.R. 887); on corporate security-giving as an object in itself (*Rolled Steel Products Holding Ltd. v. British Steel Corp.* [1985] 3 All E.R. 52).

[39] *Rolled Steel Products Holding Ltd v. British Steel Corp.* [1985] 3 All E.R. 52; *Re Introductions Ltd: Introductions Ltd. v. National Provincial Bank Ltd.* [1968] 3 All E.R. 1221.

Viewed in this light therefore, merely because a company with a *Cotman* clause lists as an object the borrowing of monies or giving of guarantees, this does not mean that the company actually has such an object.[40] In every case, the lender will have to consider whether the borrowing company can be regarded as a company that could have such purpose as its object. Alternatively, the lender must consider whether the company is a company that merely has the mere power to borrow/ grant security, exerciseable only in the pursuit of the company's genuine trading objects. If the object is either one that is incapable of being an object, or an item that cannot be an object when the constitutional documents are construed, then not even the presence of a *Cotman* clause can ensure that it is rendered a valid object of the company.[41]

(ii) Bell Houses clause

5–11   The second device employed by lawyers in an attempt to avoid the main objects principle is the *"Bell Houses"* clause.[42] Such a clause is drafted in terms which provide that the company may pursue any business that the directors believe would be advantageous to the company's business. The courts will uphold such a clause as being a successful means of allowing a company to circumvent the main objects rule provided that the following two caveats are satisfied:

(a) the clause has to be compatible with the entire articles and memorandum on their *construction*, and

(b) the directors have to be acting *bona fide* at the time they entered the particular transaction.

However, the courts are not keen to allow the directors to render every conceivable activity to be an object of the company. The directors must be able to show that the activity was beneficial to the company's general business. It is submitted that if no such limitation is expressly included in the clause, then it will be implied – otherwise a company could conceivably have as its object the doing of anything that the directors might wish.

---

[40] See *Re Introductions Ltd: Introductions Ltd. v. National Provincial Bank Ltd.* [1968] 3 All E.R. 1221 considered below.

[41] Buckley L.J. in *Re Horsley & Weight* [1982] 3 All E.R. 1045. Courtney, *The Law of Private Companies* (1994, Butterworths, Dublin) at 211 agrees with this view.

[42] *Bell Houses Ltd v. Citywall Properties Ltd* [1966] 2 All E.R. 674. Although known as the *Bell Houses* clause where it came to notorious fame, this type of clause existed in various forms in companies' constitutional documents long before the *Bell Houses* decision itself.

(3) Restrictive judicial interpretation

5–12 The decision in *Re Introductions*[43] demonstrates the limited effectiveness of circumvention devices such as *Cotman* and *Bell Houses* devices. In *Re Introductions*, a company was formed with the object of providing tourist services. It had both a *Cotman* and *Bell Houses* clause in its constitutional documents. The company engaged in the business of pig-breeding which was *ultra vires* its stated objects.

When the lender (a bank which had loaned the company funds in the knowledge that the funds were to be used for the pig business) attempted to recover its loan, it was faced with the argument that the loan was *ultra vires* the company's objects and thus void.

In response, the lender argued that the *Cotman* clause in the company's memorandum was effective in maintaining borrowing as an independent object of the company. Dismissing the *Cotman* clause, the court held that the borrowing of money cannot be an object in itself so far as a normal trading company is concerned: money is not borrowed in isolation, but for the purpose of pursuing the company's objects. Consequently, borrowing money was a mere power which could only be exercised for purposes ancillary to the attainment of the objects of the company. A *Cotman* clause could not therefore elevate such a power to the status of object.[44]

So far as the *Bell Houses* clause was concerned, the trial judge held that it could not assist the bank's case either. The directors could not be regarded as acting *bona fide* when they borrowed for the purposes of pig breeding, as it was not credible to argue that they *bona fide* believed that pursuing the pig breeding business was beneficial for the pursuit of the company's general business of tourism promotion.[45]

Therefore, normally it will be difficult for a trading company to successfully argue that it has the borrowing of funds or security-granting, as an *object*. At most, it will have either an express or implied power to borrow/grant security. Such powers are exercisable only for the purpose of facilitating the attainment of the company's proper objects. As Buckley J. stated:[46]

> "Where a company incorporated under the [U.K.] Companies Act 1948 has the power to borrow, that fact must be discovered from its memorandum of association. The power may be one which has to be inferred

---

[43] *Re Introductions Ltd: Introductions Ltd. v National Provincial Bank Ltd.* [1968] 3 All E.R. 1221 at 1227; affirmed on appeal at [1969] 1 All E.R. 887.

[44] See *dicta* from both the Chancery judgment ([1968] 3 All E.R. 1221 *per* Buckley J.) and the Court of Appeals ([1969] 1 All E.R. 887 *per* Harman L.J.).

[45] Harman L.J. agreed on appeal at [1969] 1 All E.R. 887 at 889.

[46] *Re Introductions Ltd.: Introductions Ltd. v National Provincial Bank Ltd.* [1968] 3 All E.R. 1221 at 1225.

from the objects of the company, or it may be one that is expressly conferred on the company by the terms of its memorandum. If the power to
borrow is one which is inferred, it naturally follows that the borrowing is
only within the power of the company in relation to those matters in
respect of which the inference arises. Where the memorandum is one in
which those sub-clauses of the objects clauses, which confer what are
truly powers rather than objects, are to be read as subsidiary to the main
and real objects of the company, in such a case also the borrowing power
must be read as confined to borrowing for the purposes for which the
company is formed."

Therefore, it is clear that despite the best efforts of those who draft
company constitutional documents, judicial construction of the relevant
clauses may well cut down the scope of the clauses. Irish courts adopt
a similar approach. In *Northern Bank Finance Corporation Ltd v. Quinn
and Achates Investments Co.*[47] Keane J. in the High Court ably demonstrated how overwidely drafted and ambiguously worded clauses in a
company's constitutional documents could not have the meaning contended for them when subjected to close judicial scrutiny and interpretation. For example, having identified that the company's objects
were confined to the pursuance of its own investment activities, the
court would not permit the company's memorandum (which provided
that the company could "secure payment of money in such manner
and on such terms as the directors may deem expedient") to mean that
the company thereby had the power to guarantee the liabilities of a
third party. Clearly the company had no such object, hence no such
power could be inferred from the memorandum's clauses. Similarly,
neither would a clause which permitted the directors to ". . . do and
carry out all such other things as may be deemed by the company to be
incidental or conducive to the attainment of the above objects . . ." be
interpreted to mean that the directors had the power to guarantee third
party liabilities.

Another example of how judicial interpretive techniques may narrow the purported scope of memorandum clauses is to be found in *Re
Frederick Inns Ltd.*[48] In this decision, the Revenue Commissioners contended that a number of companies had the power to make payments
towards the tax liabilities of another group of related companies. The
Supreme Court rejected such contention. The Revenue had contended
that clauses which allowed the paying companies to "promote or establish in promoting" other companies or "purchase or acquire the debts
. . . of any company", permitted the paying companies to pay the tax
debts of the other associated group of companies. Rejecting such con-

---

[47] [1979] I.L.R.M. 221.
[48] [1991] I.L.R.M. 582 (High Ct.), [1994] 1 I.L.R.M. 387 (Supreme Ct).

tention, the court found that paying another's debt is not tantamount to "purchasing" the debt, nor is it within the meaning of "promoting". Furthermore, the Court also found that a clause which permitted the companies to "advance and lend money from time to time . . . and in such manner as may seem expedient" did not encompass the paying of another's tax debts.

(4) Benefit to the company

5–13 An issue that caused much confusion in the past was the issue of whether there should be a *benefit* to the company in order for a transaction to be *intra vires*. Older case law was thought to tend towards the view that in order for a transaction to be *intra vires* there had to be a benefit to the company.[49] However, in more recent times the courts have clarified the area by drawing a distinction between objects and powers so far as the question of benefit is concerned (the question of *powers* and *benefit* will be considered further below).[50]

It would now appear, so far as *objects* are concerned, that where a company has a particular pursuit as a valid object, then the question of benefit to the company would not appear to be relevant to the legality of its pursuit. For example, in *Re Horsley & Weight Ltd*[51] the English Court of Appeal held that a company could have a non-commercial object (such as the paying of pensions) which could not be said to be of commercial benefit to the company, at least not in a narrow sense of the term. Furthermore, Keane J. remarked *obiter* in the High Court in *Northern Bank Finance v. Quinn and Achates Investment Co.*[52] that in light of more recent case law, the older authorities which might be thought to require benefit, might need to be reconsidered.[53] Also of interest is

---

[49] *Hutton v. West Cork Railway Co* [1883] 23 Ch. Div. 672 although on closer inspection it would appear that the court may have clouded the issue, by intermingling its consideration of two separate matters, the issue of the company's *vires* and the separate issue of whether the directors have abused their fiduciary duty to act in the best interests of the company: whereas questions of benefit are not relevant to the *vires* issue, they may be relevant to the issue of whether a breach of directors' fiduciary duties has occurred. In *Re Lee Behrens & Co* [1932] 2 Ch. 46 Eve J. continued this confusion by requiring benefit to be a prerequisite for a valid exercise of a company's corporate capacity. Several later decisions in both Ireland and the U.K. have cast doubt on *Lee Behrens*: see further, n.53 below and also para. 5–18.

[50] See para. 5–18 below where the question of benefit and powers is considered.

[51] [1982] 3 All E.R. 1045.

[52] [1979] I.L.R.M. 221 at 226–227.

[53] *ibid* at 227 Keane J. was referring to *Hutton v. West Cork Railway Co* [1883] 23 Ch. Div. 672 which he said may have been "extended too far" in *In re Lee Behrens & Co* [1932] 2 Ch. 46 and he observed ". . . its (*i.e Lee Behren's*) authority as a persuasive precedent would require reconsideration to-day in light of the decision

the decision in *Charterbridge Corporation Ltd. v. Lloyd's Bank Ltd.*[54] where Pennycuick J. found, that the question of benefit is not relevant to the pursuit of a company's objects, but rather is pertinent to the issue of the propriety of the directors' exercise of their powers in the context of their fiduciary duties to the company.[55] In other words, when a question arises as to whether the directors have complied with their fiduciary duties to the company whose shareholders they serve, the issue of benefit becomes relevant (not where the issue of the company's *corporate capacity* is concerned).[56] That the question of benefit does not arise when the issue of whether a company has corporate capacity arises, is clear from the decision of McWilliam J. in *Re Metro Investments Ltd.*[57] McWilliam J. observed that where a company has the requisite capacity, one need not be concerned to see whether the transaction is of benefit to the company, and approved of *Charterbridge Corporation Ltd v. Lloyd's Bank Ltd.* in this regard.[58]

B. BORROWING TRANSACTIONS TAINTED BY ABUSE OF THE DIRECTORS' POWERS:

5–14   At this point, the issue arises as to whether transactions which

---

in *Charterbridge Corporation Ltd v. Lloyd's Bank Ltd* [1970] Ch. 62." Also Slade L.J. stated in *Rolled Steel Products (Holdings) Ltd v British Steel Corporation* (1986) Ch 246 that *In re Lee Behrens & Co* is "positively misleading" in so far as it purported to require benefit as a criterion on which to assess the corporate capacity of a company, although he did concede that it "may well be helpful in considering whether or not in any given case directors have abused the powers vested in them by the company." The judgments in *Re Horsley & Weight Ltd.* [1982] 3 All E.R. 1045 and *Re Halt Garage (1964) Ltd.* [1982] 3 All E.R. 1016 have similarly restricted *Lee Behrens'* application.

[54] [1970] Ch. 62.
[55] In this event, the issue of benefit is an objective one as Pennycuick J. observed in *Charterbridge Corporation Ltd. v. Lloyd's Bank Ltd.* [1970] Ch. 62 at 74: "The proper test, I think, in the absence of actual separate consideration, must be whether an intelligent and honest man in the position of the director of the company concerned, could, in the whole of the existing circumstances, have reasonably believed that the transactions were for the benefit of the company."
[56] Some of the older case law has resulted in unnecessary confusion in this area, and was caused by judges who, when considering the issue of benefit to the company, confused corporate capacity issues (*i.e.*, *ultra vires*) with the separate issue of whether there had been a breach of directors' fiduciary duties.
[57] unreported, High Court, 25 May 1977.
[58] Other U.K. decisions which take a similar view include *Re Halt Garage (1964) Ltd* [1982] 3 All E.R. 1016 (Ch. Div.) *and Re Horsley & Weight Ltd* [1982] 3 All E.R. 1045 (C.A.).
[59] In the sense that the company had no corporate capacity in law to enter the transaction.

result from an abuse of the directors' powers are *ultra vires* on that account? This is an issue that has created confusion and requires clarification. The confusion flows from the fact that the term *ultra vires* has been used in two senses. The term *ultra vires* has been used to describe both of the following situations as being *ultra vires* situations, when in reality only the first is an *ultra vires* situation. First, *ultra vires* has been used to describe the situation where a corporate loan or security appears to be *ultra vires* the company's objects.[59] Second, *ultra vires* has also been used to describe the situation where the company had corporate capacity,[60] but the transaction originated from an improper use by the directors of their powers[61] to borrow or give security.

(1) *Ultra vires* distinguished from abuse of directors' powers

5–15 In the English Court of Appeal in *Rolled Steel Products Holding Ltd v. British Steel Corporation*[62] Slade L.J. explained that, used in its proper context, *ultra vires* properly describes anything that is beyond the corporate capacity (objects) of the company.[63] Browne-Wilkinson L.J. further observed that *ultra vires* has been confusingly used in the case law to describe an exercise of the directors' powers which, although such powers could be exercised in pursuit of the company's objects, they were in fact misused by the directors in order to pursue some other purpose.[64] The learned judge considered that the use of the term *ultra vires* to describe this situation is unhelpful, as it is inaccurate to describe as *ultra vires* what is in fact an improper use by directors of *their* powers.[65] *Ultra vires*, which properly relates to *corporate capacity* only, should not be used to describe mere misuse by the directors of their powers.

(2) Transactions tainted by abuse of directors' powers

5–16 Having clarified this confusion, the Court of Appeal in *Rolled Steel Products Holding Ltd v. British Steel Corporation* then went on to establish further important propositions that will be relevant for lenders and corporate borrowers. For example, the case is authority for the

---

[60] *i.e., intra vires.*
[61] "powers" meaning either the express powers prescribed for the directors by the company's constitutional documents, or implied powers.
[62] *Rolled Steel Products Holding Ltd v. British Steel Corporation* [1985] 3 All E.R. 52.
[63] *ibid.* at pp. 68 and 79.
[64] *ibid.* at pp. 89.
[65] Courtney, *op. cit.* agrees, stating (at p.214) that, "Using *ultra vires* in this context is inaccurate and ought to be laid to rest. "*Ultra vires*" only refers to actual corporate contractual capacity and ought never to be used in the context of an abuse of directors' powers under a company's memorandum of association."

proposition that where the directors of a company commit the company to borrowing or security-granting, then the transaction will be unenforceable where the lender knew or ought to have known that the directors were exercising their powers for purposes other than the attainment of the company's objects.[66] Crucially, such transactions are unenforceable, not because of *ultra vires*, but because the lender knew or ought to have known that the directors had abused their powers when they exercised their borrowing powers. By implication, where the lender had no such knowledge of misuse of powers on the part of the directors, the transaction may remain enforceable as there is no issue pertaining to *ultra vires*. The Irish courts have endorsed this approach.[67]

Essentially, it will be seen how the courts, relying on principles from the law of agency, do not allow a party to enforce a transaction against a company where that party knew or ought to have known that the directors of the company were exercising their legitimate powers for an improper purpose. In the present context, this means that the outsider who knows or ought to have known that the company was borrowing money to pursue a non-object objective is not permitted to enforce the transaction against the company. However, this will not be because of *ultra vires* but rather because the outsider cannot rely on agency principles to bind the company to a transaction that the company's agents (the directors) committed it to, in circumstances where the outsider knew, or ought to known, that the directors were exceeding their authority. No case demonstrates the aforegoing better than the facts of *Rolled Steel* itself.

---

[66] In this regard, the statement by Buckley J. in *Re Introductions Ltd.: Introductions Ltd. v. National Provincial Bank Ltd* [1968] 3 All E.R. 1221 at 1225 that, "Moreover, borrowing for any purpose other than the legitimate activities of the company will be *ultra vires*, and if the lender is aware of the circumstances which render the borrowing *ultra vires* he will be unable to recover the moneys as lent." does not contradict this proposition, as helpfully, Browne-Wilkinson L.J. in *Rolled Steel Products Holding Ltd v. British Steel Corporation* [1985] 3 All E.R. 52 at 91 observed that, "Buckley J. at first instance described the borrowing as being ultra vires: but, in my judgment, this was merely an unguarded use of language since he also regarded the bank's knowledge of the facts as being a crucial element rendering the debenture unenforceable (see [1968] 3 All E.R. 1221 at 1225). In my judgment, *Re Introductions Ltd.* is not a decision relating to ultra vires in the strict sense: it is an example of a case in which a third party has entered into a transaction with a company with actual notice that the transaction was an abuse of power and accordingly could not enforce the transaction against the company."

[67] See *Re Fredrick Inns Ltd* [1994] 1 I.L.R.M. 387 (S.Ct.) and *Parkes & Sons Ltd v. Hong Kong and Shanghai Banking Corporation* [1990] 1 I.L.R.M. 341 considered below shortly.

In *Rolled Steel Products Holding Ltd. v. British Steel Corporation*, the plaintiff company granted security by way of a guarantee in favour of the defendant company. The purpose of the guarantee was to guarantee a loan made to a third company by the defendant company. The defendant company was controlled by the principal shareholder (S) in the plaintiff company. It was determined at the trial that the loan was of no benefit to the plaintiff company itself, and also that S., one of directors of the plaintiff company, had not declared his interest in the contract when he was required to do so by the plaintiff company's articles of association.[68] It was further held by the trial judge that the parties were deemed to be aware of the aforegoing irregularities. Consequently, when the plaintiff company was called upon to honour the guarantee, the issue arose as to the legal status of the guarantee. A perusal of the plaintiff company's constitutional documentation demonstrated that the plaintiff company had the power to give guarantees in favour of third parties where that furthered the objects of the plaintiff company. Therefore, one of the key issues in the case was:

(a) whether the guarantee should remain enforceable against the plaintiff company even though it was given for a purpose which had nothing to do with the objects of the plaintiff company? or,

(b) whether the guarantee was *ultra vires* because granted in pursuit of an *ultra vires* object?

The English Court of Appeal held that where a company has a certain power to do something, then because such a power is capable of being exercised by the directors for *intra vires* objectives, the exercise of the power will not be rendered *ultra vires* the company merely because the directors are in fact exercising the power to pursue a non-object purpose. This is significant as, by not automatically classifying such transactions as being *ultra vires* transactions, they are not automatically void.[69] Delivering the principal judgement of the Court of Appeal, Slade L.J., explained this apparent conundrum.

Slade L.J. began by holding that the apparent attempt by the company to use various circumvention tools[70] to elevate the power to grant

---

[68] Under current law, s.194 of the Companies Act 1963 obliges a director who has an interest in a transaction involving his or her company to so declare at a meeting of the board.

[69] Though, as already noted at para. 5–16 above, they may be *unenforceable* where the outsider knew or ought to have known that the directors were abusing their powers.

[70] *e.g.*, *Cotman* clause (see above at paras 5–10—5–12 where judicial attempts to cut-down the effects of such a clause were considered).

guarantees, to the status of independent object, failed on a construction of the plaintiff company's memorandum and articles.

Slade L.J. next considered whether a transaction would be *ultra vires* the company if it ostensibly falls within the scope of the wording of the company's memorandum, but was in fact entered into for some purpose not authorised by that memorandum? Having reviewed various authorities, Slade L.J. held that the directors (according to the memorandum) had the power to grant guarantees for such purposes "as may seem expedient", which he held to mean to be a limitation not on the corporate capacity of the plaintiff company, but as a limitation on the directors' use of their power.[71] Clearly the directors had abused their powers in this case as it had been found that they knew that the granting of the guarantee would be of no benefit to the plaintiff company and indeed might well be injurious to its interests.

Having established that the directors had abused their powers, Slade L.J. then considered whether this meant their actions rendered the granting of the guarantee *ultra vires* the company, such that it was void and unenforceable against the company? Slade L.J. held that the power to grant guarantees was a power that was capable of being exercised for purposes set out in the memorandum, and therefore where it had been exercised for purposes not set out in the memorandum,[72] it could bind the company unless the recipient of the guarantee either knew or ought to have known that the guarantee was being granted by directors who were abusing their power.

The significance of this approach is that the court regarded transactions entered into by directors who were abusing the limits on their powers as *not* being *ultra vires*. Consequently, transactions originating in such circumstances were binding on the company *unless* the lender either knew or ought to have known that the directors were exercising their powers for an improper purpose. As the recipients of the funds knew that the plaintiff's directors were acting outside of their powers, it was held that they were not entitled to enforce the guarantee against the plaintiff company and hence they, rather than the plaintiff guarantor, were liable to repay the funds they had borrowed.[73]

This distinction between *ultra vires* and abuse of directors powers also seems to be accepted by the Irish courts. In *Re Frederick Inns Ltd.* Blayney J., delivering the judgment of the Supreme Court[74] referred approvingly to the distinction made in *Rolled Steel* by Slade L.J. on the

---

[71] In other words, that they could only use the power to give guarantees where that furthered the business of the company.
[72] As was the case before the court.
[73] Slade L.J. relied upon the authority of *Re David Payne & Co Ltd.* [1904] 2 Ch. 608.
[74] [1994] 1 I.L.R.M. 387 at 398–99 (O'Flaherty and Denham JJ. concurring)

distinction between *ultra vires* (the corporate capacity of the company) and abuse by directors of their fiduciary duties. Also Blayney J. had observed earlier in *Parkes & Sons Ltd. v. Hong Kong and Shanghai Banking Corporation*[75] that just because directors abuse their powers, this does not mean that it necessarily follows that the transaction thereby resulting is *ultra vires* the company.

(3) Limitations of a general and specific nature distinguished

5–17 Although the aforegoing principles are generous to the lender who neither knew nor ought to have known of the directors' abuse, there is one caveat. As Slade L.J. in *Rolled Steel* noted: if the company's constitutional documents specify that there is an express limitation on the use of a particular power and if such limitation goes to the very heart of the power, then notice of such express limitation will be imputed to the lender as it is expressly contained in the company's constitutional documents.[76] An example of such an express limitation would typically be a stipulation in the articles of association that the directors cannot borrow beyond a specific monetary limit.[77] Consequently, a lender in such a position would be precluded from asserting that borrowing, sanctioned by the directors in contravention of the specified monetary limit, was nevertheless enforceable.[78] By contrast, where limitations on the directors' powers stated in general terms[79] are breached, lenders will not be precluded from asserting that the transaction is nevertheless enforceable against the company, unless they either knew or ought to have known that the directors were exercising their powers for an improper purpose.[80]

---

[75] [1990] I.L.R.M. 341 at 349.

[76] [1985] 3 All E.R. 52 at 83–84. Where the stated limitation is specific (as in the case of a specified monetary ceiling on borrowings), then the lender cannot claim that they were not constructively aware of the clear limitation as it appears in the public documents of the company.

[77] *e.g.*, as *per* Art.79 Companies Act 1963, First Schedule Table A Model Articles.

[78] Unless of course the directors had in the interim got the members of the company to ratify the exceeding of the borrowing limits: *Re Burke Clancy & Co Ltd*, unreported, High Court, Kenny J., May 23 1974; *Irvine v. Union Bank of Australia* [1877] 2 App. Cas. 366.

[79] *e.g.*, 'in the interests of the company'; 'as may be expedient', etc.

[80] As Browne-Wilkinson L.J put it in *Rolled Steel Products Holding Ltd v. British Steel Corporation* [1985] 3 All E.R. 52 at 91: "Sometimes the drafting of the memorandum and articles may be such that they put third parties on notice of the fact that certain things can only properly be done subject to certain conditions being satisfied. If the third party is put on notice in this way, he will not be able to rely on any exercise of the power which he knew or ought to have discovered did not comply with such conditions. But a provision that a power can be exercised only 'for the purposes of the company's business' does not require a third party to satisfy himself that the power is in fact being exercised for that purpose."

As Slade L.J. stated:

> "While due regard must be paid to any express conditions attached to
> limitations on powers contained in a company's memorandum (*e.g.*,
> power to borrow only up to a specified amount), the court will not ordi-
> narily construe a statement in a memorandum that a particular power is
> exercisable 'for the purposes of the company' as a condition limiting the
> company's corporate capacity to exercise the power: it will regard it as
> simply imposing a limit on the authority of the directors. . . ."[81]

Therefore, it appears that specific and general limitations on the directors' powers must be distinguished, with the lender being in a stronger
position where the limitations are general in nature.

However, lenders themselves can sometimes themselves be the victim of *their own* abuse of powers, as was seen in *Re PMPA (Longmile)
Ltd.*[82] In that decision, PMPS was statutorily barred to make loans, but
was enabled to do so provided it had received proper security. The
High Court held that the lender's power to lend was thereby severely
curtailed by this restriction. No such security was provided when the
PMPS made loans to companies in the PMPA group of companies.[83]
Consequently, the lending was made in violation of the PMPS's own
powers to lend, and thus the transaction was unenforceable.[84]

(4) The issue of benefit to the company

5–18   As was previously discussed elsewhere above, the question of
benefit should not arise when the question of the company's *corporate
capacity* arises.[85] Furthermore, it would seem that the better view is
that the question of benefit to the company does not arise either where
the directors of the company are exercising *powers* given them by the
company's articles of association[86] (unless of course the particular

---

[81] [1985] 3 All E.R. 52 at 83–84.

[82] [1992] I.L.R.M. 337.

[83] Although the recipients of the loans, the PMPA companies, did provide guarantees, such guarantees did not constitute proper security within the meaning
of the PMPS's governing rules.

[84] Although recovery of the sums loaned was allowed in the *Re PMPA (Longmile)
Ltd. (No. 2)* decision [1992] I.L.R.M. 349 on the basis that unjust enrichment (permitting the borrower to retain the sums loaned) cannot be allowed: see further
below at para. 5–27.

[85] See para. 5–13 above.

[86] Oliver J. in *Re Halt Garage (1964) Ltd.* [1982] 3 All E.R. 1016 at 1034 highlighted
the difficulty in requiring benefit to be demonstrated, pointing out that the question of benefit, if relevant at all, was only relevant to the question of the propriety of the directors' exercise of a power, rather than the capacity to exercise it.
The learned judge explained this by observing that the courts will not imply a
power, even if beneficial for the company, where the power is not reasonably

power explicitly has such a condition attached).[87] What instead is properly of relevance when an express power is being exercised is the question of whether the power has been exercised for a purpose that is "reasonably incidental" to the attainment of the objects of the company.[88]

However, where the issue of benefit may be of relevance is when the question of the *bona fides* of the directors in called into question.[89] In other words, when an assessment is called for as to whether the directors have abused their *fiduciary duties* to the company, the question of whether they acted *bona fide* may arise. If the shareholders consider there has been an abuse, then legal action against the directors by the company may be a possibility. In this context, the issue of whether the directors considered the transaction to be of benefit to the company will be relevant to the question of their *bona fides*. This was acknowledged by the courts in several of the cases which clarified the non-relevance of the issue of benefit to the pursuit of company *objects*.[90]

---

incidental to the business (*i.e.*, the objects) of the company. Where an express power is at issue the question of benefit is similarly irrelevant, as such a power may only be exercised for purposes reasonably incidental to the objects of the company. Also, see Buckley L.J.'s observations in *Re Horsley & Weight Ltd.* [1982] 3 All E.R. 1045 at 1054 where he commented (on the issue of the scope of express powers and the issue of whether benefit was relevant for the validity of their exercise) that the issue of benefit was "quite inappropriate to the scope of express powers." The learned Judge did not express a view on benefit and implied powers, as that issue did not arise before him.

[87] As Buckley L.J. observed in *Re Horsley & Weight Ltd.* [1982] 3 All E.R. 1045 at 1054 that while the issue of benefit was "quite inappropriate to the scope of express powers. . . . Of course, if the memorandum of association expressly or by implication provides that an express object only extends to acts which benefit or promote the prosperity of the company, regard must be paid to that limitation; but, where there is no such express or implied limitation, the question whether an act done within the terms of an express object of the company will benefit or promote the prosperity of the company or of its business is, in my view, irrelevant."

[88] In *Attorney General v. Great Eastern Railway* [1880] 5 App. Cas. 473 the court held that a company has implied power to do whatever is reasonably incidental to the express objects of the company. Therefore, so far as *implied* powers are concerned, as they are also subject to the "reasonably incidental" test, the question of benefit is thought not to be of relevance, save to the extent that the directors' fiduciary duties are in issue (which is a separate issue in itself): *per* Oliver J. in *Re Halt Garage (1964) Ltd.* [1982] 3 All E.R. 1016 at 1034.

[89] *Re Halt Garage (1964) Ltd.* [1982] 3 All E.R. 1016; *Charterbridge Corporation Ltd v. Lloyd's Bank Ltd* [1970] Ch 62; *Re Metro Investments*, unreported, High Court, McWilliam J., 25 May 1977; *Northern Bank Finance v. Quinn & Achates Investment Co.* [1979] I.L.R.M. 221; *Re Horsley & Weight Ltd* [1982] 3 All E.R. 1045; *Rolled Steel Products (Holdings) Ltd. v. British Steel Corporation* [1985] 3 All E.R. 52.

[90] *ibid.*

More recently, Murphy J. in *In Re PMPA (Longmile) Ltd* [91] was called upon to consider whether the directors of a group of companies had acted *bona fide* when they caused the companies to give guarantees for the liabilities of the companies to the provider of the funds, even where some of the companies were not receiving any of the funds. The learned judge held that where companies are associated with each other, as these companies were as they had common directors and management, then they cannot safely ignore the problems of each other[92] and therefore the directors had properly exercised their power granting the guarantees where their objective was to secure the future of the group as a whole.[93]

There is one other context in which the issue of benefit may arise. So far as the outsider dealing with the company is concerned, the question of benefit may become relevant where the transaction or the surrounding circumstances are such as to give rise to a duty to enquire as to whether the directors were properly exercising their powers. *Re Frederick Inns Ltd.*[94] presents a good example of this issue. The Supreme Court held that the Revenue Commissioners, who accepted *ultra vires* payments from four companies towards discharge of the tax liabilities of six related companies, did so as constructive trustees. The Court found the Revenue were constructively aware that the company had no power to make such *ultra vires* payments, as the constitutional documents of the company were open to public inspection.[95] Not only had the company acted *ultra vires*, but also the directors were found to have abused their *fiduciary duties* as they misapplied company funds contrary to the interests of the creditors of the companies.[96] Consequently,

---

[91] [1992] I.LR.M. 337 at 341.

[92] *ibid. at* 343.

[93] However, this judgment should not be taken as authority for the proposition that benefit has to be demonstrated in order for the transaction to be within the respective *capacity* of the various companies in the group itself, as the court had earlier found that the various companies did have the power to give guarantees and furthermore had found that that the giving of the guarantees in helping secure the future of the group of companies, advanced the interests of each company. Clearly therefore, the question of benefit is not a relevant consideration in such a context.

[94] [1991] I.L.R.M. 582 (High Ct.), [1994] 1 I.L.R.M. 387 (Sup. Ct).

[95] Note that in this case, the Revenue were unable to rely on s.8(1) of the Companies Act 1963 to enforce an otherwise *ultra vires* transaction on the grounds that the transaction was not one which could have been "lawfully and effectively done" within the meaning of s.8.

[96] [1994] I.L.R.M. 387 at 399 *per* Blayney J. (Supreme Ct.). It is submitted that Lardner J.'s comments in the High Court [1991] I.L.R.M. 582 at 588 when finding that the payments were *ultra vires* and adverting to the fact that the payments were not for the benefit of the paying companies, is not a statement of authority that benefit must be shown for corporate capacity to exist, but rather that the lack of

because the Revenue were constructively aware of this breach of duty, they were ordered to repay the funds to the companies.

C. ENFORCING LOAN CONTRACTS AGAINST *ULTRA VIRES* CORPORATE BORROWER

(1) Section 8(1) of the Companies Act 1963

5–19   Section 8(1) of the Companies Act 1963 provides that although a corporate act may be *ultra vires*, a party dealing with the company may[97] choose to enforce the transaction against the company, provided that the party was not "actually aware" at the time the transaction was entered into, that the company was acting *ultra vires*. [98]

(a) *Limitations on availability of section 8(1)*

5–20   Although section 8(1) allows a party to enforce a transaction against a company, even though it is *ultra vires* the company, there are limitations on the availability of section 8(1).

First, so far as the party dealing with the company is concerned, that party cannot rely on section 8(1) to circumvent the *ultra vires* nature of the transaction if the party is shown to be "actually aware" that the company's act was an *ultra vires* act.[99]

Second, the party dealing with the company cannot successfully invoke section 8(1) if the transaction was an illegal transaction which company law prevents a company from entering.[100] The provision provides that in order to be able to avail of section 8, the transaction must be "any act or thing . . . which if the company had been empowered to do the same would have been lawfully and effectively done. . . ." Consequently, any act which the company is prohibited from engaging in, such as provision of financial assistance towards the purchase of its own shares contrary to section 60 of the Companies Act 1963, cannot

---

any obvious benefit to the paying companies made it evident that the transactions were *ultra vires*.

[97]   Of course the party dealing with the company could equally choose not to enforce the transaction as, it being *ultra vires*, he is entitled to do.

[98]   subs.8(2) provides that any member or debenture holder of the company may apply to court seeking to restrain the company from entering into any *ultra vires* act.

[99]   See further below at para 5–21 where the "actually aware" criterion is considered in detail.

[100]   In *Bank of Ireland Finance Ltd v. Rockfield Ltd.* [1979] I.R. 21 a company provided assistance for the purchase of its own shares, contrary to s.60 Companies Act 1963. The Bank was not permitted to invoke s.8 in order to permit it enforce the transaction. ·

be enforced by resort to section 8(1). However, in light of the recent High Court and Supreme Court judgments in *Re Frederick Inns Ltd.*[101] it may be that misapplications of company funds which violate general principles of company law also fall outside section 8's helping arms. If this is so, then the scope of section 8 to enforce otherwise *ultra vires* transactions has been greatly reduced.

In *Re Frederick Inns Ltd.* the respective courts held that the making of payments by a group of insolvent companies to guarantee the liabilities of related companies to the Revenue Commissioners, in circumstances where the winding-up of all of the companies was imminent, was *ultra vires*.[102] However, it was further held that although the outsider (the Revenue Commissioners) was not "actually aware" of the lack of capacity, nevertheless the outsider could not invoke section 8 to enforce the payments because the courts held that the transactions could not "have been lawfully and effectively done"[103] (within the meaning of section 8). The courts reached this decision on the basis that, once liquidation was imminent, a company, according to the general principles of company law, may not make payments which might defraud its general body of unsecured creditors.[104] Hence, the courts would not permit the tax payments to be enforced pursuant to section 8.

It remains to be seen how widely this judgment will be interpreted. It could be viewed as a minor narrowing of the scope of application of section 8 if viewed from the perspective that the companies in question were in a state of insolvency, liquidation was imminent, and thus the hopelessly insolvent nature of the companies dictated that the court was wise not to allow the outsider rely on section 8. This is appropriate, particularly in view of the finding that, although the outsider was not "actually aware" that the payments were *ultra vires*, the outsider was factually aware that the companies were hopelessly insolvent. On the other hand, if the case is thought to be authority for a wider propo-

---

[101] [1991] I.L.R.M. 582 (H.C.); [1994] 1 I.L.R.M. 387 (S.Ct.).

[102] Lardner J. in the High Court held that even if the directors had been given powers to pay the debts of other companies, such payments would have been *ultra vires* given that they were of no benefit to the payor companies and were a misapplication of the companies funds in view of the companies insolvent state. Blayney J. (O'Flaherty and Denham JJ. concurring) in the Supreme Court held they were *ultra vires* on the basis that they were not authorised by the memorandum or articles.

[103] subs. 8(1) refers to "Any act or thing done by a company which if the company had been empowered to do the same would have been lawfully and effectively done. . . ."

[104] *per* Lardner J. at 591 (High Court); and *per* Blayney J. at 397 (Supreme Court). In both courts *Kinsella v. Russell Pty (in liquidation)* [1986] 4 N.S.W.L.R. 722 was applied.

sition (*e.g.*, that any breaches of company law or its general principles will render a company's *ultra vires* actions to be actions that cannot be "lawfully and effectively done" for the purposes of section 8) then it is submitted that this may be an overwide interpretation of the case.[105] If such interpretation is correct, then section 8 may cease to have little practical use to outsiders dealing with companies who act *ultra vires*.

Third, so far as the company itself is concerned, section 8(1) is not available to it as the wording of section 8(1) implies that it is only effective for those who are not "actually aware." In this regard, it is difficult to conceive of circumstances where a company would not be deemed to be "actually aware" of the limitations imposed on its own capacity by its own constitutional documents.

Fourth, there is the issue of whether section 8(1) is available to the company's officers. While it would appear to be available to them in principle, in practice, it is unlikely that a company insider could argue they were not "actually aware" of the content of the company's constitutional documents.[106] If this is the correct view, then the final words of section 8(1) hold ominous portents for company officers, as it provides that any director of officer of the company who is responsible for committing the company to an *ultra vires* act, shall be liable to the company for any loss or damage that it may suffer as a consequence.[107]

(b) "Actually Aware"

(i) Judicial interpretation of section 8(1)

5–21   The crucial issue at the centre of section 8(1) is the "actually aware" criterion. In *Northern Bank Finance v. Quinn and Achates Investments Co.*[108] Keane J. was called upon to consider the meaning of "actually aware". The learned judge pointed out that section 8(1) was intended to eradicate the doctrine of constructive notice[109] from the

---

[105] Courtney, *op.cit* at p.222 observes that if the true meaning of "lawfully and effectively done" extends to covers all transactions contrary to company law and not merely criminal ones (or those expressly prohibited by the Companies Acts such as s.60 of the Companies Act 1963 which prohibits the company from financing the purchase of the company's own shares), then s.8 could be emasculated and effectively its availability would be severely curtailed.

[106] Forde, *op.cit* at 431 and Courtney, *op.cit* at 222.

[107] Though s.391 of the Companies Act 1963 provides that a court may decide that although an officer of a company has been guilty of negligence, breach of duty, default or breach of trust, nevertheless the court may decide to excuse the officer either wholly or partially from any liability for the breach where the court takes the view that the officer acted honestly and reasonably in all the circumstances.

[108] [1979] I.L.R.M. 221.

[109] Which prior to the enactment of s.8, deemed persons dealing with a company to be aware of the contents of the company's public documents.

field of *ultra vires.* Nevertheless, the learned judge held that one is "actually aware" for the purposes of section 8(1) where one read, but misunderstood, the contents of the company's memorandum or articles. In the case in question, a bank lender agreed to make a loan to the first named defendant provided that it was guaranteed by a mortgage created by the second named defendant, an unlimited company. The lender's solicitor received a copy of the second defendant's constitutional documents for perusal. The court found that, while in all probability the solicitor had read the documents, he had failed to appreciate from them that the second defendant had no power to give a guarantee in favour of the first named defendant. As the solicitor was the lender's agent, the lender was held to have the agent's "knowledge" imputed to it. Refusing to allow the lender to rely on section 8(1) to enforce the otherwise *ultra vires* guarantee against the company, Keane J. explained the decision of the court on the basis that:

> "I think it is clear that the section was designed to ensure that, . . ., persons who had entered into transactions in good faith with the company without ever reading the memorandum and accordingly with no actual knowledge that the transaction was *ultra vires* were not suffer. I can see no reason in logic or justice why the legislature should have intended to afford the same protection to persons who had actually read the memorandum and simply failed to appreciate the lack of *vires.*"[110]

On the face of it, although this seems to be a reasonable interpretation of what "actually aware" might mean, this interpretation of "actually aware" has been criticised on several grounds. Ussher takes the view that when the legislature enacted section 8(1), it intended to break with the past by employing the "actually aware" formula in order to rid this area of the application of constructive notice entirely, whereas Keane J.'s judgment seems to reintroduce an element of it, contrary to the legislature's apparent intention in section 8. Furthermore, Ussher suggests that:

> "Section 8 does not tell us that the outsider ought to be aware of anything: it is concerned with the actuality and it contains no words from which a duty to investigate could in any circumstances be inferred"[111]

and continues to observe that the High Court's judgment confused "notice" with "knowledge", and that this is at odds with the legislature's intent. Courtney takes a similar, if less strident view, stating that:

> " 'Notice' does not mean 'awareness'. If being 'actually aware' of the provisions of a company's memorandum of association was intended to

---

[110] [1979] I.L.R.M. 221 at 229.
[111] Ussher, *op.cit.* at p. 126.

equate with 'actual notice' of such, one would have thought that the legislature ought to have used the words 'actual notice'. As the law stands, a person who has not seen a company's memorandum and articles, will be protected by section 8(1). Ironically, a person who reads a company's memorandum and articles of association, but fails to understand the lack of vires, will not be protected by section 8(1)."[112]

Although yet another commentator's observations (Johnston) support the broad thrust of Ussher's views as to the "knock-on" difficulties that emanate from Keane J.'s dicta, at the same time a warning to be heeded by lenders' legal advisers is sounded should they wish to interpret the *dicta* as a *carte blanche* to avoid reading the memorandum and articles at all:

"The Supreme Court's decision in *Roche and Roche v. Peilow and Peilow* should be a constant reminder that the adoption of an accepted practice may not be enough to avert a successful claim for negligence. To avoid reading a company's memorandum of association would run contrary to prudent and current accepted practice and must therefore must be even more likely to result in a successful claim for negligence than the circumstances pertaining in *Roche and Roche v. Peilow and Peilow*."[113]

The question therefore arises as to whether lenders really are better served by not inspecting the borrower's constitutional documents at all? While Johnston agrees that the dicta might be open to such an interpretation, he cautions that:

"However, it would be a brave, if not foolish, banker or lawyer who, in the absence of judicial authority at the highest level, would ignore the uncomplicated task of reviewing a company's memorandum of association prior to it completing a financing transaction to ensure that the company had the power to borrow money for a purpose falling within its principal objects."[114]

Forde takes a more cautious approach to the debate, adding an interesting angle. Stating that the EEC First Company Law Directive 68/151[115] uses the formula "could not in view of all the circumstances have been unaware", Forde suggests that section 8(1)'s "actually aware" formula be interpreted in light of the Directive's formula.[116] In this

---

[112] Courtney, *op. cit.* at pp. 223/4.
[113] Johnston, "Corporate Guarantors – Capacity and Authority" (Nov 1997) C.L.P. 240 at p.243.
[114] *op. cit.* at p.242/3.
[115] Council Directive 68/151/ EEC, March 9, 1968 (also known as the First Company Law Directive).
[116] The relevant Article of the Directive will be considered in detail in para. 5–22 below. It should also be noted that although s.8 of the Companies Act 1963 was enacted some years before the Directive was adopted, and must be read in light of the Directive, it would appear to be consistent with the Directive.

way, he suggests that, "knowledge of the actual contents of the memorandum is treated as knowing what the company's objects are."[117] If
this approach is the correct one,[118] then his following comment arouses
further interest:

> "It remains to be seen whether this principle equally applies to the le-
> gally unsophisticated person who may have seen the memorandum and
> the objects clause but did not appreciate their full legal significance. An-
> other matter to be resolved is the position of the party who deliberately
> refrains from reading the memorandum which has been made available
> for his perusal."

Johnston would appear to have more definite views, which although
expressed in the context of the giving of corporate guarantees, are
equally applicable to the granting of a loan:

> ". . . for the practitioner, to be safe, the guarantor's memorandum of as-
> sociation should be reviewed to establish whether the guarantor has the
> capacity to give the guarantee and to understand the purpose for which
> the guarantee is being given in order to establish whether the power
> being exercised is in furtherance of one of the company's principal ob-
> jects."[119]

In light of the foregoing concerns, the question therefore arises as to
whether the EEC Directive 68/151 on Company Law adds to or clarifies this matter? This will now be considered.

(ii) Compatibility with Article 9 First Company Law Directive 68/151/EEC

5–22   Article 9(1) of Council Directive 68/151/EEC of 1968[120] provides
that:

> "Acts done by the organs of the company shall be binding upon it even
> if those acts are not within the objects of the company, unless such acts
> exceed the powers that the law confers or allows to be conferred on those
> organs. However, a Member State may provide that the company shall
> not be bound where such acts are outside the objects of the company, if it
> proves that the third party knew that the act was outside its objects or
> could not in view of the circumstances have been unaware of it; disclo-
> sure of the statutes [of the company] shall not of itself be sufficient proof
> thereof."

---

[117] Forde, *op.cit.* at 430.
[118] Ussher, *op.cit.* at 135 disagrees with this approach, stating that the Directive's
formula of "or could not in view of the circumstances have been unaware" is to
be regarded as mere "cautious surplusage, adding nothing to the formula already employed in s. 8(1)."
[119] *op.cit.* at p.244.
[120] March 9, 1968 reproduced in the Community's Official Journal in 1972 in O.J.
(Spec. English ed.) 1972, 1968 (I), p. 41.

Thus, the Directive clearly intended to restrict the scope of *ultra vires*. It is clear from Article 9(1) that, unlawful acts apart, *ultra vires* transactions were to be binding on, and enforceable against, the company that had acted outside its objects save where the party dealing with the company either knew of the *ultra vires*, or, could not in the circumstances have been unaware of it. Crucially, Article 9 also intended to inhibit the application of constructive notice because Article 9(1) specifically states that mere disclosure of the company's constitutional documents was not tantamount to "awareness". Something more would be required before a Member State's laws could prevent the outsider from enforcing an *ultra vires* transaction against the company. Section 8(1) of the Companies Act 1963, although it predates the Directive by several years, clearly is compatible with the aforegoing requirements. However, Keane J.'s interpretation of section 8(1) in *Northern Bank Finance Corp v. Quinn and Achates Investments Co.* may not be consistent with Article 9,[121] although in this regard it must be noted that Article 9 was not applicable in that case because the Directive has been implemented in Ireland to apply only where the enforceability of dealings with *limited* companies is in issue. *Achates Investments* was an *unlimited* company, and therefore the Directive did not arise for consideration in the judgment.

In any event, the matter is further complicated by the manner in which Article 9 was implemented in Ireland by Regulation 6 of S.I. 163 of 1973.[122]

(iii) Regulation 6 of S.I. No. 163 of 1973

5–23 Regulation 6 states that:

(1) In favour of a person dealing with a company in good faith, any transaction entered into by any organ of the company, being its board of directors or any person registered under these regulations as a person authorised to bind a company, shall be deemed to be within the capacity of the company and any limitation of the powers of that board or person, whether imposed by the memorandum or articles of association or otherwise, may not be relied upon as against any person dealing with the company.

(2) Any such person shall be presumed to have acted in good faith unless the contrary is proved.

As one commentator has observed, "It is clear that we are dealing here with a legislative blunder"[123] and urges that the courts are free to con-

---

[121] See para. 5–21 above.
[122] European Communities (Companies) Regulations 1973 [S.I. No. 163 of 1973].
[123] Ussher, *op.cit.* at 136.

strue section 8(1) without regard to Regulation 6, submitting that the "good faith" requirement in Regulation 6 goes further than Article 9 of the Directive intended, supporting this view by considering the different meanings attaching to "awareness" on one hand and "good faith" on the other. While all outsiders who are in good faith will also not be actually aware, it is not necessarily the case that the reverse is true. In this regard, Ussher concludes that an outsider who is, "not actually aware of the company's lack of capacity will not be in good faith if he allows to remain unresolved any suspicions which he may actually have about the company's capacity."[124]

An interesting observation is that Regulation 6 was not relevant to Keane J.'s decision in *Northern Bank Finance v. Quinn and Achates Investments Co.* because Regulation 6 only applies to limited companies, the company at the centre of that particular case being an *unlimited* company. Thus, any difficulties that Regulation 6 may give rise to, will only be relevant where the enforceability of transactions against *limited* companies arises.

There are also further restrictions on the availability of Regulation 6. For example, Regulation 6 is only relevant where the outsider deals with the board of directors, or, a person registered under the Regulations as a person authorised to bind the company.[125] In *Re Frederick Inns Ltd.* the Revenue Commissioners attempted to rely on Regulation 6 in order to validate *ultra vires* tax payments made by a group of companies. The Supreme Court held that Regulation 6 was not available to the Revenue as the companies had no persons "registered under the regulations as a person authorised to bind the company" and neither could the Revenue demonstrate that the *ultra vires* tax payments made to them "was a transaction entered into by the board of directors of each of the companies." The court was not prepared to hold that informal meetings between company accountants and Revenue officials satisfied the aforegoing requirements.[126]

Finally, Johnston notes about Regulation 6:

> "In practice this Regulation is not used to obviate the prudence to make certain basic enquiries and to review the information provided from such enquiries when completing a financing transaction. This is probably due to the uncertainty as to what is meant by good faith."[127]

---

[124] *op.cit.* at 136.
[125] Again, Ussher criticises this aspect of the Regulation as he asks why should one regime apply to outsiders who deal with directors or registered persons and another set of rules (Companies Act 1963, s.8(1)) apply where the outsider deals with other company agents.
[126] [1994] I.L.R.M. 387 at 394–395 *per* Blayney J.
[127] Johnston, *op.cit.* at p.245.

D. RECOVERY OF FUNDS LOANED PURSUANT TO
ULTRA VIRES TRANSACTION

5–24   With the enactment of section 8 of the Companies Act 1963, the legislature intervened in order to permit *ultra vires* transactions to be *enforced against* the *ultra vires company*. Consequently, a company that had acted *ultra vires* could be compelled to fulfill its obligations under a loan contract, even though the contract was *ultra vires* the company.

However, before such legislative reform came about, the courts too played a part in attempting to ameliorate the harsh excesses of the *ultra vires* doctrine. The assistance that the courts provided was different in emphasis. Rather than permitting *the ultra vires* transaction itself to be *enforced,* the courts were prepared to contemplate rights of recovery for the outsider, so that money furnished under an *ultra vires* contract could be *recovered* in certain circumstances. While the conceptual difficulties that the courts faced in this regard were considerable, nevertheless there were ways in which the courts sought to obviate the harshness of the *ultra vires* rule whenever possible. The traditional difficulty for the courts in this respect was that any court that attempted to come to the assistance of the adversely affected outsider risked being accused of assisting in the *enforcement of* an *ultra vires* transaction, contrary to the common law.

(1) *In personam* **contractual and quasi-contractual remedies denied**

5–25   The pinnacle of harsh judicial attitudes was seen in *Sinclair v. Brougham.*[128] In this case, a building society was set up under statute to conduct the traditional business of a building society. Its business was defined by statute to be the accepting of deposits and the granting of loans for funding house purchase/construction to depositors. However, the society expanded its activities by engaging in *ultra vires* activities such as the solicitation and acceptance of depositors funds for the purposes of granting loans for commercial purposes. When the society went into liquidation, the House of Lords was *inter alia* called upon to consider which group had the rightful claim to the commercial deposits – the society's shareholders/ creditors, or, the depositors of the funds? The House of Lords held that the moneys could not be recovered by the depositors on the basis of normal contractual remedies. This was because the building society, being a statutory body, had no powers other than those given it by statute. Consequently, it had acted *ultra vires* when it accepted deposits towards its commercial lending business, as it never had the power to enter into the relation-

---

[128] [1914] A.C. 398.

ship of debtor and creditor with such depositors. Hence, no *in personam* remedy (*i.e.* a contractual remedy) could be invoked in the courts against the society, the *ultra vires* acceptor of the funds. As Viscount Haldene, the Lord Chancellor stated:

> "To hold that a remedy will lie *in personam* against a statutory society, which by hypothesis cannot in the case in question have become a debtor or entered into any contract for repayment, is to strike at the root of the doctrine of *ultra vires* as established in the jurisprudence of this country."[129]

Illustrating the harshness of this position, the Lord Chancellor continued:

> "I think it (*ultra vires*) excludes from the law. . . any claim *in personam* based even on the circumstance that the defendant had been improperly enriched at the expense of the plaintiff by a transaction which is *ultra vires.*"

Having ruled that normal contractual remedies were not available to the disgruntled depositors, the House of Lords then considered whether the depositors could be permitted to recover their deposits by way of *quasi-contractual* remedies, such as the action for monies "had and received". The Lords refused relief, on the basis that to permit such a remedy would have amounted to indirect enforcement of what was an otherwise *ultra vires* activity. The Lords held that where a corporate body, acting *ultra vires* itself, has taken receipt of another's funds, then the provider of the funds cannot plead that recovery should be granted on the basis of a quasi-contractual remedy. The law was not prepared to impute a promise to repay on the part of the *ultra vires* recipient of the funds, as no such promise could be implied where the recipient of the funds was taking those funds *ultra vires* itself.

Having ruled out the availability of both *in personam* contractual remedies, and quasi-contractual remedies (based on the legal fiction of an implied promise to repay), the court held that the only remedy that was available to the disgruntled depositers, if at all, was a remedy *in rem, i.e.*, tracing. If the depositors could successfully trace their specific funds into the assets of the *ultra vires* holder of the funds, then they could be recovered. This would not be tantamount to *enforcing* the *ultra vires* action under which the funds were obtained in the first place, but would merely be a means of *recovery* of specific property that was the property of the depositor. The difficulty with this remedy is that if a holder of funds has mixed the funds with other funds, then the attempt to trace the funds successfully may be ineffective.

---

[129] *ibid.* at 414.

Undoubtedly, public policy grounds, and the fact that the building society was a body whose powers were defined under specific legislation, influenced the House of Lords in coming to its decision in this case. However, what is even more significant about this case as an example of judicial attitude to *ultra vires* transactions, is that it indicates that some courts were determined to ensure that no other legal stratagems (such as the implied promise to repay or the action for money had and received) were used as a means of *enforcing / permitting recovery of* monies pursuant to an *ultra vires* transaction.[130] While the intention may have been a worthy one,[131] this seems particularly harsh as innocent outsiders would not even be permitted to recover monies paid over to the company that had itself taken receipt of such funds *ultra vires*. One consequence surely was that the *ultra vires* company was permitted to be unjustly enriched by the retention of such funds.

However, as will be discussed shortly, courts in more modern times take a more enlightened view, as they consider that restitution should be permitted in order to avoid a party being unjustly enriched by reliance on another's *ultra vires*.[132]

(2) Quasi-contractual remedies rehabilitated

5–26 Not all courts were prepared to adopt the strict approach taken in *Sinclair v. Brougham*. For example, in *Flood v. Irish Provident Assurance Company*[133] a non-life insurance company entered into the business of life insurance. Customers purchased life assurance policies, paying premiums to the company. An issue arose as to the status of the premiums when it emerged that the company had acted *ultra vires* its objects in writing such life assurance policies. As such policies were *ultra vires*, they were void, and thus it was feared by the policy holders that they would be prevented from recovering their premiums paid to the company. The court held that although normal contractual remedies could not be available to the policy holders as the policies were

---

[130] Although insistent that no remedy *in personam* would lie, the House of Lords did concede that a remedy *in rem* was not automatically precluded. However, as noted above, the usefulness of this remedy was doubted by the Lords.

[131] To protect the creditors of a corporate body from being impoverished when a company liquidates by preventing *ultra vires* transactions from being enforceable against the liquidator.

[132] It should be noted that strong statements of disapproval of *Sinclair v. Brougham* were made in the House of Lords in *Westdeutsche Landesbank Girozentrale v. Islington London Borough Council* [1996] A.C. 669. Although it was not overruled as such, the fact that the Lords "departed" from it as an authority greatly diminishes its status as an authoritative precedent (see also n.143 below).

[133] [1912] 46 I.L.T.R.; [1912] 2 Ch. 597.

[134] *i.e.*, valid life assurance cover.

ultra vires, nevertheless the premiums could be recovered because they were paid to the company without the company providing any valid consideration in return.[134] In ruling that the premiums could be recovered, the court did not enforce an otherwise *ultra vires* transaction. All that was merely achieved, albeit significantly, was that the premiums paid were ordered to be returned. Yet the court's ruling in no way purported to enforce the life policies *per se.*[135]

In more modern times, the Irish courts have further enhanced the possibilities for quasi-contractual recovery in respect of *ultra vires* transactions. For example, the dicta of Henchy J. in the Supreme Court in *East Cork Foods v. O' Dwyer Steel*[136] illustrate how the principles of quasi-contractual recovery have developed to such an extent that the legal fiction of an imputed promise to repay is no longer required in order for the law to permit a party who has *provided* funds to an *ultra vires* recipient to recover such funds. Consequently, as the legal fiction of an imputed promise is no longer required by modern courts, difficulties such as those that troubled the House of Lords in *Sinclair v. Brougham* are largely obviated. In a memorable dictum, Henchy J. stated[137]:

> "The historical reason for this fiction[138] was to enable the claim to be brought as a form of *indebitatus assumpsit.* It was a pleader's stratagem. In most cases, however, it is in the teeth of the facts to impute to the debtor a promise to repay. So long as the forms of action governed the course of litigation, it was necessary for the courts to go along with this transparent fiction. Nowadays, however, when the forms of action have long been since buried, the concept of implied contract is an unreal and outdated rationale for the action for money had and received. Judges in modern times prefer to look at the reality of the situation rather than engage in the pretence that the defendant has promised to repay the debt. . . . The real reason why the courts would uphold the claim [today] is because it would be unjust and inequitable to allow the first defendant to keep the money. To refuse the claim would mean that the first defendant would be unjustly enriched."

Thus, because of the harshness of the *ultra vires* rule on innocent parties, the courts are willing to allow outsiders to have resort to quasi-contractual remedies, provided that such remedies do not lead to direct or indirect enforcement of the *ultra vires* contract. Such remedies are available because the courts are now unprepared to tolerate an *ultra vires* party relying on their own *ultra vires* and consequently be un-

---

[135] Another example of a case which demonstrates this more benevolent approach is the decision in *Re Lough Neagh Shipping Company* [1895] 1 I.R.. 533.

[136] [1978] I.R. 103.

[137] *ibid.* at 110–111.

[138] *i.e.,* that a promise to repay be imputed to the recipient of the funds.

justly enriched. Therefore, a lender, unfortunate enough to have lent funds to an *ultra vires* corporate borrower could attempt recovery provided that the *ultra vires* contract was not incidentally indirectly enforced.

These developments facilitating the availability of quasi-contractual relief demonstrate that, while the courts could not go as far as section 8(1) of the Companies Act 1963 by enforcing an *ultra vires* contract, nevertheless they are willing to play a constructive role.

(3) Basis for recovery of funds (and interest) loaned *ultra vires* the lender?

5–27   While the law was willing to provide the outsider with both statutory and judicial means to avoid the harshness of the *ultra vires* doctrine, an issue that was more problematic was whether a company which had *granted* a loan or security *ultra vires* its own objects, could recover such loan or enforce such security even though it itself was the *ultra vires* party?

This issue arose for consideration in *Re PMPA (Longmile) Ltd and Others (No. 2)*[139] in the High Court. In earlier litigation in this saga, *Re PMPA (Longmile) Ltd and Others*,[140] Murphy J. had found that the Private Motorists Provident Society had lent monies to companies in the Private Motorists Protection Association group of companies, and that in return the PMPA companies executed guarantees in favour of the PMPS. Furthermore, Murphy J. found that the loans that the PMPA companies had obtained from the PMPS were *ultra vires* the PMPS, because the relevant legislation which allowed the PMPS to grant loans only permitted the PMPS to grant loans in circumstances where some form of independent security was provided by the borrower. In this regard, the learned judge held that the PMPA guarantees, although valid, did not constitute the required independent security. Thus in *Re PMPA (Longmile) Ltd and Others (No. 2)*, the High Court was called upon to consider whether PMPS, was entitled in law to enforce the guarantees and thereby recover the loans it had granted, notwithstanding that *it* had acted *ultra vires*.

Murphy J. commenced the court's analysis by first dealing with the proposition that because the loan was *ultra vires*, it was therefore void and unenforceable. The learned judge held that it would be a monstrous injustice if the borrowers of an *ultra vires* loan could retain it and not have to repay the lender merely because the lender had granted the loan *ultra vires* itself. The court continued stating that where

---

[139] [1992] I.L.R.M. 349.
[140] [1992] I.L.R.M. 337.

a transaction is *ultra vires*, the party who has delivered property or monies pursuant to it would be entitled to recover such property or monies from the donee, whether the deficiency in capacity is that of the donor or the donee. The court also noted that where the case law differs is as to the extent of the nature of the legal action which can be taken to achieve such object.

Having set out the aforegoing, the court approved of the House of Lords decision in *Sinclair v. Brougham*, stating that the law's readiness to permit the availability of tracing remedies does not amount to a violation of the principle that *ultra vires* contracts are void and unenforceable. Furthermore, the court agreed with the proposition put forward in *Sinclair v. Brougham* that a contractual action for debt cannot be possible where a transaction is *ultra vires*. However, where the court differed with *Sinclair v. Brougham* was in the modern law's readiness to permit quasi-contractual remedies to be available. Quoting Henchy J's *East Cork Foods Ltd dicta* (which recognised that quasi-contract was no longer grounded on an implied promise to repay),[141] Murphy J. stated:

> "The significance of this development is that by eliminating the need for an express or imputed promise to pay as an ingredient of the action for money had and received it overcomes the problem faced by the House of Lords in *Sinclair v. Brougham*. If it is not necessary to infer some hypothetical or fictitious promise to pay then there is no impediment in availing of that remedy against a corporate body to recover monies received by it as a result of a transaction which was outside its corporate powers."[142]

Having referred to this "more enlightened view"[143] of recovery on a quasi-contractual basis, the court then considered authorities from several other common law jurisdictions which, although not always reconcilable, appeared to be authority for the further proposition that a party cannot be permitted to retain goods or monies received pursuant to an *ultra vires* transaction. Murphy J, in a lengthy quote reproduced here because of its clarity, stated:

---

[141] See para. 5–26 above.

[142] *ibid* at 354.

[143] *ibid*. U.K. courts now take a similar view. For example, Lord Browne-Wilkinson in *Westdeutsche Landesbank Girozentrale v. Islington London Borough Council* [1996] A.C. 669 at 710 stated that developments subsequent to *Sinclair v. Brougham* in the law of restitution demonstrate that the reasoning of *Sinclair v. Brougham* (which rejected the notion of an implied contract to repay) ". . . is no longer sound. The common law restitutionary claim is based not on implied contract but on unjust enrichment: in the circumstances the law imposes an obligation to repay rather then implying an entirely fictitious agreement to repay . . . I would overrule *Sinclair v. Brougham* on this point."

"I recognise the force of the simple cogent proposition that a body corporate cannot enforce a contract which it never has the capacity to make. It is demonstrated with equal clarity that all judicial authorities have set their face against any party who seeks to prevent the recovery from him of goods or monies which he has retained under an *ultra vires* transaction. The precise grounds on which such claims have been defeated have varied over the century during which the debate has spasmodically taken place but the result has always been the same. No court would permit the manifest injustice which such a contention would involve. [Counsel for the PMPA] has summarised this by saying that the courts have had difficulty in reconciling the intuitive desire for restitution with the strict observance of the doctrine of *ultra vires*....there is no inconsistency between the proper application of the *ultra vires* doctrine and the recovery by means of an action *in rem* or on a quasi-contractual basis of monies or goods in the hands of the party receiving the same in consequence of the transaction. The problem which must be faced is whether there is any other basis on which such goods or monies can be recovered. It seems to me that the alternative basis is something akin to an estoppel."[144]

The learned judge continued:

"There are differences of opinion as to whether the restriction imposed on the borrower is properly described as an estoppel but it seems to me that the overwhelming body of judicial opinion is to the effect that the borrower is precluded from making the point that the transaction was *ultra vires* where this would result in an injustice. In most cases, the injustice envisaged is where the competent party would retain for his own benefit the fruits of the *ultra vires* transaction."[145]

Thus, having established that the PMPS could be admitted as a guarantor on foot of each of the PMPA guarantees, the court held that the PMPS could be allowed to recover its funds.

5–28 This High Court decision must give some solace to non-bank[146] lenders who lend to corporate borrowers. The courts are no longer prepared to allow borrowers or the grantors of security to avoid their obligations merely because the lender acted *ultra vires* itself when granting

---

[144] *ibid.* at 362.

[145] *ibid.* at 363. On this issue of whether a promise to guarantee a debt, may be enforceable by a rule akin to an estoppel even if the debt itself is *ultra vires*, see discussion by O' Dell, "Estoppel and Ultra Vires Contracts" (1992) 14 D.U.L.J. 123. Also contrast contrary decision in *Credit Suisse v. Allerdale BC* [1997] Q.B. 306. For further discussion of the development of restitutionary principles in Irish law see further by the same author, "The Principles Against Unjust Enrichment" (1993) 15 D.U.L.J. 27 and "Restitution" in *Annual Review of Irish Law* (1996) (Binchy and Byrne ed.) at pp. 502–529.

[146] "Non-bank" is used as presumably a bank will not be acting *ultra vires* itself when it grants loans.

the loan. While the court cannot order the loan or guarantee to be enforced as if the contract were a valid contract, it certainly is not willing
to tolerate the borrower retaining loan proceeds and thereby become
unjustly enriched.

Although the judgment refers to the principle against unjust enrichment as the basis for allowing restitution, what precisely does this
mean as a matter of law? The judgment does not explicitly specify
whether the sums to be repaid are the sums that were *actually lent*, or
an equivalent sum. Such issue may not be of great concern where the
recipient of the funds is solvent. However if the recipient were in imminent danger of insolvent liquidation, this matter could be of the greatest importance. In other words, if a *trust* arises, the loan recipient's
creditors would be precluded from access to such funds. On the other
hand, if a trust does not arise, then the lender's right to recovery may
be effectively of little value.

The House of Lords has recently given some consideration to this
issue in *Westdeutsche Landesbank Girozentrale v. Islington London Borough Council*.[147] In that case, a bank advanced monies to a local authority under an interest rate swap arrangement entered into between the
parties in 1987. Unknown to the parties, the council was acting *ultra
vires*.[148] The lower courts found that restitution could be awarded on
the basis of a common law restitutionary action for money had and
received *and also* in equity under a *resulting trust*. On appeal to the
House of Lords, the issue was whether the lower courts were right to
find that a resulting trust[149] had come into existence (were this so, then
the bank would retain an ownership interest in the monies advanced).

The House of Lords held that there was no basis for finding that a
recipient of monies received under a contract, void on grounds of *ultra*

---

[147] [1996] A.C. 669.

[148] A few years earlier the House of Lords had held in an unrelated case that local
authorities who entered into interest rate swap agreements were acting *ultra
vires*: *Hazell v. Hammersmith and Fulham L.B.C.* [1992] 2 A.C. 1. Note that the
local authority swaps debacle in the U.K. has spawned a raft of litigation: e.g.
Kleinwort Benson v. Lincoln City Council [1997] 4 All E.R. 513 (where the House
of Lords held, inter alia, that a plaintiff could recover money paid in a failed
swap on the grounds of mistake regarding the validity of the swap; *Guinness
Mahon v. Chelsea and Kensington L.B.C.* [1998] 2 All E.R. 272 (where the Court of
Appeal held that failure of consideration is no bar to restitution, provided sufficiently total). My thanks to Eoin O'Dell, Trinity College Dublin, for drawing
these decisions to my attention and for furnishing me with an advance copy of
his forthcoming chapter, "Incapacity", to be published shortly in Birks and
Rose (eds.), *Lessons of the Swaps Litigation* (Mansfield Press, Oxford, 1999 (forthcoming)).

[149] This was particularly pertinent to the issue of whether compound, as opposed
to mere simple, interest was recoverable by the bank: on the interest issue, see
further below.

vires, held such monies under a resulting trust. The main reasons advanced for such conclusion were that (apart from the fact that there is no general principle that a resulting trust arises in such a situation in any event)[150] the recipient of the funds could not be aware that the funds were received on trust as they had no knowledge of the *ultra vires*;[151] furthermore, such a proposition would create intolerable legal uncertainty for third parties to whom the funds may have been passed on.[152]

Although this judgment is persuasive on the point that no resulting trust interest in favour of the lender arose in such circumstances, this does not however necessarily mean that no fiduciary obligation can arise out of an *ultra vires* contract. It may be that a *constructive trusteeship* may arise. In this event, fiduciary obligations will arise. Indeed in *Westdeutsche Landesbank Girozentrale v. Islington London Borough Council* itself the House of Lords did briefly address this issue, but did not consider it, as it did not arise on the facts.[153] However, the issue has been considered to a greater extent in the Irish courts. Blayney J., delivering the judgement in the Supreme Court in *Re Frederick Inns Ltd.*[154] held that the Revenue Commissioners had constructive knowledge that four companies acted *ultra vires*, and thus had no power to make payments to the Revenue in discharge of the tax liabilities of other companies.[155] Consequently, the Revenue, being held to be constructive

---

[150] [1996] 2 A.C. 669 *per* Lord Goff at 689.

[151] Such that it would be unfair to foist the obligations of trustee on such a party.

[152] *ibid. per* Lord Browne-Wilkinson at 704.

[153] *ibid. per* Lord Browne-Wilkinson who noted at p. 707 that: "Counsel for the bank specifically disavowed any claim based on a constructive trust. This was plainly right because the local authority had no relevant knowledge sufficient to raise a constructive trust at any time before the monies, upon the bank account going into overdraft, became untraceable. Once there ceased to be an identifiable trust fund, the local authority could not become a trustee. . . ." Of course, in order for a constructive trust to arise, there must be some knowledge, actual or imputed. Where this is not the case, then the constructive trust cannot arise. It is interesting to note that later in his judgment Lord Browne-Wilkinson observed at 716 that, "Although the resulting trust is an unsuitable basis for developing proprietary restitutionary remedies, the remedial constructive trust, if introduced into English law, may prove a more satisfactory road forward. The court by way of remedy might impose a constructive trust on a defendant who knowingly retains property of which the plaintiff has been unjustly deprived. Since the remedy can be tailored to the circumstances of the particular case, innocent third parties would not be prejudiced and restitutionary defences, such as change of position, are capable of being given effect."

[154] [1994] I.L.R.M. 387 at 399.

[155] The Revenue were deemed constructively aware because the court held that the memoranda of the four companies were documents of public record, which, had the Revenue inspected them would have revealed the companies were acting *ultra vires*. Consequently, such knowledge was imputed to the Revenue (as

trustees of the sums which were the subject of the *ultra vires* payments, were thus ordered to repay them to the official liquidators of the paying companies.[156]

5–29   Another issue that did not arise for decision in the *Re PMPA Longmile (No. 2)* judgment is the issue of interest repayment on *ultra vires* loans. Are such sums due to be payable as if the initial transaction had been *intra vires*? Murphy J. did not decide whether interest payments were recoverable as the matter of interest did not arise in that set of proceedings before the High Court.[157] Just as with the recovery of principal sums loaned *ultra vires*,[158] the issue arises (should interest recovery be permitted) whether this would assume the appearance and substance of "enforcement" of an *ultra vires* contract.

Further litigation arising out of the liquidation of both the PMPA and PMPS, throws light on this issue. In 1994, in *PMPA Ltd. v. PMPS Ltd.*[159] Murphy J. held that where the plaintiff had paid sums *ultra vires* itself to the defendant in 1979 and 1980, the defendant's obligation to make restitution included the obligation to pay interest to the plaintiff at the "court rate"[160] under the Debtors (Ireland) Act 1840 as set by the Minister for Justice. Although the judgment is quite brief on the issue, the learned judge held that the court may depart from the court rate where it finds that the court rate at any particular time is unrealistic.[161] However, when determining what a fair interest rate should be, the court refused to accede to the plaintiff's argument that the recipient of the sums was obliged as part of its restitutionary obligations, to pay a

---

for the reasons why the Revenue could not rely on either s.8 of the Companies Act 1963 or Regulation 6 of S.I. No. 163 of 1973 to prevent constructive notice of *ultra vires* being imputed: see further paras 5–20 and 5–30 (on s. 8) and paras 5–23 and 5–52 (on Reg. 6).

[156] Of course, in order for a constructive trust to arise, there must be some knowledge, actual or imputed. Where this is not the case, then the constructive trust cannot arise (as was the case in *Westdeutche Landesbank Girozentrale v. Islington London Borough Council* [1996] A.C. 669); and as held by Laffoy J. in *Ulster Factors Ltd v. Entonglen Ltd (in liquidation) and George Moloney*, unreported, High Court, February 21, 1997.

[157] Apart from observing that, "it is not seriously disputed that the PMPS would be entitled to interest, though not necessarily at the rate agreed between the parties. . . . I will postpone for the time being this aspect of the matter.": [1992] I.L.R.M. 349 at 354/355.

[158] Whether *ultra vires* the lender or the recipient.

[159] unreported, High Court, Murphy J., June 27, 1994.

[160] Also known as "statutory interest".

[161] Following Kenny J. in *Law v. Roberts* [1964] I.R. 306 where Kenny J. departed from the court rate of 4% and set a rate of 6%. In the instant case, Murphy J. took cognisance of the fact that the court rate was 11% in 1981 and reduced to 8% in 1989. Consequently, he set an interest rate of 10% as meeting "the justice of the case.": unreported, High Court, Murphy J., June 27, 1994 at p. 4.

rate of interest that might reflect alternative arrangements the plaintiff might have made with financial institutions had the sums been under the plaintiff's management. Even though the court did acknowledge that the recipient of sums who receives the sums from an *ultra vires* payor, holds such sums in a "fiduciary capacity"[162] and therefore is liable to account for any profits made from such funds, nevertheless, the learned judge was not prepared to hold that such obligation extended to awarding a level of interest that the plaintiff might have succeeded in obtaining in the commercial deposit market. The court held that the court rate is a sum awarded by way of restitution independently of the efforts of the parties, free from any element of risk.[163] Therefore, the only factor that would influence a court when deciding whether to grant the court rate, or alternatively an adjusted rate, was whether the court rate set by the Minister would meet the justice of the case.

Other cases have also provided for the award of interest. For example, in *Re Frederick Inns Ltd* the Supreme Court directed that, in addition to repayment of sums paid by companies *ultra vires* themselves to the Revenue Commissioners, court rate interest was also payable by the Revenue, from the date of payment to the date of repayment.

One further point should be made before concluding on the issue of interest. In *PMPA v. PMPS*, Murphy J. referred to the recipient of the *ultra vires* funds holding them in a "fiduciary capacity." In this context the learned judge's remarks were merely confined to finding that the recipient of the sums would be accountable to account for any profit made by it if evidence to that effect were available.[164] In light of the recent consideration of the issue of *ultra vires* transaction and trusts in the U.K.,[165] it is probably correct to state that Murphy J's reference to fiduciary capacity does not imply that a resulting trust had arisen, or that the recipient of the *ultra vires* payments had become a trustee. Instead it appears that the term "fiduciary" was used in a wider sense to mean that the recipient of the funds was under a obligation to repay the sums to the payor in order to prevent the recipient's unjust enrichment.[166]

In *Westdeutsche Landesbank Girozentrale v. Islington London Borough*

---

[162] As to what Murphy J. may have intended by this reference to "fiduciary capacity" see immediately below.

[163] unreported, High Court, Murphy J., June 27, 1994 at p. 3.

[164] In the event there was no such profit as all the defendant had done with the funds was to lodge them to its bank account, whereupon they were dissipated.

[165] *Westdeutsche Landesbank Girozentrale v. Islington London Borough Council* [1996] A.C. 669.

[166] Although the use of the term fiduciary in the strict sense might be justified if the circumstances were such that a constructive trusteeship arises, as was the case in *Re Frederick Inns Ltd.* [1994] I.L.R.M. 387 discussed above.

Council the House of Lords rejected the contention that there is a right to recovery of *compound* interest in aid of a bank's valid common law claim to restitution of sums paid to a recipient, a local council, who had acted *ultra vires* in receiving such sums. The Lords were not unanimous on this issue, with Lords Goff and Woolf dissenting. The majority[167] declined to allow the bank claim compound interest on the basis that in the absence of fraud, Equity has traditionally declined to award compound interest except in the case of fraud against a trustee or someone in a fiduciary position who has abused that position and thereby made improper profits. As the Lords had already held that the bank was not the beneficiary of a trust,[168] the Lords therefore declined to award compound interest in favour of the bank. Only simple interest was allowed. The Lords were also heavily influenced by the fact that the U.K. Parliament had twice this century intervened to provide the courts with the power to award interest where the common law did not so provide: in neither instance did it provide for the awarding of compound interest. The minority argued that compound interest should be allowable, as the principles of restitution dictate that the law should make available whatever is necessary to prevent one party from profiting from unjust enrichment.[169] However, for the aforementioned reasons, this did not find favour with the three majority Lords.

(4) Recovery of sums paid *ultra vires* to the Revenue authorities

5–30   This expansion of restitutionary principles can also be seen in the context of another issue that has arisen recently, which is whether a company which pays tax to the Revenue is entitled to be repaid the tax, plus interest, where either the company or the Revenue acted *ultra vires*. This issue arose recently in the Supreme Court in *Re Frederick Inns Ltd* (the company acted *ultra vires*) and in the House of Lords judgment in *Woolwich Building Society v. Inland Revenue Commissioners (No. 2)* (the U.K. Revenue acted without valid authority).

In *Re Frederick Inns Ltd,*[170] both the High and Supreme Court held that four companies in a related group of insolvent companies had acted *ultra vires* when the directors of the companies had discharged to the Revenue Commissioners the liabilities of another six related companies, using money from the first four companies. Furthermore, sec-

---

[167] Lords Browne-Wilkinson, Lloyd and Slynn. For further discussion of the interest issue, see Rose's chapter, "Interest" in Birks and Rose (eds.), *Lessons of the Swaps Litigation* (Mansfield Press, Oxford, 1999 (forthcoming)).

[168] See above at para. 5–28.

[169] The minority (Lords Goff and Woolf) considered that the common law action for restitution should permit the courts to award compound interest.

[170] [1991] I.L.R.M. 582 (H.C.), [1994] 1 I.L.R.M. 387 (S.C.).

tion 8 of the Companies Act 1963 could not be invoked by the Revenue even though the Revenue was not "actually aware" of the *ultra vires*.[171]

Having held the payments to have been *ultra vires*, the Supreme Court was then called upon to consider whether the High Court was correct in directing that the payments credited by the Revenue to the six related companies, should be re-credited towards the liabilities of the four companies, in proportion to their respective contributions. The Supreme Court overruled the High Court on this issue, and directed that as the funds were paid *ultra vires*, the sums advanced by the four companies must be returned to their respective liquidators. Blayney J. delivering the judgment of the Supreme Court, held that as the funds were paid *ultra vires*, they constituted a misapplication of company funds and the Revenue Commissioners were deemed to be *constructively aware* that the funds were being misapplied. The basis for constructive knowledge lay in the fact that the constitutional documents of the four companies were documents of public record, and the Revenue therefore were deemed constructively aware that the directors had misapplied company funds. Consequently, the Revenue was deemed to be constructive trustee of the payments, and thus held them in trust for the liquidators of the four companies.

The clear implication following this judgment is that where a company pays money *ultra vires* itself in circumstances where section 8 cannot be invoked, then the recipient of the payment who knows or ought to have known of the *ultra vires* will hold the funds as constructive trustee on the company's behalf. Furthermore, interest will also be payable, as the Supreme Court held that that interest was repayable from the date of payment, to the date of repayment.

5–31 The House of Lords has also given consideration to the repayment of sums plus interest issues, though in the context of the *recipient* of the funds being the party that acted *ultra vires*. In *Woolwich Building Society v. Inland Revenue Commissioners (No. 2)*[172] a building society paid sums to the IRC when so demanded. However, when judicially reviewed, the regulations on which the IRC sought to rely as the basis for giving it the authority to levy tax were held to be *ultra vires*. Consequently, the building society sought to have the tax paid refunded, with interest. The judgment of Lord Goff makes most interesting reading,[173] as it surveys the existing law and then powerfully comes to the

---

[171] As discussed above at para. 5–20, it was held that s.8 cannot be relied upon to give effect to *ultra vires* transactions if the transaction is of a type which a company cannot otherwise "lawfully and effectively" enter into.

[172] *Woolwich Building Society v. Inland Revenue Commissioners (No. 2)* [1992] 3 All E.R. 737.

[173] *ibid., per* Lord Goff at 752-764.

conclusion that, at common law, moneys paid to the Revenue authorities in the form of taxes are *prime facie* recoverable where levied pursuant to *ultra vires* taxation regulations. Furthermore, interest on such sums is also recoverable from the date of such payments. Alluding to the revolution that has occurred in the law of restitutionary principles during this century, Lord Goff indicated that the basis for such conclusion was that where the Revenue authorities make demands in circumstances where they have no valid statutory authority, then the demand being an *ultra vires* one, "Common justice seems to require that tax to be repaid, unless special circumstances or some principle of public policy require otherwise: prima facie, the taxpayer should be entitled to repayment as of right."[174]

III. CORPORATE BORROWING – AUTHORITY OF COMPANY AGENTS TO BIND THE COMPANY

Overview

5–32 Where a company's agents are not duly authorised to borrow on the company's behalf, the company may subsequently attempt to claim that it is not bound by the loan on the ground that its agents committed the company without due authorisation. A lender who wishes to avoid such concerns may require evidence that the borrower's agents, usually its directors, had the requisite authority to enter the transaction.[175] Evidence of the agent's actual authority may emanate from either the company's internal regulations, its articles, or from board/shareholder resolutions.

However, if for each and every transaction entered into with company agents lenders had to be satisfied as to agents' actual authority, commercial life would become intolerable. Given that all companies act through human intermediaries, the law takes a more pragmatic position, intervening in a number of different ways.

First, applying the laws of agency, although company agents may not possess actual authority, nevertheless they may be deemed to have ostensible authority. A company will be bound by the actions of its agents, provided the lender can demonstrate that the company's actions clothed the agent with ostensible authority. Such authority can

---

[174] *ibid.* at 759.
[175] In this respect, at issue is not *ultra vires* or whether the directors are borrowing for an *ultra vires* purpose. That has been considered above at paras 5–06—5–18 and is an entirely separate matter.

be implied from an amalgam of the contents of the company's internal regulations *and* the company's own conduct.

Second, the rule in *Turquand's* case may be applicable. Under the doctrine of constructive notice, knowledge of a company's constitutional documents are imputed to the public because they are public documents. Consequently, knowledge that the company's articles require the company to take certain internal steps[176] in order to perfect an agent's authority is imputed to any party dealing with the company. However, the rule in *Turquand's* case modifies the application of constructive notice in that it establishes that a party dealing with a company may presume, unless put on enquiry, that such internal company requirements have in fact been satisfied. Consequently, a lender can therefore rely on the rule to enforce a loan or security against the borrower, notwithstanding a failure by the company to comply with its own internal procedures and rules.[177]

Third, it shall also be seen how European law has had an impact on the principles that apply to transactions entered into with corporate agents. Regrettably however, the manner in which such law has been implemented has tended to obscure rather than clarify some of the key issues that arise in the area[178]

A. TYPES OF AUTHORITY

(1) Actual Authority

5–33 Company agents have *actual* authority to do whatever the memorandum or articles of association empower them to do. For example, a company that adopts Model Article 80[179] permits the directors of the company, as a board, to manage the company's business and exercise all powers of the company that do not require the authority of the general meeting. Furthermore, Model Article 79[180] allows the directors, as a board, to exercise certain borrowing powers on the company's behalf.

There are also other means by which a director could be actually authorised to enter a transaction. For example, a director could be authorised to enter into a particular transaction by a board resolution or a resolution of the members of the company.

---

[176] *e.g.*, a company resolution.
[177] However, there are limits on the availability of *Turquand's* rule, as will be explained further below.
[178] EEC Council Directive 68/151 (First Company Law Directive) of March 9, 1968: see further below.
[179] First Schedule, Table A, Companies Act 1963.
[180] *ibid.*

(2) Ostensible Authority

5–34   The law is also prepared to impute to the agent a form of *ostensible* authority. Where certain circumstances exist, the impression may have been created by the company that the agent ostensibly had authority to enter the transaction in question. The courts are prepared to impute the agent's actions to the company on the basis that the transactions entered into by the agent were within the field of the agent's *usual* authority and the company, by its actions, contributed to the impression that the agent had the requisite *actual* authority.

An agent's field of *usual* authority will be prescribed by the terms of the company's articles. Taking the Companies Act 1963 First Schedule Table A Model Articles as an example, it can be seen how the directors, as a board, have a wide field of authority as Article 80 specifically gives them wide powers to manage the company's business. However, such articles have little to say about the authority of company directors acting outside the boardroom arena. Consequently, it can be said that the field of usual authority of an individual director acting on their own is very limited, unless the company's articles are specifically modifed.

The leading case in the area of ostensible authority is *Freeman & Lockyer v. Buckhurst Park Properties (Mangal) Ltd.*[181] A company director was allowed act by his company as if he were the managing director, and as if he had all of the usual powers that a managing director usually possesses. However, even though the articles permitted a managing director to be appointed, the director was never formally appointed as managing director by the company. Nevertheless, the court held that when the director committed the company to a contract, the company was not permitted to deny that it had ostensibly clothed him with the requisite authority. This was because the company's board had, for a considerable period, allowed the director conduct himself as if he were managing director, with all of the powers that would be within the field of usual authority of such an agent.[182] Consequently, even though the board had never formally appointed him managing director nor ever formally delegated a managing director's powers to him, this did not mean that the company had not clothed him with ostensible authority by virtue of the provisions of its articles *and* its conduct.

Another example is the case of *Hely-Hutchinson v. Brayhead Ltd.*,[183] a

---

[181] [1964] 2 Q.B. 480.
[182] For example, in the First Schedule, Table A Model Articles Art. 112 provides that the board of a company can delegate any or all of the function of the board to *the managing director*.
[183] [1968] 1 Q.B. 549.

case which involved a company chairman. The company chairman traditionally has had a very limited field of usual authority because they usually have had a very limited role in the actual day-to-day running of companies. Consequently, it is not common for a company's articles to provide for large powers to be conferred on a company chairman.[184] In this case, the chairman of Brayhead Ltd. acted as if he were the managing director of the company with the acquiesence of its board. He had a stake in another company in which the plaintiff also had an interest. The chairman and the plaintiff agreed that, if the plaintiff invested in the other company, Brayhead Ltd. would guarantee the loan that the plaintiff would have to obtain for the purposes of making the investment. When the guarantee was subsequently called upon, Brayhead claimed that the chairman had no authority to commit it to the guarantee. It was held that Brayhead Ltd. was bound to honour the guarantee on the basis that chairman had actual authority to do what he did. However, this case can be criticised on the basis that while the result is correct, the reasoning is deficient.[185] In other words, the correct basis for the decision should have been that Brayhead, by its acquiecence in allowing its chairman to act as if he had all of the authority of a managing director, had held him out as having the requisite authority to commit the company to giving the guarantee.

In *Freeman & Lockyer*, Diplock LJ laid down a five[186] criteria test for the attribution of ostensible authority. This has been approved in Ireland as a correct statement of the law in *Kett v. Shannon and English* and also in *Ulster Factors Ltd v. Entonglen Ltd (in liquidation) and George Moloney*.[187] Where all of the criteria are satisfied, the agent's actions will be imputed to the company even though the agent never had actual authority.

(a) Representation of authority

5–35 The first criterion is that there must be a representation to the other party that the agent had the requisite authority to bind the company to the transaction. The representation can be either actual, or tacit.

---

[184] While Art.104 of the First Schedule, Table A Model Articles provides that a chairman can be elected by the board, it does not stipulate that the board can delegate a wide range of powers to that officer, unlike Art.112 which deals with managing directors. Thus, before a chairman can have a wide range of usual authority, the company's articles must be modified accordingly.

[185] *i.e.*, there was no evidence that the chairman ever had actual authority (Forde, *op.cit.*; Courtney, *op. cit.* also criticise the decision).

[186] Actually it was four criteria but the fourth in reality comprises of two separate criteria. Therefore, for present purposes and clarity, the author considers Diplock L.J.'s fourth criterion as the fourth and fifth criteria. See further below.

[187] [1987] I.L.R.M. 364 and unreported, High Court, Laffoy J., February 21, 1997, respectively.

A tacit representation is one that, for example, is evidenced by a course of dealing over a period of time between the company and the third party. The company, content to allow one of its directors act under the style of managing director, will be deemed to have represented that the director had all of the powers that one would expect a managing director to have.[188]

(b) *Representation must be made by the company*

5–36 The second criterion is that the representation must be made by persons who had actual authority to make such representation, or by persons who would be generally or usually be expected to have the authority to deal in the matters to which the disputed contract relates. For example, a company that has a Model Article 80 permits the directors, as a board, to have the full powers of the company. Hence, as a board, the directors are persons who, by their conduct, are capable of making the requisite actual or tacit representations. This criterion is not satisfied if the only person making the representation is the agent. Under the common law principles of agency, it is the principal, not the agent, who can clothe the agent with authority.

(c) *Reliance on the representation*

5–37 The third criterion is that there must have been reliance on the representation by the other party, and furthermore, this reliance must have caused the party to enter into the transaction with the company. Consequently, if the other party entered the transaction without reliance being placed on the representation, then they will fail to satisfy this criterion, in which case it may be open to the company to disclaim the agent's actions and hence the transaction.

(d) *Transaction must be* **intra vires**

5–38 The fourth criterion is that the company must have had the capacity to enter into the transaction. This merely is a recognition that the principles of agency cannot be used to attribute to a company an *ultra vires* representation. A company will not be deemed to have represented that its agent had authority to do something which clearly it had not the corporate capacity to do itself.

(e) *No express limitation on agent's authority to enter transaction*

5–39 The fifth criterion is that there must not be anything in the company's memorandum or articles that would deprive the agent of the

---

[188] Provided of course that the company's articles do not specifically cut down the usual authority one expects a managing director to have.

authority to enter into the transaction in question. So far as this criterion is concerned, this means that if there is any express limitation on the powers of company agents contained in the memorandum/articles of association, then naturally, the company cannot be deemed to have conferred authority on an agent when clearly this was not permitted under its articles of association. This is so because the doctrine of constructive notice deems parties dealing with the company to be constructively aware of the contents of the company's constitutional documents. For example Model Article 79 provides that the directors cannot borrow more than the value of the company's nominal share capital. Consequently, a lender that makes a loan to a company whose articles contain such a provision cannot claim that the company had in any way represented that the directors had the power to borrow in excess of that amount. Because this limitation is expressly contained in the company's constitutional documents, the lender will be deemed to be constructively aware of the limitation on the agents' powers.[189] Another example, would be if the company adopted a modified version of Model Article 112, providing that the managing director may run the company's business, but may not borrow sums on the company's behalf. Knowledge of this modified article will be deemed to any party dealing with the company, and therefore the company cannot be regarded as representing that the managing director could have had the power to borrow on the company's behalf.

B. CONSTRUCTIVE NOTICE AND AUTHORITY OF COMPANY AGENTS

5–40 Whenever the status of the authority of company agents is in issue, the doctrine of constructive notice arises for consideration. However, attempts have been made by case law and by legislation to limit its application to the area.

(1) The rule in *Turquand's* case

5–41 In its original form, the doctrine of constructive notice imputed notice to any party dealing with a company of all the public documents of a company.[190] Consequently, in the context of the present discussion, any limitation in the articles of a company that might affect the authority of any particular company agents was imputed to the party by way of constructive notice.

---

[189] Consequently, lenders will often insist that a company amends its articles so as to remove borrowing ceilings.

[190] *Ernest v. Nicholls* [1857] 6 H.L. Cas. 401.

However, the rule in *Turquand's* case modified this position some-what. Some provisions of a company's articles will not limit the agent's powers but rather will make them exercisable provided that certain in-house formalities are first completed. For example, a company's arti-cles will commonly provide that the board may only borrow in excess of certain sums if an ordinary resolution to that effect has been passed by the members. Formerly, in this situation, under the doctrine of con-structive notice, a party dealing with the company would be deemed to be aware that the resolution was required to be adopted before the directors borrowed the loan on behalf of the company. If no such reso-lution had been adopted, the lender would not have been able to bind the loan to the company. However, *Royal British Bank v. Turquand*[191] altered this situation. The court held that a lender is relieved from the duty to enquire if in-house company formalities have been satisfied, unless the lender either knew, or is put on enquiry, that they may not have been satisfied. Hence, where a company's directors have the power to borrow provided that a resolution is passed giving them the neces-sary authorisation, the lender will not be obliged to enquire if the re-quired resolution was passed, unless the lender either knows it was not passed, or, was put on enquiry by suspicious or unusual circum-stances.[192]

This rule was accepted in Ireland, in *Ulster Investment Bank v. Euro Estates Ltd.*[193] In this decision, the directors were given unlimited bor-rowing powers provided that a valid quorum of one A and one B di-rector attended any meeting of the board where the granting of security was to be sanctioned. A resolution was passed by the board, but the directors present were of the same class. The resolution did not actu-ally indicate on its face that they were of the same class. The bank seek-ing the security had seen a copy of the signed resolution, and also some months earlier had seen a shareholder agreement which had indicated that the directors who had actually signed the adopted resolution were of the same class. Notwithstanding such notice to the bank, the High Court held that the bank was entitled to rely on *Turquand's* rule as it was conceivable that the directors had changed their shareholding class in the interim.[194] Hence the bank lender was entitled to assume that the required quorum had been validly constituted.

---

[191] [1856] 6 E. & B. 327. The rule is also known as *the indoor management*, or *internal management rule*.
[192] Note that the aforegoing does not apply in the case of a special resolution. As to why *Turquand's* rule is not invocable in that situation, see para. 5–42 below.
[193] (1982) ILRM 57. Also see *AIB v. Ardmore Studios International (1972) Ltd.*, unre-ported, High Court, *per* Finlay J, 30 May 1973.
[194] *i.e.*, between the date the bank saw the shareholders agreement and the subse-quent date of the resolution's adoption.

However, it will be seen how there are serious limitations on the scope of *Turquand's* rule such that a lender who seeks to rely on it in order to enforce a loan/security against the company may find that *Turquand's* rule is not available.

(a) Limitations on the availability of Turquand's rule

(i) Where the deficiency is a matter of public record

5–42 Where a limitation on the powers of the directors is evidenced in the publicly filed memorandum or articles of association, then the party dealing with the company is deemed to be constructively aware of such limitation and therefore cannot rely on *Turquand's* rule. Furthermore, constructive knowledge of any other company requirements that have to be publicly filed will also be imputed. For example, special resolutions, which by law are required to be filed in the Companies Office, are documents of public record. Consequently, if a company's articles require a special resolution to be adopted by the borrower as a prerequisite to the company borrowing in excess of a certain stated ceiling, then knowledge that no such resolution has been filed in the Companies office will be imputed to the lender. A lender in this situation cannot rely on *Turquand's* rule to enforce the transaction against the company.[195] Ordinary resolutions, on the other hand, are not required to be filed. Consequently *Turquand's* rule can be invoked where merely an ordinary resolution is required.

(ii) Where the party dealing with the company was not in good faith

5–43 Where the party dealing with the company knew that the company had not complied with its internal requirements, then it cannot attempt to rely on *Turquand's* rule to enforce the transaction against the company. An example of such a case is *Rolled Steel Products Holding Ltd v. British Steel Corporation.*[196] In this decision, British Steel was found to be aware that a director of Rolled Steel, which was giving a guarantee in favour of British Steel, was personally interested in the contract and that therefore the Rolled Steel board meeting which granted the guarantee, was inquorate. Consequently, British Steel could not rely on *Turquand's* rule to enforce the guarantee against the company.

5–44 Furthermore *Turquand's* rule is also not available where there are circumstances which should have aroused the suspicions of the party dealing with the company that the company agent may not have been duly authorised to act. Where such circumstances exist, then that

---

[195] *Irvine v. Union Bank of Australia* [1877] 2 App. Cas. 366 (P.C.).
[196] [1985] 3 All E.R. 52; [1986] 1 Ch. 246.

party is regarded as being on enquiry. In *A.L. Underwood Ltd v. Bank of Liverpool*[197] a director of a company endorsed cheques, payable to the company, in his own favour and had lodged them to his own personal bank account. When recovery of the sums involved was sought, the bank attempted to rely on *Turquand's* rule. However, the court was not prepared to allow this as it held that the circumstances were so unusual that the bank were obliged to make further enquiries as to whether the company had ever authorised the director to act as he had so done.

The Australian courts have also pronounced on this issue. According to *Northside Developments Pty v. Registrar General*[198] the outsider may be placed on enquiry where the transaction being entered into (the giving of a guarantee) was not apparently related to the business of the company. According to dicta in that case, one may be put on enquiry where the transaction was apparently unrelated to the company's business. This decision is interesting as one member of the court, Mason C.J. took the view that this enquiry might arise even where the company seal was attached to the documents in question. Normally, the attachment of the seal to a document conveys that the transaction was entered into with the assent of the company. However, in this regard, it was suggested that where the transaction is not related to the company's business, then evidence that the directors had authorised use of the seal should be sought. This decision is not authority for the proposition that evidence of the directors' intention that the seal be used should be sought by lenders in all cases, but only where the circumstances are such that they are put on enquiry.

Brennan J. in the same decision suggested that it is not within the usual authority of a company to have the company give guarantees to guarantee the liability of another company where the transaction is not apparently connected to the guarantor's business. In such circumstances, an outsider may well be put on enquiry to ensure that the directors who caused the guarantee to be granted had the requisite authority. It is suggested that evidence be sought that the board did authorise those who executed the guarantee to do so, and that such persons were in fact the persons who executed the guarantee (or other such transaction).

5–45 Another issue that arises from the dicta in this Australian decision concerns the question of benefit to the company where it guarantees the liabilities of another. While the issue of benefit to the company has declined in significance in recent years[199] nevertheless the issue of

---

[197] [1924] 1 K.B. 775.
[198] [1990] 170 C.L.R. 146.
[199] Such that the courts now view it as an issue to do more with whether the direc-

benefit is one that may be important as to the issue of whether the outsider was placed on enquiry so that he should have ascertained whether the company officers had authority to enter the transaction in the first place. Where the transaction seems of dubious benefit, then the outsider might be well advised to see a certified copy of a board resolution. If a defect in authority is detected, then it can be cured by having the members of the company ratify in general meeting.[200]

5–46 It is debatable whether company agents should be allowed to rely on *Turquand's* rule where they have loan dealings with the company. In this respect it is submitted that it is difficult to conceive of circumstances whereby company insiders should be permitted to rely on *Turquand's* rule. In *Cox v. Dublin City Distillery (No. 2)*[201] a company's articles stated that no director of the company was to vote in favour of any matter in which he had a personal interest. Company directors granted loans to the company as did other parties. The directors convened and issued debentures in favour of themselves and the other lenders. As the directors who had a personal interest were precluded from voting, it was held that there was no valid quorum at the board meeting where the decision was taken to authorise the debentures. Consequently, the debentures in favour of the director lenders were void and they could not rely on *Turquand's* rule in an attempt to bind the company to honour them. However, the court also held that the other lenders were not in any way put on enquiry as to quorum irregularities. Therefore, they could rely on *Turquand's* rule. It is difficult to see how company insiders could ever take advantage of *Turquand's* rule in their dealings with the company as it is difficult to conceive of a situation whereby they could convince a court that there were no circumstances that would have put them on enquiry as to whether there had been internal compliance with company's own regulations. However, notwithstanding, each case will have to be looked at on its own particular facts.[202]

---

tors have abused their powers rather than whether the transaction is *ultra vires*: see paras 5–13 and 5–18 above.

[200] *Bank of Ireland v. Rockfield* [1979] I.R. 21 where Kenny J. adopted the three conditions set out in *Firth v. Staines* [1897] 2 Q.B. 70: (1) the agent whose act is sought to be ratified must have purported to act on behalf of the company, (2) the agent must have had a competent principal at the time the act was done, (3) at the time of ratification the company must be capable of doing the act itself. (Note that condition (2) no longer applies as s.37 of the Companies Act 1963 permits pre-incorporation contracts to be ratified and adopted by a company even though the company was not formally incorporated at the time the agent entered the contract).

[201] [1916] 1 I.R. 345.

[202] *Morris v. Kanssen* [1946] A.C. 459 would appear to be authority for the proposi-

(iii) Where the company agent was acting outside usual authority

5-47 *Turquand's* rule does not allow a party dealing with a company to rely on the rule as a means of expanding the usual authority of a company agent. *Kreditbank Cassell Gmbh v. Schenkers*[203] is illustrative in this regard. In this decision, a bank manager issued a bill of exchange in the name of the bank. The bank's articles did permit such power to be conferred on a manager, but this had not occurred. Consequently, a party dealing with the bank claimed that it could rely on *Turquand's* rule to bind the bank to the bill. The court held that, although the articles provided that the requisite power could be conferred on the manager, nevertheless *Turquand's* rule could not be invoked because issuing bills of exchange was not within that official's field of usual authority. This is explained on the basis that *Turquand's* rule cannot be used to clothe company officers with authority in excess of that which would be beyond their usual authority. The consequence of this is that the rule cannot be used as a means of expanding a company agent's field of usual authority merely because the articles hold out the possibility that a particular officer may have been given such "extra" authority.

This decision illustrates a vital distinction which must be appreciated whenever a party seeks to invoke Turquand's rule. Where a company's articles permit a company's agents to do something provided internal regulations have been carried out, then *Turquand's* rule may be relied on by an outsider acting in good faith. However, where the articles permit the doing of something (provided the company grants such authority) which would normally be beyond the particular agent's usual authority, then merely because such enabling provision appears in the articles does not entitle the party dealing with the agent to presume that the requisite authority has in fact been granted to that particular agent by the company. Consequently, a party dealing with the agent cannot rely on *Turquand's* rule as a means of enforcing the transaction against the company. To so allow would go beyond the rationale of *Turquand's* rule (which is to merely allow a party to assume that internal company regulations have been complied with, where such is necessary to perfect a power exerciseable on the company's behalf). Therefore, the rule does not additionally allow one also to assume that additional powers have been conferred on a company agent in excess of the officer's usual authority, even though the company's articles may so contemplate.

---

tion that a company director can never take advantage of *Turquand's* rule, whereas *Hely-Hutchinson v. Brayhead Ltd.* [1968] 1 Q.B. 549. appears to countenance this possibility in appropriate circumstances.

[203] [1927] 1 K.B. 826.

Similarly *Turquand's* rule does not allow a party to assume that, activities otherwise *prohibited* by the articles, have been duly sanctioned.

C. THE IMPACT OF EUROPEAN LEGISLATION

(1) Article 9(2)

5–48 Article 9(2) of the First EEC Company Law Directive[204] provides that

> "The limits on the powers of the organs of the company, arising under the statutes [of the company] or from a decision of the competent organs, may never be relied upon as against third parties, even if they have been disclosed".

This constitutes an attempt to reduce the impact of constructive notice when the issue arises as to whether limitations on the powers of the organs of the company could be relied upon against parties attempting to bind the company to a transaction entered into by company agents. In this respect, Article 9(2) provides that such limitations can not be relied upon by the company, even if they had been disclosed. However, as implemented in Ireland by Regulation 6 of the European Communities (Companies) Regulations 1973, Article 9(2) is of limited applicability.[205]

(2) European Communities (Companies) Regulations 1973[206]

(a) Regulation 6

5–49 Regulation 6 provides that

(1) In favour of a person dealing with a company in good faith, any transaction entered into by any organ of the company, being its board of directors or any person registered under these regulations as a person authorised to bind a company, shall be deemed to be within the capacity of the company and any limitation of the powers of that board or person, whether imposed by the memorandum or articles of association or otherwise, may not be relied upon as against any person dealing with the company.

(2) Any such person shall be presumed to have acted in good faith unless the contrary is proved.

---

[204] Council Directive 68/151/EEC of March 9, 1968.
[205] See paras 5–49—5–52 immediately below.
[206] Ireland implemented the directive by way of the European Communities (Companies) Regulations, 1973 (S.I. No. 163 of 1973). The Regulations also impact on the doctrine of corporate *ultra vires*, which being an entirely separate issue, is considered separately earlier in this chapter above at paras 5–22—5–23.

(3) For the purposes of this Regulation, the registration of a person authorised to bind the company shall be effected by delivering to the registrar of companies a notice giving the name and description of the person concerned.

At the core of Regulation 6 is the proposition that, where a person in good faith transacts with the "organs" of the company, *"being its board or any persons under these regulations as a person authorised to bind the company"*, any limitation on such organs' powers imposed by the memorandum or articles or otherwise cannot be relied upon as against a person dealing with the company (even if they have been disclosed). In this way, Regulation 6 seeks to modify constructive notice as, notwithstanding constructive (or even actual) notice of, for example, the company's articles, any limitation on the powers of the board or registered agents contained therein cannot be relied upon as against a person who deals with the company in good faith.

Before considering Regulation 6 further, Regulation 10 should also be noted. It too seeks to modify the application of constructive notice in this area. It provides that a company cannot rely on limitations contained in a specified list of company documents[207] against a person dealing with a company unless the person either had knowledge of them or unless notice of their delivery to the Companies Office has been published in *Iris Oifigiuil*.[208] Thus, if the company wishes to rely on such documents against a third party, not only must they be filed in the Companies Office, but also notice of such filing must be made in *Iris Oifigiuil*.[209]

(b) Impact of Regulation 6 on agency principles/Turquand's rule

(i) Turquand's rule[210]

5–50 The question therefore arises as to whether these regulations modify the principles of agency or the application of *Turquand's* rule in their application to transactions entered into with company agents.

So far as *Turquand's* rule is concerned, the Regulations do not affect its application. However, what Regulation 6 does do is enable the company to be bound by a transaction concluded by its agent in circumstances where *Turquand's* rule could not have been invoked. For

---

[207] Specified in Regulation 4, to include *inter alia*, the company's memorandum and articles.
[208] Responsibility for this task lies with the Registrar of Companies.
[209] Of course, if the party was aware of the content of the documents, then being aware, he would not be acting in "good faith". Consequently, whether or not the documents were advertised in the *Iris*, or not, would be irrelevant.
[210] Turquand's rule is set out at para. 5–41 above.

example, *Turquand's* rule does not extend so as to oblige a company to be bound to a transaction where the company's own internal regulations expressly prohibit the agent concluding such transaction. Where Regulation 6 applies, the company can be bound to the transaction even though its regulations prohibited the conclusion of the transaction, as Regulation 6 provides that:

> ". . . any limitation of the powers of that board or person, whether imposed by the memorandum or articles or otherwise, may not be relied upon as against any person dealing with the company [in good faith]."

Another example of a situation in which Regulation 6 would be available in principle, but *Turquand's rule* cannot be,[211] is where a special resolution is required to perfect an agent's authority.

(ii) Agency principles

5–51 So far as the principles of ostensible agency are concerned, it is submitted that the Regulations do not affect their application. What Regulation 6 modifies is the application of constructive notice *vis a vis* a person dealing with the company in respect of limitations on the powers of company "organs".[212] The Regulation provides that where a person deals with company "organs", limitations on their powers cannot be relied upon against the person dealing in good faith. This displaces the application of constructive notice of such limitations.[213] It does not seek to alter the application of agency principles. In other words the *Freeman and Lockyer* criteria[214] may additionally, depending on the circumstances, have to be satisfied before the agent's actions are *attributed* to the company. Thus, whether dealing with a company "organ" or some other type of company agent, the question of whether the agent's actions can be imputed to the company notwithstanding some limitation in the articles, will have to be considered.

(c) Limitations on the availability of Regulation 6

5–52 Notwithstanding what Regulation 6 attempts to achieve, its impact is relatively minimal as there are several limitations on its availability.

---

[211] As special resolutions are required to be registered in the Companies Office, the person dealing with the company will be deemed to be constructively aware if no such resolution is so registered. Consequently, *Turquand's* rule cannot apply: see para. 5–42 above.

[212] "being its board of directors or any person registered under these regulations as a person authorised to bind the company...".

[213] Save where the person was not in good faith.

[214] See paras 5–35—5–39 above.

First, Regulation 6 can only be invoked where one is dealing with the directors acting as a board, or a person registered as being authorised to bind the company. Thus, for example, where a transaction with a director(s) is entered into outside the board context, Regulation 6 is inapplicable.[215] In this event, the principles of agency and *Turquand's rule* are the applicable law. Similarly, where a person transacts with a company agent who is *not* registered as having authority to bind the company, Regulation 6 will be inapplicable.[216] In Ireland, it is not commonplace for persons to be registered[217] as having authority to bind the company. Hence, Regulation 6 will continue to be relatively obscure in the present context unless corporate practices in this area dramatically alter.

The second limitation on Regulation 6's applicability stems from Regulation 3, which provides that the Regulations shall only apply to limited liability companies. Thus, Regulation 6 has no application in the case of unlimited liability companies.[218]

The third limitation is that Regulation 6 can only apply where the person dealing with the company was acting in "good faith". This modifies the application of the doctrine of constructive notice. Previously, the doctrine's application would impute to the person dealing with the company knowledge that there was a limitation on the agent's power. However, under Regulation 6, a person cannot have that limitation asserted against them, unless put on enquiry. In other words, in order for a person not to be in "good faith", the person must either be actually aware of the limitation imposed by the company's constitutional documents, or at least there must have been circumstances which should have put them on enquiry. In the absence of Irish authority on the matter, the UK courts appear to take the view of the comparable UK provision that one is acting in good faith unless one actually knew that the agent had no authority, or could not in view of all the circumstances have been unaware that the agent had no such power.[219] From

---

[215] Regulation 6 refers to the directors ". . . *being the board*. . .". (author's emphasis added).

[216] As happened in *Re Frederick Inns Ltd.* [1994] 1 I.L.R.M. 387 where the Supreme Court refused to apply Regulation 6 as no one was registered as having authority to bind the company, nor was the transaction at issue entered into with the board of directors.

[217] The Regulations do not make registration mandatory in respect of such agents. Were a company to register such an agent, registration would take place by notifying the Registrar of Companies.

[218] Hence it had no relevance to *Northern Bank Finance v. Quinn and Achates Investments Co.* [1979] I.L.R.M. 221 as Achates Investments Co. was an unlimited liability company.

[219] *TCB Ltd v.Gray* [1986] 1 All E.R. 587; *International Sales and Agencies Ltd & Anor v. Marcus* [1983] 3 ALL E.R. 551.

a practical point of view, *in the current context* it would appear that a provision such as Regulation 6 would be meaningless if, notwithstanding its provisions, a person dealing with a company remained obliged to inspect the memorandum and articles in order to be in "good faith". It is submitted that such an obligation only arises where either the person knows, or is put on enquiry by virtue of a certain state of circumstances, that the agent may not have had the requisite authority from the company.

A company itself cannot invoke Regulation 6 in order to render effective a transaction that its agent had no authority to make, because Regulation 6 is only available to persons "dealing with" the company.

Interestingly, there is nothing in the Regulation that precludes company insiders who have dealings with the company from relying on Regulation 6. However, they may have difficulties demonstrating that they acted in "good faith".

IV. CORPORATE BORROWING – CHARGING BOOKS DEBTS

5–53 Although the wide range of legal issues that may arise in the context of corporate security do not properly fall within the scope of this book,[220] it is however appropriate to consider the law's treatment of the legal issues that arise when a company, in consideration of receiving a loan facility, grants a charge (or charges) over its *book debts* as security. Such charges are now a common feature and intricate element of the legal framework set up by lenders and corporate borrowers to facilitate corporate borrowings. Book debts can be a substantial asset that the borrowing company can offer as a chargeable asset to the lender. In the last few years, the use of this particular form of security has given rise to some interesting legal problems and issues for corporate lenders and borrowers.

A. TYPES OF CHARGES ON BOOK DEBTS

5–54 Charges over book debts can be either fixed or floating. The Companies Acts do not define either type. However, there have been many

---

[220] On charges and security generally, see Forde, *Company Law* (2nd ed., Mercier Press, Dublin, 1992) chap. XVI; Keane, *Company Law in the Republic of Ireland* (2nd ed., Butterworths, Dublin, 1991) chaps. 22–24, and chap. 39 on examinership; Courtney, *Law of Private Companies* (Butterworths, Dublin, 1994) chaps. 14-16; Ussher, *Company Law in Ireland* (Sweet and Maxwell, Dublin, 1986) chaps. 14 and 15; Ferran, "Floating charges-the nature of the security" (1988) Cambridge Law Journal 213.

judicial pronouncements on what distinguishes fixed and floating charges. For example, in *Re Keenan Bros*[221] Henchy J. considered the distinction as follows. A fixed charge takes effect on its creation, so that the assets charged will be encumbered by the charge, or if they are future assets once they come into existence. In either case, the company can deal with the assets only to the extent permitted by the charge. A floating charge, on the other hand, was stated to be "dormant and hovering." It does not attach to the assets expressed to be subject to the charge and thus does not prevent the company dealing with those assets in the ordinary course of its business. Only if a specified crystallisation event occurs will the company lose the freedom to deal with the charged assets. In such event, the company can only deal with the assets to the extent, if any, permitted by the charge.

(1) What is a "Book Debt"?

5–55 While the Companies Acts give no definition as to what constitutes a "book debt", the case law appears to indicate that book debts are all *trade* debts.[222] In considering whether a particular charged debt is a "book debt" or some other type of debt, the courts will consider whether the debt in question is one that the particular type of corporate borrower in question can be expected to incur as a normal trading debt.[223]

Sometimes, this can give rise to difficult legal issues as often a charge is defined as attaching to "book debts and *other debts*" of the borrowing company. The reason why it is important to ascertain whether a charged debt is a "book debt" or not, is because section 99 of the Companies Act 1963 only requires certain types of charge to be registered in the Companies Office.[224] Section 99(2)(e), which designates as registrable "a charge on book debts of the company", brings both fixed and floating charges on book debts within the section 99 registration obligation. Section 99(2)(f) additionally provides that *all* floating charges on a company's property are registrable. Therefore, if a debt item is not a "book debt", then a floating charge on it, while not registrable under section 99(2)(e), will nevertheless be registrable under section 99(2)(f). However, there is no comparable blanket mandatory registration provision in respect of fixed charges. Consequently, a fixed charge on sums owed to a company is only registrable if the debt charged is a

---

[221] [1985] I.R. 401.
[222] *Jackson v. Lombard & Ulster Bank* [1992] I.R. 94; *Re Brian Tucker: Farrell v. Equity Bank* [1990] 2 I.R. 549.
[223] In *Re Kum Tung Restaurant (Dublin) Ltd.* [1978] I.R. 446 the High Court held that a solicitor's undertaking to lodge proceeds of sale of property with a bank could not constitute a charge over book debts.
[224] The registration regime will be considered further below at para. 5–57.

"book debt" within the meaning of section 99(2)(e).

Re Brian Tucker[225] raises an interesting issue. The High Court had to consider whether a *possible* refund of insurance premiums might fall within the definition of book debt. Lynch J. held that whether an item is a book debt, or not, depends on its character at the date of creation of the charge where it is an existing item. On the other hand, the court further held that where it is not an existing item at that date, then it cannot be classified as a "book debt" merely because it might come into existence at some time in the future.[226]

5–56 Another difficult issue that may arise is whether a company may grant a charge over company deposits lodged in the bank to *the same* bank, and if so, whether such a charge constitutes a charge over book debts? These charges are known as "charge-backs" and have given rise to considerable controversy in the U.K in recent years. In *Re Charge Card Services Ltd.*,[227] Millett J. in the U.K. High Court put forward the view that such charges could not be created as they were "conceptually impossible". The learned judge took the view that it was impossible for the owner of a bank deposit to grant a charge over that deposit in favour of the bank holding the deposit, because the deposit is in reality a debt owed by the bank to the depositor and the bank cannot take a charge over something it owes to another. As a consequence of this dictum, banking lawyers were obliged to adopt what has become known as "triple-cocktail" arrangements. Such arrangements which consist of a combination of a charge, contractual rights of set-off, and a flawed asset arrangement[228] are designed to ensure that a bank has an adequate level of protection should the charge element of the arrangements fail as a charge.

Dicta in subsequent cases doubted the correctness of Millet J.'s view, as did academic debate.[229] However, notwithstanding these doubts

---

[225] *Re Brian Tucker: Farrell v. Equity Bank* [1990] 2 I.R. 549.

[226] Note however that this judgment is not authority for the proposition that a charge over future book debts cannot be created. Assuming that the future debts the charge intends to attach to will be "book debts", then such a charge can be created and will attach to the debts when they come into existence.

[227] [1986] 3 All E.R. 289.

[228] A "flawed asset" is a deposit with a flaw which is constituted by a restriction on its repayment until defined liabilities are satisfied. For further reading on these arrangements see Yeowart, "House of Lords upholds charge-backs over deposits" (January 1998) International Financial Law Review 7; Evans, "Triple Cocktail Becomes Single Malt? Some thoughts on the Practical Consequences of the Decision of the House of Lords in *Morris v. Agrichemicals Ltd*" (1998) J.I.B.L. 115.

[229] For example, dicta in *Welsh Development Agency v. The Export Finance Company Ltd.* [1992] B.C.L.C. 148. Considerable academic debate also ensued after the

expressed about the wisdom of Millett J's remarks, the Court of Appeal in *Morris and Others v. Agrichemicals Ltd. and Others, Morris and Others v. Rayners Enterprises Incorporated*[230] approved *obiter* Millet J.'s remarks in *Re Charge Card Services Ltd* by stating that "a man cannot have a proprietary interest in a debt or other obligation which he owes another".[231]

However, on appeal, the House of Lords *per* Lord Hoffman strongly doubted *obiter* that there is any legal obstacle to "preventing banks and their customers from creating charges over deposits if, for reasons of their own, they want to do so."[232] Lord Hoffman explained how:

> "The depositor's right to claim payment of his deposit is a *chose in action* which the law has always recognised as property. There is no dispute that a charge over such a *chose in action* can validly be granted to a third party. In which respects would the fact that the beneficiary of the charge was the debtor himself be inconsistent with the transaction having some of the various features which I have enumerated.[233] The method by which the property would be realised would differ slightly; instead of the beneficiary of the charge having to claim payment from the debtor, the realisation would take the form of a book entry. In no other respect, as it seems to me, would the transaction have any consequences different from those which would attach to a charge given to a third party. . . . I cannot see why it cannot properly be said that the debtor has a proprietary interest by way of charge over the debt."[234]

Lord Hoffman's strong *obiter* dicta would appear to be the nail in the coffin of *Re Charge Card Services Ltd*[235] on the issue of charge-backs.

dicta of Millett J. with notable commentators on both sides of the argument. For example, *Wood* condemned the decision in *English and International Set-Off* (Sweet and Maxwell, London, 1989) chap. 5., while Professor Goode took the opposite view in *Legal Problems of Credit and Security* (2nd ed., Sweet and Maxwell, London, 1988) at p.124. For a comprehensive overview of the arguments for and against the decision, see Downey and Grebauer, "Morris v. Agrichemicals: the Availability of Charge-Backs" (April 1998) Irish Business Law 80.

[230] [1996] 2 All E.R. 121.
[231] [1996] 2 All E.R. 121 at 130 *per* Rose L.J. Interestingly, Millet L.J. (as he now is) was a member of the panel that heard the appeal.
[232] *Morris v. Rayners Enterprises Incorporated, Morris v. Agrichemicals Ltd.* [1997] 4 All E.R. 568 at 577. This decision is also known as the *Re Bank of Credit and Commerce International SA (No. 8)* judgment. Note that Lord Hoffman delivered the unanimous judgement of the House of Lords. Therefore, his remarks on the issue of charges and book debts, although *obiter*, are nevertheless of considerable significance.
[233] Lord Hoffman was referring here to the characteristics of an equitable charge which he had just earlier outlined at p. 576 of the judgment.
[234] *ibid.* at 577.
[235] Particularly as Lord Hoffman's judgment was unanimously concurred with by the other four members of the House of Lords hearing the appeal.

Clearly the House of Lords were of the view that a company may grant a charge to the bank which holds its deposits.

Nevertheless, *Re Charge Card Services Ltd* may continue to be of significance in another respect. Lord Hoffman's judgment expressly refrained from expressing a clear view on the related issue of whether charges over deposits in favour of the bank holding the deposit constitutes a charge over "book debts" within the meaning of the U.K equivalent of section 99 of the Companies Act 1963, section 396 of the U.K. Companies Act 1985. This will be considered shortly below.[236]

(2) Statutory obligation to register charges on Book Debts

5–57   Under section 99(1) of the Companies Act 1963 certain categories of charge, including charges on book debts[237] must be registered, within 21 days of their creation by the company[238] in the Companies Office.[239] Failure to register a charge on book debts in accordance with section 99 is not only an offence,[240] but also results in the charge being void and of no effect against the liquidator of the company (should the company subsequently liquidate) or its creditors.[241] While there is provision whereby the court has discretion to permit late registration in certain circumstances such as inadvertent omission or mistake, the court, if it does exercise such discretion, cannot allow the rights of other secured creditors to be prejudiced.[242] Where a company has *actually* commenced winding-up, a late registration order will only be made in the most exceptional circumstances, and if so granted, the court will ensure that no other creditor of the company (whether secured or not) is prejudiced.[243] Where a late registration order is granted in circum-

---

[236] See para. 5–58 below.

[237] Companies Act 1963, s.99(2)(e).

[238] Security interests which arise by operation of law do not fall within the meaning of registrable charges for the purposes of s.99 as they are not created by the company. One of s.99's prerequisites is that the security interest must have been created by the company before consideration can be given to the issue of whether it falls within one of s.99's categories of registrable charge: *e.g.* liens that arise by operation of law (*Bank of Ireland Finance v. Daly* [1978] I.R. 79; *Re Farm Fresh Frozen Foods Ltd.* [1980] I.L.R.M. 131) are not registrable, whereas an equitable deposit of title deeds, being an act of the company, may be (*Welch v. Bowmaker (Ireland) Ltd.* [1980] I.R. 251).

[239] Companies Act 1963, s.99(1).

[240] Companies Act 1963, s.100.

[241] s.99(1). Although a charge that is not registered in accordance with s.99 will be ineffective against the liquidator/other secured creditors, s.99 also provides that the debt remains a valid debt and the monies (which the charge was intended to secure) become due immediately.

[242] Companies Act 1963, s.106.

[243] *Re Resinoid & Mica Products* [1983] Ch. 132; *Victoria Housing Estates v. Ashpurton Estates Ltd.* [1983] Ch. 110.

stances where a winding-up is *imminent*, then usually the court will make it a condition of the order that if the company does subsequently wind-up, the liquidator should be free to request the court to set the late registration order aside.[244]

5–58 The question arises as to whether a charge granted by a company over its bank deposits to the bank itself[245] can constitute a registrable charge for the purposes of section 99. Although U.K. company law (just like section 99 of the Companies Act 1963) requires charges over book debts to be registered,[246] this issue (whether charges over deposits in favour of the bank holding the deposits are registrable) has not been specifically considered in either an Irish or U.K. court to date. However, it has arisen in the U.K. case law in a peripheral manner in several judgments. The term "peripheral" is used because in none of the cases about to be discussed, was a judicial interpretation of the corresponding provision of U.K company law to section 99 of the Companies Act 1963 (*i.e.*, s.396 U.K Companies Act 1985) attempted. Rather what was involved in those cases were judicial attempts to define terms such as "book debts" contained in company debentures.[247]

Once again, the ubiquitous *Re Charge Card Services Ltd.* judgment is at the heart of the debate.[248] In that judgment, Millett J. expressed the view that a deposit at bank constitutes a "book debt" of the corporate depositor, and that such deposit could be charged as such in favour of a third party. However, as Millett J. then went on to controversially consider that the depositor could not however charge this deposit in favour of the bank which *held* the deposit,[249] no further consideration was given to the issue of whether it is correct to state that cash deposits in this situation constitute "book debts".

In *Northern Bank v. Ross*[250] the Northern Ireland Court of Appeal interpreted a charge document's terms to mean that "book debts" did not include cash at bank.

---

[244] *Re Telford Motors,* unreported, High Court, Hamilton J., January 29, 1978.
[245] Known as a "charge-back": see para. 5–56 immediately above where these were discussed.
[246] s.396 Companies Act 1985.
[247] Simmonds, "Charge Card Revisited (For the Last Time?)" (1998) J.I.B.L. 85 gives as excellent account on this area; as does Evans, "Triple Cocktail Becomes Single Malt? Some thoughts on the Practical Consequences of the Decision of the House of Lords in *Morris v. Agrichemicals Ltd*" (1998) J.I.B.L. 115.
[248] [1986] 3 All E.R. 289.
[249] See para. 5–56 above as to how this view has been doubted *obiter* by Lord Hoffman in the House of Lords in *Morris and others v. Agrichemicals Ltd.* [1997] 4 All E.R. 568.
[250] [1990] B.C.C 883.

While it must be emphasised that neither *Re Charge Card Services Ltd* nor *Northern Bank v. Ross* are of persuasive authority on the interpretation of the meaning of "book debts" as that term is used in the U.K section 396, nevertheless they may be of some relevance to a consideration of the matter, although to what degree is questionable. For example, some commentators have suggested that the reasoning in these authorities, while an interesting view of judicial attitudes, should not be applied when the meaning of "book debts" for the purposes of the statutory registration regime is being considered. This observation is based on the rationale that the books of a company will reflect cash at bank as being a company debt, even though labelled "cash at bank".[251]

Furthermore, it is submitted that observations such as those made by Hoffman J. (as he then was) in *Re Brightlife*[252] (when the learned judge suggested that a company bank balance does not fall within what a businessman would normally term a debt, but rather "cash at bank") demonstrates some judicial confusion as to the distinction between business parlance and accountancy practice.[253] Interestingly, Lord Hoffman (as he now is) in *Morris v. Rayners Enterprises Incorporated, Morris v. Agrichemicals Ltd.*[254] observed *obiter*, on the issue of whether a charge over a deposit in a bank granted by the corporate depositor in favour of *that* bank constitutes a charge over "book debts", "In my view, this is a matter on which banks are entitled to make up their own minds and take their own advice on whether the deposit charged is a "book debt" or not." While Lord Hoffman did not express any further view on the matter (apart from referring to *Northern Bank v. Ross* which he suggested suggests that in the case of deposits at banks an obligation to register is unlikely to arise)[255] nevertheless the fact that the House

---

[251] Calnan, "Security over Deposits Again: BCCI (No. 8)" (April 1998) Journal of International Banking and Financial Law 125 at 128 suggests that: "There is no question that such amounts constitute debts owing by the bank to its customer. It is equally clear that such debts ought to be written up in the books of the customer. The only issue is as to the precise place in the books where they should be written up. It is suggested that the mere fact that an amount standing to the credit of a bank account is to be written up as "cash at bank" rather than under the heading of "trade and other debtors" does not prevent it being a debt which ought properly be written up in the books of the company and therefore a "book debt".

[252] [1987] 2 W.L.R. 197.

[253] Although again it must be emphasised that Hoffman J. (as he then was) was not interpreting the phrase book debts as used in the U.K. Companies Act, but rather whether that term as used in a debenture could include cash at bank (as Hoffman J. subsequently himself made clear when he commented on his judgment in *Re Brightlife* in *Re Permanent Houses (Holdings) Ltd.* [1988] B.C.L.C. 563).

[254] [1997] 4 All E.R. 568.

[255] It is submitted that the *Northern Bank* case is not authority for such "suggestion" as the court was concerned with interpreting the terms of a specific de-

did not see fit to pronounce on the issue means that banks would be well advised to continue with the current practice of registering such charges in accordance with section 99.[256] It is interesting to note that several jurisdictions have adopted legislation specifically to negate any legal uncertainty that might result from *Re Charge Card Services Ltd* in this regard in the books.[257]

(3) Advantages of being a fixed charge lender

5–59   Fixed charge lenders have certain advantages that floating charge lenders do not have. For example, fixed charge lenders take priority over floating charge lenders even where the floating charge was created first in time, save where the fixed charge lender actually knew of the existence of a negative pledge covenant in a prior created floating charge.[258]

A fixed charge holder also has advantages in a liquidation. First, fixed charges rank ahead of preferential creditors, whereas floating charge lenders rank behind.[259] Second, floating charges created in the 12 months[260] prior to the charged company commencing liquidation,

---

benture rather than the term "book debts" as it is used in s. 396 U.K. Companies Act 1985.

[256] Simmonds, "Charge Card Revisited (For the Last Time?)" (1998) J.I.B.L. 85 at 86 (though that commentator also queries (at p.87) "whether there are some bank accounts over which charges are registrable and other bank accounts over which charges are not registrable."); Evans, "Triple Cocktail Becomes Single Malt? Some thoughts on the Practical Consequences of the Decision of the House of Lords in Morris v. Agrichemicals Ltd" (1998) J.I.B.L 115 although doubting that charges over bank deposits constitute charges over book debts, advises that banks will nevertheless seek to register such charges to counter legal uncertainty in the matter pending legislative or judicial clarification, and further advises that another reason why banks taking such charges should register the charges as a matter of prudence is to allow them take advantage of the rule in *Dearle v. Hall* (see Chapter 7 where this rule is considered in the context of debt factoring), *i.e.*, registration is equally relevant to ensuring that those taking equitable charges over deposits do not lose priority to an assignee of the deposit, as by giving notice (constituted by registering the charge in the Companies Office) they put any assignees of the debt on notice of their interest in the deposit); Hutchinson, "Taking Security over Cash Deposits: The House of Lords Confirms the Conceptual Possibility of Charge-Backs" (January 1998) C.L.P. 3 at 9 suggests that because charges over a company's deposits "might" be held to be registrable, any such charges should be registered pursuant to s.99.
[257] *e.g.* Hong Kong; Singapore; Bermuda; Cayman Islands.
[258] *Welch v. Bowmaker (Ireland) Ltd.* [1980] I.R. 251.
[259] Companies Act 1963, s.285(7).
[260] Or two years in the case of "connected persons" such as company directors: see s.288 of the Companies Act 1963 as amended by s.136 of the Companies Act 1990.

will be susceptible to invalidity under section 288[261] of the Companies Act 1963 unless it can be proved that the company was solvent immediately after the creation of the charge. If solvency cannot be demonstrated, then although there is some respite in that the charge remains valid in respect of sums advanced to the company at the time of and in consideration for the granting of the charge,[262] the charge will be invalid in respect of sums advanced before the date of the creation of the charge.[263]

However, one advantage that fixed charges formerly had over floating charges has now been largely obviated by legislation. Where a company is not in liquidation, but a receiver has been appointed to realise a floating charge, section 98 of the Companies Act 1963 provides that preferential creditors[264] must be satisfied first.[265] As section 98 does not apply to fixed charges, traditionally fixed charge lenders did not suffer this regime. However, much of this advantage for fixed charge lenders has now been obviated by the enactment of section 115 of the Finance Act 1986.[266] Section 115 provides that where the Revenue Commissioners are owed income tax or VAT by a company which granted a fixed charge, the Commissioners can call on the holder of the fixed charge over company book debts to pay over to the Commissioners any sums that might be obtained in the future pursuant to the charge (the maximum so payable being the sum secured by the charge). This naturally reduces the attractiveness of *fixed* charges over book debts to corporate lenders as a solid form of security over corporate borrowings.

Any charge, fixed or floating, may be invalid as a fraudulent preference if made in circumstances which contravene section 286 of the Companies Act 1963.[267]

---

[261] As amended by s.136 of the Companies Act 1990.

[262] Companies Act 1963, s.288(1).

[263] *Re Yeovil Glove* [1965] Ch. 148; *Re Creation* Printing [1981] I.R. 353; *Re Daniel Murphy* [1964] I.R. 1; *Clayton's case* [1817] 1 Mer. 572; *Re Destone Fabrics* [1941] 1 Ch. 319; *Re Matthew Ellis Ltd.* [1933] Ch. 358.

[264] As designated by s.285 of the Companies Act 1963.

[265] *cf. Re Brightlife* where it was held that if the charge actually crystallises before the appointment of the receiver, the then U.K. equivalent of s.98 would not apply because the receiver was not appointed to enforce a right *under a charge* (the charge *had already* crystallised). Thus, the U.K. equivalent of s.98 could not apply to the Receiver's activities, and thereby deprived the preferential creditors of the statutory right to call on any sums realised by the Receiver. The U.K. subsequently amended its legislation to allow the preferential creditors have a preferential claim in this situation also.

[266] As amended by s.174 of the Finance Act 1995.

[267] A charge is a fraudulent preference where made when a company is unable to pay its debts as they fall due and within six months the company commences

B. FEASIBILITY OF ATTACHING FLOATING OR FIXED CHARGES ON BOOK DEBTS?[268]

(1) Floating charges over Book Debts

5–60 In *Re Yorkshire Woolcombers Assoc Ltd (Houldsworth v. Yorkshire Woolcombers Association Ltd)*[269] it was held that an attempted assignment of book debts had in law given rise to the creation of a floating charge over book debts, and that book debts could be secured by a floating charge. Because the charged debts remained receiveable by the company and were at its disposal for use in the ordinary course of its business, the absence of control on the part of the chargeholder indicated that the charge created was a floating charge. Romer L.J. *obiter* elucidated his now-famous criteria which, if satisfied, are strongly indicative that a charge is a floating charge. While it is not necessary that all three criteria be satisfied in all cases, the third criterion appears to be the essential criterion for the purposes of determining whether a charge is floating or not. According to Romer L.J., a charge is floating in nature where:

— it charges assets present, or future, or both

— the assets are of a class that may be changing in the ordinary course of business

— it is contemplated by the charge, that, until some future step is taken the company can carry on business as normal regarding the charged assets.

These criteria have often been cited with approval in both the Irish High and Supreme Courts.[270] For the corporate borrower, the advantage of a floating charge on book debts is that the company is able to offer such debts as security when seeking further borrowings and yet have use of the charged debt assets until the charge crystallises (if ever).

---

insolvent liquidation. See further Chapter 6 where s.286's criteria are considered (in the context of debt subordination).

[268] For further reading on charges and book debts specifically, see Forde *op. cit.* at 501-503; Forde, *Law of Company Insolvency* (1993) at 361–362; Keane *op. cit.* at 223/4; Courtney *op. cit.* at 580–585.

[269] [1903] 2 Ch. 284 Court of Appeal (*a.k.a. Illingsworth v. Houldsworth* [1904] A.C. 355 in the House of Lords, where Court of Appeal was affirmed)

[270] *e.g.*, Kenny J. referred to them approvingly in *Welch v. Bowmaker (Ireland) Ltd.* [1980] I.R. 251; Keane J. in *Re Keenan Bros.* [1980] I.R. 401; Blayney J. in *Re Holidair* [1994] I.R. 481.

(2) Fixed charges over Book Debts?

5–61 Although it was accepted since the last century that book debts could be the subject of a floating charge, it is only relatively recently that it also became clear that they could also be the subject of a *fixed* charge. The two main objections to the recognition of such a charge were as follows. First, from the perspective of corporate borrowers, it was felt that if book debts could be successfully made the subject of fixed charges, then lenders would effectively, in demanding such charges, be in a position to starve the company of the everyday use of the proceeds of these important assets. Second, from the perspective of the corporate lawyer, it was considered that book debts could not be the subject of fixed charges as, being assets that are intangible in nature and constantly changing in the course of a company's business, it would be legally difficult to successfully attach a fixed charge to such assets.

However, these perceived difficulties were overcome. For example, in 1977 the U.K. High Court in *Siebe Gorman & Co Ltd v. Barclays Bank Ltd*[271] held that a charge over book debts was a fixed charge. Under the terms of the charge, the company could not deal in the debts while uncollected and the company had to pay the proceeds into the company's account with the bank. On its construction, Slade J. held the charge as drafted intended that the company could only make withdrawals from the account with the bank's permission. In Ireland, similar developments shortly followed. In *Re Lakeglen Construction (Kelly v. McMahon Ltd)*[272] in 1980, Costello J. in the High Court considered *obiter* that fixed charges could be created over book debts in an appropriate case. The matter was subsequently put beyond doubt by both the High and Supreme Courts judgments in *Re Keenan Bros.*[273] in 1985.

(3) Judicial methods for ascertaining the true nature of charges over Book Debts

(a) *The constructionist approach*

5–62 In *Re Keenan Bros.*,[274] the Supreme Court held that a fixed charge could be created over book debts, both present and future.[275] In *Re Keenan Bros.* the terms of the charge were even more restrictive than in

---

[271] [1977] 2 Lloyd's Reps. 142.
[272] [1980] I.R. 347.
[273] [1985] I.R. 401.
[274] [1985] I.R. 401.
[275] Although reversed by the Supreme Court on the substantive issue, Keane J. in the High Court had expressed similar views *obiter* in the High Court hearing of the case.

Siebe Gorman: the company could not deal in the book debts while uncollected and the proceeds once collected had to be paid into a restricted bank account from which, the charge *expressly* stated, withdrawals could only be made with the permission of the chargeholder.

Notwithstanding such terms, Keane J. held in the High Court that the charge was a floating charge. The learned judge acknowledged that there were some, though not absolute, restrictions on the company's ability to use the book debts and their proceeds. For example, the proceeds had to be paid into a special account and the company could only make withdrawals with the lender's permission. Nevertheless, the court held that, notwithstanding such restrictions, the charge was a floating charge because the company was able to access the special restricted account for use in the company's business. Consequently, the court regarded the essential third criterion of Romer L.J.'s test (that the company can use the book debts in the ordinary course of its business) as satisfied. By not depriving the company of the use of the book debts, this was consistent with the parties intention to create merely a floating charge.

On appeal, the Supreme Court took the opposite view as to the nature of the charge, holding it to be a fixed charge. However, what is interesting is that the Court, similar to the High Court, also used the constructionist approach in order to ascertain the true nature of the charge. The Supreme Court began its analysis by finding that when considering whether a charge was intended by the parties to be fixed or merely floating, the intentions of the parties can be ascertained by construing the charge documents in their entirety. Emphasising that the parties intentions at the time of creation of the charge are paramount, the Supreme Court held that the charge documents intended the charge to be a fixed charge because the terms of the charge provided for the mandatory lodgement of book debts proceeds to a special restricted bank account under the lender bank's control. This was evidence that the parties intended to create a fixed charge over the book debts, as such a mechanism was intended to deprive the company of the use of the book debt proceeds in the ordinary course of its business. Consequently, such charge terms were held to be indicative of the parties' intention to create a fixed charge.[276]

While it appeared therefore that the constructionist approach was being used by the courts to ascertain parties intentions, it did not always necessarily give results that favoured the chargeholder. In a sub-

---

[276] Merely because the company could have access to the collected book debt proceeds from the special account with the bank's permission did not prevent the Supreme Court so finding.

sequent U.K. High Court decision, *Re Brightlife Ltd.*[277] Hoffmann J. (now Lord Hoffman) distinguished *Siebe Gorman*[278] and *Re Keenan Bros.*[279] In *Brightlife, inter alia* the issue was whether a charge over company book debts attached to *collected* book debts, the proceeds of which were sitting in the bank. Hoffmann J. held that the charge, *on its construction*, attached to the book debts while uncollected but did not extend to them once converted into proceeds. The learned judge further went on to hold that, as the proceeds were at the disposal of the company once paid into the account, the charge could not be a fixed charge. Hoffmann J. thus held that a floating charge has been created.

It is difficult to determine with certainty the actual grounds on which the *ratio* of this decision rests. Two quite different interpretations are possible. The first possible interpretation is that the *terms* of the charge were drafted too narrowly, such that the charge was confined to attaching to the book debts only while they remained uncollected. If this is correct, then once the debts were collected, the charge's terms did not secure those proceeds, and so, those proceeds fell outside the charge. Alternatively, a second possible interpretation of the decision is that the decision is authority for the proposition that ordinary use of the book debt proceeds must be restricted, otherwise, any purported charge over book debts is only capable of being, at most, a floating charge. This interpretation treats the debt and proceeds elements of the debt as indivisible.

The issue of which interpretation is the correct one could be significant. The first possible interpretation would confine the decision in the case to the peculiar facts of that particular charge as drafted. However, the second possible interpretation, if it is the correct one, could have more far-reaching consequences. If it is the true *ratio* of the decision, then effectively the case could be taken to be authority for the proposition that a fixed charge cannot attach to book debts while they are *uncollected* if it does not also restrict their use when *collected*. Should this interpretation be the correct one, then for the purposes of determining the true nature of charges over book debts, the book debts would be treated as an *indivisible* asset with the debt and collected proceeds being regarded as the one asset.[280]

Whichever proposition *Brightlife* is authority for, one thing was becoming certain – the courts favoured adopting a constructionist approach in each individual case in an attempt to contrue the true intention

---

[277] [1987] 2 W.L.R. 197.
[278] Hoffman J. could not overrule Slade J. (*Siebe Gorman*) as both decisions are decisions of the English High Court.
[279] [1985] I.R. 401.
[280] *cf. Re New Bullas Trading* considered below.

of the parties as to the nature of the charge, and such approach placed reliance upon interpreting the terms of the charge documents.[281]

(b) Consolidation of the constructionist approach

5–63   The debate was further added to by the Irish High and Supreme Court decisions in *Re Wogan's Drogheda Ltd (Jenkins v. Hill Samuel (Ireland) Ltd)*.[282] In the High Court, Denham J. held that a floating charge existed over book debts in the following circumstances. Under the terms of a debenture, a lender was given the power to designate a special account into which book debts proceeds would be lodged. Interpreting *Keenan Bros.* as being authority for the proposition that a special designated account must *exist* in order to find that a charge over book debts was of the fixed variety, Denham J. admitted evidence to show that no account had ever been actually designated by the lender. As no account had been designated, the court held the charge to be a mere floating charge (though the court did add that were the special restricted account designated, then the charge would be converted into a fixed charge).

On appeal, the decision of the High Court was reversed by the Supreme Court. The Supreme Court *per* Finlay C.J. held that when assessing whether a charge was fixed or floating, the intention of the parties must be determined from the terms of the documents which created the charge. Consequently, consideration of subsequent events, such as whether a special restricted account was ever actually designated or not, was not admissible for this purpose.[283] On the construction of the terms of the debenture, the Supreme Court held that the terms of the debenture, which *inter alia* provided for a special account to be designated, was indicative of a fixed charge. Thus, the practical consequence of the decision is that a fixed charge may exist, even though control of the proceeds has not *actually* been taken from the borrower.[284] Finlay C.J. further held that the construction of the debenture deed

---

[281] For example, in *Re Armagh Shoes* [1982] N.I. Reps. 60 the court made it clear that merely because the parties describe a charge as "fixed" does not mean that it is a fixed charge on that account. The charge documents must be construed in their entirety.

[282] [1993] 1 I.R. 154.

[283] Finlay C.J. rejected the suggestion that Walsh J. had engaged any such subsequent conduct examination exercise in the Supreme Court in *Re Keenan Bros.*

[284] Fealy, "Fixed Charges over Bookdebts: A Loosening of the Reins?" (June 1993) I.L.T. p.133 criticises this decision, arguing that not only did the Supreme Court misinterpret the effect of the relevant clauses, but also, that the Supreme Court's decision runs contrary to previous caselaw which he argues required control over book debt proceeds in order to find that a fixed charge existed.

being paramount, the fact that no special account had been designated was a "mere concession" by the lender.

After this judgement, the position would appear to be that if the terms of a debenture provides the machinery for a special restricted account to be designated by the lender, then in the absence of other terms indicating to the contrary, a charge may well be held to be a fixed charge, even though in actual fact the borrowing company continues to have access to the book debt proceeds. This would seem somewhat conceptually difficult to accept in some quarters as traditionally the whole idea of a fixed charge was that the company's ability to have access to the charged assets in the ordinary course of its business was removed from the company.

Interestingly, the English Court of Appeal in a recent decision, *Re New Bullas Trading Ltd*[285] has endorsed a debenture which, on its construction, deliberately set out to create a fixed charge over book debts and, in default of instructions from the chargeholder, the collected proceeds were to be subject to a floating charge. By its very nature, such a latter charge would render the proceeds available to the company. The Court of Appeal accepted that the debenture had, by its very terms, created a fixed charge over the book debts while uncollected, and that such a finding would not be altered by the express intention of the parties to make the proceeds subject to a floating charge (and thus available to the company) once collected.[286]

(c) The importance of the terms of the designated account

5–64 *Re Wogan's*[287] demonstrates how important the terms of the charge are, particularly those that set up a special restricted account. However, it was the subsequent decision in *Re Holidair Ltd.*[288] which demonstrated how the courts will construe the terms of the charge against the lender where they are vague or unclear. In *Re Holidair* one of the issues was whether a debenture had created a fixed or floating charge over company book debts. The debenture in question stipulated, *inter alia*, that the companies (there were several related companies in the group affected by the debenture) were prohibited from dealing in the uncollected book debts and were to pay the proceeds of collected book debts into "*. . . such accounts with the (lending) banks or any of them as the trustee (of the debenture) may from time to time select. . .*". Delivering the opinion of the Supreme Court on this issue, Blayney J.

---

[285] [1994] B.C.L.C. vol. 1 485.

[286] This decision is considered further below; *cf., Re Brightlife* considered above at para. 5–62.

[287] [1993] 1 I.R. 154: for an account of the case see para. 5–63 above.

[288] [1994] I.R. 481.

held that, from a construction of the debenture's terms, the debenture created a floating charge over the book debts as the fixed element of the charge (*i.e.* lack of company freedom to deal) only applied to the debts whilst uncollected. Once collected, the clause gave the trustee a discretion to nominate the account into which the proceeds should be paid; and those accounts, on the terms of the debenture were not to be accounts in the name of the banks[289] *but merely* the companies' own accounts with the banks.[290] Thus concluded Blayney J., as the debenture imposed no restriction on withdrawals from those accounts, the assets (the proceeds) were available to the company in the normal course of its business.[291] Thus Blayney J. held that the charge was a floating charge.

In the course of his judgment, Blayney J. referred to the two previous Supreme Court judgements in *Keenan Bros.* and *Wogans*, pointing out that both of those cases held a fixed charge over book debts to exist because, in each case, the terms of their respective debentures contemplated the designation of a special bank account from which company withdrawals were restricted. Hence, he concluded, they were distinguishable from the *Holidair* charge terms.

The English Court of Appeal's recent decision in *Re New Bullas Trading*[292] represents the most creative and innovative example of judicial efforts at interpretation of complicated charge terms. The issue to be determined was whether a charge over book debts was fixed or floating. If the charge was a floating charge, then the preferential creditors could, pursuant to section 40 of the U.K. Insolvency Act 1986[293] call on the receiver appointed pursuant to the charge to pay over to them any sums collected in realisation of the charge. The debenture purported to grant a fixed charge over company book debts. It provided that the company was to deal in the uncollected debts only as directed by the chargeholder. If no directions were given, all the company was permitted to do was to collect the debts and pay the collected proceeds either into the company's own account with the bank, or else, into a separate account to be designated by the chargeholder. Furthermore,

---

[289] Had this been the situation, the companies would have no access to the proceeds.

[290] The banks had made an attempt by letter to designate a special account in their *own* name but this was rejected by Blayney J. as he held that the terms of the charge gave the trustee discretion to nominate company bank accounts only.

[291] *i.e.*, while the trustee had a discretion under the terms of the debenture to decide that the companies pay the proceeds into particular company accounts with particular banks, there was no restriction under the terms of the debenture preventing the companies' withdrawing monies from those accounts.

[292] [1994] vol. 1 B.C.L.C. 485.

[293] This is similar in this respect to s.98 of the Companies Act 1963.

the charge provided that the company was to pay out of the lodged proceeds as directed by the chargeholder from time to time. However, if no directions were given by the chargeholder regarding the proceeds, or, if no demand had been made by the chargeholder for repayment from the proceeds, then, the proceeds were to be released from the fixed charge and become subject to a floating charge.

No demand for repayment from the proceeds was made by the chargeholder, nor were directions given by the chargeholder regarding the proceeds. Furthermore, no special account was actually designated by the chargeholder for the proceeds. Thus, the company continued to collect the debts, lodged the proceeds into its own bank accounts, and used those monies in the ordinary course of its business. Knox J. in the English High Court held that the charge was a floating charge. The learned judge considered that the terms of the charge were similar to the charge held to be a floating charge by the English High Court in *Re Brightlife*. The company was free to collect its debts, free to pay the proceeds into its own bank account, and free to deal with the proceeds in the ordinary course of its business once the debts were paid into that account. None of the potential restrictions possible under the debenture's terms had been put into effect.[294] The learned High Court judge stated:

"Absent a direction (from the chargeholder) . . . there was a freedom of action conferred upon the Company which was in my judgement inconsistent with the existence of a specific charge."

Delivering the judgment of the Court of Appeal,[295] Nourse L.J. reversed the High Court decision. On appeal, it was successfully submitted that the express terms of the debenture reflected the intention of the parties, at the time of creation of the charge, that a fixed charge should attach to the debts before collection, and that the proceeds once collected would be *released* from the fixed charge and become subject to a floating charge. The existence of a floating charge depended on whether any prior direction or demand for repayment or designation of a special account had been made by the charge holder to the company. Nourse L.J. considered that the essential question was whether the law would allow the parties to make an agreement to that effect, notwith-

---

[294] For example, no direction/demand was made by the lender, nor was there any restriction on making withdrawals from the company account used, nor had a special account been designated.

[295] For further criticism of the Court of Appeal decision, see Breslin, "Company Charges over Book Debts after Holidair and New Bullas Trading" (Feb. 1995) C.L.P. p.32; Naccarato & Street, "Re New Bullas Trading Ltd: Fixed Charge over Book Debts – Two into One won't go" (March 1994) Butterworths Journal of International Banking and Financial Law p.109.

standing the fact that in the previous authorities the drafters of charge clauses had treated book debts as *indivisible*. The learned Court of Appeal judge stated:

> "Here, for the first time in a reported case, the draughtsman has deliberately . . . set out to subject them (*i.e.*, the book debts) to a fixed charge while they are uncollected and a floating charge on realisation."

Nourse L.J. went on to indicate that the question depends in the first instance on the *true construction* of the charge deed and held that the parties clearly intended the debts to be released from the fixed charge upon the payment of the proceeds into the bank account in the absence of any directions being given concerning how the proceeds might be used. Citing Lord MacNaghten's dictum from *Tailby v. Official Receiver*,[296] the learned judge stated:

> "Between men of full age and competent understanding ought there to be any limit to the freedom of contract but that imposed by positive law or dictated by considerations of morality or public policy? The limit proposed is purely arbitary, and I think meaningless and unreasonable."

Nourse L.J. then continued:

> "These observations support the view that, just as it is open to contracting parties to provide for a fixed charge on future book debts, so it is open to them to provide that they shall be subject to a fixed charge while they are uncollected and a floating charge on realisation. No authority to the contrary has been cited. . . . For these reasons I would . . . hold that the charge over book debts of the Company, as created by the debenture, was, unless and until their proceeds were paid into the specified account, a valid fixed charge."

(4) Some possible implications which merit consideration after these recent judgments

5–65   The floating charge lender over a company's book debts will not feel very comfortable *vis-à-vis* the lender who is the benficiary of a subsequently created so-called "fixed" charge, particularly if the fixed charge contemplates a restricted account, but one is never actually operated. The fixed charge lender and the borrower may well have the best of both worlds – the lender a fixed charge and thus priority over the floating charge lender; while the borrower company will have *de facto* access to book debt proceeds in the ordinary course of its business. In light of such developments, lenders may well think twice before willingly accepting floating charges over a corporate borrower's book debts.

---

[296] [1888] 13 A.C. 523.

Even the fixed charge lender will have to take care to ensure that the account into which the book debt proceeds are to be paid (whether the account is already set-up and operating, or merely contemplated) is in the name of the lender as opposed to the borrower, in order to ensure that the borrower may be potentially restricted from making account withdrawals.

Also, it is now clear that it is not legitimate for a court to look to the conduct of the parties subsequent to the charge's creation, in order to ascertain the true nature of the charge.

One issue which awaits definitive resolution in Ireland is whether it is conceptually legally possible for a debenture to create a fixed charge over book debts if the charge does not also restrict use of, or contemplate restricted use of, the debt proceeds? For the purposes of this issue, should the uncollected debts and their resulting proceeds be regarded as indivisible components? While the Court of Appeal in England has pronounced on this issue in *Re New Bullas Trading*, a definitive judgment in the Irish courts on this issue is awaited.

C. BOOK DEBTS, CHARGES AND BORROWER EXAMINERSHIP[297]

5–66 Pursuant to the Companies (Amendment) Act 1990[298] the High Court may appoint an examiner to a company in difficulties where pursuant to a petition to appoint[299] an examiner, the court is satisfied that placing the company in examinership would be likely to facilitate the survival of the company (either in whole or in part) as a going concern.[300] Where the court grants the petition to appoint, the exam-

---

[297] On the impact of the Companies (Amendment) Act 1990 examinership regime on this area, see further Connaughton, "The Kentz Case-more problems for secured lenders" (April 1994) C.L.P. 110; Johnston, "Bank Finance-Searching for suitable security" (Jan. 1994) C.L.P. 3; Tomkin, "Examinership: the Kentz Case" (May 1994) I.L.T. 110; O'Donnell, "Nursing the Corporate Patient – Examinership and Certification under the Companies (Amendment) Act 1990" (March 1994) C.L.P. 83; Lynch, "Saving jobs – at what cost?" (Sept. 1994) I.L.T. 208; Donnelly, "Is there a case for corporate rescue?" (Jan. 1994) C.L.P. 8.
[298] No. 27 of 1990.
[299] s.3 of the Companies (Amendment) Act 1990 sets outs the categories of persons who may present a petition including the directors or creditors of a company.
[300] Companies (Amendment) Act 1990, s.2. However, note that at the time of writing the Companies (Amendment) (No. 2) Bill 1999 proposes an amendment to s.2 whereby s.5(b) of the 1999 Bill proposes that the test for appointing an examiner be made more restrictive. It provides that, "The court shall not make an order [appointing an examiner to the company] unless it is satisfied that there is a *reasonable prospect of the survival* (author's emphasis) of the company and

iner duly appointed takes over the operational control of the company for a short period in order to assess whether the distressed company can be saved.[301] During this period the company is under court protection, which effectively means that the company's creditors are kept at bay. Complicated legal issues may arise for corporate borrowers and lenders where a company is under examinership.

The Supreme Court judgment in *Re Holidair*[302] provides significant guidance on some of these complex issues, particularly those that may arise for corporate book debt chargeholders. In interpreting the ambit of the statutory regime, the Supreme Court has helpfully clarified the extent to which the examinership regime may "interfere" with the rights of secured lenders, thereby favouring corporate borrowers. *Re Holidair* interpreted the 1990 Amendment Act such that during the borrower's examinership period, examinership:

— causes crystallised floating charges to de-crystallise

— renders negative pledge covenants unenforceable

— prevents lender realisation of charged debts

— permits certified borrowings to be repayable in priority to borrowings secured prior to examinership

Each of these key aspects will be considered in turn shortly. The Companies (Amendment) (No. 2) Bill 1999 should also be borne in mind. If adopted in its current form, it proposes to adopt some of the case law's interpretations of various provisions of the 1990 Amendment Act, while in others instances it seeks to overturn the case law or amend the 1990 Amendment Act generally.[303]

In *Re Holidair*, Holidair Ltd. petitioned the High Court seeking the appointment of an examiner whose task it would be to ascertain whether certain of the troubled Kentz group of companies could be restructured and saved from bankruptcy.[304] An examiner was appointed by the High Court. Notwithstanding the existence of charges

---

the whole or any part of its undertaking as a going concern." The amendment was recommended by the Company Law Review Group Report (December 1994) at p. 15. At the time of writing the Bill is proceeding to Committee Stage in the Dáil.

[301] Such period being three months (subject to further extension): Companies (Amendment) Act 1990, s.5. However, note that s.14 of the Companies (Amendment) (No. 2) Bill 1999 (which at the time of writing is proceeding to Committee Stage in the Dáil) proposes that the examinership period be shortened to 70 days.

[302] [1994] I.R. 481.

[303] At the time of writing the 1999 Bill is not yet fully debated in the Oireachtas, as it has only reached Committee Stage in the Dáil.

[304] [1994] I.L.R.M. 481.

in favour of the company's bank lenders as well as the existence of negative borrowing covenants in such charges, the examiner sought the High Court's permission to borrow funds on behalf of the troubled companies pending examination of their prospects of survival. In the High Court, Costello J. held *inter alia* that the lenders had valid fixed charges and that the examiner could only borrow with the consent of the lenders. The examiner (and the companies) successfully appealed to the Supreme Court.

(1) Crystallised floating charges de-crystallise

5–67 As has already been discussed elsewhere in this chapter, the Supreme Court held that the lenders' charges were not fixed, but floating.[305] Having decided that central issue, the Supreme Court *per* Blayney J. then proceeded to deal with the issue of whether the floating charges, which *crystallised* upon the appointment of a lender-appointed receiver,[306] had *de-crystallised* upon the appointment of the court-appointed examiner.[307] Blayney J. held that upon the appointment of the examiner, the charges de-crystallised, thereby resuming their character as floating charges.

Explaining the reasoning of the court on this point, Blayney J. outlined how the intention of the legislature in enacting the 1990 Amendment Act was to give a short period of protection to companies whilst an examiner assessed whether the company had a reasonable prospect of survival. As an essential element of this protection had to be the keeping of creditors at bay during the examinership period, it would be wholly inconsistent with this purpose the learned judge maintained, if, during the examinership period, the companies (a) were subject to the activities of a receiver,[308] and, (b) were to be deprived of their book debts.[309] The learned judge took the view that this conclusion caused no injustice to the chargeholders on two grounds.

---

[305] Judgment of Blayney J. on this issue discussed above at para. 5–64.

[306] A receiver was appointed by the banks on the same day that the companies petitioned the High Court seeking the appointment of an examiner.

[307] The examiner had been appointed the day after the receiver had been appointed. For a criticism of the de-crystallisation on the grounds that it weakens legal certainty, see Courtney, *op. cit.* chap. 17.

[308] Neither ss.3 nor 6 of the Companies (Amendment) Act 1990 were of any assistance to the bank-appointed receiver. The only way in which a receiver may continue to act in circumstances where a petition to appoint an examiner is presented to the court, is where either the receiver was appointed more than three days prior to the petition to appoint the examiner being presented (Companies (Amendment) Act 1990, s.3); or where the court so orders pursuant to s.6 of the Companies (Amendment) Act 1990.

[309] Particularly if the book debts formed an important part of the company assets, and were thus essential to any proposed survival plan for the company.

First, the continued trading activity of the company would assist the company in generating funds to pay off the charged debts. Second, allowing the company have access to its book debts would allow the company continue to create new book debts to which the charges could attach. Indeed, section 11 of the Companies (Amendment) Act 1990 expressly envisages that any company property affected by charges can be disposed of by the examiner. Where company property is subject to a *floating* charge, as created, it may be sold by the examiner as if the property was not subject to the charge (the court's permission must be obtained and will be granted where the court is of the view that the disposal is likely to facilitate the company's survival).[310] In this event, the floating charge will attach to any property of the company which, either directly or indirectly, represents the property disposed.[311] Should the property be charged with a *fixed* charge, then although the examiner may dispose of property subject to a fixed charge (provided sanction has been given by the court),[312] section 11 curtails the examiner's freedom to deal with the *proceeds* from realisation of the charge. The proceeds from such sale must be applied towards the discharge of the security.[313]

Finally, Blayney J. held that if the receiver were to insist on the charge remaining crystallised, then the receiver would be acting in breach of section 5 of the Companies (Amendment) Act 1990 which, *inter alia*, provides that, "where any claim against the company is secured by a charge on the whole or any part of the property, effects or income of the company, no action may be taken to realise the whole or part of such security, except with the consent of the examiner."[314]

5–68 This *suspension* of rights by the examinership regime (in the case of *floating* charge holders) and *dependance* of the chargeholder on the examiner acting with reasonable speed (in the case of *fixed* charge-holders) raises an interesting issue in the case of charge-backs over corporate deposits. As considered above,[315] the House of Lords has

[310] Companies (Amendment) Act 1990, s.11(1).
[311] Companies (Amendment) Act 1990, s.11(3).
[312] Companies (Amendment) Act 1990, s.11(2).
[313] Companies (Amendment) Act 1990, s.11(4).
[314] Companies (Amendment) Act 1990, s.5(2)(d). S.14(b) of the Companies (Amendment) (No. 2) Bill 1999 proposes substituting this provision of s.5 with the following more comprehensive provision: "(d) where any claim against the company is secured by a charge, mortgage or other encumbrance or a pledge of, on or affecting the whole or any part of the property, effects or income of the company, no action may be taken to realise the whole or any part of that security, except with the consent of the examiner."
[315] See para 5–56.

indicated that charge-backs can be effective in creating charges. Charge-backs are often accompanied by contractual rights of set-off.[316] Consequently, the question arises as to whether, even though the company is in examinership, the bank holder of such a charge may exercise a contractual right of set-off against the company's deposits held in the bank in view of the company's overall liabilities to the bank? Such set-off against a company in examinership is currently not possible because an express prohibition is to be found in section 5(2)(h) of the Companies (Amendment) Act 1990. It provides that no set-off between separate bank accounts of a company in examinership can be effected, except with the consent of the examiner. However, interestingly section 14(b)(ii) of the Companies (Amendment) (No. 2) Bill 1999 proposes to repeal section 5(2)(h). Should this proposed amendment eventually become law,[317] then a bank could attempt to exercise such rights without being dependent on the examiner's permission to do so. This would be particularly useful where the charge element of the charge-back failed as a charge. It is submitted that were this proposed legislative amendment adopted, then set-off could be possible against company deposits notwithstanding that they were also subject to a charge. There should be no objection to such contractual rights being enforced in such circumstances, particularly as examinership has a curious effect on floating charges as it causes them to decrystallise upon examinership, in which event the charge would be inoperable in any event.[318]

Contractual rights of set-off should not be confused with statutory rights of set-off under Bankruptcy legislation.[319] In an insolvent liquidation, lack of mutuality (*i.e.*, a charge has already crystallised on the asset) would prevent the operation of statutory set-off under the Bankruptcy legislation.[320]

---

[316] As noted above at para. 5–56 because of concern that charges would be ineffective over company deposits, banks sought to protect themselves by use of the "triple cocktail" charge-back which not only has a charge element, but also two further elements, a contractual right of set-off and a flawed asset stipulation.

[317] The Bill is currently at Committee Stage in the Dáil.

[318] Decrystallisation aside, Calnan, "Security over Deposits Again: BCCI (No. 8)" (April 1998) Journal of International Banking and Financial Law 125 at 129 goes further and suggests that under U.K. legislation the holder of the charge-back could presently opt to exercise contractual set-off rights against the company's deposit account, notwithstanding the existence of the charge and even though the company is in administratorship (U.K. equivalent of examinership).

[319] Bankruptcy Act 1988.

[320] S. 284 of the Companies Act 1963 provides that, the rules that apply to the setting-off of debts under the Bankruptcy Act 1988, also apply in the winding up of an insolvent company. In such a situation, (as opposed to an examinership situation), should an attempt be made to exercise statutory rights of set-off

Corporate Finance Law

(2) Negative pledge covenants unenforceable

5–69 On the other issues surrounding the issue of examinership and charges in *Re Holidair*, Finlay C.J. delivered the judgement of the Supreme Court. This judgment is illuminating as it demonstrates the invasiveness of the examinership regime on corporate borrower / lender arrangements. For example, one issue that arose was whether the examiner was bound by negative borrowing covenants entered into by the corporate borrowers prior to examinership.[321] The Court began by looking to the main aim of the 1990 Amendment Act.[322] The 1990 Amendment Act enacted the intention of the Oireachtas that allows a company in examinership continue to trade as a going concern during the short examinership period, while its survival prospects are assessed. Bearing this in mind, the learned judge concluded that the Amendment Act permitted the examiner to borrow on behalf of the companies without having to get the permission of the chargeholders, *notwithstanding* the contractually agreed negative borrowing covenants entered into by the corporate borrowers *prior* to examinership. Therefore, such covenants could be disregarded by the examiner as they were detrimental to a company seeking to survive under the examinership mechanism. In recognition of this aspect of the judgment, the Companies (Amendment) (No. 2) Bill 1999 proposes that the examiner's power to ignore negative borrowing or charging pledges be expressly incorporated into the Companies (Amendment) Act 1990.[323]

---

pursuant to the Bankruptcy Act 1988, it would fail on grounds of lack of mutuality as under the Bankruptcy Act 1988 statutory set-off rights can only be exercised in bankruptcy where mutuality exists. Where a charge has crystallised, then mutuality no longer exists for the purposes of statutory set-off: *Lynch v. Ardmore Studios* [1966] I.R. 133. On the other hand, were the charge to be ineffective, then mutuality may well exist. Similarly, where the rights of set-off sought to be exercised in an insolvent liquidation are contractual in nature, lack of mutuality will adversely affect contractual rights of set-off even though it can be demonstrated that such rights were in place prior to insolvency, because the (effective) charge will attach to the asset. However, it will be otherwise if the contractual right of set-off is the only exerciseable right (*i.e.* no charge exists): *Glow Heating v. Eastern Health Board* [1988] I.R. 110 held that genuine contractual rights acquired prior to liquidation do not violate *pari passu* and so can be exercised; *Dempsey v. Bank of Ireland*, unreported, Supreme Court, December 6, 1985 held that contractual rights to set-off bank accounts against each other in the event of a customer's liquidation bound the liquidator.

[321] Typically such a covenant (also known as a *negative pledge*) constitutes a promise by the borrower not to borrow or create security in favour of any party other than the lender/chargeholder without the lender/chargeholder's permission.

[322] Also considered in *Re Atlantic Magnetics Ltd (in Recevership)* [1993] 2 I.R. 561, especially *dicta* of McCarthy J. and Finlay C.J.

[323] s.18. At the time of writing this Bill is proceeding to Committee Stage in the Dáil.

(3) Lender realisation of debt charged prevented

5–70   Lender attempts to invoke mechanisms for realising a charged debt is another area where examinership can create major difficulties for the secured lender of a corporate borrower. Again, *Re Holidair* gives an excellent illustration of the typical kinds of difficulties that may arise in this regard. Subsequent to the appointment of the examiner, a lender bank attempted to designate a special restricted account in its name and instructed the company to pay all proceeds into that account.[324] The Supreme Court *per* Finlay C.J. held that such action was contrary to the 1990 Amendment Act. Once the petition for the appointment of an examiner is made to a court, a chargeholder cannot take any action to realise their charge, except with the consent of the examiner.[325] The court further held that it is only when the examinership period has ended, that the chargeholder may recommence steps to realise their charge. Thus, the court held that the bank's attempt to nominate a special restricted account in its own name, subsequent to the presentation of the petition to appoint an examiner, is a violation of the statutory examinership mechanism.[326]

(4) Certified borrowings repayable in priority to sums secured

5–71   The Companies (Amendment) Act 1990's certification mechanism allows the examiner to certify liabilities incurred by a company during the period of its examinership as being liabilities which were incurred in order not to prejudice the survival prospects of the company as a going concern.[327] The chief legal consequence of certification is that certified sums are repayable *in priority* to any sums that might have been secured by charges *before* the examinership commenced. Following dicta in *Re Atlantic Magnetics*,[328] Finlay C.J. in *Re Holidair* held

---

[324] Designating *such* an account was not possible under the terms of the charge in *Re Holidair* as Blayney J. delivering the Supreme Court's judgment on this point, held that the only type of account that the debenture permitted the banks to select was merely one of the companies' own unrestricted accounts.

[325] Companies (Amendment) Act 1990, s.5(2)(d) (and also Companies (Amendment) (No. 2) Bill 1999, s.14(b) considered above at n.314). The only way in which a receiver may continue to act is if the receiver was appointed more than three days prior to a petition to appoint an examiner being presented (Companies (Amendment) Act 1990, s.3); or where the court so orders pursuant to Companies (Amendment) Act 1990, s.6.

[326] Apart altogether from the fact that the bank's attempted designation of a special restricted account *in its own name* was never possible under the charge's terms in the first place (*per* Blayney J.).

[327] Companies (Amendment) Act 1990, s.10. S.29 of the Act permits the expenses of an examiner (which include certified liabilities of the company) to be paid in priority to all other claims.

[328] [1993] 2 I.R. 561.

that sums borrowed for the purposes of keeping the company trading during the examinership period may be certified. This is of potentially far-reaching consequence as it means that borrowings by a company under examinership, where certified by the examiner, will take priority to borrowings secured by fixed charges created in the period prior to the presentation of the examinership petition. The court explained the rationale for this far-reaching conclusion on the basis that this was consistent with the Oireachtas's intentions for the operation of the examinership mechanism. However, interestingly, section 28 of the Companies (Amendment) (No. 2) Bill 1999 proposes to radically alter this situation by an amendment to the Amendment Act 1990.[329] It proposes that while the examiner's own costs will continue to rank in priority to all other company debts, other examiner-certified liabilities incurred by the company during examinership (such as company borrowings) while continuing to rank in priority to all other claims, will not rank in priority to company liabilities that are secured by *fixed* charges. Should this proposal become law,[330] then *Re Holidair* would no longer represent the law to the extent that it currently (under the 1990 legislation as it stands) is authority for the proposition that certified corporate borrowings take priority over fixed charges notwithstanding that the charges (and the company liabilities they secure) were created prior to the examinership's commencement.

---

[329] Specifically by amending s.29 of that Act.
[330] At the time of writing this Bill is proceeding to Committee Stage in the Dáil.

6

Debt Subordination Legal Framework and Methods

I. Debt Subordination 363
   What is debt subordination? 363
   Why subordinate corporate debt? 364
      (1) The debtor company 364
      (2) The senior creditors 364
      (3) The junior creditors 364
   Some Possible Advantages of Debt Subordination to
      the Debtor Company 365
      (1) Breathing space 365
      (2) Circumvent borrowing limits 365
      (3) Group companies and group debtors 366
   Subordinated Debt – Debt or Equity? 366
      (1) Similarities 366
      (2) Differences 367
   Debt Subordination and Charges Distinguished 368
   Debt Subordination and Assignment of Debt
      Distinguished 370
**II. Legal Framework of main methods of debt
   subordination** 371
   When Will the Subordination Take Effect? 371
      (1) Complete subordination 371
      (2) Inchoate subordination 372
   Main Methods of Debt Subordination 373
      (1) Turnover subordination 373
         (a) Subordination trust: *advantages* 374
            (i) Junior creditor insolvency 374
            (ii) Avoiding debtor/junior creditor set-off 375
            (iii) Senior creditor double payment 375
            (iv) Avoids privity concerns 376
            (v) Avoids *pari passu* objections 376
            (vi) Proving the junior debt 377
            (vii) Breadth of turnover obligation 378
         (b) Subordination trust: *disadvantages* 379

         (i) Trust concept not universally
              recognised 379
         (ii) Inadvertent creation of security interest 379
         (iii)Assignment by junior creditor..................... 382
     (c) Contractual turn-over subordination:
         advantages 383
         (i) Senior creditor may receive double
              payment.. 384
         (ii) Avoids *pari passu* concerns 384
         (iii)Avoids 'inadvertent' security concerns...... 384
         (iv)Contract concept more widely recognised 385
     (d) Contractual Turn-Over Subordination:
         disadvantages.. 385
         (i) Senior creditor has no beneficial
              interest 385
         (ii) Turn-over may breach company law 386
     (2) Contractual Contingent Subordination 386
     (a) Contractual Turn-Over Subordination
         distinguished... 386
     (b) Compatibility with *pari passu*: the source of
         the confusion 387
     (c) The contingency 388
     (d) Judicial clarification 390
     (e) Legislative clarification...................................... 398
     (3) Turn-Over Subordinations and Contingent
         subordination: a comparison 400
III. Subordination: Some Company Law issues 402
     Fraudulent Trading 403
     Reckless Trading 404
     Fraudulent Preference 407

Debt Subordination Legal Framework and Methods

I. DEBT SUBORDINATION

WHAT IS DEBT SUBORDINATION?

6–01   Debt subordination[1] is a tool that is widely used in corporate[2] borrowing transactions or credit transactions, especially those of an international nature. It facilitates the raising of finance or credit by companies who find it difficult to attract fresh sources of finance because of their high level of debt. From a legal point of view, debt subordination involves one group of the debtor company's creditors ("junior creditors") agreeing to defer exercising their rights to payment until the claims of other creditors ("senior creditors") have been satisfied by the debtor company. Normally, the senior creditors will be concerned to ensure that the debt subordination will operate successfully in the event of the debtor company's liquidation. However, it is also open to the parties to agree that the subordination arrangements will also take effect before any liquidation occurs. Therefore, depending on the creditors' specific requirements, the debt subordination arrangement may be designed to either come into effect immediately[3] between the

---

[1]   For further reading on debt subordination, the following are recommended: the leading international work by Wood, *Project Finance, Subordinated Debt and State Loans* (Sweet and Maxwell, London, 1995), Chaps. 6–11; Johnston, "Debt Subordination: The Australian Perspective" (1987, April issue) A.B.L.R. p.80; Aitken, "Liquidators and the Subordinated Loan", Company and Securities Law Journal (1987) Vol. 4, p.4.

[2]   Debt subordination can equally be used with natural persons, but for the purpose of this work, the use of debt subordination by corporate bodies is what is at issue.

[3]   This is known in the literature on the subject (see footnote 1) as a *complete* subordination as it takes effect immediately upon commencement of the subordination arrangements – it's commencement is not dependent upon some further event occurring. It is considered further below at para. 6–17 in section II of this chapter.

parties, or else spring into effect upon the happening of certain specified events.[4]

WHY SUBORDINATE CORPORATE DEBT?

Debt subordination is attractive to the debtor company, the senior creditors and the junior creditors for different reasons.

(1) The debtor company

6–02   Where a number of the debtor company's creditors agree to assume the status of junior creditors by way of a debt subordination arrangement, this greatly enhances the debtor company's prospects of raising fresh finance or attracting fresh sources of credit. Financial institutions, formerly reluctant to make fresh finance facilities available to the company because of its existing debt obligations, may be more willing to make fresh facilities available to the company because the debt subordination arrangement will assuage concerns about the company's ability to meet its obligations on an on-going basis.

(2) The senior creditors

6–03   The presence of a subordination arrangement induces the senior creditors (and other credit sources) to assist the debtor company because the company now becomes a more attractive credit risk for senior creditors who will be more willing to provide fresh lines of credit or loan finance to the debtor company in this more secure environment. Senior creditors often will view subordinated debt as part of a capital pool[5] held by the debtor company from which their senior debt (owed by the debtor company) can be repaid.

(3) The junior creditors

6–04   Where a debtor company is experiencing financial difficulties, subordination arrangements may be used to give the company time in which to trade its way out of such difficulties. If the company manages

---

[4] Subordination that comes into effect upon the happening of a specified trigger event is known in the literature as *inchoate* subordination and is considered further below at para. 6–18 in section II of this chapter. For example, the debt subordination arrangements may come into effect should the debtor company default at any time in its repayments to the senior creditor.

[5] Such capital being the funds advanced to the company by other creditors, who have now agreed not to press claims for due repayment (i.e. they have become junior creditors).

to do this, then at some point in the future it should be able to commence meeting all of its creditors' claims. Where a debt subordination arrangement is in place, it makes it easier for the company to raise additional outside working finance, rather than succumb to insolvency due to the overwhelming immensity of its creditors' and lenders' claims. In this way, the junior creditors hope that the debt subordination will facilitate the company's survival and thus their prospects of repayment by the company.

SOME POSSIBLE ADVANTAGES OF DEBT SUBORDINATION TO THE DEBTOR COMPANY

There are many reasons why a debtor company might wish to have its creditors enter into a debt subordination arrangement.

(1) Breathing space

6–05 As already noted above, the overall benefit from the debtor company's perspective is that it acquires a breathing space which it can use to support its efforts to trade out of its difficulties. Once the subordination arrangement is in place, creditor pressure on the company should decrease as the senior creditors will feel more secure about their position. Accordingly, the debtor company becomes more attractive to fresh credit and loan finance sources. In this way, the debtor company may be able to successfully avoid going into either liquidation or seeking court protection under the examinership regime.[6]

(2) Circumvent borrowing limits

6–06 Once some of the debtor company's creditors agree to subordinate, the company may be able to legitimately circumvent borrowing limits imposed by the company's own memorandum and articles of asso-ciation. Although a company's constitutional documents may specify an actual monetary limit on lawful company borrowings, when appropriately drafted, the constitutional documents may be amended so as to exclude subordinated debt from the constitutional documents' definition of "borrowings." In such a case, provided that the consti-tutional documents so permit, then the company can

---

[6] The examinership regime whereby the company can be placed in examinership for a period while the examiner can assess its survival prospects was established pursuant to the Companies (Amendment) Act 1990. On examinership generally see Lynch, Marshall & O'Ferrall, *Corporate Insolvency and Rescue* (Butterworths, Dublin, 1996).

effectively increase its borrowing capacity in real terms while yet remaining within the letter of the constitutional documents' borrowing limit definition.[7]

(3) Group companies and group debtors

6–07   A debtor company may find debt subordination attractive where the company is part of a group of companies and has creditors both inside and outside its group structure. Often, the debtor company's external creditors will be more confident where the debtor company gets its internal creditors to subordinate their claims on the company in favour of the external creditors' claims. Once this subordination arrangement is in place, the outside creditors – now senior creditors – will regard the debts owed to the internal creditors – junior creditors – as postponed in their favour. This in turn will satisfy the senior creditors that any fresh credit advanced to the company will be used for the company's business, and not for the purpose of paying off the internal creditors' claims first.

SUBORDINATED DEBT – DEBT OR EQUITY?

(1) Similarities

6–08   Subordinated debt is often considered by financiers to be a debt/equity hybrid as it possesses some of the attributes of both.[8] While it is a form of debt financing, often it will be treated as if it were equity. For example, when a company is being wound up, the holders of preference shares are entitled to priority repayment of share capital over ordinary shareholders. Senior creditor debt has a similar advantage *vis-à-vis* junior creditor debt as it ranks ahead of the junior debt in the event of the debtor company's liquidation.

Another way in which the debt/equity distinction is somewhat blurred in the case of subordinated debt arises when a lender is assessing the debtor company as a credit risk. Debt that is subordinated may be regarded as part of the capital base of the company when a lender is deciding whether to loan funds to a company. According to Johnston, subordinated debt provides the debtor company with an effectively enlarged "capital" base of reserves upon which it can advance its case for the borrowing of further funds. Lenders will frequently view the subordinated debt as a "pool" of debtor company

---

[7]   Although a company whose constitutional documents so provide may yet not be able to make such additional borrowings if pledges it has given in existing loan agreements would thereby be violated by such additional borrowings.
[8]   Wood; Johnston, *op. cit.* at n.1 above.

reserves (i.e., creditor funds held by the debtor company (the repayment of which is subordinated)) which may facilitate the repayment of senior debt. Furthermore, the view is often taken that a senior creditor should treat debtor company debt which is subject to complete[9] subordination as not being reckonable when calculating the debt/equity ratio of the debtor company.

(2) Differences

6–09 The chief difference between equity and subordinated debt is that the subordination of debt does not affect control within the company in the same way that equity ownership would.[10] Debt can be incurred without diluting the rights of the shareholders whereas an issue of equity will. Unlike equity, debt gives the creditor no voting rights, unless the debt is convertible into shares.

Another difference between debt and equity concerns the respective rights of the creditor and shareholder to a return. Payment of interest on a loan or the payment of an outstanding debt is legally due regardless of the company's profitability. Whereas with equity, dividends can never be paid to shareholders unless the company has profit declared available for distribution. However, a creditor does not benefit if the company's share value rises, nor is he entitled to share in company profits.

Another example demonstrating the distinction arises when a company limited by shares wishes to reduce its equity capital by purchasing its own shares or by redeeming redeemable shares. The company must adhere to stringent company law procedures.[11] However, by contrast, there are relatively few such impediments where the company wishes to repay a creditor, apart perhaps from the situation where the company has made payments in the period pre-liquidation such that they might constitute a fraudulent preference[12] or fraudulent or reckless trading[13] under the Companies Act 1963.

---

[9] "Complete" subordination is a term that has been adopted in the literature to denote a subordination arrangement that is effective not only at the time of liquidation, but also from the time that the subordination arrangements are entered into by the parties. See further below para. 6–17 of this chapter.

[10] Keane, *Company Law in the Republic of Ireland* (2nd ed., Butterworths, Dublin, 1991), Chaps. 14, 17 (at pp.167–170) and 18; Wood, *op.cit*, at n.1 above, Chap. 6; Forde, *Company Law* (2nd ed. Mercier Press, Dublin, 1992), Chap. VI (at pp. 176–182) and Chap. IX (at pp. 301–308).

[11] ss. 72–77 of the Companies Act 1963 deals with procedures for the reduction of capital of limited companies and Pt XI of the Companies Act 1990 governs the issuing by such companies of redeemable shares.

[12] s.286 of the Companies Act 1963, prohibits the making of fraudulent preferences which can be constituted by, *inter alia*, any payment intended to give one creditor

Finally, debt can be secured by way of a charge thus giving the chargeholder priority in the event of the debtor company's liquidation over other unsecured general creditors. With shareholders on the other hand, shareholders rank in priority behind all unsecured general creditors, with the shareholders priority to repayment of capital *inter se* being determined according to the rights attaching to their shares.

DEBT SUBORDINATION AND CHARGES DISTINGUISHED

6–10 It is important to distinguish debt subordination from the granting of security. When a creditor of a company takes a charge over company property it will rank in priority over unsecured creditors of the company in the event of the company going into liquidation.[14] This is because the chargeholder acquires a security interest over the assets of the company.[15]

6–11 Debt subordination is quite different. To begin with, debt subordination does not involve the creation of a security interest. More significantly however, junior creditors who are party to a debt subordination agreement agree that in the event of the debtor company's insolvency, their debt shall not be satisfied until after the senior creditors have been satisfied. Whereas a security interest seeks to put a creditor in a preferential position ahead of unsecured creditors,

---

preference over another in the period before the company goes into insolvent liquidation. Whether or not the payment constitutes a fraudulent preference depends, *inter alia*, on whether the payment was made within certain time limits (six months in the case of creditors and two years in the case of 'connected persons' as defined in the Act) and whether there was an "intention to prefer".

[13] s.297 of the Companies Act 1963 imposes criminal liability on any person who carries out the business of a company with, *inter alia*, intent to defraud creditors of the company ("fraudulent trading"). Section 297A empowers the court to declare such person to be personally liable for all or any of the company's debts or other liabilities where the person engaged in 'fraudulent' or 'reckless' trading. See further below section III of this chapter.

[14] Though not all unsecured creditors lose priority to the chargeholder. For example, in the case of a fixed charge over book debts, s.174 of the Finance Act 1995 puts in place a mechanism whereby the Revenue Commissioners can require such a chargeholder to pay over to the Revenue amounts recovered from the company on foot of the charge. Furthermore, in the case of floating charges, s.285(7)(b) of the Companies Act 1963 makes floating charges over company property subject to the claims of preferential (unsecured) creditors such as the Revenue, employees' statutory entitlements, etc. See also s.98 of the 1963 Act.

[15] Provided that any registration requirements are satisfied, e.g. s.99 of the Companies Act 1963.

a subordination arrangement results in unsecured junior debt agreeing to rank behind other unsecured debt (senior debt).

6–12 The precise extent of the subordination, as will be further explained in this chapter, depends on which of the two main methods of subordination is chosen. In the first method, *turn-over subordination*,[16] the junior creditor proves for its debt on a *pari passu* basis in the event of the debtor company's liquidation alongside all other unsecured creditors, including the senior creditor. In that sense therefore, the subordination arrangements give the senior creditor no advantage over the junior creditor from the point of view of *pari passu* distribution. The advantage for the senior creditor arises subsequently as the junior creditor is obliged to turn-over the recoveries to the senior creditor. In this latter sense, the junior creditor ranks behind the senior creditor under the subordination arrangements.[17] By contrast, in the case of a chargeholder, the chargeholder's claims would have to be met first by the liquidator ahead of all unsecured creditors' claims.

6–13 The second subordination method is *contractual contingent subordination*.[18] Here the junior creditor agrees to rank behind the senior creditor by agreeing to opt out of *pari passu* participation. Although under this type of subordination, the junior creditor does not prove for the junior debt until the senior creditor debt has been satisfied first, it does not permit the senior creditor to jump ahead of other unsecured creditors. The senior creditor will prove for the senior debt on a *pari passu* basis with all other senior creditors and other unsecured creditors not party to the subordination arrangements. By contrast with a charge therefore, this method of subordination does not enable the senior creditor to elevate itself in the *pari passu* order over other unsecured creditors. All that happens is that the junior creditor decides not to assert its *pari passu* rights.

---

[16] See further below section II of this chapter.

[17] Although the senior creditor ultimately gets the upper hand from a repayment point of view when the junior creditor turns-over liquidation recoveries, nevertheless the subordination arrangements do not enable the senior creditor to elevate liquidator repayment of senior debt ahead of liquidator repayment of junior creditor debt.

[18] See below section II of this chapter for a detailed consideration of *contractual contingent subordination*. It should not be confused with contractual turn-over subordination , the distinction between the two being that the latter involves a turnover arrangement where the former does not: see further section II of this chapter below.

6–14 Debt subordination is also quite different from the taking of charges in another way also, in that the creditors of the company agree the subordination arrangements among themselves and in conjunction with the company. Often, such a consensual approach is not part of the process of acquiring a security interest, as the chargeholder will be anxious to quietly secure the priority advantage that the charge will bring without other creditors being involved.

For the purposes of this chapter, it will be assumed that debt subordination arrangements are entered into by unsecured creditors. In the event that the creditors are secured, then the senior creditor must ensure that the subordination arrangements subordinate as many rights that the junior secured creditor has by virtue of the security, as is possible. Otherwise the senior creditor could be faced with junior creditor attempts to use the security to hijack and subvert the agreed subordination arrangements.

DEBT SUBORDINATION AND ASSIGNMENT OF DEBT DISTINGUISHED

6–15 Finally, one may consider why a senior creditor would prefer to participate in a debt subordination arrangement (whereby the junior creditor agrees to rank behind the senior creditor) rather than acquiring all interest in the debt by way of an assignment of the junior creditor's debt? After all, it might be assumed that an assignment of all interest in the debt would place the assignee (senior) creditor in a better position than the mere agreement by some creditors to allow their debt to be the subject of a subordination? There can be many reasons why a subordination of debt may be preferable to an assignment. The chief reason is that if a creditor (the junior creditor) assigns his debt to another creditor (the senior creditor), then the former loses all prospect of ever being paid by the debtor company because all interest in the debt will have been assigned to the other creditor. By contrast, with subordination arrangements, the aim of the junior creditor is to recover payment of the junior debt eventually, albeit after the senior creditor has been fully satisfied. Also there can be other reasons why an assignment of the junior debt may not be chosen, such as: the risk that the assignment might not be a complete assignment of full legal title in the debt; or that other assignments may have previously been made of the debt, thus leading to priority problems; or the assignment may be of future interests which can be problematic.[19] Furthermore, there is always the

---

[19] See Chap. 7 on Debt Factoring where these and other issues pertaining to the efficacy of assignments of debts are discussed in detail.

risk that the assignment might, on its true construction, constitute a form of security interest, rather than a full transfer of title. This could give rise to difficulties if the charge was not duly registered pursuant to section 99 of the Companies Act 1963. Finally, another difficulty that may arise to inhibit assignment of the junior debt could be the presence of an express restriction on assignment of the junior debt. This restriction might be imposed by the junior creditors' own creditors who may be anxious to ensure that the junior creditor did not deplete its own asset-base, of which junior debt (i.e. debt owed by the debtor company to the junior creditor) forms a part.

II. LEGAL FRAMEWORK OF MAIN METHODS OF DEBT SUBORDINATION

WHEN WILL THE SUBORDINATION ARRANGEMENT TAKE EFFECT?

6–16 Normally, the senior debtors' chief concern will be that the subordination arrangement will be effective should the debtor company go into liquidation. From the senior creditors' perspective, it is imperative therefore that the arrangements work effectively upon the happening of that event. However, as noted earlier above in this chapter,[20] some subordination arrangements go further and specify that the subordination will come into effect immediately, in which case the subordination is known as a *complete* subordination. Thus, a complete subordination is effective pre-liquidation. Alternatively, the subordination may be *inchoate* in the sense that it is envisaged that it will only spring into effect upon the happening of any one of a number of specified events. Whether an inchoate subordination springs into effect pre-liquidation all depends on whether one of the specified events occurs. Before considering the legal framework of the two main methods of debt subordination, some brief consideration should be given to the issues just raised.

(1) Complete Subordination

6–17 When the subordination operates immediately from the date of the subordination agreement, it is known as *complete* subordination. This type of subordination takes effect pre-liquidation. This means that from the moment the parties agree the subordination arrangements, all debtor company repayments towards the junior creditor debt are

---

[20] Paras 6–01 and 6–08 above.

postponed in favour of the senior creditor debt. No payments either of principal or interest can be *applied in reduction of* the junior creditor debt.[21] Debt subordination of this type is very secure from the senior creditors' perspective as the funds constituting the subordinated junior debt are effectively "locked into" the debtor company's reserves. This is not often used as a form of debtor company financing in itself, but rather as a tool to facilitate and encourage other debt financing.

Once (and if) liquidation of the debtor occurs, then the junior debt repayments, previously blocked by the complete subordination, now become unblocked, in the sense that the junior creditor can now seek recovery of the junior debt under the rules of insolvency. In the event that the subordination arrangement is of the turnover variety, then any junior debt recoveries must be turned over to the senior creditors.

(2) Inchoate/Springing Subordination

6–18   With this type of subordination arrangement, the subordination will not come into actual effect until a specified event occurs. For example, it may be specified that the subordination will only come into effect on the liquidation of the debtor company. However, as will usually be the case, the list of specified events may often be much more comprehensive and include non-liquidation events.[22] In any event, this type of subordination springs into effect when a specified event occurs. Until such event(s) occur, the subordination remains dormant or inchoate.

It is common in this type of subordination for the parties to agree that until such time as a trigger event occurs, the junior creditor may receive interest repayments[23] which can be applied to reduce the junior

---

[21] For example, in a complete contractual contingent subordination, the junior creditor does not receive any repayments until and unless the senior creditor has been paid in full. While the other main method of debt subordination (the subordination trust considered at paras 6–21 *et seq.*) might at first glance appear to be at variance with the text above, in fact it is not. In a subordination trust arrangement, the junior creditor may receive repayments from the debtor towards the junior debt. *However*, although the junior creditor receives such sums, the junior creditor is not free to apply them to *reduce* the junior debt as such proceeds are subject to the subordination trust. Therefore, where a subordination trust is of the complete variety, any repayments received by the junior creditor, whether received before or during the debtor company's liquidation, will be held on trust for the senior creditor and thus cannot be used by the junior creditor to reduce the junior debt. In this sense, junior debt reduction is postponed in favour of the senior creditor. See further below in this section where both methods of subordination are considered in detail.

[22] e.g. a default in repayment of a loan instalment.

[23] Though although the junior creditor may receive such sums if a subordination trust is the model used, the trust terms may further provide that the junior

debt, but not principal repayments. Obviously, once the trigger event occurs, all such payments will become subordinated in favour of the senior debt. Because some element of the junior debt will usually be paid unless one of the specified events occur, this form of subordination is more often used than complete subordination arrangements.[24]

MAIN METHODS OF DEBT SUBORDINATION

6–19 There are two main methods of debt subordination:

(a) Turn-over Subordination
 – Subordination Trust
 – Contractual Subordination

(b) Contractual Contingent Subordination

(1) Turn-Over Subordination

6–20 Either a trust or contract can be used as the legal framework to achieve the turn-over subordination. Under a *subordination trust*, upon the occurrence of the usual subordination event, liquidation, the junior creditor agrees to turn-over to the senior creditor any monies recovered from the liquidator of the debtor company, or alternatively, the junior debt itself. Of course, if the subordination is complete, then this "turn-over" of the junior creditor's rights in respect of the junior debt repayments will have taken place at the time the subordination agreement came into effect (i.e. pre-liquidation). This will also be the position where the subordination was of the inchoate variety and a trigger event has occurred pre-liquidation.

Alternatively, *contractual turn-over subordination* could be used. Under contractual turn-over subordination, the junior creditor agrees to turn-over to the senior creditor *an amount equal to* whatever he succeeds in recovering from the debtor company's liquidator in satisfaction of the junior debt.[25]

As the subordination trust mechanism is the more effective from the senior creditors' point of view, it will be given detailed consideration.[26] The contractual turn-over subordination method, being less effective, is not as widely used.

---

creditor may not be free to apply such sums towards reduction of the junior debt: see paras 6–21 *et seq.* below where the advantages of subordination trusts are further considered.

[24] Complete subordination is discussed at para. 6–17 above.

[25] See further paras 6–38—6–45 below.

[26] It is more effective than the contractual model because the use of a trust gives the senior creditor proprietorial rights over junior creditor recoveries.

(a) Subordination trust and its advantages

6–21   In this legal framework, the junior creditors declare a trust in favour of the senior creditors. In declaring the trust, the junior creditors agree to hold any proceeds recovered from the debtor company and/ or the junior debt on trust for the benefit of the senior creditors until the senior creditors have been completely repaid by the debtor company (or its liquidator) as the case may be. The turn-over aspect of this arrangement is that the junior creditors are agreeing to turnover the subject of the trust to the senior creditors. At its most basic, the subject of the trust can be either any proceeds recovered by the junior creditors from the debtor company (or its liquidator) in satisfaction of the junior debt, or alternatively, the actual debt owed to the junior creditors. Or both.

6–22   The effectiveness of the subordination trust is most evident when the debtor company is actually in liquidation. Because the mechanism of a trust is used, this means that in the event of the senior creditors failing to recover the full amount of the senior debt from the debtor company's liquidator, then the senior creditors can call on the junior creditors to turn over to them any sums collected in satisfaction of the junior debt under the terms of the subordination trust.[27] This is permissible as the trust device gives the senior creditors a beneficial interest in the junior debt that is akin to a proprietary claim. The creation of a beneficial interest is not the only advantage that the subordination trust has for the senior creditors. There are several others. These will now be considered.

(i) Insolvency of junior creditor

6–23   An advantage of the subordination trust is that it avoids problems which otherwise may arise should the junior creditor become insolvent. The junior debt, and any sums recovered in respect of it from the debtor company by the junior creditor, are held on trust by the junior creditor for the senior creditors. The liquidator of the junior creditor cannot have access to such assets.[28]

---

[27]   And/or the junior debt if that was also declared the subject of the trust. However, as shall be seen below when subordination trusts' disadvantages are considered, there is a risk that the declaration of a trust over a debt (as opposed to a trust over any liquidation recovery proceeds) might inadvertently lead to the creation of a security interest rather than a trust.

[28]   Lynch, *et al., op. cit.* at n.6.

(ii) Debtor/junior creditor set-off

6–24 The use of the device of a trust will normally prevent the occurrence of set-off of mutual debts as between the debtor company and the junior creditor in respect of the junior debt, should either go into liquidation. As the junior debt is now the subject of a trust, beneficial rights to it no longer reside exclusively with the junior creditor. Consequently, the mutuality necessary for set-off to operate is not present.

However, as an added measure of protection, the senior creditor should get the debtor company and junior creditor to agree that pre-liquidation, they will not set-off mutual debts. This gives the senior creditor added protection against any attempts by the debtor company and junior creditor to engage in *solvent* mutual set-off.[29]

(iii) Senior creditor "double payment"

6–25 The senior creditor will be entitled to receive repayments from the debtor company's liquidator in satisfaction of the senior debt. However, in the event that such payments do not entirely satisfy the senior creditor's claims, the senior creditor will also be entitled to receive any sums[30] that the junior creditor might recover from the liquidator until the senior debt liability has been satisfied. This is because the trust extends over such sums.

Furthermore, if the subordination is a complete[31] subordination, the senior creditor will also be able to claim any pre-liquidation repayments that might have been made by the debtor company to the junior creditor in respect of the junior debt.[32]

The position is somewhat different where the subordination is of the inchoate variety and no trigger event has yet occurred. This normally means that the junior creditor will be able to receive some repayments (typically interest repayments) on the outstanding junior debt (before any trigger event occurs) and apply same towards reduction of junior debt. However, even in inchoate subordination, it can be quite common for subordination trusts to stipulate that although the subordination arrangements may be of the inchoate variety, certain repayments that the junior creditor may receive pre-trigger event will also be the subject of the trust. In this situation therefore, although the junior creditor may have been permitted to receive interest repayments before the main subordination arrange-ments were actually triggered,

---

[29] *Hong Kong and Shanghai Banking Corp v. Kloeckner & Co. A.G.* [1990] 2 Q.B. 514.
[30] e.g. principal or interest repayments.
[31] see para. 6–17 above for elaboration on "complete" subordination.
[32] e.g. interest repayments.

such sums will not have been at the free disposal of the junior creditor to apply in reduction of the junior debt as they will have been held by the junior creditor on trust for the senior creditor. In the event that the senior creditor debt remains unsatisfied, the senior creditor can call on such sums.[33] Whether or not this is the position all depends on the terms of the trust.

(iv) Avoidance of privity concerns

6–26   The use of a trust means that the senior creditor can enforce the subordination arrangements although it may not be a party to the original loan or credit agreements entered into between the debtor company and the junior creditor. It is commonplace (for example) in bond issues for the senior creditor not to be party to the agreement entered into between the debtor company (bond issuer) and the junior creditors.[34] However, when the need to put a subordination arrangement in place subsequently arises, junior creditors will declare a trust in favour of the senior creditor, thereby subordinating the junior debt. Should the junior creditors subsequently attempt to amend the subordination arrangements without the senior creditor's approval, the senior creditor could take action against the junior creditors for breach of trust.

   The doctrine of privity of contract does not apply to preclude the senior creditor from taking legal action to enforce the trust that has been declared in his favour by the junior creditor. However, where practicable, in order to give itself the greatest level of influence, the senior creditor will draw up a tripartite subordination agreement to which the junior creditors and debtor company will also be parties. Such agreement will contain many stipulations in order to ensure that no change shall be made to the subordination arrangements by either debtor company or junior creditor without senior creditor approval. However, as noted already, this may not be practicable in many cases, due to multiplicity of junior creditors. A way around this practical difficulty is for a trustee to be appointed on behalf of the senior creditor to monitor enforcement of debtor company and junior creditor covenants.

(v) No pari passu objections

6–27   The use of the trust mechanism avoids an objection that has often been made to *contractual contingent subordination*.[35] In some jurisdictions,

---

[33] In this sense therefore, the apparently "inchoate" arrangements are in substance "complete".

[34] Simply because there may be hundreds or thousands of such creditors.

[35] Note that this form of contractual subordination (see paras 6–45 *et seq.* below) is very different from contractual turn-over subordination and one should take care not to confuse them.

the courts[36] have on occasion prevented contractual contingent subordination from being enforceable on the basis that it constituted an attempt by parties to use a private contract to avoid the application of the statutory principle of *pari passu*. *Pari passu* is a principle whose objective is to ensure that, subject to the claims of preferential creditors,[37] in the event of liquidation unsecured creditors of a company should be treated equally.[38]

Such an objection does not arise in the context of the subordination trust. This is because a junior creditor who has declared a trust is not agreeing to rank behind the senior creditor in the event of debtor company liquidation. Instead, the junior creditor will prove for the junior debt *pari passu* on the debtor company's liquidation, and then turn over any proceeds recovered to the senior creditor in whose favour it had declared the trust over such proceeds. Equally, had the junior creditor declared a trust over merely the actual junior debt itself, again the junior creditor is not agreeing to rank behind the senior creditor, but merely agreeing that in the event of the debtor company going into liquidation, it will prove for the junior debt on a *pari passu* basis with the other creditors and turn-over to the senior creditor the right to receive junior debt proceeds from the liquidator.

(vi) Proving the junior debt

6–28 Consideration will also have to be given to the question of what action, if any, can a senior creditor (the beneficiary of a subordination trust) take where the junior creditor decides not to prove for the junior debt in the event of the debtor company's liquidation?[39] Properly drafted subordination trust arrangements will normally have covenants whereby the junior creditor expressly promises to prove the junior debt, within any period in which claims on the debtor company must be proven, or else, the senior creditor can prove the debt should the junior creditor fail to do so. Even if such covenants were not express, they

---

[36] See further below in this chapter below where Australian and New Zealand authorities are considered.

[37] *e.g.* Revenue Commissioners, employees entitlements, chargeholders, etc.

[38] In this respect, contractual contingent subordination is open to the criticism that it may constitute an attempt by one group of unsecured creditors (senior) to elevate themselves ahead of other unsecured creditors (junior) when the *pari passu* principle demands that all unsecured creditors be treated equally. This issue will be considered further below when contractual contingent subordination is considered at paras. 6–46 *et seq.*

[39] s.283 of the Companies Act 1963 sets out the type of debts provable on a winding-up. Note that when proving debts on a company insolvency, account should also be taken of the Bankruptcy Act 1988 as well as the Rules of the Superior Courts. See further ss. 283, 284 of the 1963 Act; also, Lynch, *et al, , op. cit.*, Chap. 2.

may well be implied under the trust. Where a junior creaditor fails to comply with any covenant it may have given regarding the proving of the junior debt, another course of action open to the senior creditor would be to sue the junior creditor for breach of trust for failure to prove the debt. However, this might not be a very attractive solution if the junior creditor is not a "good mark". Therefore, the senior creditor who wishes to avoid undue difficulties with an un-cooperative junior creditor, should ensure that the subordination agreement gives the senior creditor the right to prove for the junior debt on the debtor company's insolvency (if it so wishes). Also the senior creditor should ensure that it has power of attorney to vote in respect of the junior debt in the debtor company's insolvency.

6–29　A difficulty may arise for the senior creditor where the subordination trust is declared over junior debt liquidation recovery proceeds solely, rather than over the junior debt itself. In this situation, the view could be taken that until such proceeds actually come into existence, the senior creditor has no rights arising under the trust and hence could not claim to be a creditor capable of proving a debt on the debtor company's liquidation. The fear here is that a liquidator could attempt to deny the senior creditor the status of "creditor" for the purpose of proving the debt in lieu of the non-compliant junior creditor. In order to avoid such difficulty, the senior creditor should ensure that appropriately worded clauses are inserted into the subordination agreement so that the senior creditor is irrevocably authorised by the junior creditor to claim and prove for the junior debt, and furthermore that the senior creditor may take such steps in good time so that it does not fall foul of any deadlines set by the court in which creditors are required to prove debts.[40]

(vii) Breadth of turnover obligation

6–30　The breadth of the turn-over obligation all depends on the terms of the subordination. A well drafted subordination trust arrangement will also provide that the debtor company agrees that it will not make any payments to the junior creditor apart from defined permitted payments, and the junior creditor will covenant that it will not accept any payments from the debtor company other than such defined payments. This is designed to prevent the debtor and junior creditor from accelerating reduction of the junior debt, as the senior creditor

---

[40] Pursuant to s.241 of the Companies Act 1963 the court may fix a time by which creditors' claims must be proven, or else may order that any debts not proven by a certain time should be excluded from the benefit of any distribution made before those debts are proved.

will wish to ensure that the junior debt continues to exist (as the senior creditor may have to call upon it, in the event that the debtor company becomes insolvent without first having satisfied the senior debt fully).

Another common clause found in turnover subordinations is a clause which provides that the turnover obligation (accepted by the junior creditor) extends to cover repayments towards junior debt from any source. Typically, the objective of such a clause is to ensure that if, say a third party had guaranteed the junior debt and the guarantee was honoured, then the subordination trust (and hence turnover obligation) would attach to such proceeds.

Finally, in some instances, it is not uncommon to find clauses which direct the debtor company's liquidator to pay junior debt recoveries (once proven) directly to the senior creditor (rather than having them paid first to the junior creditor, who then in turn would turn them over to the senior creditor).

(b) Subordination Trust and its disadvantages

However the use of a subordination trust, while giving the senior creditors much comfort, may not be totally secure.

(i) Trust concept not universally recognised

6–31 One potential problem that can arise is that the concept of a trust is not recognised in some jurisdictions. Thus, in an international debt subordination which involves creditors in, for example, common and civil law jurisdictions, this may pose particular difficulties as trusts are not recognised in many civil law countries.[41]

(ii) Inadvertent creation of security interest[42]

6–32 A further difficulty that can arise is that the parties may inadver-

---

[41] *Re Maxwell Communications Corporation plc* [1993] 1 W.L.R. 1402 (a contractual subordination had to be used as part of the subordination arrangements as trusts were not recognised under Swiss law); *Re British and Commonwealth Holdings plc* [1992] 1 W.L.R. 672.

[42] *Swiss Bank Corp. v. Lloyds Bank Ltd and Others* [1982] A.C. 584 (House of Lords, affirming the Court of Appeal), the U.K. courts were called upon to consider whether an equitable charge had been created, holding that in order for such a charge to be created, the debtor must have intended no charge to arise. However, Buckley L.J. (Court of Appeal) (affirmed in the House of Lords) further held (at 595/596) that: "But notwithstanding that the matter depends upon the intention of the parties, if upon the true construction of the relevant documents in the light of any admissible evidence as to surrounding circumstances the parties have entered into a transaction the legal effect of which is to give rise to an equitable charge in favour of one of them over property of the other, the fact that they may not have realised this consequence will not mean that there is no

tently have created a security interest rather than a trust interest. This would be disastrous from the senior creditor's point of view, as the failure to create the trust would deprive the senior creditor of all of the advantages which a trust has to offer. A charge, inadvertently created, might give the senior creditor little comfort.

Apart from the fact that the senior creditor would not have obtained a proprietorial interest[43] (due to the trust being defunct), a further concern that the senior creditor may have to face would be the risk that the charge that may have come into inadvertent existence might be of the registrable variety. In this situation, the junior creditor, not being aware that the intended object (the creation of a trust) had failed, would not have taken any steps to register the "charge" with the Registrar of Companies as required by section 99 of the Companies Act 1963. Consequently, such security would be unenforceable against the liquidator and other creditors of the debtor company.

6–33 However, it is suggested that this risk may not be as potent as might at first appear. To begin with, there are principally two types of charge that could be relevant in this context.

The first is that a "charge over book debts" might be inadvertently created. Under section 99(2)(e) Companies Act 1963 a charge over book debts must be registered – otherwise it is unenforceable against the liquidator or creditors of the company. However, in order for such a charge to be registrable, the asset the subject of the charge must be "book debts". As this term has not been legislatively defined, the issue arises of whether it is possible to characterise the subject of the defunct "trust" as section 99 "book debts"? In Ireland, the courts have regarded "book debts" as meaning trade debts (although no all embracing definitive definition has been elaborated).[44] It would appear difficult to contend that "book debts" includes any liquidation proceeds that might be payable by a debtor company's liquidator to the junior creditor. Consequently, as such proceeds would be the subject of the inadvertently created charge (the defunct trust), the charge would probably not be a "charge over book debts" and hence not require registration pursuant to section 99 as such a charge.[45] While the point is not free

---

charge. They must be presumed to intend the consequences of their acts." (Note that ultimately, on the facts, the court found that there was no such charge existing).

[43] Unlike a trust, which implies a proprietorial interest on the part of the beneficiary, a change implies no proprietorial interest, but rather indicates a debt or funds (as the case may be) out of which the security may be satisfied.

[44] *Farrell v. Equity Bank* [1990] 2 I.R. 549.

[45] Wood, *op. cit.* at n. 1, p.67 takes this view under the corresponding U.K. registration legislation, s.395 of the Companies Act 1985.

from doubt, it would seem that this risk – the inadvertent creation of a charge over book debts requiring registration – would not therefore arise in this context.

On the other hand however, had the subject of the defunct trust been declared to have been *the subordinated debt itself*, then it is arguable that such a debt might well constitute a book debt of the junior creditor within the meaning of section 99. It is therefore possible that an inadvertently created charge over such debt might well fall within the meaning of a "charge over book debts".

The second type of registerable change, that might possibly be deemed to arise, could be a charge "granted for the purpose of securing any issue of debentures". Section 99(2)(a) requires such charges to be registered. Whether or not section 99(2)(a) would be applicable is debateable. The circumstances in which it might present an issue would be where an issue of subordinated debentures takes place and they are secured by a charge (inadvertently) created by the junior creditor.[46]

6–34 Wood suggests that in order to avoid the inadvertent creation of a security interest when creating a subordination trust, the parties should ensure that the trust is drafted appropriately.[47] Care should be taken to ensure that the junior creditor's liability is defined as liability to pay over to the senior creditor amounts up to the amount of outstanding senior debt, rather than all recovered proceeds being handed over to the senior creditor with any surplus being repaid to the junior creditor. The latter arrangement implies an equity of redemption could arise in respect of the surplus, whereas the former attempts to avoid such an equity being implied. The senior creditor should ensure that the trust is declared (for amounts to be turned over by the junior creditor) up to an amount equal to the amount of the unsatisfied senior debt, thereby leaving no room for an equity of redemption to be implied. Where the circumstances are such that an

---

[46] One commentator helpfully suggests that a possible means of avoiding the risk of inadvertent creation of a registrable charge is for an independent trustee to be appointed at the time of the trust's creation. In declaring the trust on behalf of the junior creditors, this trustee could not be regarded as creating a charge over book debts as any such debts could not be regarded as the book debts of the trustee and the junior creditors could not be regarded as charging their beneficial interest in the debts: Johnston, *op. cit* .at n. 1 at p. 126. The main practical advantage of having an independent trustee representing the interests of the subordinated creditors is that the senior creditors can enforce the trust against that party thereby avoiding having to enforce the trust against a multiplicity of junior creditors in hundreds of separate legal actions.

[47] Wood, *op. cit.* at n.1 at p.66, although that learned author does concede that whether the suggested form of drafting could stand up to judicial scrutiny, is undecided.

equity of redemption is implied, such a construction is likely to result in the inference that the parties intended to create a security interest, rather than a trust.

(iii) Assignment by junior creditor to third party assignees

6–35   A question arises as to whether an assignment by a junior creditor of the junior debt to a third party assignee enables the assignee to take free from the subordination trust arrangements.[48] Here, the law pertaining to the assignment of debt applies. In Chapter 7 on Debt Factoring, it is explained how a third party can take an assignment of debt and obtain priority over a previous assignee provided that the third party was (1) bona fide unaware of the prior assignment, and (2) the first to give notice to the debtor of the assignment.[49] Where a debt instrument includes provisions indicating that it is the subject of a subordination trust, this conflict will not arise. However, as many debt instruments will not have such provision, a bona fide assignee could conceivably take the junior debt free from a subordination trust provided (a) that the assignee was unaware of that prior interest at the time of the assignment, and (b) its assignment was the first interest in the debt to be notified to the debtor company. In other words, the principles of the law of debt factoring may well apply, such that if the junior creditor assigned the junior debt to an assignee without informing the assignee of the existence of the prior equitable interest (the subordination trust in favour of the senior creditor), then priority in the debt depends on which party[50] first gave notice of their interest to the debtor.[51]

In order to obviate this danger, the senior creditor would be well advised to notify the debtor company of the existence of the subordination trust declared in its favour by the junior creditor, before the junior creditor has the opportunity to attempt to assign any interests in the junior debt to third party assignees. Requiring the debtor company to be a party to the subordination agreement effectively conveys such notice.

---

[48] See para. 6–15 above where assignment and subordination are distinguished.

[49] For the purpose of deciding priority between competing assignments, all assignments are treated as if they are equitable interests under s.28(6) Supreme Court of Judicature (Ireland) Act 1877.

[50] *i.e.* the bona fide assignee or the senior creditor.

[51] See further Chap. 7 on the law of Debt Factoring. In *Pfeiffer Weinkellerei Weinenkauf Gmbh & Co. v. Arbuthnot Factors* [1988] 1 W.L.R.150, it was held that priority as between competing assignments in a debt depends not on whether the competing interests are legal or equitable, but rather on which assignee bona fide (i.e. unaware of the existence of the other) was the first to give notice of their interest to the debtor.

6–36 Where the subordination trust is over the *proceeds* of the debt, rather than the debt itself, the further question arises as to whether an assignment by the junior creditor of the proceeds to an assignee is tantamount to an assignment of the debt itself such that the assignee could get priority over the senior creditor if the assignee was the first to give notice to the debtor company? Were this to be the case, a senior creditor could protect its priority under the subordination trust against such assignees by ensuring that the debtor company had notice first of its subordination trust interest. It is suggested that were the position to be otherwise – such that notice to the debtor company of the trust over the proceeds would not confer priority on the senior creditor over a subsequent assignee of the debt itself – then severe difficulties could arise for the senior creditor. In this event, there would be no fool-proof way for a senior creditor to ensure protection of its priority unless the assignee can be put on notice of the trust at the time of the assignment.[52]

(c) Contractual Turn-Over Subordination and its advantages

6–37 The other method by which a turn-over subordination can be effected is by way of *contractual turn-over subordination*. The junior creditor and the senior creditor agree by way of a contract that in the event of the debtor company going into liquidation, the junior creditor will prove for the junior debt and then pay over to the senior creditor an amount *equal to* the amount of junior debt recovered. This sum may or may not satisfy the senior debt outstanding.

6–38 Unlike the subordination trust, this form of turn-over subordination being based on contract, does not impute beneficial rights to the senior creditor over the junior debt in the manner that a trust would. Consequently, it is not often used in preference to a subordination trust as a primary means of achieving the necessary legal framework for a turn-over subordination. However, it will often be used as a back-up to a subordination trust or contractual contingent subordination so that the senior creditor will still have some possibility of recourse to the junior creditor should either trust or contingency fail or be invalidated.

---

[52] Wood, *op. cit.* at n.1 above. Wood suggests that while the law is far from being clear on this point, the former of the two possibilities considered above is probably the correct one. On the other hand, if the latter possibility is correct – such that only the actual putting on notice of the assignee at the time of assignment of proceeds could preserve the senior creditor's priority arising out of the trust – then matters would be very difficult for senior creditors. This is because many forms of subordinated debt (such as bonds) are frequently intended to be fully marketable and consequently there will be no indication on their face that they are already the subject of a subordination trust.

Therefore, in that sense it can be quite commonly used, but not as the primary turn-over subordination tool. Contractual turn-over subordination has several advantages.

(i) Senior creditor may receive double payment

6–39　A senior creditor will expect to receive repayments from the debtor company in respect of the senior debt. In addition, under the contractual turn-over arrangement, in the event of the debtor going into liquidation, the senior creditor can also expect to receive payments from the junior debtor of sums equal to any amounts recovered by the junior creditor from the debtor company's liquidator in respect of the junior debt. In this sense, the senior creditor receives a 'double' payment. However, whether the senior creditor actually receives this double payment from the junior creditor is a risk that the senior creditor has to take. This is because the success of this form of subordination will be very much dependent on firstly, whether the junior creditor succeeds in recovering from the liquidator and secondly, whether or not the junior creditor remains solvent.

(ii) Avoids pari passu concerns

6–40　As with a subordination trust, a major advantage of contractual turn-over subordination is that the junior creditor will prove for the junior debt on the debtor company's liquidation on an equal footing *pari passu* with all other unsecured creditors. Consequently, this method avoids any objection that it constitutes an attempt to interfere with the statutory *pari passu* rule.

(iii) Avoids "inadvertent" security concerns

6–41　One possible advantage of this method over subordination trusts is that there is little concern that the arrangement could be susceptible to challenge on the grounds that it creates some kind of inadvertent security interest by default. As discussed above,[53] such a concern is always in the background where a trust is used as the trust might be construed as creating some kind of problematic security interest (instead of a genuine trust interest). Contractual subordination does not present such a risk, as the junior creditor is merely contracting to pay over to the senior creditor an amount *equal to* the amount it recovers in respect of the junior debt from the debtor company, rather than creating proprietary rights over the junior debt in the senior creditor's favour. Hence, the risk of a security interest being implied can effectively be discounted.

---

[53] See para. 6–32 *et seq.*

(iv) Contract concept more widely recognised

6–42   Often a difficulty with international subordinations is that some jurisdictions' law cannot recognise the concept of a trust. Consequently, contract may be more appropriate.[54]

(d) Contractual Turn-Over Subordination: disadvantages

(i) Senior creditor has no beneficial interest in junior debt

6–43   Unlike a subordination trust, the senior creditor has no beneficial "proprietary" claim over the junior debt. Consequently, the senior creditor will merely be just another debtor of the junior creditor. In this sense therefore, this form of subordination will only be of use from the senior creditor's point of view if the junior creditor remains solvent and fulfills its contractual obligations to the senior creditor.

Furthermore, because the senior creditor has no beneficial interest in the junior debt, the senior creditor is not in a strong position to restrain the junior creditor from assigning the junior debt to a third party, even where specific prohibitions on assignment were agreed.[55] This is because, in all probability, the assignee would have no notice that the debt was non-assignable.[56] Indeed, even if the assignee had such notice, that would not prevent the assignee taking the debt as owner, as the senior creditor would have no beneficial rights in the debt. Consequently, the only remedy that the senior creditor would have would be to sue the junior creditor for breach of contract,[57] a remedy that might be well-nigh worthless if the junior creditor was insolvent.

In reality, what will really be of concern to the senior creditor will be whether the assignee feels bound to honour the subordination. The risk that the senior creditor faces is that the assignee might attempt to accelerate payment of the debt from the debtor company and thereby leave the senior creditor with no recourse to the assignee in the event of the debtor company's subsequent liquidation. In this scenario, the senior creditor would argue that the assignee took the debt subject to equities, *i.e.* subject to the conditions attaching to the debt under the subordination in favour of the senior creditor. Hence, the senior creditor

---

[54] *Re Maxwell Communications Corporation plc* [1993] 1 W.L.R. 1402.

[55] While the U.K. courts take the view that express prohibitions on assignment are effective, the Irish courts take a different view: *International Factors Ltd v. Midland International Ltd*, unreported, High Court, Murphy J., December 9, 1993 discussed further in Chap. 7.

[56] As noted earlier, in various types of subordination, prohibition on assignment will not be evident on the document evidencing the debt.

[57] Or the assignee for inducing breach of contract.

will argue that the assignee is bound to honour the subordination's strict terms.[58]

(ii) Turn-over may breach Company Law

6–44   Where the junior creditor enters into a turn-over contract to pay sums to the senior creditor, care should be taken to ensure that company law provisions are not breached, *e.g.* fraudulent or reckless trading, fraudulent preference. This could have serious consequences for both junior and senior creditor.[59]

(2) Contractual (Contingent) Subordination

(a) Contractual Turn-Over Subordination distinguished

6–45   The other principal method of debt subordination is *contractual contingent subordination*. Care should be taken not to confuse it with another type of contractual subordination – contractual *turn-over* subordination.

Contractual contingent subordination is very different to contractual turn-over subordination. In contractual turn-over subordination, the junior creditor agrees with the senior creditor that it shall claim due debts and then turn-over to the senior creditor an amount equal to the amount of junior debt recovered. However, in contractual contingent subordination, the junior creditor agrees with the debtor company that repayment of debt owed to the junior creditor is subject first to repayment of the senior creditor's debt in full.

6–46   Such an arrangement may be complete or inchoate. Where the subordination is *complete*, the junior creditor renounces all entitlement to receive repayment from the debtor company pre-liquidation, and all entitlement to be repaid *pari passu* with the senior creditor in the event of the debtor company's subsequent liquidation. Consequently, if the senior creditor does not get fully repaid, the junior creditor will receive nothing. On the other hand, where the subordination is *inchoate*, the junior creditor may, depending on its terms, receive some repayments on the junior debt pre-liquidation as the subordination will only come into effect upon the occurrence of a specified trigger event. Should the debtor company subsequently enter into liquidation, the junior creditor's position is the same as in the case of complete subordination because the junior creditor will have agreed not to be entitled to receive any repayments *pari passu* with the senior creditor. Con-

---

[58] See further Chap. 7 where the issue of assignment of debt and subject to equities is further considered.
[59] See section III of this chapter below.

sequently, if the senior creditor does not get fully repaid, the junior creditor will receive nothing.

6–47 Thus, although the *inchoately* subordinated junior creditor is in a better position pre-liquidation than a *completely* subordinated junior creditor, both are in the same position once the debtor company goes into liquidation. This is so because in the event of debtor company insolvency, the senior creditor, as an unsecured creditor, will be entitled to repayment *pari passu* with other unsecured creditors. The junior creditor's subordination in favour of the senior creditor now effectively places the junior creditor behind not only the senior creditor but also all other unsecured creditors' whose claims rank *pari passu* with the senior creditor's claim. In this event, the junior creditor therefore has no entitlement to be repaid until all unsecured creditors (including the senior creditor) have been repaid in full.

(b) Compatibility with **pari passu**: *the source of the confusion*

6–48 There is nothing objectionable about contractual contingent subordination while the debtor company trades as a going concern. However, due to misunderstanding of judicial pronouncements on the scope of the statutory *pari passu* rule, doubts arose about the lawfulness of contractual contingent subordination in the event of the debtor company going into liquidation. This confusion resulted in conflicting judicial decisions in other jurisdictions and uncertainty for unsecured creditors who wanted to enter into contractual contingent subordination arrangements. This confusion could have been avoided if (1) the irrelevance of the *pari passu* principle to genuine subordination arrangements had been appreciated earlier, or (2) legislative change had been made to clarify the situation.

This confusion has now been resolved such that the legality of this important method of debt subordination is no longer in question where an appropriately drafted contingency clause is used. However, it is important to have an appreciation of how the confusion arose in order to ensure that such problems do not arise in future.

6–49 The confusion arose in the following context. Once a company commences liquidation, the liquidator is obliged to meet the claims of unsecured creditors on a *pari passu* basis,[60] *i.e.* all unsecured creditors of a company must be treated equally on a winding-up, subject to the payment of preferential debts as determined by the Companies Acts. This rule is designed to protect the public good. However, in some

---

[60] s.275(1) of the Companies Act 1963.

quarters, because of the broad nature of judicical pronouncements to the effect that the *pari passu* rule could not be "contracted out of",[61] the view was taken that arrangements such as contractual contingent subordination were incompatible with *pari passu*.[62] Such a view was based on a misunderstanding of the nature of contractual contingent subordination.

In this respect it was felt that contractual contingent subordination was legally suspect as it could be viewed as being tantamount to an instruction from the junior creditor to the liquidator not to pay the junior creditor until the senior creditor had been paid first. Consequently, the subordination arrangement (it could be argued), was an attempt to prevent the liquidator meeting all unsecured creditors' claims on a *pari passu* basis. Such a concern was seen to be exacerbated by the fact that as the senior creditor would have to be paid on a *pari passu* basis with all other creditors, effectively therefore, the junior creditor would not be satisfied until after all other unsecured creditors claims had been fully satisfied. Hence, this method of subordination was suspected of being an attempt to interfere, by way of a private contract, with the application of the statutory *pari passu* principle. Some judicial decisions considered such subordinations based on *contract* to constitute an illegal attempt to "contract out of" *pari passu* distribution.[63]

As will be seen below, the wisdom of such a view has now been severely questioned. It has been convincingly demonstrated, both in the courts[64] and in the literature[65] that, concerns as to the validity of attempts by private contractual agreement to "interfere" with the application of *pari passu* principle, may in fact have been misplaced.

(c) The contingency

6–50   Before considering such issues further, it is necessary to elaborate on the requirement for a contingency in this form of subordination. It

---

[61] See *National Westminster Bank v. Halsowen Presswork and Assemblies Ltd* [1972] A.C. 785 which concerned the U.K. bankruptcy rules and statutory rights relating to set-off where Lord Kilbrandon at p.824 held that the statutory rules applicable to the administration of claims in bankruptcy could not be contracted out of; and *British Eagle International Airlines Ltd. v. Air France* [1975] 2 All E.R. 390, *per* Lord Cross of Chelsea (delivering the 3:2 majority opinion) at p. 411, who held that there could be no contracting out of the *pari passu* rule. Neither case, however, involved genuine contractual subordination arrangements. Note how Vinelott J. reconsidered both decisions in *Re Maxwell Communications Corp. plc* [1993] I.W.L.R. 1402. See para. 6–58 below.

[62] See Goode, *Legal Problems of Credit and Security* (2nd ed.), pp. 95–97 where this is considered.

[63] *Re Orion Sound Ltd* [1979] 2 N.Z.L.R. 574.

[64] See below at paras 6–55—6–59.

[65] Wood; Johnston *op. cit.* at n.1 above: also para. 6–55.

is submitted by Wood that a way to get around the risk that a contract of subordination might be construed as an unlawful attempt to evade the *pari passu* regime is to ensure that it contains a contingency: to the effect that if the debtor goes into liquidation, the junior creditor debt will be expressly conditional on the debtor being able to repay the senior creditor debt.[66] Hence the inclusion of the word "contingent" in the description of this form of subordination. Where this is the case, then, where the debtor company is totally insolvent, the senior creditor will not recover and thus neither will the junior creditor. On the other hand, where the debtor company has some realiseable assets, then the unsecured creditors (including the senior creditor) will be *pari passu* repaid so much in the pound, but again the junior creditor will receive nothing as the junior debt is contingent on the senior creditor being repaid in full. Thus, where the debtor company is unable to satisfy the senior debt fully, then the junior creditor effectively has renounced the junior debt. Only if the senior creditor has been repaid in full, will the junior creditor be able to claim the right to recover in respect of its debt from the liquidator.[67]

Wood is also of the view that while there is always a risk that the drafting of the contingency might cause the arrangements to breach the statutory *pari passu* principle, nevertheless, a properly drafted contingency should minimise this risk. Notwithstanding the adoption of express legislation in Ireland, which recognizes that subordination arrangements do not violate the *pari passu* principle, this concern about the use of an appropriately drafted contingency clause remains. This will be considered further below.[68]

6–51   One further issue that arises in connection with the contingency concerns the proving of the junior debt, and the value it will be given by the liquidator on a winding-up. Section 283 of the Companies Act 1963 provides, *inter alia*, that contingent debts are provable on a

---

[66] *op. cit.* at n.1 at p. 45.
[67] Note that the learned author, the leading commentator in the area, also usefully points out that if the junior debt is *secured*, then the use of a contingency should be modified. This is because the operation of the contingency may prevent recovery by the junior creditor even though the security used is sufficient. Therefore, he suggests that the contingency should not apply to the extent that the junior debt is recoverable out of the security.
[68] See para. 6–61 *et seq*. S.275 of the Companies Act 1963 (as amended by s.132 Companies Act 1990) stipulates *inter alia* that subordination agreements do not violate the statutory *pari passu* principle. However, as will be seen below, although the amended section makes it clear that genuine debt subordination does not violate *pari passu*, the section cannot be used to validate arrangements which, while having the appearance of subordination arrangements, are in fact devices which seek to remove assets already vested in the liquidator in violation of *pari passu*.

winding-up, and that a just estimate should be made as to their value. Where the contingency has been properly drafted, the value of the junior creditor's contingent debt should be nil, or merely a nominal amount. Alternatively, the subordination arrangements could contain a commitment by the junior creditor not to prove for the junior debt until after the senior debtor has been paid in full. However, as Johnston notes, this may be difficult to enforce and in any event the remedy may only be damages (rather than an injunction), which may be worthless if the junior creditor itself is not in a healthy financial state. Hence, all the more reason why the contingency should be suitably drafted in order that the value of the contingent debt is merely nominal. Therefore, even if the junior creditor does prove for the junior debt in defiance of the subordination agreement, proving the debt should not prejudice the subordination. Section 283 further provides that in the case of insolvent winding-up, the laws of bankruptcy will apply.[69]

(d) Judicial clarification

6–52 Although the House of Lords decision, *British Eagle International Airlines Ltd v. Air France*[70] did not concern debt subordination, unfortunately, the decision was subsequently incorrectly and overwidely interpreted to the effect that the principles it enunciated were perceived as condemning contractual contingent debt subordination as illegal. In order to appreciate how this regrettable confusion occurred, it is first necessary to have some understanding of the background to the case.

A number of airlines operated a clearing house system, to settle their accounts with each other, by using the International Air Travel Association as a clearing house. Instead of making an individual payment to each other for every single transaction conducted between themselves for the provision of passenger and cargo transfer services, each airline had an account with the clearing house to which all credits and debits were entered *vis-à-vis* other airlines using the system. At the end of each balancing period, the clearing house would either owe, or be owed, particular sums. All of the airlines which took part in this system agreed contractually that by adhering to this system, they could not, in law, claim debts due from the other participating airlines. Instead they would claim from the clearing house.

---

[69] See also s.284 of the Companies Act 1963 which elaborates on this. S.75 of the Bankruptcy Act 1988 provides that all debts and liabilities including contingent claims can be proved in bankruptcy.

[70] [1975] 2 All E.R. 390. (Note that the Companies Act 1989, Part VII, attempts to obviate the *pari passu* objections raised to clearing house arrangements in *British Eagle* by taking such arrangements outside the U.K.'s statutory liquidation distribution rules.)

According to the House of Lords, this clearing house system was based on sound commercial principles and operated in good faith. The Lords also accepted that the clearing house system did not intend to deliberately interfere with the *pari passu* satisfaction of a member airline's unsecured creditors in the event of a member's winding-up. Nevertheless, the Lords held the system to be illegal and unenforceable because it was contrary to *pari passu*.

6–53 At issue was the claim of the liquidator of British Eagle Airlines to the sum of £6,000. The liquidator claimed that this sum due from Air France to British Eagle was his to claim for the purpose of satisfying British Eagle's liabilities to its creditors. The lower courts dismissed the liquidator's claim, holding that the airlines had clearly and expressly agreed not to be liable to each other once they became part of the clearing house system. Any monies in the clearing house system or debts owed through it were for the benefit of the system's participant airlines, not the creditors of British Eagle. On appeal to the House of Lords the essential issue was whether British Eagle (through its liquidator), could still claim that it itself was legally owed the debt and thus entitled to collect it in order to distribute it to its creditors notwithstanding its contractual membership of the clearing house system. The liquidator claimed the United Kingdom statutory *pari passu* principle would be violated if the clearing house system was upheld, as the debt could not be applied for the benefit of all the company's unsecured creditors, but only the clearing house creditors.

In a 3:2 decision, the Lords held that the contract setting up the clearing house system was a violation of the *pari passu* principle which is a rule of public policy, given effect by the law. Hence the clearing house system, which was based on contractual agreement between the airlines, was void. To permit otherwise, according to the Lords, would be tantamount to saying that the distribution of a company's assets (in this instance debts owed to the company) could be determined by some arrangement other than the *pari passu* arrangement which existed for the protection of company creditors.

6–54 If the scope of the Lords' decision was clearly confined to this domain, there would be no conceptual problem as the statutory *pari passu* principle and the reason for its existence (to protect creditors in a winding-up) is well recognised.[71] However, the decision was subsequently interpreted in some quarters as being authority for the wider proposition that *any* attempt to subordinate company debts constitutes a *per se* infringement of *pari passu*, and therefore is void. Thus, after this

---

[71] Goode, *Legal problems of Credit and Security op. cit.* at n.62 above.

case, doubts remained about the efficacy and indeed validity of contractual subordination attempts.[72]

In a New Zealand decision, *Re Orion Sound*[73] the New Zealand Supreme Court had to consider the legality of a deed that had been entered into by a company's creditors allowing the company to freeze their accounts. The immediate objective was to allow priority to be given to subsequent creditors so that they could be paid in full. Ultimately, the company hoped that such arrangement would allow it trade out of its difficulties, so that the creditors who agreed to defer their claims would be paid subsequently. As not all of the creditors had formally indicated their acceptance in writing of the arrangements, when the company went into liquidation an issue arose as to whether this agreement was valid. *Inter alia*, it was held that the deed was inoperative because it represented, in the court's view, an attempt to contract out of the statutory mandatory *pari passu* regime. However, Mahon J. was urged by counsel to permit the deed to be given effect, on the basis that it is not incompatible with the statutory principle of pari passu if some creditors agree to defer their claims on the company and merely give other unsecured creditors a priority position.[74] Mahon J. rejected this submission, citing *British Eagle* as an authority for the proposition that there could be no contracting out of the statutory *pari passu* principle. Mahon J. then went on to hold that the debt deferral arrangement in the case before him constituted such an illegal attempt. It has been suggested that this decision is not correct on this point[75] as it is submitted that the debt deferral arrangement does not constitute a contracting out of the *pari passu* principle. Therefore, such subordination does not violate the principles set out in *British Eagle*.

The author would agree with this view. It would appear that the true ground for Mahon J.'s decision is that the arrangement was unenforceable because, as noted by the court, not all of the creditors had assented to it. It would be generally difficult to enforce arrangements of this type in situations where not all of the creditors had been involved or aware of it.[76]

Another decision which contains dicta supportive of the overwide

---

[72] Another Lords' decision cited in support of the overwide interpretation of *British Eagle* is *National Westminster Bank v. Halsowen Presswork and Assemblies Ltd* [1972] A.C. 785 where the House of Lords held that the statutory rule regarding the operation of set-off of debts on bankruptcy was mandatory and could not be altered by private contractual agreement.

[73] [1979] 2 N.Z.L.R. 574.

[74] *ibid.* at p. 578.

[75] Wood, *op. cit.*

[76] Aitken, "Liquidators and the Subordinated Loan", Company and Securities Law Journal (1987) Vol. 4, p.4.

interpretation of *British Eagle* is *Carreras Rothmans Ltd v. Freeman Matthews Treasure Ltd*[77] where Gibson J., while extolling the virtues of how a trust avoids *pari passu* objections, *obiter* expressed the view that the *pari passu* rule's operation cannot be altered by contract.[78] Consequently, as a result of judicial decisions along these lines, it was thought that contractual contingent debt subordination was suspect as being an attempt, by way of a contract, to contract out of *pari passu*.

6–55 However, not all courts accepted this view. In an Australian decision, *Horne v. Chester & Fein Property Developments Pty Ltd*[79] it was held that under Australian insolvency law the statutory *pari passu* principle is not offended where the deferment of a debt does not result in prejudice to the equal ranking of other creditors.

Another instructive case is the New Zealand case *Re Walker Construction Co Ltd*,[80] which although it predates *British Eagle*, appeared to take this alternative line also.[81] A company and its creditors agreed that debts incurred by the company in a certain period would be preferred and that debts incurred by the company prior to that would be deferred, all in the hope that this would assist the company to trade out of current difficulties. It was held that the creditors could validly agree to such an arrangement and that if they did, it would be unconscionable to allow them plead *pari passu* and thereby renege on their agreement to defer some of the debts. Thus, this case established that a creditor could by way of a contract agree to waive its right to invoke *pari passu* and a court would give effect to it where to do otherwise would be contrary to the legitimate interests of other creditors who might have supplied goods to the company on the understanding that existing creditors had contractually agreed not to invoke *pari passu*.

Leading commentator Wood submits that it is conceptually incorrect to assume that contractual contingent debt subordinations automatically offend the *pari passu* principle. They do not violate the principle because the object of *pari passu* is to ensure that one group of unsecured creditors is not paid ahead of the general body of unsecured creditors – whereas in a contractual contingent debt subordination, an unsecured creditor(s) merely agrees to rank behind the others. Sub-

---

[77] [1985] 1 All E.R. 155.
[78] However, upon closer inspection it becomes clear that the learned judge was in fact saying something that is in substance quite different, i.e. that a contract cannot be permitted to remove an asset from the hands of the liquidator if it was the company's at the commencement of the liquidation: *per* Costello J. in *Glow Heating Ltd v Eastern Health Board & Others* [1988] I.R. 110 at 119.
[79] [1987] A.C.L.R. 485.
[80] [1960] N.Z.L.R. 523.
[81] Note that in *Re Orion Sound* Mahon J. refused to follow the earlier (1960) New Zealand decision *Re Walker Construction*, instead "preferring" *British Eagle*.

mitting that the *British Eagle* case concerned a contract to take away an asset (a debt owed) of an insolvent company after liquidation had commenced, he considers the clearing house rules (the contract) constituted an attempt to snatch away the company's asset (the debt) after liquidation commenced. Accordingly, Wood concludes, *British Eagle* was properly concerned with preventing that occurring. Accordingly, *British Eagle* should not be interpreted as authority for the wider proposition that contractual contingent debt subordinations *per se* are a violation of the statutory *pari passu* rules.

6–56   The scope of *British Eagle* was considered in the Irish courts by Costello J. in *Glow Heating Ltd v. Eastern Health Board & Others* in 1988.[82] In this case, a building contractor ("the main contractor") went into liquidation. The plaintiff, a sub-contractor, sued the Eastern Health Board claiming its entitlement to be paid out of monies in the hands of the awarder of the building contract. A clause in the works contract provided that the EHB should pay monies due direct to the sub-contractors in the event that the main contractor had withheld monies (which had been paid to the main contractor on behalf of all of the sub-contractors by the awarder of the contract). The main contractor's liquidator claimed that this clause was an illegal contractual attempt to defeat the statutory *pari passu* principle, as it sought to divest the liquidator of funds already vested in the main contractor's hands in breach of the *pari passu* as provided for in section 275 of the Companies Act 1963.[83]

Costello J. held for the plaintiff.[84] He held that the liquidator took the property in the funds subject to the liabilities that affected it in the main contractor's hands.

Costello J. approved of *British Eagle* to the extent that it was, in his view, authority for the proposition that, if an asset is vested in a company at the commencement of liquidation and the effect of a contract would be to prevent the liquidator from dealing with such property other than on a *pari passu* basis, then, such a contract would be void because it would be contrary to public policy reflected in the statutory *pari passu* principle. Thus, Costello J. adopted the narrow

---

[82] [1988] I.R. 110.
[83] s.275 of the Companies Act 1963 which enunciates the *pari passu* principle. At the time of this decision (1988) s.275 had still not been amended by s.132 of the Companies Act 1990 which now makes it clear that genuine debt subordination arrangements do not violate *pari passu* (s.275(2)).
[84] According to the learned judge, the clause did not dispose of the main contractor's assets but instead imposed a contingent liability on the main contractor's entitlements such that its monies would suffer a reduction in the event of a specified default by the contractor.

interpretation of *British Eagle* as being the correct one. The learned judge then went on to examine the case before him in light of this. He found that the liquidator took the asset (the funds) under the terms of the contract subject to existing liabilities, defects or prior contingencies. Thus he made it clear that section 275 of the Companies Act 1963 (as it then was) did not render all contracts which *appear to* interfere with *pari passu* void. The effect of Costello's judgment thus was significant as his interpretation of *British Eagle* meant that genuine debt subordination did not violate *pari passu* (as expressed in section 275). So that there is no doubt in the matter, some two years later in 1990, section 275 was expressly amended to recognise that debt subordination does not violate *pari passu*.[85]

In *Glow Heating,* the funds were subject to a contingent liability which came into being before the liquidation, and therefore the liquidator took the funds subject to that prior liability. In such an event the asset was not the liquidator's to distribute on a *pari passu* basis. Hence, it could not be said that the contingency clause conflicted with the *pari passu* principle. Thus, while Costello J. did not apply *British Eagle* on the facts of the case, he did agree that it was authority for the proposition that if an asset – meaning a debt in this context – is the company's property at the commencement of the liquidation, then it must be available to the liquidator to distribute on a *pari passu* basis. Any contractual attempt to interfere with this would be an interference with the statutory principle and so would be contrary to public policy and void. It is submitted that this narrow interpretation of *British Eagle* is correct and that *British Eagle* does not provide authority for the wider proposition that all attempts to contractually subordinate debts are a violation *per se* of the *pari passu* principle.

6–57 In light of this clarified judicial assessment, it is interesting to note that *British Eagle* has been reassessed recently in the English courts. Noted commercial law expert, Vinelott J. has re-examined the question of whether *British Eagle* is authority for the wide proposition (that because it is not permissible to contract out of *pari passu*, contractual contingent debt subordinations are consequently a violation of the *pari passu* principle *per se*). In *Re Maxwell Communications Corporation plc*[86] the learned judge considered the whole issue of contractual debt subordination and *pari passu*. Maxwell Communications Corporation had guaranteed the debts of Maxwell Finance Jersey Ltd under certain bonds. Maxwell Communications Corporation's obligation to those

---

[85] See further below.

[86] [1993] 1 W.L.R. 1402; case comment by Fealy in (1993) C.L.J. pp.396–399 and by Bean, *The Company Lawyer* (1994) Vol. 15 No. 2, pp.52–54.

bondholders was subordinated until all other unsecured debts were paid. Maxwell Communications Corporation became insolvent and an administrator was appointed to restructure the Maxwell companies.

In this case, a key issue was whether the administrators of Maxwell Communications Corporation could exclude from a proposed senior creditor scheme of arrangement several unsecured subordinated creditors of Maxwell Communications Corporation, amongst them the bondholders. The subordinated creditors argued, relying on *British Eagle*, that the *pari passu* principle is mandatory on a company's insolvency and that it cannot be contracted out of. Consequently, they argued that as the debt subordination arrangement had been effected by a *contract*, the attempt to subordinate had been ineffectual in law. Vinelott J. noted that if English law would not give effect to contractual debt subordination, then the entire global restructuring of the Maxwell empire would be jeopardised. Swiss law and United States law recognised contractual debt subordination.[87]

6–58 Vinelott J. held that the *pari passu* principle did not prohibit contractual contingent debt subordination. In order to reach such a conclusion, the learned judge considered *inter alia*, the *Halsowen*[88] and *British Eagle*[89] decisions. In *Halsowen* the House of Lords had held that the mutual set-off rules in the Bankruptcy Act 1914 which incorporated *pari passu* principles were mandatory and could not be circumvented by private arrangements. In other words, contracting out of the statutory insolvency rules was not permitted. The learned judge took the view that this decision has been overwidely interpreted such that it was considered that contractual contingent debt subordination was tantamount to a contracting out of *pari passu*. The learned judge took the view that the statutory principle of *pari passu* was not offended where a creditor agreed with the debtor that a debt would be subordinated. Explaining that a creditor who refuses to prove its debt in a winding up does not violate *pari passu, a fortiori*, why should the creditor not be able to agree to merely subordinate payment to it by the debtor company if that was the creditor's wish? In Vinelott J.'s view, as the former does not violate the *pari passu* principle, then he could see no reason of public policy why the latter should either.

6–59 The learned judge then proceeded to examine *British Eagle* and took the view that what was at issue in *British Eagle* was the way in

[87] It is interesting at this point to note that a subordination trust had not been used because the governing law was Swiss law and under Swiss civil law the concept of a trust presents certain difficulties.
[88] [1972] A.C. 785.

which one group of unsecured creditors had attempted, by way of a contract, to elevate themselves above other unsecured creditors[90] once liquidation had begun. Furthermore, he stated that the House of Lords had been quite correct to prevent such an attempt from succeeding as otherwise it would create havoc with the public policy of the law which was to rank all unsecured creditors equally in a liquidation. In adopting this view of *British Eagle*, Vinelott J. thereby favoured the narrow interpretation of *British Eagle*. Thus, in effect, *British Eagle* was distinguished from the *Maxwell* case on the basis that the issue before him – whether a contractual debt subordination *per se* violated *pari passu* – was an issue that *British Eagle* was not concerned with. Vinelott J. stated:

> "In my judgment I am not compelled by the decisions of the House of Lords in the *Halsowen* and *British Eagle* cases ... to conclude that a contract between a company and a creditor, providing for the debt due to the creditor to be subordinated in the insolvent winding up of the company to other unsecured debt, is rendered void by the necessary legislation."[91]

Thus, he held the fact that a key English law of insolvency principle – *pari passu* cannot be contracted out of – did not prevent the contractual subordination of debt. He also supported his decision by adverting to the fact that as the courts were now prepared to hold that subordination trusts did not violate the *pari passu* principle, there was no good reason of policy why the use of contractual subordinations should not be recognised. Otherwise, the law would be giving more importance to form rather than to substance. In addition, the learned judge took cognizance of *dicta* from other jurisdictions where contractual debt subordination was not seen to be prohibited by mandatory *pari passu* rules.[92] Finally, the learned judge also opined that in light of his interpretation of the caselaw, there was no good reason why English law respected subordination effected by way of a trust, whereas a subordination effected by way of a contract was questionable. While a trust and a contract are very different mechanisms, in the context of debt subordination, the objective of both is similar. Fealy[93] suggests that as the *Maxwell* decision is a decision of the English High Court and *British Eagle* a decision of the House of Lords, English law should be amended so as to explicitly recognise contractual debt subordination as being valid *vis-à-vis* the *pari passu* rule.[94]

---

[89] [1975] 2 All E.R. 390.
[90] By reference to the clearing house agreement: see paras 6–53 *et seq*. above.
[91] [1993] 1 W.L.R. 1402 at 1416.
[92] *e.g. Horne v. Chester and Fein* [1987] A.C.L.R. 485.
[93] (1993) C.L.J. pp. 396–399.
[94] Other common law jurisdictions that have taken this route apart from Ireland are the USA, France, New Zealand and Australia.

(e) Legislative clarification

6–60   In 1990 section 275 of the Companies Act 1963[95] was amended
by section 132 of the Companies Act 1990. A new subsection (2) was
inserted into section 275 expressly recognising that creditors can agree
to subordinate their debts in favour of other creditors without violating
the *pari passu* principle. It provides as follows:

> (1) Subject to the provisions of this Act as to preferential payments, the
> property of a company on its winding up –
>
>> (a)   shall, subject to subsection (2), be applied in satisfaction of its
>> liabilities *pari passu*, and
>>
>> (b)   shall, subject to such application, and unless the articles otherwise
>> provide, be distributed among the members according to their
>> rights and interests in the company.
>
> (2) Nothing in paragraph (a) of subsection (1) shall in any way affect any
> rights or obligations of the company or any other person arising as a
> result of any agreement entered into (whether before or after the
> commencement of *section 132 of the Companies Act 1990*) by any person
> under which any particular liability of the company to any general
> creditor is postponed in favour of or subordinated to the rights or claims
> of any other person to whom the company may be in any way liable.
>
> (3) In subsection (2) –
> "liability" includes a contingent liability; and
> "person" includes a class of persons.

In effect therefore, section 275(2) now expressly permits any agreement
under which any particular liability of the company to any creditor is
postponed in favour of the rights or claims of any other creditor,
notwithstanding the *pari passu* principle (section 275(1)). A creditor may
waive its entitlement to be treated in the same way as other unsecured
creditors without the arrangements running the risk of being accused
of offending the statutory *pari passu* principle.[96]

---

[95] s.275 originally read:
"Subject to the provisions of this Act as to preferential payments, the property
of a company shall, on its winding up, be applied in satisfaction of its liabilities
pari passu, and, subject to such application shall, unless the articles otherwise
provide, be distributed among the members according to their rights and
interests in the company."

[96] s.275(1) provides, *inter alia,* that in a voluntary liquidation, the liabilities and
debts of the company shall be satisfied on a *pari passu* basis. According to Forde,
Law of Company Insolvency this rule also applies on a compulsory liquidation
(*Att. Gen. of New Zealand v. McMillan & Lockwood Ltd* [1991] 1 N.Z.L.R. 53) and
Lynch, *et al. op.cit.* at n.6 take a similar view citing s.284 of the Companies Act
1963 in support as it provides that in the event of a winding-up of an insolvent

6–61   However, although section 275(2) now removes any doubt that genuine contractual subordination agreements do not violate the *pari passu* principle, care should be taken to ensure that the arrangement concerned is in fact a *genuine* subordination agreement. Section 275(2) cannot validate an arrangement that seeks to prevent the liquidator from distributing, on a *pari passu* basis, a debt asset which is properly vested in the company at the time of winding-up. Such an asset must be available to the liquidator to distribute to the general body of creditors, as opposed to only those creditors claiming the benefit of the "subordination" agreement.

6–62   Costello J.'s decision in *Glow Heating* is not affected by section 275(2). Apart from its usefulness in illuminating *British Eagle*, the decision is helpful as it illustrates the type of examination that is required when seeking to ascertain whether an arrangement is a genuine subordination arrangement meriting the protection of section 275(2), or whether it is a covert attempt to subvert the *pari passu* principle. *Glow Heating* was a pre-1990 Act decision and in order to assess the true nature of the contract in that case, Costello J. examined two issues. First, whether the clause in question constituted a contractual imposition of a liability on the debtor company's monies before liquidation, thereby preventing the liquidator from claiming unencumbered rights to such monies once liquidation commenced. Second, whether, on the other hand, the clause constituted an attempt to divest assets, already fully vested in the debtor company, out of the liquidator's hands once liquidation had commenced. If it were the *latter* then the *pari passu* principle would prevent the arrangement taking effect. In *Glow Heating* Costello J. held, on the facts, that the first situation prevailed and thus *pari passu* was irrelevant. The enactment of section 275(2) in 1990 would therefore not affect Costello J.'s decision as his decision recognised in effect the irrelevance of *pari passu* in the first

---

company, the same rules shall apply as apply in bankruptcy *vis-à-vis* the rights of creditors.

[97] At p.120 of the judgement, Costello J held: "The House of Lords decision (British Eagle) in no way conflicts with the well established principle of insolvency law that a liquidator takes the company's property subject to the liabilities which affected it in the company's hands. Neither the main contract nor the sub-contract in this case can properly be regarded as a contract for the disposal of an asset of the company, and so the contracts are not ones subject to the criticisms applied in *British Eagle International Airlines v Companie National Air France* [1975] 1 W.L.R. 758. It is clear that clause 55(a) of the main contract imposes a contingent liability on an asset of the main contract or. . . . The liquidator, in my opinion, took the retention fund subject to this liability. Neither contract in my view involved an attempt to contract out of the provision of s.275, and neither is therefore contrary to public policy."

situation and thus is consistent with the present version of section 275(2). This is because both the section as amended and the judgment[97] recognise that a genuine subordination, as described, does not arouse *pari passu* concerns.[98] Of course, if an arrangement sought to remove an asset, vested in the liquidator, from the liquidator, then neither *Glow Heating* nor section 275(2) would save it from invalidity.

6–63 By legislating expressly in this area (thereby dispelling invalidity doubts), similar problems to those that have arisen in other jurisdictions should not arise in this jurisdiction, thereby increasing certainty for unsecured creditors who wish to enter into effectual subordination arrangements *vis-à-vis* a common corporate debtor.

(3) Turn-Over Subordinations and Contractual Contingent Subordination – a comparison

6–64 In a turn-over subordination, the senior creditors benefit from the turnover of monies from the junior creditors, in effect therefore receiving a double payment, because, not only do the senior creditors receive repayments from the debtor company in respect of the senior debt, but in addition, the junior creditors turn-over repayments received in respect of the junior debt.[99] On the other hand, in a contractual contingent subordination no such double payment is possible as the junior creditor has no obligation to turn-over to the senior creditor because the junior creditor will not be receiving anything in the event of the debtor company's liquidation until the senior debt has been repaid in full. Even if the latter arrangements were inchoate – in which event the junior creditor would receive some form of repayments pre-liquidation – the junior creditor would be under no obligation to turn them over to the senior creditor.

6–65 With contractual turn-over subordination, there is always the

---

[98] On the other hand, sums held under a trust are recognised as being free from *pari passu*-type concerns because a sum which is held under any kind of trust for a specific purpose, is not available for distribution by a liquidator and thus it cannot be subject to the application of the *pari passu* rule or to objections that it interferes with the rule's application: *Carreras Rothmans Ltd v.Freeman Matthews Treasure Ltd* [1985] 1 All E.R. 155. Note that while Carreras did not involve a subordination trust *per se*, the principle is just as applicable to demonstrate why subordination trusts cannot be accused of violating the statutory *pari passu* principle. See section II of this chapter above.

[99] This would be the case where the form of turn-over is the subordination trust. Where the other form of turn-over is used, contractual turn-over subordination, then the turn-over is not of the actual repayments received by the junior creditor, but rather of sums equivalent to such repayments.

risk that the junior creditor's insolvency will jeopardize the turn-over, whereas with contractual contingent subordination the senior creditor will receive its repayments directly from the debtor company without junior creditor involvement.

6–66 In a turnover subordination, the junior creditors are only subordinate to the senior creditors. Whereas in a contractual contingent subordination the junior creditors are subordinate to both the senior creditors and also all creditors entitled to participate *pari passu* with the senior creditors because the junior creditors agree not to be paid until after the senior creditors are paid. Therefore, in the event of debtor insolvency, as the senior creditors are merely unsecured creditors and thus will only be paid on a *pari passu* basis with *all* other unsecured creditors, the junior creditors can only hope to be paid once this *pari passu* distribution has been completed.

The issue of whether a debt subordination might violate the *pari passu* principle does not arise in regard to turnover subordinations because the junior creditors prove their debts with the debtor company on a *pari passu* basis along with all of the other creditors including the senior creditors. On the other hand, in a contractual contingent subordination, the junior creditors agree not to accept any payment from the company until the senior creditors have been fully paid. It is for this reason that until recently, doubts arose that such arrangements might be contrary to public policy.

6–67 Neither contractual contingent nor contractual turn-over subordinations should give rise to the issue of whether a security interest requiring registration has been inadvertently created by the parties. However, this issue could arise in the case of an inappropriately drafted subordination trust. This might arise where the "trust" was drafted so that, in substance, the junior creditors make a security assignment of the *entire* junior debt or its proceeds in favour of the senior creditors, instead of the junior creditors agreeing to hold in trust for the senior creditors an amount equal to the senior debt outstanding. Where this happens, a charge may well be created, as the junior creditors will be entitled to claim back any surplus from the senior creditors in excess of the senior debt amount. Therefore it is advised that, when drafting the trust document, one should ensure that the trust obliges the junior creditors to hold on trust for the senior creditors amounts up to the amount of the senior debt outstanding, as opposed to the entire junior debt. Where a charge has been inadvertently created, then apart from the fact that it achieves something other than what was intended, it may further require registration under section 99 of the Companies Act 1963.

6–68 With a subordination trust, the fact that the senior creditor may not be a party to the arrangement does not prevent the senior creditor from taking legal action to restrain the junior creditor from departing from the terms of the trust. Lack of privity is not a barrier to the taking of legal ation against a junior creditor who chooses to depart from the terms of the trust. However where practicable, the senior creditor will attempt to become a party to the subordination trust agreement itself. By contrast, in contractual contingent subordination, the senior creditor will be less able to restrain the junior creditor or the debtor company from departing from the terms of the subordination because the senior creditor typically is not a party to the arrangements. Thus, in order to strengthen his position, the senior creditor will encourage the junior creditor and debtor company to set up an estoppel in his favour by the making of a covenant not to alter the terms of the subordination arrangements, on the basis that they are aware that it is only because of the subordination that the senior creditor continues to grant fresh credit to the debtor company in the first place. Such covenant would be part of the debtor company/junior creditor subordination contract. While this may give some comfort to the senior creditor, there is no guarantee that it will act as a sufficient deterrent to deter either junior creditor or debtor company from departing from the terms of the subordination.[100]

III. SUBORDINATION: SOME COMPANY LAW ISSUES

6–69 Depending on the particular method of debt subordination chosen, one or other or all of the parties (debtor company, junior creditor and senior creditor) should take care to ensure that company law is not violated by the debt subordination arrangements. Of particular relevance in this regard are the provisions relating to fraudulent trading, reckless trading and fraudulent preference. As such provisions have been amply considered from a general company law perspective in other works, it is not proposed to duplicate such efforts.[101] However, it

---

[100] Wood, *op. cit.* at n.1 suggests at p. 276 that this covenant constitutes an "attempt to create an estoppel in favour of the senior creditors who rely on the [subordination] Agreement". While that learned commentator does not suggest it is foolproof, at least its presence in the subordination agreement may encourage the debtor company and junior creditor not to breach the terms of the subordination to the detriment of the senior creditor.

[101] See Forde, *Company Law* (2nd ed., Mercier Press, Dublin, 1992); Keane, *Company Law in the Republic of Ireland* (2nd ed., Butterworths, Dublin, 1991); Courtney, *The Law of Private Companies* (Butterworths, Dublin, 1994); Lynch, *et al, op. cit.* at n.6 above.

may be useful to analyse their relevance in the specific context of their potential impact on debt subordination. At the outset however, it should be emphasised that, in general, instances of successful enforcement of fraudulent and reckless trading have been quite rare.

FRAUDULENT TRADING

6–70 Depending on which method of debt subordination is chosen, the possibility may arise that either the debtor company, the senior creditor or the junior creditor could be found to have engaged in fraudulent trading contrary to the Companies Act 1963. However, while the following discussion no doubt will be of interest to parties to debt subordination arrangements, it should be noted that to date, fraudulent trading has only been found by the courts to exist where there was obviously clearly fraudulent activity being pursued.

Under section 297(1) of the Companies Act 1963 where a person knowingly is a party to the carrying on of a company's business with intent to defraud, *inter alia*, creditors of the company or of any other person, that person is guilty of the offence of fraudulent trading. Summary conviction can lead to a one year jail term or a £1,000 fine, or both. Conviction on indictment attracts heavier penalties of up to seven years in jail or a fine of up to £50,000, or both. Furthermore, because of the form of words used in the Act, the range of parties that can be guilty of fraudulent trading is not confined merely to officers of the company which agree to subordinate its debt. Consequently, other parties to the transaction could also be guilty of breaching the section if they had the required state of knowledge.

6–71 Thus for example, in the case of turn-over subordination, assume that a junior creditor was in a poor financial state. A debt is owed to it by a debtor company. The junior creditor then decides to declare a subordination trust over that debt in favour of another creditor of the debtor company, the latter creditor thereby effectively becoming a senior creditor. Or perhaps the junior creditor instead chooses to subordinate the debt by way of a contractual contingent subordination. In either situation, there may be a risk that the officers of the junior creditor have engaged in fraudulent trading in agreeing to facilitate the senior creditor, rather than retaining access to the debt for the purposes of meeting the junior creditor's liability to its own creditors. It may well be that the junior creditor continued to incur debts to its own creditors, while knowing that the likelihood of such debts ever being repaid was all the less likely given the subordination it was making in favour of the senior creditor. It would of course have to be demonstrated that the officers of the junior creditor were aware that, in incurring the obligation to the senior creditor, this would be likely to adversely affect other creditors of the junior creditor. Were this to be the case, then the junior creditor officers might well be guilty of fraudulent trading. In addition, so also would the senior creditor officers if it could be shown that they too had the requisite degree of knowledge. It would be arguable that they were party to a transaction which they knew would be to the detriment of the creditors of the junior creditor.[102]

6–72   In addition, under section 297A(1), a person guilty of fraudulent trading can also attract civil liability in a personal capacity under section 297A(1) for all or any of the company's debts. Furthermore, a person declared to have engaged in fraudulent trading can be disqualified from acting as a director of a company for a period as may be determined by the court.[103]

RECKLESS TRADING

6–73   Section 297A of the Companies Act 1963 provides for civil liability in respect of reckless trading. Unlike fraudulent trading, the Act does not make reckless trading a criminal offence. As reckless trading does not require fraudulent intent, it might be thought to be of more concern to parties involved in debt subordination merely because the risk of infringement might be more likely given the apparently lower standard of proof.[104] However, in practice there have been few successful reckless trading actions in Ireland since the section was introduced by the Companies Act 1990.[105]

Nevertheless, parties to a debt subordination should be aware of the risk of reckless trading, particularly the junior creditor. Section 297A(1) stipulates *inter alia* that in the winding-up[106] of a company, any officer[107] can be held liable without limitation of liability for all or any debts or other liabilities of the company, if he knowingly carried

---

[102] The Irish courts have held outsiders personally liable for some or all of the insolvent company's debts: *Re Hunting Lodges* [1985] I.L.R.M. 75 (although this was not specifically a debt subordination situation).
[103] s.160(2)(c) Companies Act 1990.
[104] Fraudulent trading is considered in detail in Keane; Forde; Lynch, *et al.*; Courtney, *op. cit.* at n.74.
[105] The section did arise for consideration in *Re Hefferon Kearns* [1993] 3 I.R. 191 (though not in the context of debt subordination).
[106] Or in the course of proceedings under the Companies (Amendment) Act 1990, *e.g.* examinership.
[107] 'Officer' includes not only company officers but also auditors, liquidators, receivers and shadow directors (s.297A(10)).

on the business of the company in a reckless manner. Not only can the liquidator or examiner be an applicant in such proceedings, but also, *inter alia*, creditors.

In order for a court to have jurisdiction to make a declaration that reckless trading has taken place, the section[108] requires that it must be shown that:

- a creditor has demanded in writing that an indebtedness of the company of more than £1,000 be satisfied and such indebtedness remains unsatisfied for more than three weeks; or

- a judgment executed on the company has been returned unpaid; or

- the company is unable to pay its debts, which includes the company's contingent and prospective liabilities.

and that, loss or damage occurred to an applicant as a result.[109]

Once these criteria have been satisfied, the court may then declare that there has been reckless trading if an officer of the company was either:

- carrying on the business of the company in a manner in which a person of his skill and experience ought to have known that his actions or those of the company would cause loss to any company creditors; or

- a party to the contracting of a debt by the company and did not reasonably believe that the company would be able to pay its debts as they fell due as well as all its other debts. When considering such "other debts" contingent and prospective liabilities must be taken into account.[110]

So far as the latter possibility is concerned, section 297A(4) goes on to provide that when considering whether to declare that the officer traded recklessly, the court shall have regard to whether the creditor was, at the time the debt was incurred, aware of the company's financial state of affairs, and notwithstanding such awareness nevertheless assented to the incurring of the debt. Finally, it should be noted that section 297A(6) provides a defence whereby if the person accused of reckless trading can show that he acted honestly or reasonably, then, the court has discretion to relieve him of some or all liability for reckless trading.

---

[108] s.297A(3) of the Companies Act 1963 by reference to s.214.

[109] s.297A(3) of the Companies Act 1963. Because of this damage or loss requirement, it will effectively be the creditors rather than say, the liquidator, who will have standing to bring this action.

[110] Companies Act 1963, s.297A(2)(b).

6–75   An application for a declaration of civil liability for fraudulent or reckless trading can also be made where a company cannot be wound up due to an insufficiency of its assets in circumstances where the company either cannot satisfy a judgment or cannot pay its debts as they fall due (which includes the company's contingent and prospective liabilities).[111]

6–76   So far as debt subordination is concerned, reckless trading may be a potential risk for officers of the junior creditor in the following context. Turn-over subordination will involve the junior creditor incurring a turn-over obligation in favour of the senior creditor. Consequently, officers of the junior creditor could be exposed to civil liability for reckless trading contrary to section 297A if it appears in the course of the subsequent winding-up of the junior creditor that the junior creditor's officers had traded recklessly by entering into the subordination with the senior creditors. This could arise where, for example, the junior creditor officers, at the time they incurred the debt to the senior creditor, did not reasonably believe that the company would be able to pay either that debt or all its other debts. The Act defines "other debts" as including its contingent or prospective liabilities.[112]

Contractual contingent subordination would arouse similar concerns if it could be demonstrated that the officers of the junior creditor, given their experience and position, ought to have known that the subordination arrangement would cause loss to its creditors in the event of the debtor company's subsequent liquidation.[113] For example, this could arise where the decision to enter into the contractual contingent subordination effectively meant that the junior creditor would renounce all chances of recovering anything from the debtor company. Thus, if the debtor company was already in poor circumstances, it is arguable that the junior creditor officers should have maintained the junior creditor's position as an unsecured creditor ranking *pari passu* with the other unsecured creditors in the hope of recovering something, rather than assuming a back seat position under the subordination arrangement behind all other creditors and recovering nothing. In subordinating, the junior creditor's chances of recovering anything could effectively be wiped out as it cannot recover until the senior creditors (and all other unsecured creditors) have been paid in full.

6–77   Officers of the debtor company also need to be aware of the

---

[111] s.251 of the Companies Act 1990.
[112] s.297A(2)(b) of the Companies Act 1963.
[113] s.297A(2)(a) of the Companies Act 1963.

reckless trading provisions. Particularly when they are considering whether to incur new debt, they should be wary of disregarding debt that junior creditors have agreed to subject to a contractual contingent subordination in favour of a senior creditor. Although such debt is not due or payable until all other debt has been paid, section 297A(2)(b) provides that contingent and prospective liabilities must be taken into account when deciding whether or not the officers honestly believed that the company could repay its debts at the time they contracted new debt.

Unlike fraudulent trading, liability for reckless trading can only be imposed on an errant company's officers, such term being defined to include auditors, liquidators, receivers or shadow directors.[114] Hence, other parties to the transaction are not liable under this section. As with fraudulent trading, a person declared to have engaged in reckless trading can be disqualified from acting as a director of a company for a period as determined by the court.

FRAUDULENT PREFERENCE

6–79 Section 286 of the Companies Act 1963 is another provision that the parties to debt subordination arrangements should be aware of when entering into a subordination arrangement. Section 286 prohibits the making of fraudulent preferences which can be constituted by, *inter alia*, any payment intended to give one creditor of a company preference over another in the event that the company subsequently goes into insolvent liquidation within a specified period. Under the section, fraudulent preferences are invalid.

In order for the section to be applicable, four criteria need to be satisfied. First, at the time the payment was made, the company must be unable to pay its debts as they fall due. Second, the company must be insolvent at the time of liquidation which is defined to mean that it must have been unable to pay its debts taking into account its contingent and prospective liabilities. Third, in order for the preference to be fraudulent there must have been an "intention to prefer". Fourth, the preference must have been made in the six months prior to winding-up, or two years in the case of "connected persons".[115]

---

[114] s.297A(10) of the Companies Act 1963.

[115] S.286(5) of the Companies Act 1963 defines a range of persons to be "connected persons" such as directors, shadow directors, family members, etc. A group company also falls within the definition of "connected person" which includes, *inter alia*, related companies.

In order for the requisite intent to be found, the company that made the preference in favour of the creditor must have had as it sole or dominant intention the preference of that creditor over others. In the case law it has been held that where the motive of the debtor in making the preference was to avert massive creditor pressure rather than to prefer that creditor over others, then there will not be an "intention to prefer".[116]

Subsection 4 provides that the prohibition on fraudulent preferences shall not affect the rights of any person making title in good faith and for valuable consideration "through or under a creditor of the company".

6–80 A distinction has to be drawn between the entering of the subordination arrangements and the actual payment that constitutes the fraudulent preference. Entering into the subordination arrangements will not constitute the preference as, ordinarily, no payment will be turned over at that time (i.e. no preference has occurred). However, any payments that are turned-over pursuant to the subordination arrangements will constitute fraudulent preferences if the four section 286 criteria (outlined above) are met. Therefore the implications of the fraudulent preference regime for debt subordination are as follows.

In a turn-over subordination, care should be taken to ensure that the junior creditor's insolvent liquidation is not imminent in the six months following payment to the senior creditor. Otherwise, there is a risk that any turn-over payment to the senior creditor might constitute a fraudulent preference. *A fortiori,* in a group company subordination intra-group, there is a risk that turn-over payments made in the two years preceding the insolvency of the group member (junior creditor) might be a fraudulent preference.

Normally, contractual contingent subordination itself does not raise a concern for the debtor company from a fraudulent preference perspective as it only requires that the debtor's liquidator not repay the junior debt until the senior creditor has been paid. Section 286 would not be applicable as such subordination usually is intended to come into effect upon the occurrence of the debtor company's liquidation, not in advance of it. Thus, the issue of whether the debtor company was making preferential payments to the senior creditor in violation of section 286 should not ordinarily arise. However, the position may be otherwise if the subordination is *complete.* In this scenario, the debtor will be required to make payments to the senior creditor *in advance of* liquidation, and, none perhaps to the junior creditor. The risk of fraudulent preference might arise in the event of the debtor's

---

[116] *Corran Construction v. Bank of Ireland Finance* [1976] I.L.R.M. 175.

subsequent insolvency within the period specified in section 286. In other words, although the point is undecided, the view could be taken that a fraudulent preference arose because, pre-liquidation, the senior creditor was receiving repayments but the junior was not. Again it should be noted that were this scenario to be realised, it is not the debt subordination contract *per se* that would constitute the fraudulent preference, but the actual payments made on foot of the contract. In order to rebut allegations of fraudulent preference it might be arguable that such payments do not constitute illegal preferences if it could be demonstrated that the senior creditor had forced the debtor company to participate in the subordination arrangements by subjecting it to overbearing pressure.[117]

It must be reiterated that, whether or not the risk of fraudulent preference arises in any of the aforementioned situations depends on whether the four criteria in section 286 are all satisfied.

6–81 One further interesting issue arises. Under section 286, solvency has to be assessed at two different stages using different criteria. Both must be satisfied in order for fraudulent preference to have occurred.

First, it will have to be shown that, at the time the suspect payment was made, the debtor company or the junior creditor (as the case may be) was "unable to pay its debts as they become due". This can be rebutted if it can be shown that the company (or junior creditor, as the case may be) either had the cash to pay due debts at the time of the suspect payment, or, that it would have been able to raise finance to pay such debts. It is submitted that debts, which by virtue of contractual contingent subordination are not due, should not be counted as debts for the purposes of this liability test. Thus, while debt that is the subject of a turn-over subordination will be 'due' (as debtor pays both junior and senior debts, and junior turns-over to the senior), on the other hand, debt which has been subordinated by way of a contractual contingency will not be "due". It only becomes due in the event that the debtor company goes into liquidation *and provided* that the senior creditors have been paid in full. (For the purposes of this discussion, it is assumed that the contractual contingent subordination is of the *complete* variety.)

However, were it to be *inchoate*, then of course some or all of the junior debt would be "due" in advance of any liquidation and such portions of it as were mature would be "due" for the purposes of the solvency test and thereby reckonable notwithstanding the contingency.

Second, it must be further established that at the time of the debtor

---

[117] In the eyes of the court, such pressure negates the inference of an 'intention to prefer'.

company or the junior creditor's liquidation (as the case may be) the debtor company or the junior creditor (as the case may be) also failed the section's second solvency test. It would have to be shown that the debtor company or the junior creditor was, at the time of liquidation "unable to pay its debts (taking into account the contingent and prospective liabilities)". Here, it is clear – contingent and prospective liabilities will have to be taken into account for the purposes of assessing solvency.

7

Debt Factoring

I.   **Debt Factoring as a Source of Corporate Finance** 413
II. **Assignment of Debt – A Brief History** 418
    Law and Equity – Two systems 418
    Choses in Action – Historical difficulties at
    Common Law 418
III. **Debt Factoring – The Legal Framework** 420
    Assignment in Law 420
        (1) "Absolute" assignment 422
        (2) Express notice to debtor 424
        (3) Written requirement 428
        (4) Section 28(6) "Subject to Equities" 429
        (5) Notice of assignment and the rule in
            Dearle v. Hall 432
        (6) Failure to comply with section 28(6) and
            whether assignment may take effect
            in equity 433
    Assignment in Equity 433
        (1) Necessary requirements 434
        (2) Recommended requirements 435
           (a) Assignment in writing 435
           (b) Notice of assignment to debtor 435
IV. **Competing Assignments – Priority Rules** 437
    Priority nightmare 437
        (1) *Dearle v. Hall* 437
        (2) Section 28(6) and *Dearle v. Hall* 439
    Case Study 440

7

Debt Factoring

I. DEBT FACTORING AS A SOURCE OF CORPORATE FINANCE

7–01 Factoring of corporate book debts can provide a fruitful short term source of finance for companies. Instead of a company waiting for the credit period it has granted its trade debtors to expire, the company can receive cash immediately from the factor by selling its uncollected invoices to the factor[1] who purchases them outright from the company. The legal framework in which this sale of book debt assets takes place is called an assignment.[2] Before considering the legal issues which arise when book debts are factored (*i.e.* assigned), it first may be useful to briefly consider the way in which debt factoring operates.[3]

For the assignor company there are many advantages which flow from having a good relationship with a debt factor. For instance, the company may obtain an improved predictable cash flow when the factor buys its debts. Where the factor agrees to be "without recourse", the additional benefit to the company is that bad debt exposure is reduced and so the company can be more generous to its other trade customers.

---

[1] This chapter concerns assignment of debts to the debt factor, the relevant legal framework and issues arising therefrom. The *debt factor* should not be confused with the *goods factor*. Debt factoring, which is an entirely different activity to goods factoring, involves the outright purchase of corporate debts (intangible assets) by the debt factor as owner, whereas the goods factor trades in goods (tangible assets) in a quasi-agency capacity on behalf of others. A goods factor is a party who acts as an agent with customary authority to negotiate the sale of goods on behalf of a third party. Historically the role of the goods factor developed from being a mere agent for the sale of goods, to a party who often assumed extra responsibilities, *e.g. a del credere* agent, etc. See further An Act to amend and consolidate the Factors Acts 1889, 52 & 53 Victoria.

[2] On assignment of debt generally, see also Salinger, *Factoring Law & Practice* (2nd ed., Sweet and Maxwell, London, 1995); Burgess, *Corporate Finance Law* (2nd ed., Sweet and Maxwell, London, 1992), pp.99–128. The assignment of *choses-in-action* is considered in detail in Bell, *Modern Law of Personal Property in England and Ireland* (Butterworths, Dublin, 1989), Chap. 15.

[3] See Kennedy and Others, *Financial Management* (4th ed., Gill and MacMillan, Dublin, 1988) for a business perspective.

A factoring arrangement may save the assignor the trouble and diversion of resources normally deployed in collecting difficult debts. Factoring may also be more feasible for a company than granting a charge. It may be easier for the company to sell its debts by way of assignment to a factor instead of trying to persuade lenders to accept a charge, particularly in circumstances where the company has granted several charges already over its assets.[4]

Once debts are assigned to the factor by the company, the collecting responsibility may be removed from the company and assumed by the factor.[5] Trade debtors will be instructed to make all payments to the factor. In return, the factor pays the assignor a purchase price equivalent to a generous percentage of the uncollected debt on the date of assignment. The balance, as agreed between the parties, would be payable either in stages or by an agreed date (normally the date the invoice would become due).

Sometimes however, the company continues to collect the debts, and immediately passes the collected proceeds over to the assignee factor.[6] Where this is the preferred arrangement, the factor will have obliged the company to hold collected proceeds on trust, as its agent. Debtors may, or may not be aware of the factor's involvement, depending on the company/factors' desire for confidentiality.

An interesting case is *International Factors Ltd. v. Roderiguez*. A factoring arrangement was put in place whereby the plaintiff factors purchased the book debts of a company of which the defendant, Roderiguez, was a director. A term of the factoring agreement stipulated that if any assigned debt was directly paid to the company instead of to the factor, then it was to be held on trust for the factor and

---

[4] Although in this situation, the factor should ensure that the chargeholders waive any negative pledge clauses prohibiting assignment of the charged debts that the charges may contain, as otherwise the factor might face an action for inducing the company to breach its contract with the chargeholder. Furthermore, if the circumstances were such, such that the factor was deemed aware of the negative pledges, then the factor who disregarded such pledges could not take good title.

[5] Sometimes however, a tactic that is used is that the factoring company will incorporate a company with an identical name to the assignor company except that the word "(sales)" will appear in the company name. This gives the impression to third parties that the company responsible for collecting debts owing to the company is merely an offshoot of the (assignor) company, when in fact it is the vehicle that the factor controls. This technique is used where both factor and assignor company agree that to overtly use the factor would send negative signals to company creditors.

[6] Some companies prefer to do this as in some quarters open use of a factor's services may be regarded as a sign of credit or liquidity frailty. See Kennedy and Ors. *op.cit.* at n.2 above, at 79.

immediately handed over to it. Company invoices were stamped to indicate that the debts had been factored. This arrangement was breached when the company lodged four debtors' cheques to its own bank account on the defendant's orders despite the fact that each invoice clearly indicated that all trade debts were now owned by the factors. The court held that the trust in favour of the plaintiffs arose as soon as the cheques arrived at the company thus giving the factors sufficient title to sue Roderiguez in conversion.[7]

7–02 Where a company wishes to use the factor in a discreet manner, notice of the factor's interest in the debt will not have been given to the debtor.[8] While this secrecy may suit the company, it may not be favoured by factors for several reasons.

First, although it is not necessary to give notice to the debtor of the factor's rights in the assigned debt in order to make the assignment legally complete in *equity* as between assignor company and assignee factor,[9] notice is required in order to make the assignment of a debt one that is effective at law.[10] This is because section 28(6) of the Supreme Court of Judicature (Ireland) Act 1877 requires notice of the assignment of debt to be given to the debtor in order for the assignment to be effectual at law. Until notice is given, the assignment (*i.e.* the transfer of all rights to the debt) will only be recognised in equity between the assignee factor and the assignor company. Should the assignee wish to enforce the debt, this can only be done provided that the assignor is joined as a party to the action. However, once notice has been received by the debtor of the fact that the assignment has taken place, subsection 28(6) declares the assignment to be effectual in law. *Inter alia*, this endows the assignee as the party having the sole right to enforce the debt against the debtor because, once notice is given, section 28(6) declares that the assignee can take action to enforce all rights in the debt.[11] This has several practical consequences. For example, it prevents

---

[7] [1979] Q.B. 351. Goode, *Commercial Law* (2nd ed., Penguin, Harmondsworth, 1995), p. 815 points out that this case demonstrates that not only will the assignor company in such circumstances be liable in conversion, but so also will the company director who caused the company to commit the act of conversion.

[8] Where notice is given, the usual mode of giving it to the debtors is by affixing the factor's name to the invoice stating that the factor is now the owner of the debt.

9 *Holt v. Heatherfield Trust* [1942] 2 K.B. 1; *Gorringe v. Irwell India Rubber and Gutta Percha Works* (1886) 34 Ch.D. 128.

[10] s.28(6) of the Supreme Court of Judicature (Ireland) Act 1877, 40 & 41 Vict., Chap. 57. Where notice is not given in accordance with the subsection, the assignment may take effect in equity only. This is considered further below in section III, Debt Factoring – the legal framework.

[11] As Gibson J. put it in *Conlon & Coyle v. Carlow County Council* [1912] II I.R. (K.B.D.)

the debtor from paying the debt to the assignor as the debtor is now aware that the factor, as the new owner of the debt, is the only party who can discharge the debtor from its obligations.[12] Furthermore, should the debtor default, the debtor will now be aware that the factor can take direct action against the debtor in law in the factor's own name without the need to join the assignor company as a party to the action.

Second, the giving of notice to the debtor of the factor's ownership of the debt may give the factor certain protection which he cannot have where notice is not given to the debtor.[13] Notice not only lets the debtor know that the only party who can give good discharge for the debt is the factor (and not the assignor company)[14] but it also may protect the factor's claim to the debt against other interests that might otherwise arise in the debt. For example, it may help prevent the assignor company

---

535 at 542, "The object of the section was to enable the legal assignee to sue and enforce legal and all other remedies without joining the assignor. . . . The section appears intended to make debts and legal choses in action . . . legally assignable so as to be recoverable without joining the assignor. . . ."

[12] As Parker L.J. observed in *Walter & Sullivan Ltd. v. J. Murphy & Sons Ltd* [1955] 2 Q.B. 584 at 588, "The whole object of the notice to the debtor is to protect the assignee. After receipt of that notice, the debtor pays the assignor at his peril." Furthermore, it appears that this holds good in Irish law even where the original assignor/debtor contract (out of which the assigned debt arose) had a clause in it prohibiting the assignment of the debt contract to a third party: in *International Factors (Ireland) Ltd v. Midland Factors Ltd,* unreported, Lynch J., High Court, December 9, 1993, Lynch J. held that a clause in the assignor/debtor contract prohibiting the assignment of the contract or any interest or payment thereunder was not permitted to render the contract incapable of assignment to the factor. Lynch J. adverted to the fact that the factor had no notice of such prohibition at the time of assignment, and furthermore that the debtor, having already co-operated with the factor by making payments to the factor, was estopped by such conduct from relying on the prohibition. Courts in the U.K. however take a different view, adopting the position that where a debt is assigned contrary to a contractual prohibition, then the assignee (the factor) does not acquire the right to be paid by the debtor because it has been held that the assignment is ineffective as an assignment: *Helstan Securities Ltd. v. Hertfordshire Co. Council* [1978] 3 All E.R. 262; *Linden Garden Trust Ltd. v. Lenesta Sludge Disposals Ltd. & Others* [1994] 1 A.C. 85. Should this U.K. position be a correct view of the law, then it is submitted that notwithstanding that the assignor's rights may not be transferred to the assignee, the assignor holds any proceeds paid by the debtor, for the assignee (*dicta* in *Linden Garden* support this view). For this reason, and for the avoidance of doubt, a well drafted factoring agreement will expressly declare that should the debtor pay proceeds to the assignor, the assignor agrees to hold such proceeds on trust for the assignee.

[13] This will be the case irrespective of whether the particular assignment mandatorily requires notice be given to the debtor (a s.28(6) assignment at law) or not mandatory (an assignment recognisable at equity). See further para. 7–18 below.

[14] *Walter & Sullivan Ltd v. J. Murphy & Sons Ltd* [1955] 2 Q.B. 584.

from attempting to assign the same debt subsequently to someone else; or it may prevent the debtor from attempting to create interests in the debt in favour of itself,[15] or in favour of third parties who might attempt to gain priority over the factor's claim to the debt.[16]

7–03 The factor may purchase debts "with recourse". In such a factoring arrangement, if the factor fails to collect from the debtor, the factor can have recourse to the company (the assignor) who was the original creditor. Alternatively the factor may purchase the debts "without recourse" in which event the factor who fails to collect from the debtor has no recourse to the company. In such a situation, the company is not responsible for bad debts as responsibility for bad debts is effectively assumed by the factor. Usually, the assignment agreement will restrict this to situations where the debtor genuinely cannot pay up.

The factor will agree to purchase certain present debts and arrangements may be made for the company to forward certain future invoices to the factor from time to time. At this point the factoring arrangement will usually assume one of two forms. Either the factor agrees to accept all invoices that the company will issue in certain sectors or to certain specified customers, or alternatively, the factor may instead retain the right to refuse any particular invoice that is forwarded by the company at any particular time. The former arrangement is known as a whole turnover factoring arrangement, and the latter as a facultative factoring arrangement.

The factor will charge a service charge as often it will take over management of the company books which detail the assigned debts, as well as an additional fee where it is an assignee "without recourse".

7–04 Finally, it should be noted that the following practice does not constitute factoring. This involves a factor, or more usually a bank, advancing sums to a company on the strength of its customer invoices. Often, a charge over the invoices (book debts) may accompany the arrangements. However, the critical difference between this type of arrangement, and factoring of invoice debts *per se*, is that there is no assignment of the company's ownership of the invoice debt.

---

[15] Such as rights of set-off or counterclaim which the debtor could assert against the assignee on the basis that such rights came into existence before it got notice of the assignee's interest: precisely such a situation was held to prevail in *International Factors (Ireland) Ltd v. Midland International Ltd*, unreported, High Court, Lynch J., December 9, 1993 where a debtor was permitted to counterclaim for defective products against the factor on the basis that the debtor's right arose before notice of assignment was given by the factor.

[16] See further sections III and IV of this chapter below.

II. ASSIGNMENT OF DEBTS – A BRIEF HISTORY

LAW/EQUITY – TWO SYSTEMS

7–05 In order to understand the requirements of the law both for the recognition of, and the enforceability of, assignments of debt made in favour of a factor, it is necessary to have an understanding of the historical "development" of the law in this area. Historically, there were two sets of courts in our legal system: courts of common law where common law disputes were adjudicated and courts of equity where equitable relief could be obtained under the principles of equity. Equity was developed by the judges as a response to the rigidity of the common law in an attempt to ameliorate the common law's overly legalistic approach. In addition, equity sought to cater for the common law's inadequacy both in terms of the somewhat limited range of legal remedies offered by the common law, and also the types of commercial transactions the common law could not "recognise". Over time, two courts made it their business to offer the necessary relief: the Court of Chancery and the Court of Exchequer (but only on its so-called "equity-side").[16a] While the courts of equity could deal with matters not amenable to adjudication in the courts of common law, at the same time, they could not grant a result that would conflict directly with the common law position on any particular legal matter. This did not however prevent courts of equity from granting forms of relief[17] or recognizing transactions which were not possible under the common law.[18]

CHOSES IN ACTION: HISTORICAL DIFFICULTIES CONCERNING THEIR ASSIGNMENT AT COMMON LAW

7–06 The strict demarcation between courts of common law and of equity was formally abandoned in the last century when, pursuant to section 27 of the Supreme Court of Judicature (Ireland) Act 1877 a new High Court of Justice was created which had both common law and equitable jurisdiction. Before this "merger" however, the common law/equity distinction meant that, subject to certain limited instances, the

---

[16a] Osborough, *Studies in Irish Legal History* (Four Courts Press, Dublin, 1999), p. 252.

[17] For example, the equitable remedy of specific performance, or relief by way of injunction.

[18] *e.g.* assignments of *choses in action*, such as debts.

common law courts would not give effect to assignments of choses in action[19] whereas the courts of equity had no such difficulty giving effect to assignments of many (though not all) *choses in action*.[20] Unlike courts of equity, the courts of common law had great conceptual difficulty in giving effect to assignments of debts. The common law had difficulty dealing with "items" of intangible property such as debts, other than by enforcing the debt in favour of the original creditor. Thus, courts of common law had difficulty recognising claims to enforce the assignment of a debt by an assignee because it considered the debt to be personal in nature, *i.e.* personal as between debtor and creditor and no other party could sue on foot of the debt. To permit a third party (the assignee) to enforce against the debtor, what was before the purported assignment the personal right of another (the creditor assignor), was not considered possible by the courts of common law.

On the other hand, while courts of equity had no difficulty enforcing the assignment of non-personal *choses*, courts of equity could not give effect directly to an assignment of *personal choses* (such as an assigned debt) as this would run contrary to the position of the courts of common law. However, the courts of equity found a way to circumvent this obstacle. On the application of the assignee, equity could compel the assignor (the original creditor) to be joined as a plaintiff to the action by the assignee against the debtor to enforce the debt.[21] In effect therefore, by joining the original creditor (the assignor), equity was permitting the action to be grounded on the fiction that the original owner of the personal right at common law was enforcing that right on behalf of himself. Of course, when the action succeeded, it would be the new owner of the debt, the assignee, and not the assignor, who would be receiving the debt due.

---

[19] Although it must be conceded that even before 1877 the courts of common law had begun to recognise that the common law should recognise assignments of debt at common law by at least enabling the assignee to sue the debtor in the name of the creditor: see *dicta* of Cozens-Hardy L.J. in *Fitzroy v. Cave* [1905] 2 K.B. 364 at 372 and *dicta* of Atkinson J. in *Holt v. Heatherfield Trust Ltd* [1942] 2 K.B. 2 where Atkinson surveyed the older authorities and came to the same conclusion.

[20] A *chose in action* is defined as:
"a right of proceeding in law to procure the payment of a sum of money . . . A *legal chose* in action is a right of action which could be enforced in a court of law, *e.g.* debts; an *equitable chose in action* is a right which formerly (*i.e.* before 1877 in Ireland or 1873 in England) could only be enforced in a Court of Chancery, *e.g.* an interest in a trust."
Murdoch, *A Dictionary of Irish Law* (2nd ed., Topaz, Dublin, 1993), p. 89.

[21] In *Conlan & Coyle v. Carlow County Council* [1912] II I.R. 535 at 541 and 542, Gibson J. explains how in equity suits all interested parties were joined. See also *dicta* of Atkinson J. in *Holt v. Heatherfield Trust* considered in section III below.

7-07   Gradually, the common law resistance to giving effect to assignments of debts and other types of *choses in action* lessened, but it was up to the legislature to put matters beyond doubt. In 1877, the Supreme Court of Judicature (Ireland) Act created a High Court having both common law and equitable jurisdiction.[22] Furthermore, in section 28(6)[23] of the 1877 Act it recognised that debts could be assignable at law provided the assignment fulfilled certain criteria as prescribed by the subsection.[24] From a practical point of view, this permitted, *inter alia*, the assignee of a debt to sue a debtor at law in the assignee's own name. Therefore, unlike previously, it would not be necessary to join the assignor as a party to the action in order to pursue the debtor. This development however does not mean that the rules of equity concerning assignments of debts became obsolete. These rules are still highly relevant today when an assignment of a debt fails to fulfill the section 28(6) criteria (assignment effective at law) as it may still be able to take effect as an assignment effective in equity. This is discussed further below.

III. DEBT FACTORING – THE LEGAL FRAMEWORK

7-08   Debt can be factored either by way of an assignment that complies with the section 28(6) criteria or, notwithstanding the assignment's failure to comply with the section 28(6) criteria, it may yet be effective in equity. The former is known as an assignment effective at law. The latter is known as an assignment effective at equity. Both will now be considered in turn.

ASSIGNMENT IN LAW

7-09   Section 28(6) of the Supreme Court of Judicature (Ireland) Act 1877 sets out the requirements to be satisfied in order to give effect to an assignment of a debt at law. An assignment that complies with these

---

[22] ss. 4 and 5. S. 27 provided for law and equity to be administered in the High Court of Justice. There had been earlier legislative attempts to give courts of equity a common law jurisdiction and common law courts an equitable jurisdiction, but these were not entirely satisfactory.

[23] Discussed in detail in section III below.

[24] Note that the English equivalent of s.28(6) was s.25(6) of the Supreme Court of Judicature Act 1873, 36 & 37 Vict. which was subsequently repealed and replaced by (with some minor changes) s.136(1) of the Law of Property Act 1925, 15 Geo. 5, Chap 20.

statutory requirements is an assignment effective in law.[25] Section 28(6) provides:

> "Any absolute assignment, by writing under the hand of the assignor (not purporting to be by way of charge only), of any debt or other legal[26] chose in action, of which express notice in writing shall have been given to the debtor, trustee, or other person from whom the assignor would have been entitled to receive or claim such debt or chose in action, shall be and be deemed to have been effectual in law (subject to all equities which would have been entitled to priority over the right of the assignee if this Act had not passed,) to pass and transfer the legal right to such debt or chose in action from the date of such notice, and all legal and other remedies for the same, and the power to give a good discharge for the same, without the concurrence of the assignor: Provided always, that if the debtor, trustee, or other person liable in respect of such debt or chose in action shall have had notice that such assignment is disputed by the assignor or anyone claiming under him, or of any other opposing or conflicting claims to such debt or chose in action, he shall be entitled, if he think fit, to call upon the persons making claim thereto to interplead concerning the same, or he may, if he think fit, pay the same into the High Court of Justice under and in conformity with the provisions of the Acts for the relief of trustees."

The essential elements required by section 28(6)[27] for an assignment in law are:

(a) the assignment must be absolute. This means that ownership of the debt must be transferred outright. Section 28(6) states that any

---

[25] Hereinafter, an assignment "effective in law" shall be understood to mean a "statutory assignment" within the meaning of s.28(6), *i.e.* an assignment of a debt satisfying all of the s.28(6) assignment criteria.

[26] In *Torkington v. Magee* [1902] K.B.D. 427 at 430–431, Channell J. held that the word "legal" in this context means "debt or right which the common law looks on as not being assignable by reason of its being a *chose in action*, but which a Court of Equity deals with as being assignable." In other words, it refers to *choses* which were, before the enactment of s.28(6), not assignable at law but were at equity. In *Tolhurst v. Associated Portland Cement Manufacturers (1900) Ltd* [1903] A.C. 415 at 424, Lord Lindley made similar observations stating (when commenting on the analogous U.K. provisions that had practically identical wording to s.28(6)), "The Judicature Act 1873, s. 25, clause 6, has not made contracts assignable which were not assignable in equity before....." According to Bell, *op. cit.* at n.2, p.363 "legal" means *choses* that were "lawfully assignable." In other words, any *chose* that can lawfully be assigned can be assigned under the section except those *choses* which the law does not permit to be assignable at all, or, those *choses* which the law prescribes must be assigned pursuant to a different legal framework. In *Torkington v. Magee,* Channell J. instanced the assignment of company shares pursuant to the Companies Acts as an example of the latter. (Note that although Channell J.'s judgment was overturned on appeal in [1903] 1 K.B. 644, it was reversed on other grounds).

assignment which is in fact a charge cannot constitute an assignment at law because a charge does not transfer all ownership rights to, and in, the debt; and,

(b) express notice of the assignment must be given to the debtor in writing. In practice such notice is normally given by affixing it to the company's invoices that are sent to trade debtors. The Act does not specify which party should give notice to the debtor; and,

(c) the assignment must be in writing.

Various aspects of these criteria shall now be considered in more detail.

(1) Assignment must be absolute

7–10   According to section 28(6) the assignment must be "absolute". This means that first, the assignment must cover the whole debt.[28] Second, all rights of the assignor to the debt must be unconditionally and irrevocably[29] assigned to the assignee factor such that the assignee obtains all rights absolutely to sue for, and give discharge for, the debt.

An assignment of part only of the debt causes the assignment to fall

---

[27] Note that s.136(1) of the English Law of Property Act 1925 is similar to s.28(6) though there are some minor differences: see Bell, *op. cit.* at n.2, pp. 362 *et seq.* where a brief comparison is made between the Irish and United Kingdom provisions. The United Kingdom courts' interpretation of s.136 or its forerunner, s.25(6) of the U.K. Judicature Act 1873 (referred to in pre-1925 cases) are of assistance in interpreting s.28(6) should no Irish authority exist. S. 136(1) states that:

"Any absolute assignment by writing under the hand of the assignor (not purporting to be by way of charge only) of any debt or other legal thing in action, of which express notice in writing has been given to the debtor, trustee, or other person from whom the assignor would have been entitled to claim such debt or thing in action, is effectual in law (subject to equities having priority over the right of the assignee) to pass and transfer from the date of such notice –
(a) the legal right to such debt or thing in action;
(b) all legal and other remedies for the same; and
(c) the power to give a good discharge for the same without the concurrence of the assignor:
Provided, that if the debtor, trustee, or other person liable in respect of such debt or thing in action has notice:
(a) that the assignment is disputed by the assignor or any person claiming under him; or
(b) of any other opposing or conflicting claims to such debt or thing in action; he may, if he thinks fit, either call upon the persons making claim thereto to interplead concerning the same, or pay the debt or other thing in action into court under the provisions of the Trustee Act, 1925."

[28] *Conlan and Coyle v. Carlow Co. Council* [1912] II I.R. 535.

[29] *Re Williams: Williams v. Ball* [1917] 1 Ch. 1.

outside section 28(6) according to a 1912 decision of the Irish Kings Bench. In *Conlan & Coyle v. Carlow County Council,*[30] the court held that an assignment of part of a debt causes the assignment to fall outside section 28(6). Gibson J. held that:

> "The section appears intended to make debts and legal choses in action, previously in equity transferable, legally assignable so as to be recoverable without joining the assignor, subject to specific conditions. 'Any debt or other legal choses in action' must be read as descriptive of the entire debt and choses in action, and not part of them."[31]

Gibson J. explained that this was the only conclusion possible. Were it otherwise, such that the debt could be assigned in several different parts to several assignees, then the absurdity that could arise would be that the debtor would be sued separately by the assignees for their respective portions of the debt. Apart from this imposing an unfair burden of a multiplicity of legal actions on the debtor, the absurd result that might occur could be that the debtor might successfully resist some of the claims, and not others. Clearly the section did not intend to facilitate such a possibility.

In the United Kingdom decision of *Skipper & Tucker v. Holloway and Howard*[32] Darling J. held that assignment of part of a debt was within the former United Kingdom equivalent of section 28(6). However, this decision has not been followed in several subsequent decisions in the United Kingdom.[33]

7–11 The requirement that the assignment of the assignor's rights in the debt must be "absolute" also means that it must not be granted subject to any conditions. Therefore, the assignor must not retain any rights to the debt as against the debtor. The assignor must alienate his rights irrevocably.[34] So, for example, the granting of a charge over company book debts (as opposed to selling them outright to the factor) cannot constitute an assignment at law because a charge does not effect an outright transfer of ownership of the book debts to the factor. Instead, all that a charge does is indicate the debts out of which the charge will

---

[30] [1912] II I.R. 535.

[31] At 542 *per* Gibson J. As a practical consequence therefore, because an assignment of part of a debt cannot be a statutory assignment pursuant to s.28(6), the assignee (*i.e.,* of the part of the debt assigned) will have to join the assignor as a party to the action to recover that part of the debt from the debtor.

[32] [1910] 2 K.B. 630.

[33] Bray J. did not follow it in *Forster v. Baker* [1910] 2 K.B. 636 (that learned judge's reasoning was similar to that employed by Gibson J. in *Conlan & Coyle v. Carlow Co. Council); Williams v. Atlantic Assurance Co. Ltd* [1933] 1 K.B. 81; *Walter & Sullivan v. J. Murphy & Sons Ltd* [1955] 2 Q.B. 584.

[34] Failure to do so causes the assignment to fail: *Re Williams* [1917] 1 Ch. 1.

be satisfied if the sums which the charge secures are not repaid. This is not tantamount to a transfer of outright ownership in those debts. For the avoidance of doubt, section 28(6) specifically states that a charge does not constitute an absolute assignment.

Assigning debt may constitute an assignment within the meaning of section 28(6) where ownership of the debt is conveyed even though it is envisaged that the debt will be reassigned to the assignor once a loan advanced to the assignor by the assignee, is paid off. This is because until that condition is met, the assignee owns all rights in the debt and therefore it constitutes an absolute assignment. The mere fact that the assignee's interest is subject to a reversionary interest in favour of the assignor, will not prevent an absolute assignment taking effect.[35]

Other arrangements can also look like assignments and may, or may not, depending on their terms, constitute assignments. If they do, they may be of the legal or equitable variety. For example, an authorisation to a factor from a company authorising the factor to collect a debt from a debtor will not, if it is revocable, be effective as an assignment because there is no absolute transfer. Where irrevocable, it might merely constitute an equitable assignment, rather than one effective in law (because (for example) the arrangement was not in writing). Another situation that could arise would be where the company, without having any arrangement with the factor, informed the debtor that all payments should be made to the factor as new owner of the debt. Of itself, this is not an assignment. However, if on the other hand, the factor indicated willingness to be a party to the company/debtor arrangements when subsequently contacted by the debtor, then an equitable assignment will have come into effect provided that the company's direction to the debtor was demonstrated to be irrevocable. It cannot however constitute an assignment effective in law under section 28(6) as there was no assignment between the company and the factor prior to the receipt of notice, as required by 28(6).[35a]

(2) Express notice of the assignment must be given to the debtor in writing

7–12   Notice to the debtor is a statutory requirement to effect an

---

[35] *Hughes v. Pump House Hotel Co.* [1902] 2 K.B. 190; *Tancred v. Dalagoa Bay & East Africa Rly. Co.* [1889] 23 Q.B. 239. Also note *Burlinson v. Hall* [1884] 12 Q.B.D. 147: a charge differs from a mortgage in that no title is transferred for any period of time by a charge, it merely indicates the funds out of which the debt shall be satisfied. In *Hughes v. Pump House Hotel Co.*, Cozens-Hardy L.J. approved of the idea that a mortgage of a debt can be an assignment as it constitutes a passing of the entire interest of the assignor to the mortgagee.

[35a] Notice in this instance being the debtor contacting the factor and informing him of the company's instruction.

assignment at law under section 28(6).[36] The section does not actually stipulate which party should give notice to the debtor.[37] Notice must be clear and unambiguous to the effect that the factor is now owner of the debt and is the only party who can discharge the debtor's indebtedness. In practice, notice is often given by actually stamping notice of the existence of factoring arrangements on the invoices as they are issued. In *Denney Gasquet & Metcalfe v. Conklin*,[38] Atkin J. held that notice must bring to the attention of the debtor that the debt has been assigned and that the debtor is now required to discharge the debt in favour of the assignee, not the assignor. One of the issues in *Holt v. Heatherfield Trust Ltd*,[39] was whether for the purposes of the modern U.K. equivalent of section 28(6),[40] notice became effective on the date it was sent or the date it was received? It was held that the assignment cannot be complete at law as between the assignee factor and the debtor until notice of the assignment is actually received by the debtor. Finding the date of receipt of notice to be the correct date, Atkinson J. went on to explain that until the debtor actually receives notice of the assignment, even if the assignment satisfies the statutory requirements in every other respect, the assignment can only take effect in equity as between assignor and assignee. The learned judge noted that:

> "Absence of notice to the debtor does not affect the efficacy of the transaction as between the assignor and the assignee. Until notice be given the assignment is an equitable assignment, but it is an assignment which requires nothing more from the assignor to become a legal assignment. The assignee may himself give notice at any time before action brought, and, further than that, even before notice he may sue in his own name, provided that he makes the assignor a party to the action, a plaintiff if he consents, and as defendant if he does not consent."[41]

---

[36] Notice to debtors is not necessary to effect an assignment at equity but, in practice there is good reason why notice to debtors should be given of equitable assignments also. This shall be considered when assignments in equity are considered in section III below.

[37] In *Bateman v. Hunt* [1904] 2 K.B. 539 Stirling L.J. observed at 538 (of the anologous U.K. provision, s.25(6)): "The Statute prescribes no limit of time within which notice must be given, nor does it lay down that notice must be given by any particular person. . . ." The same has been held to be true of the successor to s.25(6), s.136(1) U.K. Law of Property Act 1925: per Jenkins L.J. in *Curran v. Newpark Cinemas Ltd* [1951] 1 All E.R. 295 at 299.

[38] [1913] 3 K.B. 177.

[39] [1942] 1 All E.R. 404, where s.136(1) of the United Kingdom Law of Property Act 1925, was considered.

[40] *i.e.* s.136(1) of the Law of Property Act 1925.

[41] *ibid.* at 407. In *Gorringe v. Irwell India Rubber and Gutta Percha Works* [1887] 34 Ch. Div. 128 considered later in this chapter in section III below, the court took a similar view.

Therefore, while the absence of notice to the debtor does not affect the efficacy of the transaction as between the assignor and the assignee, a failure to give such notice will prevent the assignee taking the full legal title to the debt such that, in order for the assignee to enforce the debt, it will be necessary to join the assignor to the action.[42]

Until notice is received by the debtor, the debtor can validly discharge its payment obligation on foot of the debt, by making payment to the assignor. However, once notice is received by the debtor, the debtor is not discharged if it pays the assignor (except in the case where the factor continues to use the assignor as the debt-payment collection agent). Therefore, a practical consequence flowing from notice-giving is that the debtor will be under no illusions as to which party it is to pay.

7–13   In order to be effective as a section 28(6) notice, notice to the debtor must be received by the debtor after the assignment has taken place and not before.[43] In whole turnover factoring, the factor agrees to buy all of the trade debt owed to the assignor, or a particular section of the assignor's invoices. Whereas in facultative factoring the factor instead insists that each debt is offered to the factor by the assignor and the factor remains free to refuse to take an assignment of any particular debt that the company might offer. Salinger[44] points out that a danger inherent in facultative factoring arrangements is that while the company may have already notified the debtor that the debt is to be assigned to the factor, the factor's acceptance of the offered debt might only occur after the company had given notice to the debtor. Such a practice does not comply with the United Kingdom legislation,[45] and it is submitted that neither would it constitute compliance with the Irish section 28(6). In both provisions, the reasonable interpretation appears to be that notice must be received by the debtor after the assignment has occurred between the assignor company and the assignee factor, in order to satisfy the legislative requirements for assignments of debt to be effective at law.

This point is demonstrated as follows. A company presents an invoice to the factor and it is intended that the factor will present it to

---

[42] And also (as was noted earlier above at para. 7–02) until notice is given to the debtor, the debtor is free to set up counterclaims against the assignor, which in turn can be asserted against the assignee also: International Factors (Ireland) Ltd v. Midland International Ltd, unreported, High Court, Lynch J., December 9, 1993.

[43] *A fortiori* the notice must be communicated to the debtor before the debt has extinguished itself: see *Lee v. McGrath* [1882] 10 L.R. (Ir) 313 C.A..

[44] *Factoring Law and Practice, op. cit.* at n.2 above.

[45] S.136(1) of the U.K. Law of Property Act 1925.

the debtor for payment. This may take effect as an assignment in law under section 28(6) provided that (a) the factor agrees to accept the offered assignment; and, (b) the assignment is intended to be irrevocable; and, (c) the invoice is either furnished to the debtor "dressed" with notice of the factor's title, or alternatively, a letter is furnished to the debtor which makes it clear that the factor is now the new owner of the invoice debt and thereby the only party who can give good discharge for the debt. Section 28(6)'s terms will have been satisfied by such a course of action because the arrangements are in writing, intended to be irrevocable and the furnishing of the "dressed" invoice (or alternatively, a letter acknowledging the factor's assigned title) to the debtor will constitute written notice to the debtor of the assignment.

However, as Salinger points out, if notice to the debtor of the assignment is to be given by the alternative method (*i.e.* by way of letter), then the factor must be careful to ensure that this notice document is received by the debtor after the assignment was actually made. Otherwise, the letter will not be effective as section 28(6) notice. This difficulty usually arises where the company (the assignor) "jumps the gun" and gives notice without checking to ensure that the factor has in fact accepted the debt offered for assignment. This problem can arise particularly with "facultative factoring" arrangements as the factor may only have accepted an assignment of a particular debt offered by the company after notice had already been given by the company to the debtor in respect of the particular debt.[46] However, by contrast this difficulty does not arise with "whole turnover" factoring arrangements as the factor in such an arrangement has already agreed to accept all invoice debts specified in the factoring agreement. Furthermore, it is common practice to "dress" such invoices with notice of the assignment rather than to send a separate notice letter to the debtor. Such invoice-dressing constitutes notice to the debtor which, as a matter of course, cannot arrive to the debtor before the invoice because it is stamped or attached to the invoice itself.

7–14 A further difficulty that can arise in factoring arrangements is that the factor may attempt to give notice to debtors by way of a letter of introduction stating that future debts that the debtors may incur by reason of their doing business with the assignor, are to be paid to the

---

[46] Facultative factoring is briefly considered above in para. 7–03. "Jumping the gun" is of course less likely to arise where the factor sends the notice letter rather than the assignor company as the prudent factor will be careful to ensure that the letter of notice is not sent until the factor has actually accepted the debt which is the subject of the notice letter.

factor as owner of those future debts. The difficulty with this arrangement is that, as those debts have not yet come into existence, they are incapable of being assigned to the factor at the time the letter of introduction (*i.e.* notice) was sent out to the debtors. An "assignment" of a *future chose* – a debt not yet in existence – is not capable of being a present assignment. An assignment will only come into effect once the debt comes into existence. As a result, a factor in this position runs the risk that the notice letter would constitute notice given prior to the assignment of those future debts coming into effect, with the result that the letter could not be effective notice pursuant to section 28(6).[47] Thus, the factor would be well advised to modify the factoring arrangements so that this risk is eliminated.[48]

(3) Assignment must be in writing

7–15   According to section 28(6), the assignment must be "by writing under the hand of the assignor." Failure to comply with this condition will prevent the assignment from being effective at law though it may take effect at equity. No prescribed form of words is required. What is required is that the document makes it clear what is being assigned, and to whom.[49] Where one is signing an assignment in a representative capacity on behalf of another, there are conflicting views as to whether an agent of the assignor can satisfy the statutory wording by signing the assignment instead of the assignor.[50] The better view appears to be that provided it is made clear that one is acting in such a capacity, and on behalf of whom, the statutory requirement should be satisfied.

Historically, a major disincentive to committing debt factoring arrangements to the form of written executed documents was that they could be subject to the levying of stamp duty, such duty being payable by the purchaser (the assignee factor). A direct consequence of this was that, in order to avoid duty, many debt assignments were not committed to the form of executed written documents. A consequential drawback of this practice was that such arrangements were incapable of constituting section 28(6) assignments, as they were not in writing. However, the adoption of section 207 of the Finance Act 1992 declared

---

[47] In which event, an assignment in equity would arise.

[48] *Johnstone v. Cox* [1881] 16 Ch. Div. 571. Future debts must be distinguished from the situation where debts, already in existence, have been assigned although not due until some time in the future. These latter debts are not future debts and are capable of present assignment. However, as noted in the previous paragraph above, the factor must ensure that the debtor does not receive notice until after assignment in order to satisfy s.28(6). See also Salinger; Bell, *op. cit.* at n.2.

[49] *William Brandt's Sons Ltd v. Dunlop Rubber Company* [1905] A.C. 454.

[50] Bell; Burgess, *op. cit.* at n.2 above.

"debt factoring agreements" exempt from stamp duty. A "debt factoring agreement" is defined for the purposes of the 1992 Act as being "an agreement for the sale, or a transfer on sale, of a debt or part of a debt where such sale occurs in the ordinary course of the business of the vendor or the purchaser." However, the scope of this definition may not alleviate some parties' fears that their assignment arrangements may fall outside the exemption. Consequently, in practice, many factoring agreements continue not to be evidenced in written executed form in order to avoid the risk of incurring duty, with the result that a factor in this position is not able to take full advantage of section 28(6)'s regime.

It is common for a factor in this position to require the assignor to execute a written assignment in favour of the factor, *but* the factor itself leaves such document unexecuted on its part. The factor will refrain from executing the document on its part unless the prospect of the assignor (or the debtor) going into liquidation arises (if ever). Should such a prospect arise, then the factor will execute the assignment document, and give notice to the debtor that the factor (as assignee) is the only party who can give a good discharge for the debt. It is important to note that the execution of a written assignment by the factor in this situation does not give the factor title to the debt. The factor already has title because (notwithstanding the factor's lack of execution heretofore) the arrangements *as executed by the assignor* constitute a perfectly valid equitable assignment by the assignor in the factor's favour.[51] What belated execution on the part of the factor (importantly) does achieve, is that it permits the factor to sue the debtor *directly* for the debt, because now the factor has satisfied all of the requirements of section 28(6).[52]

(4) Compliance with section 28(6) "subject to equities"

7–16　Where all of the requirements of section 28(6) have been satisfied, then the assignment shall be effective at law from the date of receipt of notice by the debtor. According to section 28(6), this means that full legal ownership of the debt shall pass to the assignee (the factor) so

---

[51] Because in executing the documents for its part, the assignor has clearly signalled to the factor that it is the assignee of the debts.

[52] It is quite common for factors not to require fulfillment of all of s.28(6)'s requirements for a variety of other reasons also. For example, where the assignor does not wish the factor's ownership of the debtor's debt to be revealed to the debtor, the factor may be happy for the assignor to act as the collecting agent from the debtors. To protect against a breakdown in this collection arrangement, the factor will require the assignor to deposit an assignment executed on the part of the assignor (only). The factor will only execute such assignment, for its part, in the event of the failure to collect by the assignor.

that the assignee alone is the party entitled in law to enforce the debt.[53] This includes the right to pursue all legal remedies regarding the debt as well as the power to give discharge for the debt to the debtor.

However, the taking of a section 28(6) assignment does not mean that the factor necessarily takes title to the debt free from pre-existing equities, as section 28(6) provides that a section 28(6) assignee take an assignment subject to all equities which would have been entitled to priority over the right of the assignee as if the Act had never been enacted.[53a] The statutory phrase "subject to all equities" is a caveat of great significance. In effect this means that even though the assignee may take legal title to the debt (*i.e.* ownership), the assignee's interest in the debt may still be subordinate to interests ("equities") which others may claim, affect the debt in their favour. Such equities may arise in several different contexts.

One such situation would be where there is a defect in the assignor's actual title to the debt such that the assignor would have been unable to recover the debt from the debtor had recovery been attempted. Such a situation might arise for example, where the debtor alleges fraud on the part of the assignor. The assignee cannot hope to be assigned a flawless title free from such a defect. The assignee can only take as "clean" a title as the assignor had to give. In fact this holds whether the assignment is effective at law or equity: the assignee will take the debt subject to any equities that the debtor could have invoked against the assignor which would vitiate the debt itself. Such an equity will come into existence at the time of creation of the debt and will affect its very existence. So, if the debtor could have resisted the assignor if it had attempted to collect the debt while it was the owner of the debt, the debtor can also resist the assignee factor. The assignee can take no better title than the assignor had to give.

Another context in which the subject to equities principle may arise is where, instead of trying to vitiate the debt, the debtor argues instead that there is some equity in its favour which arises out of the same contract as that which created the debt. Goode points out that where the debtor asserts that the goods or services furnished by the assignor are not in conformity with the contract, the debtor is not precluded by the factor's assumption of title to the contract debt from asserting against the factor any valid claim that the debtor might have had against the assignor pre-assignment.[54] The debtor can exercise the equity against the assignee just as the debtor could have done against the

---

[53] Although note that the factor (assignee) is regarded as the owner in equity from the time the assignment was entered into between assignor and assignee: *Holt v. Heatherfield Trust Ltd* [1942] 2 K.B. 1; [1942] All E.R. 404.

[53a] See para. 7–09 above for the precise form of wording used in s.28(6).

[54] *op. cit.* at n.6 above, p.815.

original assignor. In *International (Factors) Ireland Ltd v. Midland International Ltd*, unreported, High Court, December 9, 1993 Lynch J. held that a debtor was entitled to counterclaim for damages against the assignee factor (who was insisting on payment by the debtor of trade debts assigned by the assignor). The court held that the goods supplied were defective at the time of delivery to the debtor, and therefore the debtor was entitled to set-off such claims against the assignee (even though the defects did not manifest themselves until after notice of assignment). Another decision which demonstrates how the debtor may be permitted to assert claims arising out of the assigned contract against the assignee is *Newfoundland Government v. Newfoundland Railway Co. and Others*.[55] A company was awarded a government contract to build a railway and assigned subsidies due to it under the contract to assignees. The company breached the contract by failing to complete the railway line's construction. The government counterclaimed for damages against the company and the assignees (who were seeking payment of the subsidies for existing work done by the company). Delivering the judgment of the Privy Council, Lord Hobhouse stated:[56]

> "It would be a lamentable thing if it were found to be the law that a party to a contract may assign a portion of it, perhaps a beneficial portion, so that the assignee shall take the benefit, wholly discharged of any counterclaim by the other party in respect of the rest of the contract, which may be burdensome".

While Hobhouse made it clear that there is no universal rule that claims arising out of a contract may be set-off against each other in all circumstances, he held that set-off of claims were allowable in this case because the competing claims had their origin in the same contract and were intertwined in the closest manner.

The Privy Council held that the government could counterclaim for damages against the assignee because the equity (the counterclaim) arose out of the same contract as the debt.[57]

In light of the above concerns therefore it would be advisable for the factor to enquire of the assignor company before the assignment of a debt, whether the original company/debtor contract (under which the debt arose) contained a clause stipulating that any assignee of the debt would take free from any equities arising in favour of the debtor.

---

[55] [1883] 13 App. Cas. 198.

[56] *ibid.* at 213.

[57] On the other hand if the equity is not closely connected to the debt, then the equity can only be asserted by the debtor against the assignee where it was invoked by the debtor before he received notice of the assignment – afterwards is too late: See *Roxburghe v. Cox* [1881] 17 Ch. Div. 520.

7–17 The subject to equities principle may also arise where a third party (not the debtor) claims that it is the beneficiary of a prior equitable assignment of the debt. In this situation, the rule in the case of *Dearle v. Hall*[58] will determine the question of which party's assignment in the debt has priority. In this respect, it shall be seen next below how the giving of notice to the debtor may give the factor some measure of protection from this sort of competing claim.

(5) Giving notice of the assignment to the debtor and the rule in *Dearle v. Hall*

7–18 The notice that section 28(6) requires to be given to the debtor has a significant spin-off effect where competing assignees claim a superior interest to the debt. This stems from the application of the rule in *Dearle v. Hall*. The issue that arises here is, whether an equitable assignment of the debt made by the assignor in favour of a third party before it was assigned to the factor pursuant to section 28(6) could affect the factor's title in the debt, even though the debt was assigned to the factor in accordance with section 28(6).

In the case of determining priorities as between competing interests in intangible property such as a *chose in action* (*i.e.* a debt), *Dearle v. Hall* stipulates that interests rank in priority based not on the date of their creation, but from the date of their notification to the debtor.

Originally, the rule in *Dearle v. Hall* governed the issue of determining priority where several equitable assignments of the same interest arising under a will were competing for priority. It was held that priority amongst the competing equitable assignees depended not on which assignee's assignment arose first in time, but on which assignee's assignment was the first to be *bona fide* notified to the trustee of the will. Accordingly, it was held that the third assignee of the *chose*, who bona fide[59] was the first to notify the debtors of his interest, took priority over the earlier assignees who had neglected to give any such notice of their respective interests. However, the rule's application was subsequently extended to also determine priority between prior created equitable assignments and subsequently created assignments effective at law, in the same *debt*.[60] Hence, a section 28(6) factor assignee's title in a debt will prevail against the holder of a prior existing equitable

---

[58] [1824–1834] All E.R. 28.

[59] *i.e.* was unaware at the time of notification of either of the earlier two assignments.

[60] As will be explained more fully in section IV of this chapter below, the "subject to all equities" proviso in s.28(6) expands the scope of application of the rule in *Dearle v. Hall* in this fashion such that it also applies to determine priority between competing prior equitable and subsequent s.28(6) assignments in a debt.

assignment of the debt, provided that the factor was bona fide[61] and provided that the debtor had not received notice of such prior equitable assignment.

Failure by an equitable assignee (whose interest in the debt arose first in time) to give notice to the debtor will enable the subsequent bona fide section 28(6) assignee to gain priority under *Dearle v. Hall*, because notice to the debtor is a mandatory requirement for section 28(6) assignments (and so will be given as a matter of course). Conversely, while notice to the debtor is not necessary in order to actually create a valid assignment of a debt in equity, there is therefore good reason why an equitable assignee should give notice. The rule in *Dearle v. Hall* will give an equitable assignee who, as a matter of prudence gives notice to the debtor, priority over a subsequent section 28(6) assignee.[62]

(6) Assignments which do not satisfy section 28(6) criteria may yet take effect in Equity

7–19   An assignment, which does not fully comply with section 28(6)'s requirements, may yet be given effect in equity[63] provided that the assignor has made it clear by its actions that the assignee was to have the benefit of the debt.[64] This means that it is necessary that the actions of the parties, particularly the assignor, clearly demonstrate that the assignee was irrevocably intended to become the owner of the debt. Assignments in equity will now be considered.

ASSIGNMENTS IN EQUITY

7–20   Where an assignment takes effect in equity it may be necessary for the factor (the assignee) to join the company (the assignor) as a plaintiff if instituting legal proceedings against the debtor because the

---

[61] *i.e.* had no notice of the prior equitable assignment at the time of notification of the s.28(6) assignment to the debtor.

[62] And of course, priority also over other prior equitable assignees who have failed to notify the debtor of their interest in the debt, provided that the assignee was bona fide (*i.e.* unaware of those earlier assignments) at the time of notification.

[63] A failure to meet s.28(6) criteria means, in practical terms, that the assignee cannot sue the debtor in his or her own name as the law will only regard the assignee as the full legal owner of the debt where its terms are met. To get around this obstacle, a court wearing its equity hat, on the application of the assignee will join the assignor's name as a party to the action against the debtor, thereby allowing the assignee to recover from the debtor.

[64] *William Brandt's Sons & Co. v. Dunlop Rubber Company* [1905] A.C. 454.

factor is not the sole "owner" of all rights in the debt.[65] However, in practice this may not be necessary as the debtor may waive the need for the assignor to be joined.

(1) Necessary requirements

7–21   In order for an assignment to be effective in equity there must be a clear intention to assign manifested by the assignor, and assent by the assignee. The assignor's actions must clearly demonstrate that the assignor intended to assign the debt to the assignee, thereby rendering the assignee the owner of all rights in the debt.[66]

The assignor has to irrevocably demonstrate that all rights in the debt are to be assigned to the assignee as sole owner. However, as considered earlier above,[67] notice of such intent may come to the intended assignee *via* the debtor rather than from the assignor. Assuming that the intended assignee wishes to be bound to the purported assignment in such circumstances, the intending assignee would be well advised to take steps to ensure that the assignor communicates notice of assignment to the assignee directly because there is a risk that the view could be taken that the assignor has not evidenced a clear intention to assign irrevocably where the assignor has not directly notified the assignee (*i.e.* the factor) that he or she will be the beneficiary of the assignment.

Valuable consideration is not required in order to effect a section 28(6) assignment.[68] However, its absence will be detrimental to an assignee of an attempted equitable assignment as "equity cannot assist a volunteer".[69] In other words, in the event that all of section 28(6)'s requirements are not fulfilled, equity cannot assist an assignee who has given no valuable consideration for the assignment.

---

[65] *Holt v. Heatherfield Trust Ltd. op. cit.* In *Whittingstall v. King* [1882] 46 L.T. 520 the notice of assignment had an incorrect date of assignment, therefore it was ineffective as a statutory assignment but yet could be enforceable in equity.

[66] Note the observations of Lord MacNaghten in *William Brandt Son & Co v. Dunlop Rubber Co* [1905] A.C. 454 at 462: "It may be addressed to the debtor. It may be couched in the language of command,. It may be a courteous request. It may assume the form of mere permission. The language is immaterial if the meaning is plain".

[67] See paras 7–11 and 7–13 above.

[68] Commenting on the analogous U.K. legislation (the Supreme Court Judicature Act 1873) to the Supreme Court of Judicature (Ireland) Act 1877, Atkinson J. in Holt v. Heatherfield Trust Ltd [1942] 1 All E.R. 404 at 407 stated: "Neither the Supreme Court of Judicature Act 1873 nor the Law of Property Act 1925, says a word about consideration". As s.28(6) of the 1877 Act is practically identical to s.25(6) of the 1873 Act, this statement is persuasive.

[69] *Lee v. McGrath* [1882] 10 L.R. (Ir) 313 C.A.; *William Brandt's Sons & Co. v. Dunlop Rubber Company* [1905] A.C. 454.

While these are the minimum requirements necessary for the assignment to be effective in equity, in practice a number of other issues arise for consideration and these will now be examined.

(2) Recommended requirements

(a) Assignment in writing

7–22   Equity does not require that the assignment (or notice of it) be in writing. However, there are at least two prudent reasons why both the assignment and notice of it should be evidenced in writing.

First, written evidence of the assignment often helps from an evidential point of view to prove that an assignment was in fact actually made. Second, where either the assignment, or notice of it, are not in writing, the assignment will not possess the potential under section 28(6) to ever become (should the parties so desire) an assignment effective in law.[70]

Notwithstanding the foregoing, there appears to be one situation where an assignment must be in writing in order to be enforceable in equity. Where the *chose* being assigned is in the form of a trust, then the assignment of that *chose* has to be in writing. This requirement is laid down by section 6 of the Statute of Frauds 1695:

> "... all grants and assignments of any trust ... shall be in writing signed by the party granting or assigning the same ... or else shall..be utterly void and of no effect."

Thus, while assignments of choses ordinarily need not be in writing in order to be effective in equity as equitable assignments, assignments of *trust* interests must be evidenced in writing.

(b) Notice of assignment to debtor

7–23   It is not necessary that notice be given to the debtor in order for the assignment to be enforcable in equity as between assignor and assignee.[71] However, notice should be given as a matter of prudence so that:

(a) the debtor will be made aware that the factor is the new debt owner and thus the party to be paid (not the assignor company).[72] Once notified, only the factor can give the debtor a good discharge for the debt; and

---

[70] S.28(6) requires both the assignment, and notice of it, to be in writing.

[71] See observations of Atkinson J. in *Holt v. Heatherfield Trust Ltd* considered above in para. 7–12, and the *Gorringe* decision considered hereafter.

[72] As Lord MacNaghten observed: "If the debtor ignores such a notice he does so at his peril": *William Brandt's Sons & Co. v. Dunlop Rubber Company, op. cit.* at 462.

(b) notice to the debtor ensures that the bona fide factor will get priority over other competing third party equitable assignments in the debt that have not been previously notified to the debtor;[73] and

(c) notice prevents the debtor setting up further equities in favour of itself *vis-à-vis* the assignor and thus against the factor's rights in the debt ; and

(d) notice helps prevent the assignor attempting to assign the same debt to a second unsuspecting assignee, particularly where the unsuspecting party makes enquiries with the debtor; and

(e) where there is no written evidence of the assignment, the giving of notice to the debtor may, in the eyes of the court, be evidence that an assignment was actually made.

Gorringe v. Irwell India Rubber and Gutta Percha Works[74] is an instructive case on the giving of notice. A. Ltd owed money to B. Ltd. It sent a letter to B. Ltd stating that it held, ". . . at your disposal £425 due from C. & Co. for goods delivered by us to them... ." Notice of this assignment was given by B. Ltd to the debtor (C) but only after presentation of a petition to wind up the assignor (A. Ltd). At issue was the question of the status of this assignment. Had it been validly created? Should the fact that no notice was given to the debtor until after the assignor had presented a petition to wind itself up prevent the assignee claiming that a valid assignment had been made in its favour by the assignor? It was held that the letter indicating that A. Ltd was holding a sum of money at the disposal of the recipient, B. Ltd, was an immediate equitable assignment and therefore, giving notice to the debtor, C. Ltd, was not necessary to give the assignee equitable title as against the assignor. In other words, notice to the debtor is not necessary to create an equitable assignment. In this context, the fact that the assignor petitioned to wind-up before notice was given to the debtor of the assignment was irrelevant. The court pointed out that the relevance of giving notice to the debtor does not have anything to do with the creation of an equitable assignment but, it would of course be required in order to make the assignment effective at law (*i.e.* one that would comply with the statutory conditions of section 28(6)).

---

[73] *Dearle v. Hall* [1824–34] All E.R. 28.
[74] [1887] 34 Ch.D. 128.

IV. PRIORITY BETWEEN COMPETING ASSIGNMENTS OF THE SAME DEBT

THE PRIORITY NIGHTMARE

7–24 This concerns conflict between parties who have assignments competing for priority over the same debt. One of the assignees will be the factor who will be unaware that another assignee has already been assigned the debt by the assignor at some time prior to the assignment to the factor. Who may claim that their assignment has priority?

As noted above in section III of this chapter, when a factor takes an assignment of a debt, a potential concern will be whether there are any other interests affecting the debt which might be superior to the rights which the factor assumes the assignment will confer. A particular concern for the factor is whether the debt has already been assigned to someone else.[75]

The priority problem is most acute where an equitable assignment has been made by the assignor, A., in favour of B. A. then (deliberately or otherwise) purports to create in the same debt either:

- a subsequent equitable assignment in favour of unsuspecting factor C., or, alternatively,

- a subsequent assignment effective at law under section 28(6) in favour of unsuspecting factor C.

In either situation, the priority conflict with B. may become the factor's nightmare. Because the factor is now dealing with competing interests in intangible property, *i.e.* debts, the priority rules that apply are determined by the interplay between two different elements: (1) the rule in *Dearle v. Hall*[76] and (2) section 28(6) Judicature Act 1877.[77]

(1) *Dearle v. Hall*

7–25 In order to appreciate the impact of the rule in *Dearle v. Hall*, it is necessary to understand the background to that case. In *Dearle v. Hall*, Z. was a beneficiary under his father's will. Under the will, Z. was to be paid annual dividends by the executors of the will from the funds of the deceased's estate. Z.'s right to receive the dividends annually was an equitable *chose in action*, the legal title of which remained vested

---

[75] Of course, if the initial assignment was one *effective at law* (i.e. a s.28(6) assignment) then these problems cannot arise as the entire assignor's interest will have been alienated – there would be nothing left for the original assignor to attempt to further assign.

[76] [1824–1834] All E.R. 28.

[77] Supreme Court of Judicature (Ireland) Act 1877.

in the executors. Thus Z. was the beneficiary of an equitable interest. Z. then assigned his equitable right to benefit to Dearle but neither party gave notice to the executors of this transaction. Subsequently, Z. assigned the same right to Shering, but neither party gave notice to the executors of this transaction either. Z. then assigned his interest to Hall. However, before he paid Z., Hall made inquiries with the executors as to whether there were any prior interests in the *chose*. The executors replied in the negative as they were genuinely not aware of either of the other two previous assignments' existence. Thus the court had to determine which of the assignees' assignments had superior title to the dividends.

The court held that assignee Hall had priority over the prior assignees because he had given notice to the debtors (the executors) of the equitable assignment in his favour, and furthermore was unaware of those prior assignments. By failing to give notice, Dearle and Shering had permitted Z. to appear as if he were entitled to transfer the *chose* free of any other interests. Had Dearle or Shering given notice to the executors of the equitable assignments in their favour, then the executors would have been in a position to inform Hall of the prior interests.

In order to place this precedent in its legal and historical context, it should be noted that this case concerned priorities as between assignments effective in equity only. As the case took place in the early part of the nineteenth century, all of the assignments were equitable in nature because Z. could not have made an assignment of the *chose* effective in law because the 1873/1877 Acts[78] were not yet enacted. Before section 28(6) or its United Kingdom equivalent were adopted, assignments of *choses* (debts) were largely possible in equity only.[79]

The "rule" in *Dearle v. Hall*, as it came to be known, originally governed the law relating to the assignment of equitable interests held under a trust set up by a will. Then its applicability was extended by the courts[80] such that it applied to equitable assignments of *choses* generally, in particular to the question of determining *priority* as between an equitable assignment and a subsequently created equitable assignment in the same *chose*.

---

[78] The U.K. equivalent legislation was the Supreme Court Judicature Act 1873, which is the analogue of the Supreme Court Judicature (Ireland) Act 1877.

[79] As described earlier in section II of this Chapter. Note that even if it was post the Judicature Acts, an assignment effective in law would not be possible in any event because Z. would not be able to assign the entire legal title in the *chose* as he did not have it vested in him in the first instance. It was vested in the executors under the will. Z. only ever had an equitable interest in it.

[80] *e.g., Marchant v. Morton, Down & Co* [1901] 2 K.B. 829.

7–26 Before proceeding to consider *Dearle v. Hall's* interplay with section 28(6), it must be emphasised that *Dearle v. Hall* is not authority for the proposition that notice must be given to the debtor in order to create an equitable assignment. Notice to the debtor is not required in order to create an assignment effective in equity as between assignor and assignee.[81] However, as adverted to above in Section III of this Chapter the giving of notice to the debtor can obtain valuable protection for the assignee of an equitable assignment. What *Dearle v. Hall* itself specifically demonstrates is that the giving of notice to the debtor of the assignee's equitable assignment will ensure that the bona fide assignee gets priority over prior created equitable assignments of the debt where the existence of the prior assignments was never notified to the debtor.

Also, it should be borne in mind that *Dearle v. Hall* is of no consequence where the first created assignment of the debt was one effective at law. This is because, in creating an assignment effective at law under section 28(6), the legal title to the debt is fully assigned according to the requirements of the law and there is therefore nothing left to the assignor to attempt to further assign to anybody else (whether at law or at equity). As the assignee will have in such a case given notice to the debtor as required by section 28(6), no subsequently "created" interest in the debt can take priority over the notified assignment.

(2) Section 28(6) of the Judicature Act 1877 and its relationship with *Dearle v. Hall*

7–27 It has been seen how *Dearle v. Hall* is relevant where there is an equitable assignment followed by a subsequently created equitable assignment in the same debt. However, *Dearle v. Hall* is also relevant for resolving priority disputes where there is an equitable assignment followed by a subsequently created assignment effective at law under section 28(6) in the same debt. Even after the enactment of section 28(6), the principles elucidated in the case of *Dearle v. Hall* are of central concern to the factor in the modern business world. Far from the subsection relegating the rule in *Dearle v. Hall* to the sidelines, the case continues to be more relevant than ever.

Section 28(6) stipulates that assignments effective in law are, ". . . (subject to all equities which would have been entitled to priority over the right of the assignee if this Act had not passed). . . ." The significance of this "subject to equities" proviso in this context is that it permits

---

[81] As seen above in *Holt v. Heatherfield Trust Ltd* and *Gorringe v. Irwell India Rubber and Gutta Percha Works, op. cit..* Notice is legally required on the other hand to give effect to a s.28(6) assignment in law.

Dearle v. Hall to apply to a priority dispute between an equitable
assignment followed by a subsequently created assignment effective
at law under section 28(6) in the same debt. Normally, the legal interest
holder in tangible property would expect to have priority over a prior
created equitable interest provided he had no notice of that prior
interest. However, with intangible property, different rules apply.
Section 28(6) combined with *Dearle v. Hall* ensures that the prior
equitable assignee of the debt will not lose priority to the subsequent
bona fide section 28(6) assignee who had no notice of the earlier
equitable interest in the debt, provided the equitable assignee had gone
beyond the strict requirements required to effect an equitable
assignment by actually giving notice to the debtor. In such a situation,
Dearle v. Hall will permit the equitable assignee's assignment to have
priority over a subsequently created 28(6) assignment at law.[82]

The factor assignee who has a section 28(6) assignment will only
get priority over a prior created equitable assignment of the debt provided that, at the time the section 28(6) assignment was being effected,
the factor was *unaware* of the equitable assignee's prior interest *and* the
equitable assignee had not given *notice* to the debtor. Thus *Dearle v.
Hall* not only determines priority between competing equitable assignments in the same debt, but it also determines priority as between an
equitable assignment and a subsequently created assignment effective
in law in the same debt. (Of course, no such priority issue can arise
where the assignment effective at law is created first in time because
the entire legal interest will have been assigned, and in any event, notice
will have been given to the debtor as required by section 28(6)).

CASE STUDY

Pfeiffer Weinkellerei v. Arbuthnot Factors Ltd[83]

7-27 The significance of the combination of the "subject to equities"
proviso in section 28(6) and the rule in *Dearle v. Hall* can be seen and
appreciated by reference to the following United Kingdom decision in
Pfeiffer Weinkellerei v. Arbuthnot Factors Ltd where the U.K. High Court
considered the analagous United Kingdom legislation[84] which is similar

---

[82] In other words, the assignee at law under s.28(6) will not take the assignment of
the debt free from the prior created equitable assignment provided the equitable
assignee had already given notice to the debtor of the equitable assignment. See
section III of the Chapter above for further elaboration.
[83] [1988] I W.L.R. 150.
[84] S.136(1) of the Law of Property Act 1925 (which replaced s.25(6) Supreme Court
of Judicature Act 1873).

to section 28(6) in substance. Applying a combination of the "subject to equities" rationale and the rule in *Dearle v. Hall,* the court held that a prior created equitable assignment competed for, and lost, priority to a subsequently created assignment effective at law.

The plaintiff, a wine producer, supplied wine to a wine importer, S., under a contract of sale. S. subsequently entered into a factoring agreement with the defendant, Arbuthnot Factors. Under this factoring agreement the defendant agreed to purchase debts owed to S. by S.'s wine customers. Pursuant to the agreement, the defendant in due course purchased a number of the debts by way of assignment effective in law in accordance with all the requirements of section 136(1)[85] of the United Kingdom Law of Property Act 1925. At the time of entering into the factoring agreement, the defendant factor was unaware that any adverse third party claims or interests might affect the wine. Indeed, in the factoring agreement S. warranted that ". . . no reservation of title by any third party will apply to . . . the goods. . . ."

However, there was already such a claim because the plaintiff, the original supplier of the wine, had inserted a purported retention of title clause in the contract of sale to S.. That clause purported to retain property in the wine to the plaintiff until paid for, but yet at the same time, permitted S. to sell the wine provided that S. passed on any proceeds collected or claims to such proceeds to the plaintiff up to the amount of S.'s outstanding indebtedness to the plaintiff. Clearly therefore, S. was in breach of its warranty to the defendant factor.

In due course S. failed to pay the plaintiff sums due for wine. Accordingly, the plaintiff claimed under the purported retention of title clause that it was the beneficial owner of the debts arising from each subsale made by S. of the wine; and furthermore, that any title to those subsale debts that the defendant factor received by way of the assignment from S. was subordinate to the plaintiff's prior title. To resolve the dispute as to who had priority to the debts, the plaintiff, the wine producer, instituted legal proceedings against the defendant, the factor.

7–29 The first issue was to determine the exact nature of the plaintiff's interest. The plaintiff submitted that the reservation of title clause retained title in the goods to the plaintiff while in S.'s possession, and allowed him obtain title in the debts/proceeds once S. had sold the goods. The defendant claimed that the clause merely created some sort

---

[85] s.136(1) of the United Kingdom Law of Property Act 1925 is referred to in the following discussion. Its terms are almost identical in substance to the equivalent Irish provision, s.28(6) of the Judicature Act 1877, and so Phillips J.'s judgment will be of assistance in interpreting the "subject to equities" proviso in s.28(6).

of security interest in the goods and in the proceeds/ debts arising from their subsale. Phillips J. held that the terms of the purported reservation of title clause did not retain title to the plaintiff as it permitted S. to sell the goods in the ordinary course of business. Title to the goods and proceeds from subsales could only be reserved to the plaintiff where a fiduciary relationship was deemed to exist and the clause did not, by its terms, give rise to such a relationship. So, if the clause did not reserve title, what was its effect? Phillips J. held that the clause gave rise to a charge over the wine while in S.'s possession and over the subsale book debts when S. sold that wine. However, such a charge required registration under the United Kingdom Companies legislation,[86] and because it was never registered, it was void for want of registration.[87]

So, if the clause did not reserve title, and was void as a charge, was it of any effect? Phillips J. held that the clause, a security interest, *inter alia,* in effect gave rise to a form of equitable assignment by S. to the plaintiff of S.'s rights in future debts owed to S. by S.'s customers for the wine, to the extent that the plaintiff could claim out of such debts up to the amount of S.'s indebtedness to the plaintiff, *but not* that the entirety of such debts were assigned to the plaintiff absolutely.

Once subsale debts came into existence the clause created an assignment in equity of the sub-sale debts' proceeds in favour of the plaintiff, but only up to the amounts owing to him at any one time by S. This assignment was not the same as an outright assignment absolutely of all S.'s rights in those subsale debts because S. could retain the surplus balance of any particular debt once the sum due to the plaintiff was discharged.

The plaintiff could not argue that even if the clause did not reserve title to him, it constituted an assignment effective at law (thereby defeating the defendant) because the actual debts themselves were not assigned to the plaintiff absolutely by the clause. In any event, this argument was not open to the plaintiff as notice of the clause had never been given to the debtors of S. (as is required by section 136(1)).[88]

The second issue therefore was to determine which party's assignment had priority. The defendant's primary submission was that, being the holder of legal title to the debts under an assignment effective at law,[89] its interest in the debt should defeat the plaintiff's equitable

---

[86] A charge over book debts is a registrable charge in Ireland also, see s. 99 of the Companies Act 1963.

[87] It never occurred to the plaintiff to register the clause as a charge because it thought it had a totally different effect, *i.e.* that of reserving title.

[88] It is also a requirement of the 1877 Irish Judicature Act, s.28(6).

[89] Agreement in writing, absolute transfer of all rights, written notice to debtors etc.

assignment even though created subsequent to the plaintiff's, purely because a legal interest is a superior title to a merely equitable one.

In reply, the plaintiff submitted that while section 136(1) permitted an assignee of debt to take a title effective in law, section 136(1) does not affect the determination of priorities. In other words, in so far as priorities between competing interests are concerned, a section 136(1) assignee is in no better position than if the assignment had been effective in equity because the proviso in section 136(1) states that, "Any absolute assignment . . . shall be subject to equities having priority over the right of the assignee. . . ." At this point it is appropriate to point out that the proviso in the Irish legislation, section 28(6), is even more emphatic:

> "Any absolute assignment . . . shall be . . . (subject to all equities which would have been entitled to priority over the right of the assignee if this Act had not passed). . . ."

Thus the plaintiff submitted that the equivalent United Kingdom proviso meant that: (a) for priority determination purposes an assignment in law must be considered as if it were an equitable assignment, and (b) consequently under normal equity principles the first interest created in time prevails, so that the plaintiff's equitable rights took priority because they were created first in time.

Phillips J. accepted the plaintiff's first submission (that the statutory proviso meant that an assignment in law should be regarded as an assignment in equity for priority determination purposes). In effect therefore, the priority rules were not altered by the enactment of section 136. In other words, while section 136 allows debt assignments to be effective at law, it did not, however, permit a subsequently created assignment effective in law to have priority over a prior created assignment in equity merely because the subsequent assignment was effective at law and the prior created assignment only effective in equity. Thus, the court rejected the defendant's primary argument that a subsequently created assignment effective in law is by definition superior to a prior created assignment effective in equity when determining priorities between such competing interests in a debt.

However, the learned judge could not agree with the plaintiff's second argument for priority based on the first-in-time rule. Phillips J.'s held that this was the wrong rule to apply when dealing with priorities and intangible property such as debts. Instead, he agreed with the defendant's argument.

The defendant submitted that the first-in-time rule gave way to the rule in *Dearle v. Hall*. Phillips J. accepted this argument, holding that the rule in *Dearle v. Hall* is an exception to the general principle that equitable interests take priority in the order in which they were created.

It applies, in particular, where priority between equitable assignments of *choses in action* is in issue, or assignments effective at law (such as the defendant's) which must be treated, for priority determination purposes as merely an assignment effective in equity. Under the *Dearle v. Hall* rule, priority depends not on whether the interest was created first in time, but on the order in which notice of the interest is given to the party affected by it.

Having resolved the preliminary issues, which assignment would have priority? Applying *Dearle v. Hall*, the defendant's assignment at law took priority because the defendant had notified the debtors of S. of the assignment of the debts, whereas no such notification had ever been given by either the plaintiff or S. of the plaintiff's "reservation of title" clause (which itself in reality was no more than an assignment in equity). On the other hand, had notice of the plaintiff/S.'s equitable assignment been given either by the plaintiff or by S. to S.'s debtors, then it would have had priority instead. But of course, this never occurred to the plaintiff or S., as they assumed that the clause reserved title to the plaintiff. They never suspected that it was ineffective for that purpose (instead taking effect as an equitable assignment). Hence, under the rule in *Dearle v. Hall*, the defendant took priority.

This English judgment while not binding on Irish courts, would be nonetheless very persuasive if the issue of priority determination as between competing assignments in the same debt were to arise under the similar Irish proviso found in section 28(6) of the 1877 Irish Judicature Act.

8

Legal Framework of Main Sources of State-Provided Corporate Finance

I. **Institutional Framework** 448
    (1) Forfás 448
    (2) The IDA 449
    (3) Institutional Reforms 451
        (a) Forbairt (1993) 451
        (b) Reform of Agency Framework and the
            establishment of Enterprise Ireland 452
II. **Part III Industrial Development Act, 1986 –
    Industrial Incentives** 456
    (1) Legal Framework of financial incentives 456
        (a) Fixed asset purchase grant 458
        (b) Additional persons employed grant 459
        (c) Leased fixed assets grant 460
        (d) Reduction of fixed asset loan interest grant 460
        (e) Fixed asset loan guarantee grant 460
        (f) Employment grants to service industries 461
        (g) Loan guarantees and Interest subsidies grant to
            promote corporate restructuring 461
        (h) Loan guarantees and interest subsidies grant to
            promote enterprise development 462
        (i) Training grants 462
        (j) Research and development grants 462
        (k) Technology acquisition grants 463
        (l) Acquisition of shares 463
        (m)Rent subsidies grant 465
        (n) Land acquisition grant 465
    (2) Statutory Limits on Aggregate of Certain grants 465
    (3) Government's Power to Override grant Limits 466

III. Grant Contract – Legal Framework and Terms 466
    (1) Agreement 466
IV. Other State Agencies 468
    (1) County Enterprise Boards 468
    (2) ICC Bank plc 458
    (3) Údarás na Gaeltachta 469
    (4) FÁS 470
    (5) Shannon Development 470
    (6) EU 471
    (7) Sectoral agencies 471

Legal Framework of Main Sources of State-Provided Corporate Finance

8–01 The State can provide financial assistance to companies in a variety of forms. For example, the form that the finance takes can be as diverse as fixed asset acquisition grants, loans or loan grants, loan guarantees, rent subsidies, equity participation, training grants, employment grants, working capital loan grants, technology acquisition grants.[1]

Traditionally, many different State agencies and initiatives have been involved in the administering of corporate finance and financial assistance under various State sponsored schemes.[2]

In this Chapter, what shall be considered is the legal framework for the administration of State finance to the corporate sector with particular reference to the statutory legal framework concerning two main State agencies, Industrial Development Agency (Ireland) and Enterprise Ireland. The role and functions of their umbrella body, Forfás, will also be considered. Later in the Chapter consideration will be given to the legal conditions likely to accompany the grant of assistance. Finally, brief consideration will be given to the role of some of the other State

---

[1] While historically the State provided "hard" supports, such as capital grants, in late years the emphasis has moved towards the provision of "soft" supports such as employment grants, training grants and research and development grants in order to boost employment and enhance the quality of the workforce.

[2] It is outside the scope of this work to attempt to define the many varied and changing operational programmes by which the State makes finance available to the corporate sector. According to a Department of Enterprise, Trade and Employment policy statement released at the time of the enactment of the Industrial Development (Enterprise Ireland) Act in mid–1998, a serious need for rationalisation existed as there were over 45 different State sponsored schemes operating. Neither is a consideration of the minutae of all agencies operating in the area within the scope of the present work, changing as they tend to do as frequently as changes of government occur. Such a task falls more properly within the scope of a contemporary work on Irish industrial policy.

created agencies who service the financial needs of distinct sectors of the economy or defined geographical areas of the country.

I. INSTITUTIONAL FRAMEWORK

(1) FORFÁS

8–02 Pursuant to the Industrial Development Act 1993 (the "1993 Act") Forfás was established as part of an overall restructuring by the State of its mechanisms for assisting industry generally following the recommendations of the Culliton Report in 1991. Forfás assumed many of the policy functions formerly performed by the Industrial Development Authority.[3] Under this new structure, Forfás oversaw two new agencies, the Industrial Development Agency (Ireland) (the "IDA")[4] and Forbairt (Forbairt was dissolved in 1998 and replaced by Enterprise Ireland[5]).

8–03 The 1993 Act provides that Forfás (and each of its agencies)[6] shall comply with such general directives given by the Minister relating to the policy to be followed by it in the exercise of its functions.[7] It[8] further provides that any such order made by the Minister must be laid before the houses of the Oireachtas.

Forfás's statutory objectives are specified in section 6(1) of the 1993 Act:

(a) to advise the Minister on matters relating to the development of industry within the State;

(b) to advise on the development and co-ordination of policy for Enterprise Ireland, the IDA, and such other bodies (established by or under statute) as the Minister may by order designate;[9]

---

[3] see para. 8–04 below. Pursuant to s.6 of the 1993 Act. Also Forfás assumed all Industrial Development Authority rights and liabilities that the Industrial Development Authority had contracted prior to the establishment of Forfás.

[4] see para. 8–04 below.

[5] The Industrial Development (Enterprise Ireland) Act 1998 (no. 34 of 1998) (the "1998 Act") dissolved Forbairt in 1998 and created a new agency, Enterprise Ireland. Along with the IDA, Enterprise Ireland is an agency of Forfás. See further paras 8–05—8–08 below.

[6] Currently known as the IDA and Enterprise Ireland.

[7] s. 6(2).

[8] s.6(3) as inserted by s.45(1)(c) of the 1998 Act.

[9] subs. (b) inserted by s.45(1)(a) of the 1998 Act.

(c) to encourage the development of industry, science and technology, innovation, marketing and human resources in the State;[10]

(d) to encourage the establishment and development of industrial undertakings from outside the State;

(e) to advise Enterprise Ireland and the IDA in relation to their functions.

Under current legislation, Forfás, the IDA and Enterprise Ireland may have made available to them up to £2,000,000,000 to enable them to perform their statutory functions.[11] Section 6(1) of the Industrial Development Act 1995 gives Forfás the power to invest in bodies corporate, partnerships or other bodies which are established for the purpose of investing in industry in the State by administering an investment fund for that purpose. However, as a matter of practice, it is Forfás's operational agencies who deal with companies, rather than Forfás itself. Consequently, section 6(2)[12] provides that this power shall be assigned to either Enterpise Ireland or the IDA in respect of specific schemes, which, once they have received Ministerial sanction, must be laid before the houses of the Oireachtas. Forfás' role therefore is chiefly that of a policy-making body, and also that of a supervisory body as it "oversees" the two operational agencies' operations.

(2) THE INDUSTRIAL DEVELOPMENT AGENCY (IRELAND)

8–04 The IDA was originally constituted in 1950 as the Industrial Development Authority.[13] The Authority's original role was to act in an advisory capacity to the Government on matters pertaining to the creation and development of Irish industry. However, over the years the Authority was transformed into an agency whose responsibility was to attract foreign investment into Ireland with the help of assistance in various forms provided by State resources. The Industrial Development Act 1986 (the "1986 Act") repealed much of the older IDA legis-

---

[10] subs. (c) inserted by s.45(1)(a) of the 1998 Act.

[11] Note that in this respect, s.11 of the 1993 Act was amended by s.33 of the 1998 Act to drastically increase the maximum funds available from £750,000,000 to £2,000,000,000. It should also be noted that grants provided by the State pursuant to s.14(3) of the Industrial Development Act 1986 for the purposes of honouring liabilities arising from guarantees the IDA or Enterprise Ireland may have given on behalf of client companies, are not included in the £2,000,000,000 ceiling.

[12] As amended by s.48(1)(b) of the 1998 Act.

[13] Industrial Development Act 1950.

lation.[14] Section 18 of the 1993 Act[15] abolished the Authority and replaced it with the Industrial Development Agency (Ireland). The functions[16] of the Industrial Development Agency (Ireland) ("IDA"), an agency of Forfás, are:

(a) to promote the establishment and development in the State of industrial undertakings from outside the State;

(b) to make investments and provide supports to such industrial undertakings;

(c) administer schemes, grants and other financial facilities requiring the disbursement of EU funds as authorised by the Minister for Finance;

(d) carry out functions assigned to it by Forfás with the Minster's consent.

Although the powers and functions of the former Industrial Development Authority were vested in Forfás,[17] the abolished Authority's investment incentive powers[18] are vested directly in either Enterprise Ireland[19] or the IDA.[20]

As will be discussed further below,[21] Enterprise Ireland has responsibility for manufacturing companies and services companies where services are traded internationally, while IDA is responsible for attracting inward investment and for companies whose Irish operations are not autonomous of their foreign parents.

---

[14] Twenty Acts were repealed (going back to the 1950 Act).

[15] Industrial Development Act 1993.

[16] *ibid.*, s.8.

[17] s.9(1) of the 1993 Act: in which event they may, subject to Ministerial direction, be exercised by the IDA or Enterprise Ireland (see s.44(3) of the 1998 Act which inserted Enterprise Ireland in place of Forbairt) as Forfás (and the Minister) may determine.

[18] Described in Part III of the 1986 Act considered further below at para. 8–09 *et seq.* Part III of the 1986 Act concerns industrial incentives, *i.e.* grants, loan guarantees, rent subsidies, training subsidies, equity acquisitions, etc.

[19] s.44(2) of the 1998 Act substituted Enterprise Ireland in s.9(2) in place of Forbairt.

[20] In which event they may be exercised by the two agencies to such an extent and in accordance with such directions as Forfás (with the concurrence of the Minister) may from time to time determine.

[21] See paras 8–06—8–07.

(3) INSTITUTIONAL REFORMS

(a) Forbairt – forerunner of Enterprise Ireland

8–05   In 1998 the Industrial Development (Enterprise Ireland) Act 1998 (the "1998 Act") established a new agency, Enterprise Ireland. Enterprise Ireland was created in order to streamline the existing agency framework so that companies operating in Ireland could have their needs met more efficiently by the State's employment creation agencies. As part of this response, the IDA would continue to operate, but its client base of companies would change. Forbairt was abolished and many of its functions were transferred and assumed by Enterprise Ireland.[22]

In order to appreciate the division of labour between Enterprise Ireland and the IDA which the 1998 Act brings about, it is first necessary to describe the previous legal framework which divided statutory responsibilities between Enterprise Ireland's forerunner, Forbairt, and the IDA.

Forbairt was established by the Industrial Development Act 1993. Until 1998, Forbairt and the IDA were the two main implementation agencies of Forfás, the State policy-making body charged with developing State industrial development policy. Section 7 of the 1993 Act provided that Forbairt was to be responsible for

– developing industry within the State;

– strengthening industry's technological base;

– providing services which support such development;

– making investments and providing support to industrial undertakings;

– administering schemes, grants and other financial facilities requiring the disbursement of EU funds as authorised by the Minister for Finance;

– carrying out functions assigned to it by Forfás, with the Minster for Enterprise, Trade and Employment's consent.

Essentially therefore, Forbairt was charged with providing business and development support for domestic manufacturing companies or

---

[22] Following the bringing into force of the 1998 Act which created Enterprise Ireland, Forbairt was dissolved by s.4 of the 1998 Act with effect from July 23, 1998, the date the 1998 Act came into force pursuant to the Industrial Development (Enterprise Ireland) Act 1998 (Establishment Day) Order 1998 (S.I. No. 252 of 1998).

internationally traded services companies operating in the State. The IDA, on the other hand, focused on attracting inward investment into Ireland.[23]

In order to be eligible for Forbairt support, a company had to have had its focus on either export markets or the displacement of imports coming into Ireland. Forbairt was particularly concerned with fostering start-up support for new ventures. In this regard, Forbairt operated three principal start-up programmes: the regional small business programme; the enterprise development programme; and the international services programme.[24]

On the other hand, the IDA was the main agency charged with administering State financial assistance to inward industries. Since it originally came into existence in 1950, the IDA had traditionally been charged with attracting inward investment into Ireland as well as supporting domestic industry. However, the 1993 Act reorientated the IDA's focus, so that it focused exclusively on attracting overseas companies (inward investment). As part of this plan, Forbairt assumed many of the domestic industry functions previously performed by the IDA.[25]

Effectively therefore, the State had created distinct agencies to deal with a client base of companies which more or less depended on the nationality of shareholder ownership. Companies that were domestically owned fell with Forbairt's remit,[26] and companies that were attracted into the State under foreign control fell within the IDA's remit. However, from the client companies' perspective, this was not the most satisfactory way in which to divide responsibility between the agencies.

(b) Reform of agency framework and establishment of Enterprise Ireland

8–06 In 1998 the Department of Enterprise, Trade and Employment published a policy statement to announce details of the creation of a new agency, Enterprise Ireland. In this policy statement, the Department pointed out several factors that lay behind the reform of the

---

[23] Companies that provided domestically traded services fell within the remit of other sectoral State agencies, such as Bord Fáilte (tourism), Bord Iascaigh Mhara (fishing), etc.

[24] However, where a proposal was very small in terms of its employment-generating prospects (*i.e.* less than 10 employees), then applicants would be advised to approach a local County Enterprise Board. See further para. 8–28 below.

[25] And also of Eolas, a State agency which promoted science and technology in Irish industry. Eolas was dissolved by s.18 of the 1993 Act.

[26] Although an exception to this were the food and timber sectors which remained within Forbairt's remit even where the companies were foreign-owned.

existing agency structure. In particular, the Department was concerned that globalising forces in world industry meant that distinctions applied by the State based on the simplistic nature of company ownership were being called into question for both legal and business reasons.

First, the document observed that, under international law the World Trade Organisation was already being asked to consider whether criteria based on the nationality of a company's owners, used by many States' to determine how a State should treat companies who seek State assistance, were compatible with international trade anti-discrimination rules.[27]

Second, such legal concerns aside, the Department considered that a new approach was also required for business reasons. The policy statement pointed out that newly established foreign branches of multinationals often faced the same competitive pressures as equivalent Irish owned companies operating in the same sector.[28] Yet, these two groups of companies, although operating in the Irish State, were served by different agencies merely on the basis that one was domestically controlled, and the other was not. Consequently, if Irish-based (rather than merely Irish-owned) industry was to thrive, a new unified agency approach was required. The Department observed that it was not necessarily in any company's interest to, for example, commence its trading life within Forbairt's remit at its start-up stage, and then have to transfer to the IDA's bailiwick once the company was bought out by foreign interests. Such a transfer would not be of benefit to a company still experiencing the challenges of establishment and development. In light of these concerns, the Department proposed a new approach under the Industrial Development (Enterprise Ireland) Act 1998. All manu-facturing companies and all services companies whose services are traded internationally henceforth fall within the remit of a new agency, Enterprise Ireland, irrespective of whether the ownership of the company is domestic or foreign, save where the Irish management does not have autonomous decision-making powers.[29]

8–07 The statutory basis for Enterprise Ireland was provided by the Industrial Development (Ireland) Act 1998. Section 25(1) provided that the formerly separate State agencies Forbairt and An Bord Tráchtála[30]

---

[27] Department of Enterprise and Employment policy statement on Enterprise Ireland (1998), pp. 10–11.

[28] *ibid.*, p. 11.

[29] In the case of such companies, they fall within the remit of the IDA.

[30] An Bord Tráchtála was set up by the Trade and Marketing Promotion Act 1991 (as amended by the Trade and Marketing (Promotion) Act 1994) following the merger of Coras Tráchtála (originally set up by the Export Promotion Act 1959) and the Irish Goods Council. Both Acts have now been repealed by the 1998

were to be dissolved[31] and their functions were brought together under the umbrella of Enterprise Ireland.[32] The policy statement further elaborated, providing that companies which are foreign owned will fall within the remit of Enterprise Ireland where the Irish management has autonomous decision making power in relation to a majority of the following activities:

– strategy formulation;

– research and development;

– marketing;

and, provided management has a high degree of autonomy in funding investment decisions as a consequence of these strategic decisions.

Only foreign owned companies whose management in Ireland has no autonomous decision making powers in relation to a majority of the above listed activities will remain within the remit of the IDA. In other words, only those companies whose long term strategy is determined by their foreign parents will continue to be dealt with by the IDA.[33]

8–08 Section 6 of the 1998 Act provides that Enterprise Ireland shall be a body corporate and its functions shall be as follows:

– to develop industry and enterprise in the State;

– to promote, assist and develop in the marketing of goods;

Act. The Bord's primary function was to assist companies based in the State attempting to target and develop international export markets. As well as providing practical assistance in foreign markets, the Bord could also award grant finance to companies attempting to market their products in new international markets. As the Bord is now subsumed by Enterprise Ireland pursuant to the 1998 Act, the new agency has assumed the Bord's rights and liabilities pursuant to Part III of the 1998 Act, and its functions pursuant to s.7 of that Act.

[31] Upon the declaration of the Minister for Enterprise, Trade and Employment of 'the establishment day' of Enterprise Ireland. Pursuant to s.3 of the 1998 Act and the Industrial Development (Enterprise Ireland) Act 1998 (Establishment Day) Order 1998 (S.I. No. 252 of 1998), the Minister declared Enterprise Ireland to have come into formal existence on July 23, 1998. Consequently, both Forbairt and An Bord Tráchtála were dissolved from that date.

[32] However, note that while all of An Bord Tráchtála's functions are assumed by Enterprise Ireland, Forbairt's functions in the metrology areas are transferred to the National Standards Authority of Ireland (see Part VIII of the 1998 Act) rather than to Enterprise Ireland. It should also be noted that Enterprise Ireland assumed responsibility for certain functions of FÁS, the State agency charged with developing manpower and training skills for the national workforce.

[33] Department of Enterprise and Employment policy statement on Enterprise Ireland (1998), p.11.

- to promote, assist and develop the marketing of service industries within the meaning of the 1986 Act;[34]
- to assist enterprises in strategy assessment and formulation;
- to develop the technological base and the capacity of enterprises to innovate and under take research, development and design;
- to strengthen the skills base of industry;
- to provide services which support such development;
- to make investments in and provide supports to industrial undertakings which comply with the requirements of the enactments for the time being in force;
- to administer such schemes, grants and other financial facilities requiring the disbursement of European Union and such other funds as may from time to time be authorised by the Minister with the concurrence of the Minister for Finance;
- to apply for and receive, in the State and elsewhere, any trade marks, licences, protections or concessions in connection with trade or the marketing of goods or services, and in relation thereto, to do all such things as it considers necessary for the purposes of its functions;
- to carry out such other functions as may from time to time be assigned to it by Forfás, with the consent of the Minister.

Section 8 provides that the Minister may give directives to Enterprise Ireland concerning general policy. However, the Minister may not give a directive whose effect is to apply to any individual company or which would give preference to one area of the country over another, otherwise than as part of a general review of industrial policy for the country as a whole. Section 23 provides that the agency shall supply such information to the Minister or to Forfás, as such parties may require from time to time.

---

[34] s.3 of the of the Industrial Development Act 1986 permits the Minister to provide by order that any service specified by the Minister is to be regarded as a service industry for the purposes of the 1986 Act. Pursuant to Industrial Development (Service Industries) Order 1998 (S.I. No. 253 of 1998) the Minister specified a list of services that are deemed to be service industries for this purpose: software development; data processing and electronic commerce; technical and consultancy services; commercial laboratory services; administrative centres, co-ordination and headquarters services; research and development services; media, multi-media and recording services; entertainment and leisure services; training services; publishing services; international financial services; healthcare services; construction related services; environmental services; logistics management services.

II. PART III INDUSTRIAL DEVELOPMENT ACT 1986 – INDUSTRIAL INCENTIVES [35]

(1) LEGAL FRAMEWORK OF FINANCIAL INCENTIVES

8–09 Part III of Industrial Development Act 1986 (the "1986 Act") sets out the legal parameters on the granting of incentives by both Enterprise Ireland and the IDA. The various statutory provisions found in Part III (as amended[36]) shall now be considered.

Under Part III of the 1986 Act, the now abolished Industrial Development Authority was empowered to make the incentives available to "industrial undertakings." "Industrial undertakings" are defined in section 2(1) as including "an undertaking ancillary to industry and a service industry . . .". While manufacturing industry easily satisfies the definition of industrial undertaking for incentive eligibility purposes, the position appears somewhat restrictive regarding service industries although, as shall be seen when the 1998 Ministerial Order is considered, many more service industries quality than heretofore.[37]

---

[35] Note that the monetary limits of many of the financial ceilings described below have been recently increased by s.34(2) of the 1998 Act. While the ceilings mentioned reflect these increases, individual reference will not be made in every specific case (where the ceiling has been raised) to the corresponding ceiling originally proposed in the 1986 Act (or where further amended by the 1993 Act).

[36] By, *inter alia*, the Industrial Development Act 1998.

[37] Indeed historically service industries were generally treated less favourably by the State, e.g. a corporate taxation treatment of "manufacturing" companies was (and still is) a 10% rate, whereas service industries were taxed at a significantly higher rate. However, since the 1980's many companies whose activities might not strictly be classified as *manufacturing of goods* activities, have been permitted to be regarded as manufacturing activities and thereby become eligible for the lower corporate taxation regime currently applicable to manufacturing companies. Section 443 of the Taxes Consolidation Act 1997 ("the 1997 Act"), consolidates the tax legislation in this area. It defines many business activities carried on in the State as "*manufacturing*" (even though ordinarily speaking they may not appear to be so in common parlance). For example, film making, newspaper production, fish farming, plant biotechnology, meat processing, design and planning services for engineering works intended for projects outside the EU, ship repairs, etc. are classified as manufacturing activity for corporation tax purposes. Of particular significance in this regard is s.443(10), which provides that "computer services" (defined to mean data processing services, software development services, or technical or consultancy services relating to either activity) are to be regarded as *manufacturing* activity *where an employment grant* is awarded (see para. 8–15 below where employment grants to service industries under s.25 of the Industrial Development Act 1986 and s.12(2) of the Industrial

In order for a company to qualify as a service undertaking, it is first necessary that the particular industrial sector in which the company operates has been so designated by Ministerial Order pursuant to section 3 of the 1986 Act. The latest order in force for this purpose is the order made by the Minister for Enterprise, Trade and Employment on 22 July 1998.[38] Under this order, any undertaking engaged in the provision of a service specified in the following list shall be a service industry for the purposes of the 1986 Act: software development; data processing and electronic commerce; technical and consultancy services; commercial laboratory services; administrative centres, co-ordination and headquarters services; research and development services; media, multi-media and recording services; entertainment and leisure services; training services; publishing services; international financial services; healthcare services; construction related services; environmental services; logistics management services. Because the current order is so wide-ranging in scope, service industries (whose services are traded internationally, are much more likely to qualify for industrial incentives then was the case heretofore.

It should be noted that between 1993–1998 Forbairt and the IDA had responsibility for the grant of the incentives about to be considered below.[39] Since Forbairt's dissolution in July 1998, Enterprise Ireland

---

Development Act 1993 are discussed). As the software and data processing sectors are such valuable parts of the national economy at present, subs.10 is therefore highly significant because it means that once the IDA or Enterprise Ireland award a "computer services" undertaking an employment grant, the undertaking becomes classified as a *manufacturing* undertaking for corporate taxation purposes. (Note that subs. (10) makes similar provision in the case of certain types of grants and/or financial assistance that may be granted to companies that fall within the remit of either the Shannon Development or Údarás na Gaeltachta agencies: see paras 8–32 and 8–30 respectively below where the role of these agencies are briefly considered).

Undertakings engaged in the provision of certain designated types of financial services, on behalf of persons not resident in the State, can qualify as *manufacturing* undertakings for corporation tax purposes where they satisfy specified criteria for operating at the International Financial Services Centre in Dublin (see s.446 of the 1997 Act).

Undertakings operating in the Shannon Airport Zone may qualify for the preferential corporate tax regime applicable to undertakings operating in the Zone where, pursuant to s.445 of the Act, the Minister is satisfied that "the activities in question contribute to the use of the airport *or* otherwise constitute *manufacturing* as defined in the Act." Note however, that under current government plans, the State aspires to taxing all manufacturing *and* service companies at a corporate tax rate of 12½% in 2003.

[38] Industrial Development (Service Industries) Order 1998 (S.I. No. 253 of 1998) with effect from July 23, 1998.

[39] paras 8–10 *et seq.*

now shares responsibility for administering these incentives, along with the IDA.[40]

While the maximum ceilings on the incentives about to be described appear generous, it should not be overlooked that in current times they are rarely approached, as the favourable corporate taxation climate currently prevailing in the State reduces the need for maximum level grants to be awarded to recipients.

Another point to be borne in mind is that the State also has to be conscious of its State Aid obligations under EC law. Indeed, the European Commission has indicated that it intends to take a less sanguine view of Ireland as a peripheral location than was the case heretofore. For example, the European Commission's latest guidelines on State Aid demonstrates that State assistance will be more tightly scrutinised in future.[41]

Finally, over the last decade, the agencies have moved from a position of granting "hard" supports (*i.e.* capital grants) to a position whereby employment grants and similar such "soft" supports are predominantly the bulk in terms of value of grants awarded.[42] Consequently, it should be borne in mind that while all of the legal frameworks and statutory provisions grounding the incentives about to be described all remain *in situ*, in practice the incentives that are "soft" in nature are those that are most likely to be granted nowadays.

(a) Fixed asset purchase grants

8–10   Section 21(2) of the 1986 Act provides that fixed asset purchase grants may vary between a maximum of 45–60% of the cost of the asset, depending on whether the asset is located in a designated area or not.[43]

In order to qualify for such a grant, the awarding agency must be satisfied pursuant to section 21(3) *inter alia* that the undertaking will, in the case of a manufacturing entity:

(a) produce primarily for international markets, or

(b) produce advanced products for supply to internationally trading or skilled sub-supply firms within the State, or

(c) produce products for sectors of the Irish market that are subject to international competition.

---

[40] s.9 of the 1993 Act (as amended by s.44(3) of the 1998 Act).
[41] European Commission Regional Aid Guidelines on State Aids.
[42] See paras 8–15 and 8–18—8–20 below.
[43] Pursuant to s.4 of the 1986 Act, the Minister may (in addition to those localities specifically named in the Act's Third Schedule) designate certain areas of the country for the purposes of the Act.

In the case of an undertaking engaged in the provision of a service, the Minister must have designated the sector the company is operating in as a "service industry" by order pursuant to section 3.[44] Unless the sector the company operates in is designated, the particular company concerned will not be regarded as an "industrial undertaking" and therefore will be ineligible for many of the various Part III incentives.

In addition, before eligibility is established in the case of either a manufacturing or a service company, section 21(4) criteria must be satisfied:

(a) the assistance is necessary[45] to ensure the establishment or development of the undertaking's business;

(b) the investment proposed is commercially viable;

(c) the undertaking has an adequate capital base;

(d) the undertaking concerned has a suitable development plan; and

(e) the undertaking will provide new employment (or maintain existing employment) which could not be done without State incentive assistance.

It should be emphasised that these criteria are not applied on a singular basis but rather they illustrate that before an applicant will receive funding, a viable business plan must be produced and the prospect for creating employment must appear realistic.

Furthermore, as noted earlier above, the current trend is for the awarding agencies not to grant substantial "hard" supports such as fixed asset grants, but rather instead to grant employment grants on a "grant-per-job" basis. In this way, taxpayers money is being used to develop and enhance the quality of the national workforce, rather than to subscribe to the capital start-up costs of companies developing or expanding their plant.

(b) Additional persons employed grant

8–11 The 1986 Act[46] provides that the agency concerned may make a grant on such terms as it thinks proper in respect of any additional persons employed by an industrial undertaking. The agency concerned

---

[44] Pursuant to s.3 of the 1986 Act the Minister may designate that a particular undertaking is a service provider for the purposes of making it eligible to receive assistance. In this regard, see the service sectors designated by S.I. No. 253 of 1998 considered at para. 8–09 above.

[45] Although, in reality, "necessary" may be taken to equate with what is politically necessary or desirable.

[46] s.21(5)(a) as amended by s.9 of the Industrial Development Act 1991.

is obliged to ensure that any grant that is awarded is subject to such limits and conditions as the Minister may from time to time specify.[47]

(c) Leased fixed assets grant

8–12   Grants may be obtained to assist with the cost of leasing fixed assets under the 1986 Act.[48] Again, similar maximum grant limits apply as outlined in the case of fixed assets grants. Criteria for eligibility are as *per* section 21(3) and (4).[49] Where the undertaking is leased land by an agency, any difference between commercial rent rates and the rent actually charged, shall be treated as a grant to the undertaking concerned.[50] Given the shift in emphasis over the last number of years from "hard" to "soft" supports, leased fixed asset grants tend to be directed more towards machinery rather than building assets.

(d) Grants towards reduction of loan interest on fixed assets

8–13   Grants may also be awarded towards the reduction of bank interest payable on fixed assets utilised by the undertaking.[51] The awarding agency is obliged to ensure that any grant remains within 45–60% of the value of the fixed assets, depending on whether the recipient is located in a designated area, or not. Furthermore, the agency must conform with any Ministerial terms and conditions governing such grants. However, in the current climate, which leans against the granting of "hard" supports, these grants are rarely granted.

(e) Loans guarantees for fixed assets

8–14   The 1986 Act permits the agencies to guarantee loans that undertakings have taken out in order to pay for fixed assets.[52] The agencies are permitted to guarantee up to 80% of either the principal or interest repayable, or both. Where the amount of the principal of the money guaranteed exceeds £1,200,000, grant assistance in this form cannot be given without the permission of the Government. The awarding agency is obliged to respect any terms or conditions as may be

---

[47] s.21(1)(5)(b).
[48] s.22 of the 1986 Act.
[49] *i.e.* 45-60% discussed above at para. 8–10.
[50] s.22(4) of the 1986 Act.
[51] s.23 of the 1986 Act. Eligibility criteria are as *per* s.21(3) and (4), discussed above at para. 8–10.
[52] s.24. Eligibility criteria are as *per* s.21(3) and (4) discussed above at para. 8–10. However, it should be noted that the current climate which leans against the granting of "hard" supports, this kind of grant tends not to be granted as fully as before.

specified by the Minister, with the concurrence of the Minister for Finance.

(f) Employment grants to service industries[53]

8–15   Employment grants to service industries may be based on two sets of legislative provisions, the more recent of which allows more discretion to the awarding agency. First, section 25 of the 1986 Act allows employment grants to be made to service industries where, in the opinion of the agency concerned, the service industry would contribute significantly to regional and national development and would not be developed without grant assistance. Limits on the amounts of such assistance will be set from time to time by the Minister. Employment grants in excess of £2,000,000 (in aggregate) may not be granted without prior Government permission.[54] Second, section 12(2) of the 1993 Act[55] provides that Enterprise Ireland and the IDA may make grants on such terms and conditions as they think proper towards employment of persons in a service industry.

For the purposes of either grant, the term "service industry" refers to service industries designated by the Minister under the 1986 Act.[56]

As already discussed at par. 8-09 above, the awarding of either of the aforegoing grants to a "computer services" undertaking[57] has an added vital significance. Section 443 of the Taxes Consolidation Act 1997 provides that the award of an employment grant to a computer services undertaking entitles the undertaking to be classified as a "manufacturer of goods". As a consequence, such undertaking when in receipt of an employment grant, becomes eligible to pay the significantly lower corporate tax rate applicable to *manufacturing* industry.

(g) Loan guarantees and interest subsidies to promote corporate restructuring

8–16   The 1986 Act provides a legal basis by which grants can be given in circumstances where a loan was incurred by an industrial undertaking as part of a takeover of, or amalgamation with, another industrial undertaking.[58] The grant may cover loan interest or, alter-

---

[53] See also para. 8–11 which concerns *additional* persons employed grants.
[54] s.25(4).
[55] As amended by s.34 (1) of the 1998 Act.
[56] See para. 8–09 above where list of industries so designated by S.I. No. 253 of 1998 are specified.
[57] Meaning a data processing or software development undertaking or an undertaking providing consultancy services in relation to either activity.
[58] s.26.

natively the grant may take the form of a guarantee in respect of loan principal, or interest, or both.[59] Such grants or guarantees may not be given without the permission of the Government where the aggregate of the value of the grant and the guarantee exceeds £1,200,000.

(h) Loan guarantees and interest subsidies to promote enterprise development

8–17   The 1986 Act provides a legal basis for the payment of grants[60] to assist the establishment of industrial undertakings by "suitably qualified persons" who have never been to a significant extent involved in the ownership of an industrial undertaking.[61] This assistance can range from grants to assist with the reduction of interest repayable on a loan raised to provide working capital for the undertaking, to guarantees (subject to an 80% limit) in respect of working capital loans. The prior permission of the Government is required where guarantees and grants as described would exceed £480,000 in aggregate.

(i) Training grants

8–18   The 1986 Act provides for training grants,[62] which are designed to contribute towards an industrial undertaking's costs when it engages consultants and technical advisers to train its staff in its processes, or where persons are trained for positions of supervision and management. The grant can cover salaries, wages, fees or expenses paid. An awarding agency cannot award assistance in this form exceeding a limit of £3,200,000 in aggregate without prior Government permission.[63] In the current climate which favours "soft" supports which are directed at improving the quality of the national workforce, training grants are widely granted to eligible applicants.

(j) Research and development/feasibility grants

8–19   Research grants are also provided for in the 1986 Act. Section 29 provides that such grants may be awarded in respect of projects which have as their primary object the promotion or development of new or improved industrial processes, methods or products in the State, and which are carried out wholly or mainly in the State by one or more

---

[59] Although in the current climate, these grants, which are regarded as "hard" supports, tend not to be granted.
[60] Eligibility criteria are as *per* s.21(3) and (4), discussed above at para. 8–10.
[61] s.27.
[62] s.28 of the 1986 Act. Eligibility criteria are as *per* s.21(3) and (4) discussed above at para. 8–10.
[63] The £3,200,000 ceiling was increased from £2,000,000 by the 1998 Act.

industrial undertakings. The amount of a research grant may not exceed 50% of the approved costs of the project or £400,000, whichever is the lower sum. Government approval is required for the awarding of higher sums. However, where any such approval is obtained, the amount awarded cannot exceed a maximum of 50% of the approved costs of the project.[64]

Section 29(5) includes a provision specifically designed to assist "small industrial undertakings". Under this provision, research grants of up to one third of the approved costs may be granted even before they are incurred, on condition that such sums are repaid in the event of the research not being carried out to the awarding agency's satisfaction. The awarding agency is precluded from awarding such assistance unless it is satisfied that the industrial undertaking has available to it sufficient assets to cover its potential liability under this provision. Finally, section 29(7) provides that, in respect of any particular industrial undertaking, grant assistance exceeding the higher sum of £800,000 or £800,000 in excess of the aggregate amount of research grants previously approved by the Government, may not be granted unless Government permission is obtained.

In the current climate, where the State is actively seeking to promote innovation and add value to national industry's research base, these grants are readily granted to eligible applicants.

(k) Technology acquisition grants

8–20   Section 30 provides a legal basis for the award of grant assistance to assist an industrial undertaking acquire product or process technology which has as its primary object the improvement of the technological capability of production or application of advanced industrial processes or products in the State. "Product or process technology" is defined to include patents, designs, trademarks, trade secrets, copyright, proprietary and non-proprietary information and techniques. Similar financial ceilings apply as in the case of research and development grants.[65]

In the current climate, where the State is actively seeking to promote innovation and add value to national industry's research base, these grants are readily granted to eligible applicants.

(l) Power to acquire shares

8–21   Under the 1986 Act,[66] the agencies have the power to purchase

---

[64] s.29(3)(b). A description of items likely to qualify as approved costs is given in the Act.

[65] See para. 8–19 above.

[66] s.31 of the 1986 Act.

or take shares in a body corporate that owns, controls or manages an industrial undertaking[67] or to purchase shares in a body corporate which participates in such ownership, control or management.[68] In addition, an agency may also form or take part with others in the formation of such bodies corporate.[69] However, in all instances, shares may not be purchased or taken unless the agency concerned has consulted with any State sponsored body that the Minister may have specified. This consultation obligation also applies where the holding held by the agency together with the holdings of other State-sponsored bodies would exceed more than half the equity share capital[70] or more than half of the nominal value of shares carrying voting rights. However, Ministerial permission can be obtained permitting these limits to be exceeded. The agencies may not invest more than £2,500,000 in a body corporate by way of a purchase or taking of shares unless the Government has consented.[71]

Section 4 of the Industrial Development Act 1995 provides that any securities[72] held by Forfás shall, as determined by Forfás, be deemed to have been assigned to either Forbairt or the IDA. Any transfer of securities so transferred pursuant to section 4 shall not be affected by any provision of any corporate body's memorandum or articles of association which would otherwise purport to restrict the transfer of the securities.[73] Enterprise Ireland assumes ownership of any property, including securities, formerly held by Forbairt.[74]

This power to invest in companies by way of taking an equity participation has been very successful in many instances resulting in substantial dividends being earned by the agencies. Investment is only made where the company is agreeable.

---

[67] Provided the undertaking otherwise satisfies the criteria for the award of assistance set out in s.21(3) and (4) as set out in para. 8–10 above.

[68] s.31(1)(a).

[69] s.31(1)(b).

[70] "Equity share capital" is defined by s.155(5) of the Companies Act 1963. S.31(1) of the 1986 Act was amended in this regard by s.9(d) of the Industrial Development (Amendment) Act 1991.

[71] s.31(4) of the 1986 Act as amended by s.34(2)(j) of the 1998 Act. This includes any amounts invested by the National Development Corporation before its abolition by s.11 of the Industrial Development (Amendment) Act 1991. The Corporation was set up pursuant to the National Development Corporation Act 1986. Upon its abolition, its functions and liabilities were assumed by the former Industrial Development Authority pursuant to s.3 of the 1991 Act. S.7 of the 1991 Act permitted the IDA to take shares in companies.

[72] Defined to include stocks, shares, debentures and loans by s.4(9)(a). S.4(8) excludes Forfás shares held in International Development Ireland Limited from the application of s.4.

[73] s.4(6) of the 1995 Act.

[74] s.26 of the 1998 Act.

(m) Rent subsidy grants

8–22   Grants may be made to the lessors of factory premises with the objective of encouraging the lessor to lease the factory to an industrial undertaking[75] at a reduced rent.[76] Alternatively, the grant can be made directly to the industrial undertaking concerned. This grant shall not exceed the amount of the grant which may be made in respect of a factory building under section 21.[77] Recent practice would indicate that rent subsidies are no longer granted to any significant extent.

(n) Grants to assist acquisition of land

8–23   Section 16(1)(g) of the 1986 Act permitted the former Industrial Development Authority to give grants to aid persons to acquire land, construct and adapt buildings, and provide services and facilities in connection with land. Although section 9(1) of the 1993 Act provided that Forfás assumed all of the powers of the dissolved Authority (and also provided that it in turn may assign such powers to either of its two agencies), section 3(3) of the Industrial Development Act 1995 added a qualification in the case of section 16 powers. Section 3(3) provides that the IDA may exercise all of the section 16(1) powers formerly exercised by the dissolved Authority.[78]

(2) STATUTORY LIMITS ON AGGREGATE OF CERTAIN GRANTS

8–24   In addition to the ceilings or limits specified in connection with the various forms of assistance outlined above, section 33 of the 1986 Act specifically provides that where grants or loan guarantees have been made pursuant to two or more of the following sections, the aggregate amount of such grants together with the capitalised value of any guarantee given under section 24 (fixed asset loan guarantees)[79] shall not exceed the 45–60% percentage limits specified in section 21(2).[80]

---

[75] Which otherwise satisfies the eligibility criteria are as *per* s.21(3) and (4).

[76] s.32 of the 1986 Act.

[77] s.32(3). See para. 8–10 above where s.21(2) was considered.

[78] Note that s.16 concerns the dissolved Authority's powers generally to acquire lands for the purposes of fostering industrial development. Consideration of such powers are outside the scope of this work, apart from s.16(1)(g) which concerns the provision of financial assistance to acquire land for industrial development (see para. 8–23 below).

[79] See para 8–14 above.

[80] See para. 8–10 above.

The relevant sections are: section 21 grants (fixed asset[81] but not additional employment[82]); section 22 grants (leased fixed assets);[83] section 23 grants (reduction of interest on fixed asset loans);[84] and, section 32 grants (rent subsidies).[85]

Section 34[86] of the 1986 Act provides that the total amount of money granted to a particular industrial undertaking under any section referred to in section 33 shall not exceed, in the aggregate, the higher of £4,000,000, or, £4,000,000 in excess of the aggregate amount of grants for which Government permission has previously been obtained. Government permission may be sought to exceed these limits.

(3) GOVERNMENT'S POWER TO OVERRIDE GRANT LIMITS

8–25 Section 35 provides that where Government permission to exceed limits set in Part III of the 1986 Act[87] is required, the Government has the power, in lieu of granting permission, to either grant permission subject to conditions, or grant permission for lower amounts.

III. GRANT AGREEMENT – LEGAL FRAMEWORK AND TERMS

(1) GRANT AGREEMENT

8–26 The terms and conditions attaching to the provision of grant assistance, in whatever form, will be agreed in a grant contract between the undertaking receiving the assistance and the relevant agency. Where an undertaking receiving assistance has a parent company, then the parent company will also be involved, giving assurances and performance guarantees together with the undertaking directly concerned. While the contract which governs the parameters under which assistance is given will vary from case to case,[88] the following five

---

[81] s.21(1).
[82] s.21(5)(c).
[83] See para. 8–12 above.
[84] See para. 8–13 above.
[85] See para. 8–22 above.
[86] s.12 of the 1993 Act raised the limits originally specified in s.34 of the 1986 Act, and s.12 was in turn further amended by s.34(1) of the 1998 Act.
[87] As set out in paras 8–09—8–24 above.
[88] This all depends on the content of the applicant's business plan and the type of grant assistance it is seeking.

categories illustrate matters which are likely to be covered in every grant contract.

First, the grant contract will require assurances from the grant recipient concerning how the grant assistance will be utilised: (a) a detailed plan on how the recipient intends to raise matching finance and how it will be repaid,[89] and (b) a detailed plan outlining the activities, assets or purposes on which the grant assistance will be expended.[90]

Second, recipient assurances will form part of the grant contract on matters such as the attainment of targets regarding: (a) employment creation targets promised, and (b) a timeframe for the achievement of employment targets.

Third, obligation clauses in the grant contract will oblige the recipient to obtain agency consents in respect of matters such as: (a) any future change in the ownership or control of the recipient,[91] or (b) a recipient's future wish to dispose of grant assisted assets, or (c) a recipient's future wish to pay royalties to a related third party in respect of assisted assets or processes.[92]

Fourth, the grant contract will also require recipient assurances concerning: (a) the transfer of investment funds from parent to recipient,[93] and (b) that the recipient will not incur or guarantee loans other than for the purpose of its business, and (c) that all grant aided assets will be fully insured against loss.

Fifth, the grant contract will permit the grant agency to reclaim assistance already granted or halt assistance promised in the event of: (a) a failure to reach promised employment targets within agreed timeframes, (b) a blatant breach of assistance utilisation terms, (c) an unauthorised change in control of the recipient, (d) the liquidation of the recipient, (e) the cessation of assisted activities, (f) a failure to make matching investment promised, or (g) a distribution of grants by way of dividend or loan payments. However, apart from the situation where the grant recipient is faced with a closure situation, the grant awarding

---

[89] In other words, the business plan of the applicant must demonstrate viability, and also satisfy the grant agency that grant funds will not be improperly used to repay outside financiers of the applicant.

[90] The applicant's business plan will have given elaborate information on this issue, which is then incorporated as an essential term of the grant contract.

[91] In this regard, the contract will invariably provide that if consent is given, it will only be on the basis that the new parent becomes a party to the grant agreement.

[92] In this regard, the contract will provide that restrictions will not be imposed where royalties are paid to independent third party entities, but may be imposed if the grant recipient proposes to make such payments to related entities.

[93] Although in practice the grant agency will not even consider awarding assistance unless this finance is already in place.

agency will normally not seek the repayment of grant assistance immediately unless the recipient has failed to remedy the breach, when called upon to do so. Therefore, the grant contract will invariably contain terms which provide that the repayment obligation will arise only in the event of a failure to correct a material breach of the contract terms. Also, it is common for the contract to provide that until such time as the breach is remedied in accordance with the contract's terms, the grant agency is entitled to withhold outstanding grant instalments.

8–27 Section 37 of the 1986 Act provides that whenever there is a contravention of a term or condition attached to a grant or other payment, the amount of such grant or payment shall be repayable to the grant agency concerned.[94] It further provides that where there is default of repayment, the grant shall be recoverable as a simple contract debt. It is common for the grant contract to provide that liability to repay grant in the event of failure to correct a material contravention shall subsist for a number of years (typically, five years) after the final payment of grant assistance.

Irish law will always be chosen as the governing law of the grant contract.

IV. OTHER STATE AGENCIES

(1) COUNTY ENTERPRISE BOARDS

8–28 Under the Industrial Development Act 1995 the County Enterprise Boards were established for the purpose of promoting and assisting economic development within limited geographical areas of the country.[95] An Enterprise Board confines its activities to the county in which it is based. Thirty five such boards were incorporated as companies limited by guarantee. The boards were set up in response to the needs of small businesses which were not suitable for funding by the larger State agencies, who focus on medium to larger size companies. Undertakings employing fewer than ten persons are the types of undertakings that the boards are intended to assist. For this purpose, section 10(3) of the 1995 Act permitted the Minister to allocate up to £100,000,000 for the purpose of allowing the boards to discharge their obligations. Each board is obliged to prepare a county enterprise plan and identify ways in which local enterprise can be fostered and

---

[94] However, in practice, as noted already, the awarding agency will first call on the grant recipient to remedy the default.
[95] s.10.

assisted. Boards are not permitted to allow their liabilities and obligations to exceed the amount of grant made available to them by the Minister.

Section 10(4) details the types of financial assistance that a board may make available. These can take the form of loans, grants or equity investments. Section 10(5) provides that any of these forms of assistance shall be in a form and on such terms and conditions as may be specified by the Minister. The boards are precluded from having the power to give loan guarantees, nor has a board the power to borrow or give security.

(2) ICC BANK PLC

8–29 ICC Bank plc is a State owned bank. It was established pursuant to the Industrial Credit Acts 1933 *et seq.* with the objective of assisting Irish companies, primarily those which aim at targeting export markets. The ICC was also given responsibility for administering funds by way of loans which have been made available to the State by the European Investment Bank. Loans granted by the ICC are State guaranteed and often the recipient of the assistance will be required to put up matching funds. The ICC may also take an equity participation in the recipient.

According to the Annual Report on Small Business in Ireland 1997,[96] in 1996 the State, through ICC, made £100,000,000 available to small businesses at long term low fixed interest rates under the Small Business Expansion Loan Scheme. This scheme was followed by the Access to Finance Scheme which amounted to £208,000,000. This funding was provided by the State in partnership with Irish banks and also the European Commission. At the time of writing, the State plans to divest itself of its interest in the ICC bank.

(3) ÚDARÁS NA GAELTACHTA[97]

8–30 Undertakings operating in Gaeltacht areas of the country may qualify for assistance from Údarás na Gaeltachta, a State agency whose statutory brief is to foster industrial development in the gaelic speaking parts of the country. Údarás can provide corporate finance in a number of ways such as grants for fixed asset acquisition, financing via the acquisition of equity holdings in undertakings, financing grants for training employees or promoting employment of additional employees.

---

[96] Published by Department of Enterprise, Trade and Employment.
[97] Údarás na Gaeltachta Acts 1979-1987.

Given that the gaelic speaking parts of the country tend to be concentrated along the less developed western seaboard, Údarás continues to grant the more traditional "hard" support grants (such as rent subsidies or building grants) alongside a full range of "soft" supports such as employment and training grants.

(4) FÁS

8–31   FÁS was set up by the State in 1988 with the aim of providing training schemes for workers, in particular those seeking to acquire skills in order to enter the labour market.[98] FÁS is permitted to make grants to companies who provide training for employees, typically by taking on additional employees and providing them with job training.

(5) SHANNON DEVELOPMENT

8–32   The Shannon Free Airport Development Company Limited was originally formed to promote the creation of industry in the immediate vicinity of Shannon Free Airport, Co Clare in 1959.[99] Since then, various Acts of the Oireachtas have greatly expanded the role of Shannon Development (as it is known) such that it now also has responsibility in several counties (or parts thereof) which border the river Shannon for the development of indigenous small and large industry alike (known as the Shannon Development region). Shannon Development's grant-giving powers are similar to those of Enterprise Ireland.[100] The IDA retains responsibility for attracting inward investment into the Shannon Development region.[101] Companies located in the Shannon Airport zone benefit from a special tax regime which traditionally has treated service companies in the zone much more favourably than service companies operating outside the zone by subjecting them to a much more favourable tax regime.[102] The significance of Shannon

---

[98] Its predecessor was known as AnCo, the national manpower agency.

[99] Shannon Free Airport Development Company Limited Act 1959.

[100] See paras 8–09—8–23 above. Enterprise Ireland does not tend to operate in the Shannon Development region.

[101] Although in certain sectors, Shannon Development, in co-operation with the IDA, seeks to attract inward investment into the region. However, within the Shannon Airport Zone, Shannon Development is autonomous, *i.e.* the IDA does not operate there.

[102] S.445 Taxes Consolidation Act 1997. Although, it should not be forgotten that companies located outside the Airport Zone *but yet within* the wider geographical area of Shannon Development's region of responsibility (the "Shannon Development region"), can nevertheless qualify for the relatively low manu-

Development's impact should not be understated. For example, the 1998 Act provided that the amount of grant finance that the Minister may make available to Shannon Development was to be increased from £200,000,000 to £250,000,000.[103]

(6) EU

8–33 Although there have been very significant wealth transfers to Ireland arising from EU membership (such as, for example, the transfer of Structural Funds), the amount of funds transferred in order to directly foster enterprise has been relatively insignificant, being confined mainly to certain types of training grant and limited technology development grants. The vast bulk of the funding for assisting enterprise development has come from the Irish taxpayer. However, where EU enterprise assistance of the types mentioned is available, the normal way that such assistance is administered is via the relevant State agencies, local authorities, or via local partnerships set up to administer such funding.[104]

(7) OTHER SECTORAL AGENCIES

8–34 Companies operating in the domestic sector may seek assistance from sectoral agencies such as Bord Iascaigh Mhara (fishing industry), Bord Fáilte (tourism) and other relevant agencies.

---

facturing tax rates applicable generally throughout the State if they qualify as *manufacturing* undertakings under the broad definition of manufacturing provided by s.443 of the 1997 Act (briefly considered in para. 8–09 above). Similarly, where a "computer services" undertaking receives certain types of grant or financial assistance from Shannon Development within the terms of s.443 of the 1997 Act, it can qualify as a manufacturing undertaking for corporate taxation purposes.

[103] s.35.
[104] It is outside the scope of this work to describe the various EU operational programmes, changing as they do, from time to time.

Legal Regulation of Mergers

I.   The Different Legal Regimes 477
II. The Mergers Act Regime 479
     (1) What is a Merger or Take-Over? 479
     (2) What criteria make a Merger or Take-Over notifiable
         under the Mergers Act? 482
     (3) Notification 482
         (a) Form 482
         (b) Contents 483
     (4) Power to request further information 485
     (5) Time limit for Ministerial consent or refusal 485
     (6) Courses of action open to Minister 485
         (a) Minister takes no action 485
         (b) Minister refers proposal to Competition Authority
             and makes Section 9 Order 486
         (c) Minister declines to make any order under
             Section 9 488
     (7) Appeal to High Court against Section 9 Order
         of Minister 488
     (8) Enforcement of Section 9 Orders 488
     (9) Title to shares or assets cannot pass unless Minister
         makes favourable decision within relevant period
         (or else makes no decision within that period) 489
         (a) Title cannot pass 489
         (b) Purported vendor has right to damages 489
     (10) Failure to notify 491
III. The Competition Acts Regime 491
     (1) The Competition Authority 492
     (2) Could a Merger or Take-Over be an anti-competitive
         arrangement contrary to section 4(1)? 494
     (3) 1997 Category Certificate 497
         (a) Authority's definition of a 'Merger' 498
         (b) Assessment of state of the market in which the
             Merger is located 498
             (i) The Hirfindahl/Hirschmann index (HHI) 499
             (ii) The Four-Firm Concentration Ratio (FFC) 502

(iii) The HHI and FFC compared 502
(iv) The HHI and FFC ignored 503
(c) Category Certificate inapplicable 503
  (i) Dominant position created or strengthened
    by merger 503
  (ii) Actual level of competition in relevant market
    already weak 503
  (iii) Ancillary restraints on competition 504
(4) Vertical Mergers 510
IV. **EC Mergers Regulation Regime** 511
The Merger Regulation: An Overview 511
(1) Concentrations 514
(a) Acquisition of control or decisive influence 514
(b) Joint Ventures as Concentrations: clarification
  or confusion 516
(c) Extra-territorial Concentrations 518
(2) Notifiable concentrations – 'Community Dimension' 519
(a) The original thresholds 519
(b) Additional thresholds 520
(c) Revised Turnover Rules for Credit and Financial
  Institutions 521
(3) "One-Stop Shop" 524
(a) Exclusive Regulator 524
  (i) National Competition/Merger Law
    disapplied 524
  (ii) Notification-triggering event 525
  (iii) Suspensive effect 525
  (iv) Regulation deadlines and legal bases for
    Commission decisions 526
(b) Appraisal test – compatible with the common
  market? 531
  (i) Collective Dominance 533
  (ii) Failing Firm Defence 537
  (iii) Full-Function Joint Ventures 537
(c) Exceptions to exclusive regulation 538
  (i) The German clause 538
  (ii) Legitimate interests 543
  (iii) The Dutch clause 544
(4) Full-Function Joint Ventures 545
(5) Powers of Commission to enforce Regulation 550
V. **The Takeover Panel Rules Regime** 552
A. Institutional Background 552
(1) Replacement of London Panel 552
(2) Irish Takeover Panel Act 1997 553

B. The Takeover Rules 554
    (1) General principles 554
    (2) Takeovers and Control 555
    (3) Influence of Principles on Rules 557
    (4) Restrictions on acquisitions 559
    (5) Exceptions 560
    (6) Mandatory Offer 561
    (7) Interplay with Mergers Act/EC Merger Regulation
        Regimes 562
C. Substantial Acquisition Rules 563
    (1) Prohibition 563
    (2) Exceptions 565
    (3) Prompt Disclosure Obligation 566
D. The Panel 567
    (1) Composition and Legal Form 567
    (2) Powers of Panel 567
        (a) Rulings and Directions 567
        (b) Censure 568
        (c) Hearings 568
    (3) Judicial Review of Panel 569
    (4) Liability of Panel 571
E. The Proposed Takeovers Directive 572
    (1) Mandatory Bid 573
    (2) Defensive Measures 573
    (3) Cross-Border Takeovers and determination of
        Supervisory Authority Competency 574
    (4) Impact of the Directive on national
        appeal systems 575
    (5) Forms of Consideration in a Takeover 575
    (6) Information requirements 576

Legal Regulation of Mergers

I. THE DIFFERENT LEGAL REGIMES

9–01 Depending on the scale and effects of a proposed merger or take-over, one or more different legal regimes and regulatory authorities may have jurisdiction over the transaction. In this chapter, each of these regimes will be considered in turn. However, before considering each regime, a brief overview will be instructive.

First, the provisions of the Mergers, Take-Overs and Monopolies (Control) Act 1978[1] (as amended) will apply where the merger or take-over satisfies certain asset or turnover thresholds set out in the 1978 Act. Where these thresholds are met, then the merger or take-over will have to be notified to the Minister seeking clearance under the Act.

Second, ever since the *Woodchester* decision of the Competition Authority in 1992, a merger or take-over which is suspected of restricting competition in the State contrary to the provisions of the Competition Acts 1991–1996, will have to be notified to the Competition Authority seeking clearance. Consequently, the merger or take-over may be subject to dual regulation: by the Minister under the Mergers Act regime, and the Competition Authority under the Competition Acts regime. Furthermore, even if the merger or take-over does not require notification to the Competition Authority under the Competition Acts regime, the Competition Authority may yet be involved in the regulation of the transaction because the Minister may call upon the Competition Authority to assess the merger or take-over before the Minister reaches a final decision on whether to permit or prohibit the transaction under the Mergers Act.

Third, additional regulations may apply to mergers under national legislation in certain sectors.[2]

---

[1] Mergers, Take-Overs and Monopolies (Control Act) 1978 No. 17 of 1978 (hereafter referred to as "the Mergers Act" for ease of reference).

[2] For example, a merger or take-over of an Irish insurance company requires the permission of the High Court; mergers or take-overs of banks operating under an Irish Banking Licence require the consent of the Central Bank. The Central Bank Act 1989 provides that the approval of the Central Bank is required where a bank, the holder of a licence to operate from the Central Bank, acquires or

Fourth, the European Community Merger Regulation regime may apply. Where a merger or take-over satisfies the EC Merger Regulation thresholds, it will fall within the ambit of the Community's Merger Regulation, in which event the Merger Task Force of the European Commission will have exclusive competition/merger control jurisdiction over the transaction. This is because the Merger Regulation[3] precludes the application of national mergers, take-overs and competition legislation to mergers or take-overs which are above a certain size and which have cross-border implications within the E.U. Consequently, where such a merger is taking place, any part of it that involves enterprises operating in the State will fall outside the jurisdiction of both the Mergers Act and the Competition Acts' regimes.

Fifth, Articles 81 and 82 EC may apply where the merger or take-over affects trade within a substantial part of the European Union.[4] Although the suitability of these articles for the regulation of mergers has been questioned,[5] nevertheless the European Commission and the European Court of Justice held, prior to the EC Merger Regulation's adoption, that Articles 81[6] and 82[7] may be applicable to certain types of merger transactions. While the adoption of the Merger Regulation altered this position by disabling the European Commission from applying Articles 81 or 82 to mergers that satisfy the Merger Regulation's thresholds,[8] the European Commission nevertheless stated that it reserved its position on whether it may apply Articles 81 or 82

---

controls 10 per cent of the total shares or total voting rights attaching to shares following an acquisition. Furthermore, Central Bank approval is also required under the Act where any person (including a corporate entity) proposes to make an acquisition, the effect of which would be that 20 per cent of the total assets in the State of all holders of licences would be controlled by that person.

[3] Council Regulation (EEC) 4064/89 December 31, 1989 on the control of concentrations between undertakings (O.J. L. 395/1 [1989], as rectified in [1990] O.J. L. 257/13, 21.09.1990, and amended by the 1994 Act of Accession) and as amended by Council Regulation (EC) 1301/97 of June 30, 1997 ([1997] O.J. L.180/1).

[4] The Treaty of Amsterdam changed the numbering of these two Articles from 85 and 86, respectively.

[5] For a sample of various views on this matter, see Elland "The Merger Control Regulation and its Effect on National Merger Controls and the Residual Application of Articles 85 and 86" (1991) 1 E.C.L.R. 19; Bright, "The Merger Control Regulation: Do Member States Still Have an Independent Role in Merger Control?" (1991) 5 E.C.L.R. 184; Brittan, "The Law and Policy of Merger Control in the E.E.C." (1990) 15 E.L.R. 351; Levitt "Article 88, the Merger Control Regulation and the English Courts: BA/Dan-Air (1993) 2 E.C.L.R. 73.

[6] Joined Cases 142 & 156/84 *BAT and Reynolds v. Commission* [1987] E.C.R. 4487.

[7] Case 6/72 *Europemballage Corp. and Continental Can Co. Inc. v. Commission* [1973] E.C.R. 215.

[8] *i.e.* very large mergers which affect a substantial part of the common market: see section IV of this chapter below where the EC Merger Regulation thresholds are considered.

to sub-threshold mergers.[9] In practice, the Commission has not attempted to apply 81 or 82 to such transactions. However, while the Commission may no longer have neither the legal competence or the political will to apply Articles 81 and 82, the position may be otherwise were private party enforcement of those Articles to be attempted. Several leading commentators take the view that although Article 81 has lost its 'direct effectiveness' once the European Commission's competence[10] to apply Article 81 has been disabled *vis-à-vis* mergers, Article 82 on the other hand does not suffer from such infirmity.[11] Consequently, private parties may yet be able to invoke Article 82 against a sub-threshold transaction.

Sixth, where a takeover involves a company whose securities are listed, the regime introduced by the Irish Takeover Panel Act 1997 and the Panel's Takeover Rules may be applicable.[12]

II. THE MERGERS, TAKE-OVERS AND MONOPOLIES (CONTROL) ACT REGIME[13]

(1) What is a Merger or Take-Over?

9–02 Although used in the 1978 Mergers Act's title and in the body of the Act, neither the term "merger" nor "take-over" are given a specific definition under the Act. Instead, the notion of *control* lies at the heart

---

[9] The Commission's competence to apply Arts. 81 or 82 arises out of Art. 83 (formerly Art. 87) and Council Regulation 17/62/EEC (O.J. Sp. Ed. 1962 No. 204/62, p. 87). Art. 22.1 of the Merger Regulation disables Regulation 17/62 *vis-à-vis* mergers and thus the Merger Regulation effectively prevents the Commission from applying those Articles to mergers. However, in the minutes to the 1989 meeting where the Council adopted the Regulation, the Commission expressly reserved its position on whether it may apply Arts. 81 and 82 to sub-threshold ('small') mergers using its residual powers under Art. 85 (formerly Art. 89) of the Treaty (see text of Statements Accompanying minutes, reproduced at (1990) 4 C.M.L.R. 314). Given the cumbersome nature of Art. 85, it is questionable whether it could ever be used by the Commission as an effective mechanism for merger control.

[10] *i.e.* Regulation 17/62/EEC.

[11] Once Regulation 17/62 has been disabled, then the Commission is no longer competent to grant exemptions under Art. 81(3). Consequently, as national courts cannot grant exemptions, Art. 82(1) loses its direct effectiveness.

[12] No. 5 of 1997. (Note that, at the time of writing, the proposed 13th E.C. Directive on Company Law has still not been finally adopted. It seeks to put in place a regime with elements which all Member States must implement *vis-à-vis* takeovers of public companies presenting cross-border implications).

[13] Hereafter referred to as the Mergers Act for ease of reference. Note that certain provisions of the Act were amended by the Competition Act 1991.

of the legislative definition of whether a "merger" or "take-over" has
occurred. According to section 1(3)(a) of the Mergers Act, a "merger or
take-over shall be taken to exist where two or more enterprises,[14] at
least one of which carries on business in the State, come under common
control."

It is clear that control can be acquired in a number of ways. Section
1 proceeds to define "common control" situations:

– where the decision as to how, or by whom, each enterprise shall be
  managed can be made by either the same person, or by the same
  group of persons acting in concert (section 1(3)(b)), or

– where the right to appoint or remove a majority of the board or
  management committee of an enterprise has been acquired (section
  1(3)(c)(i)), or

– where an enterprise acquires shares carrying voting[15] rights in
  another enterprise, except where the voting rights in the second
  enterprise which are controlled by the first enterprise (i) are not after
  the acquisition more than 25 per cent of the total of such voting rights,
  or (ii) are before the acquisition more than one-half of the total of
  such rights (section 1(3)(c)(ii)), or

– where the assets, including goodwill (or a substantial part thereof)
  of an enterprise are acquired by another enterprise, the acquisition
  shall be deemed to constitute a merger or take-over for the purposes
  of the Act if, upon the acquisition a result of the acquisition is to
  place one enterprise in a position to replace the other in the business
  in which the other was engaged in immediately before the acquisition

---

[14] Subs. 1(1) defines an "enterprise" as being a person or partnership engaged for
profit in the supply or distribution of goods or the provision of services, including
a society (including a credit union, registered under the Industrial and Provident
Societies Acts 1893 to 1978); a society registered under the Friendly Societies
Acts 1896 to 1977; a society established under the Building Societies Act 1989; a
holding company within the meaning of s.155 of the Companies Act 1963.
"Service" is defined as including any professional service, but does not include
any service provided by the holder of a licence under s.9 of the Central Bank
Act 1971; nor any service provided by a trustee savings bank certified under the
Trustee Savings Bank Acts 1989; nor any service provided under a contract of
employment; nor any service provided by a Local Authority within the meaning
of the Local Government Act 1941. S.15(1) of the Competition Act 1991 further
provides that "service" as defined in subs. 1(1) of the Mergers Act shall not
include the owning and transfer of land where this activity is the sole activity of
the enterprise in which control is being sought.

[15] s.1(3)(d) provides that "voting rights" shall be deemed to be controlled by an
enterprise when it can determine how the votes concerned shall be cast, and
further that "voting rights" do not include voting rights which arise only in
specified circumstances.

(section 1(3)(e)). (Hence a "merger" or "take-over" can occur merely where an enterprise merely acquires the business of another enterprise, rather than acquiring the actual shares or tangible assets of the other enterprise).

Section 1(3)(f) and (g) provides that certain situations cannot be regarded as "common control" situations. Consequently they do not constitute mergers or take-overs within the meaning of the Mergers Act.

Section 1(3)(f) provides that where enterprises come under common control under a receiver or liquidator in the manner described in section 1(3)(b),[16] then no merger or take-over has occurred. It further provides that where the person acquiring common control is an underwriter or jobber (acting as such), then the transaction cannot be regarded as a merger or take-over where control, as defined in section 1(3)(c)(i) or section 1(3)(c)(ii),[17] is acquired by such person. Finally, where a person acquires control in the manner described in section 1(3)(e) in their capacity as a receiver or liquidator, the transaction will not be a merger or take-over.[18]

Section 1(3)(g) provides that transactions between bodies corporate are not a merger or take-over where each is a wholly owned subsidiary of the same company.[19] Section 2(3) provides that the Act shall not apply to enterprises coming under common control where this occurs solely as a result of a testamentary disposition or an intestacy.

---

[16] Where the decision as to how, or by whom, each enterprise shall be managed can be made by either the same person, or by the same group of persons acting in concert (section 1(3)(b)).

[17] Where the right to appoint or remove a majority of the board or management committee of an enterprise has been acquired (section 1(3)(c)(i)), or where an enterprise acquires shares carrying voting rights in another enterprise, except where the voting rights in the second enterprise which are controlled by the first enterprise (i) are not after the acquisition more than 25 per cent of the total of such voting rights, or (ii) are before the acquisition more than one-half of the total of such rights (section 1(3)(c)(ii)).

[18] Where the assets, including goodwill (or a substantial part thereof) of an enterprise are acquired by another enterprise, the acquisition shall be deemed to constitute a merger or take-over for the purposes of the Act if, upon the acquisition a result of the acquisition is to place one enterprise in a position to replace the other in the business in which the other was engaged in immediately before the acquisition (section 1(3)(e)). (Hence a "merger" or "take-over" can occur merely where an enterprise merely acquires the business of another enterprise, rather than acquiring the actual shares or tangible assets of the other enterprise).

[19] s.1(3)(g).

(2) What criteria make a Merger or Take-Over notifiable under the Mergers Act?

9–03   Under the Mergers Act, where there has been a "merger" or "take-over" then it becomes notifiable to the Minister where at least one of the enterprises carries on business within Ireland[20] and provided certain asset or turnover thresholds are met.

Section 2(1)(a) provides that the Act applies only if the value of the gross assets of each of two (or more) of the enterprises involved was not less than £10 million in the most recent financial year, or, if the turnover of each of those two (or more) enterprises is not less than £20 million.[21] However, notwithstanding these thresholds, the Minister may, by order, apply the Act to a proposed merger or take-over where, in the Minister's opinion, the exigencies of the common good so warrant. In respect of such transactions, section 2(5)(a) provides that the Minister may by order declare that a proposed merger or take-over will be subject to the jurisdiction of the Act, which will arise upon the making of the order. Section 2(1)(b) provides that "turnover" does not include any payments in respect of VAT on sales or any excise duties.

(3) Notification

(a) Form

9–04   Section 5(1) requires that each of the enterprises involved in the proposed merger or take-over shall notify the Minister in writing of the proposal and provide full details within "the specified period" of "the offer capable of acceptance" having been made, the effect of which would bring the enterprises under common control. This clearly intends that the notification be made *in advance* of any deal being completed. Section 5(4) provides that the "specified period" shall be one month or such other period as the Minister may specify.

Unlike a notification under the European Community Merger Regulation,[22] there is no prescribed format that a notification should

---

[20] s.1(3)(1).

[21] These thresholds, set out in S.I. No. 135 of 1993 update the original thresholds which were significantly lower.

[22] s.19 of the Competition Act 1991 provides that the transmission to the Minister by the E.C. Commission of a copy of a merger notification made to the Commission under the E.C. Merger Regulation 4064/89 shall constitute a notification under s.5 of the Mergers Act. However, it also provides that the "relevant period" under s.5 of the Mergers Act shall not commence until the Commission makes a decision under either Arts. 9 or 21 of that Regulation. Under Art. 9 the Commission may decide to allow the Minister regulate a merger which would otherwise fall within the Commission's exclusive competence to regulate, where the Commission takes the view that the notified transaction

follow. A fee of £4,000 must accompany the merger notification.[23] It is not entirely clear from the fee regulations that the fee is payable per transaction as opposed to per notification. Thus, it appears that where parties notify separately, rather than jointly, then a separate fee must accompany each notification that is made to the Minister even though they all concern the same transaction.[24]

(b) Contents

9–05 A well prepared notification should provide the following information to the Minister[25]: the identify of the parties involved, whether they are subsidiaries, holding companies or are controlled by other entities or person; up to date audited accounts for the enterprises; details of the proposed transaction[26] including means of control, the consideration involved and the period within which the transaction is to take place; details of any future acquisition, whether already under way, or planned for the future; the beneficial effects of the merger for the enterprises, the consumer, the goods or services sector concerned; the estimated market shares of the enterprises before the merger, and the merged entity after the merger; identification of other players in

---

poses a distinct threat to the Irish market. Under Art. 21, the Commission may, at the request of the Minister, permit the Minister to take appropriate measures to protect legitimate interests notwithstanding the Commission's exclusive jurisdiction under the Regulation. Article 21 lists public security, plurality of the media and prudential rules as "legitimate interests". Where a Member State seeks to invoke any other public interest as a ground for justifying regulating a merger in some respect, the State must first communicate its intention to the Commission, which shall recognise such interest provided it is comparable with E.C. law.

[23] S.I. No. 381 of 1996 (The Merger or Take-over (Notification Fee) Regulations 1996) adopted pursuant to s.5(1A) which was inserted into the Act by the Competition Act 1996, thereby permitting the Minister to specify notification fees for merger notifications under the Mergers Act.

[24] Interestingly, a bulletin from the Company Law committee of the Law Society reveals that informal contacts between the committee and the competition policy section of the Department of Enterprise and Employment indicate that in "grey area" cases the £4,000 fee need not be tendered. For example, such a situation might arise where the enterprises involved in the transaction have assets and turnover far in excess of the Act's thresholds but their assets and turnover in the State do not meet the thresholds in respect of their assets or turnover within the State. Such enterprises may nevertheless notify the proposed transaction to the Minister as a precaution in which case the Department may decide that the fee need not accompany the notification (*Law Society of Ireland Gazette*, January/ February 1997, p.34).

[25] According to a Department circular available to the public, on what types of information are normally required by the Department.

[26] The Department will accept a draft legal contract, or, where applicable in the case of a publicly quoted company, an offer document.

the same markets; any increases in employment numbers; the motivation of the merging enterprises for the proposal; details of any changes in operation of any of the participating enterprises such as levels of employment, purchase or distribution patterns, geographical location; terms and conditions of employees, product changes. Where foreign companies are involved, details of any other merger clearances that are required in any other jurisdiction should be supplied, as well as details of whether such enterprises have been the subject of competition law proceedings in any other jurisdiction.

However, since the enactment of the Competition Act 1991 parties may have to address additional matters in the notification as well. Under the amended section 7 of the Mergers Act, the Minister may refer a merger or take-over to the Competition Authority for its "views" and "opinion" before making a final decision on the notified transaction. Should the Minister involve the Competition Authority, the risk increases that the Minister, who as a merger regulator has adopted a benevolent approach to merger regulation traditionally, may be swayed by a negative Competition Authority assessment of the proposal. Therefore, in order to minimise such a risk, the merging parties may, in their Mergers Act notification, address the criteria under which the Competition Authority would assess the merger or take-over (were it to be asked to do so). Such a pre-emptive strategy is designed to foreclose any potential Competition concerns that the Minister might have about the notified transaction and thereby may successfully dissuade the Minister from making a referral to the Authority in the first place.

Although section 7 of the Mergers Act does not state on what grounds the Minister may base the decision to refer the proposed transaction to the Competition Authority, presumably the Minister will refer if she thinks that there may be concerns about the merger's effects on competition in the State. In any event, the criteria by which the Competition Authority may consider a merger are set out in section 8(2) of the Act and consequently, parties are well-advised to address these criteria in the notification made to the Minister.

Section 8(2) of the Mergers Act[27] provides that the Competition Authority shall be required to give:

(a) its "opinion" on whether or not the proposed merger or take-over concerned would: be likely to prevent or restrict competition or restrain trade in goods or services and would be likely to operate against the common good.

(b) its "views" on the likely effect of the proposed merger or take-over

---

[27] As inserted by s.17(4) of the Competition Act 1991.

on the common good in respect of: continuity of supplies or services; levels of employment; regional development; rationalisation of operations in the interests of greater efficiency; research and development; increased production; access to markets; shareholders and partners; employees; consumers.

Accordingly, where parties feel that the Minister might be liable to refer the proposal to the Competition Authority, they would be well advised to address these criteria in the Mergers Act notification.

(4) Power to request further information

9–06 Section 5(2) of the Mergers Act provides that when the Minister has received a notification from each of the enterprises involved, the Minister has one month from the date of the receipt of the last notification to request the parties, or any of them, to furnish further information. The Minister additionally has the power to specify the time in which such information must be provided. The one month period that the Minister has, in which to request further information, does not begin to run until the last notification is received. Therefore, in this respect, it may be to the parties' advantage for the parties to arrange to make a joint notification in order to expedite the Minister's consideration of the transaction.

(5) Time limit for Ministerial consent or refusal

9–07 The Minister has three months from the commencement of the "relevant period" in which to make a decision in respect of the notified transaction. Section 6(1) provides that this three month period ("the relevant period") commences from either the date on which the Minister first receives a notification – or, where she requests further information, three months from the date she receives the requested information. If the Minister fails to prohibit the merger within the three month period, the merger or take-over may proceed by default.[28]

(6) Courses of action open to Minister

9–08 The Minister can take one of several courses of action as follows.

(a) Minister takes no action

9–09 Where the Minister has taken no decision by the end of the relevant period, section 3(1)(c) provides that the proposed merger or take-over may proceed by default.

---

[28] s.3(1)(c).

(b) Minister refers proposal to Authority and makes section 9 order

9–10 Under section 7(b) the Minister has 30 days in which to decide whether to refer a notified merger or take-over to the Competition Authority for consideration. Where this course of action is chosen, then the Competition Authority shall investigate the proposal referred and shall make its report to the Minister by a date specified by the Minister. The criteria that the Competition Authority will assess the proposal under are those set out in section 8(2).[29] The minimum period permitted by the Act for the Competition Authority to conduct its deliberations is 30 days from the date of reference by the Minister. Upon receipt of the Competition Authority's report, the Minister, having due regard to commercial confidentiality, shall publish the Competition Authority's report within two months of it being furnished to her by the Authority.[30]

Having received the Competition Authority's report, the Minister can make two types of order under section 9: either prohibit the proposed transaction (absolute prohibition order) or else prohibit it subject to certain conditions (conditional prohibition order).

The criteria on which the Minister will base either type of order are set out in section 9. Section 9(1)(a) of the Act provides that the Minister – having considered the Competition Authority's report on the matters referred to in section 8(2) – may[31] if she thinks the exigencies of the common good so warrant, either prohibit the proposed transaction absolutely (absolute prohibition order) or else prohibit it subject to conditions (conditional prohibition order). In providing that the Minister's decision must be in furtherance of the common good, section 9 makes it clear that the Minister may base the ultimate decision on matters extraneous to the Authority's report, if the exigencies of the common good so warrant.[32]

A Minister who wishes to take either course of action will have to ensure that the notified transaction was referred to the Competition

---

[29] At para. 9–05 above.

[30] s.17(5) of the Competition Act 1991 which amends s.8 of the Mergers Act, obliges the Minister to publish. On 9 April, 1998, the Minister, having considered the Authority's report, prohibited the take-over of Balcas Ltd by Coillte Teoranta. Under the proposed acquisition, Coillte, which already held a 97 per cent market share of roundwood sales in the State, would have further strengthened its dominance.

[31] The section also provides that this decision may be taken by the Minister "after consultation with any other Government Minister appearing to him to be concerned."

[32] s.9(1)(a) (as amended by s.18 of the Competition Act 1991) specifies that the Minister's decision shall include, but is not confined to, the s.8(2) criteria (which the Competition Authority had considered the proposal under).

Authority within 30 days[33] of the commencement of the relevant period. Thus, where a Minister has doubts about a notified transaction, prompt action is required. If the Minister fails to refer to the Competition Authority within the 30 day period (from the commencement of the relevant period), the Minister's power to make a section 9 prohibition order or a conditional prohibition order will be lost. This reality was starkly demonstrated in the recent *Guinness Ireland Group Limited/United Beverages Holdings Ltd* acquisition of the entire share capital of the latter by the former. The Minister failed to refer the transaction within the 30 days from the commencement of the relevant period with the result that the Minister effectively was precluded from being able to act under section 9 to either prohibit the transaction, or at least require that the merger arrangements be modified.[34]

Where the Minister makes a conditional prohibition order, the order shall include a condition requiring the merger or take-over to be completed within 12 months of the making of the order.[35]

Where an order is made under section 9, the order shall state the reasons upon which it is based. In the case of a conditional prohibition order, it may have retrospective effect.[36] It is further provided that the Minister may revoke[37] an order made pursuant to section 9, and may amend such order where the enterprises concerned agree.[38] Every order made under section 9 must be laid before the Oireachtas and may be annulled by a resolution of either House where adopted in the 21 days after the order was laid before that House. However, this is stated to be without prejudice to the validity of anything done thereunder in the intervening period.

---

[33] s.7(b).
[34] This concerned a take-over which raised potentially serious competition implications. The parties decided to notify the arrangements to the Competition Authority under the Competition legislation, thereby granting the Competition Authority Competition Act (but not Mergers Act) jurisdiction. One reason why the parties may have taken this route is that the enactment of the Competition Act, 1996 gave the Competition Authority power to investigate, of its own volition, anti-competitive transactions and practices. Consequently, had the parties decided not to notify the Competition Authority, they may well have been faced with an investigation by the Competition Authority. However, it is interesting to note that had the notified transaction occurred before the adoption of the 1996 Act, the parties would not have had to be concerned about a Competition Authority investigation and so the State would effectively have been unable to regulate the transaction. (In the event, the Competition Authority indicated that it would approve the transaction, subject to the parties divesting themselves of certain interests): Decision No. 512, June 17, 1998.
[35] s.9(1)(b).
[36] s.9(2).
[37] s.9(4).
[38] s.9(4).

488 Corporate Finance Law

(c) Minister declines to make any order under section 9

9–11 It should not be overlooked that the Minister may decide not to make any order under section 9.

Where the Minister decides, after having received the Competition Authority's report, not to make an order under section 9, the Minister, as soon as practicable after receipt of the notification, is obliged by section 7(a) to inform the enterprises which made the notification[39] that the Minister has decided not to make an order under section 9 in relation to the proposed merger or take-over. Effectively, this amounts to clearance of the notified transaction. Should the Minister in this situation fail, for whatever reason, to notify the parties that she does not propose making a section 9 order,[40] the merger or take-over will in any event take effect pursuant to section 3(1)(c) once the relevant period has elapsed.[41]

(7) Appeal to High Court against section 9 order of Minister

9–12 Section 12 of the Mergers Act provides that where the Minister makes an order under section 9, an appeal on a point of law may be made to the High Court against the order within one month of the coming into effect of the order, by any enterprise referred to in the order. Where the High Court allows any such appeal, the Minister shall, by order, amend or revoke as may be appropriate the order appealed against, as soon as practicable. Unlike a section 9 order,[42] it is not required that this subsequent order be laid before the Houses of the Oireachtas.[43]

(8) Enforcement of section 9 orders

9–13 Section 13 of the Mergers Act provides that the Minister or any other person may seek an injunction to enforce compliance with the terms of an order under section 9. Criminal proceedings may also be instituted.

Where a person contravenes a section 9 order, whether by act or omission, that person shall be guilty of an offence.[44] The criminal penalties vary depending on whether the offence is prosecuted

---

[39] s.7(a) also provides that the Minister shall similarly inform "any other enterprise involved which enquires of him."

[40] *i.e.* the Minister neither intends to prohibit the transaction nor prohibit it conditionally.

[41] *i.e.* proceeds by default. See para. 9–09 above.

[42] s.9(5).

[43] s.12(4).

[44] s.13(2).

summarily or on indictment. Upon summary conviction, the fines vary from a £500 maximum fine (with a £100 maximum fine for every day the offence is continuing), and/or a prison term of six months maximum duration, or both. Where a conviction on indictment is secured, the fines range to a maximum of £5,000 (together with a maximum of £500 for each day the offence continues), and/or a prison term of up to two years. Further penalties are provided where a person who has been convicted fails to comply with an order requiring him to perform a specified act.[45] Persons who aid, abet, assist or conspire with another, to do anything which might be an offence as described, are themselves guilty of an offence,[46] and liable to the penalties described, just as the person who was convicted was liable. Section 13(6) provides that where an offence under section 13 committed by either a body corporate, or a person acting for a body corporate or an unincorporated body, is proved to have been committed with the consent of, connivance of, or to be attributable to any neglect on the part of any person who is a director, manager, secretary, or member of the management committee or other controlling authority of any such body,[47] that person shall also be guilty of an offence.

(9) Title to shares or assets cannot pass unless Minister makes favourable decision within relevant period (or makes no decision within that period)

(a) Title cannot pass

9–14 It will be of vital interest for the parties whether the Minister acts (and if so, how) within the relevant period. This is because section 3 of the Mergers Act provides that title to shares or assets[48] shall not pass until the earlier of the following occurs:

(i) the Minister has stated in writing[49] pursuant to section 7(a) that

---

[45] s.13(3).

[46] s.13(4)

[47] Or who is any other similar officer of any such body.

[48] s.1(3)(e) defines the term "assets" to include "goodwill" such that a merger or take-over is deemed to have occurred where upon the acquisition by one party of another's business, the acquiring party replaces that other party in the business. From this definition, it would appear therefore that a merger or take-over may occur merely where the asset acquired is the business of another without any acquisition of tangible physical assets or shares actually taking place. Consequently, presumably any ownership rights to such a business cannot pass until s.3(1) has been satisfied as outlined above.

[49] s.3(2) provides that this statement shall cease to have effect at the end of the 12 month period beginning on the date of the statement if the enterprises the subject of the proposed merger or take-over referred to in the statement have not come under common control during that period.

she has decided not to make a section 9 order in relation to the proposed merger or take-over, or

(ii) the Minister has stated in writing that she has made a conditional order[50] in relation to the proposed merger or take-over in which event the proposed transaction may proceed subject to compliance with the Ministerial conditions, or

(iii) the relevant period – three months[51] – has elapsed without the Minister having made an order under section 9 in relation to the proposed merger or take-over.

Should the Minister fail within the relevant period to make a statement either in terms of (i)[52] or else (ii),[53] then the merger or take-over may proceed pursuant to (iii) upon the expiry of the relevant period. Of course, if on the other hand, the Minister has instead made an absolute prohibition order under section 9, the aforegoing is moot.

Parties who fail to notify in accordance with the Act will face very grave difficulties in view of the Act's stipulation that title to assets or shares may not pass. There appears to be no provision in the Mergers Act, which requires the Minister to accept a late notification, i.e. notification of a merger or take-over, which has already been put into effect. Should the Minister accept such a notification, although the point is undecided, it may be that the Minister, where favourably disposed to the merger notwithstanding the failure to notify on time, might clear the merger by way of a conditional prohibition order. Section 9(2) provides that such orders can have retrospective effect. Whether a Minister would be acting properly in accepting a late notification for the purposes of giving it retrospective approval using a section 9(2) conditional prohibition order, is another matter.[54]

(b) Purported vendor has right to damages

9–15 Where a purported sale of shares is rendered invalid under section 3, the purported vendor shall be entitled to recover from the purported purchaser any damages that the vendor suffers by reason

---

[50] Pursuant to s.9(1)(a).

[51] s.6(1) defines the relevant period as being three months beginning on the date on which the Minister first receives the notification under s.5(1) or, where the Minister requests further information under s.5(2), the date of receipt of such information.

[52] *i.e.* no s.9 order will be made.

[53] *i.e.* conditional order has been made.

[54] The possibility (and uncertainty) of resorting to a s.9(2) conditional prohibition order in this situation is raised by O'Connor, "Notifying the Irish Regulatory Authorities of a Merger or Take-Over" (1994) I.L.T. 156.

only of the invalidity.[55] However, the purchaser will have a defence to such an action if he can satisfy the court that, before the purported sale he had notified the vendor of circumstances relating to the proposed sale which gave rise to the possibility of such invalidity.

(10) Failure to notify

9–16 Where the proposed transaction has not been notified in accordance with the Act, section 3 provides that no title to shares or assets[56] may pass. In addition to preventing title passing, the Act also provides criminal penalties for failure to notify. Section 5(3) provides that where there has been a contravention of section 5(1) (obligation to notify) or 5(2) (obligation to provide further information), then upon summary conviction, the person in control of the enterprise which failed to notify the Minister in accordance with either 5(1) or (2) shall be liable:

- upon summary conviction to a fine not exceeding £1,000, and for continued contravention a daily default fine not exceeding £100, or

- upon conviction on indictment, a fine not exceeding £200,000 and, for continued contravention, a daily default fine not exceeding £20,000.

Section 5(3)(c) provides that a person is a "person in control" for the purposes of these offences who: in the case of a body corporate, is an officer of that body who knowingly and wilfully authorises or permits the contravention; in the case of a partnership, is a partner who knowingly and wilfully authorises or permits the contravention; in the case of any other form of enterprise, is any individual in control of that enterprise who knowingly and wilfully authorises or permits the contravention.

III. THE COMPETITION ACTS REGIME

9–17 As already discussed above, one impact of the enactment of the Competition Act 1991 was to give the newly established Competition Authority a role in the Minister's activities when the Minister assesses proposed mergers or take-overs under the Mergers Act.[57]

---

[55] s.4.

[56] As noted above at para. 9–14, assets includes goodwill.

[57] Where the Minister so wishes, she may involve the Competition Authority by making a s.7 reference to the Competition Authority, asking it to give its "views" and "opinions" on a wide range of matters concerning the notified merger, before making her final decision on the merger or take-over under s.9 of the Mergers' Act: see paras 9–05 and 9–10 above.

However, from an early stage in its life, the Competition Authority asserted an independent jurisdiction for itself over mergers.[58] The Competition Authority based this jurisdiction on its view that a merger or take-over could potentially be regarded as an anti-competitive arrangement within the meaning of section 4(1) of the 1991 Competition Act, *i.e.* an agreement that prevented, restricted or distorted competition within the State. Section 4 prohibits as void and unenforceable any such arrangements between undertakings where they may affect trade within the State. Consequently, after 1991, parties to mergers or take-overs now had to consider whether their proposed transactions were compatible not only with the Mergers Act regime, but also with section 4(1) of the Competition Act.[59] Notwithstanding this potential for "duplicity" to arise between the two regimes, in practice, chaos has not resulted as the Authority, as will be explained below, will only require mergers to be notified to it where a competition issue arises.

(1) The Competition Authority

9–18 When the Competition Authority first indicated that mergers could potentially constitute anti-competitive arrangements within the meaning of section 4(1), it certainly came as a surprise to many. This was particularly so as it was not readily evident from the 1991 Competition Act that the Competition Authority was intended to have any role in merger control under that Act. A brief overview on what

---

[58] *i.e.* independent of the Mergers Act 1978. Though it should be noted that while the Authority asserted that mergers with anti-competitive elements were within the scope of the Competition Act 1991's s.4 prohibition, such mergers were not obliged to be notified to the Authority. In other words, unlike the Mergers Act, there is no obligatory time limit in the Competition Act 1991 in which notifications have to be made to the Authority. However, in practice, parties will notify the Authority if there is a fear that the competition rules of the Competition legislation might be infringed. In this event, the merger should be notified to the Authority for the purposes of seeking the grant of a Certificate. A Certificate is a Decision by the Authority to the effect that a transaction, although it might appear anti-competitive, is not in fact so in substance. The award of a Certificate gives the holder an immunity in damages should any party subsequently challenge its award as being contrary to s.4. In recent times, legal advisers have to be more cautious in advising clients not to make a notification to the Authority because under the 1996 Competition Act, the Authority acquired its powers to investigate, of its own motion, suspected breaches of the 1991 Act. However, it must be emphasised, that in practice, many mergers notified to the Minister under the Mergers Act, are not notified to the Authority under the Competition Act, as the parties' legal advisers obviously take the view that the risk of the merger being anti-competitive (and thus requiring notification to the Authority for the purposes of being awarded a Certificate) are minimal.
[59] The notification fee required by the Competition Authority is £250 per notification (S.I. No. 379 of 1996). Parties may notify separately or jointly.

the Act appeared to intend the Competition Authority to do is instructive in this regard. Section 4(1) of the 1991 Act prohibits as void and unenforceable all agreements which prevent restrict or distort competition within the State. The Competition Authority's chief task under the Act was (and is) to award Certificates or Licences in respect of arrangements notified to it. A Certificate is awarded where the Competition Authority is of the view that although the notified arrangements might appear to have as their object or effect the prevention, restriction or distortion of competition in the State contrary to section 4(1), the arrangements do not in fact have such object or effect, and therefore merit the award of a Certificate. Effectively, the award of a Certificate meant that, even if the Certificate was subsequently struck down by a Court, the parties to the arrangements would have an immunity from damages for the period while the Certificate was in force. The Competition Authority was also empowered to issue Licences in respect of arrangements which, although they had anti-competitive features, overall led to improvements in the production or distribution of goods and services and imposed no more than indispensable restrictions on the parties freedom of action. Consequently, such arrangements, although ineligible for a Certificate, would merit the award of a Licence. Where the Competition Authority saw fit to grant a Licence, unlike a Certificate, it would be granted for a specific finite period of time and would not necessarily be renewable.

Thus, the Competition Authority's chief functions under the 1991 Act appeared to be confined to considering whether to award Certificates or Licences in respect of apparently anti-competitive trade practices. Mergers or take-overs did not appear to be contemplated as anti-competitive trade practices within the meaning of the Act, and therefore, it was assumed that they did not require notification to the Competition Authority (under the 1991 Act). This assumption seemed to be bolstered by the fact that – by contrast with the Mergers Act which had a mandatory prior notification requirement and demanded regulatory clearance as a prerequisite – parties to section 4(1) transactions were not required to seek Licences or Certificates before they could transact with each other. The 1991 Act regime imposed no legal obligation to engage in prior notification of proposed arrangements, something which one would expect to find in an effective merger control regime. Thus, apart from its involvement in regulating proposed transactions *under the Mergers Act* when requested to do so by the Minister, there was no hint that the Competition Authority was to engage in the regulation of mergers under the 1991 Competition Act.

(2) Could a Merger or Take-Over be an anti-competitive arrangement contrary to section 4(1)?

9–19 However, in retrospect, the view taken by the Competition Authority – that section 4(1) could be interpreted so as to cover mergers or take-overs which had anti-competitive features or implications – was hardly that surprising. In this regard, it was already the view of the European Commission and the European Court of Justice that section 4(1)'s European forerunner, Article 81(1),[60] could be applied in order to prohibit mergers which actually or potentially distort competition in the Community.[61] Although the correctness of the Community view was severely questioned in certain quarters,[62] it continued to maintain this view until it was given a specific merger control tool in the form of the European Merger Regulation in 1989. Until then, the European Commission used the threat of Article 81(1) as a legal mechanism for the control of mergers that might adversely affect trade in the Community. However, for many reasons Article 81 was quite unsuitable for this purpose, principally because (like section 4(1)) it has no prior notification mechanism, nor in-built time limits to assure speedy clearance/prohibition decision-making, both of which are essential features of any effective merger control regime.

Therefore, while there was nothing overt in section 4(1) which might indicate that mergers or take-overs violated section 4(1)'s prohibition, nevertheless, there was European precedent for such an interpretation arising out of the Article 81 caselaw. In *Woodchester Bank Ltd/UDT Bank Ltd*,[63] the Competition Authority held that, because section 4(1) prohibits "all agreements" which restrict competition in the State, in principle there was nothing in the section 4(1) prohibition to preclude mergers from being classified as section 4(1) "agreements" where their object or effect was the restriction of competition in the State.[64]

Woodchester Bank Ltd was acquiring all of the share capital in UDT Bank Ltd. The merger was notified to the Minister under the Mergers Act, and was approved. The parties had also notified the transaction to the Competition Authority, though they maintained that because the Minister had already approved it under the Mergers Act regime,

---

[60] Formerly Art. 85, now renumbered as Art. 81 (but without substantive amendment) by the Treaty of Amsterdam 1997 which came into effect in 1999.

[61] Joined Cases 142 & 156/84 *BAT and Reynolds v. Commission* [1987] E.C.R. 4487.

[62] Korah, "The Control of Mergers under EEC Competition Law" (1987) 8 *E.C.L.R.* 239; Venit, "The Merger Control Regulation: Europe comes of Age . . .or Caliban's Dinner" (1990) *C.M.L.Rev.* 7; Cagney, "The Competition Act and Mergers – The EEC Analogy" (1993) *I.L.T.* p.23; Fine, "The Philip Morris Judgment: Does Article 85 now extend to Mergers" (1987) *E.C.L.R.* 333.

[63] Decision No. 6, August 4, 1992.

[64] *ibid.*, para. 49.

the transaction therefore was not reviewable by the Authority under the Competition Act. Therefore it came as a surprise when the Competition Authority announced its Decision. Although it did not inhibit the merger from proceeding,[65] the Competition Authority found that mergers could violate the section 4(1) prohibition if they restricted competition. The immediate implication of this appeared to be that parties to mergers would have to notify their arrangements to two authorities for approval in future – the Minister *and* the Competition Authority, with the possibility that one could approve the merger and the other might prohibit.

The Competiton Authority indicated that it was taking the view that mergers, where anti-competitive, fell within the jurisdiction of the Competition Act 1991 because section 4(1) provides that "all agreements" that are anti-competitive are prohibited. Therefore, according to the Competition Authority, as some mergers may restrict competition (whether intrinsically or because they effect ancillary anti-competitive restraints) they can be categorised as falling within the term "all agreements." The Competition Authority stated that if the legislature wished to exclude mergers from the application of section 4, it could have done so, but had not.[66] The Competition Authority supported its view by pointing out that mergers frequently include a number of ancillary clauses which may themselves involve some restriction of competition. Consequently, the Competition Authority was of the view that should mergers not be reviewable under the Competition Act, then a number of practices, which would be prohibited under section 4(1) in other circumstances, would escape that prohibition if they were part of a merger.[67]

Having adopted the view that mergers – where anti-competitive – fall within section 4, the Competition Authority then explained why it could not accept that any distinction should be drawn between threshold and non-threshold mergers for the purpose of confining its section 4 jurisdiction.[68] The Competition Authority pointed out that, if a distinction was drawn between small and large mergers, then section 6 of the 1991 Act – which permits aggrieved parties[69] to take legal action[70] against parties to anti-competitive practices – could only be

---

[65] As the Authority granted the transaction a Certificate.

[66] *ibid.*, para. 49.

[67] *ibid.*, para. 50.

[68] *i.e.* mergers that are sufficiently large are notifiable to the Minister under the Mergers Act on the grounds that they meet the financial thresholds set out in that Act: see further para. 9–03 above.

[69] And also the relevant Minister.

[70] The Competition Authority itself had no such powers until s.6 was amended by the Competition Act 1996, granting the Competition Authority its own enforcement powers for the first time.

enforced by aggrieved parties where the merger was not notifiable to the Minister[71] (whereas, large mergers which had anti-competitive effects could not be so challenged). Such a distinction was not acceptable to the Competition Authority. Finally, the Competition Authority indicated another inconsistency would also arise if small and large mergers were treated differently. While the Minister may approve a merger because the Minister (under the Mergers Act) took the view that it was in the "common good",[72] the Competition Authority requires much stricter criteria to be satisfied when considering whether to grant a Licence. Consequently argued the Competition Authority, if section 4 was not to apply to threshold-size mergers, a further inconsistency in the treatment of large and small mergers would arise.[73]

However unsettling this Decision of the Authority was for legal advisers and their clients, there was ample "food for thought" in the Competition Authority's reasoning. In the debate that followed, it was somewhat overlooked that the Competition Authority had continued near the end of its Decision to state that although mergers may frequently result in a reduction of the number of competitors in the market, this did not, in the Competition Authority's view, necessarily constitute a restriction of competition.[74] The Competition Authority continued to state that before a merger or acquisition could be found to violate section 4(1), it must be shown that it would, or would be likely to, result in a diminution of competition in the market concerned.

Furthermore, the Competition Authority indicated that merely because a merged entity thereby increased its market share than its separate individual members had before the merger, this was not necessarily indicative of a restriction or diminution of competition either.[75] In the Competition Authority's view, a merger would offend against competition (section 4(1)) where it resulted, or would be likely to result, in a lessening of competition in the relevant market.[76] Examples of situations were given which would indicate such a lessening of competition, such as, where the merged undertakings might either on their own or in conjunction with the remaining operators in the market raise their prices; or, where new competitors could not enter the market easily after the merger.[77]

---

[71] Because it fell below the Mergers Act threshold.

[72] The common good is discussed at para. 9–10 above.

[73] Decision No. 6, August 4, 1992 (*Woodchester/UDT*), para. 52.

[74] *ibid.*, para. 77.

[75] Reaffirmed at para. 11 of the Authority's 1997 Category Certificate (December 2, 1997) .

[76] Reaffirmed at para. 10 of the 1997 Category Certificate (December 2, 1997) .

[77] *ibid.* (*Woodchester/UDT*), para. 79.

(3) 1997 Category Certificate

9–20 The Competition Authority published a Category Certificate in respect of agreements involving a merger and/or sale of a business[78] in late 1997. In it, the Authority reaffirmed its view in *Woodchester* that mergers or sales of a business are not automatically outside the scope of section 4(1) of the 1991 Act. Furthermore the Competition Authority reaffirmed its view that merely because a merger or take-over fell within the Minister's jurisdiction under the Mergers Act, that did not preclude the merger from also being subject to section 4(1) of the 1991 Act. The Competition Authority made it clear that the Category Certificate is relevant to all mergers without limitation of the size or turnover of the undertakings involved.[79]

Where a merger satisfies the terms of the Category Certificate, it does not require to be notified to the Competition Authority seeking an individual Certificate.[80]

However, helpfully, the Competition Authority reaffirmed its view that in many cases, a merger will not have any adverse effect on competition and so will not contravene the prohibition on anti-competitive agreements contained in section 4(1) of the 1991 Act.[81] Consequently, such arrangements fall outside the Competition Act, and thus notification to the Competition Authority is not necessary because such mergers, being mergers which satisfy the terms of the Category Certificate, need not be notified to the Competition Authority. However, the Competition Authority also made it clear that just because a merger satisfies the Competition Authority's Category Certificate, this in no way affects the requirement to notify mergers under the Mergers Act where that Act applies.[82]

---

[78] Category Certificate, Competition Authority Decision No. 489, December 2, 1997.

[79] *ibid.*, para. 8.

[80] In practice, if merging parties cannot satisfy the terms of the Category Certificate, they may apply to the Authority for an individual Certificate. Note that a Licence will not interest merging parties as, unlike Certificates, Licences are granted by the Authority only for a finite period. In this regard the *Guinness Ireland Group/ United Beverages Holdings Ltd* Decision of the Authority is of interest (Decision No. 512, June 17, 1998). The Authority refused to grant a Certificate to Guinness' acquisition of a 100 per cent stake in UBH as the acquisition of such control by a producer of a significant downstream player (wholesaler) was anti-competitive given the concentrated state of the beer wholesale market, the lack of potential competition and Guinness' stake in another major wholesaler, C&C. However, the Authority was prepared to grant a licence to the arrangements provided Guinness reduced its 49 per cent shareholding in C&C to below 10 per cent.

[81] Category Certificate, para. 2.

[82] *ibid.*, para. 40.

(a) Competition Authority's definition of a "Merger"

9–21   Article 1 of the Competition Authority's Category Certificate defines a merger as the transaction which occurs when two or more undertakings, at least one of which carries on business in the State, comes under "common control." Common control exists in any circumstances where the decision as to how, or by whom, each of the undertakings is to be managed can be made either by the same person, or by the same group of persons acting in concert.[83] Examples given to illustrate how such control may be acquired include the right to appoint or remove a majority of the undertaking's board or management committee, or the acquisition of shares which carry 25 per cent or more of the voting rights in the undertaking.[84]

However, the Certificate continues to make it clear that common control exists in any circumstances where one undertaking controls the commercial conduct of another,[85] and with this in mind, the Competition Authority elaborated by listing some innovative examples of how common control may be acquired. For example, control may be acquired where the conditions of a loan or other contract give an undertaking the right to veto some or all of the specified commercial decisions of another undertaking.[86] However, while the Competition Authority made it clear that the acquisition of an undertaking's assets by a receiver, liquidator or examiner does not constitute a merger,[87] it also provided that where an undertaking makes a loan to another undertaking with the result that it may have the right to appoint a receiver over that other should it default on the loan, then this could constitute an "agreement between undertakings" for the purposes of section 4(1).[88]

(b) Assessment of state of the market in which the Merger is located

9–22   According to the Competition Authority Category Certificate,[89] before a merger can be regarded as one that may give rise to anti-competitive concerns, first it must be determined that it either gives rise to, or potentially gives rise to, a diminution of competition in the market concerned. Only mergers which give rise to such concern are to be notifiable to the Competition Authority.

---

[83] *ibid.*, Art. 1(c).
[84] *ibid.*, Art. 1(d).
[85] *ibid.*, Art. 1(d).
[86] *ibid.*, Art. 1(d).
[87] *ibid.*, Art. 1(e) and para. 7.
[88] *ibid.*, Art. 1(e) and para. 7.
[89] *ibid.*, para. 10.

In the 1992 *Scully Tyrrell/ Edberg*[90] Decision, the Competition Authority had further elaborated upon the *Woodchester*[91] test in this regard. In *Scully Tyrrell/ Edberg*, it held that in order to assess whether a merger would impact adversely upon competition in a particular market, the Competition Authority would consider the following factors:

– the level of competition in a market

– the level of concentration in the market and how the merger might impact on it

– the ease with which new competitors may enter the market

– the extent to which imports may provide a measure of competition.[92]

For the purposes of assessing whether competition in the market was likely to be diminished after the merger, the Competition Authority focused on the level of market concentration before and after the merger. For this purpose, the Competition Authority introduced two tests as a measure of market concentration: the *Hirfindahl/Hirschman index* and the *Four-Firm Concentration ratio*. These tests provide a formula for measuring market concentration both before, and after, a merger. Applying the formulae in *Scully/Tyrrell*, the Competition Authority concluded that the transaction under assessment in that Decision did not result in a significant diminution of competition in the post-transaction market.

The Competition Authority has now adopted both tests in its 1997 Category Certificate.[93] In so doing, the Competition Authority stated in the Category Certificate's explanatory paragraphs that it hoped to clarify for business parties those circumstances in which an agreement for a merger or sale of a business will not prevent, restrict or distort competition. According to the Authority, these two tests are easy to apply for the purpose of determining the level of concentration in a market and whether a merger would be likely to adversely affect the level of competition. Both tests will now be considered further.

(i) The Hirfindahl/Hirschman (HHI) index

9–23 Article 2(a) of the Category Certificate provides that a merger which involves competitors in one or more markets does not contravene

---

[90] Decision No. 12, 1992.
[91] Decision No. 6, 1992: see para. 9–19 above.
[92] All of these factors are referred to also in the Competition Authority's Category Certificate, para. 11 (Decision No. 489, 1997).
[93] Decision No. 489, 1997.

section 4(1) of the Competition Act 1991, if the level of market concentration is

- below 1,000 points; or

- between 1,000 and 1,800 points but has increased by less than 100 points as a result of the merger; or

- above 1,800 points but has increased by less than 50 points as a result of the merger.

The index is defined as the sum of the squares of the market shares of all firms in the relevant market. Where the HHI is below 1,000, the market is regarded as unconcentrated. Where the HHI is between 1,000 and 1,800, the market is regarded as being moderately concentrated. Mergers which increase the HHI in this region above 100 points are considered to raise potentially significant competitive concerns, depending on other factors.[94] Where the HHI is above 1,800, the market is highly concentrated, although mergers which increase the HHI by less than 50 points in this Category are not regarded as having an adverse effect.

While the Competition Authority acknowledges that this index (which is used in the United States market) may be more suited to a larger economy, nevertheless it submits that it is useful as a guide. This is somewhat curious as on one hand the Competition Authority is acknowledging that in a small economy like Ireland, market concentration may be relatively high, unlike in larger economies like the United States. As the position currently stands, the Competition Authority has effectively legislated the HHI into law, as it has adopted it in Article 2 of the Category Certificate. While it will of course be open to parties, whose index calculations exceed the HHI parameters, to apply for an individual Certificate from the Competition Authority[95] one wonders if the Competition Authority might not have been wiser to modify the HHI in order to make it more useful for Irish economic conditions.

Where there is a significant degree of competition from imports in the relevant market, the Competition Authority is prepared to accept that although the merger may result in levels of market concentration

---

[94] While the Authority did not specify what these other factors might be, it appears from the Certificate that the absence or presence of significant barriers to entry and whether competition may be possible from imports, would be relevant factors in determining this issue.

[95] As the Competition Authority recognises that although market concentration may be high after a merger, it does not necessarily follow that competition is adversely affected.

above those specified in the HHI (*i.e.* Article 2(a)), nevertheless the merger does not restrict competition. The Competition Authority based its view on the assumption that any attempt by the merger parties to raise prices would be unsustainable due to competition from imports where there was significant import competition already before the merger.[96]

Where a merger involves potential competitors and the HHI is below 1,800, the merger will not contravene section 4(1).[97] On the other hand, if at the time merger takes place the market concentration is already high enough to exceed the HHI index thresholds, then this could have an adverse effect on competition because the removal of a potential competitor removes a potential check on the market power of existing market competitors.[98] In such circumstances, the Competition Authority considers that where the thresholds are exceeded, then a merger involving potential competitors will not contravene section 4(1) provided there are no significant barriers to entry or where there is a realistic prospect of competition from imports.[99]

An interesting decision is *TDI Worldwide/Metro Poster Advertising Ltd.*[100] In this Decision, the Authority found that after the parties had merged, concentration in the relevant markets (outdoor advertising using 48 sheet posters, and other poster sizes) had increased beyond the levels set out in the HHI index. Furthermore, there were significant barriers to entry and no competition from imports. Nevertheless, the Authority granted the arrangements a Certificate on the basis that the increase in market concentration was more than offset by the potential of the new merged entity to act as a check on the market power of the two largest players in the relevant markets. The merged entity had a 15 per cent market share in the 48 sheet poster market, and 20 per cent in the other size posters market. Its two largest competitors had combined market shares of 59 per cent and 68 per cent in the respective

---

[96] *ibid.*, n.93, para. 19.

[97] Note that as the potential competitors have no market share in the relevant market, their market share is zero for the purposes of the index calculations.

[98] The Competition Authority explained that often the existence of a potential competitor acts as a significant check on the market power of existing competitors who may be reluctant to raise their prices for fear that it will give the potential competitor the incentive to enter the market. In *David Allen Holdings Ltd/Adsites Ltd* (Decision No. 378) and *Adsites Ltd/David Allen Holdings Ltd* (Decision No. 381), the Authority refused both a Certificate or a Licence in circumstances where a highly concentrated market was further concentrated by a proposed merger, and there were no positive implications for competition.

[99] *ibid.*, para. 20. However, see *TDI Worldwide/Metro Poster Advertising* (Decision No. 501, 1998) immediately below where the Authority granted an individual Certificate notwithstanding barriers to entry and no possibility of imports.

[100] Decision No. 501, 1998. I am grateful to my colleague, Ms Oonagh Breen, for bringing this Decision to my attention.

markets. Hence the Authority considered that the merged entity would increase competition because now it presented a more substantial threat to the larger incumbents than was the case before the merger.

(ii) The Four-Firm Concentration ratio (FFC)

9–24 Article 2(b) of the Category Certificate provides that a merger which involves competitors in one or more markets does not contravene section 4(1) of the Competition Act 1991, if the combined market share of the four largest firms in the market (in terms of market share) does not exceed 40 per cent of the total relevant market.

The Competition Authority is prepared to accept FFC ratios which exceed the 40 per cent levels where there is a strong liklihood of competition from imports and this would be likely to continue should the merger parties decide to raise prices.[101] Furthermore, where a merger involves potential competitors, the Competition Authority is also prepared to allow the FFC ratio to be exceeded where mitigating factors (similar to those considered under HHI above) are present.[102]

In *IDG/Cooley*,[103] the Authority refused to grant a Certificate to the proposed take-over by Irish Distillers ("IDG"), the dominant producer of Irish whiskey, of Cooley, a new small market entrant. Applying the FFC ratio test, the Authority found that the market was highly concentrated and that IDG intended to eliminate Cooley, once it had acquired it, by closing it down. Consequently, the Authority refused to grant a Certificate to the proposed acquisition, thereby preventing the take-over going ahead.[104]

(iii) The HHI and the FFC compared

9–25 The Competition Authority considers that the HHI is in many respects a better measure of market concentration than the FFC ratio, since it takes into account the relative size of all firms in the market. However, a potential drawback in using HHI is that specific information on the market shares of all firms in the market may be either unavailable, unreliable, or difficult to obtain. Nevertheless, the Competition Authority has indicated that it will use HHI whenever possible, resorting to use of the FFC ratio where inadequate information on

---

[101] *ibid.*, para. 19.

[102] *ibid.*, para. 20.

[103] Decision No. 285, 1984

[104] This is a particularly interesting Decision in light of the fact that the take-over was not notifiable under the Mergers Act 1978 because Cooley's turnover was too small for the purposes of triggering Mergers Act jurisdiction. By contrast, IDG's turnover was £200 million within the State alone.

market shares makes use of HHI unreliable.

(iv) The HHI and the FFC ignored

9–26 Article 2(d) of the Category Certificate provides that where a merger involves two competitors, then irrespective of the level of market concentration post-merger, the Competition Authority takes the view that such a merger will not contravene section 4(1) unless it can be shown that there are barriers to entry such that other firms are prevented from entering the market or there is little prospect for purchasers of the products concerned to obtain supplies from outside the State. This provision and sentiment is likely to be of tremendous significance in the future, particularly in light of the integration of European national economies.

(c) Category Certificate not applicable

(i) Dominant position created or strengthened by merger

9–27 Article 2(c) provides that, irrespective of the market concentration post-merger, where a merger involves competitors and it leads to the creation or strengthening of a dominant position, then the Category Certificate cannot apply. Such a merger will require individual consideration.[105] The Certificate also provides that where any of the parties to a merger already had a market share of 35 per cent or more, the Category Certificate cannot apply.[106]

(ii) Actual level of competition in relevant market is already weak

9–28 The Competition Authority has made it clear that where the actual level of competition in the market is already weak, then a merger between actual or potential competitors poses a high risk that competition will be further diminished.[107] Consequently, the Authority takes the view that the Category Certificate could not be availed of by

---

[105] Note that s.5 of the Competition Act 1991 prohibits the abuse of a dominant position in the State. In Case C–6/72 *Europemballage Corp. & Continental Can v. E.C. Commission* [1973] E.C.R. 215, the European Court of Justice held that it is an abuse of a dominant position contrary to Art. 82 E.C. where a competitor, already dominant, takes over another competitor. Furthermore, Art. 2 of the E.C. Merger Regulation prohibits mergers or take-overs which, *inter alia, create* a dominant position. No doubt, this kind of thinking as well as the principles espoused by the Authority in its *IDG/Cooley* (Decision 285, 1994) have prompted the Authority to be vigilant against mergers between competitors which either create or strengthen a dominant position in the State.

[106] As such a market share (or greater) may indicate the possibility of dominance.

[107] Category Certificate, para. 22.

a merger in such a market – the merger will merit more detailed analysis in order to establish whether or not it has any adverse effect on competition. The Competition Authority indicated that when considering whether there is evidence of non-competitive performance in the market, it will have regard to all relevant evidence, in particular:

– the existence of stable relative market shares of the leading firms in recent years;

– the existence of declining combined market shares of the leading firms in recent years, and

– the profitability of the leading firms over substantial periods of time that significantly exceed that of firms in industries comparable in capital intensity and risk.

(iii) Ancillary restraints on competition

9–29 Sometimes a merger will result in the owner of one of the merged companies ceasing to be involved with the new merged entity. The party who has acquired the former owner's business may wish to prevent the former owner (*i.e.* the vendor) from re-entering the market as a competitor. Where mergers contain restrictions on the vendor preventing the vendor competing in the market for a period of time, the Competition Authority is concerned that such restrictions may be more than is necessary to ensure a transfer of the goodwill and/or technical know-how attaching to the business. Therefore, the Competition Authority's Category Certificate is not available where a merger contains such ancillary restraints, unless such restraints do not restrain competition for more than is necessary to ensure a transfer of the business's value to the purchaser. In this regard, Articles 4 and 5 of the Category Certificate are instructive. Article 4(a) provides that the Category Certificate shall not apply unless the merger[108] agreement includes the sale of goodwill of the business and the restriction on the vendor from competing does not:

– exceed two years from the date of completion of the merger;

– apply to any location outside the territory where the products concerned were manufactured, purchased or sold by the vendor at the time of the merger;

---

[108] Note that the term merger is used in this context to describe a merger, take-over or the acquisition of a business by a purchaser (either in whole or in part) in circumstances where the vendor of the business ceases to have any connection or role in the business after the acquisition.

– apply to goods or services other than those manufactured, purchased
  or sold by the vendor at the time of the merger.

Any such non-competition restraints are compatible with the Category
Certificate because the Authority regards them as being ancillary to
the transfer of the goodwill of the business being sold.[109] Consequently,
such restraints do not require to be notified to the Authority in order
to benefit from the Category Certificate. Where the restraint on the
vendor exceeds two years, it will not be eligible for the Category
Certificate. However, it may nevertheless be eligible for the award of
an individual Certificate[110] provided the Authority is satisfied that a
period in excess of two years is necessary to transfer the goodwill
attaching to the business.[111]

Similar principles apply to restraints on the vendor from soliciting
customers of the sold business, i.e., the Category Certificate is available
provided that the restriction on the vendor does not:

– exceed two years from the date of completion of the merger;

– apply to any location outside the territory where the products
  concerned were manufactured, purchased or sold by the vendor at
  the time of the merger;

– apply to goods or services other than those manufactured, purchased
  or sold by the vendor at the time of the merger.[112]

Where any such non-solicitation restraint is set to last for more than
two years, it may be eligible for an individual Certificate if the Authority
can be satisfied that it is necessary to protect the goodwill transferring
on the merger.[113] The Category Certificate is not available where a

---

[109] At paragraphs 24-29 of the explanatory memorandum accompanying the
Category Certificate.

[110] In order to obtain a individual Certificate, notification of the arrangements
would have to be made to the Authority.

[111] Some of the Authority's pre-Category Certificate Decisions illustrate how such
restraints may be acceptable, e.g., Decision No. 1, *Nallen/O'Toole*, 2 April 1992
(where a three year post-sale of business non-competition restraint was accepted
as necessary to transfer goodwill in video shop business); Decision No. 8, *ACT/
Kindle*, 4 September 1992 (where a three year non-competition restraint was
accepted where vendors possessed specialised technical know-how).

[112] Article 4(a).

[113] e.g., in Decision No. 6, *Woodchester Bank/UDT Bank*, 4 August 1992, the Authority
accepted a three year restraint on soliciting former customers who were customers in the three year period prior to the business being transferred. This
was accepted on the basis that given the nature of the business concerned (motor
leasing and instalment credit) this restriction was no more than was necessary
to ensure the transfer of the goodwill. In Decision No. 8, *ACT/Kindle*, 4 September

restriction on soliciting extends to customers who were not customers of the business at the time of the merger or who were not customers in the two years preceding the sale or merger.[114]

So far as restraints on soliciting employees of the business are concerned, the Category Certificate utilises similar principles as apply to soliciting customers. Should a restraint exceed the parameters set by the Category Certificate, it is open to the parties to apply for an individual Certificate.[115]

Where the merger involves the transfer of *technical know-how*, then longer periods of restraint are acceptable according to the Category Certificate's explanatory memorandum.[116] Article 4(b) of the Category Certificate recognises that the two year restraints acceptable under Article 4(a) (as discussed immediately above) may be important where the business transfer involves the use of "technical know-how." The explanatory memorandum to the Category Certificate defines technical know-how as a body of technical information that is secret, substantial and identified in an appropriate form. A restraint of up to five years may be acceptable.[117] However Article 4(b) also provides that such a restraint must cease to apply should the technical know-how enter the public domain before the end of the restraint's duration. For the

---

1992, a three year non-solicitation of customers was acceptable as it was confined to only customers who were customers in the 12 months before transfer of the business and was regarded as being no more than was necessary to ensure transfer of the goodwill attached to the business.

[114] Paragraph 30 of the explanatory memorandum to the Category Certificate.

[115] In Decision No. 6, *Woodchester Bank/UDT Bank*, 4 August 1992, the Authority found a three year non-solicitation restraint acceptable on the grounds that it only applied to employees employed at the time of the business transfer; it did not prevent employees offering themselves to their former employer unsolicited; nor did it prevent the employees from responding to general non-directed job advertisement placed by the (former employer) vendor, nor did it prevent the vendor soliciting an employee whose employment with the purchaser was terminated before the end of the restraint period. However, in Decision No. 9, *Phil Fortune/Budget Travel Ltd*, 14 September 1992, the Authority refused to grant a Certificate to a restraint which sought to prevent the vendor from soliciting employees employed at the time of the transfer of the business for a four year period, on the grounds that a four year restraint was more than was necessary to transfer the goodwill attaching to the employees' knowledge and association with the business transferred (a travel agency).

[116] And also as reflected in the Authority's pre-Category Certificate Decisions, e.g. in Decision No. 8, *ACT/Kindle*, 4 September 1992, the Authority granted an individual Certificate for a restraint which prevented the vendors disclosing or using technical know-how for a five year period after the transfer of the business, on the grounds that it was necessary in order to transfer the value of the know-how to the purchaser.

[117] In this circumstance, Art. 4(b) permits restraints on customer and employee solicitation for a similar period.

avoidance of doubt, knowledge concerning a particular line of business does not, in the Authority's view, constitute technical know-how for the purposes of the Category Certificate.[118]

In contrast, Article 4(c) of the Category Certificate provides that the Certificate shall also apply where agreements include restrictions on the vendor using or disclosing *confidential information* about the merged business for an unlimited time.[119] In the Category Certificate's explanatory memorandum, the Authority explained its difference in treatment between technical know-how and confidential information. In general, the Authority considers restrictions on the use or disclosure of confidential information regarding the business as not being anti-competitive, as they are merely designed to prevent the vendor using confidential commercial information about the business (such information being properly the property of the business that was merged). Therefore, a restriction on its use for an unlimited time would not normally contravene section 4(1), except where in exceptional circumstances the restriction could be demonstrated to have the effect of preventing the vendor re-entering the market once a legitimate non-compete provision had expired.[120] On the other hand, if the confidential information is actually technical know-how (as discussed above), then an unlimited restraint is not acceptable to the Authority because it would effectively prevent the vendor from ever re-entering the market even after all of the goodwill had transferred effectively to the purchaser.[121] For this reason, the Category Certificate shall not apply where the agreement includes a restriction on the vendor using or disclosing technical know-how for a period exceeding five years.[122]

The Category Certificate also sets out principles regarding permissible restraints where the vendor retains an involvement[123] with the business merged or transferred (in all of the instances examined thus far, the restrained vendor has ceased to have any role in the

---

[118] Article 4(b).

[119] Article 4 (c). However, it is clear from Authority Decisions that this is qualified in the sense that if the confidential information loses it value over time, then an unlimited restraint will not be permissible: in Decision No. 9, *Phil/Fortune*, 14 September 1992, the Authority refused to grant a Certificate to a four year restraint on disclosure or use of confidential information on the basis that the information would lose its value quickly. The Authority accepted a proposal from the parties to reduce the restraint to two years.

[120] Paragraph 31 of explanatory memorandum. The Authority had expressed similar views in its pre-Category Certificate Decision, *Scully Tyrrell/Edberg Ltd.*, No. 12, 29 January 1993.

[121] *ibid.*

[122] Article 4(c).

[123] Whether as an employee, shareholder or director.

business post-sale). According to the explanatory memorandum to the Category Certificate, restraints can be imposed preventing the vendor from competing with the business in an active capacity provided that they are not an artificial construction designed to obtain a longer restraint on vendor competition than would otherwise be permissible.[124] Such restraints can cover non-competition, non-solicitation of customers and employees.

Article 5(a) provides that the Category Certificate shall apply[125] where, following the sale of the business, the vendor remains engaged in the business either as an employee, shareholder or director and is prevented from competing, soliciting customers or employees *for as long as* the vendor remains engaged with the business.

However, as the Authority elaborates in the explanatory memorandum,[126] where a vendor's only involvement with the business after the merger is a *passive shareholding*, the vendor cannot be so restrained.[127]

However, if the vendor continues to hold a 10 per cent or greater shareholding, then Article 5(b) provides that a restraint on competing or soliciting for a period of up to two years from the sale of such a shareholding shall be acceptable. The Authority explains in its memorandum that such a restraint is not incompatible with section 4(1) of the 1991 Act because it is necessary to ensure that the remainder of the goodwill transfers to the purchaser. (Presumably, a shareholder with a shareholding of 10 per cent, or more, would be in a position to exert at least some degree of control over the business and therefore, the post-share-sale restraint is justifiable).[128]

However, where a vendor does not retain a shareholding, but continues involvement with the business whether as an employee or a director, restraints on competition which extend beyond the date of the vendor's *employment or association with* the business, will offend

---

[124] Paragraph 37.

[125] *i.e.*, the Category Certificate is available.

[126] Paragraph 37.

[127] Apart of course from the generally accepted Article 4 Category Certificate restraints set out above (these are acceptable because they *run from the date of the merger*, not from the date the ex-vendor sells his shares.

[128] While the Authority did not refer to the 10 per cent threshold in its pre-Category Certificate *Scully Tyrell/Edberg Ltd.*, Decision No 12, the Authority indicated that post-share-sale restraints are compatible with s.4(1) on the basis that a substantial shareholder would normally have, by virtue of such shareholding, exerted a measure of control over the business, and therefore it was compatible with s.4(1) to restrain such a party from competing for a period after they sold their shares so that the remaining goodwill could transfer effectively to the purchaser.

section 4(1).[129] The Category Certificate will not legitimise such restraints. Paragraph 37 of the Category Certificate's explanatory memorandum states that restraints on mere directors or employees
post-termination of their employment are anti-competitive and contravene section 4(1).[130] However, of course this does not prevent the
vendor being restrained in another way, i.e., pursuant to Article 4
Category Certificate. As described above, when Article 4 was considered, a vendor may be restrained from competing for a period after
the merger *because* of their status as vendor.

A brief examination of the Authority's pre-Category Certificate
Decision, *Scully Tyrell/Edberg Ltd.* will illustrate the approach adopted
by the Authority. In *Scully Tyrell/Edberg Ltd*[131] the directors of a loss
adjusting business sold their business to Edberg Ltd, and in return
received, *inter alia* a 38 per cent shareholding in Edberg Ltd.
Furthermore, all of the vendors (bar one) became directors of Edberg
Ltd. Under the terms of the shareholding, this gave the vendors
considerable control over Edberg Ltd. The vendors covenanted *inter
alia* not to compete with the company for three years post-sale and
furthermore not to compete for two years post-employment (whichever
was the longer).

The Authority refused to grant an individual Certificate on the
grounds that such restraints could potentially exclude the vendors from
re-entering the market for a period of time of between three and five
years – a period which in the view of the Authority was more than was
necessary to transfer the goodwill attached to the business.[132] Thus for

---

[129] As established by the Authority in the *Apex Fire Protection/Murtagh*, Decision in
1993, the Competition Authority will not grant a Certificate to a restraint which
seeks to prevent an employee leaving to set up a competing business against
the employer in the employee's own right (although, note that the Authority
also held in the Decision that the employee may be restrained from using or
disclosing confidential information in their new business, or from soliciting
customers or other employees of the employer who were such at the time of the
employee's departure). However, note that where the employee is *also* a vendor
of the business which merged, then the employee may be restrained from
competing, but this is because of their status as vendor (*i.e.*, Article 4, Category
Certificate applies) rather than their status as employee (not permitted).

[130] Interestingly, the Authority added (at para. 37 of the Category Certificate
explanatory memorandum) that a restriction on soliciting customers for a period
of one year post-employment is acceptable. This does not appear however in
the operative part of the Category Certificate (*i.e.* Article 5).

[131] Decision No. 12, 29 January, 1993.

[132] The Authority took the view that the directors' arrangements with Edberg were
so structured such that it would be very difficult for the directors to terminate
their involvement with the company until the maximum restraint period had
expired.

example, if the vendors left after only a year, they would still be restrained for at least two more years from competing. According to the Authority this exceeded the two years normally required to effect a transfer to the purchaser of the goodwill attached to the business.

Thus the parties agreed to restrict the duration of the restriction to the period while the directors remained as directors and employees, and for two years after they would dispose of their shareholdings. The Authority was prepared to accept that the directors could rightly be restrained from competing while they were directors and substantial shareholders who enjoyed a degree of control over Edberg Ltd, whereas they could not be if their shareholding was purely for investment purposes or was an artificial arrangement designed to evade section 4(1).

The parties agreed to amend the arrangements. The Authority granted a Certificate as the parties agreed that they would not compete while retained as employees, and would not compete for a two year period after the sale of their shares. As the shareholding gave the vendors considerable control over the company, it was felt that such a shareholding was not a mere passive investment, in which event a two year restraint post-sale-of-shares was acceptable.[133]

(4) Vertical Mergers

9–30 The Competition Authority does not consider that vertical mergers pose the same degree of risk to competition as are posed by horizontal mergers. Vertical mergers are mergers that take place between operators at different levels in the same industry, *e.g.* producers and distributors or retailers. Consequently, the Competition Authority has provided in Article 3 of the Category Certificate that, a vertical merger does not in the Competition Authority's opinion, contravene section 4(1) of the 1991 Act unless it can be shown that the agreement would result in foreclosure of a relevant market by denying other undertakings access to sources of supply or distribution outlets which are independent of the undertakings which are parties to the sale of a business agreement.

In *Guinness Ireland Group/United Beverages Holdings Ltd*,[134] the Authority was called upon to consider whether a Certificate should be granted to a beer producer, Guinness, which was acquiring a 100 per cent interest in UBH, a beer wholesaler. Applying the U.S. Dept. of

---

[133] Some other pre-Category Certificate Decisions which elaborate similar principles to those discussed here are *John D. Carroll Catering Ltd/Sutcliffe Ireland Ltd* (9 September, 1993) and *IAWS-Agri Society Ltd/Unigrain* (6 September, 1994).
[134] Decision No. 512, 17 June 1998.

Justice 1984 merger guidelines, the Authority refused to grant the acquisition a Certificate. Under those guidelines, three conditions must be considered before objectionable barriers to entry are created by vertical integration. (1) The degree of vertical integration between the two markets must be so extensive that entrants to the primary market also would have to enter the secondary market simultaneously. (2) The requirement of entry at the secondary level must make entry at the primary level more difficult and less likely to occur. (3) The structure and other characteristics of the primary market must be otherwise so conducive to non-competitive behaviour that the increased difficulty is likely to affect its performance.

The Authority went on to find that only about 35 per cent of the relevant market was vertically integrated and that the three conditions were not satisfied, *i.e.*, a beer producer wishing to launch a new product on the Irish market would have plenty of other undertakings through which to wholesale and distribute its product. Nevertheless, the Authority refused to grant a Certificate to the acquisition as the Authority considered that the acquisition was anti-competitive, *inter alia* on the grounds that Guinness already had a substantial shareholding (49 per cent) in another leading drinks distributor, C&C.[135]

IV. EC MERGERS REGULATION REGIME

The Merger Regulation: an overview

9–31 In 1989 the European Community adopted Council Regulation 4064/89[136] (the "Merger Regulation"). The aim of the Regulation was twofold.

First, it provided a mechanism whereby large mergers would be regulated by one merger control authority (the EC Commission Merger Task Force) and single legal regime (the Merger Regulation), rather than subjecting the merger to multiple notifications and national merger regimes in the different Member States concerned.

Second, any such mergers that would lead to the strengthening or creation of a domination position, and thereby have an adverse effect

---

[135] Other factors included the limited number of significant competitors, the limited nature of potential competition from imports, and the concentrated nature of the market. The Authority granted a Licence to the acquisition on condition that Guinness reduced its holding in C&C to less than 10 per cent.

[136] [1989] O.J. L 395/1, December 30, 1989, rectified by [1990] O.J. L 257/13, Sept. 21, 1990 and amended in 1997 by amending Regulation 1301/97 of June 30, 1997, [1997] O.J. L 180/1, July 9, 1997 (with effect from March 1, 1998). The Commission has also in 1998 published a series of non-binding Notices which assist in the interpretation of the amended regime.

on competition in the common market or a substantial part of it, were to be prohibited.

It had become evident that neither national merger control regimes on the one hand, nor Articles 81/82 EC (formerly Articles 85 and 86) on the other, were appropriate regulatory regimes for dealing with large cross-border mergers. National merger control rules were ineffective as they could only deal with a merger's effect within the State concerned. Articles 81 and 82 were not effective either. For example, neither Article has a prior notification mechanism (an essential requirement in any effective merger control regime), nor was either Article capable of prohibiting the attainment of dominance that a merger might occasion (while Article 82 prohibits the abuse of dominance, it does not prohibit the attainment of a position of dominance in a market by two merging competitors in circumstances where neither of them was dominant before the merger).

Consequently, the need for a specific legal regime to deal with mergers that had European Community cross-border implications was acute. However, in answering this need by adopting the Merger Regulation in 1989, the European Community authorities do not acquire regulatory jurisdiction over all mergers that would have an effect on trade across Member State borders.

Under the Regulation, the Commission only acquires jurisdiction over mergers (known as "concentrations" in the Regulation[137]) which are very large in terms of financial size, *i.e.* those that have a "Community Dimension".[138] On the other hand, concentrations that are not financially large enough to have a Community Dimension, continue to be subject to national regulatory control. Thus, whether a concentration has a Community Dimension or not assumes huge significance. Where a Community Dimension is demonstrated, Article 21 precludes Member States from applying domestic national competition or merger control laws to the concentration, even though parts of the concentration take place within the borders of the Member State.[139] In this way, the Commission can exercise exclusive regulatory competence over large concentrations, to the exclusion of national regulatory authorities. This is known as a "one-stop-shop" regime as the parties only have to deal with one regulatory authority (the Commission) rather than having to

---

[137] Art.3.

[138] "Community Dimension" is defined in Art. 1 and considered further below at para. 9–36.

[139] In other words, the Mergers, Take-Overs and Monopolies (Control) Act 1978 and the Competition Acts 1991 – 1996 are not applicable to a Community Dimension concentration (save where the Commission agrees to refer the Irish part of the concentration to the Irish authorities pursuant to Art. 9 Art. 9 is considered below at para. 9–53.

notify, and obtain regulatory clearance from, several national regulatory authorities. As a consequence, parties involved in such a concentration need not be concerned about obtaining merger or competition clearance from the individual Member State national competition authorities.

To facilitate regulation as described, the Regulation operates a prior notification mechanism whereby Community Dimension-size concentrations must be notified to the Commission. Furthermore, the concentration is suspended from coming into effect until the Commission has issued its decision on the concentration's compatibility with the common market.[140] Finally, notwithstanding the exclusive competence of the Commission over concentrations which meet the Community Dimension thresholds, the Merger Regulation does recognise that Member States may take appropriate measures to protect their legitimate interests in certain circumstances such as, public security, plurality of the media and prudential rules provided that it is in a manner compatible with Community law.[141]

The Commission set up a separate unit to deal with concentrations, the Merger Task Force. To date, it has been regarded as being quite successful in its operations as it has succeeded in operating an effective and speedy clearance process for Community Dimension concentrations.[142] The adoption of the Regulation finally provided the European Commission with an effective legal tool for the regulation of large mergers that may adversely affect competition within the Union territory. As this regime overcame many of the inadequacies of Articles 81 and 82 of the Treaty as inappropriate merger control tools, it was considered best in the interests of legal certainty, for the Regulation (Article 22) to disapply the Commission's Regulation 17/62 powers[143] to apply Articles 81 and 82 to concentrations. Despite Commission reservations that it could still apply 81 and 82 to sub-threshold concentrations,[144] it has not done so in practice.[145]

---

[140] Art.7.

[141] Art.21.

[142] The latest statistics available on the DGIV Commission web-site indicate that in the period January 1, 1999 to May 31, 1999, 115 concentrations have been notified to the Merger Task Force. 235 concentrations were notified in 1998. This represented an increase of 30 per cent on the number of notifications made in 1997.

[143] The Commission's powers to apply Art.81 and Art.82 to concentrations pursuant to Reg. 17/62 has been suspended by the Merger Control Regulation (Art.22.1).

[144] By using its Art.85 powers. The Commission's capacity to exercise such powers is seriously questionable in light of Art.85's cumbersome mechanisms.

[145] For a range of views on this matter, see Elland, "The Merger Control Regulation and its Effect on National Merger Controls and the Residual Application of Arts. 85 and 86" (1991) 1 E.C.L.R. 19 (note 85 and 86 are now 81 and 82 since Treaty of Amsterdam); Bright, "The European Merger Control Regulation: Do

However, while Articles 81[146] and 82 will not be invoked by the Commission, it may still be possible for the prohibition in Article 82 to be applied in national courts by other parties opposed to a concentration as, under the doctrine of "direct effect", Article 82 is capable of being invoked by parties in national courts against abuses of a dominant position which affect them adversely.[147]

In 1997, an amending Regulation was adopted which amended the Merger Regulation.[148] The amendments effected by this amending Regulation came into legal effect from March 1, 1998. The impact of these amendments to key provisions of the Merger Regulation's initial regime will now be considered in more detail, and their likely impact assessed.

(1) "Concentrations"

(a) Acquisition of control or decisive influence

9–32 In order for the Merger Regulation to apply, one of the prerequisites is that a "concentration" must have occurred. Under Article 3 of the Regulation, a "concentration" occurs whenever either a simple merger occurs[149] between two or more independent undertakings or when an undertaking(s)[150] acquire(s) the right to exercise "decisive influence", whether directly or indirectly, over another undertaking(s)'s (or parts of an undertaking(s)) strategic management in any way whatsoever, whether by way of purchase of shares, assets, contractual rights or otherwise. A concentration therefore results whenever structural change occurs in a market as a result of a change in control of an undertaking.

In so far as the simple merger situation is concerned, Commission Notice 98/C 66/02[151] on the concept of a concentration, makes it clear

---

Member States still have and Independent Role in Merger Control?(1991) 5 E.C.L.R. 184 (Pt. II).

[146] Though under the newly inserted Art.2.4 of the Merger Regulation, Art.81 may be applicable in respect of elements of a joint venture which facilitate co-ordination between the venture's parent undertakings. This is considered below in further detail.

[147] Case 66/86 *Ahmed Saed Flugreisen and Silver Line v. Z.B.U.W.* [1989] E.C.R. 803. The position is more complicated with Art.81, as there are difficulties in asserting that it too could be directly invoked in this particular context. It would seem that it cannot be directly effective since Regulation 17/62 is disapplied, such that the Commission's 81(3) exemption-granting power is disabled: Case 13/61 *Bosch v. Van Rijn* [1962] E.C.R. 45.

[148] Reg.1301/97 of June 30, 1997, [1997] O.J. L 180/1, July 9, 1997. The main changes brought about by this reform will be considered further below.

[149] Defined as occurring when previously independent undertakings merge.

[150] Or person(s) who already control at least one undertaking.

[151] [1998] O.J. C 66/5 2.3.98, replacing an earlier Notice 94/C/385/02, [1994] O.J. Dec. 31, 1994, p.5.

that a concentration occurs when, for example, a new entity is formed and the merging entities cease to exist as legal entities. Alternatively, a concentration occurs where one entity absorbs another, such that only the acquiring party continues to exist as a legal entity. However, the Notice also indicates that a concentration can also occur in less obvious ways. For example, a concentration will also be deemed to have taken place where the merging parties have merged in a de facto sense, such as where they form a single economic entity by combining their activities (previously carried out independently) so as to appear to be acting as a single economic unit. In such an arrangement, the fact that they still retain separate legal identity does not prevent the arrangements from being regarded as a concentration.

In so far as the "decisive influence" situation is concerned, the acquisition of the ability to exercise control over another undertaking's strategic decisions leads to a "concentration" occurring. Examples given in the Regulation include the right to exercise decisive influence over matters such as all or part of the assets of an undertaking, or the composition of its board or management committee, or over voting and key decisions of the undertaking.[152] It does not matter whether such decisive influence is actually exercised as long as the acquirer has "the possibility"[153] of exercising such control. Under the Regulation, it does not matter how control is acquired. While the Regulation lists examples such as the acquisition of control by way of share or asset acquisition, it makes it clear that control can be acquired by any means — what is essential is that it allows the holder(s) ". . . having regard to considerations of fact or law [to have] the possibility of exercising decisive influence on an undertaking . . .".[154]

9–33 Article 3(5)(a) is of specific relevance to credit or financial institutions whose normal activities include dealing in securities either on their own account or on behalf of others. Provided they hold such securities on a temporary basis with a view to reselling them within a one year period, then the acquisition of securities as part of such activities will not be deemed to be an acquisition of control (i.e. a concentration). In order for such institutions to be able to take advantage of this provision, no voting rights attaching to such securities may be exercised with a view to determining the competitive behaviour of the issuer of the securities. However, voting rights may be exercised where

---

[152] Commission Notice 98/C 66/02, [1998] O.J. C 66 of 1998, p.5, on the concept of a concentration elaborates further.
[153] Art. 3.3 of the Merger Regulation.
[154] *ibid*.

this is a preparatory step in respect of the eventual disposal of the securities.

(b) Joint Ventures as Concentrations: clarification or confusion

9–34 Particular problems arose in the early years of the Merger Regulation's operation in so far as joint ventures were concerned.[155] By their nature, joint ventures may inevitably give rise to competitive restraints ranging from necessary restraints to encourage the parents of the venture to create the venture on the one hand, to active co-ordination (*i.e.* non-competition) amongst the parent undertakings on the other. When the Merger Regulation was adopted, the issue arose as to whether, from a regulatory point of view, all joint ventures were to be regulated under Article 81[156] rather than under the Regulation even though some joint ventures consequentially effected structural change in the market (*i.e.* they were concentrative in nature). This issue caused particular difficulties where a joint venture had both concentrative and co-operative elements.[157]

Resolution of this issue was important for two reasons. First, the compatibility criteria used in Article 81 EC are very different from the compatibility criteria used in the Merger Regulation (as originally enacted). Hence, whether a joint venture was likely to be cleared could all depend on whether it fell to be regulated under Article 81 or the Merger Regulation. Second, if parts of a joint venture transaction were concentrative in nature, and other parts were not, the timeframe for the grant of regulatory clearance by the Commission could vary greatly. For example, the Merger Regulation regime obliges the Commission to give its final decision on a notified concentration within relatively short time limits,[158] whereas the Commission is not constrained by any comparably strict time limits when operating its normal Article 81

---

[155] Hawk, "Joint Ventures under EEC law," (1991/92) Fordham Int'l Law Journal 303; Sibree, "EEC Merger Control and Joint Ventures," (1992) E.L.R. 91; Pathak, "The EC Commission's Approach to Joint Ventures: A Policy of Contradictions," (1991) 5 E.C.L.R. 171; Picat and Zachmann, "Community Monitoring of Concentration Operations: Evaluation After Two Year's Application," (1993) 6 E.C.L.R. 240; Fine, "The Appraisal Criteria of the EC Merger Control Regulation," (1991) 4 E.C.L.R. 148.
[156] As joint ventures by their nature would contain restrictions on competition.
[157] As is evidenced by the fact that the Commission has issued no fewer than three Notices on the matter, and further has amended the Regulation by adopting the new Art. 2.4 considered shortly below when "Full-Function Joint Ventures" are assessed at para. 9–58.
[158] Five months maximum from date of submission of complete notification information to the Commission. See further para. 9–45 below.

jurisdiction. This uncertain state of affairs frustrated legal certainty and regulatory efficacy.

The amending Regulation 1301/97 has now attempted to deal with this situation in two ways.[159] First, the Commission has amended Article 3.2 of the Merger Regulation by abandoning the distinction between "concentrative" and "co-operative" joint ventures which the original 3.2 used for the purpose of delimiting Merger Regulation jurisdiction over joint ventures. Under the original Article 3.2, where a joint venture promoted co-ordination between the parent undertakings, it was deemed to be a co-operative joint venture, and therefore could not be regulated under the Regulation's regime. Instead it fell to be regulated under Article 81. This was much criticised as effectively two different legal regimes were applicable to joint ventures, depending on whether they were "concentrative" or "co-operative". A joint venture that might well otherwise look like a concentration would be precluded from being regulated under the Regulation if it's creation promoted co-ordination between the parent companies.

However, now the amended Article 3.2 no longer resorts to use of the concentrative/co-operative distinction. Instead, it provides that if a joint venture performs all of the functions of an autonomous economic entity, then it shall constitute a concentration within the meaning of the Regulation. In order to be concentrative in nature, the joint venture must be in a position to operate on a day to day basis largely autonomously of its parents by having sufficient economic and human resources devoted to its operations. Such a concentration is known as a "full-function joint venture". In 1998, the Commission published a Notice[160] specifically explaining the concept of "full-function".[161]

The second way in which the amending Regulation has intervened is by the enactment of Article 2.4. Should a "full-function" joint venture have co-operative elements, (*e.g.* it may promote co-ordination in some respects between the parents) then Article 2.4 provides that the Commission will consider the compatibility of those co-operative elements with Article 81 within the strict timeframes set out in the Regulation (as apply to the concentrative element of the joint venture). In other words, a decision on the compatibility of such elements will be given within the same time period as is allowed for the consideration of the concentrative elements under the Merger Regulation. Conse-

---

[159] What follows is a brief outline, as the matter is discussed in further detail below when "Full-Function Joint Ventures" are discussed at para. 9–58.

[160] Commission Notice 98/C 66/1, March 2, 1998 on the concept of full-function joint ventures which replaces Commission Notice 94/C 385/1, Dec. 31, 1994 on the distinction between concentrative and co-operative joint ventures.

[161] Considered below when "Full-Function Joint Ventures" are discussed at para. 9–58.

quently, the Commission's view on the compatibility of all elements of the joint venture will be made known within a legally definite period.[162]

The aforegoing does not apply to restrictions on competition that are neither ancillary to, nor a direct consequence of, the creation of the joint venture. Such restrictions will be regulated under Regulation 17/62, according to the Commission Notice.

(c) Extra-territorial Concentrations

9–35   Concentrations will fall under the Merger Regulation's jurisdiction if they affect competition within the EU territory. Therefore, parties to a concentration outside the EU must notify the concentration to the Merger Task Force where the concentration affects the market within the EU. A review of some recent Commission Decisions will illustrate the scope of the Regulation's extra-territorial grasp.

In *Gencor v. EC Commission*[163] the parties argued in the European Court of First Instance that the Commission had no jurisdiction over the parties' concentration. Gencor and Lonrho proposed taking over a South African mining company, Impala. The Commission prohibited the concentration because the post concentration market in the platinum and rhodium markets would have been dominated by two entities, the concentration and one other undertaking. The companies involved, and their mining operations, were based entirely outside of the EU territory. Nevertheless, the Commission asserted jurisdiction under the Merger Regulation on the basis that it is substantive factors (i.e. sales), rather than formal presence within the EU, that triggers the Regulation's jurisdiction. The CFI held that the Commission was correct in regarding the parties as being subject to the Regulation's regime on the basis that their turnover based on sales into the EU territory was sufficient to give the concentration a "Community Dimension" for the purposes of Article 1 of the Regulation.[164]

In *United Technologies Corporation/Sundstrand Corporation*[165] the Commission cleared a take-over of Sundstrand by UTC even though both undertakings are based in the USA. Both are active in the aerospace markets in different areas and conduct substantial business in the EU. *United States Surgical Corp/Tyco International*[166] is another example of a

---

[162] Of course, where a joint venture is not *concentrative* in nature, the Merger Regulation is not relevant and, in this event, Article 81 (or national competition law) will be the applicable regime(s).

[163] Case T–102/96 *Gencor Ltd v. EC Commission*, March 25, 1999.

[164] Art. 1, considered in detail at para. 9–36 below, details how a concentration must be of significant financial and geographical size ("Community Dimension") in order for the Regulation's jurisdiction to apply.

[165] M. 1943 (26 May 1999) (IP/99/356).

[166] O.J. [1998] C. 282/5 (11.09.98).

concentration between two US companies operating in the surgical products market whose concentration was cleared by the Commission in 1998. Both companies are US based, but have significant activities and sales in the EU territory.

An example of extra territorial "dis-application" arose in the Commission's non-opposition to the acquisition of joint control over UAB Omnitel, a Lithuanian mobile phone operator by Amber Mobile Teleholding (a joint venture between Telia of Sweden and Sonera of Finland) and Motorola Lithuania Telecom Inc (a subsidiary of U.S. Motorola Corp). The Commission found that as the acquired entity was operating in a market outside the EU, the assessment of the acquisition with EC competition rules was not warranted as mobile phone markets are not assessed, as yet, on a European-wide basis.[167]

(2) Notifiable Concentrations "Community Dimension"

9–36 In order for a concentration to come within the "one-stop-shop" regulatory regime provided for by the Merger Regulation, it must have a "Community Dimension".[168] A concentration has a Community Dimension where its financial size meets the Regulation's thresholds. The Regulation provides that a concentration which has a Community Dimension is notifiable to the Commission not more than one week after the conclusion of the agreement, or the announcement of the public bid, or the acquisition of a controlling interest, which ever is the earlier.[169]

The Community Dimension thresholds have been modified by the 1997 amending Regulation. First, new lower thresholds have been added, and second, there has been a major revision of financial thresholds for banking undertakings.

(a) *The original thresholds*

9–37 However, before examining these amendments, the original thresholds, still retained in the Regulation, must be considered. The

---

[167] Case JV.9, 18 August 1998 (IP/98/772 of August 20, 1998).

[168] Failure to demonstrate a Community Dimension means that the concentration is not notifiable to the Commission. In this event, the concentration may be notifiable (depending on the requirements of individual Member State legislation) to the national competition or merger control regulatory authorities, in which event the relevant national competition/merger laws may apply.

[169] Article 4.1. Concentrations which arise due to the merger of two or more previously independent undertakings or which arise when there has been an acquisition of joint control over an undertaking, are to be notified jointly by the parties to the merger or those acquiring joint control, as the case may be. In all other cases, notification is to be by the undertaking or person acquiring control(Art. 4.2).

original thresholds are set out in Article 1 as follows: Article 1.2 provides that a concentration has a Community Dimension where:

(a) the combined aggregate world-wide turnover of all the undertakings concerned is more than 5,000 million euros, and

(b) the aggregate Community-wide turnover of each of at least two[170] of the undertakings concerned is more than 250 million euros,

unless each of the undertakings concerned achieves more than two thirds of its aggregate Community-wide turnover within one and the same Member State.[171]

9–38 Article 5 indicates items that are reckonable as turnover for the purposes of determining aggregate turnover. Article 5.1 provides that aggregate turnover shall comprise the amounts derived by the undertakings concerned in the preceding financial year from the sale of products and the provisions of services; ordinary activities after deduction of sales rebates and VAT and other direct turnover-related taxation. Intra-group sales shall not be reckonable.

Article 5.4 provides that reckonable turnover not only includes that of the undertakings immediately involved in the concentration, but also, the turnover of any undertakings controlled by the undertakings, or any parent or sister undertakings, or any joint ventures in which either of the aforementioned undertakings are involved as joint controllers. Consequently, a relatively insignificant Irish subsidiary of a large multinational could find its turnover being aggregated with "related" undertakings for the purposes of determining if the concentration has a Community Dimension. In such event, Irish Competition and Mergers and Take-Over legislation may be rendered inapplicable to the Irish elements of the concentration, unless a Community Dimension was eventually determined not to exist.

(b) Additional thresholds

9–39 With the adoption of the amending Regulation 1301/97 in 1997, the Council expanded the definition of Community Dimension. The Commission was of the view that the original thresholds were too high,

---

[170] Case IV/M.053 *Aerospatiale-Alenia/de Havilland* O.J. [1991] L.334/42 demonstrates how this criterion is satisfied even if the two undertakings are on the *same* side of the merger transaction. The Commission made it clear that it is not necessary that there be a significantly large player on *both* sides of the transaction.
[171] In the event that this proviso applies, the concentration does not have a Community Dimension because the bulk of its activity is confined to just one Member State.

such that many significant mergers did not qualify for inclusion in the Merger Regulation's regime. According to the Commission, many large non-Community Dimension concentrations, which have a significant impact in several Member States, were being regulated under a number of national merger control systems with the consequence that multiple notification and regulation increases legal uncertainty, costs and sometimes leads to conflicting assessments. To address this concern, the EC Council of Ministers agreed to amend the original Merger Regulation by providing that the scope of the Regulation be expanded in order to allow more concentrations take advantage of the "one-stop shop" regime of the Regulation (and thereby avoid the need for multiple notification to different regulatory authorities in the different Member States concerned by the same transaction).

Consequently, the amending Regulation 1301/97 inserts a new Article 1.3 into the Merger Regulation. Article 1.3[172] provides that a concentration which does not meet the Article 1.2 thresholds (which remain intact) nevertheless has a Community Dimension where:

(a) the combined aggregate world-wide turnover of all the undertakings concerned is more than 2,500 million euros; and

(b) in each of at least three Member States, the combined aggregate turnover of all the undertakings concerned is more than 100 million euros; and

(c) in each of at least three Member States included for the purpose of (b), the aggregate turnover of each of at least two of the undertakings concerned is more than 25 million euros, and

(d) the aggregate Community-wide turnover of each of at least two of the undertakings concerned is more than 100 million euros;

unless each of the undertakings concerned achieves more than two thirds of its aggregate Community-wide turnover within one and the same Member State.

(c) Revised Turnover Rules for Credit and Financial Institutions

9–40 Article 5 of the Regulation provides special rules for calculating turnover for the purposes of assessing whether banking concentrations have a Community Dimension.[173] In order to assess whether a banking

---

[172] According to the new Article 1.4 inserted by the amending Regulation, the Commission is obliged to report on the operation of the thresholds to the Council of Ministers by July 1, 2000, and the Council may revise them, if necessary.

[173] Special rules are also provided in respect of insurance undertakings: see Art.5 (as amended by the 1997 Reg.).

concentration has a Community Dimension, a two-stage process must be undertaken. First, the "turnover" of the respective merger parties must be determined. Certain items of banking income are reckonable for this purpose. Second, once determined, the relevant turnover figure will then be applied in the Article 1 Community Dimension formula in order to assess whether the concentration is sufficiently large in order to attract the "one-stop-shop" jurisdiction of the Merger Regulation regime.

9–41   However, before looking at the new version of the Community Dimension rules applicable to banking concentrations it is instructive to have an appreciation of the regime they replaced. In its form originally adopted, the Merger Regulation did not provide such a two stage process for assessing whether a banking concentration had a Community Dimension. Originally, Article 5 of the Regulation stipulated that in order for a concentration between "credit institutions"[174] or "financial institutions"[175] to satisfy the "Community Dimension" thresholds, the following criteria had to be satisfied:

- one tenth of the combined worldwide assets of the merging parties (which included those of associated companies, subsidiaries, parents) must have been worth more than 5,000 million euros, and,

- one tenth of the combined worldwide assets, when multiplied by the ratio between loans and advances to credit institutions and customers located within the Community and the total of loans and advances made to credit institutions and customers worldwide, must have been worth more than 250 million euros for each of at least two of the undertakings concerned in the merger.[176]

---

[174] Institutions which receive deposits from the public and grant loans, as defined in the First Banking Directive 77/780/EEC, O.J. [1977] L 322/30.

[175] Institutions, other than "credit institutions", whose principal activity is to grant credit facilities or to acquire holdings or make investments, as further elaborated upon in the Second Banking Directive 89/646/EEC O.J. [1989] L 386/1.

[176] However, the Regulation did not seek to bring within its jurisdiction mergers whose main effect was felt within a single Member State. Consequently, a proviso was attached: if each undertaking concerned found that one tenth of its combined worldwide assets, when multiplied by the ratio between loans and advances to credit institutions and customers located within one and the same Member State and the total of loans and advances made to credit institutions and customers worldwide, was more than two thirds, then the concentration would not satisfy the Merger Regulation's Community Dimension thresholds. Where the aforegoing proviso applied, then the concentration would be deemed to have most of its effect within a single Member State's territory, thereby not prompting Community-wide concern. In this event, it was felt that regulation of the concentration was more properly left to the national competition authorities of that State rather than the Commission whose focus

In 1997, the amending Regulation 1301/97 amended this Community Dimension calculation test, replacing it with the new two-stage test. According to the amending Regulation's preamble, the reason for the change was that, for the purpose of calculating the turnover of credit and financial institutions, banking income is a better measure than asset measurement because it reflects more accurately the economic realities of the whole banking sector.[177] Consequently, in place of the original Article 5 Community Dimension test, instead the following two stage test applies:

Stage one requires that the sum of the following items[178] will comprise the turnover for credit institutions and other financial institutions:

(i) interest income and similar income

(ii) income from securities

(iii) commissions receivable

(iv) net profit on financial operations

(v) other operating profit.

As amended, Article 5 further elaborates by providing that the turnover of a credit or financial institution shall comprise the aforementioned income items which are received by the branch or division of that institution established in the Community or in the Member State in question, as the case may be.[179] (This domicile qualification becomes relevant when the Community Dimension formula is applied in stage two, as it shall be seen how certain criteria in the Community Dimension test require bank turnover in both the Community and in individual Member States to be ascertained).

Once the relevant turnover sums have been calculated in accordance with the aforegoing criteria, stage one is complete. Now stage two commences, using the relevant turnover sums. The Article 1 Community Dimension formula uses those turnover sums in order to assess whether the concentration has a Community Dimension.

It should be noted that, for the purposes of calculating "aggregate turnover" of "undertakings concerned" under Article 1, Article 5 pro-

---

is on the Community market rather than the national market of just one Member State.

[177] A specific Commission Notice, the Notice on Calculation of Turnover under Council Regulation 4064/89 ([1998] O.J. C-66/25), elaborates on how these turnover rules are to be applied.

[178] Minus value added tax and other direct taxes related to those items, as per the amended Article 5.

[179] Separate criteria provided for insurance undertakings. Article 5 (as amended) should be consulted to ascertain these requirements.

vides that the turnover of the respective "undertakings concerned" is to be aggregated with *inter alia* the turnover of undertakings controlled by those undertakings[180] and also with that of undertakings which control the undertakings concerned[181] in the respective worldwide, Community and Member State areas as specified by the Community Dimension formula.

(3) One-Stop Shop

(a) Exclusive Regulator

(i) National Competition/Merger law disapplied

9–42 The advantage for merger or take-over parties in falling within the Merger Regulation's thresholds is that once their concentration meets the thresholds, it is deemed to have a Community Dimension. As a consequence, it is only notifiable to one merger control authority, namely the Commission's Merger Task Force in Brussels. Article 21.2 of the Regulation provides that no Member State shall apply its national competition legislation to any concentration that has a Community Dimension. Consequently, where a concentration has a Community Dimension, the Commission is the only regulator that has competition jurisdiction over the concentration. Hence, the difficulties traditionally associated with multiple notifications to several national competition/merger control authorities in several States, are obviated. The major advantage of the regime is that the risk that different national merger regulation authorities might reach conflicting decisions is now no longer a possibility, as they have no jurisdiction once the Regulation's thresholds are met.

The takeover by Tesco of the Quinnsworth and Crazy Prices chains in Ireland in 1997 provides a good example of how the Commission had exclusive regulatory competence over the concentration. Once the Community Dimension was established, neither the Irish Competition Authority nor the Minister for Enterprise and Employment had jurisdiction to regulate the transaction, despite vigorous opposition to the takeover from some quarters here in Ireland.[182]

---

[180] Whether solely or jointly.
[181] And also with that of other undertakings which the controlling undertaking controls.
[182] The Commission did not oppose the take-over on the grounds that it was unlikely that Tesco would achieve dominance in the Irish grocery retail market in either the short or medium term: Case No. IV/M.914 Tesco/ABF (May 5, 1997).

(ii) Notification-triggering event

9–43   A concentration which possesses a Community Dimension must be notified to the Commission within seven days of the earlier of any of the following:[183]

(a) the acceptance of the offer; or

(b) the announcement of a public bid; or

(c) the acquisition of a controlling interest.

The amendments made to the Merger Regulation by the amending Regulation do not affect any transactions agreed, notified, or effected before March 1, 1998, nor to any concentrations that were the subject of investigation by national regulatory authorities before that date.

(iii) Suspensive effect

9–44   The provisions on suspensive effect have also been changed by the amending Regulation. Under the original Article 7.1, a Community Dimension concentration could come into effect three weeks after initial notification, unless the Commission at its discretion opted to continue the suspension period for a further period pursuant to Article 7.2. Heralding a major change in the operation of this suspension regime, Article 7.2 has been repealed and the new Article 7.1 provides that notifiable concentrations shall not come into effect in law neither before nor after notification until the Commission has either delivered a compatibility decision or the Commission has failed to make a decision within the prescribed time limits (in which event the concentration is deemed to be compatible).

Article 7.3 provides that Article 7.1 shall not have the effect of preventing a notified public bid from being implemented, provided that the acquirer does not exercise the voting rights acquired.[184] Article 7.4 has also been amended. It provides that a derogation may be granted, at the Commission's discretion, from the application of the obligations imposed by Article 7.1 or Article 7.3. In considering such a request, the Commission may consider the effects of the suspension on a third party, or on one of the concentrating parties, or the threat to competition posed by the concentration. The derogation may be requested either before or after notification and may be subject to such conditions as the Commission considers appropriate.

The amended Article 7.5 provides that where a transaction is carried

---

[183] Art. 4.

[184] By way of exception to this, Art. 7.3 further provides that the voting rights may be exercised in order to maintain the full value of those investments, provided that a derogation in this respect has been granted by the Commission.

out in violation of Article 7.1, its validity shall ultimately depend on whether the Commission has either made a clearance decision, a prohibition decision, or has failed to adjudicate upon the concentration within the prescribed time limits. Importantly, it is also provided by Article 7.5 that Article 7 shall not affect the validity of any transactions in securities, including those convertible into other securities admitted to trading on a market which is regulated and supervised by authorities recognised by public bodies, which operates regularly and is accessible directly or indirectly to the public, unless the buyer and seller knew or ought to have known that the transaction was carried out in contravention of Article 7.1.

(iv) Regulation deadlines and legal bases for Commission appraisal decisions

Phase One and Phase Two

9–45 A notable feature of the regime is that it operates under tight time limits. In phase one, the Commission has one month[185] from the date of receipt of the notification in which to decide whether to declare that the concentration either does not fall within the scope of the Regulation or, if it does, it does not raise serious doubts in regard to its compatibility with the common market.[186] In either case, the Commission's consideration of the notification concludes and the parties are free to proceed with the concentration.

Alternatively, should the Commission decide that the concentration does raise serious doubts, it must initiate proceedings within this one-month period to investigate whether the serious doubts warrant the prohibition of the concentration. Where this phase two investigation takes place, it must be concluded within four months of the decision to open the investigation and the Commission must deliver its final decision within that time limit.[187] The Commission can decide to either make a decision approving the concentration subject to modifications proposed by the parties,[188] or to prohibit the concentration on the grounds that it is incompatible with the common market.[189]

---

[185] Art. 6.1 and Art. 10.1. Note that Art. 10.1 also provides that this period shall be increased to six weeks if the Commission receives an Art. 9 request from a Member State to refer the concentration to the Member State for regulation by its authorities. Also note that this may also be the case where the parties submit commitments after notification intended to render the concentration acceptable to the Commission.

[186] Art. 6.1 and Art. 10.1.

[187] Art. 10.

[188] Arts 8.2 and 10.2. For an example of a modified transaction, see Commission Decision 92/553/EEC, Nestle/ Perrier: [1992] O.J. L356/1, discussed below at para. 9–49.

[189] Arts 8.3 and 10.3.

Decisions that may close a phase two investigation

9–46 Where a four-month investigation is initiated,[190] such an investigation will be closed by way of a Commission Decision along the lines set out in Article 8.2–8.5, as appropriate to any particular case as follows.

Under Article 8.2, paragraph 1, the Commission may declare a concentration to be compatible with Article 2.[191] Under Article 8.2, paragraph 2, the Commission has the power to attach "conditions and obligations" on the parties to ensure that they comply with any commitments they may have furnished to the Commission. Such a decision will usually be prompted by the parties having made modifications to the concentration, thereby rendering it acceptable to the Commission.

Since the coming into force of the amending Regulation's amendments, the Merger Task Force now has the jurisdiction to consider concentrative joint ventures with co-operative elements also (Article 2.4). Article 8 has been amended, largely to allow the Commission, for the first time, to have the legal power under the Merger Regulation to clear or prohibit a concentrative joint venture that raises Article 81 concerns. Consequently, the amended Article 8.2 enables the Merger Task Force to consider such transactions under the Merger Regulation and grant an Article 8.2 clearance decision in circumstances where the parties have proposed modifications which render the joint venture compatible with Article 81(3) criteria.

9–47 Under Article 8.3, the Commission may declare a "concentration" to be incompatible with Article 2 on the basis that it creates or strengthens a dominant position contrary to Article 2.3, in which event the concentration is prohibited.[192] As amended, the Commission may now also decide under Article 8.3 to prohibit an Article 2.4 concentration (a concentrative joint venture with co-operative elements) where the co-operative elements do not fulfil Article 81(3) criteria.

---

[190] DGIV statistics on the Commission's web-site indicate that 12 phase two-four month investigations were opened in 1998. Ten were closed, the remaining two resulting in prohibition orders: see para. 9–50 below.

[191] Article 2.2 provides that a concentration which does not create or strengthen a dominant position as a result of which effective competition would be significantly impeded in the common market, or a substantial part or it, shall be declared compatible with the common market.

[192] Article 2.3 provides that a concentration which does create or strengthen a dominant position as a result of which effective competition would be significantly impeded in the common market, or a substantial part of it, shall be declared incompatible with the common market.

9–48   Under Article 8.5(b), the Commission may revoke a prior favourable decision previously made under 8.2 where undertakings concerned commit a breach of an obligation attached to the prior decision. Article 8.5(a) provides that the Commission may also revoke compatibility decisions taken under Article 8.2 where undertakings concerned originally provided false information.[193] Article 8.4 provides that where a concentration already has been implemented, the Commission may require divestiture of assets or the cessation of joint control (whichever is appropriate) in order to restore effective competition.

Modifications and Commitments

9–49   It is seen from the Commission practice that the Commission much prefers to accept commitments from the parties to either modify their concentration or to agree to comply with conditions and obligations, rather than to prohibit the concentration outright. This enables the Commission to grant compatibility decisions, rather than declare concentrations (as notified in their original form) to be incompatible (*i.e.* prohibited). This very pragmatic approach adopted by the Commission accounts in large measure for the low number of incompatibility decisions. A brief review of some recent of the Commission's practice in this area is instructive.

In *Danish Slaughterhouses*[194] the Commission granted clearance subject to conditions to a merger between two of Denmark's largest pig slaughtering undertakings, Danish Crown and Vestjyske Slagterier. The Commission took the view that the concentration would create a duopolistic dominant position between the concentration and another main operator in the fresh pork market, as structural links existed between them. However, the Commission cleared the concentration after the parties proposed several structural and behavioural modifications and commitments. First, the undertakings agreed to release pig suppliers from their current exclusive agreement to supply pigs for slaughter – henceforth suppliers could supply up to 15 per cent of their pigs to competitors. Second, a commitment was given to cease supplying weekly quotes on pig prices to the Danish association of slaughterhouse operators (this would make price transparency less obvious for competitors post-concentration). Third, the merging parties agreed to terminate their interests in an export undertaking in which its two remaining competitors had a minority stake. Fourth, assurances

---

[193] Art. 8.6 provides that where Art. 8.5 applies, the Commission is not bound by Art.10 four-month deadline.
[194] M. 1313 IP/99/165 (March 9, 1999).

were given that in the event that either other main competitor decides to sell its stake in a meat-trading undertaking jointly owned with the merged undertakings, then such competitor will be given full value for their interest. Fifth, the parties agreed to sell one slaughterhouse to a competitor, other than a main competitor.

In the Commission's view the commitments and modifications proposed will ensure that the links between the concentration and the other main competitor in the market will terminate, thereby promoting a greater chance that competition will be maintained. Furthermore, the termination of supplying weekly price quotes should help ease fears of price collusion amongst remaining competitors in the market.

Another example of a decision where clearance was granted subject to conditions is the *Total/Petrofina*[195] concentration whereby Total (French) acquired control of Petrofina petrochemical company (Belgian).[196] Clearance was possible because the Commission required the parties to structurally modify the concentration. For example, they undertook to divest certain depots in northern France to a competitor. Also commitments as to future behaviour were given, such as the offering of standard supply contracts to regular wholesale customers for a period of three years in order to assure continuity of supplies.

A most interesting clearance is that which was made in *WorldCom/ MCI*[197] whereby the Commission granted a conditional clearance in respect of the merger between WorldCom and MCI telecommunications corporations. This concentration involved both the Commission and the U.S. Department of Justice, which co-ordinated their approach to assessing the concentration under their respective regimes. Of particular concern was the fear that the concentration might lead to dominance in the market for universal connectivity over the Internet. The Commission found that very few undertakings, apart from the merging undertakings, had the ability to offer connectivity over any part of the Internet without having to rely on other service providers. Although technically, smaller undertakings could provide such a service, the reality of the market was such that the size of an undertaking dictated actual market power in this area, and so for practical purposes customers were not attracted to an undertaking because of its technical abilities, but rather its size and ability to offer universal connectivity.

---

[195] M. 1464 IP/99/197 (March 29, 1999).
[196] Certain elements of the concentration raised competition concerns in southern France and so those elements of the concentration that pose particular concerns to that market were referred to the French competition authorities under Article 9 Merger Regulation: see further below where Article 9 referrals are considered at para. 9–53.
[197] M. 1069 IP/98/639 (July 8, 1998).

The Commission feared that the concentration, if allowed proceed, would give the concentration a 50 per cent market share which would allow it dictate terms to competitors and customers. As both undertakings were competitors in this field, the Commission agreed to clear the concentration on condition that MCI divest itself of its Internet business to a third party who must be approved by both the Commission and the DOJ. Effectively this third party will assume the role formerly occupied by MCI in the marketplace. The extent of co-operation between the US/EU authorities was quite significant in this notification.

However, the Commission will not always be satisfied by modifications and commitments proposed by the parties. In *Gencor Ltd v. EC Commission*[198] a concentration in the platinum market was prohibited and the Commission refused to accept modifications proposed by the parties as an incentive to grant clearance. The parties proposed to make capacity available to a new competitor; maintain output at existing levels; and develop additional capacity. These proposals were not sufficient in the Commission's view to negate its finding that the concentration would be incompatible with Article 2 of the Regulation as such commitments did not alter the *structure* of the concentration, and hence could not alleviate the Commission's concerns about competition in the relevant market.

This is most interesting by contrast with the first Commission Decision on collective dominance, *Nestle/Perrier*.[199] In that Decision, although the Commission found that the merged entity would be in a position of collective dominance in the French mineral water market with the remaining main competitor, BSN, nevertheless it cleared the concentration as Nestle proposed to alter both its behaviour *and* the structure of the concentration. It is submitted that the reason why the *Gencor* situation is different is because the parties were not modifying *the structure* of the notified concentration in any way, but only their *post-concentration* behaviour. Monitoring compliance with commitments may not be something the Commission has resources to undertake. However, this does not mean that the Commission will never be happy with behavioural commitments only, as the CFI stressed that each case must be examined on its own merits.

Because of this practice of accepting modifications and commitments by the Commission, most notified concentrations never get to the Article 8 stage (*i.e.* four months, phase-two investigation). Instead, they are disposed of at the Article 6.1(b) stage (*i.e.* one month, phase-one). In

[198] Case T–102/96 *Gencor Ltd v. EC Commission*, March 25, 1999.
[199] Case No. IV/M.190 [1992] O.J. L356/1.

other words, the Commission finds that the concentration does not raise serious doubts *vis-à-vis* its compatibility with the European Community's common market. Consequently, no four-month investigation is necessary. In the original Regulation, there was no competence given to the Commission by Article 6.1(b) to act as it could under Article 8.2, *i.e.* to grant approval *subject* to the parties either proposing modifications or accepting the imposition of Commission conditions/obligations. However, the Commission developed such a practice under Article 6.1(b), approving concentrations upon the entering of the parties into commitments during the initial one-month post-notification period. On the basis of such commitments, the Commission would declare the concentration to be compatible with the common market without ever opening a full four-month investigation.

The amending Regulation has now amended Article 6 such that the amended Regulation now expressly provides the Commission with the above-described competence.[200] In this regard, the Regulation now expressly provides that the Commission has the power to impose conditions and obligations in respect of commitments entered into by the parties as the "price" of obtaining a clearance decision during the initial one-month post-notification period. Consequently, concerns about the legality of the Commission's former practices[201] have now largely abated in this area.[202]

(b) Appraisal Test – Compatibility with the Common Market?

9–50 Article 2 of the Merger Regulations provides the legal test for the appraisal of Community Dimension concentrations by the Commission. Article 2.2 provides that a concentration which does not create or strengthen a dominant position as a result of which effective competition would be significantly impeded in the common market, or a substantial part of it, shall be declared compatible with the common market. Article 2.3 provides, on the other hand, that a concentration which does create or strengthen a dominant position as a result of which effective competition would be significantly impeded in the common

---

[200] Art. 6.1a.

[201] Krause, "Article 6(1)b EC Merger Regulation: Improving the reliability of Commitments," (1994) 4 E.C.L.R. 209; Fine, "The Appraisal Criteria of the E.C. Merger Control Regulation," (1991) 4 E.C.L.R. 148; Doran, "Reflections on the Du Pont E.C. Merger Regulation Case," (1993) 2 E.C.L.R. 70.

[202] Commission statistics on the DGIV web-site indicate that in 1998 alone, the Commission closed nine investigations at the end of the one-month period on the basis that commitments made by the parties in the one-month period were satisfactory.

market, or a substantial part of it, shall be declared incompatible with the common market.[203]

It can be readily seen how Article 82 is deficient as a merger control tool in light of Article 2 of the Regulation. For example, Article 2 prohibits the *creation* of a dominant position where such a dominant position would impede effective competition in a substantial part of the common market. Article 82, which is drafted much more narrowly than Article 2, could not apply to prohibit such an occurrence.

Whether or not a dominant position exists within the meaning of Article 2.3 is ascertained by the Commission determining the relevant product market(s) and the relevant geographic market(s).[204] This analysis will determine the size of the concentration's economic and market power. Where "dominance" is the conclusion, the concentration will be prohibited, unless it can be demonstrated that there will be no impediment to effective competition.[205] On the other hand, where a concentration does not result in the creation or strengthening of a dominant position, Article 2.2 provides that it shall be declared compatible with the common market.

The compatibility test is based on whether the concentration is compatible with the common market. In making this appraisal, the Commission is obliged to take into account factors such as the need to maintain and develop effective competition within the common market in view of the structure of markets concerned and the actual or potential competition from undertakings located inside or outside the Community.[206] Examples given of other factors to be taken into account include: the market position of the undertakings concerned; their economic and financial power; whether there are alternatives available to suppliers and users; access to markets; any legal or other barriers to entry; the interests of consumers; and the development of technical or

---

[203] On the whole, the Commission has prohibited few notified concentrations. At the time of writing only ten concentrations have been prohibited: *e.g.* Commission Decision 91/619/EEC in Case IV/M.053 *Aerospatiale-Alenia/De Havilland* [1991] O.J. L334/42; Commission Decision 94/922/EC in Case IV/M.469 *MSG Media Service* [1994] O.J. L364/1; *Bertelsmann/Kirsch/Premiere* (Commission Decision 99/153, Case IV/M.933) and *Deutsche Telecom/Beta Research* (Commission Decision 99/153, Case IV/1027), May 27, 1998.

[204] Pathak: "Market Definition, "Compatibility with the Common Market," and Appeals from the Commission Decisions under the Merger Regulation during 1993," (1993) ELR (Competition Checklist Volume, Chap IX).

[205] Downes & MacDougall, "Significantly Impeding Effective Competition: Substantive Appraisal under the Merger Regulation," (June 1993) ELR vol. 19, no. 3, 286.

[206] Hawkes, "The EC Merger Control Regulation: Not an Industrial Policy Document – The De Havilland Decision" (1992) 1 E.C.L.R. 24.

economic progress, provided it is to consumers' advantage and does not form an obstacle to competition.

Since the Regulation came into force in 1990, ten concentrations have been prohibited on the basis of incompatibility with Article 2 of the Regulation. The last two of these Decisions were delivered in 1998 in *Bertelsmann/Kirch/Premiere* Decision 99/153[207] and *Deutche Telecom/Beta Research*[208] where two proposed concentrations were prohibited by the Commission arising out of the German pay-tv and digital-tv market.

In *Bertelsmann/Kirch/Premiere*, Kirch and CLT-UFA proposed taking joint control of the German pay-tv provider Premiere, and Beta Digital. In *Deutche Telecom/Beta Research*, Kirch and DT proposed gaining joint control of Beta Research. Before these proposed concentrations, Kirch had sole control over both target undertakings. The Commission prohibited the concentrations on the basis that if they had been allowed proceed, Premiere would have become dominant as a programme platform in Germany; Beta Digital would become dominant over the provision of technical services for pay-tv in Germany in the satellite sector; and DT would have become the only supplier of technical services for pay-tv in the German cable network.

(i) Collective Dominance

The notion of collective dominance has also been established under the Merger Regulation, such that a concentration which leads to the creation of collective dominance and which thereby impedes effective competition in the common market or a substantial part of it, will be declared incompatible with Article 2 of the Regulation.[209] Collective

---

[207] Case IV/M.933 (May 27, 1998).

[208] Case IV/M.1027 (May 27, 1998).

[209] Winckler, "Collective Dominance under the EC Merger Control Regulation", 30 (1993) C.M.L.R. 787; Alonso, "Economic Assessment of Oligopolies under the Community Merger Control Regulation" (1993) 3 E.C.L.R. 118; Ridyard, "Economic Analysis of Single Firm and Oligopolistic Dominance Under the Merger Control Regulation" (1994) 5 E.C.L.R.; Rodger, "Oligopolistic Market Failure: Collective Dominance versus Complex Monopoly" (1995) 1 E.C.L.R. 21; Whish and Sufrin,"Oligopolistic Markets and EC Competition Law" 12 (1994) Y.E.L. 59; Brown,"Judicial Review of Commission Decisions under the Merger Regulation - The First Cases" (1994) 6 E.C.L.R. 296; Ridyard, "Joint Dominance and the Oligopoly Blind Spot under the EC Merger Regulation" (1992) 4 E.C.L.R. 161; Pope, "Some Reflections on Italian Flat Glass" (1993) 4 ECLR 172; Mobley, "Watering down the power of duopolies", International Corporate Law (September 1992) p.8; Bright, "Nestle/Perrier: new issues in EC Merger Control" (September 1992) International Financial Law Review p.22; Briones, "Oligopolistic Dominance: Is there a common approach in different jurisdictions? A review of Decisions adopted by the Commission under the Merger Regulation" (1995) 6 E.C.L.R. 334; Maitland-Walker, "The Unacceptable Face of Politics in

dominance means that two or more firms collectively exercise such significant market power that they are dominant in the particular market concerned. This issue arose most recently for consideration in the European Court of First Instance judgment in *Gencor Ltd v. EC Commission*.[210] The applicants sought to have the Commission's prohibition of the concentration (on the ground that it gave rise to collective dominance contrary to Article 2 Merger Regulation[211]) overturned. The CFI upheld the Commission's Decision prohibiting the concentration, and accepted the notion that a concentration could be prohibited on grounds of collective dominance.

Before any further consideration is given to this judgment of the CFI, it is appropriate at this point to consider the Commission's acceptance in 1992 that collective dominance could constitute valid grounds for prohibiting a concentration under the Regulation. In Commission Decision *Nestle/Perrier*[212] the concept of collective dominance was found by the Commission to fall within the prohibition in Article 2 of the Regulation.[213] Article 2.3 prohibits concentrations which either create or strengthen a dominant position in the common market as a result of which competition is impeded in the common market or a substantial part of it. In *Nestle/Perrier*, the Commission found that dominance for the purposes of Article 2 was not confined to the exercise of market power by a single firm, but could also cover dominance exercised collectively by two or more firms in an oligopolistic market. At paras 113 and 114 of the Decision the Commission had stated that:

> "... The restriction of effective competition which is prohibited if it is the result of a dominant position held by one firm cannot become permissible if it is the result of more than one firm. If, for instance, as a result of a merger, two or three undertakings acquire market power and are likely to apply excessive prices this would constitute an exercise of a collective market power which the Merger Regulation is intended to prevent by the maintenance of a competitive market structure. The dominant position is only the means by which effective competition can be impeded. Whether this impediment occurs through single firm power or collective power cannot be decisive for the application or non-application of Article 2(3) of the Merger Regulation.
>
> In the absence of explicit exclusion of oligopolistic dominance by Article 2(3) it cannot be assumed that the legislator intend to permit the

---

Competition Cases" (1991) 1 E.C.L.R.; Krause, "Article 6(1)b EC Merger Regulation: Improving the reliability of Commitments" (1994) 4 E.C.L.R. 209.

[210] Case T-102/96 *Gencor Ltd v. EC Commission*, March 25, 1999.

[211] Commission Decision 97/26 of 1997.

[212] Case No. IV/M.190, O.J. [1992] L356/1.

[213] *ibid.* at para. 113.

impediment of effective competition by two or more undertakings holding the power to behave together to an appreciable extent independently
of the market...."

The Commission went on to find that a position of collective dominance
would exist as the merged entity (Nestle/Perrier) would find itself in a
duopoly with the other main competitor, BSN, where due to the
structure of the particular market (mineral water in France), competition
between the two main duopolists was unlikely. However, the Commission cleared the concentration eventually after a full investigation
as Nestle gave major commitments which effectively modified the
structure of the concentration and ensured that after the concentration
took place, there would be brands and sources available to facilitate
entry by a significant third competitor in the market place. In this
regard, Nestle agreed to divest itself of several brands and mineral
water sources in order to facilitate the entry of a viable competitor into
the French market. Furthermore, it agreed to modify its behaviour after
the concentra-tion.[214]

It remained to be seen whether the European Community courts
would accept the notion that Article 2 covered collective dominance
concentrations. In 1998, the notion that the concept of collective
dominance is applicable under the Merger Regulation was endorsed
by the European Court of Justice in *France v. EC Commission*[215] and
more recently in 1999 by the Court of First Instance in *Gencor Ltd v. EC
Commission*.[216]

In *Gencor* the CFI has clearly indicated that it is not necessary that
"economic links" between the main players in a market be established
as a prerequisite to a finding of collective dominance. In this sense
therefore, the difference in legal tests for the establishment of collective
dominance under Article 82 EC and Article 2 Merger Regulation appear
to be different.[217] In *Gencor* the Commission prohibited a concentration

---

[214] e.g. Nestle agreed not to supply trade associations with latest sales figures so
that its few competitors would no longer have access to its most up to date
sales information. This was designed to prevent competitors adjusting their
behaviour and thereby not compete with Nestle.

[215] Cases C–68/94 & 30/95 [1998] ECR I–1375.

[216] Case T–102/96 *Gencor Ltd v. EC Commission*, March 25, 1999.

[217] When recognising that the notion of collective dominance existed under Article
82 EC in 1992, the CFI referred to the presence of "economic links" between
undertakings whereby the existence of such links could give the undertakings
concerned a position of collective dominance (such as by way of licences or
agreements between the undertakings): see Case T-68/89 & T-77-78/89 *Societa
Italiano Vetro and Oths v. Commission* ("*Italian Flat Glass*") [1992] E.C.R. II-1403,
where the CFI accepted the concept of collective dominance could exist under
Article 82 EC (although it overturned the Commission's findings on the facts
as an insufficient market analysis had been conducted).

Corporate Finance Law

on the grounds that it was incompatible with Article 2 Merger
Regulation. A question arose in a challenge to the Commission's
decision in the CFI as to whether economic links of some nature must
exist between the parties before collective dominance can be established
under the Merger Regulation? The CFI held that it is *not a prerequisite*
that economic links of a *formal* or *structural* nature exist before collective
dominance can be established. The CFI found that the prior Merger
Regulation case law's reference to economic links (i.e. *France v.
Commission*[218]) was merely illustrative, rather than being a prerequisite
condition. However, in order to "underpin" its decision, the CFI also
expressed the view that the interdependent relationship which arises
in an oligopolistic market may well constitute "links" within the
meaning of that term, as used in the prior case law.

The CFI pointed to the fact that the Commission had found that
after the concentration, the merged entity and the other main competitor
would have large market shares in the platinum market; similar cost
structures; growth in the platinum market in general was slow; and
the likelihood of a new competitor entering the market was low. Hence,
the CFI found that the Commission did not err in law when it found
that interdependent collusion, rather than competition, in this
duopolistic market was more likely. All of these factors created a
duopolistic interdependence between the parties such that it could be
said that in economic and legal terms, there were "economic links"
between them.

After *France v. Commission* and *Gencor v. Commission*, it now can be
taken that the notion of collective dominance is firmly established in
Merger Regulation jurisprudence. It is an essential weapon in the
Commission's arsenal.

Whish[219] points out, the Commission does not make any reference
to economic links when considering whether collective dominance
exists under the Merger Regulation. For example, in *Nestlé/Perrier*,
collective dominance was established on the basis that after the concentration a duopoly would exist, and given the particular market conditions a position of collective dominance was almost inevitable. The
CFI in *Gencor* appears to adopt this reasoning, and in so doing, clarifies
confusion that arose after *France v. Commission*. After *France v.
Commission* there was some uncertainty in that the ECJ did not explicitly
state that economic links were not a prerequisite condition for
establishing collective dominance under the Regulation, but rather it
found that collective dominance was not established as the links found

---

[218] Cases C-68/94 & 30/95 [1998] ECR I-1375.
[219] *Competition Law* (1993) (3rd ed., Butterworths, London) at p. 489.

by the Commission between one of the merging parties (German potash producer Kali und Salz) and another undertaking (SPCA, France) were not sufficient to indicate collective dominance. However, now the CFI has made it clear that, in its view at any rate, economic links are not a prerequisite, and this would appear to be in line with the Commission's thinking on the matter.

(ii) Failing Firm Defence

9–51 In *France v. EC Commission*[220] the ECJ adopted the notion that a "failing firm defence" exists in Community law for the purposes of Article 2 of the Merger Regulation. This provides that where a company takes over a competitor, it may justify its actions (which would otherwise be prohibited under the Merger Regulation on the basis that the take-over leads to either the creation or strengthening of a dominant position adverse to competition) if it can demonstrate that the target company was a failing company whose market share would have been subsumed by the stronger undertaking in any event, over time. In Decision 94/449[221] the Commission had cleared a concentration between top German potash producer Kali und Salz and another potash undertaking based in the former East Germany, provided that Kali und Salz terminated its links with a French potash producer (SPCA). Although the ECJ had annulled that Decision on the basis that the Commission had incorrectly found collective dominance to exist,[222] it nevertheless agreed with the Commission's findings that the "failing firm defence" may be invoked to negate the prohibition in Article 2 Merger Regulation if it can be demonstrated that there is no other means of saving the failing competitor, other than for it to be taken over by the stronger competitor.[223]

(ii) Full-Function Joint Ventures

9–52 Where a concentrative joint venture gives rise to the risk of parent co-ordination, then the concentrative element be assessed under Article 2 of the Regulation, and additionally, any such co-ordinative elements

---

[220] Cases C-68/94 & 30/95 [1998] E.C.R. I–1375.

[221] O.J. 1994 L.186/38.

[222] As noted immediately above, the Court found that the Commission had not demonstrated satisfactorily that collective dominance existed (note that this was the first time the ECJ had annulled a Commission Decision under the Merger Regulation).

[223] Note that the Commission re-examined the concentration in light of the ECJ's ruling and cleared it on October 3, 1998 (Case No. IV/M.308 [1998] O.J. C.275/3).

it may give rise to will have to be assessed under Article 81(3) criteria within the strict Regulation time limits.[224]

(c) Exceptions to exclusive regulation

(i) The "German clause"[225]

9–53   Article 9 of the Merger Regulation provides that the Commission may refer a Community Dimension concentration to a Member State for adjudication where the Member State informs the Commission that the particular concentration threatened to create or strengthen a dominant position as a result of which competition would be significantly impeded on the market in the Member State. This request is not one that the Commission is likely to accede to easily, as it is not in general anxious to hand over jurisdiction to the Member States.[226] To reflect this, the Article 9 handing-over mechanism is cumbersome and biased in favour of the Commission retaining jurisdiction. Before looking in detail at the intricacies of Article 9 in this regard, it is first instructive to give an overview of what Article 9 purports to achieve and then consider how its operation has been amended by the amending Regulation.

In order to make its case, the Member State must argue either that the affected Member State market is a distinct market in itself, or that it is a distinct market which is not a substantial part of the common market.[227] The Member State is required to make its request within three weeks of being notified by the Commission that a notification has been made.[228] It is at the Commission's discretion whether or not it

---

[224] This is considered further below when Full-Function Joint Ventures are discussed at para. 9–58.

[225] Art. 9 is known as the "German Clause" because it was inserted at the behest of larger Member States such as Germany, who, having had a long tradition of competition enforcement and merger control, wished to have a mechanism in the Regulation whereby a merger, or part of it, which proved a distinct threat to competition within a Member State, could be referred by the Commission to the national authorities for regulation under national competition/merger control law, notwithstanding that it had a Community Dimension.

[226] Although, in the last year, the Commission has acceded to Article 9 requests in a number of instances. In 1998 four referral requests were acceded to, and in the first half of 1999, two further requests were acceded to. See further below.

[227] Art. 9.2.

[228] Art. 9.2. The Commission is obliged to notify the Member States of all notifications made to it under the Regulation, Art. 19 of which obliges the Commission to transmit copies of notifications within three working days of their receipt by the Commission. Note that s. 19 Competition Act 1991 provides that the transmission to the Minister by the Commission of a copy of the notification shall constitute a notification under s. 5 Mergers Act 1978. However,

accedes to the Member State's arguments that there is a distinct market. Even if the Commission sees merit in the Member State's argument it need not accede to the application as the wording of Article 9 makes it clear that the Commission refers at its discretion.[229] However, as amended, the Regulation now further provides that if the Commission does conclude that a distinct market is affected *and* that market *is not* a substantial part of the common market, it *must* refer.[230] These mechanisms shall now be considered in more detail.

9–54 As amended, Article 9 provides as follows. Article 9(2) provides that, within three weeks of being informed of the notification by the Commission, the Member State concerned may inform the Commission that either:

(1) the concentration threatens to create or strengthen a dominant position which will lead to a significant impeding of effective competition in that State which presents all of the characteristics of a distinct market (Article 9(2)(a)); or

(2) that the concentration will significantly impede effective competition in that State which presents all of the characteristics of a distinct market and which does not constitute a substantial part of the common market (Article 9(2)(b)).[231]

Where a Member State makes either a paragraph (a) or (b) referral request to the Commission, the Commission is then obliged under Article 9(3) to consider whether the claimed "distinct market" exists and whether the claimed competition threat to the "distinct market" exists. Upon considering these matters, Article 9(3) provides that the Commission may then decide to either:

(1) deal with the concentration itself; or

(2) refer the whole or part of the concentration to the Member State's

---

the clock does not start to run under s. 5 unless the Commission makes a decision to either remit the merger (or the Irish part of it) back to the Minister pursuant to Article 9 of the Regulation; or alternatively, until the Commission indicates to the Minister (pursuant to Art. 21.3 of the Regulation) that any measure the Minister proposed to take on prudential grounds to protect legitimate public interests, is compatible with E.C. law.

[229] Art. 9.

[230] Art. 9(2)(b). This is a new element introduced into the Merger Regulation for the first time by the amending Regulation.

[231] Note the differences between Art. 9(2)(a) and 9(2)(b). For example, Art. 9(2)(b) does not require consideration of whether a dominant position will be created or strengthened.

competent authorities[232] in order to allow that State's national competition law to be applied.

Unlike the position under the original Article 9, which was that the Commission retained absolute discretion on whether to refer, the amended Regulation now provides that in the specific instance where the Commission considers that situation 9(2)(b) applies,[233] then it "shall refer" to the Member State the whole or part of the concentration which relates to the distinct market. This amendment therefore removes an element of the Commission's previous discretion. Notwithstanding this change, it nevertheless remains the case that (as is clear from the final sentence of Article 9(3)) it is the Commission which has the discretion to first decide whether the market affected is a "distinct" market.

Where an Article 9 request is made by a Member State, the Commission must make its decision on whether to refer, within the following time limits:

(1) where the request is made and the Commission has not initiated a four-month investigation, within six weeks of the notification having been made to it originally (Article 9(4)(a));

(2) where the Commission has initiated an Article 6(1)(c) four-month investigation, within three months of the original notification where it has not taken any preparatory steps to either:
  (a) attach conditions or obligations;[234] or
  (b) to prohibit the concentration;[235] or
  (c) take measures to restore effective competition[236] (Article 9(4)(b)).[237]

The above demonstrates how the Commission should exercise its discretion where requested by a Member State within the initial six-week period. Where a four month (phase two) investigation has been initiated by the Commission, then the Commission is obliged to take a decision within three months of the date of receipt of the notification unless it has taken preparatory steps to clear, or prohibit, the concen-

---

[232] *i.e.* national merger regulatory authorities.
[233] *i.e.* that a distinct market exists and it does not constitute a substantial part of the common market.
[234] Pursuant to Art. 8(2), sub para. 2.
[235] Pursuant to Art. 8(3).
[236] Pursuant to Art. 8(4).
[237] In absence of a decision not to refer in response to a request, the Commission is deemed to have decided to refer. However, there must be a Member State "reminder" to the Commission before such referral can be deemed to have occurred.

tration. It is further provided that if the Commission has neither taken a decision on the referral issue in this period nor taken the preparatory steps required to make either a clearance or prohibition decision, then where the Member State has reminded it of the referral request within that period, the Commission is deemed to have taken a decision to refer the concentration to the Member State concerned.[238]

Where the Commission refers a concentration to a Member State, the Member State's competent authorities have a maximum of four months from the date of referral by the Commission to decide on the compatibility of the concentration with national competition law.[239] The Member State exercising such jurisdiction "may take only the measures strictly necessary to safeguard or restore effective competition on the market concerned".[240]

Although in general, the Commission is not overly willing to relinquish jurisdiction when requested to do so by Member States, however, interestingly, in the last year, the Commission has referred a number of notified concentrations, either fully or partially, back to the Member States on foot of Article 9 requests. In June 1998, the Commission decided to refer part of a concentration to the Bundes-kartellampt in Germany. *Kruass-Maffei AG* and *Wegmann & Co GmbH*[241] proposed to acquire joint control of a joint venture set up to operate in the armoured car market in Germany. While the Commission cleared other aspects of the joint venture which concerned simulation technology, it felt that so far as the venture's activities relating to the construction of armoured cars was concerned, the venture raised particularly national issues and hence referred the concentration back to the national competition authority for review under national competition law.

There have also been further references back to the Bundes-kartellampt even more recently. According to Commission Press Release of 9 April 1999[242] the proposed acquisition of delicatessen

---

[238] Art. 9.5.

[239] This in effect is about the amount of time the Minister has to deliver a decision on a merger ordinarily notified under the Mergers Act, although where the Minister does not request further information, the Minister must deliver a decision within a short time, *i.e.* within three months of the clock starting to run. See para. 9–07 above. So far as the Competition Authority is concerned, should the parties decide to notify an Article 9-referred merger to it, then it obviously has to respect the four month time limit set by the Regulation. This is interesting, principally because no such time limit is ordinarily applicable to mergers notified to the Authority in circumstances where the Merger Regulation is not applicable.

[240] Art. 9(8).

[241] O.J. [1998] C.217/08 (11.07.98) (IP/98/555).

[242] (IP/99/220, 9 April 1999).

products supplier *Fritz Homann Lebensmittelwerke GmbH* by *Beeck Feinkost GmbH* which was notified to the Commission pursuant to the Merger Regulation, has been referred by the Commission to the *Bundeskartellamt* for examination. The Commission acceded to the German request, which was based on concern that the concentration may lead to the merged entity becoming dominant in the Germany in the market for self-service salad products and for salad products served at delicatessen counters.

Another concentration that has been the subject of an Article 9 referral is the take-over of *KBB* by *Vendex*.[243] Both undertakings operate in the food and non-food retail sectors in several Member States. The Dutch authorities were particularly concerned that as both were the only retail operators that also owned department stores in the Netherlands, that a dominant position might arise in the non-food retail sector in the Netherlands as a result of the concentration given that both undertakings operate in the sector respectively *via* several retail chains. The Commission indicated that it was willing to accede to the request as the concentration raised particularly national concerns for the Member State's non-food retail sector, and it did not have a Community interest in this regard. The Commission cleared the concentration in relation to the parties operations in other areas.

In *Total/Petrofina*,[244] certain elements of a concentration whereby Total (French) acquired control of Petrofina petrochemical company (Belgian) were referred by the Commission to the domestic competition authorities in France, as it raised competition concerns in southern France and so those elements of the concentration that pose particular concerns to that market were referred to the French competition authorities under Article 9.

An example of a concentration in which an Article 9 referral request was refused by the Commission is the acquisition of *London Electricity* by *Electricité de France*.[245] The UK had requested that the purchase of London Electricity (which supplies about 0.5 per cent of national demand) by the French State owned electricity undertaking (which supplies 6 per cent of UK demand *via* the Franco/British inter-connector cable) be referred to it for regulation as the UK wished to ensure that the UK Director of Electricity Supply should have seisin of the purchase in order to ensure that certain measures applicable in the deregulated UK energy generation and supply market were applied as conditions

[243] M.1060, O.J. [1998] C.280/5 (IP/98/494, June 2, 1998).
[244] M. 1464 (IP/99/197, March 26, 1999).
[245] M. 1346 (IP/99/49, January 27, 1999).

of the purchase. The Commission refused the request as it found that the concentration was unlikely to have an adverse effect on competition in the common market, and the UK had not established that there was a purely national competition problem arising out of the concentration other than that it wished to ensure that general transparency conditions apply to the concentration, as apply generally in the UK energy industry. Consequently, held the Commission, the UK had not made out a case under Article 9 of the Regulation warranting Article 9 referral to the domestic regulatory authorities. Any concerns the UK did have, could be addressed by the DGES in due course.

(ii) Protection of legitimate interests

9–55 Although Article 21.1 of the Regulation provides that the Commission shall have sole jurisdiction to take the decisions provided for in the Regulation, and Article 21.2 precludes the application by Member States of their national competition legislation to any concentration that has a Community Dimension, nevertheless Member States are permitted to take certain measures to protect "legitimate interests". In this regard, Article 21.3 provides that Member States may take appropriate measures to protect "legitimate interests", provided they are compatible with the general principles and other provisions of Community law. The Article lists public security, plurality of the media, and prudential rules as examples of legitimate interests. Article 21.3 provides that any other public interest must be communicated to the Commission by the Member State concerned before any Member State measures may be taken. The Commission must have the opportunity to assess whether the interest being claimed is compatible with the general principles of Community law. The Commission has one month in which to make its assessment. The Competition Act 1991[246] amended the Mergers Act 1978 such that if the Minister prepares to act under the 1978 Act in order to protect the common good, then the clock under the Mergers Act will not begin to run until the date that the Commission has made its decision under Article 21(3). For this purpose, the transmission by the Commission to the Minister of the concentration notification, shall constitute a notification under 5.5 of the 1978 Act, such that the parties will not be requested to make a separate notification to the Minister.

---

[246] s.19.

(iii) Referral to the Commission of a non-Community Dimension concentration (the "Dutch" clause)[247]

9–56   Although a concentration may not be of sufficient size to have a Community Dimension, the Commission can be requested by a Member State, pursuant to Article 22(3), to assume Merger Regulation jurisdiction over the concentration in order that the Commission could take measures outlined in Article 8(2), paragraph 2, Article 8(3), or Article 8(4). In order for the Commission to be able to take such measures, the concentration must, in its view, create or strengthen a dominant position within the Member State making the request. Any action that the Commission does take must be limited to dealing with those aspects of the concentration that affect trade between Member States. Member States will be likely to make Article 22(3) requests to the Commission in circumstances where, for either logistical or domestic political reasons, the Member State would prefer the Commission to deal with the concentration, rather than the national authorities. This procedure has also been modified by the amending Regulation, which amends Article 22(3) to provide that a request can now also be made "at the joint request of two or more Member States",[248] provided the concentration affects those Member States.

9–57   The Commission has an absolute discretion whether to refuse to assume Article 22(3) jurisdiction. Where an Article 22(3) request is made, Article 22(4) provides that certain Articles of the Merger Regulation shall apply to the concentration, particularly Article 7 (suspensive effect). Article 22(4) provides that once the Commission informs the parties to the concentration that a referral request has been made to it by a Member State, then any elements of the concentration that have not been put into effect, are suspended pursuant to Article 7. Article 22(4) further provides that the relevant time limits under the Regulation shall run from the day following the receipt of the request from the Member State(s) concerned. The Member State must make the request to the Commission within one month of the earlier of either the date the concentration was made known to the Member State or to all of the States making a request or affected.

---

[247] Art. 22.3 is known as the "Dutch Clause" as it was inserted at the behest of smaller Member States such as Holland also wished to have a mechanism in the Regulation to enable them refer concentrations to the Commission in the event that the State did not feel it had sufficient reasons to deal with a sizeable concentration.

[248] This addition to Art. 22(3) is known as the "Scandinavian Clause" as it was inserted at the behest of the new Nordic members of the Union.

Where the Commission accedes to an Article 22(3) request, Article 22(5) provides that the Commission may only take such measures as are necessary to restore effective competition within the State(s) at whose request it has intervened.

(4) Full Function Joint Ventures

9–58 Joint ventures posed a particular difficulty for the Commission in the early days of the operation of the Merger Regulation.[249] As originally drafted, Article 3.2 of the Regulation provided that a distinction had to be drawn between *concentrative* and *co-operative* joint ventures.

9–59 Concentrative joint ventures were defined as joint ventures that were created on a lasting basis and which would perform all of the functions of an autonomous economic entity, and which did not give rise to the co-ordination of the competitive behaviour of the parties amongst themselves, or between them and the joint venture.

9–60 Co-operative joint ventures were defined as joint ventures which have as their object or effect the co-ordination of the competitive behaviour of undertakings which remain independent. Because a joint venture that is co-operative in nature serves to allow the parents to co-ordinate their competitive behaviour, it was not regarded as an autonomous economic entity. Consequently, the creation of such a joint venture was not regarded as effecting change in the market from a structural point of view (unlike a concentrative joint venture). Thus, a co-operative joint venture, not being a concentration by nature, would be regulated under Articles 81 and 82 EC, and not under the Regulation's regime.

9–61 In practice, the Commission found that the Article 3.2 criteria were difficult to apply. In 1994 it adopted a new replacement interpretative Notice[250] which, in turn, paved the way for the amendment of

---

[249] Hawk, "Joint Ventures under EEC law," (1991/92) Fordham Int'l Law Journal 303; Sibree, "EEC Merger Control and Joint Ventures," (1992) E.L.R. 91; Pathak, "The EC Commission's Approach to Joint Ventures: A Policy of Contradictions," (1991) 5 E.C.L.R. 171; Picat and Zachmann, "Community Monitoring of Concentration Operations: Evaluation After Two Year's Application," (1993) 6 E.C.L.R. 6 E.C.L.R. 240; Fine, "The Appraisal Criteria of the EC Merger Control Regulation," (1991) 4 E.C.L.R. 148.

[250] Commission Notice 94/C385/01 ([1994] O.J. C.385/2. 31.12.94) on the distinction between concentrative and co-operative joint ventures which replaced an earlier 1990 Notice. The 1994 Notice in turn has now been replaced by Commission

Article 3.2 by the amending Regulation. Particular difficulty was posed by the stipulation in the original Article 3.2 that joint ventures would be deemed to be co-operative if they gave rise to co-ordination between the joint venture and the parents. As some venture/parent co-ordination is inevitable in many joint ventures, this criterion seemed excessive. Furthermore, another difficulty arose from the fact that, where a joint venture had concentrative and co-operative elements, the concentrative part was assured of speedy decision making under the Merger Regulation,[251] whereas there was no such guarantee of speedy Commission action when it considered the co-operative part under Article 81[252] (*i.e.* under Regulation 17/62).

9–62   Thus, the Commission attempted to remedy these difficulties in the replacement Notice adopted at the end of 1994.[253] The 1994 Notice provided that in order to ascertain whether a venture is concentrative or not, attention should focus on, first, the economic autonomy of the venture and, second, whether the joint venture is merely a vehicle for co-ordinating the competitive activity of the parents who remain independent.

So far as the first criterion (economic autonomy) is concerned, issues to be considered are whether the joint venture has sufficient resources to act as an autonomous entity; whether it has been set up for a short specific period/project or whether it is set up on a longer lasting basis; and whether parent influence over the venture amounts to no more than a role in strategic decision-making or whether it also extends into day-to-day commercial operations. Helpfully, the Notice also accepted that while it is inevitable that a joint venture, in the first few years of life, will be involved in transactions with the parent, possibly as its major customer or supplier, this will not affect the autonomy of the joint venture provided that such a heavy degree of interaction does not normally exceed a period of three years post start-up.[254] A venture which satisfied the foregoing requirements was described by the Commission as being a "full-function joint venture". This "full function" test has been retained in the 1998 Notice on the concept of a full function joint venture.

Notice 98/C66/01 ([1998] O.J. C.66/1, 2.3.98) in light of the amendments made by the 1997 amending Regulation 1301/97.

[251] Because the Regulation imposes strict time limits for Commission decision-making.

[252] Because no time limits are imposed under Article 81.

[253] Commission Notice 94/C385/01 ([1994]O.J. C.385/1, 31.12.94) on the distinction between concentrative and co-operative joint ventures replacing Commission Notice C203/10 (O.J. 14.8.1990).

[254] Also stated to be of relevance is whether sales are made to the parents on a commercial basis.

9–63 However, so far as the second criterion is concerned (whether the venture reinforces co-ordination between the parents) there have been major changes. The 1994 Notice effectively went "half the way" but it took the amending Regulation and the 1998 Notice (which replaces the 1994 Notice) to complete the task. Re-interpreting the original Article 3.2, the 1994 Notice provided that the Commission is only concerned with joint venture/parent co-ordination where the venture is an instrument for producing or reinforcing co-ordination *between the parents*. This was an important development, as it clarified that the Commission accepted that it is inevitable that there will be some co-ordination between parent(s) and the venture, and this should not affect the concentrative quality of the venture unless the venture is a vehicle through which the parents (who have remained independent) may co-ordinate their activities. However, the 1994 Notice nevertheless maintained the position that if the venture gave rise to co-ordination between the parents, then, although apparently "full-function", it nevertheless could not be regarded as a concentration and would therefore fall under the jurisdiction of Article 81, and not the Merger Regulation.[255]

Regulation 1301/97 (the amending Regulation) (and the 1998 Notice which replaces the 1994 Notice) has now gone further in this regard in two key respects.

First, the amending Regulation totally deleted all reference to co-operative joint ventures in Article 3.2. The 1998 Notice was adopted on the concept of the full-function joint venture, replacing the 1994 Notice on the distinction between concentrative and co-operative joint ventures. Effectively, this heralds the abandonment, both as a matter of law and as a matter of Commission policy and practice, of the concentrative/co-operative distinction for the purposes of delimiting Merger Task Force jurisdiction under the Merger Regulation. The 1998 Notice gives insight into this new thinking. The Commission is no longer concerned with ascertaining whether a joint venture is concentrative or co-operative: instead, what it wishes to ascertain for the purposes of establishing jurisdiction under the Regulation is whether the joint venture is "full-function". Where the joint venture is "full function", then it will fall within the Regulation's jurisdiction (provided it has, like all other concentrations, a Community Dimension). Furthermore, paragraph 16 of the 1998 Notice explains that where such a joint venture has as its direct consequence the co-ordination of the

---

[255] Unless the parent co-ordination elements could be separated from the creation of the venture itself. In such event, the venture would be regulated under the Merger Regulation and the parent co-ordination elements would be regulated under Regulation 17/62: the 1994 Notice, para. 17.

competitive behaviour of the parent undertakings, this will not prevent the joint venture from being regulated under the Merger Regulation regime. The newly adopted Article 2.4 provides that such a joint
venture will have to satisfy two tests: (a) the Article 2 Merger Regulation dominance/threat to effective competition test, which all concentrations must satisfy; and (b) the criteria of Article 81(3) EC in respect
of those elements that concern co-ordination between the parents.

Second, the amending Regulation by the enactment of Article 2.4
obliges the Commission to regulate all aspects of a full function joint
venture under the Merger Regulation's time limits.

9–64 Therefore the amending Regulation's impact can be summarised
as follows. Article 3.2 is now merely concerned with establishing the
criteria for what constitutes concentrative joint ventures: *i.e.* joint
ventures that perform on a lasting basis all of the functions of an
autonomous economic entity. Additionally, the new Article 2.4 will
provide the legal base for the regulation of concentrative joint ventures
whose creation may (as a direct consequence) lead to the co-ordination
of the competitive behaviour of the parent undertakings which remain
independent. Such co-ordination will be assessed (*within* the Merger
Regulation time limits and framework) under Article 81 with a view to
establishing whether the operation is compatible with the common
market. In particular, Article 2.4 provides that the Commission shall
take into account whether two or more parent companies retain, to a
significant extent, activities in the same market as the joint venture; or
activities in a market which is downstream or upstream from that of
the joint venture; or activities in a neighbouring market closely related
to this market.

These amendments herald a major change in regulatory competence.
Particularly, Article 2.4 which provides that if the joint venture is
concentrative, then any directly consequential co-ordinative[256] elements
it promotes will be assessed under Article 81 and this will not prevent
the transaction from falling within the jurisdiction of the Regulation.
No longer is the concentrative/co-operative distinction relevant as the
basis for deciding whether to regulate the venture under the Regulation
(Article 2 dominance test and tight clearance deadlines) or under Article
81 (different legal test and no clearance deadlines). Now the emphasis
is on whether the venture is "full function". Once it is deemed to be
"full function", then the fact that it may lead to parent co-ordination
does not preclude it from being regulated under the Regulation's

---

[256] A joint venture has co-ordinative qualities where it appears to be a means of
reinforcing co-ordination between the parent companies of their independent
competitive behaviour.

regime. Significantly also, any such co-ordinative elements will be assessed under Article 81 in the same time frame as the concentrative part of the joint venture.

For example, Article 8.2 provides that the Commission shall declare such a concentration to be compatible with Article 2.2 of the Regulation and Article 81(3) of the Treaty if the parties modify their arrangements in order to render it compatible. Alternatively, the Commission may declare it incompatible where Article 81(3) or Article 2.2 cannot be fulfilled. As Article 10 requires that these decisions be made by the Commission in the same time frame that apply to the concentrative parts of the joint venture, effectively this imposes a legal obligation on the Commission to assure speedy decision making for both elements of the joint venture.

From March 1998 when Article 2.4 came into effect, the Commission began considering full-function joint ventures in accordance with this new regime. Its first clearance was in the *Telia/Telenor Nextel/Schibsted* Decision.[257] The three parties involved came together for the purposes of creating a joint venture which would provide internet services in Sweden. The Commission cleared the venture, finding that it was compatible with Article 2. Furthermore, it did not reinforce parent co-ordination to any appreciable extent, hence it was compatible with Article 81. Other similar decisions reached in the past year where Article 2.4 clearance was granted include Decisions such as *@HomeBenelux BV/ Palet Kabelcom/Edon*[258] (internet provision); *British Telecom/Air Touch/ Grupo Acciona, Torreal/CFA/Airtel*[259] (where a consortium led by BT and AT increased their minority stake to acquire joint control over Spanish mobile telephony provider, Airtel); *Amber Mobile Teleholding/Motorola Lithuania Telecom Inc/ UAB Omnitel*[260] (acquisition of joint control over UAB Omnitel, a Lithuanian mobile phone operator). It is of interest to note that the first ten notifications considered pursuant to Article 2(4), all concerned either the telecommunications or internet sectors. Up until the end of 1998, of 76 joint ventures notified, 26 merited some degree of Article 2(4) examination.[261]

9–65 The new Article 2.4 regime does not apply to restrictions that are neither ancillary[262] to, nor a direct consequence of, the creation of

---

[257] Case IV/JV.1 (May 27, 1998).

[258] Case JV.11 (September 15, 1998) (IP/98/825).

[259] Case JV.3 (July 8, 1998) (IP/98/656).

[260] Cases JV.9 (August 18, 1998) (IP/98/772 of August 20, 1998).

[261] DGIV Competition Policy Newsletter No. 1 of 1999, p. 42.

[262] Restrictions that are directly related and necessary for the implementation of the concentration are known as "ancillary" restrictions. Para. 16 of the 1998 Notice provides that such restraints shall be assessed with the concentration

the joint venture. Such restrictions will be regulated under Regulation 17/62, according to the 1998 Notice.

9–66 Finally, the question arises as to the appropriate legal tools for the regulation of restraints attached to a "full function" joint venture that does not have a Community Dimension. It cannot be regulated by the Merger Regulation, as it falls below the Community Dimension thresholds. National competition and merger law is applicable, as the concentration, being of non-Community Dimension size, is more properly a concern of the national authorities of the Member States concerned. On the other hand, where such a concentration is of the variety that has co-ordination risk elements, then Regulation 17/62's regime is potentially applicable as well because Article 22.1 of the Merger Regulation (as amended) has only disapplied Regulation 17/62's applicability to concentrations, *but not* to "joint ventures that do not have a Community Dimension and which have [as] their object or effect the co-ordination of the competitive behaviour of undertakings that remain independent".[263] Therefore, it would appear that Article 81 is still potentially invocable by the Commission, under Regulation 17/62, against restraints attaching to non-Community Dimension concentrations which have co-ordinative elements.[264]

(5) Power of Commission to enforce Regulation

9–67 The Commission has extensive enforcement powers. Apart from extensive powers to request information from the undertakings concerned (Article 11), it can also request information from the competent authorities and governments of the Member States.[265] Article 13 empowers the Commission to undertake investigations with wide powers of search. Article 14 provides that the Commission can impose fines ranging from 1,000–50,000 euros where, either intentionally or negligently, any of the following have occurred:

(1) failure to notify a concentration in compliance with the regulation;[266] or

---

itself in accordance with the principles set out in the 1990 Commission Notice regarding restrictions ancillary to concentrations: [1990] O.J. C203/5 (14.08.1990).

[263] Art. 22(1).

[264] Commission Information Statement 98/C/66/06 (O.J. 2.3.98).

[265] Art. 11. Art. 12 further provides that, in addition, the Commission can request competent authorities in the Member States to undertake investigations on its behalf.

[266] Danish undertaking AP Moller was fined 219,000 euros (M. 969/IP/99/100, 10 February 1999) by the Commission for implementing a concentration without

(2) notification of incorrect or misleading information; or

(3) failure to supply information, or supply of incorrect information in circumstances where it was requested under an Article 11 request for information; or

(4) undertakings being unable to produce complete sets of books during Article 12 or 13 investigations, or where they refuse to submit to Article 13 investigations.

Where other breaches occur, the potential penalties are far more grievous than the foregoing. Article 14.2 provides that the Commission may fine undertakings sums up to 10 per cent of their aggregate turnover[267] where they either intentionally or negligently:

(1) fail to comply with commitments they gave in return for an Article 8.2 clearance decision, or where they fail to honour commitments given in return for the Commission granting a derogation from suspensive effect pursuant to Article 7.4; or

(2) put into effect a concentration contrary to Article 7.1 (which suspends all notifiable concentrations from coming into effect both before they are notified and also after notification until they have been declared to be compatible with the common market); or where in return for a clearance decision under Article 8.2, modifications were proposed by the parties and commitments given, and these have been breached; or

(3) put a prohibited concentration into effect contrary to a declaration of incompatibility by the Commission; or do not take the de-merging measures ordered by the Commission under Article 8.4 in respect of a merger which has already taken effect.

Furthermore, Article 15 provides that the Commission shall have the further power to impose periodic penalties of up to 25,000 euros per day where the parties have not complied with their Article 11 (information) obligations or submitted to an Article 13 investigation.

---

notifying it to the Commission under the regulation. The Commission levied the fine pursuant to Article 14 of the Regulation. The relative lightness of the fine is attributed to the fact that the Commission ultimately cleared the concentration; the undertaking voluntarily notified the Commission of its failure to notify; no harm was found to have been done to Competition; and the infringement occcurred before the Commission had announced its first fine in this area (in the Samsung Decision in February 1998 – on that occasion a very light fine was imposed (33,000 euros) for similar reasons).

[267] Defined in Art. 5. See above.

Article 15.2 provides that even more heavy daily fines of up to 100,000 euros per day may be imposed where undertakings do not comply with the measures of Articles 7.4, 8.2, or 8.4 as noted above.

Conclusion

9–68   The Merger Regulation regime has been well received by lawyers, business parties, and regulators alike since its inception. The amendments effected by the amending Regulation have improved some of the original regime's defects. These amendments can only be welcomed as, by clarifying previously unclear issues, legal certainty is promoted. Hence confidence in the regulatory regime is enhanced. The Merger Regulation regime is a key example of how a supranational regulatory regime can operate successfully across different Member States in an efficient and legally effective fashion.[268]

V. THE TAKEOVER PANEL RULES REGIME

A. INSTITUTIONAL BACKGROUND

(1) The replacement of the London Takeover Panel

9–69   The separation of the London and Irish Stock Exchanges occurred with the enactment of the Stock Exchange Act 1995.[269] A consequence of this separation was that the Irish Stock Exchange ceased to be supervised by the International Stock Exchange based in London. In its place, the Central Bank of Ireland assumed this role.[270] The "separation" of the two Exchanges from a unified supervisory structure led to further supervisory separation, as shortly after the Exchanges' separation the London Panel on takeovers ceased to regulate the conduct of takeovers involving Irish listed companies. It was considered that the time was appropriate for the creation of an Irish Takeover Panel

---

[268] This section of the chapter on EC Merger Control also drew on the author's paper "Recent Developments in EC Merger Regulation Jurisprudence" delivered at the 4th Annual Summer Academy of the European Lawyers Association at the College of Europe, Bruges, July 1999 as well as the author's article, "The EC Merger Regulation – Recent Amendment and Reform" (1998) CLP, pp. 193–197 (Sept. 1998) and pp. 229–335 (Oct. 1998).

[269] See Chap. 1 above. The separation was prompted by the EC Investment Services Directive's (Directive 93/22/EC) requirement that each Member State establish a regulatory authority or authorities with competence to regulate firms that provide investment services and provide for their authorisation to operate under the Home State supervision principle.

[270] As well as the role of regulating the member firms of the Stock Exchange.

as a "knock-on" effect following the separation of the two Exchanges. Consequently, the London Panel, a self regulatory body which applies the City Code on Takeovers,[271] was replaced by the Irish Takeover Panel with effect from 1997.

(2) Irish Takeover Panel Act 1997

9–70   In 1997 the Irish Takeover Panel Act was enacted.[272] It provided for the creation of the Irish Takeover Panel, a domestic body charged with the orderly regulation of takeovers of listed companies in accordance with rules of fair conduct and good commercial standards. In effect, the Irish Panel was to fulfil the role previously undertaken by the London Panel[273] which before the 1997 Act had continued to apply the City Code rules to takeovers involving Irish listed companies.[274] With the coming in to force of the 1997 Act, the Irish Panel adopted its own rules, the Takeover Rules, to govern the orderly conduct of takeovers. It also adopted another set of rules, the Substantial Acquisition Rules, to govern the acquisition of "substantial interests"[275] in listed companies.

While as a matter of law, the Irish Panel's rules have been drawn up in accordance with a set of 12 general principles appended to the 1997 Act's Schedule, in reality however the Irish Panel's rules mirror to a large extent the substantive content of the City Code.[276]

---

[271] The purpose of the Code is to ensure that takeovers of listed companies takes place in an orderly fashion in order to protect the interests of shareholders and companies.

[272] Irish Takeover Panel Act 1997 (No. 5 of 1997). The Act came into effect in various stages by way of the Irish Takeover Panel Act 1997 (Commencement) Order 1997 (S.I. 158 of 1997) and the Irish Takeover Panel Act 1997 (Commencement) Order (No. 2) 1997 (S.I. 256 of 1997) with effect from April 14 and July 1, 1997 respectively.

[273] Although the legal form of the Panels is different as the London Panel is a self regulatory body, whereas the Irish Panel is a statutory body.

[274] And also Irish companies that had been listed in the previous ten years before a relevant transaction.

[275] See below where the Substantial Acquisition Rules ("SARs") are considered.

[276] The City Code on Takeovers has ten general principles, and the Irish code has twelve. In substance the extra two principles (no.'s 11 and 12) are already reflected in the substantive rules of the London Panel's City Code. For the most part (though there are some variations), the Irish general principles and rules are very much based on the City Code.

B. THE TAKEOVER RULES

(1) General principles applicable to Conduct of Takeovers

9–71 The general principles[277] are as follows:

1. All shareholders of the same class of the offeree shall be treated similarly by an offeror.

2. Where information is tendered by the offeror or offeree or their respective advisers to shareholders of the offeree in the course of any offer it shall be made available equally to all of the shareholders who may accept the offer.

3. No offer shall be made and no announcement of a proposed offer shall be made save after careful and responsible consideration of the matter by the offeror and any advisers of the offeror, and only if the offeror and any advisers of the offeror are satisfied that the offeror will be able to implement the offer if it is accepted.

4. Shareholders to whom an offer is made shall be entitled to receive such information and advice as will enable them to make an informed decision on the offer. For that purpose the information and advice should be accurate and adequate and be furnished to the shareholders in a timely fashion.

5. It is the duty of all parties to a takeover or other relevant transaction to prevent the creation of a false market in any of the securities of the offeror or offeree and to refrain from any statement or conduct which could mislead shareholders or the market.

6. It is the duty of the directors of an offeree when an offer is made or when they have reason to believe that the making of an offer is imminent, to refrain from doing anything as respects the conduct of the affairs of the offeree which might frustrate that offer or deprive shareholders of the opportunity of considering the merits of the offer, except upon the authority of those shareholders given in the general meeting.

7. Directors of the offeree shall give careful consideration before they enter into any commitment with an offeror (or any other person) which would restrict their freedom to advise shareholders of the offeree in the future.

8. The directors of the offeree and (if it is a company) of the offeror owe a duty to the offeree and the offeror respectively and to the

---

[277] These principles are found in the Schedule to the 1997 Act.

respective shareholders of those companies to act in disregard to personal interest when giving advice and furnishing information in relation to the offer: in discharging that duty the said directors shall be bound to consider the interest of the shareholders as a whole.

9. Rights of control must be exercised in good faith and the oppression of a minority is not acceptable in any circumstance.

10. Where an acquisition of securities is contemplated as a result of which a person may incur an obligation to make an offer, he or she must, before making the acquisition, ensure that he or she can and will continue to be able to implement such an offer.

11. An offeree ought not to be disrupted in the conduct of its affairs beyond reasonable time by an offer for its securities.

12. A substantial acquisition of securities (whether such acquisition is to be effected by one transaction or a series of transactions) shall take place only at an acceptable speed and shall be subject to adequate and timely disclosure.

(2) Takeovers and Control

9–72 The statutory objects[278] of the Takeover Panel are:

(a) to monitor and supervise *takeovers* and *other relevant transactions* concerning a *relevant company* so as to ensure that the provisions of the Act and any rules adopted thereunder are complied with

(b) to make rules under the Act in relation to takeovers and other relevant transactions concerning a relevant company

The term *"takeover"* means any agreement or transaction (including a merger) whereby control of a relevant company is or may be acquired.[279] It also may mean any invitation, offer[280] or proposal made, or intended or required to be made, with a view to concluding or bringing about a takeover. *"Control"* is defined[281] to mean the holding whether directly or indirectly, of securities of a relevant company (*i.e.*

---

[278] Irish Takeover Panel Act 1997, s.5.

[279] Irish Takeover Panel Act 1997, s.1(1).

[280] "Offer" is defined in s.1(1) of the Irish Takeover Panel Act 1997 to mean an offer to the holders of the securities in a relevant company to acquire some or all of their securities by the payment of cash or other valuable consideration or in exchange for other securities or by means of both such a payment and such an exchange.

[281] Irish Takeover Panel Act 1997, s.1(1).

a company to which the Act applies) that confer in aggregate not less than 30 per cent (or such other percentage as may be prescribed) of the voting rights of the company.

This raises the question as to what is meant by the term *"relevant company"*? From the Act, it is evident that the Panel does not have jurisdiction to supervise the conduct of takeovers or other relevant transactions in respect of all kinds of companies. The Act primarily confines its jurisdiction to "relevant companies", which is defined to mean public limited companies or other incorporated bodies in the State who have securities trading on a recognised stock exchange.[282] However, the Act also gives the Panel jurisdiction to adopt rules in relation to public limited companies or other incorporated bodies in the State whose securities traded on a recognised stock exchange in the last five years prior to a takeover or relevant transaction.[283] In this regard therefore, the Panel can to the extent stated, regulate transactions concerning companies or bodies not listed on the exchange at the time of the takeover or relevant transaction. Furthermore, the Act allows the Minister to empower the Panel to have jurisdiction over "any other public limited company which, in order to secure more fully the protection of shareholders" the Minister may prescribe.[284] There is no provision to allow the Panel regulate transactions involving the takeover or acquisition of substantial interests in private companies.

The Panel also has the power to regulate and specify rules in respect of *"other relevant transactions"*. This is statutorily defined[285] to mean any offer, agreement or transaction in relation to the acquisition of securities conferring voting rights in a relevant company (including a substantial acquisition) which the Panel specifies[286] to be a relevant transaction for the purposes of the Act. The Panel has in fact specified what "relevant transactions" are in concrete terms by specifying in the Takeover Rules[287] that the following shall be regarded as relevant transactions: (a) a substantial acquisition[288] of securities (b) a partial or

---

[282] Irish Takeover Panel Act 1997, s.1(2)(a). At the time of writing the only "recognised stock exchange" is the Irish Stock Exchange Limited in Dublin as per the Irish Takeover Panel Act 1997 (Prescribed Stock Exchange) Regulations 1997 (S.I. No. 256 of 1997).

[283] Irish Takeover Panel Act 1997, s.1(2)(a).

[284] Irish Takeover Panel Act 1997, s.1(2)(c). Note that s.1(2)(c) expressly excludes UCITS and investment companies (as defined in Part XIII Companies Act 1990) from this category.

[285] Irish Takeover Panel Act 1997, s.1(1). It also includes any proposal or action made or contemplated which may be consequent or incidental to such matters.

[286] Pursuant to s.8 of the Irish Takeover Panel Act 1997.

[287] Rule 3.1 Takeover Rules (Preliminary Rules, Part A).

[288] As will be seen below at paras 9–78 *et seq.*, the Panel has made separate rules to deal with "substantial acquisitions."

tender offer which could result in the acquiring party holding less than 30 per cent of the voting rights in the company (c) a reverse takeover transaction (not constituting a takeover of the relevant company which enters into the reverse takeover transaction) and (d) any other offer, not being a takeover, to acquire voting securities of a relevant company.

In order to comply with its statutory obligations, in 1997 the Panel published two sets of rules, the Takeover Rules and the Substantial Acquisition Rules.[289] Each shall now be considered in turn.

(3) Influence of the General Principles on the Panel's Rules

9–73 The Panel is charged with making the Takeover Rules by the 1997 Act.[290] The Panel also is empowered under section 7 of the Act to monitor and supervise takeovers[291] and other relevant transactions[292] so as to ensure that the provisions of the Act are respected. This is bolstered by section 8(1)(b) which provides that the Panel shall ensure that takeovers comply with the general principles set out in the Act's Schedule as well as the principles of the Act generally. Allied to this, the Panel is also charged under section 5 of the Act with making rules to ensure that takeovers are conducted in an orderly fashion. In accordance with this statutory obligation, the Panel published the Takeover Rules on July 1, 1997.

The Takeover Rules are designed to ensure that takeovers and other relevant transactions involving relevant companies comply with the general principles set out in the Schedule to the 1997 Act.[293] Throughout the Takeover Rules the influence of the general principles can be observed. For example, Rule 6.1 is illustrative of the discipline demanded by the general principles. It provides *inter alia* that where a "voluntary" offer of securities is made, then the offeror[294] shall offer

---

[289] Pursuant to s.8(3) of the Irish Takeover Panel Act 1997, as approved by the Minister for Enterprise and Employment pursuant to subs.8(5).

[290] Irish Takeover Panel Act 1997, ss. 5 and 8.

[291] The term "takeover" means any agreement or transaction (including a merger) whereby control of a relevant company is or may be acquired. It also may mean any invitation, offer or proposal made, or intended or required to be made, with a view to concluding or bringing about a takeover. "Control" is defined to mean the holding whether directly or indirectly, of securities of a relevant company (*i.e.* a company to which the Act applies) that confer in aggregate not less than 30 per cent (or such other percentage as may be prescribed) of the voting rights of the company: see further para. 9–72 above.

[292] Defined in s.1(1) to mean any offer, agreement or transaction in relation to the acquisition of securities conferring voting rights in a relevant company (including a substantial acquisition) which the Panel specifies to be a relevant transaction for the purposes of the Act: see further para. 9–72 above.

[293] See para. 9–71 above where the twelve principles are set out.

[294] And any parties acting in concert with the offeror.

the holders of securities in the class in which the offeror has previously acquired securities in the months prior to the announcement of the current offer, terms no less favourable than those offered the sellers of the previously acquired securities.[295] This is to ensure that if an offeror has been offering generous terms initially when building up a sizeable stake in the company, it must offer similar terms to other shareholders when it seeks to increase its stake.[296]

The Rules also deal with the "mandatory offer" situation. This provides that where an offeror has acquired a stake above a certain size, it is obliged to make an offer for the rest of the shares in the company, or in that class, depending on the nature of the shares.[297] The offeror's general obligation to give sufficient information to shareholders of the offeree company in order to enable the shareholders reach an informed decision as to the merits or demerits of the offer, is reflected in Rule 23.[298]

The Rules also deal with matters such as the revision of offers, in order to prevent the offeror using unfair tactics to entice the necessary number of offeree shareholders to accept the offer.[299] In this regard, Rule 32 *inter alia* provides that the offeror cannot make an improved offer in the final fourteen day period during which the original offer may be accepted.[300] Similarly, another Rule provides that an offeror may not[301] make a new offer for an offeree in circumstances where the offeror withdrew a previous offer in the prior 12 months.[302]

The Rules also provide for certain standards of care to be maintained throughout the conduct of the offer. For example, any advertisements, documents or statements issued during the offer must be clear, accurate, complete and fairly presented. Great care must be taken to avoid the making of misleading statements.[303] Rule 20 provides for equality of information whereby all shareholders of companies involved in the offer should have information made equally available to them as nearly as possible at the same time and in the same manner in order to avoid one group of shareholders being given an unfair advantage.[304] From

---

[295] The respective periods may be the previous three months, or the previous twelve months if the Panel considers that more appropriate: rule 6.1(b).
[296] Reflecting General Principle 1.
[297] Takeover Rules, rule 9. See further below.
[298] Reflecting General Principles 2, 4, 5 and 8.
[299] Reflecting General Principle 5.
[300] Reflecting General Principle 1.
[301] Unless the Panel otherwise permits.
[302] Takeover Rules, rule 35. This is to minimise the disruption caused to the offeree's business by a predator in accordance with General Principle 11.
[303] Takeover Rules, rule 19.
[304] Reflecting General Principle 2.

the foregoing overview of the Rules, it should be evident that the Rules are not concerned with the financial or commercial soundness of a takeover, nor are they concerned with issues such as competition or mergers policies which are regulated by different legislation.[305]

(4) Restrictions on acquisitions

9–74 Rule 5.1(b)(i) provides that, except in certain circumstances, a person holding voting securities in a company (or rights over such securities) may not, either alone or acting in concert with other parties holding any such securities or rights, acquire voting securities (or rights over same) where the aggregate of such securities and rights would confer more than 30 per cent of the voting rights in the company. This is to prevent a person or persons acquiring a controlling interest in the company by stealth, *i.e.* without first having (for example) made an announcement of the offer to the company.

Rule 5.1(b)(ii) further provides that, except in certain circumstances, where a person either alone or in concert with others, already holds 30 per cent (or more) but less than 50 per cent of the voting securities[306] in the company, then the person may not acquire any more voting securities[307] where such securities[308] when aggregated to those acquired by the person[309] would exceed 1 per cent of the voting rights of the company when aggregated to any such holdings acquired by the person[310] in the last 12 months.[311]

However, this Rule does not prevent persons acquiring new voting securities in the company,[312] nor new or existing voting securities under an established share option scheme, nor existing voting securities pursuant to the exercise of an option.[313]

Furthermore, the restrictions of Rule 5.1 do not apply to an acquisition of voting securities of a relevant company or of rights over such securities by a person who holds securities conferring more than

---

[305] That the Panel is not concerned with such matters is stated in the Introduction to the Takeover Rules, para. 1.
[306] Or rights over same.
[307] Or rights over same.
[308] Or rights over same.
[309] And those (if any) acting in concert with them.
[310] And those (if any) acting in concert with them.
[311] Takeover Rules, rule 5.1(b)(ii). Although note that any voting rights acquired by virtue of the person having to make a rule 9 "mandatory offer" do not count as additional securities acquired in this regard (rule 9 is considered at para. 9–76 below).
[312] Or of rights to subscribe for such securities or rights convertible into same.
[313] However, such voting securities or right to same will be aggregable where subsequent acquisitions are made.

50 per cent of the voting rights in the company concerned.[314] This is because such person already has majority control in the company. Also, where a person has acquired such a stake by a permitted acquisition, then again Rule 5.1 does not apply to restrict their acquisition of further securities.[315]

Finally, in addition to Rule 5.1, the Substantial Acquisition Rules will apply unless there has been an announcement by the person making the acquisition of a firm intention to make an offer in respect of the company the posting of which is not, or has ceased to be, subject to the fulfilment of any condition.[316]

(5) Exceptions

9–75   Rule 5.2 provides for a number of exceptions where the restriction on acquisitions of voting securities or of rights over such securities may be permitted. Common to several of these situations is that each involves the making of a "firm intention announcement" either immediately before or after the substantial acquisition, and furthermore there is a friendly reception on the part of the offeree's board towards the offer. Acquisition is permitted by a person

(a) who acquires voting securities (or rights over same) from a single[317] securities holder and it is the only such acquisition the person has made in the last seven days,[318] or

(b) immediately before the announcement of the person's firm intention to make an offer under the Takeover Rules for the company in circumstances where either the acquisition is made with the agreement of the offeree board, or the offer will be publicly recommended for acceptance by board, and the acquisition is conditional on the announcement of the offer, or

(c) immediately after the person announces a firm intention to make an offer in respect of the company, provided such acquisition satis-

---

[314] Note 2 on Takeover Rules, rule 5 (appended to the Takeover Rules).

[315] *ibid.*

[316] Note 5 on Takeover Rules, rule 5 (appended to the Takeover Rules).

[317] Takeover Rules, rule 5.2(b) elaborates further on the issue of "single securities holder" to provide that acquisitions from persons who are members of the person's immediate family or from related group companies will be regarded as being from a single holder.

[318] Rule 5.2(a)(i) elaborates by providing that this exception shall not apply if such person has announced a firm intention to make an offer in respect of the company and the posting of the offer is not subject to any pre-condition. Also see further Rules 5.3 and 5.4 which deal further with acquisitions from a single securities holder *vis-à-vis* consequences and disclosure requirements in certain circumstances.

fies a precondition of the posting of the offer and that the offer has been publicly recommended for acceptance by the offeree board, or the acquisition is made with its agreement, or

(d) after the person has announced a firm intention to make an offer in respect of the company, provided that the posting of the offer is not, at the time of acquisition subject to a pre-condition, and the acquisition is either made with the agreement of the offeree board, or that offer or any competing offer has been publicly recommended for acceptance by the offeree board,[319] or

(e) if the acquisition is by way of acceptance of an offer made in accordance with the Rules.

(6) Mandatory Offer

9–76 The Rules require a person to take specific action where a person[320] acquires "control"[321] of a relevant company,[322] or where the person[323] already controls the company and the person within a specified period acquires a further specified amount of securities in that company.[324] In this regard Rule 9 provides that a person must make what is known as a "mandatory" offer. It provides that where a person[325] either

(i) acquires a holding of 30 per cent or more of the voting rights in a relevant company or a holding of less than 30 per cent of such rights increases to 30 per cent or more, or,

(ii) controls a relevant company (*i.e.* has a holding of 30 per cent or more) but does not hold more than 50 per cent of the voting rights

---

[319] Furthermore, in the case of this fourth situation, there must be no Ministerial consent awaiting or approval from any other body in the State (*e.g.* Competition Authority) or the European Commission by either the first closing date of the offer or of any competing offer.

[320] Acting either alone or in concert with others: Irish Takeover Panel Act 1997, s.8(3).

[321] "control" is defined to mean the holding whether directly or indirectly, of securities of a relevant company (i.e. a company to which the Act applies) that confer in aggregate not less than 30 per cent (or such other percentage as may be prescribed) of the voting rights of the company.

[322] "relevant company" defined in s.1(1): see para. 9–72 above where this was considered.

[323] *ibid.*

[324] Note that rule 37 of the Takeover Rules provides a separate modified mandatory offer regime in the specific instance of persons who acquire control of a company (*i.e.* a holding of 30 per cent or more, and less than 50 per cent) by virtue of the redemption or purchase by that company of its own shares.

[325] Acting either alone or in concert with others: Takeover Rules, rule 9.1(a).

in a relevant company and increases the holding by more than 1 per cent within any 12 month period:

then in either situation the person is obliged to make an offer to the holders of each class of equity share capital of the company to acquire their shares as well as an offer to acquire all voting non-equity shares in the company in any class in which the person holds any such shares.

The rationale for Rule 9 is that it seeks to protect shareholders' interests. They may be unhappy that a person is building up a significant stake in the company, and so if that person is deemed to control the company by Rule 9, the person has to offer to buy them out rather than merely establish control.

(7) Interplay with other legal regimes: Mergers Act and EC Merger Regulation

9–77 The Takeover Rules provide that where a mandatory offer is required, it shall also be subject to Rule 12 if either the jurisdiction of the Minister under the Mergers Act 1978, or the European Commission under the EC Merger Regulation 5064/89, are relevant to the transaction.

So far as the Mergers Act regime is concerned, Rule 9.3 provides that the offer must be made subject to the condition that if the Minister does either of the following:

(i) makes a section 7(a) Mergers Act order to the effect that no order will be made under section 9 of the Mergers Act, or

(ii) states that a section 9 Mergers Act conditional prohibition order has been made, or

(iii) fails to make a section 9 Mergers Act order within the period allowed by section 6 of the Mergers Act

then the offer may proceed.

On the other hand, Rule 9.3 provides that if the Minister does none of the above, the condition is not satisfied, in which event the offer lapses. In such a case, the Panel may order the offeror and any parties acting in concert to reduce their aggregate holdings in the company to

---

[326] Pursuant to Art. 6(1)(c) EC Merger Regulation.

[327] For the purposes of the EC Merger Regulation, mergers and takeovers are known as "concentrations."

[328] Pursuant to Art. 9(1) Merger Regulation the EC Commission may refer a concentration to the national regulatory authorities where it considers that the concentration raises more national, than EC, concerns: see para. 9–53 above.

[329] Whichever is the later.

below 30 per cent, or in the case where their holdings were in the 30-50 per cent range to the original percentage level held before the mandatory offer obligation arose.

So far as the EC Merger Regulation regime is concerned, Rule 9.3 provides that a mandatory offer must be made subject to the condition that it will lapse if the Commission either initiates an Article 6 Merger Regulation (four month) investigation[326] in respect of the concentration[327] (or if the Commission refers the concentration to a competent authority of a Member State[328]) before the first closing date of the offer, or the date when the offer becomes or is declared unconditional as to acceptances.[329] However, if the proposed transaction is eventually allowed proceed by the regulatory authorities, then the obligation to make a mandatory offer shall continue. On the other hand, if the transaction is prohibited by the Minister/EC Commission, then the Panel may direct the parties to reduce their holdings below the 30 per cent level, or where the persons had an original level in the 30-50 per cent range, to that original level held before the obligation to make a mandatory offer was incurred.

C. SUBSTANTIAL ACQUISITION RULES

9–78 The Substantial Acquisition Rules ("SARs") reflect General Principle 12[330] which provides that a substantial acquisition of securities, whether effected by single or multiple transactions, shall take place only at an acceptable speed and shall be subject to adequate and timely disclosure. These Rules are designed to restrict the speed with which a person may increase a holding of voting securities, and rights over such securities, of a relevant company to an aggregate of between 15-30 per cent of the voting rights of the relevant company. Also, subject to certain exceptions, they require the accelerated disclosure of acquisitions of rights related to such holdings. The Panel is charged with elaborating rules to regulate the acquisition of substantial acquisitions by section 8(2) of the Act.

(1) Prohibition

9–79 Rule 4 of the SARs prohibits any person from making "a substantial acquisition" of securities except as permitted by the SARs.[331]

---

[330] The General Principles Applicable to the Conduct of Takeovers are to be found in the Schedule to the 1997 Act: see para. 9–71 above.

[331] Special provision is made for "dealers" whereby the prohibition in Rule 4 shall not apply to dealers who acquire substantial acquisitions and dispose of sufficient of them as determined by Rule 4 thresholds by 12 noon next day to

According to Rule 3(a) of the SARs, an acquisition by a person of voting securities of a relevant company[332] (or of rights over voting securities) shall be regarded as "a substantial acquisition" if

(a) any voting securities or rights so acquired confer in the aggregate 10 per cent or more of the voting rights in the company; and

(b) any voting securities (and rights over same) so acquired by that person confer 15 per cent or more but less than 30 per cent of the voting rights in the company when aggregated with any voting rights already held by that person.[333]

Should the person engage in a series of acquisitions of voting securities of a relevant company (or of rights over voting securities), then all such transactions will be aggregated within a *seven day period* for the purpose of assessing whether the acquisitions constitute "a substantial acquisition" in that period.

Essentially therefore, it is necessary for a person, before making an acquisition of voting securities in a relevant company, to identify and aggregate the acquisitions of such securities of that company made by him or her in the preceding six days with the acquisition about to be made.[334] If the acquisition represents less than 10 per cent of the total voting rights, then the proposed acquisition may be made.

On the other hand, if more than 10 per cent, then it is all a question of whether that amount when aggregated with existing holdings would elevate the person's interest to between 15-30 per cent. Should that be the case, then the acquisition may not proceed.[335] Of course if the 30 per cent threshold would be met or exceeded, then the Takeover Rules, in particular Rules 5 and 9, may come into play.[336]

It is noteworthy that neither the acquisition of new voting securi-

---

persons unconnected with the seller, or where the dealer inadvertently purchases a substantial acquisition.

[332] "relevant company " is defined in s.2 of the 1997 Act: see para. 9–72 above when the Takeover Rules were considered, for further elaboration.

[333] Note that if the person is acting in concert with other persons, then their holdings will be aggregated for the purposes of Rule 3 SARs calculations.

[334] And of course, any acquisitions made by any person acting in concert with that person during that period must be aggregated also: Rule 3(b)(i) SARs.

[335] Subject to one of the exceptions of Rule 5 SARs being applicable: see para. 9–80 below.

[336] In this regard, Note 5.5 on Rule 5 Takeover Rules provides that in addition to Rule 5 Takeover Rules applying where "control" is an issue, the SARs will also apply unless there has been an announcement by the person making the acquisition of a firm intention to make an offer in respect of the company the posting of which is not, or has ceased to be, subject to the fulfilment of any condition.

ties,[337] nor of new or existing voting securities[338] under an established share option scheme, nor the acquisition of existing voting securities by the exercise of an option, shall be treated as an acquisition of voting securities (or rights over same) for the purposes of Rule 3(a) of the SARs. However, the acquisition of any such rights will count for aggregability purposes should the person subsequently acquire further voting securities (or rights over same) in the company at any time in the future.

(2) Exceptions

9–80 A proposed transaction which is deemed to be a "substantial acquisition"[339] may not be made, unless it falls within one of the exceptions permitted by Rule 5 of the SARs. These exceptions are where "a substantial acquisition" is made of voting securities (or rights over same) in a relevant company by a person who

(a) acquires voting securities (or rights over same) from a single securities holder[340] and it is the only acquisition the person has made in the last seven days, or

(b) is engaged in a tender offer,[341] or

(c) immediately after the acquisition, announces a firm intention to make an offer under the Takeover Rules for the company concerned in circumstances where either the acquisition is made with the agreement of the offeree board, or the offer will be publicly recommended for acceptance by board, and the acquisition is conditional on the announcement of the offer, or

(d) before the acquisition announced a firm intention to make an offer for the company concerned and the posting of the offer was not subject to a precondition.

Where a person or those acting in concert with him hold 30 per cent or more of the voting rights of the company, such a person will be subject

---

[337] Which also includes in this context acquisition of securities convertible into new voting securities, or of rights to subscribe for new voting securities (other than the purchase of rights arising pursuant to a rights issue): Rule 3(a) SARs.

[338] Which also includes in this context acquisition of rights over such securities: Rule 3(a) SARs.

[339] As defined in Rule 3 SARs: see above.

[340] Rule 5(b) SARs elaborates further on the issue of "single securities holder" to provide that acquisitions from persons who are members of the person's immediate family or from related group companies will be regarded as being from a single holder.

[341] Rule 7 SARs applies in this event.

to the Takeover Rules, rather than the SARs.[342] In such event, the Takeover Rules will apply, and the person may be obliged to make a "mandatory offer" under Rule 9 of the Takeover Rules.[343]

(3) Obligation of Prompt Disclosure

9–81   A person who acquires voting securities (or rights over same) is obliged by Rule 6 of the SARs to disclose the acquisition as well as that person's total holding of voting securities (or rights over same) not later than 12 noon on the business day following the acquisition in the following circumstances[344]:

(a) where the aggregate of all voting rights[345] held by the person before the acquisition was less than 15 per cent, and after the acquisition has increased to, or is greater than 15 per cent,[346] or,

(b) the aggregate of the voting rights[347] held by the person before the acquisition was between 15 per cent and less than 30 per cent, and after the acquisition has increased by more than one whole percentage.[348]

The notification must be made to several specified parties being the company concerned, the Company Announcements Office of the Stock Exchange, and the Irish Panel.

Acquisition of new voting securities,[349] or of new or existing voting securities[350] under an established share option scheme, or the acquisition of existing voting securities by the exercise of an option shall not be required to be disclosed by Rule 6. However, the acquisition of any such rights will count for aggregability purposes should the person acquire a disclosable acquisition of voting securities (or rights over same) at any time in the future.

---

[342] Note 5.1 on Rule 5 SARs (in Notes appended to the SARs).
[343] See above para. 9–76.
[344] Rule 6 SARs.
[345] Whether of voting securities or of rights over such securities.
[346] Rule 6(a)(i) SARs.
[347] Whether of voting securities or of rights over such securities.
[348] Rule 6(a)(ii) SARs.
[349] Which also includes in this context acquisition of securities convertible into new voting securities, or of rights to subscribe for new voting securities (other than the purchase of rights arising pursuant to a rights issue): Rule 6(a) SARs.
[350] Which also includes in this context acquisition of rights over such securities: Rule 6(a) SARs.

D. THE PANEL

(1) Composition

9–82 The Irish Takeover Panel is a public company limited by guarantee formed and registered under the Companies Acts.[351] Its memorandum and articles of association are approved by the Minister for Enterprise, Trade and Employment. It must have seven directors, the chairman and deputy chairman being the nominees of the Central Bank.[352] It may also have members designated by the following bodies: the Consultative Committee of the Accountancy Bodies (Ireland), the Law Society of Ireland, the Irish Association of Investment Managers, the Irish Bankers Federation, and the Irish Stock Exchange.[353] Essentially therefore, the members of the Panel are made up of persons likely to have experience relevant to the conduct of takeovers.[354] Unlike its predecessor, the London Takeover Panel, the Irish Takeover Panel is a statutory body.[355]

(2) Powers of Panel

(a) Rulings and Directions

9–83 The Panel has extensive powers pursuant to section 9 of the 1997 Act. For example, the Panel may of its own volition, or on the application of interested parties, make a *ruling* as to whether any activity or proposed activity is, or would be, in conformity with the general principles or its own Rules.[356] It is clear therefore that it can act of its own motion if it wishes. It is also provided that its rulings will have immediate effect.[357] Whether it decides to publish its rulings is a matter for the Panel.[358]

To accompany its power to make rulings as described, the Panel also has the power to give *directions*[359] to persons for the purpose of ensuring compliance with the general principles and its own rules. *Inter*

---

[351] Irish Takeover Panel Act 1997, s.3.

[352] Irish Takeover Panel Act 1997, s.6.

[353] *ibid.*

[354] The Act also allows for members of the Panel to be nominated for specific takeovers where necessary.

[355] The Introduction to the Rules states that the decision to have a statute based Panel in Ireland resulted mainly from concern about the legal difficulties which would arise from the exercise of its functions by an Irish Panel which did not have adequate powers derived from legislation.

[356] *i.e.* the Takeover Rules or the Substantial Acquisitions Rules.

[357] Irish Takeover Panel Act 1997, s.9(1)(a).

[358] Irish Takeover Panel Act 1997, s.9(1)(b).

[359] Irish Takeover Panel Act 1997, s.9(2).

alia, this may include a wide variety of measures such as the power to direct in respect of a takeover or other relevant transactions any of the following: an acquisition of securities; an issue of securities; an allotment or disposal of securities; a restraint on exercising voting rights or any other rights attaching to the securities; an offer upon such terms as it may specify; an announcement that an offer has lapsed; a renewal of any offer that has lapsed; the disclosure of any information specified in the direction; the disclosure of shareholdings, transactions or identities of involved parties.[360]

Where the Panel considers that a party is not complying with its rulings or directions, it may apply to the High Court seeking an order to require any party to the transaction to do, or refrain from doing any act. It may also request the court to annul any transaction that has been carried out otherwise than in accordance with its ruling or direction or, it may request the Court to provide for any consequential or restitutionary relief.[361]

(b) Censure

9–84   The Panel also has the power, either of its own volition, or on the application of a party to a takeover or other relevant transaction, to enquire into the conduct of any person where it has reasonable grounds for believing that a contravention of the general principles or its rules has occurred, or may occur.[362] As a sanction, the Panel may "advise, admonish or censure"[363] and may publish the terms of the sanction as it considers appropriate.[364] A person so sanctioned has a right of appeal to the High Court, which may confirm the Panel's decision, annul it, or order such fresh enquiry as the Court deems appropriate.[365]

(c) Hearings

9–85   The Panel has the statutory power to hold hearings for the purposes of exercising its section 9 and 10 powers.[366] Hearings shall be conducted in private if the Panel considers it appropriate in view of the interests of either the parties concerned, or the securities which may be affected by the relevant transaction.[367] The Act gives the Panel

---

[360] rish Takeover Panel Act 1997, s.9(3).
[361] Irish Takeover Panel Act 1997, s.12(1).
[362] Irish Takeover Panel Act 1997, s.10(1).
[363] Irish Takeover Panel Act 1997, s.10(2).
[364] Irish Takeover Panel Act 1997, s.10(3).
[365] Irish Takeover Panel Act 1997, s.10(4).
[366] Irish Takeover Panel Act 1997, s.11(1).
[367] Irish Takeover Panel Act 1997, s.11(2).

considerable powers. For the purposes of hearings the Panel shall have "the powers, rights and privileges" vested in a High Court judge in respect of the compellability and the attendance of witnesses and documents.[368] Proceedings shall be conducted under oath.[369] It is an offence to fail to attend the Panel when summonsed, or to refuse to testify under oath, perjure oneself, or otherwise obstruct the Panel in the conduct of its hearings.[370] In such circumstances, the Panel may refer the person to the High Court, which may make such order as it deems appropriate. The Act also gives the Panel the power to prosecute[371] the person, and if the prosecution is successful, the punishment is a fine of up to £1,500 or imprisonment for up to 12 months, or both.[372] Where a prosecution is sought, it must be initiated within two years from the date of the offence.[373]

(3) Judicial Review of Panel's Acts

9–86 In providing for a right of judicial review, the Act seeks to ensure that on the one hand parties rights are protected from an abuse of power by the Panel, while on the other it seeks to limit the "opportunity" for parties to use the courts as a battleground for diversionary tactics designed to disrupt a takeover. Consequently, section 13 of the Act provides for a right of judicial review with very defined parameters.[374] It provides that the only way in which the Panel's rules (or derogations or waivers from the rules pursuant to section 8(7)) or its section 9 rulings or directions can be challenged, is by way of a judicial review action.[375] This is to ensure speedy judicial resolution as it confines legal challenge to the judicial review form of action, where expedited court procedures may apply. If parties were given the right to initiate substantive forms of legal action, this would be much more time consuming and would be detrimental to the prospects of the contested transaction being successfully completed within a relatively expeditious timeframe.

However, section 13(2) goes even further, as it also provides that such judicial review challenges may only be brought by a *party to* the takeover or relevant transaction. It restricts the scope of any such

---

[368] Although this compellability does not apply to documents normally entitled to legal professional privilege: Irish Takeover Panel Act 1997, s.18.

[369] Irish Takeover Panel Act 1997, s.11(3).

[370] Irish Takeover Panel Act 1997, s.11(5).

[371] Irish Takeover Panel Act 1997, s.25(2).

[372] Irish Takeover Panel Act 1997, s.25(1).

[373] Irish Takeover Panel Act 1997, s.25(3).

[374] Note that so far as the London Panel is concerned, a limited right of judicial review was recognised in *R. v. Panel on Takeovers, ex p. Datafin*.

[375] Pursuant to Order 84 of the Rules of the Superior Courts (S.I. No. 15 of 1986): Irish Takeover Panel Act 1997, s.13(1).

challenge to those Rules which formed the *basis of* a section 8(7) or section 9 decision.

To bolster this restrictive regime, the Act also provides an extremely short timeframe in which a party may seek judicial review. This is a mere seven days from the date the Panel made its relevant ruling or direction.[376] Given that takeovers need to take place within a definitive timeframe, the requirement for such a short time limit is under-standable. Yet one wonders if it is not a little too brief because often in complex transactions all relevant information may not be to hand or may not be in a comprehensible form until later in the transaction process. One suspects that in order to protect the short time limit from constitutional challenge, the Act also provided that the Court may extend the seven day time limit as it sees fit where it is evident that the failure by the applicant to make its challenge was not due to any neglect on the applicant's part, and that it would not result in an injustice to any other party.[377] The Act also provides that the Court shall not grant leave to apply for judicial review unless it is satisfied that there are substantial grounds for contending that the contested Rule, derogation, waiver, ruling or direction is invalid, or should be quashed.[378] Also it provides that the High Court's decision shall be final, and that appeal to the Supreme Court will only be permitted where the High Court certifies that its decision involves a point of "exceptional importance."[379] Court hearings will as far as possible all involve the same judge, and shall take place otherwise than in public if the Court so decides.[380]

The Act also provides another way in which to limit judicial intervention in takeovers or relevant transactions. Section 15 of the Act provides that nothing in the Act shall operate to invalidate any transaction that was made in violation of the Rules or the rulings or directions of the Panel.[381] Furthermore, it also provides that nothing in the Act shall operate to invalidate any transaction made in violation of the Rules or the Panel's rulings or directions even where the Rule, ruling or direction was quashed by way of judicial review.[382] This is most draconian and is designed to prevent parties attempting to have completed transactions undone. The only way in which this may be achieved,[383] is if *the Panel itself* makes an application to the Court

---

[376] Irish Takeover Panel Act 1997, s.13(3).
[377] Irish Takeover Panel Act 1997, s.13(5).
[378] Irish Takeover Panel Act 1997, s.13(3).
[379] Although this will not apply where a constitutional issue is raised: subs 13(7) Irish Takeover Panel Act 1997, s.13(7).
[380] Irish Takeover Panel Act 1997, s.14.
[381] Irish Takeover Panel Act 1997, s.15(a).
[382] Irish Takeover Panel Act 1997, s.15(b).
[383] As permitted by s. 5 of the Irish Takeover Panel Act 1997.

pursuant to section 12(2) seeking an annulment of its own earlier rulings or directions on the basis that its earlier decision was based on false or materially misleading information. In these circumstances, the Panel may request the Court to annul any transaction carried out by the transgressor and order restitutionary relief.

Finally, it is clear from the Act that the Panel is largely to be the master of its own destiny. In this regard, section 7 of the Act provides that while the Panel is under a duty to monitor takeovers and other relevant transactions and to carry out other functions, nothing in the section shall be construed as imposing on the Panel any duty or liability to which it would not otherwise be subject. It is clear from this that the legislature wished to make it clear that the courts should not be used to force the Panel into acting, or not acting, when the Panel felt otherwise. In this way it is hoped that parties will be prevented from seeking a hearing at the High Court if unhappy with the conduct of a takeover or other relevant transaction.

(4) Liability of Panel

9–87   The Panel's members, employees and advisers are under a duty to observe obligations of professional secrecy in respect of its functions, and may only disclose confidential information thereby gained in accordance with the Act.[384] However, this does not prevent the foregoing persons from making disclosure to the Minister for Enterprise, Trade and Employment, the police, the Director of Public Prosecutions, an inspector appointed in accordance with any enactment, a stock exchange for prudential supervision purposes, the Central Bank, or any person performing analogous functions to a Takeover Panel in another State, or such other persons as may be prescribed.[385] Contravention of the obligation to maintain professional secrecy shall be an offence[386] punishable by a fine of up to £1,500 or imprisonment for up to 12 months years, or both.[387] Curiously, section 25(2) provides that prosecutions for breach of the secrecy obligation may be brought by the Panel, which seems a little odd given that it would be prosecuting its own employees and this may give rise to a conflict of interest. Where a prosecution is taken, it must be initiated within two years from the date of the alleged offence.[388]

---

[384] For example, the members and staff of the Panel do not breach this obligation if they publish otherwise confidential information for the purpose of giving a section 9 Irish Takeover Panel Act 1997 ruling or direction.

[385] Irish Takeover Panel Act 1997, s.17(2).

[386] Irish Takeover Panel Act 1997, s.17(3).

[387] Irish Takeover Panel Act 1997, s.25(1).

[388] Irish Takeover Panel Act 1997, s.25(3).

The Act also gives immunity from liability in damages to the Panel, its members and employees in respect of their functions.[389] However, this does not apply if the act or omission complained of was done in bad faith. The Panel may also give its staff an indemnity from damages or costs awarded by a court in respect of any act or omission carried out as part of their duties.[390]

E. THE PROPOSED TAKEOVERS DIRECTIVE

9–88 At the time of writing, the proposed 13th EC Directive on Company Law[391] which concerns take-over bids, is proceeding through the legislative process in Brussels and Strasbourg (the proposed Directive is a Commission proposal and has been considered by both the EU Council of Ministers and the European Parliament). The aim of the Directive, which is expected to be adopted in final form before the end of 1999, is to co-ordinate the takeover rules that apply in the EU Member States to a minimum extent in order to promote legal certainty and ensure that cross-border takeover activity is not hindered by widely varying national takeover regimes. In this respect, the Directive does not propose to harmonise national takeover regimes in every respect, but rather seeks the elimination of several major obstacles to cross-border takeovers, which emanate from divergent national rules, by requiring Member States to comply with the Directive's harmonising rules in these key areas.

In particular, the Directive seeks to ensure that the mandatory bid rule applies in every Member State, in order to ensure the protection of minority shareholders. Furthermore, the Directive will seek to ensure the protection of employees' interests by requiring the board of the offeree (the target company) to reveal to employees that a takeover attempt is under way. Also, the Directive proposes that the board of the offeree cannot take defensive measures in a takeover without shareholder consent.

In the amended draft of the Directive as of June 21, 1999, it is proposed that Member States shall have four years after the date of adoption of the Directive in which to implement the Directive. In the

---

[389] Irish Takeover Panel Act 1997, s.20(1).

[390] Irish Takeover Panel Act 1997, s.20(5).

[391] June 21, 1999 Council of Ministers reached political agreement on almost all aspects of the proposed Takeover Directive. The only outstanding point concerned disagreement between Spain and the UK concerning the definition of takeover authorities in Gibraltar. At the time of writing the Directive has still not been finally adopted: see Commission Website, DG15, Company Law section.

matters which it concerns, the Directive's regime has been modelled to a large extent on the UK takeovers regime, and so its impact on the Irish takeovers regime will not be as significant as on some other Member States.

(1) Mandatory bid

9–89 Currently some Member States such as Germany and the Netherlands do not require a mandatory bid to be made where a transfer of control occurs as a result of a takeover. Furthermore, some other Member States require a bid to be made only for a certain percentage of the offeree's shareholders' securities. The Directive proposes that all Member States will have to introduce a mandatory bid regime (if this is not already so) whereby the offeror will have to make a mandatory bid for all of the offeree's shareholders' securities. The Directive further proposes that national supervisory authorities shall have the power to grant derogations from this requirement in individual cases to the extent that, instead of requiring an offeror to bid for all of the shares of the minority shareholders, the offeror can be permitted to bid for a "substantial part" of the shareholders' securities, being not less than 70% of their securities.[392] While the Directive does not specify rules for determining what the mandatory bid price should be, it requires that it must be at an "equitable price".

The introduction of the mandatory bid rule regime will prevent States, who currently prefer to provide alternative means (than the mandatory bid rule) to protect minority shareholders, from maintaining such rules in preference to the mandatory bid regime. Any State which utilises such rules currently, may retain them, but only as an additional protection to the mandatory bid regime. The Directive proposes that States, which currently only have alternative protection regimes, will have two years from the date they transpose the Directive into national law in which to introduce the mandatory bid rule as the primary method of protecting minority shareholders. This principally appears to affect Germany to the greatest extent, as it appears to be the State with the most highly developed alternative protection regime.

(2) Defensive measures

9–90 Another major area that will be affected by the proposed Directive shall be the ability of the offeree's board to take defensive measures during the period of acceptance of the bid. Currently, some

---

[392] However the Directive further provides that the supervisory authority can permit lower levels than 70% if such can be duly justified by the supervisory authority.

Member States allow such measures to be taken without consultation with the shareholders,[393] while in other Member States the taking of such measures is prohibited.[394] The Directive proposes to deal with this matter by prohibiting the board of the offeree from taking any defensive measures during the period of acceptance of the bid once it has received formal notice of the bid, unless it had authorisation from the shareholders in a general meeting convened for this specific purpose. However, the Directive also proposes that the Member States shall have the option to permit the offeree's board to increase the share capital of the company during the bid acceptance period, provided that a general meeting of the shareholders had so approved such a course of action in the 18 months prior to the launch of the takeover bid. In order for an offeree to so act, it is further provided that the shareholders pre-emption rights must not be prejudiced.

To facilitate the operation of this regime, the Directive proposes that the minimum period for acceptance of a takeover bid cannot be less than four weeks (but not more than ten). This will allow sufficient time for a shareholders meeting to be called to authorise defensive measures, should the need arise. By involving the shareholders in this way, the board is effectively obliged to take the shareholders' interests, rather then the board members' own personal interests, into account when seeking to put defensive measures in place.

(3) Cross-border takeovers and determination of Supervisory Authority Competency

9–91   The proposed Directive also lays down rules for determining which takeover supervisory authorities have competence to regulate various aspects of a cross-border takeover in the case of an offeree which is not listed in its country of origin. The Directive proposes that matters relating to the procedure and price shall be dealt with in accordance with the market rules of, and be supervised by the supervisory authority in, the Member State where the offeree is listed. On the other hand, matters relating to the information to be given to employees and also company law matters, shall be dealt with by the supervisory authority in the Member State where the offeree has its registered office. The Commission concedes that this may not be a perfect solution, and so the latest draft of the proposed Directive proposes that three years after the adoption of the Directive, this regime will be reviewed.

---

[393] e.g the Netherlands.
[394] e.g Italy.

(4) Impact of the Directive on national appeal systems

9–92   The Directive will not seek to interfere with national judicial review or administrative appeal systems *vis a vis* the review of takeover supervisory authorities' decisions under national law or regulations. The Commission has acknowledged that some fears were expressed by certain Member States that the Directive might be used by parties to invoke a "euro-defence" in order to frustrate a takeover (by forcing the national supervisory authority or court concerned with the takeover, to refer the matter to the European Court of Justice in Luxembourg, for resolution). The Commission has emphasised in the Directive's preamble that nothing in the Directive seeks to require national courts or administrative review bodies to suspend a takeover merely on the basis of anything that is contained in the Directive. However, it does concede, that by introducing the Directive, the Member State authorities will have to respect the general principles of Community Law. It remains to be seen whether the Commission's optimistic view (that the Directive will not provide a basis for parties who wish to use litigation as a means of tactically frustrating takeovers) will be proven to be correct.

(5) Forms of Consideration in a Takeover

9–93   The proposed Directive also deals with the question of what form of consideration may be offered in a takeover. Some Member States indicated that cash should be imposed as an alternative form of consideration. These States had several concerns in this regard, the principal one being that cash gives the offeree's shareholders the choice of either leaving the company or becoming a shareholder of the offeror. Other Member States disagreed, principally on the grounds that requiring cash as an alternative form of consideration would increase the transaction cost of mergers, particularly in those States where a mandatory bid rule did not already exist. Furthermore, a requirement to pay cash would increase transaction costs, in comparison to an exchange of shares as consideration in a takeover. As a compromise, the proposed Directive does not require a cash consideration as an alternative where the consideration offered consists of "liquid" shares, such shares being shares that are listed on a regulated market in an EU Member State. However, if the consideration consists of shares which are not "liquid" in this sense, then a cash alternative must be provided. The Directive does not prevent States, which already require a cash alternative from retaining such a requirement, nor States which wish to introduce such a requirement, from introducing such rules.

(6) Information requirements

9–94   The Directive requires that information must be provided on a wide variety of matters, if the national takeover regime does not already so require. For example, in order to dissuade corporate raiding using unsound financing methods such as junk bonds, the Directive requires the offeror to disclose information about the methods that are being used to finance the takeover bid. Furthermore, the Directive will require that the bid is only announced after the offeror forms the view that the financing methods to be used are sound.

   The Directive will also require the board of the offeree to disclose to the representatives of its employees that a bid has been made. This must occur as soon as the bid has been made public. It was decided not to require such disclosure prior to the bid being made public as this could encourage the occurrence of insider dealing. The offeror's offer document must also be disclosed to the employees' representatives by the offeree's board. This is particularly significant as the Directive proposes to oblige the offeror to state in the offer document its intentions regarding the future of the target company, in particular its plans for the employees and whether there will be a material change in their employment. The Directive also proposes that the board of the offeree draw up a response document, where *inter alia*, it will set out its views on the takeover bid including its view of whether the bid is in the best interests of the employees. In the event that there are no employee representatives, then communication of all of the foregoing information must be made to the employees directly.

Index

admission conditions for securities and shares
Admissions Directive 1–13
  optional exceptions 1–14, 1–22a
debt securities 1–21—1–22
mutual recognition among Member States 1–35—1–36
shares
  minimum market capitalisation 1–18
  Schedule A of Admissions Directive 1–19
  Yellow Book 1–20
Stock Exchange
"competent authority" 1–14
conditions for admission 1–14
decision must be given within six months 1–17
enforcement powers 1–16
investor protection 1–15
judicial review of decisions 1–17
non-discrimination between member states 1–15
refusal of admission 1–14
agents *see* **authority of company agents**
Alternative Investments Market [AIM] 1–12, 1–27
assignment of debts
advantages for assignor 7–01
debts collected by assignor despite factoring agreement 7–01
in equity *see* assignment of debts in equity
in law *see* assignment of debts in law

assignment of debts—*contd.*
priority between competing assignments 7–24
notice to debtor gives priority (*Dearle v. Hall*) 7–25—7–26
Section 28(6) and *Dearle v. Hall* rules 7–27—7–29
whole turnover factoring 7–03, 7–13
assignment of debts in equity
7–02, 7–08, 7–19, 7–20
assignment in writing 7–22
clear intention to assign 7–21
joinder of assignor in proceedings against debtor 7–20
notice to debtor 7–23
trust interests 7–22
valuable consideration 7–21
assignment of debts in law 7–02, 7–08, 7–09
charge over book debts does not constitute 7–11
must be absolute 7–10—7–11
must be in writing 7–15
practical consequences 7–02
reversionary interest 7–11
revocable assignment does not constitute 7–11
stamp duty exemption 7–15
subject to equities (section 28(6))
  counterclaims by debtor 7–16
  priority to first assignee to notify debtor 7–18
  third party claims 7–17
written assignment not executed by factor 7–15
written notice to debtor 7–12

authority of company agents
5–32
actual authority 5–33
constructive notice 5–40
  agent outside field of usual
    authority 5–47
  circumstances placing outsider
    on enquiry 5–44
  deficiency on public record
    5–42
  European Communities
    (Companies) Regulations
    1973 (Regulation 6)
    5–49, 5–50
  good faith 5–43
  liabilities of another company
    guaranteed 5–45
  Turquand's rule 5–41
  whether company agents may
    rely on 5–46
EEC Company Law Directive
  5–48
  agency principles 5–51
  European Communities
    (Companies) Regulations
    1973 5–49
  limitations 5–52
  Turquand's rule 5–50
ostensible authority 5–34
  intra vires requirement 5–38
  no express limitation 5–39
  reliance on representation
    5–37
  representation by company
    5–36
  representation of authority
    5–35

book debts
charge-backs 5–56, 5–68
classification of debts as 5–55
examinership of borrower
  5–66
  charge-backs 5–68
  crystallised floating charges
    de-crystallise 5–67
  lender realisation of charged
    debt prevented 5–70

book debts—*contd.*
examinership of borrower—
  contd.
  negative pledge covenants
    5–69
  priority of certified borrowings
    5–71
fixed and floating charges
  5–54
  advantages of fixed charge
    lender 5–59
  constructionist approach to
    classifying 5–62—
    5–63
  criteria for floating charge
    5–60
  designated account 5–64
  floating charge and
    subsequently created
    "fixed" charge 5–65
  historical objections to fixed
    charges on book debts
    5–61
  statutory obligation to register
    charges on 5–57—5–58
Bord Fáilte 8–34
Bord Iascaigh Mhara 8–34
Bord Trachtála, An 8–07
borrowing *see* **assignment of debts;
  book debts; debt factoring;
  debt subordination; loans;**
  ultra vires **borrowing**

Capital Adequacy Directive
Central Bank as "competent
  authority" 1–05
Central Bank of Ireland
supervision of FINEX
  1–11
supervision of Irish Stock
  Exchange 1–03—1–04
"churning" 4–112
Competition Acts regime
Category Certificate of 1997
  9–20—9–21
"common control" 9–21
compatibility with Mergers Act
  regime 9–17

Competition Acts regime—*contd.*
diminution of competition 9–22
Four-Firm Concentration
(FFC) ratio 9–24—9–26
Hirfindahl/Hirschmann (HHI)
index 9–23, 9–25—9–26
expanded role of Competition
Authority 9–18—9–20
inapplicability of Category
Certificate
ancillary restraints on
competition 9–29
competition already weak
9–28
dominant position 9–27
merger as defined by
Competition Authority
9–21
vertical mergers 9–30
County Enterprise Boards 8–28
criminal liability for prospectuses
Companies Act 1963
failure to register prospectus
3–51
material falsehood in
statement or document
3–52
untrue statements (s. 50)
3–49
violating expert's consent
3–50
Larceny Act 1861 3–60
Listing Particulars Regulations
breach of professional secrecy
3–54
failure to produce Listing
Particulars 3–56
late delivery of Listing
Particulars 3–55
publishing false or misleading
information 3–54
publishing "untrue statement"
3–56
withdrawal of expert's consent
3–56
Prospectus Regulations
breach of professional secrecy
3–58

**criminal liability for
prospectuses**—*contd.*
Prospectus Regulations—*contd.*
failure to produce prospectus
conforming to
Regulations 3–59
failure to register prospectus
3–59
publishing false or misleading
information 3–58
untrue statements 3–59
violation of expert's consent
3–59

debt *see* **assignment of debts; book
debts; debt factoring; debt
subordination; loans**
debt factoring
advancing sums on customer
invoices distinguished 7–04
assignment of debts at law or
equity (*see* assignment of
debts)
debts collected by assignor
despite factoring agreement
7–01
facultative factoring 7–03, 7–13
historical development 7–05—
7–07
choses in action 7–06—7–07
with or without recourse 7–03
debt subordination
assignment of debt distinguished
. 6–15
charges distinguished 6–10—
6–11
consensual character of
subordination 6–14
contractual contingent
subordination 6–13
turn-over subordination 6–12
commencement of arrangement
6–16
company law provisions 6–69
fraudulent preference 6–79—
6–81
fraudulent trading 6–70—6–72
reckless trading 6–73—6–77

debt subordination—*contd.*
  complete subordination 6–17
  contractual contingent
    subordination
    British Eagle 6–52—6–59
    Companies Act 1990 6–60—
      6–63
    contingency 6–50—6–51
    contractual turn-over
      compared 6–64—6–67
    contractual turn-over
      distinguished 6–45—
      6–47
    pari passu 6–48—6–49
    turnover subordinations
      compared 6–64—6–68
  contractual turn-over
    subordination 6–20, 6–37—
    6–38
    company law provisions 6–44
    contractual contingent
      compared 6–64—6–67
    contractual contingent
      distinguished 6–45—
      6–47
    lack of beneficial interest for
      senior creditor 6–43
    pari passu 6–40
    recognition in other
      jurisdictions 6–42
    security creation risk avoided
      6–41
    senior creditor double
      payment 6–39
    subordination trust compared
      6–68
  debtor company 6–02
    "breathing space" 6–05
    circumvention of borrowing
      limits 6–06
    group companies and group
      debtors 6–07
  definition 6–01
  hybrid of debt and equity 6–08
    features distinguishing from
      equity 6–09
  inchoate subordination 6–18
  junior creditors 6–04

debt subordination—*contd.*
  senior creditors 6–03
  subordination trust 6–20—6–22
    assignment by junior creditor
      6–35—6–36
    breadth of turnover obligation
      6–30
    contractual contingent
      subordination compared
      6–68
    debtor/junior creditor set-off
      6–24
    insolvency of junior creditor
      6–23
    pari passu 6–27
    privity of contract 6–26
    proving junior debt 6–28—
      6–29
    recognition difficulties in some
      jurisdictions 6–31
    security interest may be
      inadvertently created
      6–32—6–34
    senior creditor double
      payment 6–25
**Developing Companies Market
  [DCM]** 1–27
  alternative to full stock market
    listing 1–10
  and exemptions from listing
    particulars requirements
    1–47, 1–50, 1–56

EASDAQ index 1–12
EC Mergers Regulation regime
  9–31
  "concentrations" 9–31
    credit or financial institutions
      9–33, 9–40—9–41
    "decisive influence" 9–32—
      9–33
  enforcement powers of
    Commission 9–67
  joint ventures 9–34
    co-operative defined 9–60
    concentrative and co-operative
      distinguished 9–58—
      9–62

EC Mergers Regulation regime—
contd.
joint ventures—*contd.*
concentrative defined
9–59
"full-function" 9–63—9–66
notification requirement and
Community Dimension
9–36
collective dominance 9–50
credit and financial turnover
rules 9–40—9–41
deadlines and legal bases for
decisions 9–45—9–48
event triggering notification
9–43
failing firm defence 9–51—
9–52
financial thresholds 9–37—
9–39
modifications and
commitments preferred
to prohibition 9–49
suspensive effect 9–44
test for compatibility with
Common Market 9–50
"one-stop shop"
national regimes inapplicable
in case of Community
Dimension 9–42
outside EU 9–35
referral by Commission to
Member State
"German clause" 9–54
legitimate interests of Member
States 9–55
referral by Member State to
Commission ("Dutch
clause") 9–56—9–57
Enterprise Ireland
establishment 8–05—8–07
purposes and functions 8–07—
8–08
**Exploration Securities Market
[ESM]** 1–11

FÁS 8–31
FINEX 1–11

Forbairt 8–21
Enterprise Ireland replaces 8–07,
8–09
establishment 8–05
Forfás 8–21
and Enterprise Ireland 8–08
establishment 8–02—8–03

grants *see* **industrial incentives**

ICC Bank plc 8–29
**Industrial Development Agency
(Ireland) (IDA)** 8–21
and Enterprise Ireland 8–06,
8–07, 8–09
and Forbairt 8–05
replaces Industrial Development
Authority 8–04
industrial incentives
Bord Fáilte 8–34
Bord Iascaigh Mhara 8–34
corporate restructuring etc. 8–16
County Enterprise Boards 8–28
employment
additional persons employed
grant 8–11
service industries 8–15
enterprise development etc.
8–17
EU 8–33
FÁS 8–31
fixed assets
loan guarantees 8–14
purchase grants 8–10
reduction of loan interest
grants 8–13
grant agreement terms 8–26—
8–27
ICC Bank plc 8–29
land acquisition grant 8–23
leased fixed asset grants 8–12
legal framework 8–09
power of state agencies to acquire
shares 8–21
rent subsidy grant 8–22
research and development/
feasibility grants 8–19
Shannon Development 8–32

industrial incentives—*contd.*
  statutory limits on aggregate of
      grants 8–24
    government power to override
        8–25
  technology acquisition grants
      8–20
  training grants 8–18
  Údarás na Gaeltachta 8–30
insider dealing 4–01
  causing or procuring 4–51
    communication of insider
        information
        distinguished 4–56
  civil liability 4–71—4–73
    account for profit 4–79—
        4–81
    compensation for loss 4–74—
        4–78
  common law (fiduciary duty)
      4–02—4–06
  communication of inside
      information 4–52—4–55
    causing or procuring
        distinguished 4–56
  companies as insider dealers
      4–58—4–59
    "Chinese wall" 4–60
    company dealing in own
        securities 4–62
    mere information that
        company proposes to
        deal 4–61
  criminal liability
    agents 4–84
    annual report of recognised
        stock exchange
        4–93
    court's discretion 4–90
    direction of relevant authority
        by Minister 4–88
    duty to co-operate with other
        Member State stock
        exchanges 4–92
    duty to report 4–87
    investigation powers 4–89
    offences 4–82
    penalties 4–83

insider dealing—*contd.*
  criminal liability—*contd.*
    professional secrecy 4–91
    relevant authority 4–86
    whether tainted transactions
        void or voidable 4–85
  "dealing"
    definition 4–08—4–09
  directors and securities options
      4–57
  exempt transactions 4–64
    execution-only agents 4–66—
        4–68
    seven-day window 4–69
  "inside information"
    definition 4–17, 4–30—4–31
    "information of a precise
        nature" 4–26—4–29
    "likely materially to affect
        price of securities"
        4–23—4–25
    "not generally available"
        4–18—4–22
  Irish Association of Investment
      Managers (IAIM) code of
      practice 4–21, 4–23
  primary insiders
    "connected to the company"
        4–34—4–35
    "connected" to the State
        4–36
    information acquired by virtue
        of "connection" to
        company 4–33
    mere "possession" sufficient
        4–37
    two types of 4–32
    United Kingdom 4–38—4–41
  "recognised stock exchange"
      4–13
  secondary insiders ("tipees")
      4–42
    "awareness" test 4–44—4–46
    connection with company not
        required 4–43
    "directly or indirectly" and
        tipee's tipee 4–47
    United Kingdom 4–48—4–50

insider dealing—*contd.*
"securities"
definition 4–12, 4–15
foreign incorporated
companies 4–15
"off-market" dealings 4–14
"transactions involving
professional
intermediaries" 4–16
statutory regime 4–07
stock market manipulation *see*
stock market manipulation
territorial scope 4–11
Yellow Book Model Code 4–70
Interim Reports Directive 1–13
Investment Services Directive 1–03
Central Bank as "competent
authority" 1–05
EASDAQ index and 1–12
'Home State' supervision
principle 1–03
Irish Takeover Panel
censure 9–83
composition 9–82
directions 9–83
hearings 9–85
judicial review of acts 9–86
liability of members, employees
and advisers 9–87
London Takeover Panel replaced
by 9–69—9–70
rulings 9–83
ISEQ index 1–09

liability for prospectuses 3–01
common law remedies 3–02
damages against company
3–21
criminal liability *see* criminal
liability for prospectuses
deceitful misrepresentation 3–03
active misrepresentation or
fraud necessary 3–03
connection between maker of
representation and
parties relying upon it
3–06
measure of damages 3–07

liability for prospectuses—*contd.*
negligent misstatement or
omission 3–08
analogy of auditors' liability
for accounts 3–12—3–14
contractual or fiduciary
relationship necessary
3–09
liability to subsequent allottees
of shares 3–15—3–16
purpose of documents 3–09—
3–11, 3–13, 3–15
omission 3–03
liability under s. 44 3–40
Listing Particulars Regulations
3–41
Prospectus Directive
Regulations 3–42
whether grounds for action
3–04
promoter *see* promoter and
company
Registrar of Companies' liability
3–46
rescission, action for by allottee
fraud not necessary 3–17
not available in winding up
3–20, 3–21
preconditions 3–18
truthful disclosure of material
information 3–19
statutory remedies
"offer to the public" necessary
3–22
Stock Exchange liability 3–43—
3–45
"untrue statements," liability
under s. 49 of Companies
Act 1963 3–23
companies not exposed to
liability 3–25
defence of expert 3–32
defence of official statement
3–31
defence of reasonable belief in
truth of statement 3–29
defence of statement based on
expert's statement 3–30

liability for prospectuses—*contd.*
  "untrue statements," liability
    under s. 49 of Companies
    Act 1963—*contd.*
  defence of withdrawal of
    consent 3–28
  possible defendants 3–24
  possible plaintiffs 3–26
  Prospectus Directive
    Regulations 3–38
**listed companies' continuing
  obligations**
  additional requirements in
    specific transactions
    1–86
  disclosure of new developments
    1–83
  equal treatment of holders of
    shares and debt securities
    1–84
  equivalence of information
    1–84
  notification of acquisition or
    reduction of substantial
    interest 1–85
  notification of alterations to
    capital structure 1–85
  Stock Exchange powers 1–81—
    1–85
listing application procedures
  listing particulars *see* listing
    particulars
  time for application 1–55
listing markets
  admission conditions for
    securities *see* admission
    conditions for securities
  domestic 1–09
    Developing Companies
      Market [DCM] 1–10
    Exploration Securities Market
      [ESM] 1–11
    FINEX 1–11
  foreign
    Alternative Investments
      Market [AIM] 1–12
    EASDAQ index 1–12
    NASDAQ index 1–12

listing methods 1–23
  acquisition or merger issue 1–31
  "best efforts" placing 1–25
  bonus issue 1–32
  capitalisation issue 1–32
  "clawback" placing 1–25
  combined offer for sale and
    subscription 1–24
  conversions of securities 1–33
  exercise of options or warrants to
    subscribe securities 1–33
  intermediaries offer 1–26
  introduction 1–27
  issue for cash 1–33
  offer for sale 1–24
  offer for subscription 1–24
  open offer 1–30
    distinguished from rights issue
      1–30
  placing 1–25
  "private" placing 1–25
  "reasonable efforts" placing
    1–25
  rights issue
    definition 1–28
    distinguished from open offer
      1–30
    statutory pre-emption rights
      1–29
    Yellow Book 1–28—1–29
  vendor consideration issue 1–31
  "vendor consideration" placing
    1–25
listing particulars
  approval
    prior approval by Stock
      Exchange 1–42, 1–56
    supplementary particulars
      1–43
  contents 1–37
    certificates representing shares
      1–40
    debt securities 1–39
    responsibility statement and
      responsibility letters
      1–41, 3–04, 3–09
    shares or convertible debt
      securities 1–38

listing particulars—*contd.*
contravention of regulations does
not void transaction 3–47
document
informed assessment 1–34,
1–41
minimum information 1–34
exemption by Stock Exchange
from requirement to
publish 1–44
company listed in another
Member State 1–46,
1–49
Developing Companies
Market (DCM) company
1–47, 1–50
"exceptional circumstances"
excepted 1–51
exempt listing particulars
document 1–48—1–50
omission of information
1–54
previously published
documents 1–45, 1–48
shelf registration 1–53
summary particulars 1–52
mutual recognition 1–59
competent authorities required
to co-operate 1–67—
1–68
partial exemption or
derogation 1–60
prospectuses, and 1–61
listing particulars deemed to
be prospectus 1–62
mutual recognition of
prospectus as listing
particulars 1–63—1–66,
1–77
publication and circulation
1–56—158
Stock Exchange
competent authority 1–34
"untrue statements,"
damages for breach of
regulations 3–35—3–36
disapplication of some
provisions 3–33

listing particulars—*contd.*
"untrue statements,"
"informed assessment"
3–34
liability under s. 49 of
Companies Act 1963
3–23
possible plaintiffs 3–37
loans
debentures 5–05
definition 5–01
facility agreement 5–03
overdraft 5–04
revolving facility 5–03
standby facility 5–03
syndicated loan arrangement
5–03
term facility 5–03
ultra vires see ultra vires
borrowing

mergers and take-overs
9–01
"common control" 9–02
Competition Acts regime *see*
Competition Acts regime
Competition Authority 9–05
definition 9–02
EC Mergers Regulation regime
see EC Mergers Regulation
regime
Minister's consideration of
notification
absolute prohibition order
9–10
appeal to High Court against
s. 9 order 9–12
conditional prohibition order
9–10
declines to make order
9–11
enforcement of s. 9 order
9–13
failure to make decision means
approval by default
9–09
purported vendor's right to
damages 9–15

mergers and take-overs—*contd.*
Minister's consideration of
notification—*contd.*
referral to Competition
Authority (s. 9 order)
9–10
request for further information
9–06
time limit for consent or
refusal 9–07
title cannot pass without
favourable decision
9–14—9–15
notification
contents 9–05
criteria for 9–03
fee 9–04
form 9–03
penalties for failure to notify
9–16
period of notice 9–04
pre-emptive approach to avoid
referral to Competition
Authority 9–05
Takeover Panel Rules regime *see*
Irish Takeover Panel;
Takeover Panel Rules
regime

NASDAQ index 1–12
**National Treasury Management
Agency** 1–09

promoter and company 3–61
company action against promoter
who makes secret profit
rescission of contract 3–66—
3–67
return of secret profits 3–65
fiduciary relationship 3–62
whether release from
obligations possible 3–64
plcs
excluded transactions 3–72
independent valuation of
assets 3–68
"initial period" 3–70
"relevant person" 3–69

promoter and company—*contd.*
plcs—*contd.*
sanctions 3–73—3–74
size of transaction and valuer's
report 3–71
sale of promoters' property to
company 3–63
prospectuses
Companies Act Third Schedule
companies registered outside
State 2–10
exemptions 2–08, 2–30—2–31
form of application for shares
or debentures must be
accompanied by 2–02
form of application not issued
to public 2–31
genuine secondary
transactions 2–31
new shares and debentures
only affected 2–03
whether oral offer constitutes
"form of application"
2–12, 2–31
Companies Act Third Schedule
regime subsumed by
Prospectus Directive 1–71,
2–03—2–07
only three years' audited
accounts published
2–05
principal differences 2–07
companies incorporated outside
the State 2–10
United Kingdom derogation
2–10
content of prospectuses 1–73—
1–75
categories of information
which may be omitted
1–75—1–76
debt securities 1–74
contravention of regulations does
not void transaction
3–47
definition 2–11
giving of information
distinguished 2–12

prospectuses—*contd.*
  documents deemed to be
    prospectuses
    shares offered with a view to
      being offered to public
      2–13
    where Listings Particulars
      Directive applies 2–15
    where Prospectus Directive
      applies 2–14
  EASDAQ index 1–12
  exemptions 2–16, 2–32
  insider dealing 4–51
  level of disclosure 1–70
  liability *see* liability for
    prospectuses
  listing particulars, and 1–61,
    1–72—1–73, 1–77—1–80
  mutual recognition among
    Member States 1–36
  mutual recognition of
    prospectuses 1–36, 1–77—
    1–79
    "full" and "following"
      prospectuses 1–77
    provision of local information
      1–77
    translation of prospectuses
      1–77
  mutual recognition of
    prospectuses as listing
    particulars 1–36, 1–80,
    2–08
  offer to "the public" 2–17—2–26
    definitions 2–17—2–18
    offer for subscription or
      purchase 2–27—2–29
    offers not constituting 2–19,
      2–26
    offers of debentures to dealers
      not 2–26
    private companies 2–16, 2–25
    whether offers constitute
      2–19—2–24
  placing, whether required for
    1–25
  prior approval by Stock Exchange
    1–72

prospectuses—*contd.*
  public offers of transferable
    securities 1–69
  publication and registration
    1–42, 1–72
  registration with Registrar of
    Companies 1–72, 2–02
    companies registered outside
      State 2–10
  Regulations (S.I. No. 202 of 1992)
    2–09

Securities and Exchange
  Commission [SEC] 1–12
Securities and Futures Authority
  [SFA] 1–03
Shannon Development 8–32
state aids *see* **industrial incentives**
Stock Exchange (of Ireland)
  Central Bank supervision
    1–03—1–04
  complaints system 1–07
  definition of "stock exchange"
    1–04
  Developing Companies Market
    [DCM] 1–10
  Exploration Securities Market
    [ESM] 1–11
  member firms
    authorisation by Central Bank
      1–05, 1–08
    branches outside State
      1–05
    complaints system 1–07
    definition 1–05
    directions from Central Bank
      1–08
    primary dealers 1–09
    revoking of authorisation
      1–06
  securities market 1–09
  "Yellow Book" and "Green
    Pages" 1–02
Stock Exchange (of London)
  Alternative Investments Market
    [AIM] 1–12
  listing of Irish companies
    1–12

Stock Exchange of United Kingdom and Ireland
Irish and London Stock Exchanges merged to form 1–02
separation of Irish and London Stock Exchanges (1995) 1–02—1–03, 9–69 *see also* Stock Exchange (of Ireland)
"Yellow Book" and "Green Pages" 1–02
stock market manipulation 4–94
stabilisation rules 4–95
action ancillary to stabilising action 4–103
disclosure of relevant share capital not applicable 4–110
limits on stabilisation price 4–104—4–107
preliminary steps 4–99—4–101
recording of stabilisation transactions 4–109
"relevant securities" 4–96
stabilising action 4–102
stabilising periods 4–97—4–98
termination of stabilisation period 4–108
Stock Exchange regime 4–111
"churning" 4–112
subordination *see* **debt subordination**

Takeover Panel Rules regime
control
definition 9–72
general principles 9–71, 9–73
Irish Takeover Panel *see* Irish Takeover Panel
other relevant transactions
definition 9–72
relevant company
definition 9–72

Takeover Panel Rules regime— *contd.*
Substantial Acquisition Rules (SARs) 9–78
exempted transactions 9–80
prohibited transactions 9–79
prompt disclosure required 9–81
takeover
definition 9–72
Takeover Rules 9–73
acquisition of voting securities 9–74—9–75
equality of information 9–73
mandatory offers 9–73, 9–76
and other regulatory regimes 9–77
revision of offers 9–73
standards of care 9–73
voluntary offers 9–73

Údarás na Gaeltachta 8–30
ultra vires **borrowing** 5–06
abuse of directors' powers 5–14—5–16
distinguished from *ultra vires* 5–15
authority of company agents *see* authority of company agents
Bell Houses clauses 5–08, 5–11—5–12
benefit to the company 5–13, 5–18
"borrowing" cannot be object of trading company 5–07
Cotman clauses 5–08, 5–10—5–11, 5–12
enforcing contracts against *ultra vires* borrowers
Article 9 First Company Law Directive 5–22
interest rate 5–29, 5–31
in personam quasi-contractual remedies 5–25—5–26
recovery of funds 5–24—5–31
Regulation 6 of S.I. No. 163 of 1973 5–23

***ultra vires* borrowing**—*contd.*
  enforcing contracts against *ultra*
      vires borrowers—***contd.***
    Revenue Commissioners 5–30
    section 8(1) and "actually
        aware" criterion 5–19—
        5–23
    trusteeship 5–28
  general and specific limitations
      distinguished 5–17
  main objects principle 5–09—
    5–11